Lecture Notes in Computer Science 16337

Founding Editors

Gerhard Goos
Juris Hartmanis

Editorial Board Members

Elisa Bertino, *Purdue University, West Lafayette, IN, USA*
Wen Gao, *Peking University, Beijing, China*
Bernhard Steffen, *TU Dortmund University, Dortmund, Germany*
Moti Yung, *Columbia University, New York, NY, USA*

The series Lecture Notes in Computer Science (LNCS), including its subseries Lecture Notes in Artificial Intelligence (LNAI) and Lecture Notes in Bioinformatics (LNBI), has established itself as a medium for the publication of new developments in computer science and information technology research, teaching, and education.

LNCS enjoys close cooperation with the computer science R & D community, the series counts many renowned academics among its volume editors and paper authors, and collaborates with prestigious societies. Its mission is to serve this international community by providing an invaluable service, mainly focused on the publication of conference and workshop proceedings and postproceedings. LNCS commenced publication in 1973.

Adela Coman · Simona Vasilache ·
Abbas Moallem

Editors

HCI International 2025 – Late Breaking Papers

27th International Conference on
Human-Computer Interaction, HCII 2025
Gothenburg, Sweden, June 22–27, 2025
Proceedings, Part VII

 Springer

Editors
Adela Coman
University of Bucharest
Bucharest, Romania

Abbas Moallem
San Jose State University
San Jose, CA, USA

Simona Vasilache
University of Tsukuba
Tsukuba, Japan

ISSN 0302-9743   ISSN 1611-3349 (electronic)
Lecture Notes in Computer Science
ISBN 978-3-032-12800-3   ISBN 978-3-032-12801-0 (eBook)
https://doi.org/10.1007/978-3-032-12801-0

This Springer imprint is published by the registered company Springer Nature Switzerland AG
The registered company address is: Gewerbestrasse 11, 6330 Cham, Switzerland

If disposing of this product, please recycle the paper.

Foreword

The HCI International (HCII) conference was founded in 1984 by Gavriel Salvendy (Purdue University, USA, Tsinghua University, P.R. China, and University of Central Florida, USA) and the first event of the series, "1st USA-Japan Conference on Human-Computer Interaction", was held in Honolulu, Hawaii, USA, on 18–20 August. Since then, HCI International has been held jointly with several Thematic Areas and Affiliated Conferences, with each one under the auspices of a distinguished international Program Board and under one management and one registration. Twenty-seven HCI International Conferences have been organized so far (every two years until 2013, and annually thereafter).

Last year, we celebrated 40 years since the establishment of the HCII conference, which has been a hub for presenting groundbreaking research and novel ideas and collaboration for people from all over the world. Over the years, this conference has served as a platform for scholars, researchers, industry experts, and students to exchange ideas, connect, and address challenges in the ever-evolving HCI field. The conference has evolved itself, adapting to new technologies and emerging trends, while staying committed to its core mission of advancing knowledge and driving change.

The 27th International Conference on Human-Computer Interaction, HCI International 2025 (HCII 2025), was held as an 'on-site' conference at the Gothia Towers Hotel and Swedish Exhibition & Congress Centre, in Gothenburg, Sweden, on June 22–27, 2025, with the additional option for 'on-line' participation. It incorporated the 21 thematic areas and affiliated conferences listed below.

A total of 7972 individuals from academia, research institutes, industry, and government agencies from 92 countries submitted contributions. 1430 papers and 355 posters (as short research papers) were included in the volumes of the proceedings published just before the start of the conference. Additionally, 439 papers and 104 posters were included in the volumes of the proceedings published after the conference, as "Late Breaking Work". The contributions thoroughly cover the entire field of human-computer interaction, highlight the evolving role of computers in diverse contexts, and demonstrate how HCI research is shaping and improving user experiences across a wide range of domains, influencing technological progress and its effective integration into various sectors. The volumes constituting the full set of the HCII 2025 conference proceedings are listed on the following pages.

I would like to thank the Program Board Chairs and the members of the Program Boards of all thematic areas and affiliated conferences for their contribution towards the high scientific quality and overall success of the HCI International 2025 conference. Their manifold support including paper reviews (via a single-blind review process, with a minimum of two reviews per submission), session organization, and their willingness to act as goodwill ambassadors for the conference is most highly appreciated.

This conference would not have been possible without the continuous and unwavering support and advice of Gavriel Salvendy, founder, General Chair Emeritus, and Scientific Advisor. For his outstanding efforts, I would like to express my sincere appreciation to Abbas Moallem, Communications Chair and Editor of HCI International News.

September 2025   Constantine Stephanidis

HCI International 2025 Thematic Areas and Affiliated Conferences

- HCI: Human-Computer Interaction Thematic Area
- HIMI: Human Interface and the Management of Information Thematic Area
- EPCE: 22nd International Conference on Engineering Psychology and Cognitive Ergonomics
- AC: 19th International Conference on Augmented Cognition
- UAHCI: 19th International Conference on Universal Access in Human-Computer Interaction
- CCD: 17th International Conference on Cross-Cultural Design
- SCSM: 17th International Conference on Social Computing and Social Media
- VAMR: 17th International Conference on Virtual, Augmented and Mixed Reality
- DHM: 16th International Conference on Digital Human Modeling & Applications in Health, Safety, Ergonomics & Risk Management
- DUXU: 14th International Conference on Design, User Experience and Usability
- C&C: 13th International Conference on Culture and Computing
- DAPI: 13th International Conference on Distributed, Ambient and Pervasive Interactions
- HCIBGO: 12th International Conference on HCI in Business, Government and Organizations
- LCT: 12th International Conference on Learning and Collaboration Technologies
- ITAP: 11th International Conference on Human Aspects of IT for the Aged Population
- AIS: 7th International Conference on Adaptive Instructional Systems
- HCI-CPT: 7th International Conference on HCI for Cybersecurity, Privacy and Trust
- HCI-Games: 7th International Conference on HCI in Games
- MobiTAS: 7th International Conference on HCI in Mobility, Transport and Automotive Systems
- AI-HCI: 6th International Conference on Artificial Intelligence in HCI
- MOBILE: 6th International Conference on Human-Centered Design, Operation and Evaluation of Mobile Communications

Conference Proceedings – Full List of Volumes

1. LNCS 15766, Human-Computer Interaction — Part I, edited by Masaaki Kurosu and Ayako Hashizume
2. LNCS 15767, Human-Computer Interaction — Part II, edited by Masaaki Kurosu and Ayako Hashizume
3. LNCS 15768, Human-Computer Interaction — Part III, edited by Masaaki Kurosu and Ayako Hashizume
4. LNCS 15769, Human-Computer Interaction — Part IV, edited by Masaaki Kurosu and Ayako Hashizume
5. LNCS 15770, Human-Computer Interaction — Part V, edited by Masaaki Kurosu and Ayako Hashizume
6. LNCS 15771, Human-Computer Interaction — Part VI, edited by Masaaki Kurosu and Ayako Hashizume
7. LNCS 15772, Human-Computer Interaction — Part VII, edited by Masaaki Kurosu and Ayako Hashizume
8. LNCS 15773, Human Interface and the Management of Information: Part I, edited by Hirohiko Mori and Yumi Asahi
9. LNCS 15774, Human Interface and the Management of Information: Part II, edited by Hirohiko Mori and Yumi Asahi
10. LNCS 15773, Human Interface and the Management of Information: Part III, edited by Hirohiko Mori and Yumi Asahi
11. LNAI 15776, Engineering Psychology and Cognitive Ergonomics: Part I, edited by Don Harris and Wen-Chin Li
12. LNAI 15777, Engineering Psychology and Cognitive Ergonomics: Part II, edited by Don Harris and Wen-Chin Li
13. LNAI 15778, Augmented Cognition, Part I, edited by Dylan D. Schmorrow and Cali M. Fidopiastis
14. LNAI 15779, Augmented Cognition, Part II, edited by Dylan D. Schmorrow and Cali M. Fidopiastis
15. LNCS 15780, Universal Access in Human-Computer Interaction: Part I, edited by Margherita Antona and Constantine Stephanidis
16. LNCS 15781, Universal Access in Human-Computer Interaction: Part II, edited by Margherita Antona and Constantine Stephanidis
17. LNCS 15782, Cross-Cultural Design: Part I, edited by Pei-Luen Patrick Rau
18. LNCS 15783, Cross-Cultural Design: Part II, edited by Pei-Luen Patrick Rau
19. LNCS 15784, Cross-Cultural Design: Part III, edited by Pei-Luen Patrick Rau
20. LNCS 15785, Cross-Cultural Design: Part IV, edited by Pei-Luen Patrick Rau
21. LNCS 15786, Social Computing and Social Media: Part I, edited by Adela Coman and Simona Vasilache

85. CCIS 2772, HCI International 2025 — Late Breaking Posters: Part II, edited by Constantine Stephanidis, Margherita Antona, Stavroula Ntoa, George Margetis and Gavriel Salvendy
86. CCIS 2773, HCI International 2025 — Late Breaking Posters: Part III, edited by Constantine Stephanidis, Margherita Antona, Stavroula Ntoa, George Margetis and Gavriel Salvendy

https://2025.hci.international/proceedings

27th International Conference on Human-Computer Interaction (HCII 2025)

The full list with the Program Board Chairs and the members of the Program Boards of all thematic areas and affiliated conferences of HCII 2025 is available online at:

http://www.hci.international/board-members-2025.php

HCI International 2026 Conference

The 28th International Conference on Human-Computer Interaction, HCI International 2026, will be held jointly with the affiliated conferences at the Montréal Convention Centre (Palais des congrès de Montréal), in Montreal, Canada, 26–31 July 2026. It will cover a broad spectrum of themes related to Human-Computer Interaction, including theoretical issues, methods, tools, processes, and case studies in HCI design, as well as novel interaction techniques, interfaces, and applications. The proceedings will be published by Springer (part of Springer Nature) in a multi-volume set. More information will become available on the conference website: https://2026.hci.international/.

General Chair
Constantine Stephanidis
University of Crete and ICS-FORTH
Heraklion, Crete, Greece
Email: general_chair@2026.hci.international

https://2026.hci.international/

Contents

LLMs and Intelligent Agents in Social Computing and Security

Understanding User Behavior in Social Computing

Security, Privacy, and Trust in Digital Environments

Social Media, Society, and Digital Communities

Consumers' Use of Social Media Platforms as Sources of Restaurant Information: A Comparison of Google Maps, TripAdvisor, Instagram, and TikTok

Michael Beier[(✉)] [iD]

University of Applied Sciences of the Grisons, Chur, Switzerland
`michael.beier@fhgr.ch`

Abstract. Many consumers are influenced by social media platforms when choosing a restaurant, or search for restaurant information on them. However, these platforms vary considerably in how they present restaurant information, for instance, in terms of content, format, media types, and recommendation mechanisms. Based on a survey of 1004 people in Germany and Switzerland, this study compares how consumers use four different social media platforms as sources for restaurant information. The findings show how often consumers use the different platforms for restaurant information and how this usage differs between their application in known and unknown areas. Finally, the results show how people differ in their use of the four social media platforms for restaurant information depending on their age, gender, education, and the individuality of their restaurant preferences. The study's findings provide restaurant marketing and management practitioners with a better understanding of how consumers search for restaurant information. This knowledge helps them to develop and implement better strategies and measures that increase their reach and customer acquisition on different social media platforms.

Keywords: Social Media · Online Reviews · Restaurant Search · Restaurant Marketing · Information Search

1 Introduction

Social media platforms, especially online review sites, are important sources for consumers to find inspiration and recommendations for restaurant visits (Beier and Schillo 2025). In contrast to channels that restaurants own or pay for, social media are often referred to as "earned media" or "word of mouth" (Grange and Benbasat 2018, Lepkowska-White 2019). Since users share their personal experiences on social media, consumers tend to trust it more than commercial communications on corporate websites, advertisements, or professional media (Schmidt and Iyer 2015, Zhang et al. 2014). People can post and find restaurant reviews on relevant online platforms such as Google Maps, TripAdvisor, or Yelp (Cassar et al. 2020, Lee and Kim 2020, Li and Hecht 2021, Mathayomchan and Taecharungroj 2020). Additionally, they can post text, photos, or videos

© The Author(s), under exclusive license to Springer Nature Switzerland AG 2026
A. Coman et al. (Eds.): HCII 2025, LNCS 16337, pp. 3–20, 2026.
https://doi.org/10.1007/978-3-032-12801-0_1

about their restaurant experiences on social media platforms such as Instagram, Facebook, or TikTok (Azman and Mustaffa 2023, Bitter and Grabnerkräuter 2016, Lian et al. 2025). This study aims to understand how consumers use such social media platforms as a source of restaurant information.

Most studies on social media and restaurants only analyze one platform in the context of word of mouth or usage behavior (e.g., Liu and Shih 2021, Menon 2022, Scherr and Wang 2021). Furthermore, a few studies include two online review platforms, e.g., to compare rating scores (Li and Hecht 2021) or to infer consumer preferences for restaurants from more than one review platform (Garner and Kim 2022). In contrast, this study analyzes consumers' use of four different online platforms as a source of restaurant information by comparing two online review platforms (Google Maps and TripAdvisor) and two social media platforms (Instagram and TikTok). In addition, this study includes the important distinction between using social media platforms for information about restaurants in known areas (e.g., city of residence) and unknown areas (e.g., on travel or vacation) (Beier and Schillo 2025, Yarış and Aykol 2022). For example, one might expect a map service (with online review features) like Google Maps to be used differently in a known area than in an unfamiliar one. Similarly, having many contacts in a known area on Instagram or sharing dining and vacation experiences regarding unknown areas could affect how restaurant information is shared and perceived on the platform.

With this in mind, this study aims to answer the following three research questions (RQ):

- **RQ1:** To what extent do consumers use social media platforms to inform themselves about restaurants?
- **RQ2:** How do consumers use social media platforms differently to inform themselves about restaurants in known and unknown areas?
- **RQ3:** How does the use of the social media platforms for restaurant information differ by age, gender, education, and individuality of restaurant preferences?

2 Literature

The following sections present the technical and theoretical fundamentals relevant to this study. First, the four social media platforms analyzed are briefly introduced. Then, four theoretical approaches offering different perspectives on social media platforms and their potential use for finding and choosing restaurants are presented.

2.1 Social Media Platforms and Restaurant Information

This study analyzes the use of four online platforms as sources of restaurant information. Therefore, it compares the usage of two online review platforms (Google Maps and TripAdvisor) and two social media platforms (Instagram and TikTok) for restaurant information. Google Maps is a widely used mobile mapping application in many regions of the world (Horbiński et al. 2020, Huertas and Orden-Mejía 2022). One of its main uses is helping people find their way in unfamiliar areas or locate unknown places (Ghita 2024). Google Maps also lets users post reviews and ratings of places, like restaurants, directly on its maps and they can filter restaurants by attributes such as area, distance to location, average rating, or topic (Li and Hecht 2021). TripAdvisor has similar features. However, on this platform restaurant reviews and ratings are emphasized more than map features. Accordingly, the focus is on user-generated content from reviews and ratings (Cassar et al. 2020). Similar to Google Maps, TripAdvisor can also be used to search for restaurants in specific areas or cities based on certain criteria (Filieri et al. 2021).

Unlike online review platforms, other social media platforms offer additional opportunities to find information about restaurants that might interest one. These platforms allow users to connect with other parties, including private contacts, social media contacts, influencers, and restaurant channels. Through these connections, users can find information about restaurants and what they offer (Ballester et al. 2023, Beier and Schillo 2025, Kumsawat et al. 2024). In this regard, in this study Instagram and TikTok are included. On both platforms short videos are important content formats (Duan et al. 2024). However, the two platforms differ significantly in two respects. First, in addition to short videos, Instagram offers classic social media post formats with photos and text. Second, Instagram is more of a social network where users can connect with each other and share content. TikTok, on the other hand, is more of a content network where users can follow accounts (Beier and Schillo 2025). Unlike Instagram, on TikTok the algorithm of the news feed plays a much greater role in determining which videos are displayed, particularly those from accounts that are not followed (Klug et al. 2021).

2.2 Information Seeking Behavior Models

In the context of this study, information-seeking behavior models provide valuable insights into how consumers select restaurants and seek information. These models are important for understanding how tourists, travelers, and guests learn about and select potential offers in the hospitality sector (Fodness and Murray 1999, Varotsis and Mylonas 2024). Early models of information seeking behavior consisted of individuals as information users, their personal information needs and their information environment, where they attempt to satisfy their information demand (Knight and Spink 2008). As development progressed, more and more aspects of emerging digital technologies were incorporated. Researchers have examined strategies and behaviors related to online and mobile technologies, such as online social networks, online review platforms, and video platforms (Cheng et al. 2024, Ho et al. 2016, Huertas and Orden-Mejía 2022). Against this backdrop, information search behavior models have been widely applied to consumer restaurant searches. For instance, these models have been employed to analyze how people search for and process information on online review platforms (Wan and Nakayama 2025), how people seek and share dining-related information on social networks (Bilgihan et al. 2014), and how consumers engage with user- and marketer-generated content on social media when selecting restaurants (Uthaisar et al. 2024).

In addition to this general approach, two specific aspects of information seeking behavior models provide further guidance for this study. First, dual processing theories differentiate information types and the cognitive processes that handle them into two categories: (1) rapid autonomous processes and (2) higher-order reasoning processes (Evans and Stanovich 2013). More specifically, the Elaboration Likelihood Model (ELM) is an influential dual-processing model of consumer behavior. It distinguishes between two ways consumers process information: central routes and peripheral routes (Petty et al.

1983). Central routes involve thinking carefully about the arguments of an information and considering the advantages and disadvantages of each one. On the other hand, peripheral routes require less mental effort. People can rely on simple cues to make decisions. For example, they might look at how others act, their own experiences, or whether they trust the source (Wang 2015). Furthermore, studies applying the ELM have revealed many variables that influence the route consumers take (Kitchen et al. 2014). In our context, the ELM allows to analyze how users weigh different types of information on different platforms when choosing a restaurant (Kwon et al. 2021, Lee et al. 2021a, Steur et al. 2022).

Secondly, when consumers find and select restaurants, it is important to note that information search models do not only deal with consumers actively searching for information. Rather, there is a distinction between information that is actively sought ("pull") and information that reaches consumers even though they did not search for it ("push") (Beier 2018, Boyd 2004, Foster and Ford 2003). This distinction is important when comparing platforms that facilitate active restaurant searches in specific areas (like Google Maps and TripAdvisor) to platforms where users often unintentionally discover restaurants while not actively searching for them (like Instagram and TikTok).

2.3 Media Richness Theory

Media richness theory originally dealt with the uncertainty and ambiguity of communication within organizations (Daft et al. 1987). More broadly, however, the theory has been used to explain how receiving direct feedback and using multiple forms of communication, such as text, audio, voice, gestures, and body language, influence the quality of relationships and interactions (Beier and Wagner 2015, Ishii et al. 2019). Because the theory originates from management research of the pre-digital era, it originally describes an ascending order of communication formats with increasing levels of media richness: (1) unaddressed documents (e.g., standard reports); (2) addressed documents (e.g., notes, memos, or letters); (3) telephone calls involving direct audio interaction; and (4) unmediated face-to-face interaction between people in direct proximity (Daft et al. 1987). The fundamental principles of media richness theory have been applied to modern communication technologies and are now commonly used to study social media communication. This includes the new photo and video communication options on social media, particularly on online social networks and review platforms (Beier and Wagner 2015, Ishii et al. 2019, Oba and Berger 2024). Thus, media richness theory enables the analysis of how the medium influences what and how information is communicated (Berger et al. 2022, Berger and Iyengar 2013). In the hospitality sector, media richness theory has been used to analyze how communication through photos and videos affects customers' intentions and choices, as well as their perception of the communication itself (e.g., Lee et al. 2021b, 2021b, Li et al. 2023, Li and Yan 2024, Zhang et al. 2025). Media richness theory is a valuable perspective for this study because it provides a theoretical framework for distinguishing Google Maps and TripAdvisor (which mainly provide online reviews with text and photos) from Instagram and TikTok (which are social media platforms that mainly provide photo and video content).

2.4 Uses and Gratifications Theory

Another valuable theoretical perspective on usage of social media platforms is the Uses and Gratifications Theory (UGT) (Katz et al. 1973). This theory examines how people deliberately seek out and use media to fulfill specific needs or desires and has been widely used in communication research to identify the motives behind individuals' use of specific media (Garner and Myers 2025). UGT has been extensively used to analyze motivations for using online and social media. However, these studies adapted the original motives to the context of the new application. This resulted in various catalogs of motives that are often only specific to one social media platform and a specific user group (Choi et al. 2016, Curras-Perez et al. 2014, Ko and Yu 2019). Nevertheless, UGT has also been used to analyze differences in the motives of people from different demographic groups for using TripAdvisor (Liu and Shih 2021), Instagram (Menon 2022), and TikTok (Scherr and Wang 2021). The theory has also been applied to compare various social media platforms (Alhabash et al. 2024). In hospitality research, UGT has been used to analyze the reasons why people engage with social media posts from tourism destinations and hotels (e.g., Choi et al. 2016, Garner and Myers 2025), to understand why Chinese travelers use WeChat to find and choose hotels (Gamage et al. 2022), and to determine what motivates young travelers to use social media to plan their trips (Kim and Cake 2025). UGT might be able to assist with this study by offering insights into the motivations behind using the analyzed social media platforms or suggesting different weightings for them.

2.5 Information Technology Acceptance Models

Finally, another group of theories explains the adoption and use of digital technologies based on underlying motivations. The Technology Acceptance Model (TAM) is the foundation of this line of research. TAM posits that individuals are motivated to use new technologies based on their individual perception of its usefulness and ease of use (Davis 1989, Legris et al. 2003). Further research successfully employed the Unified Theory of Acceptance and Use of Technology (UTAUT) to incorporate additional relevant factors into a more comprehensive model (Venkatesh et al. 2003). UTAUT2 expanded on this model. It incorporates seven main factors that influence the intention to use and the actual use of digital technology: performance expectancy, effort expectancy, social influence, facilitating conditions, hedonic motivation, price value, and habit. UTAUT2 also addresses differences among users in terms of age, gender, and experience (Venkatesh et al. 2012). TAM, UTAUT, and UTAUT2 have been extensively used in hospitality research to analyze the motivation behind the use of digital technologies and to identify demographic differences in this regard (El Archi and Benbba 2023). However, the models in these studies usually included additional factors tailored to their specific contexts. For instance, UTAUT2 has been applied to analyze the usage of Google Maps (Gupta and Dogra 2017), TripAdvisor (Assaker 2020), Instagram (Järvinen et al. 2016), and TikTok (Wang et al. 2025) in tourism and hospitality.

3   Data and Methods

3.1   Questionnaire

For this study, an online questionnaire was developed that asked respondents to indicate how often they use specific apps/platforms (Google Maps, TripAdvisor, Instagram, TikTok) to get information about restaurants. For each app/platform, respondents were asked to indicate how often they use it on a 5-point scale: (1) never (2) rarely (3) sometimes (4) often (5) very often. The rating questions were asked twice: once for restaurants in known areas ("in the area where you live (or in an area that you know well)") and a second time for restaurants in unknown areas ("when traveling (or in an unfamiliar region)"). Respondents were also asked about certain demographic characteristics (age, gender, education) and had to rate their restaurant preferences on 33 evaluation criteria (also on a 5-point rating scale). These data on restaurant preferences were used to calculate the individuality of restaurant preferences for each respondent. To do this, the average distance between each respondent's own preferences (based on the individual ratings on the 33 evaluation criteria) and the restaurant preferences of all the other respondents was computed by applying a city block metric (Backhaus et al. 2006, Beier 2011, Beier 2025). The greater the average distance, the greater the individuality of the respondent's restaurant preferences. Finally, respondents were asked how often they eat out at restaurants in their everyday life (frequency). This variable is coded inversely, so a higher category indicates that they visit restaurants less frequently.

3.2   Survey Procedure

The questionnaire was extensively pre-tested with different people. Imprecise questions were adjusted. The final questionnaire was distributed through a panel provider to German-speaking people in Germany and Switzerland. The survey was conducted from May to June of 2024. The panel provider is a renowned market research institute in Germany and distributed the survey in its representative market research panels in Germany and Switzerland. All participants were well informed and their data protection, privacy, and confidentiality were guaranteed. The researcher received only anonymized data from the survey without any personal information. Against this background, no further ethical review was obtained.

3.3   Sample Description

A total of 1004 responses were received. Since there were no missing values in the sample, all data sets could be applied to the analyses. Table 1 provides an overview of the sample with regard to all nominal and category variables.

Table 1. Sample overview (nominal and categorial variables).

Item	Option	Number	Percentage
Country	Germany	504	50.2
	Switzerland	500	49.8
Age	1: 18–29	181	18.0
	2: 30–39	203	20.2
	3: 40–49	195	19.4
	4: 50–59	230	22.9
	5: 60–69	195	19.4
Gender	Female	493	49.1
	Male	507	50.5
	Diverse	4	0.4
Education	1: Still in vocational training	25	2.5
	2: Without a vocational qualification	57	5.7
	3: Completed apprenticeship/vocational training	485	48.3
	4: Technical college qualification, master craftsman/technician training	126	12.6
	5: Bachelor's degree	125	12.5
	6: Master's degree (incl. Magister, Diploma)	159	15.8
	7: Doctorate	9	0.9
	8: Other professional qualification	18	1.8
Frequency (Reverse-coded)	1: (Almost) daily	5	0.5
	2: Several times a week	50	5.0
	3: Once a week	125	12.5
	4: 2–3 times a month	262	26.1
	5: Every 1–2 months	259	25.8
	6: Less than once every 2 months	209	20.8
	7: (Almost) never	94	9.4

4　Results and Discussion

4.1　RQ1: Use of Social Media Platforms for Restaurant Information

The results for RQ1 are shown in Fig. 1. The results are presented in two parts, one for restaurants in known areas and one for restaurants in unknown areas. In each part, the four platforms studied are ranked by the mean of platform usage (based on the categories between (1) never and (5) very often). The rank and standard deviation (SD) are also shown. Finally, the percentage distributions of the five usage categories are shown. This makes it possible to distinguish between unimodal and bimodal distributions that would not be detected by the mean value. The percentage distributions are color-coded between white and blue. Deeper blue indicates higher percentages.

For Restaurants in Known Areas

Platform	Rank	Mean	SD	(1) never	(2) rarely	(3) sometimes	(4) often	(5) very often
Google Maps	1	3.206	1.187	10.7%	15.6%	30.7%	28.5%	14.5%
Instagram	2	2.223	1.388	47.2%	14.5%	16.0%	13.1%	9.1%
TripAdvisor	3	1.976	1.098	46.7%	21.4%	21.7%	7.9%	2.3%
TikTok	4	1.665	1.207	71.1%	9.5%	7.0%	6.7%	5.8%

For Restaurants in Unknown Areas

Platform	Rank	Mean	SD	(1) never	(2) rarely	(3) sometimes	(4) often	(5) very often
Google Maps	1	3.212	1.253	12.5%	15.6%	27.3%	27.5%	17.1%
TripAdvisor	2	2.171	1.255	44.2%	17.0%	20.9%	13.0%	4.8%
Instagram	3	2.054	1.295	51.8%	14.4%	16.3%	11.5%	6.0%
TikTok	4	1.613	1.124	71.3%	10.4%	8.5%	5.5%	4.4%

Color Coding: MIN   MAX

Fig. 1. Social media platform usage for information on restaurants in known and unknown areas.

The results show that Google Maps is clearly the most used platform for restaurant information in both known and unknown areas. The majority of respondents say they often or sometimes receive relevant information from Google Maps. In contrast, TikTok is clearly the least used platform. The majority of respondents report never using TikTok to inform about restaurants. Instagram and TripAdvisor are used moderately. However, Instagram ranks second in known areas, while TripAdvisor ranks second in unknown areas. This suggests that people tend to actively search for restaurants and use online review platforms (TripAdvisor) when they are in unknown areas, such as when traveling. In contrast, social networks (Instagram) seem to be a more useful source of information about restaurants in known areas, such as at home, where the need to actively search for new restaurants might be weaker (Beier and Schillo 2025). RQ2 explores these differences further.

4.2   RQ2: Usage Differences Between Known and Unknown Areas

The results for RQ2 are shown in Fig. 2. Here, the studied platforms are ranked according to the differences in platform usage between known and unknown areas. These differences are calculated as the mean value of platform usage in unknown areas minus the mean value of platform usage in known areas (see Fig. 1 for both mean values). The statistical significance of the mean differences was also tested. This was done using a nonparametric paired sample test, as each respondent rated each platform for both known and unknown areas. Because numerical rating scale data are used, a nonparametric test

(Wilcoxon's signed rank test) was applied (Goss-Sampson 2024). In this context, the effect sizes of the test (based on the rank-biserial correlation) and its significance (Sig.) are presented. The following thresholds provide an estimation of how to interpret the displayed effect sizes: <0.10 very small, 0.10–0.29 small, 0.30–0.49 moderate and ≥ 0.5 large (López-Martín and Ardura-Martínez 2023).

Positive differences indicate that a platform is used more often in unknown areas, while negative differences in this regard indicate higher usage in known areas. Finally, the distribution of percentage differences across the five usage categories is shown. These are color-coded in three colors: Green for positive differences, red for negative differences, and white for no differences. Deeper colors indicate larger differences.

Differences between Unknown and Known Areas

Platform	Rank	Mean	Effect Size	Sig.	(1) never	(2) rarely	(3) sometimes	(4) often	(5) very often
TripAdvisor	1	0.195	0.501	<.001	-2.5%	-4.4%	-0.8%	5.2%	2.5%
Google Maps	2	0.006	0.019	0.717	1.8%	0.0%	-3.4%	-1.0%	2.6%
TikTok	3	-0.052	-0.211	0.009	0.2%	0.9%	1.5%	-1.2%	-1.4%
Instagram	4	-0.169	-0.382	<.001	4.6%	-0.1%	0.3%	-1.7%	-3.1%

Color Coding: MIN (negative values)　　0.0%　　(positive values) MAX

Fig. 2. Differences of platform usage for restaurant information between unknown and known areas.

The analysis of the differences in the usage of the social media platforms for restaurant information shows a significantly higher usage of TripAdvisor in unknown areas compared to known areas. In contrast, the results also show significantly lower usage for Instagram and TikTok in unknown areas compared to known ones. These results further confirm the observations regarding TripAdvisor and Instagram from RQ1. In this regard, TikTok shows a similar pattern to Instagram, although somewhat weaker. Here, too, people use a social media platform for video communication (TikTok) less for restaurant information in unknown areas than in known ones. In general, social media platforms appear to be less useful for restaurant information in unknown areas than in known areas, compared to online review platforms (Beier and Schillo 2025).

Interestingly, the average usage of Google Maps is almost the same in unknown and known areas. However, in unknown areas, its usage is more concentrated in the extreme usage levels ((1) "never" and (5) "very often") compared to known areas. Some people tend to use Google Maps more frequently to search for restaurants in unknown areas (compared to known ones), while others use it less often.

4.3 RQ3: Usage Differences Between Subgroups of the Sample

RQ3 analyzes how the use of the social media platforms for restaurant information differs by age, gender, education level, and the individuality of restaurant preferences. To analyze these differences, two groups of comparable size were formed for each criterion. Nonparametric independent samples tests (Wilcoxon-Mann-Whitney tests) were then applied to compare the two groups. The results present the mean rating and its rank for the entire sample (all cases), as presented in RQ1, as well as for each of the two groups. The results of the group comparisons with independent samples tests are presented by effect size (based on the rank-biserial correlation) and significance (Sig.). Again, the effect sizes can be interpreted by the following thresholds: <0.10 very small, 0.10–0.29 small, 0.30–0.49 moderate and ≥0.5 large (López-Martín and Ardura-Martínez 2023).

Age. Two age groups were formed for the analysis of age differences. The younger group consists of people aged 18 to 49 (N = 579). The older group comprises individuals aged 50 to 69 (N = 425). The results are presented in Fig. 3.

Comparison by Age Groups		All Cases Rank	Mean	Age 18-49 Rank	Mean	Age 50-69 Rank	Mean	Difference Rank	Mean	Effect Size	Sig.
Known Areas	Google Maps	1	3.206	1	3.423	1	2.911	0	-0.512	-0.235	<.001
	Instagram	2	2.223	2	2.627	3	1.673	1	-0.954	-0.386	<.001
	TripAdvisor	3	1.976	3	2.190	2	1.685	-1	-0.505	-0.260	<.001
	TikTok	4	1.665	4	1.893	4	1.355	0	-0.538	-0.210	<.001
Unknown Areas	Google Maps	1	3.212	1	3.470	1	2.861	0	-0.609	-0.262	<.001
	TripAdvisor	2	2.171	2	2.446	2	1.798	0	-0.648	-0.287	<.001
	Instagram	3	2.054	3	2.408	3	1.572	0	-0.836	-0.352	<.001
	TikTok	4	1.613	4	1.836	4	1.308	0	-0.528	-0.220	<.001
		N = 1004		N = 579		N = 425					

Fig. 3. Comparison between older and younger people.

The results show that older people use all platforms significantly less often than younger people do to find restaurant information in both known and unknown areas. In known areas, TripAdvisor is more important to older people than Instagram is, but the opposite is true for younger people. Furthermore, the difference between older and younger respondents is largest for Instagram: The difference is −0.386 in known areas and −0.352 in unknown areas. These are the only moderate effects. All other effects are small.

This finding aligns with previous studies indicating that older adults generally utilize social and digital media less frequently than younger adults (e.g., Auxier and Anderson 2021, Hruska and Maresova 2020, Perrin 2015, Yates et al. 2015). However, the percentage of older adults using social media platforms has increased significantly over time (Perrin 2015). Additionally, a study on Google Maps showed that older people use it differently than younger people (Li et al. 2020) and findings from Switzerland indicate that older tourists are less likely to use mobile apps while traveling (Beier and Aebli 2016). However, a deeper look at the data shows that younger people tend to eat out more often in their daily lives than older people do ($\chi^2(6) = 34.865$, p < .001; Kendall's Tau-b = −0.156). Therefore, older people generally seem to need less restaurant information than younger people. This might be one reason why they use social media less for restaurant information.

Gender. To analyze gender differences, with men (N = 507) and women (N = 493) two groups have been formed for the group comparison. Only four cases involving people of diverse genders were found in the sample. Therefore, they could not be included in the group comparison analysis. The results are presented in Fig. 4.

Comparison by Gender Groups		All Cases		Men		Women		Difference		Effect Size	Sig.
		Rank	Mean	Rank	Mean	Rank	Mean	Rank	Mean		
Known Areas	Google Maps	1	3.206	1	3.158	1	3.258	0	0.100	0.040	0.257
	Instagram	2	2.223	2	1.996	2	2.448	0	0.452	0.178	< .001
	TripAdvisor	3	1.976	3	1.923	3	2.034	0	0.111	0.062	0.072
	TikTok	4	1.665	4	1.600	4	1.730	0	0.130	0.036	0.224
Unknown Areas	Google Maps	1	3.212	1	3.134	1	3.292	0	0.158	0.063	0.076
	TripAdvisor	2	2.171	2	2.069	2	2.280	0	0.211	0.099	0.004
	Instagram	3	2.054	3	1.858	3	2.247	0	0.389	0.168	< .001
	TikTok	4	1.613	4	1.554	4	1.669	0	0.115	0.050	0.085
		N = 1004		N = 507		N = 493					

Fig. 4. Comparison between women and men.

The statistical analysis shows that, in known areas, women use Instagram significantly more than men to find restaurant information. In unknown areas, women rely on Instagram and TripAdvisor more than men do for this purpose. However, the effect sizes are rather small, particularly for TripAdvisor.

These results are consistent with previous findings that women tend to use social networks in general (Hargittai 2008, Hwang et al. 2016) as well as Instagram specifically (Laor 2022) more intensively than men. Findings from another study also show that women place greater value on social media when it comes to planning trips (Osei et al. 2018). This fits well to the findings of this study on unknown areas. Finally, a detailed analysis of the relationship between gender and how often people dine out in their daily lives shows no significant correlation ($\chi^2(6) = 10.085$, p = .121).

Education. To examine differences between people of higher and lower education two groups were formed from the eight education categories surveyed. The higher education group consisted of categories 4 to 7 (N = 419). The lower education group was formed by the categories 1 to 3 and category 8 (N = 585). The results are shown in Fig. 5.

Comparison by Education Groups		All Cases		Higher Ed.		Lower Ed.		Difference		Effect Size	Sig.
		Rank	Mean	Rank	Mean	Rank	Mean	Rank	Mean		
Known Areas	Google Maps	1	3.206	1	3.391	1	3.074	0	-0.317	-0.148	< .001
	Instagram	2	2.223	2	2.377	2	2.113	0	-0.264	-0.096	0.006
	TripAdvisor	3	1.976	3	2.260	3	1.773	0	-0.487	-0.237	< .001
	TikTok	4	1.665	4	1.711	4	1.632	0	-0.079	-0.030	0.311
Unknown Areas	Google Maps	1	3.212	1	3.403	1	3.075	0	-0.328	-0.143	< .001
	TripAdvisor	2	2.171	2	2.494	2	1.940	0	-0.554	-0.241	< .001
	Instagram	3	2.054	3	2.212	2	1.940	-1	-0.272	-0.102	0.003
	TikTok	4	1.613	4	1.711	4	1.542	0	-0.169	-0.064	0.031
		N = 1004		N = 419		N = 585					

Fig. 5. Comparison between lower and higher educated respondents.

People with lower education use TripAdvisor, Google Maps, and Instagram significantly less for restaurant information than people with higher education. This applies to both known and unknown areas. The differences are most pronounced for TripAdvisor and Google Maps. However, the effect sizes are rather small overall. Furthermore, it is evident that people with lower levels of education use TikTok less frequently to find restaurant information in unknown areas than those with higher levels of education. While these differences are significant, they are also very small.

These results can be explained in part by the fact that people with lower levels of education tend to eat out less frequently. An analysis of eating out frequency in everyday life revealed that people with lower levels of education ate out significantly less frequently ($\chi^2(6) = 70.813$, $p < .001$; Kendall's Tau-b $= -0.211$).

In addition, these results align with those of other studies indicating that people with lower levels of education are less likely to use social media platforms (Auxier and Anderson 2021, Hruska and Maresova 2020, Perrin 2015). However, one of these studies found the opposite to be true for TikTok, showing that respondents with a college degree or higher used the platform the least (Auxier and Anderson 2021). This makes TikTok different from other social media platforms, and the results of this study support this.

In contrast, other studies have shown that people with higher education tend to use Instagram more frequently (Auxier and Anderson 2021, Laor 2022) and perceive online reviews, such as those on TripAdvisor, as a more trustworthy resource for travel information than people with lower education (Munar and Jacobsen 2013). Finally, further findings showed that, according to the Elaboration Likelihood Model (ELM), people tend to use online restaurant reviews differently depending on their educational level. Individuals with higher education levels tend to focus more on detailed review content, while those with lower education levels tend to rely more on quantitative restaurant ratings (Steur et al. 2022).

Individuality of Restaurant Preferences. In a final step, it was examined how people with higher individuality in their restaurant preferences differ from those with lower individuality when using social media platforms to find restaurant information. To create two equally sized groups, the sample was split based on the median individuality score calculated in this study. The results are presented in Fig. 6.

Comparison by Individuality Groups		All Cases		Higher Ind.		Lower Ind.		Difference		Effect Size	Sig.
		Rank	Mean	Rank	Mean	Rank	Mean	Rank	Mean		
Known Areas	Google Maps	1	3.206	1	3.279	1	3.133	0	-0.146	-0.082	0.020
	Instagram	2	2.223	2	2.345	2	2.102	0	-0.243	-0.077	0.024
	TripAdvisor	3	1.976	3	2.082	3	1.871	0	-0.211	-0.082	0.016
	TikTok	4	1.665	4	1.779	4	1.552	0	-0.227	-0.075	0.010
Unknown Areas	Google Maps	1	3.212	1	3.255	1	3.169	0	-0.086	-0.052	0.143
	TripAdvisor	2	2.171	2	2.267	2	2.076	0	-0.191	-0.069	0.047
	Instagram	3	2.054	3	2.177	3	1.930	0	-0.247	-0.070	0.039
	TikTok	4	1.613	4	1.747	4	1.478	0	-0.269	-0.082	0.005
		N = 1004		N = 502		N = 502					

Fig. 6. Comparison between respondents with lower and higher individuality of restaurant preferences.

The results show significant but very small differences in all comparisons, except for one. People with higher levels of individuality in their restaurant preferences tend to use social media platforms slightly more for restaurant information than those with lower levels. The exception is Google Maps in unknown areas, where no significant differences were found. The results can be partially explained by the fact that greater individuality in restaurant preferences also correlates slightly with the frequency of eating out ($\chi^2(6)$ = 47.807, $p < .001$; Kendall's Tau-b = -0.066).

However, it is also plausible that people with higher individuality in their restaurant preferences pay closer attention to restaurant-related information on social media, especially firsthand experiences shared via reviews, photos, and videos. This information appears more valuable to them when choosing a restaurant (Beier and Schillo 2025). In contrast, many people primarily use Google Maps to find places, particularly in unfamiliar areas, aside to its online review features (Ghita 2024, Horbiński et al. 2020). Accordingly, individual restaurant preferences might play a smaller role when using Google Maps in unknown areas than they do on other social media platforms or in known areas.

5 Conclusion and Outlook

The results of this study demonstrate how people use different social media platforms to find information about restaurants in known and unknown areas. The findings illustrate how valuable it is to apply the theoretical perspectives of information seeking behavior, media richness, uses and gratification, and technology acceptance in an integrated way to understand how people use social media platforms for specific purposes. In particular, this study shows why people use online review platforms and other social media platforms for restaurant information, based on their specific needs and the type of content that is used. It also demonstrates how information is shared, both when people actively seek it out (information pull) and when it is shared with them (information push). In this regard, the study shows how consumers apply social media platforms differently to find information about restaurants in known and unknown areas. It also explains how consumers use social media differently for restaurant information depending on their age, gender, education, and the individuality of their restaurant preferences.

The results might help people think about how they use different social media platforms to find information about restaurants. Making changes could help them use the platforms more effectively so that the available restaurant information better fits their needs and they finally have better restaurant experiences. Furthermore, the results of this study help restaurant marketing and management professionals understand how to use various social media platforms to reach consumers and attract new customers to their venues. This knowledge can be used to develop and implement more effective social media strategies for customer acquisition. For instance, the differences in social media application patterns for restaurant information in known and unknown areas could help to develop specific marketing measures in regard to TripAdvisor, Google Maps, Instagram and TikTok while distinguishing between local and non-local guests. The measures and strategies could also be better tailored to specific target groups based on the results of this study, taking into account age, gender, educational level, and the individuality of restaurant preferences.

The study has two notable limitations, which offer directions for future research. First, it is important to acknowledge that the findings are based on self-reported data. The respondents were asked to retrospectively rate the frequency of their use of four different platforms for restaurant information. Therefore, there is a possibility of inaccurate responses due to biased recall or perception. In this regard, future research could attempt to apply observational data to complement the findings of this study. Second, the study's findings are generally expected to be applicable to a wide range of countries. However, the study is closely tied to a specific Western European context, particularly the German-speaking regions. There may be significant differences in how social media and mobile services are used in other countries. Also, different social media platforms are more popular in other parts of the world, and these might differ in their functionalities from the platforms examined in this study. Conducting comparative studies with other European countries as well as with those in other regions, such as the USA or Asia, would be a fruitful direction for future research.

Acknowledgments. Parts of this research have been funded by Innosuisse (Swiss Innovation Agency) through an Innocheque grant (69124.1 INNO-ICT).

Disclosure of Interests. The author has no competing interests to declare that are relevant to the content of this article.

References

Alhabash, S., Smischney, T.M., Suneja, A., Nimmagadda, A., White, L.R.: So similar, yet so different: how motivations to use Facebook, Instagram, Twitter, and TikTok predict problematic use and use continuance intentions. SAGE Open **14**(2), 1–20 (2024)

Assaker, G.: Age and gender differences in online travel reviews and user-generated-content (UGC) adoption: extending the technology acceptance model (TAM) with credibility theory. J. Hosp. Market. Manag. **29**(4), 428–449 (2020)

Auxier, B., Anderson, M.: Social media use in 2021. Pew Research Center. https://www.pew research.org/internet/wp-content/uploads/sites/9/2021/04/PI_2021.04.07_Social-Media-Use_ FINAL.pdf. Accessed 13 June 2025

Azman, F.A.M., Mustaffa, N.: The impact of user generated content on food purchase intention through TikTok platform. Al-i'lam J. Contemp. Islam. Commun. Media **3**(2), 1–23 (2023)

Backhaus, K., Erichson, B., Plinke, W., Weiber, R.: Multivariate Analysemethoden, 11th edn. Springer, Berlin (2006)

Ballester, E., Ruiz-Mafé, C., Rubio, N.: Females' customer engagement with eco-friendly restaurants in Instagram: the role of past visits. Int. J. Contemp. Hosp. Manag. **35**(6), 2267–2288 (2023)

Beier, M.: Evaluation of restaurants and restaurant experiences - general weightings and individual deviations in the underlying evaluation criteria. University of Applied Sciences of the Grisons, Chur, Switzerland (2025)

Beier, M.: Digitale Strategien für Nonprofit-Organisationen Anfang des 21. Jahrhunderts. In: Vilain, M., Wegner, S. (eds.) Crowds, Movements & Communities?! Potentiale und Herausforderungen des Managements in Netzwerken, pp. 101–118. Nomos Verlag, Baden-Baden (2018)

Beier, M.: Die Entwicklung Sozialer Netzwerke von Gründerteams. Formulierung, Implementierung und Anwendung eines kognitionsbasierten Simulationsmodells. Universität zu Köln. Dissertation (2011)

Beier, M., Aebli, A.: Who uses mobile apps frequently on vacation? Evidence from tourism in Switzerland. In: Inversini, A., Schegg, R. (eds.) Information and Communication Technologies in Tourism 2016, pp. 549–562. Springer, Cham (2016). https://doi.org/10.1007/978-3-319-28231-2_40

Beier, M., Schillo, K.: Sources of restaurant recommendations and their importance for consumers in known and unknown areas: evidence from Germany and Switzerland. In: Nixon, L., Tuomi, A., O'Connor, P. (eds.) Information and Communication Technologies in Tourism 2025, pp. 411–422. Springer, Cham (2025). https://doi.org/10.1007/978-3-031-83705-0_34

Beier, M., Wagner, K.: Crowdfunding success of tourism projects. Evidence from Switzerland. SSRN Electron. J. (2015) http://ssrn.com/abstract=2520925. Accessed 13 June 2025

Berger, J., Iyengar, R.: Communication channels and word of mouth: how the medium shapes the message. J. Consum. Res. **40**(3), 567–579 (2013)

Berger, J., Rocklage, M.D., Packard, G.: Expression modalities: how speaking versus writing shapes word of mouth. J. Consum. Res. **49**(3), 389–408 (2022)

Bilgihan, A., Peng, C., Kandampully, J.: Generation Y's dining information seeking and sharing behavior on social networking sites: an exploratory study. Int. J. Contemp. Hosp. Manag. **26**(3), 349–366 (2014)

Boyd, A.: Multi-channel information seeking: a fuzzy conceptual model. In: Aslib Proceedings, vol. 56, no. 2, pp. 81–88 (2004)

Bitter, S., Grabner-Kräuter, S.: Consequences of customer engagement behavior: when negative Facebook posts have positive effects. Electron. Mark. **26**(3), 219–231 (2016)

Cassar, M.L., Caruana, A., Konietzny, J.: Wine and satisfaction with fine dining restaurants: an analysis of tourist experiences from user generated content on TripAdvisor. J. Wine Res. **31**(2), 85–100 (2020)

Cheng, W., Tian, R., Chiu, D.K.: Travel vlogs influencing tourist decisions: information preferences and gender differences. Aslib J. Inf. Manag. **76**(1), 86–103 (2024)

Choi, E.K., Fowler, D., Goh, B., Yuan, J.: Social media marketing: applying the uses and gratifications theory in the hotel industry. J. Hosp. Mark. Manag. **25**(7), 771–796 (2016)

Curras-Perez, R., Ruiz-Mafe, C., Sanz-Blas, S.: Determinants of user behaviour and recommendation in social networks: an integrative approach from the uses and gratifications perspective. Ind. Manag. Data Syst. **114**(9), 1477–1498 (2014)

Daft, R.L., Lengel, R.H., Trevino, L.K.: Message equivocality, media selection, and manager performance: implications for information systems. MIS Q. **11**(3), 355–366 (1987)

Davis, F.D.: Perceived usefulness, perceived ease of use, and user acceptance of information technology. MIS Q. **13**(3), 319–340 (1989)

Duan, Y., Khoury, C., Joh, U., Smith, A.O., Cousin, C., Hemsley, J.: Comparing climate change content and comments across Instagram reels, TikTok, and YouTube shorts and long videos. Proc. Assoc. Inf. Sci. Technol. **61**(1), 103–114 (2024)

El Archi, Y., Benbba, B.: The applications of technology acceptance models in tourism and hospitality research: a systematic literature review. J. Environ. Manag. Tour. **14**(2), 379–391 (2023)

Evans, J.S.B., Stanovich, K.E.: Dual-process theories of higher cognition: advancing the debate. Perspect. Psychol. Sci. **8**(3), 223–241 (2013)

Filieri, R., Acikgoz, F., Ndou, V., Dwivedi, Y.: Is TripAdvisor still relevant? The influence of review credibility, review usefulness, and ease of use on consumers' continuance intention. Int. J. Contemp. Hosp. Manag. **33**(1), 199–223 (2021)

Fodness, D., Murray, B.: A model of tourist information search behavior. J. Travel Res. **37**(3), 220–230 (1999)

Foster, A., Ford, N.: Serendipity and information seeking: an empirical study. J. Doc. **59**(3), 321–340 (2003)

Ghita, C.: Through the looking screen: exploring familiar places through Google maps street view. Postdigital Sci. Educ. **6**(3), 978–997 (2024)

Goss-Sampson, M.: Statistical Analysis in JASP: A Guide for Students, 6th edn. JASP, Amsterdam (2024)

Grange, C., Benbasat, I.: Opinion seeking in a social network-enabled product review website: a study of word-of-mouth in the era of digital social networks. Eur. J. Inf. Syst. **27**(6), 629–653 (2018)

Hargittai, E.: Whose space? Differences among users and non-users of social network sites. J. Comput. Mediat. Commun. **13**(1), 276–297 (2008)

Ho, C.I., Lin, Y.C., Yuan, Y.L., Chen, M.C.: Pre-trip tourism information search by smartphones and use of alternative information channels: a conceptual model. Cogent Soc. Sci. **2**(1), 1–19 (2016)

Hruska, J., Maresova, P.: Use of social media platforms among adults in the United States - behavior on social media. Societies **10**(1), 1–14 (2020)

Huertas, A., Orden-Mejía, M.: Do tourists seek the same information at destinations? Analysis of digital tourist information searches according to different types of tourists. Eur. J. Tour. Res. **32**, 1–22 (2022)

Hwang, K.H., Chan-Olmsted, S.M., Nam, S.H., Chang, B.H.: Factors affecting mobile application usage: exploring the roles of gender, age, and application types from behaviour log data. Int. J. Mob. Commun. **14**(3), 256–272 (2016)

Gamage, T.C., Tajeddini, K., Tajeddini, O.: Why Chinese travelers use WeChat to make hotel choice decisions: a uses and gratifications theory perspective. J. Glob. Scholars Mark. Sci. **32**(2), 285–312 (2022)

Garner, B., Kim, D.: Analyzing user-generated content to improve customer satisfaction at local wine tourism destinations: an analysis of Yelp and TripAdvisor reviews. Consum. Behav. Tour. Hosp. **17**(4), 413–435 (2022)

Garner, B., Myers, S.: Exploring how language drives engagement: an analysis of social media engagement on Facebook and Instagram in wine tourism destinations. Curr. Issues Tour. (2025)

Gupta, A., Dogra, N.: Tourist adoption of mapping apps: a UTAUT2 perspective of smart travellers. Tour. Hosp. Manag. **23**(2), 145–161 (2017)

Horbiński, T., Cybulski, P., Medyńska-Gulij, B.: Graphic design and button placement for mobile map applications. Cartographic J. **57**(3), 196–208 (2020)

Ishii, K., Lyons, M.M., Carr, S.A.: Revisiting media richness theory for today and future. Hum. Behav. Emerg. Technol. **1**(2), 124–131 (2019)

Järvinen, J., Ohtonen, R., Karjaluoto, H.: Consumer acceptance and use of Instagram. In: Proceedings of the 49th Hawaii International Conference on System Sciences (HICSS), New York, pp. 2227–2236. IEEE (2016)

Katz, E., Blumler, J.G., Gurevitch, M.: Uses and gratifications research. Public Opin. Q. **37**(4), 509–523 (1973)

Kim, W., Cake, D.A.: Gen zers' travel-related experiential consumption on social media: integrative perspective of uses and gratification theory and theory of reasoned action. J. Int. Consum. Mark. **37**(2), 89–116 (2025)

Kitchen, P.J., Kerr, G., Schultz, D.E., McColl, R., Pals, H.: The elaboration likelihood model: review, critique and research agenda. Eur. J. Mark. **48**(11/12), 2033–2050 (2014)

Klug, D., Qin, Y., Evans, M., Kaufman, G.: Trick and please. A mixed-method study on user assumptions about the TikTok algorithm. In: Proceedings of the 13th ACM Web Science Conference, New York, pp. 84–92. ACM (2021)

Knight, S.A., Spink, A.: Toward a web search information behavior model. In: Spink, A., Zimmer, M. (eds.) Web Search. ISKM, vol. 14, pp. 209–234. Springer, Heidelberg (2008). https://doi.org/10.1007/978-3-540-75829-7_12

Ko, H.C., Yu, D.H.: Understanding continuance intention to view Instagram stories: a perspective of uses and gratifications theory. In: Proceedings of the 2nd International Conference on Control and Computer Vision, New York, pp. 127–132. ACM (2019)

Kumsawat, P., Suttikun, C., Mahasuweerachai, P.: Does credibility matter on TikTok: the influence of food content creator types on restaurants' social media engagement and purchasing intentions. J. Glob. Mark., 1–18 (2024)

Kwon, W., Lee, M., Back, K.J., Lee, K.Y.: Assessing restaurant review helpfulness through big data: dual-process and social influence theory. J. Hosp. Tour. Technol. **12**(2), 177–195 (2021)

Laor, T.: My social network: group differences in frequency of use, active use, and interactive use on Facebook, Instagram and Twitter. Technol. Soc. **68**, 1–10 (2022)

Lee, S., Bae, G., Kim, H.: A study on the sustainable use intention of restaurant companies using the information attributes of SNS: the dual process theory. Sustainability **13**(22), 1–18 (2021a)

Lee, M., Hong, J.H., Chung, S., Back, K.J.: Exploring the roles of DMO's social media efforts and information richness on customer engagement: empirical analysis on Facebook event pages. J. Travel Res. **60**(3), 670–686 (2021b)

Lee, J., Kim, Y.K.: Online reviews of restaurants: expectation-confirmation theory. J. Qual. Assur. Hosp. Tour. **21**(5), 582–599 (2020)

Legris, P., Ingham, J., Collerette, P.: Why do people use information technology? A critical review of the technology acceptance model. Inf. Manag. **40**(3), 191–204 (2003)

Lepkowska-White, E., Parsons, A., Berg, W.: Social media marketing management: an application to small restaurants in the US. Int. J. Cult. Tour. Hosp. Res. **13**(3), 321–345 (2019)

Li, M.L., Chen, M.S., Sato, K.: Digital map design elements for local tourism: comparing user cognition between age of 20s and above 60. In: Shoji, H., et al. (eds.) KEER 2020. AISC, vol. 1256, pp. 55–65. Springer, Singapore (2020). https://doi.org/10.1007/978-981-15-7801-4_6

Li, H., Hecht, B.: 3 Stars on Yelp, 4 stars on google maps: a cross-platform examination of restaurant ratings. Proc. ACM Hum. Comput. Interact. **4**(3), 1–25 (2021)

Li, C., Kwok, L., Xie, K.L., Liu, J., Ye, Q.: Let photos speak: the effect of user-generated visual content on hotel review helpfulness. J. Hosp. Tour. Res. **47**(4), 665–690 (2023)

Li, H., Yan, J.: Does visual review content enhance review helpfulness? A text-mining approach. IEEE Access **12**, 27633–27647 (2024)

Lian, Q.L., Wong, I.A., Xiong, X.: Motivating social media sharing of food user-generated content on Instagram: how incentives drive social commerce. Tour. Rev. (2025)

Liu, W., Shih, H.P.: How do search-based and experience-based information matter in the evaluation of user satisfaction? The case of TripAdvisor. Aslib J. Inf. Manag. **73**(5), 659–678 (2021)

López-Martín, E., Ardura-Martínez, D.: The effect size in scientific publication. Educación XX1 **26**(1), 9–17 (2023)

Mathayomchan, B., Taecharungroj, V.: "How was your meal?" examining customer experience using Google maps reviews. Int. J. Hosp. Manag. **90**, 1–13 (2020)

Menon, D.: Uses and gratifications of photo sharing on Instagram. Int. J. Hum. Comput. Stud. **168**, 1–12 (2022)

Munar, A.M., Jacobsen, J.K.S.: Trust and involvement in tourism social media and web-based travel information sources. Scand. J. Hosp. Tour. **13**(1), 1–19 (2013)

Osei, B.A., Mensah, I., Amenumey, E.K.: Utilisation of social media by international tourists to Ghana. Anatolia **29**(3), 411–421 (2018)

Oba, D., Berger, J.: How communication mediums shape the message. J. Consum Psychol, **34**(3), 406-424 (2024)

Petty, R.E., Cacioppo, J.T., Schumann, D.: Central and peripheral routes to advertising effectiveness: the moderating role of involvement. J. Consum. Res. **10**(2), 135–146 (1983)

Perrin, A.: Social Networking Usage: 2005–2015. Pew Research Center. http://www.pewinternet. org/2015/10/08/2015/Social-Networking-Usage-2005-2015/. Accessed 13 June 2025

Scherr, S., Wang, K.: Explaining the success of social media with gratification niches: motivations behind daytime, nighttime, and active use of TikTok in China. Comput. Hum. Behav. **124**, 1–9 (2021)

Schmidt, K.N., Iyer, M.K.S.: Online behaviour of social media participants' and perception of trust, comparing social media brand community groups and associated organized marketing strategies. Procedia Soc. Behav. Sci. **177**, 432–439 (2015)

Steur, A.J., Fritzsche, F., Seiter, M.: It's all about the text: an experimental investigation of inconsistent reviews on restaurant booking platforms. Electron. Mark. **32**(3), 1187–1220 (2022)

Uthaisar, S., Eves, A., Wang, X.L.: Tourists' online information search behavior: combined user-generated and marketer-generated content in restaurant decision making. J. Travel Res. **63**(6), 1549–1573 (2024)

Varotsis, N., Mylonas, N.: A systematic literature review on information service management and information-seeking behavior in tourism. Cogent Bus. Manag. **11**(1), 1–20 (2024)

Venkatesh, V., Morris, M.G., Davis, G.B., Davis, F.D.: User acceptance of information technology: toward a unified view. MIS Q. **27**(3), 425–478 (2003)

Venkatesh, V., Thong, J.Y., Xu, X.: Consumer acceptance and use of information technology: extending the unified theory of acceptance and use of technology. MIS Q. **36**(1), 157–178 (2012)

Wan, Y., Nakayama, M.: Analyzing consumer decision-making patterns in online restaurant selection: a study of information processing styles on Yelp. Int. J. Hosp. Manag. **131**, 1–12 (2025)

Wang, P.: Exploring the influence of electronic word-of-mouth on tourists' visit intention: a dual process approach. J. Syst. Inf. Technol. **17**(4), 381–395 (2015)

Wang, Z., Kamarudin, S., Yaakup, H.S.: The travel trend in the age of TikTok: how older Chinese tourists choose their travel destination - an empirical study using the UTAUT2 model. Stud. Media Commun. **13**(2), 234–249 (2025)

Yarış, A., Aykol, Ş: The impact of social media use on restaurant choice. Anatolia **33**(3), 310–322 (2022)

Yates, S., Kirby, J., Lockley, E.: Digital media use: differences and inequalities in relation to class and age. Sociol. Res. Online **20**(4), 71–91 (2015)

Zhang, Y., Li, Q., Yan, J.: Exploring multimodal factors in online reviews: a machine learning approach to evaluating content effectiveness. J. Retail. Consum. Serv. **84**, 1–16 (2025)

Zhang, Z., Zhang, Z., Law, R.: Positive and negative word of mouth about restaurants: exploring the asymmetric impact of the performance of attributes. Asia Pac. J. Tour. Res. **19**(2), 162–180 (2014)

Revitalizing Community Ecology: The Impact of Gamified Interfaces on the Renewal of Green Spaces in Aging Communities

Xingyu Chen[1] and Jun Zhang[2(✉)]

[1] College of Design and Innovation, Tongji University, Shanghai 200092, China
[2] Hubei Institute of Fine Arts, Wuhan 430205, China
`80464662@qq.com`

Abstract. Against the backdrop of rapid urbanization, the issue of neglected green spaces in aging communities has become increasingly prominent, with traditional top-down governance approaches failing to sustain resident engagement. Using the Tielu Third Village community in Chongqing as a case study, this research designed and implemented a gamified platform interface incorporating map visualization, task systems, and a points-based reward mechanism. Through qualitative research methods, combining user behavior data and in-depth interviews, the study analyzes the platform's impact on resident behavior and community residual green spaces. The results demonstrate that gamification mechanisms significantly enhanced residents' motivation to participate, shifting their engagement from initial curiosity to ongoing and proactive task execution, and fostering a sense of emotional attachment and responsibility toward community green spaces. In addition, the platform's social interaction features effectively built stable neighborly collaboration, thereby strengthening community cohesion. The study also found that an age-friendly interface design with large font sizes and simplified operations improved user satisfaction among older adults. Overall, the research shows that gamification strategies provide a digital, low-intervention, and sustainable pathway for community micro-regeneration, with important application value in activating spontaneous resident participation, optimizing community ecological environments, and reshaping neighborhood interactions.

Keywords: Gamification · Aging communities · Neglected green space renewal · Resident engagement · Digital interaction · Community cohesion

1 Introduction

Against the backdrop of rapid urbanization, green spaces in aging communities are facing a crisis of degradation. Many plots of land that once held ecological and social value have gradually become overrun with weeds and litter due to long-term neglect and the absence of participatory mechanisms, turning into forgotten spaces. The abandonment of such green spaces not only undermines the quality of the community environment but also diminishes residents' willingness to interact and their sense of belonging [1].

A. Coman et al. (Eds.): HCII 2025, LNCS 16337, pp. 21–36, 2026.
https://doi.org/10.1007/978-3-032-12801-0_2

Traditional top-down renovation approaches led by government or property management may achieve initial improvements, but often fail to inspire sustained resident engagement, resulting in a cycle of neglect after redevelopment, especially in communities dominated by elderly populations [2]. Therefore, finding effective ways to motivate residents to care for and consistently invest in the development of green spaces has become a pressing issue.

Gamification, as a design strategy that stimulates behavioral motivation by incorporating game mechanics, has been increasingly applied in fields such as public services and environmental governance. By introducing task objectives, real-time feedback, and reward systems, it can enhance users' sense of participation and engagement [3]. However, research and practical application of gamification in the governance of neglected green spaces within communities remain limited. In particular, there is a lack of systematic exploration and empirical study on how to design gamified platforms that are both motivational and tailored to the behavioral characteristics of older adults. This study focuses on the renewal of neglected green spaces in aging communities. It involves designing and deploying a gamified platform interface to explore how digital, engaging, and collaborative approaches can stimulate residents, especially older populations, to care for, claim, and consistently participate in the revitalization of underutilized green areas. Through the introduction of task systems, point rankings, and social interaction features, the study attempts to construct a sustainable model of community green space co-creation and evaluate its effectiveness in enhancing behavioral motivation, improving the community ecological environment, and strengthening neighborhood interaction.

Based on the research objectives, four different research questions need to be addressed: Can gamification mechanisms effectively enhance residents' attention and motivation to participate in the revitalization of neglected green spaces in aging communities? How do residents develop a sustained participation behavior path when using the gamified platform? Does the collaborative mechanism of the platform interface effectively promote neighborhood interaction within the community? How do users evaluate the user experience of the gamified interface in practical use?

The gamified interface in this study provides a digital, low-intervention, and sustainable path for the micro-regeneration of green spaces in urban aging communities. Compared to traditional renovation models, this approach better activates internal community resources, enhances interaction among residents, and is especially suitable for the long-term governance needs of aging communities. It effectively demonstrates its practical value in stimulating spontaneous resident participation, activating internal community resources, and revitalizing neglected green spaces, offering a new practical reference for micro-regeneration.

2   Literature Review

In recent years, gamification, as a strategy that incorporates game mechanics into non-game environments to stimulate user participation, has been widely adopted. Deterding defined it as the use of game design elements in non-game contexts, emphasizing that it does not rely on a complete gaming experience but instead enhances user behavior motivation and participation sustainability through elements such as rewards, feedback, leaderboards, and challenges [4]. In urban and community planning, gamification is gradually becoming an important technological path to promote public engagement. For instance, the Game.UP project at the Technical University of Munich developed a gamified participation platform that integrates architectural design and human-computer interaction. Empirical evidence shows that gamification not only increased citizens' curiosity and social interaction but also enhanced user participation motivation, task engagement, and a sense of community belonging through features such as avatars [5]. In the context of green behavior intervention, Huang and colleagues conducted a systematic review of 56 studies and pointed out that the core mechanism of gamification as a green learning tool lies in setting challenging goals and incorporating feedback mechanisms. Key elements include point systems, leaderboards, achievement badges, collaborative tasks, and contextual feedback [6]. This provides theoretical support for the design of platforms aimed at promoting green behaviors, particularly in stimulating resident participation in environmental actions, reducing carbon emissions, and advancing low-intervention green renewal strategies. From the perspective of urban governance, gamification is seen as a way to break the traditional government-led, passive resident participation model. Fox proposed that embedding game elements into community resilience planning decision support systems (DSS) helps enhance residents' collaborative involvement in green space design, climate adaptation, and other areas, overcoming governance bottlenecks caused by green refinement and urban alienation [7]. Kavouras emphasized that through low-cost 3D modeling and open engines to build digital twins of cities, combined with game engines and co-creation mechanisms, non-professional residents' cognitive engagement and their ability to co-build urban spaces can be significantly enhanced [8].

It is worth noting that the effectiveness of gamified platforms is highly dependent on users' behavioral characteristics and technological adaptability. For older adults, researchers emphasize the importance of incorporating simplicity, supportiveness, and emotional feedback mechanisms into interaction design to reduce cognitive load and enhance willingness to use the platform. Thiel et al. point out that although older users initially express skepticism toward gamification, their participation frequency and satisfaction can increase significantly when provided with clear guidance and social feedback [9]. Koivisto and Malik highlight that although most gamification research focuses on younger users, existing evidence suggests that older populations can also benefit from well-adapted gamified interventions in areas such as health, social engagement, and cognitive stimulation. However, current research remains limited, and further studies are needed to explore interaction mechanisms and task design systems suited to older users [10].

In summary, gamification is evolving into an integrated urban governance strategy that combines participation activation, community interaction, and co-creative design. Although multiple international studies have demonstrated its positive impact on public engagement in urban renewal, further contextualized and localized research is needed, especially in aging communities, micro-scale spatial interventions, and technology-mediated environments.

3 Method

3.1 Research Framework

This study primarily adopts qualitative research methods, including case study, field observation, and resident interviews. A simplified gamified platform was developed featuring a visualized map of neglected green spaces. The interface enables residents to access information on the location, size, and ecological planting status of each plot, aiming to evaluate the platform's effectiveness in encouraging community participation in green space renewal. The research site is the Tielu Third Village in Jiulongpo District, Chongqing, China—a former staff housing area built in the 1950s by the Chengdu Railway Bureau. Characterized by significant elevation differences and a variety of green space types, the community presents a typical mountainous terrain environment and is considered representative for the study (see Fig. 1). The research is conducted in three main stages: platform interface development, field investigation and data collection, and data analysis. Special attention is given to the usability and long-term engagement of elderly users. By integrating technical deployment with user perspectives, the study explores how digital tools can stimulate resident participation in the transformation of neglected green spaces in aging communities, and systematically evaluates the usability of the platform and its ecological impacts on the community.

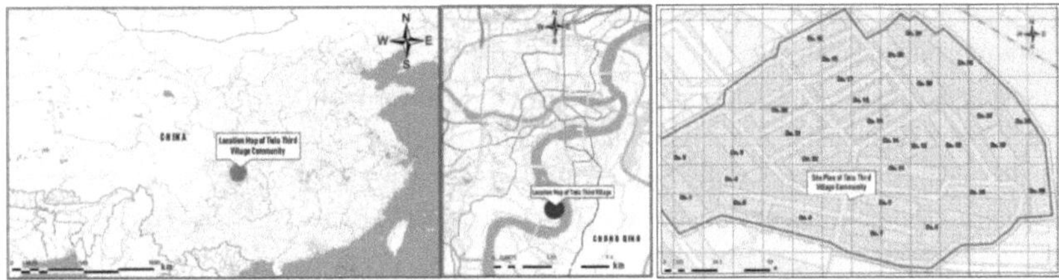

Fig. 1. Location Map of Tielu Third Village, Jiulongpo District, Chongqing, China.

3.2 Platform Interface Construction

The platform interface is based on a visualized community map module, integrating information on 18 representative residual green spaces within the neighborhood, including their locations, spatial forms, and ecological vegetation characteristics (see Fig. 2). This allows residents to intuitively identify and select suitable spatial units for participatory renovation. The system incorporates functions such as green space map browsing, task and incentive mechanisms, communication, and display features. Elements like leaderboards and honorary titles are used to enhance residents' sense of achievement and tangible feedback. To accommodate elderly users, the platform optimizes font size, icons, and relevant assistive features in the interface, improving operational accessibility and ease of use. Through these measures, the platform establishes a locally grounded system for community-based ecological renovation participation (see Fig. 3).

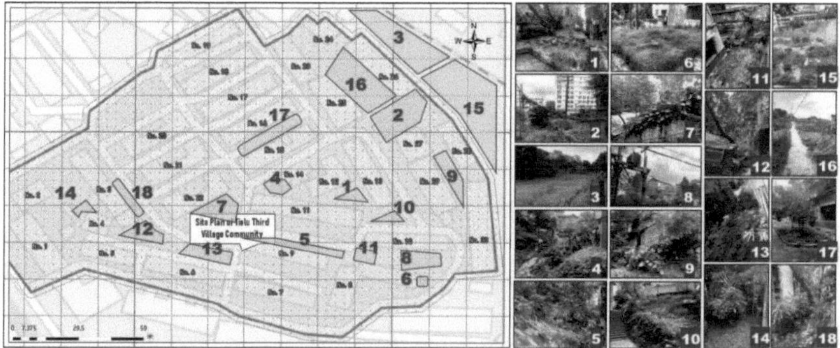

Fig. 2. Map of residual Green Spaces in the Railway Third Village Community.

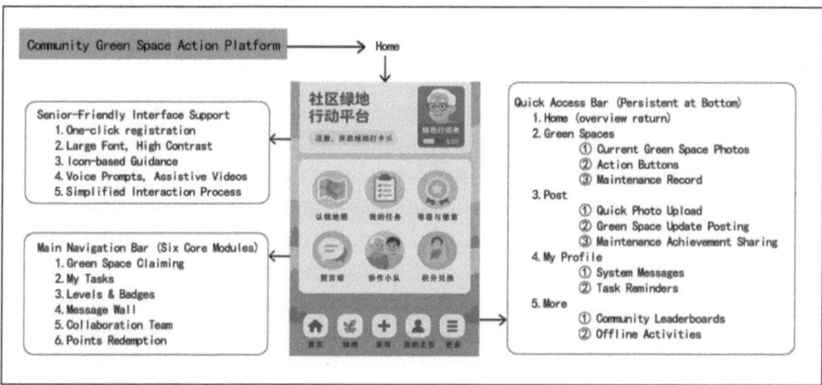

Fig. 3. Interface Design of the Community Green Space Gamification Platform.

Core Functional Modules. The platform interface comprises six core functional modules that together shape the basic user interaction flow. First, the Green Space Map Browsing Module displays the distribution of residual green spaces, allowing residents to click on each plot to view its location, form, current condition, and plant-related information. Second, the Task System Module offers a variety of tasks such as cleaning, planting, and maintenance, which residents can voluntarily claim and complete. Third, the Incentive System Module assigns points to each task and features a ranking system and honorary titles to encourage ongoing participation. Fourth, the Team Collaboration Module allows residents to invite others to join and co-manage specific green spaces. Fifth, the Message Board Module serves as a communal space where users can communicate freely, share achievements and experiences, initiate collaboration requests, and ask or answer questions. Sixth, the Point Redemption Module enables residents to exchange accumulated points for physical items such as seeds, watering cans, and fertilizers, thereby enhancing motivation to participate (see Fig. 4). This visualization- and collaboration-based interface design effectively improves residents' spatial awareness and enthusiasm for cooperative green space renewal [11].

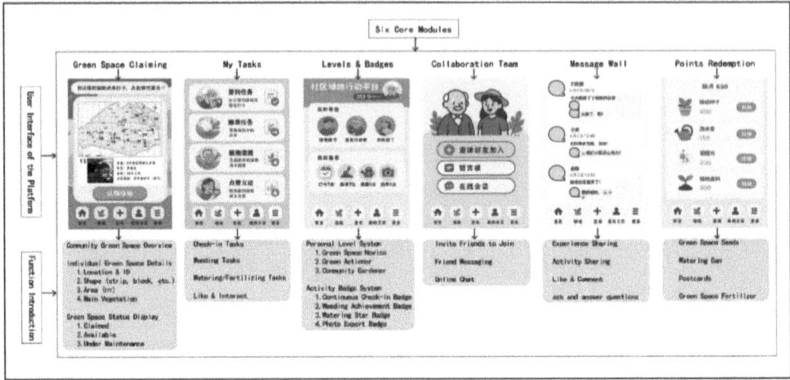

Fig. 4. Six Core Functional Modules of the Platform.

Gamification Mechanism Design.   To enhance residents' sustained willingness to participate, the platform interface integrates a gamification mechanism centered on task incentives, point-based feedback, and honor-based recognition (see Fig. 5, 6). First, green space renewal actions are broken down into quantifiable task units—such as cleaning, planting, documenting, and collaborating. Completing these tasks earns users points and experience, enabling progression within a green space level system. Second, an honor leaderboard is introduced to foster a sense of social recognition through friendly competition. Furthermore, the point system is directly linked to the incentive mechanism, forming a feedback loop between virtual rewards and tangible benefits. The overall framework embeds game logic (see Fig. 7) to establish a sustainable pathway for long-term community participation.

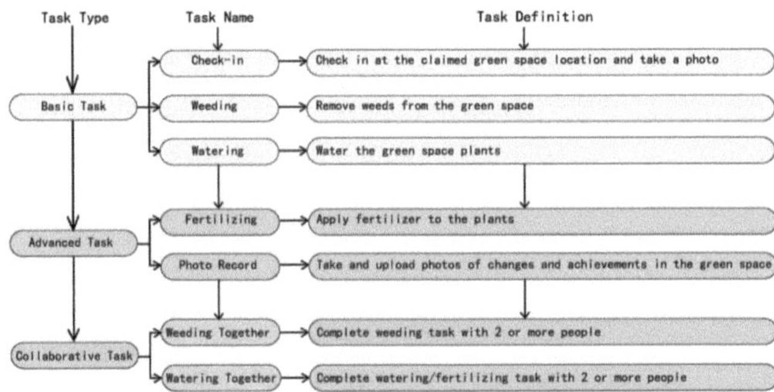

Fig. 5. Game Mechanics and Task Configuration.

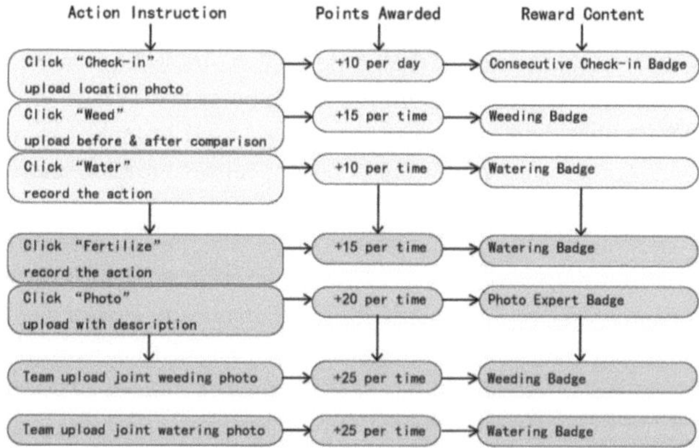

Fig. 6. Game Mechanics and Point Allocation.

Fig. 7. Game feedback loop process.

User Interaction Design. To enhance the usability and accessibility of the platform interfaces in aging communities, the interaction design adopts a simplified and intuitive modular digital layout. Large icons, enlarged fonts, and high-contrast color schemes are employed to reduce visual and operational burdens. Each task process is equipped with step-by-step guidance to assist users in efficiently completing green space claiming and task submission. Meanwhile, the interaction section includes message boards and achievement displays to encourage neighborly communication and experience sharing. Shortcut buttons are placed at the bottom of the main interface to minimize operational steps and ensure comprehensive support for elderly users.

3.3 Research and Data Collection

This study adopted a qualitative-oriented data collection strategy that combined user behavior logs with in-depth interviews to comprehensively analyze residents' experiences and perceptions of participation through the gamified platform interfaces. The platform is currently in pilot operation, targeting permanent residents of the Tielu Third

Village community, with elderly users constituting the majority of participants. The system automatically recorded users' basic behaviors, including green space claiming, task completion, and interactive communication. The aim was to uncover shifts in user motivation, interface adaptability, interaction habits, and potential barriers during use. A total of 10 residents were interviewed in depth, representing a range of age groups, usage frequencies, and levels of engagement. The interviews focused on initial impressions, cognitive understanding, emotional responses, social interaction features, overall functionality acceptance, and suggestions for improvement. All interviews were conducted with informed consent, anonymized, and carried out in accordance with ethical review standards. These data provide valuable user insights and help to understand how gamification mechanisms translate into real participatory actions in community settings, offering essential feedback for platform refinement.

3.4 Data Analysis

This study employed thematic analysis to examine interview transcripts and user message content, aiming to uncover residents' deeper experiences and behavioral logic when interacting with the gamified platform interfaces. The analysis began with line-by-line coding of interview data, focusing on individual experiences, emotional expressions, and behavioral responses related to platform usage. Based on initial open coding, recurring action patterns and expressions were identified through constant comparison and categorization of emerging concepts. In addition to interview transcripts, selected user messages were incorporated into the analysis to further investigate how users interpret and engage with key platform features, including task mechanisms, reward feedback, and social functions. All coding processes were independently conducted by the research team to ensure analytical rigor. This analytical approach not only reveals authentic user reactions but also provides insights into how individuals construct connections between digital interfaces and community actions. The findings offer theoretical support and practical implications for optimizing digital platform interfaces in ecological governance and neighborhood interaction within aging urban communities.

4 Result

In this process, the researchers focused on how users understood and responded to key components of the platform interfaces, including task mechanisms, reward feedback, and social functions. Through systematic analysis, several core themes were identified: the evolution of participation motivation, improvements in the green space environment, the formation of collaborative relationships and community cohesion, and the effectiveness of the platform interfaces and their feedback mechanisms.

4.1 Evolution of Residents' Participation Motivation

During the two-month pilot period, the gamified platform interfaces designed in this study effectively stimulated residents' spontaneous willingness to participate in the revitalization of residual green spaces. Most residents reported that features such as point rewards, level progression, and task feedback significantly increased their interest and initiative in green space renewal. Interview data indicated that many residents' motivations evolved from initial curiosity to a proactive approach to task completion. One interviewee (female, age 60) noted, "At first, I just thought it was something new, but gradually I really wanted to finish the tasks, because every time I completed one, I would get points and a level notification. It reminded me of the online farming games I played 20 years ago, and made me want to take care of it". The clarity of tasks and the immediacy of feedback played a key role in strengthening residents' sense of efficacy and sustaining their engagement. Additionally, residents shared that the activity encouraged greater participation in specific maintenance tasks, such as green space care, weeding, planting, and collaboration (see Fig. 8). One participant (male, age 65) stated, "I really enjoy planting flowers or cleaning up the surroundings. Seeing the changes in the environment with my own eyes brings me a sense of peace". These findings suggest that well-defined task design is especially effective in motivating long-term resident involvement.

Fig. 8. Community Residents Performing Green Space Maintenance Tasks.

4.2 Improvement of Community Green Spaces

Through active resident participation, several previously neglected and residual green spaces within the community have been improved. Specific renewal actions included plant removal and cultivation, facility repair, and spatial organization. Observations indicated that the visual quality and usability of these formerly neglected green spaces have increased to some extent. The renewed green spaces gradually transformed into daily leisure areas for residents, who now enter and use these spaces more frequently, demonstrating a stronger sense of spatial belonging (see Fig. 9). One resident involved in the green space renewal (female, age 68) remarked, "In the past, that green space was full of weeds, and everyone avoided it. Now, after we cleaned it up and planted flowers, a few of us can take a walk or chat there when we have free time".

Fig. 9. Improved Residual Green Space in the Community.

4.3   Collaborative Relationships and Community Cohesion Among Residents

The social interaction functions embedded within the platform interfaces effectively facilitated both online communication and offline collaboration among residents. Interview data revealed that following the commercial upgrade of surrounding areas, a growing number of rental tenants had moved into the community. The platform provided a new medium through which long-term residents could connect with unfamiliar neighbors, including renters, to jointly participate in the regeneration and maintenance of residual green spaces. These interactions gradually fostered stable collaborative relationships. Residents frequently gathered at the mobile community office point in Tielu Third Village to discuss strategies (see Fig. 10), engaging in mutual assistance, resource sharing, and experience exchange. These interactions led to the development of a grassroots support network centered around green space care. Several interviewees noted that the platform's interactive features helped transform formerly superficial neighborly greetings into meaningful cooperative relationships, enhancing the collective identity of the community. One resident (female, age 66) commented, "I met the tenant living downstairs through this platform, and we found we shared similar interests. Now we talk more and help each other regularly". This demonstrates how the platform interfaces significantly enhanced collaborative willingness and strengthened community cohesion.

4.4   Effectiveness of Platform Interfaces and Feedback Mechanisms

The user experience of the platform interfaces received positive recognition from residents, particularly in terms of operational simplicity and functional effectiveness. Interviewees consistently noted that the interface was clear and easy to navigate, with large font sizes and icon-based task guidance that significantly lowered the technological barriers for older users. For example, one elderly user (male, age 72) remarked, "The font on the platform interface is large and easy to read, and the operations are simple". In addition, the feedback provided through the point system and leaderboard allowed users to clearly perceive their contributions and personal progress, resulting in a strong sense of achievement and recognition. One resident (male, age 73) stated, "I used to just watch from the sidelines, but now after completing tasks, I always take the initiative to do more". Most residents believed that participating in the green space renewal through the platform was not only enjoyable and meaningful but also physically beneficial. The process enhanced their sense of belonging and responsibility toward the community, while also increasing their confidence in sustaining long-term engagement.

Fig. 10. Collective Consultation Among Community Residents on Planting Strategies.

5   Discussion

5.1   Behavioral Incentive Effects of Gamification Mechanisms

The findings of this study confirm that gamification elements such as points, levels, and leaderboards effectively motivate residents to take initiative in claiming and maintaining residual green spaces within the community (see Fig. 11). These elements reinforce users' intrinsic motivation by providing immediate behavioral feedback [3]. Unlike traditional approaches to community green space governance that rely heavily on external organizations or administrative interventions, the use of platform interfaces enables residents to perceive a direct connection between their actions and environmental improvements, thereby enhancing their sense of agency and sustained engagement. Notably, this mechanism is particularly effective in managing small-scale, fragmented, and under-governed spaces, where responsibilities are diffused and formal management is lacking. It demonstrates the unique value of gamification strategies in addressing governance challenges of neglected green spaces in aging urban neighborhoods. However, the study also found that the motivational effects of different task types varied. More specific and clearly defined tasks were more likely to encourage long-term participation. This suggests that residents prefer engagement activities that lead to tangible and goal-oriented outcomes [12], indicating that future gamified green space interventions should pay greater attention to the practicality and experiential quality of task design.

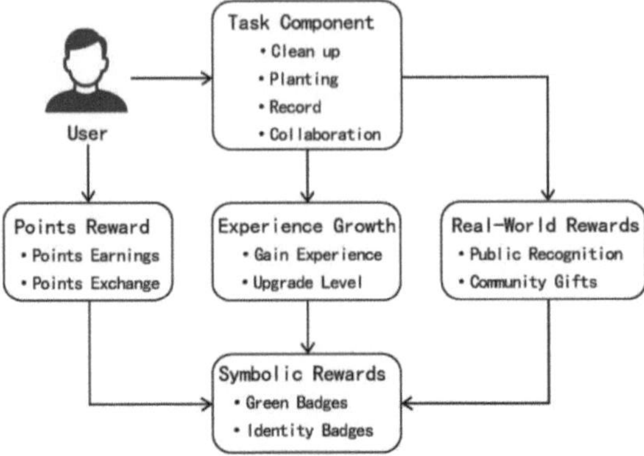

Fig. 11. Platform Incentive Logic and Task Points Diagram.

5.2   User Participation Pathway and the Construction of Continuity

The study reveals that residents' participation behavior followed a gradual transformation: from initial curiosity-driven engagement to stable task-oriented involvement, eventually culminating in a sense of emotional attachment and self-affirmation toward the community. This finding indicates that gamified platform interfaces can effectively guide residents from sporadic involvement to sustained commitment through well-designed task mechanisms, thereby enhancing a sense of belonging and community identity among users [13]. As residents engaged in specific tasks, they gradually developed emotional bonds with the green spaces. These bonds, in turn, fostered social identification and a sense of belonging through neighborhood interaction. Gamification not only increased engagement but also allowed residents to perceive the possibility of co-creating experiential community environments [14]. Furthermore, motivational elements such as point rankings—rarely adopted in traditional community governance—proved highly effective within the gamified design. The platform interfaces incorporated level-based rankings to mitigate the decline in user enthusiasm over time, thereby establishing a sustainable model for community participation. This design strategy not only sets residents' expectations for long-term engagement but also creates contextual conditions for ongoing social interaction.

5.3   Restructuring Social Relationships Through the Platform Interface

This study reveals the potential of gamified platform interfaces to reshape social networks and neighborhood relationships through the regeneration of residual green spaces in the community (see Fig. 12). Through interactive functions such as message boards, collaboration invitations, and achievement displays, originally loose community ties gradually evolved into stable cooperative networks. Residents shifted from individual actions to collective collaboration, forming green-space-centered social relationships. This emerging social network not only enhanced the overall engagement on the platform interfaces but also opened new possibilities for neighborhood interaction in aging communities. The findings further validate existing theoretical perspectives that gamified interactions can promote collaborative behaviors among residents [15] and enhance community resilience [16]. The study proposes that platform interfaces should not merely be regarded as technical tools, but as foundational structures for emotional connection and social interaction. Accordingly, future platform development should focus on strengthening the stickiness and integration of platform interfaces within the community's social fabric.

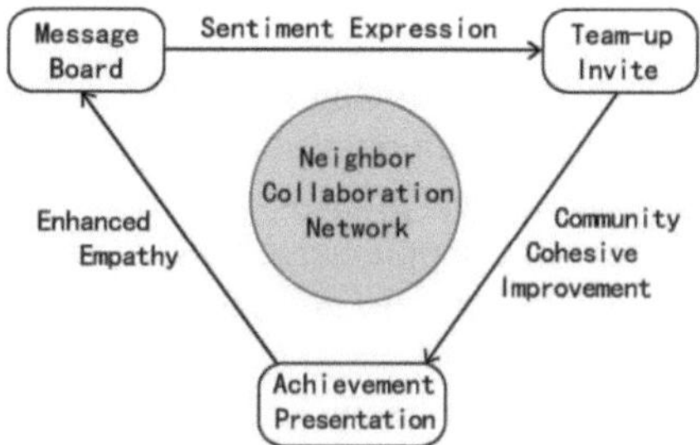

Fig. 12. Transformation Path of Neighborhood Relationships through Gamification.

5.4 Effectiveness of Adaptation Strategies for Elderly Users

This study pays special attention to the adaptability of elderly users when interacting with the gamified platform interfaces. Both operational experience and interface feedback indicate that design features such as large font sizes, icon prompts, and guided instructions effectively lowered the entry barriers and improved participation rates and satisfaction among older users. These results demonstrate that gamification is not exclusively a motivational mechanism for younger users; instead, through user-friendly and guided interface design, it can be extended to elderly populations, especially in low-tech, community micro-regeneration settings where adaptability is crucial. However, the study also found that, even with interface optimizations, some very elderly users still faced difficulties with technical operations, indicating that the digital divide remains a significant challenge for this demographic [17]. This finding suggests that future research and platform interface optimization should consider more diverse forms of support, such as further simplifying operations and exploring strong integration between online and offline activities to enhance the effectiveness of age-friendly design.

5.5 Limitations and Directions for Improvement

Although the platform interfaces have demonstrated certain positive outcomes within the pilot community, several limitations remain. First, the current incentive system focuses primarily on quantifiable user actions, while lacking in-depth evaluation of action quality and long-term ecological benefits. Second, the platform interfaces do not yet fully accommodate non-digital users, such as elderly residents with limited digital literacy or those unwilling to engage with digital tools. Moreover, due to the limited time span of data collection during the pilot phase, the long-term behavioral patterns and ecological transformations of the community remain insufficiently examined. Future improvements should aim to enhance the comprehensiveness and longitudinal depth of the evaluation system. Integrating intelligent features—such as AI-generated planting recommendations, AR-based greening simulations, and sensor-driven behavior tracking—can further improve the platform's precision and user adaptability. Additionally, more inclusive participation channels should be explored to support non-digital community members.

6 Conclusion

This study addresses the persistent challenges of neglected green space management and resident engagement in aging communities by providing a digital and gamified exploratory pathway. By transforming green space claiming and maintenance behaviors into a structured task system supplemented by incentive mechanisms, the approach emphasizes that residents can gain stronger motivation to participate through "play," while online interactive features facilitate neighborly support and communication. This model effectively fosters residents' spontaneous involvement and sustained action. The findings demonstrate that the gamified platform interfaces not only improve the environmental quality of community green spaces, but also stimulate collaboration and social awareness among residents—particularly increasing elderly residents' attention to and willingness for long-term stewardship—showing dual benefits in ecological co-construction and community interaction.

By encouraging individual initiative, the platform interfaces effectively activate the internal resources and innovative capacity of the community. The system offers multi-dimensional drivers of achievement, belonging, and social identity, facilitating a shift from passive acceptance to proactive co-creation among residents. This practice fully demonstrates that gamification is not only an effective tool for behavioral intervention, but also an important technological support for reconstructing grassroots social governance and community collaboration. It provides a flexible and interactive alternative to traditional community management models.

Future research can be further expanded in three directions: First, at the platform function level, integrating intelligent technologies such as AR visualization, sensor monitoring, and AI can enhance task precision and enrich personalized resident experiences. Second, at the incentive level, introducing long-term metrics such as behavioral quality assessment can strengthen the platform's ecological governance capacity. Third, in terms of application and dissemination, conducting empirical research across multiple communities, types, and generations can test the adaptability and value of gamification in different sociocultural contexts.

In summary, the gamified platform interfaces proposed in this study offer a digital governance pathway for the renewal of neglected green spaces in aging communities, combining playfulness, sustainability, and social cohesion, and demonstrating the innovative potential of gamification in community ecology and public space micro-regeneration.

Acknowledgments. The authors gratefully acknowledge the residents of Tielu Third Village in Chongqing for their enthusiastic participation and invaluable insights during fieldwork and platform testing. We also thank the design practitioners and academic experts who provided practical support on the study. Finally, we appreciate the research assistants who assisted with data collection and interview transcription.

Disclosure of Interests. The authors declare no competing interests. This study was conducted purely for academic research, with no commercial funding, or external institutional influence.

References

1. Wolch, J.R., Byrne, J., Newell, J.P.: Urban green space, public health, and environmental justice: the challenge of making cities 'just green enough' Landsc. Urban Plann. **125**, 234–244 (2014)
2. Xing, Y., Gan, W., Chen, Q.: Artificial intelligence in landscape architecture: a survey. Int. J. Mach. Learn. Cybern. (2025)
3. Seaborn, K., Fels, D.I.: Gamification in theory and action: a survey. Int. J. Hum. Comput. Stud. **74**, 14–31 (2015)
4. Deterding, S., Dixon, D., Khaled, R., Nacke, L.: From game design elements to gamefulness: defining "gamification". In: Proceedings of the 15th International Academic MindTrek Conference, pp. 9–15 (2011)
5. Muehlhaus, S.L., Eghtebas, C., Seifert, N., Schubert, G., Petzold, F., Klinker, G.: Game.UP: gamified urban planning participation enhancing exploration, motivation, and interactions. Int. J. Hum. Comput. Interact. **39**(2), 331–347 (2023)
6. Huang, M., Saleh, M.S.M., Zolkepli, I.A.: Gamification as a learning tool for pro-environmental behavior: a systematic review. Malays. J. Soc. Sci. Humanit. **7**(12), e001881 (2022)
7. Fox, N., Campbell-Arvai, V., Lindquist, M., Van Berkel, D., Serrano-Vergel, R.: Gamifying decision support systems to promote inclusive and engaged urban resilience planning. Urban Plan. **7**(2), 239–252 (2022)
8. Kavouras, I., Sardis, E., Protopapadakis, E., et al.: A low-cost gamified urban planning methodology enhanced with co-creation and participatory approaches. Sustainability **15**(3), 2297 (2023)
9. Thiel, S.K., Fröhlich, P.: Gamification as motivation to engage in location-based public participation?. In: Gartner, G., Huang, H. (eds.) Progress in Location-Based Services 2016. LNGC, pp. 399–421. Springer, Cham (2017). https://doi.org/10.1007/978-3-319-47289-8_20
10. Koivisto, J., Malik, A.: Gamification for older adults: a systematic literature review. Gerontologist **61**(7), e345–e357 (2021)
11. Lindquist, M., Campbell-Arvai, V.: Co-designing vacant lots using interactive 3D visualizations—development and application of the Land.Info DSS. Landsc. Urban Plan. **210**, Article no. 104082 (2021)
12. Poplin, A.: Playful public participation in urban planning: a case study for online serious games. Comput. Environ. Urban Syst. **36**(3), 195–206 (2012)
13. Morschheuser, B., Werder, K., Hamari, J., Abe, J.: How to gamify? Development of a method for gamification. In: Proceedings of the 50th Hawaii International Conference on System Sciences, pp. 1298–1307 (2017)
14. Özden, S., Arslantürk, E., Senem, M., As, İ.: Gamification in urban planning—experiencing the future city. Archit. Plann. J. **28**(3), Article no. 44 (2023)
15. Ng, P., Zhu, S., Li, Y., van Ameijde, J.: Digitally gamified co-creation: enhancing community engagement in urban design through a participant-centric framework. Des. Sci. **10**, e17 (2024)

16. Devisch, O., Poplin, A., Sofronie, S.: The gamification of civic participation: two experiments in improving the skills of citizens to reflect collectively on spatial issues. J. Urban Technol. **23**(2), 81–102 (2016)
17. Raban, Y., Brynin, M.: Older people and new technologies: towards a comprehensive model. Inf. Commun. Soc. **9**(1), 24–59 (2006)

Multimodal Speed Dating Dataset: Behavioral Cues, Psychological Ratings, and Empirical Findings

Ryo Ishii[✉][iD], Yoko Ishii[iD], Atsushi Otsuka[iD], Kazuya Matsuo[iD], and Junichi Sawase[iD]

Human Informatics Laboratories, NTT Corporation, Kanagawa, Japan
`ryoct.ishii@ntt.com`

Abstract. This paper introduces the Multi-Modal Speed Dating (MMSD) dataset, a large-scale corpus designed to support research on romantic impression formation and interpersonal interaction. MMSD contains 1,250 dyadic interactions between 147 Japanese-speaking men and women, along with synchronized multimodal recordings (audio, video, transcripts), detailed profile data, and responses to 33 psychometric scales. Participants engaged in a structured series of speed dates mimicking real-world dating scenarios and rated their impressions—including love and like—at four time points. Final preferences and mutual contact decisions were also recorded. The dataset is suitable for a wide range of research applications, from predictive modeling of romantic impressions based on pre-date attributes to exploratory analysis of verbal and nonverbal behaviors that contribute to romantic outcomes. Prior studies using MMSD have shown that features such as psychological profiles, facial traits, and interaction behaviors are effective for predicting romantic attraction, and that linguistic behavior is particularly predictive of final outcomes. We detail the construction of the dataset, summarize findings from previous analyses, and outline future research opportunities enabled by its richness—including time-series modeling, personalized prediction, and cross-cultural comparisons. MMSD represents a novel benchmark for interdisciplinary research across psychology, affective computing, and human-centered AI, offering deeper insights into the dynamics of romantic connection.

Keywords: Speed dating · Multimodal interaction · Dataset

1 Introduction

The pursuit of romantic partners is a fundamental aspect of human social behavior. In this context, *speed dating* has become a widely adopted research paradigm that offers both naturalistic social interactions and experimental control through structured, time-limited interpersonal encounters [12]. This setting enables researchers to investigate the mechanisms of romantic impression formation in sociologically valid contexts.

A. Coman et al. (Eds.): HCII 2025, LNCS 16337, pp. 37–49, 2026.
https://doi.org/10.1007/978-3-032-12801-0_3

Prior studies on speed dating have primarily focused on whether pre-encounter attributes—such as personality traits, physical appearance, and personal values—can predict post-date romantic interest (e.g., [29]). For example, research has examined associations between impression formation and various psychometric variables, including the Big Five personality traits, attachment styles, and sociosexual orientation. However, Joel et al. [22] reported that such traits account for only a small portion of the variance in mutual attraction formed during real interactions. Similarly, Eastwick et al. [10] argued that romantic evaluations are shaped more by partner-specific interactions than by general preferences.

These findings collectively suggest that speed dating outcomes are driven less by static trait-matching than by dynamic interpersonal processes. In response, recent research has increasingly examined how multimodal behaviors—such as backchannels, turn-taking, gaze, smiles, and linguistic alignment—contribute to romantic attraction [16,41,54]. For instance, linguistic style matching has been shown to reflect interpersonal rapport and predict romantic compatibility in early interactions [16].

Despite these advances, current research still lacks comprehensive, multimodal datasets that capture the full complexity of speed dating interactions. Existing corpora are often limited in size, scope, or modality, and rarely provide paired data on participant traits, psychological profiles, multimodal behaviors, mutual impressions, and decision outcomes. This limitation hinders both the development of predictive models and the deeper understanding of the behavioral dynamics underlying romantic decisions.

To address these gaps, we introduce a novel multimodal corpus of speed dating interactions that serves two central research purposes. First, it enables the prediction of romantic impressions, such as *love* and *like* scores [45], using information available before and during the interaction. Second, and more broadly, it supports the exploration of speed dating as a rich site of social interaction, allowing researchers to investigate what kinds of verbal and nonverbal behaviors contribute to romantic success.

To address these gaps, we introduce a novel multimodal corpus of speed dating interactions, the **Multi-Modal Speed Dating (MMSD) dataset**, which serves two central research purposes. First, it enables the prediction of romantic impressions, such as *love* and *like* scores [45], using information available before and during the interaction. Second, and more broadly, it supports the exploration of speed dating as a rich site of social interaction, allowing researchers to investigate what kinds of verbal and nonverbal behaviors contribute to romantic success.

Our dataset is characterized by the following features:

- **Multimodal behavioral recordings**, including speech, video, facial imagery, and biometric data captured in naturalistic speed dating settings.
- **Detailed participant profiles**, including demographics, interests, and multiple psychometric assessments (e.g., Big Five, self-esteem, social desirability).

- **Bidirectional impression ratings**, such as love, like, perceived similarity, and behavioral impressions collected before and after each date.
- **Outcome variables**, including whether participants chose to exchange contact information.

This corpus enables not only impression prediction tasks but also exploratory analyses of social dynamics, such as identifying the nonverbal cues and interactive sequences that predict romantic interest. Specifically, it supports both predictive modeling—e.g., estimating *like* and *love* scores based on participants' profile information—and exploratory investigations into which multimodal behaviors (e.g., gaze shifts, turn-taking patterns, prosodic modulation, facial expressions) play a key role in eliciting romantic interest or facilitating mutual liking during brief first encounters. Through such dual applications, the dataset provides a foundation for uncovering not only *who* is attractive to *whom*, but also *why* certain interactions succeed in fostering romantic interest, while others do not.

Moreover, in addition to releasing the corpus, we have already conducted a set of representative studies using this dataset. These include both (1) predictive experiments on *like/love* impression scores based on pre-date profiles, and (2) exploratory analyses that identify interactional behaviors—such as eye gaze, turn order, and backchannels—that significantly correlate with mutual interest. In this paper, we present the corpus along with findings from these initial investigations, offering practical demonstrations of the corpus's research utility.

We believe that our dataset will serve as a benchmark resource for computational modeling of romantic attraction, while contributing to interdisciplinary work across psychology, affective computing, and computational social science.

2 Dataset

2.1 Participants and Procedure

We constructed a large-scale multimodal corpus, the **MMSD dataset**, comprising 1,250 dyadic interactions between Japanese-speaking male-female pairs. A total of 147 participants (75 women, 72 men), aged between 19 and 60 years ($M = 31.9$, $SD = 8.6$), were recruited. All were native Japanese speakers and expressed a high level of motivation to meet potential partners, similar to typical speed dating participants.

Participants were assigned to 25 mixed-gender groups, each consisting of five women and five men. To increase diversity in pairings, 36 women and 40 men participated in more than one group. Pairings were arranged to minimize age disparities by taking into account both applicants' availability and their ages, thereby reducing the risk of mismatches due to extreme age gaps. The overall structure followed a standard Japanese speed dating format designed under the supervision of a domestic matchmaking organization, though its name is not disclosed here.

At the beginning of each session, all participants gathered in the same room for an orientation. They received instructions about the full procedure and

Fig. 1. Example of video acquired in MMSD dataset.

exchanged brief ceremonial greetings as a group. This initial phase corresponds to the "greeting phase" in the subsequent impression evaluations.

Each participant then engaged in face-to-face conversations with all five opposite-gender members in their group. The conversations followed a two-turn structure: a first round of 5-minute conversations with each partner, followed by a second round of 10-minute conversations with the same partners. All interactions were conducted in a seated face-to-face format.

2.2   Multimodal Data Collection

During each session, we recorded a total of 1,250 conversations: 625 five-minute interactions and 625 ten-minute interactions. For each dialogue, high-quality frontal video was recorded using overhead cameras, and clear audio was captured via headset microphones. In addition, manual transcriptions of the spoken content were produced for downstream linguistic analysis. Figure 1 shows a sample scene from the video data. Participants wore an Empatica E4 wristband[1], which continuously recorded heart rate (HR), electrodermal activity (EDA), skin temperature, and three-axis acceleration as physiological indicators.

2.3   Impression Ratings and Decision Outcomes

Participants evaluated their romantic impressions of each partner using the *Love-Liking Scale* [45]. The scale consists of 26 items divided into two subscales: 13 items for **Love** (romantic/affectionate feelings) and 13 for **Liking** (general fondness). Each item is rated on a 9-point Likert scale (1 = Not at all true, 9 = Very true), yielding subscale totals ranging from 13 to 117.

Impressions were collected at four key time points for each partner:

1. After the initial group greeting (pre-conversation baseline)
2. After the 5-minute conversation

---

[1] https://www.empatica.com/en-gb/research/e4/.

3. After the 10-minute conversation
4. After all sessions were completed (final report)

In the final report, participants also ranked the five partners they interacted with in order of romantic preference (1st to 5th) and indicated whether they would like to exchange contact information with each one (Yes/No). If both members of a pair selected "Yes" for each other, contact details were mutually shared by the organizers—replicating real-world speed dating procedures.

The Love and Liking subscales showed excellent internal consistency across all time points (Cronbach's $\alpha > 0.9$). For modeling purposes, we use the average of the 13 "Love" items as the *love-like score*, which serves as the main prediction target.

2.4   Profile Cards and Psychometric Measures

Table 1. Example of obtained profile items.

Items	Example
Age	28
Gender	Male
Blood type	A
Highest educational attainment	Bachelor's degree
Place of residence	Tokyo
Birth place	Osaka
Job	Salesperson
Interests	Film appreciation
Special characteristic	Not shy of meeting new people
Favorite food	Ramen
Favorite music	Hip hop
Places to go on date	Outdoor camping
My recent interest	Outdoor camping
Preferred characteristics	Cute smile
Free-text self-introduction	I am a 28-year-old male. I would like to meet a nice woman who is fun and relaxing to be with. (Omitted)

Before each conversation session, participants were provided with profile cards containing the self-reported background of their partner. These one-page cards included basic demographic and personal information such as age, gender, education, occupation, and interests. During both the 5-minute and 10-minute conversations, each participant held and referred to their partner's profile card to facilitate natural interaction. This method, commonly utilized in Japanese speed dating, was designed to support smoother exchanges and mutual understanding. See Table 1 for examples.

In addition to profile data, participants completed a comprehensive battery of psychological assessments. On a separate day, they answered 90 items drawn from 33 psychometric scales. These scales cover a wide range of constructs, including personality traits, values concerning family and relationships, interpersonal attitudes, communication styles, and views on life and romantic partnership. Table 2 summarizes representative scales included in the assessment battery, along with their subcomponents, number of dimensions, item counts, and scale types.

2.5   Ethical Considerations

All experimental procedures were reviewed and approved by the ethics and personal information protection committee of NTT. Participants were thoroughly informed of the study's objectives, data usage, and handling of personal information. Written informed consent was obtained from all participants prior to data collection. In return for their time and cooperation, participants received adequate monetary compensation.

3   Previous Studies Using the MMSD Dataset

To illustrate the utility of the MMSD dataset, we introduce two representative studies that leveraged different aspects of the corpus to explore impression prediction and behavioral analysis in romantic contexts. These studies exemplify how MMSD enables both static, trait-based modeling and dynamic, interaction-based analyses to understand the mechanisms underlying romantic interest and decision-making.

3.1   Predicting Romantic Impressions from Pre-date Information

One line of research examined whether post-date romantic impressions—specifically, Love and Like scores—could be accurately predicted using only pre-interaction data available prior to face-to-face meetings [17]. The researchers built regression models using three categories of features: (1) demographic and personal profile information (e.g., age, occupation, hobbies), (2) facial appearance features extracted from photographs, and (3) responses to 33 psychometric scales covering a broad range of individual differences.

Their analysis demonstrated that the most accurate predictions of women's Love scores were achieved when combining all three feature types, while predictions for women's Like scores and for both Love and Like scores of men were most accurate when using only psychometric features. This suggests that personality- and value-related traits play a central role in impression formation, particularly among male participants. The study also reported which specific features—such

Table 2. Representative psychometric scales with subscales, dimensionality, item counts, and response formats.

Scale	Subscales / Dimensions	Dims.	Items	Scale Type
Rosenberg Self-Esteem Scale (RSES) [42]	• Global Self-Esteem	1	10	5-point Likert
Self-Consciousness Scale [48,51]	• Public Self-Consciousness • Private Self-Consciousness • Social Anxiety	3	23	7-point Likert
Immersion Scale [47]	• Self-Preoccupation • External-Preoccupation	2	19	5-point Likert
Big Five Scale [43]	• Openness • Conscientiousness • Extraversion • Agreeableness • Neuroticism	5	60	7-point Likert
Sex Role Egalitarianism Scale—Short Version for Japanese Adults (SESRA) [53]	• Egalitarian Attitudes	1	15	5-point Likert
Gender Identity Scale [9]	• Acceptance of One's Own Gender • Identification with Parents • Intimacy with the Opposite Sex	3	30	5-point Likert
Trait Shyness Scale [1]	• Trait Shyness Scale	1	16	5-point Likert
Self-Monitoring Scale [3,21]	• Extraversion • Other-Directedness • Expressive Self-Presentation	3	25	5-point Likert
Importanceof Clothing Questionnaire [5,23]	• Clothing Interest as a Means of Enhancing Individuality • Clothing Interest for Achieving Psychological Stability • Clothing Interest in Pursuit of Aesthetic Suitability • Clothing Interest for Achieving Social Conformity • Clothing Interest in Pursuit of Comfort • Clothing Interest for Theoretical Justification • Clothing Interest for Expressing Modesty • Clothing Interest for Enhancing Interpersonal Appearance	8	22	5-point Likert
Romantic Love Attitude Scale [55]	• Romanticism toward Love • Marriage-Oriented Love • Belief in the Power of Love	3	41	5-point Likert
Lee's Love Type Scale 2nd version (LETS-2) [15,32,34]	• Eros • Ludus • Storge • Pragma • Mania • Agape	6	53	5-point Likert
Interpersonal Trust Scale [44]	• Interpersonal Trust	1	17	5-point Likert
Family Adaptability and Cohesion Evaluation Scale III (FACES III) [30,39]	• Cohesion • Adaptability	2	20	5-point Likert
Friendship Orientation Scale [38]	• Group-Oriented Type • Interpersonal Withdrawal Type • Empathy-Oriented Type	3	21	4-point Likert
Kikuchi's Social Skills Scale (KiSS-18) [25]	• Basic Skills • Advanced Skills • Emotional Regulation • Alternative to Aggression • Stress Management • Planning Skills	6	18	5-point Likert
Value Orientation Scale [46,50]	• Theoretical Value • Economic Value • Aesthetic Value • Religious Value • Social Value • Political (Power) Value	6	72	5-point Likert
TBS General Preference Survey [56]	• Family-Centered Values • Present-Oriented Lifestyle • International/Overseas Orientation • Outdoor Leisure Orientation • Visual Media Preference • Traditional Values Revival • Nature Orientation • Energy & Resource Conservation • Lifestyle Enrichment Orientation • Interpersonal Affinity • Interest in Life After Retirement • Simple Life Orientation	16	16	Yes/No
Yutori (Leeway) Scale [14]	• Pleasure Orientation • Environmental Comfort • Challenge Orientation • Temporal Autonomy • Competence • Affluence • Satisfaction and Stability • Spontaneity	8	50	7-point Likert
Ikigai (Life Purpose) Feeling Scale [26]	• Satisfaction with Current Life • Hedonic Enjoyment of Life • Sense of Existential Value • Motivation	4	31	3-point Likert
Way of Life Scale [18]	• Active and Practical Attitude • Self-Creation and Development • Coexistence with Others • Lack of Obsession/Non-Attachment • Respect for Others	5	28	5-point Likert
Privacy Orientation Scale [20,33,40]	• Solitude Preference • Autonomous Will • Intimacy with Friends • Expectation of Consideration • Intimacy with Family • Detached Life • Isolation	7	21	7-point Likert
Multidimensional Empathy Scale [7,8,36]	• Empathic Concern • Personal Distress • Fantasy • Perspective Taking	4	30	5-point Likert
Goal Orientation Scale in Friendship Situations [11,28]	• Experience and Growth Orientation • Evaluation-Approach Orientation • Evaluation-Avoidance Orientation	3	25	4-point Likert
Affiliation Motivation Scale [52]	• Rejection Anxiety • Affiliative Tendency	2	18	5-point Likert
Loneliness Scale by Ochiai (LSO) [6]	• Loneliness in Unstructured situations (LSO-U) • Loneliness in Everyday social situations (LSO-E)	2	16	5-point Likert
Divorce Attitudes Scale [37]	• Negative Image of Divorced Parents • Negative Image of Children from Divorced Families • Negative Evaluation of Divorce • Personal Growth through Divorce • Increase in Divorce Due to Women's Economic Independence	5	32	4-point Likert
Friendship Relationship Measurement Scale [57]	• Self-Disclosure and Trust • Deep Involvement and Concern • Commonality • Intimacy • Mutual Encouragement and Refinement	5	27	4-point Likert
Love Image Scale [24]	• Importance and Necessity • Rationality and Added Value • Mutual Relationship • Exclusivity and Possessiveness • Impulsivity and Blindness • Devotion • Growth	7	27	7-point Likert
Self-Concealment Scale [27,31]	• Tendency to Conceal Personal Information	1	10	5-point Likert
Communication Skills Scale (ENDCOREs) [13]	• Self-Control • Expressiveness • Decoding Skills • Assertiveness • Acceptance of Others • Relationship Coordination	6	24	7-point Likert
Daily Life Skills Scale [4,49]	• Affiliation • Leadership • Planning • Sensitivity • Information Summarization • Self-Esteem • Positive Thinking • Interpersonal Manners	8	24	4-point Likert
Subjective Well-Being Scale (SWBS) [19]	• Positive Feelings Toward Life • Sense of Accomplishment • Self-Confidence • Disappointment in Life	4	12	4-point Likert
Situational Interpersonal Anxiety Scale [35]	• Anxiety in Presentations and Public Speaking • Anxiety with Unfamiliar People • Anxiety in Opposite-Gender Interactions • Anxiety in Silence During Interactions • Anxiety Around Superiors	5	30	5-point Likert

as romantic attitudes, self-esteem, and emotional openness—were most informative for prediction. These findings support the feasibility of impression prediction in speed dating contexts and offer insights for improving algorithmic partner-matching systems.

3.2 Multimodal Behavioral Prediction of Speed Dating Outcomes

Another study focused on behavioral dynamics observed during the speed dating interactions themselves [2]. Specifically, it aimed to determine whether multimodal features—visual, acoustic, and linguistic—could predict whether two participants would mutually choose to exchange contact information at the end of the session.

Rather than using entire 10-minute interactions, the study analyzed specific temporal segments and found that behavioral patterns observed during the 2–4-minute and 9–10-minute windows were particularly predictive. This suggests that both early impressions and final interaction moments carry heightened importance in romantic decision-making.

Among the analyzed modalities, linguistic behaviors emerged as the strongest predictors, followed by acoustic and visual cues. These findings emphasize the value of speech-based interaction signals in forecasting dating outcomes. The researchers also proposed directions for improvement, such as incorporating sequential modeling techniques and features that capture interactional synchrony.

Together, these studies underscore the richness and flexibility of the MMSD dataset. The first demonstrates how pre-date individual characteristics can forecast romantic evaluations, while the second reveals how subtle behavioral dynamics during conversation contribute to interpersonal outcomes. Taken together, they show how MMSD supports both predictive and exploratory research on romantic interaction.

4 Future Directions and Broad Potential

The MMSD dataset offers a promising foundation for advancing research in romantic interaction, impression formation, and interpersonal communication. Its unique strengths lie not only in its multimodal nature but also in the richness of data capturing individual psychological traits, behavioral signals, and reciprocal evaluations. Building on the insights from prior studies, we outline here several avenues for future exploration and development.

4.1 Multimodal Temporal Modeling of Interaction Dynamics

One promising direction is to treat conversational data as time-series and develop models that capture temporal dynamics across modalities. While initial studies have relied on aggregated features or fixed time slices, future work may leverage

RNNs (e.g., LSTM), Transformers, and multimodal fusion networks to track fine-grained patterns in gaze, facial expressions, and prosody over time.

In particular, capturing synchrony—such as the timing of backchannels, gaze alignment, and lexical entrainment—can help explain why certain interactions are more romantically successful than others.

4.2   Personalized Modeling Based on Individual Differences

The inclusion of 33 psychometric scales allows for personalized modeling of impression formation. For example, participants with high versus low self-disclosure tendencies may respond differently to the same utterance or behavior.

Future research could focus on personalized impression prediction that incorporates personality traits and values, enabling the development of more adaptive and psychologically grounded matching systems.

4.3   Causal Inference and Intervention Strategies

The dataset's design—including multiple impression measurement points (after greetings, 5 min, 10 min, and final decision)—provides opportunities for studying impression change. Techniques such as difference-in-differences or structural equation modeling could be applied to answer causal questions like: What behaviors lead to improved impressions? Can first impressions be overturned?

Such insights could inform the design of conversation coaching tools or interaction support systems.

4.4   Cross-Cultural and Cross-Linguistic Extensions

While all MMSD participants are native Japanese speakers, this cultural consistency also opens the door to comparative studies. Collecting similar data in other countries or languages would enable analysis of cross-cultural differences in romantic behavior, impression dynamics, and communication norms.

This line of work could contribute to cross-cultural psychology and the development of universal or culture-sensitive computational models.

4.5   Applications in Affective Computing and Human-AI Interaction

The MMSD dataset is well-suited for training emotion-aware systems and dialogue agents. Applications may include romantic coaching robots, virtual dating simulators, or impression analysis tools that provide feedback based on behavioral patterns.

Its inclusion of bidirectional impression ratings also enables dyadic modeling—i.e., jointly predicting the impressions of both participants—which could be critical in estimating mutual compatibility.

4.6 Ethical Considerations and Responsible Use

Modeling romantic preferences and attraction raises issues of privacy and bias. Future work should prioritize fairness, transparency, and consent, ensuring that system design is ethically informed and aligned with user values.

4.7 Toward a Comprehensive Understanding of Romantic Interaction

Altogether, the MMSD dataset offers a rare opportunity to bridge psychology, social science, and computational modeling. Its scale and richness enable not only the prediction of romantic outcomes but also deeper investigation into the mechanisms of human connection.

We envision future research leveraging this resource to explore why certain conversations spark interest and others fall flat, thus contributing to a scientific understanding of how people connect in brief but meaningful encounters.

5 Conclusion

This paper introduced the Multi-Modal Speed Dating (MMSD) dataset, a large-scale and richly annotated corpus designed to support research on romantic impression formation and interpersonal behavior. The dataset comprises 1,250 dyadic interactions between 147 Japanese-speaking men and women, accompanied by detailed multimodal recordings, psychological profiles, and mutual evaluations across multiple time points. All data were collected in a setting supervised to simulate realistic speed dating procedures, ensuring high sociological validity and strong participant engagement.

We have outlined how MMSD supports both predictive and exploratory research paradigms. Previous studies using this corpus have demonstrated that romantic impressions (e.g., love and like scores) can be effectively predicted from a combination of pre-date profiles, psychometric attributes, and behavioral cues during interactions. Moreover, the dataset enables fine-grained analyses of interactional dynamics, such as the role of linguistic, acoustic, and visual behaviors in shaping romantic outcomes.

In addition to reporting empirical findings, we have discussed broad future directions made possible by the corpus, including personalized modeling, multimodal time-series analysis, causal inference, and culturally comparative research. The dataset also opens pathways toward practical applications in affective computing, AI-mediated communication, and interpersonal training systems.

We believe that MMSD represents a foundational resource for interdisciplinary research at the intersection of psychology, computational social science, and human-centered AI. By capturing the rich complexity of early romantic interactions, the dataset provides not only a benchmark for modeling romantic compatibility but also a lens through which to better understand the fundamental question of how people connect.

References

1. Aikawa, A.: A study on the reliability and validity of a scale to measure shyness as a trait. Jpn. J. Psychol. **62**(3), 149–155 (1991)
2. Azuma, N., Shikama, D., Ogushi, A., Onishi, T., Ishii, R., Miyata, A.: What timing and behavior patterns determine speed dating success in Japan? In: Extended Abstracts of the 2025 CHI Conference on Human Factors in Computing Systems (CHI EA '25), pp. 594:1–594:6. Association for Computing Machinery, New York, NY, USA (2025). https://doi.org/10.1145/3706599.3720028
3. Briggs, S.R., Cheek, J.M., Buss, A.H.: An analysis of the self-monitoring scale. J. Pers. Soc. Psychol. **38**, 679–686 (1980)
4. Brooks, D.K.J.: A life-skills taxonomy: defining elements of effective functioning through the use of the Delphi technique. Unpublished Doctoral Dissertation, University of Georgia, Athens, GA (1984)
5. Creekmore, A.M.: Methods of measuring clothing variables, Technical report Project No. 783, Michigan Agricultural Experiment Station, Michigan State University, East Lansing (1971)
6. Russell, D., Peplau, L.A., Ferguson, M.L.: Developing a measure of loneliness. J. Pers. Assess. **42**(3), 290–294 (1978)
7. Davis, M.H.: A multidimensional approach to individual differences in empathy. JSAS Catalog Sel. Doc. Psychol. **10**, 85 (1980)
8. Davis, M.H.: Empathy: A Social Psychological Approach. Brown and Benchmark, Madison, WI (1994)
9. Doi, I.: Development of the gender identity scale. Jpn. J. Educ. Psychol. **44**, 187–194 (1996). In Japanese with English abstract
10. Eastwick, P.W., Finkel, E.J.: Sex differences in mate preferences revisited: do people know what they initially desire in a romantic partner? J. Pers. Soc. Psychol. **101**(3), 513–530 (2011)
11. Elliot, A.J., Church, M.A.: A hierarchical model of approach and avoidance achievement motivation. J. Pers. Soc. Psychol. **72**(1), 218–232 (1997)
12. Finkel, E.J., Eastwick, P.W.: Speed-dating as an invaluable tool for studying romantic attraction: a methodological primer. Pers. Relat. **15**(2), 149–166 (2008)
13. Fujimoto, M., Daibo, I.: Endcore: a hierarchical structure theory of communication skills. Jpn. J. Pers. **15**(3), 347–361 (2007)
14. Furukawa, H., Yamashita, K., Yagi, R.: The structure of Yutori (Leeway). Jpn. J. Soc. Psychol. **9**, 171–180 (1993)
15. Hendrick, C., Hendrick, S.: A theory and method of love. J. Pers. Soc. Psychol. **50**(2), 392–402 (1986)
16. Ireland, M.E., Slatcher, R.B., Eastwick, P.W., Scissors, L.E., Finkel, E.J., Pennebaker, J.W.: Language style matching predicts relationship initiation and stability. Psychol. Sci. **22**(1), 39–44 (2011)
17. Ishii, R., et al.: Prediction of love-like scores after speed dating based on pre-obtainable personal characteristic information. In: Human-Computer Interaction – INTERACT 2023. LNCS, vol. 14145, pp. 551–556. Springer (2023). https://doi.org/10.1007/978-3-031-42293-5_71
18. Itatsu, H.: A study on the "way of life": scale construction and its relation to self-attitudes. Jpn. J. Couns. Sci. **25**, 85–93 (1992)
19. Itou, H., Sagara, J., Ikeda, M., Kawahora, Y.: Development and validation of the subjective well-being scale (SWBS). Jpn. J. Psychol. **74**(3), 276–281 (2003)

48   R. Ishii et al.

20. Iwa, Y.: Privacy orientation and personality traits among Japanese college students. J. Soc. Psychol. Res. **3**, 11–16 (1987). in Japanese
21. Iwabuchi, C., Tanaka, S.: A trial toward revising the self-monitoring scale. In: Proceedings of the 28th Annual Meeting of the Japanese Society of Social Psychology, p. 67 (1987), in Japanese
22. Joel, S., Eastwick, P.W., Finkel, E.J.: Is romantic desire predictable? Machine learning applied to initial romantic attraction. Psychol. Sci. **28**(11), 1478–1489 (2017)
23. Kamiyama, S.: Concept and measurement of clothing interest: a replication study of Gurel's research. J. Text. Prod. Consum. Sci. **24**(1), 35–41 (1983). In Japanese with English abstract
24. Kanemasa, Y.: Development and validation of the love image scale: associations with close heterosexual relationships and adult attachment styles. Jpn. J. Interpers. Soc. Psychol. **2**, 93–101 (2002). In Japanese with English abstract
25. Kikuchi, A.: Development of the KiSS-18 scale: a shortened version of the Kikuchi's scale of social skills. Jpn. J. Psychol. **69**(6), 472–479 (1998). In Japanese with English abstract
26. Kondo, T., Kamata, J.: Ikigai feelings and scale development among contemporary university students. Jpn. J. Health Psychol. **11**, 73–82 (1998)
27. Kono, K.: Relationships among the Japanese version of the self-concealment scale, sensation seeking scale, and subjective somatic symptoms. Jpn. J. Exp. Soc. Psychol. **40**, 115–121 (2000)
28. Kuroda, Y., Sakurai, S.: Relationship between goal orientation and depression in friendship situations among junior high school students. Jpn. J. Educ. Young Child. **49**, 129–136 (2001)
29. Kurzban, R., Weeden, J.: Hurrydate: mate preferences in action. Evol. Hum. Behav. **26**(3), 227–244 (2005)
30. Kusada, H., Okado, T.: Family relationship assessment method. In: Okado, T. (ed.) Psychological Testing, pp. 573–581. Kakiuchi Publishing (1993), in Japanese
31. Larson, D.G., Chastain, R.L.: Self-concealment: conceptualization, measurement, and health implications. J. Soc. Clin. Psychol. **9**, 439–455 (1990)
32. Lee, J.A.: The Colours of Love. New Press, Ontario (1973)
33. Marshall, N.J.: Privacy and environment. Hum. Ecol. **1**, 93–110 (1972)
34. Matsui, Y., et al.: Development of a measurement scale for romantic love among Japanese youth. Bull. Tokyo Metrop. Tachikawa Junior Coll. **23**, 13–23 (1990). In Japanese with English abstract
35. Mouri, I., Tanno, Y.: Development and validation of the situational interpersonal anxiety scale. Jpn. J. Health Psychol. **14**, 23–31 (2001)
36. Nobori, M.: The development of empathy in adolescence: a study based on a multidimensional perspective. Jpn. J. Dev. Psychol. **14**, 136–148 (2003)
37. Odagiri, N.: Survey report on divorce in Japan. J. Fac. Hum. Soc. Sci. Tokyo Int. Univ. **7**, 105–119 (2001)
38. Okada, T.: A study on youth attitudes toward friendship. J. Adolesc. Psychol. Res. **5**, 43–55 (1993). in Japanese
39. Olson, D.: Circumplex model : validation studies and faces. Fam. Process **25** 337–351 (1986)
40. Pedersen, D.M.: Dimensions of privacy. Percept. Mot. Skills **48**, 1291–1297 (1979)
41. Pentland, A.: Honest Signals: How They Shape Our World. MIT Press (2008)
42. Rosenberg, M.: Society and the Adolescent Self-Image. Princeton University Press (1965)

43. Rothmann, S., Coetzer, E.P.: The big five personality dimensions and job performance. SA J. Ind. Psychol. **29**(1) (2003)
44. Rotter, J.B.: A new scale for the measurement of interpersonal trust. J. Pers. **35**(4), 651–665 (1967)
45. Rubin, Z.: Measurement of romantic love. J. Pers. Soc. Psychol. **16**(2), 265–273 (1970). https://doi.org/10.1037/h0029841
46. Sakai, K., Yamaguchi, A., Kuno, M.: A study on the unidimensionality of the value orientation scale: an application of item response theory. Jpn. J. Educ. Psychol. **46**(2), 153–162 (1998). In Japanese with English abstract
47. Sakamoto, S.: The preoccupation scale: its development and relationship with depression scales. J. Clin. Psychol. **54**(5), 645–654 (1998)
48. Scheier, M.F., Carver, C.S.: The self-consciousness scale: a revised version for use with general populations. J. Appl. Soc. Psychol. **15**(8), 687–699 (1985)
49. Shimamoto, K., Ishii, M.: Development of a daily life skills scale for university students. Jpn. J. Educ. Psychol. **54**, 211–221 (2006)
50. Spranger, E.: Types of Men: The Psychology and Ethics of Personality. Max Niemeyer, Halle (1928)
51. Sugawara, K.: An attempting to construct the self-consciousness scale for Japanese. Jpn. J. Psychol. **55**(3), 184–188 (1984)
52. Sugiura, K.: Two types of affiliation motives and their developmental changes: relationships with interpersonal alienation. Jpn. J. Educ. Psychol. **48**, 352–360 (2000)
53. Suzuki, J.: Development of the short version of the sex role egalitarianism scale (sesra-s). Jpn. J. Psychol. **65**(1), 34–41 (1994)
54. Tan, C., Niculae, V., Danescu-Niculescu-Mizil, C., Lee, L.: Winning arguments: interaction dynamics and persuasion strategies in good-faith online discussions. In: Proceedings of the 25th International Conference on World Wide Web, pp. 613–624. ACM (2016)
55. Wada, M.: Development of a scale for attitudes toward romantic love. Jpn. J. Exp. Soc. Psychol. **34**, 153–163 (1994). In Japanese with English abstract
56. Watanabe, H.: Changes in consumer behavior and value orientation. In: Ato, H. (ed.) Social Psychology of Consumer Behavior, Chap. 7, pp. 152–172. Fukumura Publishing (1994). Based on Analysis of the TBS General Preference Survey (TBS Sōshikō Chōsa)
57. Yoshioka, K.: Satisfaction in friendship as seen from discrepancies between ideal and reality and from self-acceptance. Jpn. J. Adolesc. Psychol. **13**, 13–30 (2001). In Japanese

Cross-Cultural Interaction on Social Media Health Platforms: Challenges and Opportunities from Africa

Helina Oladapo[1]([✉]), Eric Owusu[2], and Ralitsa Diana Debrah[3]

[1] Department of Computer and Information Technology, Miami University,
1601 University Blvd., Hamilton, OH 45011, USA
oladaph@miamioh.edu

[2] Department of Computing Sciences, State University of New York, Brockport,
350 New Campus Drive, Brockport, NY 14420, USA
eowusu@brockport.edu

[3] Department of Communication Design, Kwame Nkrumah University of Science and
Technology, KNUST, CABE, FOA, DECODE, Kumasi, Ghana
rddebrah.art@knust.edu.gh

Abstract. This study investigates how social media health platforms facilitate or hinder cross-cultural interactions, evaluates the effectiveness of platform features in promoting meaningful engagement, and identifies strategies that healthcare communities can adopt to foster inclusiveness across diverse cultural groups, with a particular emphasis on African users. A mixed-methods design was used to analyze data from 155 Nigerians and Ghanaians of African descent in the U.S. engaged in health-related discussions on social media platforms. Findings reveal that while social media health platforms enable cross-cultural interactions, challenges such as cultural misunderstandings, misinformation, and language barriers remain prevalent. Platform features—including automatic translation, multimedia sharing, topic-based discussions, and culturally sensitive moderation—substantially support cross-cultural engagement. These strategies enhance the quality of interactions and promote a sense of belonging among users from diverse backgrounds. By implementing these approaches, social media health platforms can further bridge cultural divides and create a more inclusive online environment. This study concludes that integrated approaches combining technical design, and community involvement are crucial for maintaining inclusive global health communities, especially in Africa.

Keywords: Cross-cultural interaction · cultural misunderstanding · cultural sensitivity · Facebook groups · inclusivity · online health communities · social media health platforms · WhatsApp platforms

1 Introduction

Engaging in cross-cultural interactions on social media health platforms presents challenges and opportunities, especially when connecting with non-Western cultures in healthcare contexts. Much of the existing research has been concentrated in Western contexts, leaving significant gaps in understanding cross-cultural interaction and engagement on social media health platforms. Enhancing user interactions is essential to improving engagement within online health communities, such as Facebook groups.

Digital platforms that facilitate and encourage social interaction are commonly referred to as social media [1]. Social media has become an indispensable platform in today's interconnected world, bringing together individuals from diverse cultural backgrounds to engage, interact, and exchange their values, beliefs, and traditions [1]. Its rapid growth recently has transformed how people connect and communicate globally. The globalization of healthcare discourse has increasingly shifted health-seeking behaviors to social media platforms, where patients, caregivers, and professionals engage in information exchange and peer support. These platforms bring together individuals from diverse linguistic, cultural, and geographic backgrounds, generating both opportunities for cross-cultural interaction and challenges related to cultural misunderstandings, communication barriers, and inclusiveness.

For many African communities, where access to formal healthcare infrastructure may be limited, social media health platforms present significant opportunities for health education, peer support, and cultural exchange. However, the diversity of Africa's cultures, languages, and healthcare beliefs also introduces unique challenges that must be carefully navigated by platform designers, moderators, and healthcare professionals. This study identifies how social media health platforms can either facilitate or hinder interactions among individuals from diverse cultural backgrounds. Much of the existing research has been concentrated in Western contexts, leaving significant gaps in understanding cross-cultural interaction and engagement on these platforms. Social media health platform interactions among non-Western cultures have received limited attention. Enhancing user interactions is critical for fostering engagement in online health communities, such as Facebook groups. Online health communities provide valuable resources by offering continuous access to information and emotional assistance. Unlike traditional social networks, online health communities are accessible at any time, ensuring timely help when needed [2]. Therefore, expanding research to encompass more diverse cultural contexts in underrepresented regions is critical [3].

This will enable a deeper understanding of how cultural differences affect user behavior and preferences on these platforms. By integrating insights from non-Western cultures, researchers and developers can create more inclusive and effective health resources that cater to a broader audience. This study examines the following research questions:

- RQ1: To what extent do social media health platforms facilitate or hinder cross-cultural interaction among users?
- RQ2: To what extent do the features of social media health platforms promote meaningful cross-cultural interactions while respecting local communities?
- RQ3: How can healthcare communities foster inclusiveness and promote engagement across diverse cultural groups?

2   Literature Review

Social media comprises a spectrum of digital technologies that allow individuals to establish an online presence, engage in communication and networking, and disseminate user-generated content across diverse platforms [4, 5]. In 2000, 80 million African adults over 25 had hypertension, with projections reaching 150 million by 2025, illustrating the potential benefits of social media-based health interventions [6]. Online health communities serve as platforms where individuals engage with peers facing shared health challenges, enabling medical knowledge exchange through online discussions and personal experience sharing [7]. Facebook groups are online platforms that provide "a space to communicate about shared interests with certain people," fostering community building, knowledge sharing, and interaction [8, 9]. They serve as a significant platform for health communities. Groups may be public, private, or secret. In health contexts, private or secret groups are often used to maintain confidentiality due to privacy concerns when discussing health information online, with membership typically requiring an invitation to join [10].

Using personal Facebook accounts, designated administrators manage these groups, supervising membership and activities [8]. Facebook groups facilitate interaction between patients and healthcare professionals, offering support and educational resources [10]. These groups serve as valuable platforms for individuals to share experiences, ask questions, and receive guidance from others who may be facing similar health challenges. In addition to peer support, healthcare professionals can provide trusted information, helping to bridge the gap between patients and medical knowledge.

Social media serves as a prominent platform for various health-related purposes [11]. While social media enables rapid information dissemination, the COVID-19 pandemic amplified the spread of misinformation. Researchers recommend that health institutions issue timely refutations [12], share personal experiences to counter rumors [13], and engage patients in discussions about misinformation [14]. For example, it was reported that theory-based correction messages on Facebook by health authorities were more effective than standard messages in addressing vaccine misinformation [15]. Beyond combating misinformation, social media also supports health interventions by providing health information [16]. Health professionals use these platforms to communicate with patients, respond to inquiries [17], and share medical advice [18], thereby enhancing doctor-patient relationships. Additionally, social media facilitates participant recruitment for health studies, particularly among hard-to-reach populations such as immigrants [19]. All contribute to the health-related functions of social media.

2.1   Cross-Cultural Interaction Challenges and Opportunities

Cross-cultural interactions involve the mutual influence that occurs when individuals from different cultural backgrounds engage with one another, requiring at least two participants from distinct cultures [20, 21]. Social media health platforms serve as global spaces where people from diverse cultural backgrounds exchange information, experiences, and support. Additionally, they tend to offer support primarily to users from similar cultural backgrounds, which reflects a degree of cultural alignment in their interactions [22]. This information indicates that while social media facilitates cross-cultural exposure, cultural identity significantly influences interaction patterns.

In a similar vein, longitudinal research focusing on international students has shown that engagement primarily with home-nation groups on social media fosters identity and psychological adaptation [23]. Conversely, interactions with host-nation groups can sometimes create challenges or provide comfort [23]. These findings suggest that social media platforms can both facilitate and hinder cross-cultural health engagement, depending on the structures of the groups and the comfort levels of users. This duality highlights the importance of understanding user motivations and preferences when navigating these online spaces. As such, tailored interventions that leverage the benefits of both home-nation and host-nation interactions could enhance cross-cultural communication and support among international students.

2.2 Social Media Platform Features and Design

The design and features of social media health platforms are important because they influence cross-cultural interactions. Platform design influences how users from diverse cultural backgrounds engage, express themselves, and interpret health information. According to [24], essential platform features include automatic translation, cultural metadata tagging, customizable privacy settings, and culturally aware moderation tools. These features support respectful interactions among various cultures. Without them, interactions might reinforce dominant cultural narratives while sidelining minority voices.

Multimedia sharing such as videos, images, and infographics has gained importance in cross-cultural contexts, as visual content helps users navigate linguistic challenges often associated with textual content [25]. This relevance is particularly pronounced in African contexts, where multiple languages and varying literacy levels coexist [25]. Platforms that facilitate multimodal communication can enhance the accessibility of health knowledge for individuals from diverse educational and linguistic backgrounds.

Additionally, structured dialogue features—including topic-based discussion threads, Q&A forums, and event scheduling—have been found to promote deeper engagement across cultural groups [22]. These features create organized health discussions that directly address culturally specific concerns, fostering clarity and reducing conflict.

Accessibility and inclusive user interface (UI) design are also essential for users in African contexts who may access platforms through mobile devices with limited data connectivity or inconsistent network infrastructure. [26] emphasize that simple interface design, offline capabilities, and culturally adaptive UI significantly enhance usability and inclusivity for African users.

Finally, moderation systems must be sensitive to cultural differences in health norms, communication styles, and sensitive topics. Poorly moderated platforms may unintentionally amplify misinformation or contribute to cross-cultural conflict [27]. Therefore, it is crucial for platform developers to engage with local communities and experts to understand these nuances, ensuring that moderation practices are not only effective but also respectful of diverse cultural contexts. By prioritizing these considerations, platforms can foster a safer and more supportive environment for all users.

2.3 Engagement, Inclusivity, and Cultural Sensitivity

Creating inclusive health communities on social media requires more than just well-designed technical features. True inclusivity comes from fostering culturally sensitive engagement strategies that actively involve diverse users in shaping content and governing the platforms. As [25] argue, inclusiveness must be rooted in participatory approaches that value cultural humility and collaboration with users—especially in regions like Africa, where cultural diversity is immense, even within individual countries.

Encouraging users to share their own health practices, beliefs, and stories not only increases engagement but also builds trust and promotes mutual learning among communities. As [22] note, this kind of participation allows often-overlooked knowledge—such as traditional medicine, community-based care, and spiritual health beliefs common in many African contexts—to be acknowledged and integrated into digital health discourse, which is typically shaped by Western biomedical perspectives [28].

Involving culturally diverse healthcare professionals further supports this goal. As highlighted by [29], these professionals can play a vital role as cultural mediators, helping to interpret and translate biomedical information into culturally meaningful terms while honoring patients' beliefs and values.

Lastly, platform moderators and administrators must be trained in cultural sensitivity. As [24, 27] suggest, well-trained moderators are key to maintaining respectful dialogue, preventing cultural misunderstandings, and ensuring safe spaces for discussion. They can guide conversations, set inclusive norms, and de-escalate conflicts that may arise from differing worldviews. Together, these strategies form a foundation for more inclusive, culturally respectful engagement on social media health platforms—making them more effective and equitable for diverse African users.

3 Methodology

A mixed-methods approach was used to study how social media health platforms affect interactions between different cultures, evaluate how well the platform features encourage meaningful engagement across cultures, and find ways to make healthcare communities more inclusive, especially for Nigerians and Ghanaians living in the United States. We recruited a total of 155 participants through convenience and snowball sampling methods. The participants represented a variety of cultural backgrounds, primarily individuals of African descent, namely Nigerians and Ghanaians, including both males and females who participated in health-related discussions regarding hypertension management and engaged in online communities hosted on social media health platforms, such as Facebook groups.

Eligibility criteria included being 18 years or older and either living with hypertension or seeking health information on behalf of individuals affected by the condition. The questionnaire was crafted to explore experiences related to cross-cultural interactions, the effectiveness of platform features, and strategies for fostering inclusiveness. The survey was conducted online over a two-month period, utilizing various distribution channels such as email invitations, word-of-mouth, congregational gatherings, personal referrals, and social media platforms. Data were collected using Qualtrics and incorporated a mix of demographic items, multiple-choice questions, Likert-scale items, and both open- and closed-ended questions.

Participation was voluntary and anonymous, allowing respondents to skip questions or withdraw at any time. Electronically informed consent was secured prior to participation, with an estimated completion time of 15 to 30 min. We analyzed open-ended responses to identify key themes, while for closed-ended questions, we employed basic statistics like counts and averages, as well as more advanced techniques such as chi-square tests and logistic regression. No identifiable information was collected; any inadvertent identifiers were eliminated. Data were securely stored on encrypted Google Cloud servers, accessible only to the Principal Investigator and Secondary Investigators. The Miami University Research Ethics & Integrity Program approved the study and obtained electronic informed consent.

4 Results and Discussions

Socio-demographic Characteristics of Respondents. The majority of respondents were aged 18 to 24 years (36.8%), followed by those aged 25 to 34 years (27.1%) and 35 to 44 years (21.9%). A significant portion of the respondents (67.1%) were male, and nearly half (48.4%) held a bachelor's degree. In terms of nationality, most of the sample was Ghanaian (76.1%), while Nigerians accounted for 23.9%.

The findings reveal that the participants, primarily young adults aged 18 to 24 years with a higher level of education, exhibit strong digital engagement. This engagement may enhance health literacy and promote ongoing participation in online health communities. Additionally, the predominance of male participants suggests potential gender disparities, which may be influenced by cultural norms or differences in health-seeking behavior (see Table 1).

Membership of Social Media Health-Related Group or Community. The majority of respondents (78.7%) were members of at least one social media health group or community focused on health-related topics concerning hypertension management (Table 2).

The most frequently used platforms were WhatsApp (55.7%), followed by Facebook (23.8%), TikTok (5.7%), and Instagram (5.7%) (Fig. 1).

Frequency of Usage of Social Media Platform Types for Health-Related Topics on Hypertension Management. 22.6% of respondents used Facebook weekly, while 18.1% used it daily. 27.7% of the respondents used WhatsApp daily, while 24.5% used it rarely. Other platforms like TikTok, YouTube, and Instagram saw the highest weekly usage at 41.9%, although 23.9% never used them (Table 3).

22.6% of respondents used Facebook weekly and 18.1% daily for hypertension-related topics. In contrast, WhatsApp demonstrated higher daily engagement at 27.7%, with 24.5% of users reporting rare usage. Other social media platforms focused on health, including TikTok, YouTube, and Instagram, experienced the highest weekly engagement at 41.9%, although 23.9% of respondents indicated they never used these platforms. These patterns reveal distinct engagement behaviors across various social media health platforms. When designing hypertension interventions, it is crucial to consider these

Table 1. Socio-demographic information of respondents (N = 155).

Socio-demographic	Frequency (N)	Percentage (%)
Age		
18–24	57	36.8
25–34	42	27.1
35–44	34	21.9
45–54	14	9.0
55 and older	8	5.2
Gender		
Male	104	67.1
Female	51	32.9
Level of Education		
Bachelor's degree	75	48.4
Doctoral degree	13	8.4
Master's degree	43	27.7
Some college	8	5.2
High school or equivalent	16	10.3
Country of origin		
Nigeria	37	23.9
Ghana	118	76.1

Table 2. Membership of social media health-related group or community

Membership of social media health-related group or community	N	%
Yes	122	78.7
No	33	21.3
Total	155	100.0

platform-specific usage patterns to enhance user participation, interaction, and sustained engagement within online health communities.

Social Media Platforms Engaged with for Discussions About Hypertension Management. The majority of respondents engaged in discussions on WhatsApp (46.5%), followed by Facebook (14.2%) (Fig. 2).

The findings indicate that WhatsApp (46.5%) serves as the primary platform for engaging in discussions about hypertension, highlighting its accessibility and daily use. In contrast, lower engagement on Facebook (14.2%) suggests differences in usability,

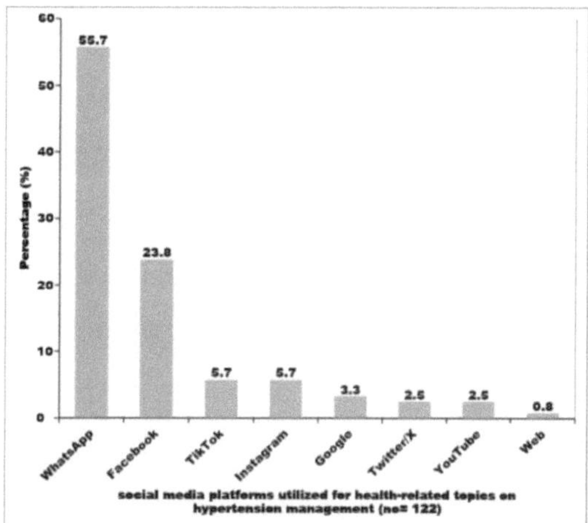

Fig. 1. Types of social media platforms utilized for health-related topics on hypertension management.

user preferences, and perceived relevance. These insights illustrate the value of considering user behavior and platform design when creating social media-based health interventions for managing hypertension.

Frequency of Interaction with Groups or Communities on Health-Related Issues About Hypertension. Respondents interacted most frequently on WhatsApp, with 24.5% engaging sometimes, 16.8% often, and 11.0% always. In contrast, Facebook exhibited lower levels of interaction, as 32.3% of users engaged sometimes, 9.0% often, and only 4.5% always. On other platforms, 23.9% reported interacting sometimes, while 12.3% did so always. Overall, Facebook had a relatively lower frequency of interaction, with 35.5% of respondents indicating they never engaged and just 4.5% stating they "always" interacted (Table 4).

WhatsApp emerged as the primary platform for hypertension-related interactions in online health communities, likely due to its accessibility and daily use. Facebook showed lower interaction, with many respondents not engaging. These findings suggest that usability, trust, and communication habits influence platform preferences. Leveraging familiar platforms like WhatsApp may enhance engagement and interaction in health interventions, while less-utilized platforms may require targeted design strategies to address engagement and barriers (See Table 4).

Reasons for Participating in Social Media Health Groups on Facebook. Respondents' overall key motivations for participation in social media health groups or communities on hypertension management included staying informed (28.0%), sharing information (21.7%), seeking advice (16.1%), providing support (16.1%), and sharing personal experiences (12.2%). Only 5.9% did not use social media for health purposes (Table 5).

Designing interventions that align with these motivations can enhance engagement and participation in hypertension management.

Table 3. Frequency of usage of social media platform types for health-related topics on hypertension management.

Usage of social media platform types	N	%
Facebook		
Never	34	21.9
Rarely	30	19.4
Daily	28	18.1
Weekly	35	22.6
Monthly	28	18.1
WhatsApp		
Never	33	21.3
Rarely	38	24.5
Daily	43	27.7
Weekly	24	15.5
Monthly	17	11.0
Others [*][+]		
Never	37	23.9
Rarely	13	8.4
Daily	19	12.3
Weekly	65	41.9
Monthly	21	13.5

[*]*Multiple responses.*
[+]= TikTok, Twitter/X, Web, YouTube, Instagram, Google.

4.1 RQ1: To What Extent Do Social Media Health Platforms Facilitate or Hinder Cross-Cultural Interaction Among Users?

Challenges in Cross-Cultural Interactions. Common challenges encountered when interacting with users from different cultural backgrounds on social media health platforms include cultural misunderstandings (25.9%), health misinformation (22.3%), and language barriers (22.0%) (see Table 6). Additionally, challenges faced within social media health groups or communities, such as Facebook groups, consist of misunderstandings of cultural norms (33.1%) and language or communication barriers (27.3%) (see Table 7). These challenges highlight significant communication and inclusion barriers on social media (Tables 6 and 7).

Cross-Cultural Interaction and Comfort. Over half (55.5%) of respondents had interacted with culturally different users. Of these, (37.4%) felt very comfortable and (30.45%) felt somewhat comfortable. The majority (73.9%) of respondents admitted that social media platforms facilitated cross-cultural interactions (see Table 8).

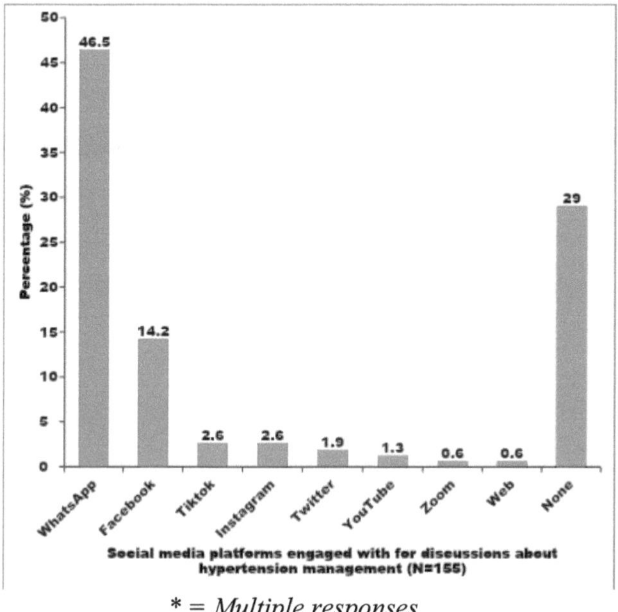

= Multiple responses

Fig. 2. Types of social media platforms engaged with for discussions about hypertension management.

Despite the potential benefits, significant barriers still exist. Survey data shows that 25.9% of respondents reported experiencing cultural misunderstandings, 22.3% encountered health misinformation, and 22.0% faced language barriers during cross-cultural health discussions on social media health platforms (see Table 6). These challenges are often exacerbated within online health communities, such as Facebook groups, where 33.1% of participants noted misunderstandings of cultural norms, along with language or communication barriers 27.3% (see Table 7). These findings illustrate that, although social media health platforms provide opportunities for cross-cultural exposure, significant inclusion barriers persist, hindering the depth and quality of interactions.

Overall, the comfort levels among users are relatively positive. More than half (55.5%) reported having interactions with individuals from different cultural backgrounds, and of those users, 67.85% expressed feeling either very or somewhat comfortable. Additionally, 73.9% of respondents believed that social media platforms promote cross-cultural interactions (see Table 8). These findings indicate that, despite the presence of structural and interpersonal barriers, many users can engage with diverse cultures with a moderate to high level of comfort when suitable design features and community norms are established.

Table 4. Frequency of interaction with groups or communities on health-related issues about hypertension on different social media platform types.

Interaction with different social media platform types	N	%
Facebook		
Never	55	35.5
Rarely	29	18.7
Sometimes	50	32.3
Often	14	9.0
Always	7	4.5
WhatsApp		
Never	46	29.7
Rarely	28	18.1
Sometimes	38	24.5
Often	26	16.8
Always	17	11.0
Others [*+]		
Never	51	32.9
Rarely	26	16.8
Sometimes	37	23.9
Often	22	14.2
Always	19	12.3

[*]*Multiple responses.*
[+]= TikTok, Twitter/X, Web YouTube, Instagram, Google.

Table 5. Perceived inspiration to participate in social media health groups or communities on hypertension management.

Choice types	N	%
Staying informed about health topics	85	28.0
Sharing personal experiences	37	12.2
Seeking medical advice	49	16.1
Providing support to others	49	16.1
Information sharing and exchange	66	21.7
I do not use social media for health management	18	5.9
Total*	304	100.0

[*]*Multiple responses.*

Table 6. Challenges encountered when interacting with users from different cultural backgrounds on social media health platforms.

Challenges	N	%
Cultural misunderstandings	87	25.9
Health Misinformation	75	22.3
Language barriers	74	22.0
Digital literacy	48	14.3
Exclusion from group dynamics	30	8.9
Total	336	100.0

Multiple responses.

Table 7. Challenges encountered when interacting with social media health groups or communities, such as Facebook groups.

Challenges	N	%
Misunderstanding of cultural norms	81	33.1
Language or communication barriers	67	27.3
Feeling excluded or marginalized	50	20.4
Difficulty finding culturally relevant groups	47	19.2
Total	245	100.0

* *Multiple responses.*

4.2 RQ2: To What Extent Do the Features of Social Media Health Platforms Promote Meaningful Cross-Cultural Interactions While Respecting Local Communities?

Effectiveness of Social Media Features for Cross-Cultural Interaction. Respondents' perceptions regarding how specific features on social media health platforms facilitate meaningful cross-cultural interaction vary. A significant majority (67.1%) of respondents acknowledged that the automatic translation features on these platforms enhance effective communication among users from different cultural backgrounds, with 30.3% strongly agreeing and 36.8% agreeing. More than half (54.8%) of respondents believed that moderation tools, which help prevent culturally insensitive or offensive interactions, were viewed positively (21.3% strongly agree, 33.5% agree). Furthermore, 65.2% of respondents agreed that social media health platforms foster meaningful cross-cultural interactions through features like webinars, forums, and group discussions, with 29.7% strongly agreeing and 35.4% agreeing. Additionally, 61.9% of respondents indicated that health-related content on social media demonstrates understanding and respect for diverse cultural practices (28.4% strongly agreed and 33.5% agreed). Over two-thirds (65.8%) of respondents appreciated the opportunity to share their own cultural health practices while learning from others, with 24.5% strongly agreeing and 41.3% agreeing.

Table 8. Interacted with users from different cultural backgrounds in health-related online groups or communities and its comfortability.

Variables	N	%
Interaction		
Yes	86	55.5
No	69	44.5
Total	155	100.0
Comfortability (n = 115)		
Very comfortable	43	37.4
Somewhat comfortable	35	30.4
Neutral	29	25.2
Somewhat uncomfortable	7	6.1
Very uncomfortable	1	.9
Felt that social media health platforms facilitate cross-cultural interactions (n = 115)		
Strongly agree	29	25.2
Agree	56	48.7
Neutral	28	24.3
Strongly disagree	2	1.7

More than half of the respondents (23.2% strongly agree, 35.5% agree) considered the design and layout of social media health platforms to be inclusive. Moreover, live events and Q&A sessions were viewed as effective means of incorporating diverse cultural perspectives, with 32.3% strongly agreeing and 27.1% agreeing.

Facebook Features Enhancing Cross-Cultural Interactions. Respondents' acceptance of various features within Facebook groups aimed at fostering cross-cultural engagement in health-related discussions was analyzed. The most effective features identified included multimedia sharing (70.3%), automatic translation (65.2%), topic-based discussions (67.8%), and event scheduling (66.5%). Each of these features received positive feedback from approximately two-thirds of respondents, who either agreed with or strongly agreed with their usefulness.

About two-thirds of respondents (32.3% strongly agree, 32.9% agree) recognized the significance of automatic translation for posts and comments. Additionally, multimedia sharing, which encompasses images, videos, and links, was considered particularly effective, with 29.7% strongly agreeing and 40.6% agreeing. Over two-thirds of respondents (28.4% strongly agreed and 38.1% agreed) confirmed that live Q&A sessions enhance cross-cultural interactions. Support for polls and surveys was also notable, with 29.0% strongly agreeing and 36.1% agreeing. Furthermore, a majority (31.0% strongly agreed and 36.8% agreed) believed that topic-based discussions, such as threads and comments focused on hypertension management, foster cross-cultural interactions. A significant proportion (26.5% strongly agreed and 40.0% agreed) acknowledged that event scheduling and participation contribute to improved cross-cultural interactions. Lastly, pinned posts or announcements were favored by more than half of the respondents, with 25.8% strongly agreeing and 38.7% agreeing.

Specific platform features play a crucial role in enabling cross-cultural interactions and engagement. Translation tools received support from 67.1% of respondents on general platforms and 65.2% in Facebook groups, aligning with [24] analysis that translation technologies help reduce language barriers and enhance access to diverse cultural content. Multimedia sharing garnered the highest endorsement at 70.3% among Facebook group users, as visual formats transcend linguistic differences, allowing culturally diverse users to universally share health experiences, consistent with [25]. Structured interaction features, such as topic-based discussions (67.8% in Facebook groups), webinars, forums, and live Q&A sessions (which received 65.2% to 66.5% approval across general platforms and Facebook groups), facilitated focused dialogue among cultural groups. Moderation tools, supported by 54.8% of respondents on general platforms, helped mitigate culturally insensitive interactions. Additionally, inclusive design elements—such as polls, pinned posts, and adaptive layouts—were positively evaluated, highlighting further opportunities to enhance inclusivity in platform design.

4.3   RQ3: How Can Healthcare Communities Foster Inclusiveness and Promote Engagement Across Diverse Cultural Groups?

Best Strategies for Cultural Inclusiveness. Table 9 presents respondents' opinions on strategies to enhance inclusiveness and engagement in online health communities. The most endorsed strategy for fostering inclusiveness and promoting engagement among diverse cultural groups in these online health groups was providing multilingual support or translation tools, with 22.8% of respondents in favor. The suggestions that received close support included encouraging users to share cultural health practices (22.2%) and hosting culturally relevant events or discussions focused on hypertension management (21.5%). Additionally, partnering with diverse healthcare professionals received support from 19.6% of participants. 13.9% of participants chose to train moderators in cultural sensitivity, indicating a recognized need for effective management that ensures respectful and inclusive interactions.

This study emphasizes the need for healthcare communities to consider cultural inclusiveness in design to engage diverse users. Key strategies included multilingual support (22.8%), encouraging users to share cultural health practices (22.2%), and hosting culturally relevant events or discussions (21.5%), emphasizing both linguistic access and cultural engagement. Partnerships with diverse healthcare professionals (19.6%) support cultural alignment and trust by involving stakeholders in intervention design [25]. Although moderator training in cultural sensitivity was less endorsed (13.9%), it remains essential for managing cultural misunderstandings [24]. These findings align with participatory design principles that emphasize community representation, shared authority, and cultural humility [25]. It is recommended that platform designers and healthcare communities adopt an approach to inclusivity, incorporating participatory engagement and culturally responsive moderation.

Table 9. Best strategies for cultural inclusiveness and promote engagement among diverse cultural groups in online health groups or communities.

Best strategies	N	%
Providing multilingual support or translation tools	107	22.8
Hosting culturally relevant events or discussions on hypertension management	101	21.5
Encouraging users to share cultural health practices	104	22.2
Partnering with diverse healthcare professionals	92	19.6
Training moderators in cultural sensitivity	65	13.9
Total	469	100.0

* *Multiple responses*

Inclusiveness of Facebook Groups. Table 10 assesses respondents' perceptions of inclusiveness for individuals from different cultural backgrounds within Facebook groups. The majority (62.6%) of respondents reported positive perceptions: 27.1% described the groups as very inclusive, while 35.5% considered them somewhat inclusive. A smaller proportion found Facebook groups less inclusive, with 9.0% indicating they were not very inclusive and only 0.6% reporting they were not inclusive at all.

Table 10. Facebook groups inclusive feeling for people from different cultural backgrounds.

Inclusive feeling for people from different cultural backgrounds	N	%
Very inclusive	42	27.1
Somewhat inclusive	55	35.5
Neutral	43	27.7
Not very inclusive	14	9.0
Not inclusive at all	1	0.6
Total	155	100.0

Perceptions of inclusiveness within Facebook groups reflect that 62.6% of respondents experienced inclusivity (27.1% very inclusive; 35.5% somewhat inclusive), while 9.6% reported exclusion. The large number of people who said "somewhat inclusive" shows there are chances to improve cultural representation, add features for handling conflicts, and encourage active participation from underrepresented user groups to create fairer online interactions.

Relationship between users' comfortability in engaging/interacting with other users from different cultural backgrounds and inclusiveness of social media like Facebook in health-related online groups or communities.

Table 11. Relationship between users' comfortability in engaging/interacting with other users from different cultural backgrounds and inclusiveness of social media such as Facebook in health-related online groups or communities.

Users' comfortability in engaging/interacting with other users from different cultural background	Inclusiveness of social media				Chi-square (χ^2)	df	p-value
	Inclusive (n = 78) (%)	Neutral (n = 26) (%)	Not inclusive (n = 8) (%)	Total (N = 112) (%)			
Comfortable	61(62.9)	10(23.3)	7(46.7)	78(50.3)	19.865	–	$f = 0.000$*
Neutral	32(33.0)	30(69.8)	7(46.7)	69(44.5)			
Uncomfortable	4(4.1)	3(7.0)	1(6.7)	8(5.2)			
Total	97(100)	43(100)	15(100)	155(100)			

f = Fisher exact test; Significant at 0.05.

Comfortable users were more likely to view the platform as inclusive (62.9%). (p = 0.000). Users' comfort in intercultural interaction is significantly related with perceived inclusiveness of the platform (p < 0.05).

Table 12. Logistic regression analysis for prior interaction with different cultural backgrounds against users' comfortability in engaging/interacting with other users from different cultural background in health-related online group or communities.

Predictor		B (β)	SE	Wald	OR (Exp(B))	p-value
Prior Interaction	Comfortable	4.53	0.84	28.98	**92.7**	**<0.001**
	Not comfortable	*Ref*				

Significant at 0.05.

Users who have previously interacted with culturally diverse individuals are 92.7 times more likely to report being comfortable in such interactions. This is a highly significant predictor (Table 12).

Comfortable users are significantly more likely to view the social media environment as inclusive. The odds are 8.3 times greater compared to those who are uncomfortable, showing that user comfort plays a crucial role in perception of inclusivity.

The findings underscore both the opportunities and persistent challenges faced by culturally diverse users on social media health platforms. While platforms have facilitated cross-cultural interactions for many African users, significant barriers remain, including cultural misunderstandings, language difficulties, and misinformation. Technical features such as translation tools, multimedia sharing, structured discussions, and moderation systems serve as critical enablers of meaningful cross-cultural health discourse, in line with prior research [24, 25, 22, 23]. However, the data also demonstrate

Table 13. Logistic regression analysis for perception of platform inclusiveness against interaction with culturally diverse users.

Predictor		B (β)	OR (Exp(B))	p-value
Comfortable	Inclusive	2.12	8.32*	0.004
	Not inclusive	*Ref*		
Comfortable	Neutral	1.97	7.12*	0.011
	Not inclusive	*Ref*		

Significant at 0.05.

that fostering inclusiveness requires more than design features alone. Culturally responsive governance, healthcare professional diversity, moderator training, and culturally relevant programming are essential to sustaining long term inclusiveness.

5   Conclusion

This study revealed both the promise and complexity of using social media health platforms for cross-cultural interaction across Africa. While platforms like Facebook offer spaces for people to share health concerns and find support, challenges around representation, language, and cultural sensitivity remain. Difficulties in recruiting Nigerian participants, highlight the need for more inclusive, regionally balanced studies. In addition, the study sample included both individuals with hypertension and those seeking health information on behalf of others without the condition, which may have impacted participant diversity.

Despite these limitations, the findings suggest that social media can be a powerful tool for fostering health dialogue, especially when the platforms are intentionally designed to be culturally responsive. Language barriers, varied health beliefs, and unequal digital access all shape how people interact online and addressing these differences is crucial for meaningful engagement. To move forward, designers and healthcare communities should consider: improving translation tools to be more culturally adaptive and accessible, encouraging visual and multimedia health communication to bridge literacy gaps, creating discussion spaces that reflect cultural values and lived experiences, equipping moderators with cultural competence training, including diverse health professionals to reflect different understandings of care, and involving users in the co-creation and governance of online health spaces.

Future research should take a long-term and holistic view looking beyond Facebook and including a broader mix of platforms. It should also prioritize experimental and qualitative methods, and draw on disciplines such as public health, Human Computer Interaction (HCI), and cultural psychology to better understand how social media shapes health behaviors in diverse African contexts. Designing with empathy, cultural insight, and collaboration at the core will help transform social media health platforms into truly inclusive, supportive communities for all.

References

1. Wibowo, G.A., Hanna, F., Ruhana, F.M., Arif, U.: The influence of social-media on cultural integration: a perspective on digital sociology. Int. J. Sci. Soc. **5**(4), 363–375 (2023)
2. Clapton-Caputo, E., Sweet, L., Muller, A.: A qualitative study of expectations and experiences of women using a social media support group when exclusively expressing breastmilk to feed their infant. Women Birth **34**(4), 370–380 (2021)
3. Alsaleh, D.A., et al.: Cross-cultural differences in the adoption of social media. J. Res. Interact. Mark. **13**(1), 119–140 (2019)
4. Carr, C.T., Hayes, R.A.: Social media: defining, developing, and divining. Atl. J. Commun. **23**(1), 46–65 (2015). https://doi.org/10.1080/15456870.2015.972282
5. Kaplan, A.M., Haenlein, M.: Users of the world, unite! The challenges and opportunities of social media. Bus. Horiz. **53**(1), 59–68 (2010). https://doi.org/10.1016/j.bushor.2009.09.003
6. Van de Vijver, S., et al.: Status report on hypertension in Africa-consultative review for the 6th session of the African union conference of ministers of health on NCD's. Pan Afr. Med. J. **16**(1) (2014)
7. Yang, B., et al.: The influences of social support expressed from doctors and disclosed from peers on patient decision-making: an analysis from the online health community. Sci. Rep. **15**(1), 2703 (2025)
8. Facebook Help Centre: Groups. https://www.facebook.com/help/1629740080681586/?hel pref=hc_fnav (Archived by the Internet Archive at https://bit.ly/33HJevN) (2019a)
9. Sahin, E., Ertepinar, H., Teksoz, G.: University students' behaviors pertaining to sustainability: a structural equation model with sustainability-related attributes. Int. J. Environ. Sci. Educ. **7**(3), 459–478 (2012)
10. Hale, K.: Benefits and challenges of social media in health care. Crit. Care Nurs. Q. **44**(3), 309–315 (2021). https://doi.org/10.1097/CNQ.0000000000000366
11. Chen, J., Wang, Y.: Social media use for health purposes: systematic review. J. Med. Internet Res. **23**(5), e17917 (2021)
12. Steffens, M.S., et al.: How organisations promoting vaccination respond to misinformation on social media: a qualitative investigation. BMC Public Health **19**, 1–12 (2019)
13. Mheidly, N., Fares, J.: Leveraging media and health communication strategies to overcome the COVID-19 infodemic. J. Public Health Policy **41**(4), 410–420 (2020)
14. Southwell, B.G., et al.: Roles for health care professionals in addressing patient-held misinformation beyond fact correction. Am. J. Public Health **110**(S3), S288–S289 (2020)
15. Gesser-Edelsburg, A., Diamant, A., Hijazi, R., Mesch, G.S.: Correcting misinformation by health organizations during measles outbreaks: a controlled experiment. PLoS ONE **13**(12), e0209505 (2018). https://doi.org/10.1371/journal.pone.0209505. [Medline: 30566485]
16. Diddi, P., Lundy, L.K.: Organizational Twitter use: content analysis of Tweets during breast cancer awareness month. J. Health Commun. **22**(3), 243–253 (2017)
17. Birnbaum, M.L., et al.: Role of social media and the Internet in pathways to care for adolescents and young adults with psychotic disorders and non-psychotic mood disorders. Early Interv. Psychiatry **11**(4), 290–295 (2017)
18. Benetoli, A., et al.: Do pharmacists use social media for patient care? Int. J. Clin. Pharm. **39**, 364–372 (2017)
19. Cudjoe, J., et al.: Recruiting African immigrant women for community-based cancer prevention studies: lessons learned from the AfroPap study. J. Community Health **44**, 1019–1026 (2019)
20. Rozkwitalska, M.: Barriers of cross-cultural interactions according to the research findings. J. Intercult. Manag. **3**(2), 127–142

21. Neuliep, J.W.: The relationship among intercultural communication apprehension, ethnocentrism, uncertainty reduction, and communication satisfaction during initial intercultural interaction: an extension of anxiety and uncertainty management (AUM) theory. J. Intercult. Commun. Res. **41**(1), 1–16 (2012)
22. Pendse, S.R., Niederhoffer, K., Sharma, A.: Cross-cultural differences in the use of online mental health support forums. In: Proceedings of the ACM on Human-Computer Interaction, vol. 3, pp. 1–29. CSCW (2019)
23. Gaitán-Aguilar, L., et al.: Social media use, social identification and cross-cultural adaptation of international students: a longitudinal examination. Front. Psychol. **13**, 1013375 (2022)
24. Li, L.: Addressing cross-cultural design challenges in social media platforms: a human-computer interaction perspective. In: Rau, P.-L.P. (ed.) HCII 2024. LNCS, vol. 14700, pp. 75–88. Springer, Cham (2024). https://doi.org/10.1007/978-3-031-60901-5_6
25. Naderbagi, A., et al.: Cultural and contextual adaptation of digital health interventions: a narrative review. J. Med. Internet Res. **26**, e55130 (2024)
26. Afolayan, O., et al.: Designing mobile health applications for low-resource African contexts: an inclusive UX framework. Int. J. Hum. Comput. Interact. **40**(1), 45–58 (2024)
27. Duna, J., et al.: Cross-cultural communication on social media: integrating neuroscience and cultural psychology. Front. Psychol. **13**, 1–14 (2022)
28. Okonofua, F.: Integrating traditional and biomedical healthcare approaches in Africa. Lancet Glob. Health **11**(5), e631–e633 (2023)
29. Adebayo, S., et al.: The role of culturally competent healthcare professionals in African public health systems. Afr. J. Health Sci. **34**(2), 112–123 (2023)

Exploring HIV Conversations: Social Media Interactions and Social Institutions in the LGBTQIA+ Community in the Philippines

Bryan O'Nomerp Payawal[(⊠)], Ryan Ebardo, and Francis Marlon Cabredo

De La Salle University, Manila, Philippines
`bryan.payawal@dlsu.edu.ph`

Abstract. Social media has significantly broadened the scope of digital engagement, facilitating more dynamic and diverse interactions between humans and computers. These interactions are not standalone but interwoven within the broader framework of social institutions. These institutions shape the context in which social interactions occur, establishing the rules, expectations, and power dynamics underpinning these exchanges. Social institutions have been central in various significant topics where interactions through discourse among social media users have occurred. Similarly, when social media users interact in discussions about sensitive or taboo issues, social institutions subtly influence the conversation—often guiding it or being referenced in the background, even if they are not the primary focus. These advantages are evident in how members of a Philippine LGBTQIA+ subreddit engage with each other when discussing HIV. This study employed a qualitative approach grounded in Social Institutional Theory to explore the social institutions in HIV discussions within a Philippine LGBTQIA+ subreddit, r/phlgbt. The research extracted threads containing the term 'HIV,' yielding 3,496 interactions from the subreddit, including both original posts and comments posted from 2014 to 2024. The results revealed that there are 264 relevant interactions, with health and the Internet being the social institutions most prominently mentioned in the threads. Furthermore, the intersection of health and Internet institutions in the discussions presents the existence of techno-social institutions. Users provide guidance with technological support and utilize the same technological advancements to support their claims. Lastly, users would also deter others from relying solely on Internet-based information.

Keywords: Social Media · LGBTQIA+ · HIV · Institutions · HCI

1 Introduction

Social media has climbed up on everyone's list of essential daily activities. As more and more platforms become available, more and more people are using them. The latest statistics show about 5.24 billion social media users worldwide [51]. Users that adopted this technology now vary in demographic, whether in age, race, and sex.

As the diversification of users inflates, social media platforms have started to target the usability of their technology for a broad range of users. Curiously, one of these

A. Coman et al. (Eds.): HCII 2025, LNCS 16337, pp. 69–81, 2026.
https://doi.org/10.1007/978-3-032-12801-0_5

diversified groups is the sexual minorities, which consideringly have a dearth of studies examining their behavior when using social media [30]. This assertion amplifies the need to investigate further.

The LGBTQIA+ community has found a "safe space" to discuss various topics, including those that others might consider taboo [24]. Such is the case of HIV, which, as a sexual condition, is still considered taboo in many places [12]. Using social media and its various functionalities, LGBTQIA+ community members have been able to discuss, debate, and raise awareness of this epidemic.

Social media communities have become the haven for these discussions, where, little by little, norms, values, and processes become more established through the members' interactions [4]. These emulate the institutions that influence and shape their conduct through collected beliefs and practices, evolving into accepted norms [5]. Social media interactions, through the form of language and discourse, constitute institutions that are susceptible to the influence of other institutions [32]. This notion opens the discussion of the levels of institutions present in this dynamic, where macro-institutions are assumed to influence micro-institutions [1]. This study aims to identify and make sense of the macro-institutions present and prominent in Reddit HIV discussions.

2 Literature Review

2.1 Social Media and LGBTQIA+

Burdened by the difficulties LGBTQIA+ community members experience in their daily lives, they have shifted to social media to communicate better [6]. These adversaries include harassment, discrimination, and even physical violence that promulgated their transition to online platforms [10, 42, 44]. These reasons transformed social media as the "safe space" for community members where they can safely and proudly express and manage their identities [17]. As such, when the population of users grows on various social media platforms, their motivations and barriers to using these technologies also expand.

A recent review found that these motivations and barriers to social media use of the LGBTQIA+ community can be categorized into diverse patterns [18]. The LGBTQIA+ community uses social media primarily for information, support, and connection. Others may say that these are available in physical settings; however, LGBTQIA+ community members find it challenging to access these, which prompts them to see them elsewhere. However, this afforded safe space does not come without a catch. Even when using social media, community members are still subjected to stigmatization, discrimination, unintended disclosure, and harm to their well-being. Community members struggle to balance these benefits and burdens as they continue to grow in parallel with the technology.

2.2 Social Institution Theory

Social institutions exist in long-lasting structures of social beliefs and organized rules linked to different functional spheres within societal frameworks [49]. Oftentimes, studies would layer these social institutions into the macro and micro institutions. Macro-institutions are understood to encompass broad institutional spheres, such as medicine, religion, and law, as well as more nuanced aspects like cultural values and racism [9, 28]. While micro-institutions are recognized as behaviors acted during social interactions [50]. Extending these interpretations to the aspect of technology, we offer an interesting perspective on the application of this theory. From a macro-institutional standpoint, another broad context is the Internet, which was recently identified as an institution [36]. From the viewpoint of micro-institutions, interactions by social media users are present in various engagements, such as posting media, reacting, and commenting [47]. This interesting dynamic enables us to examine the practices of social media users in an institutional context.

Considering these assumptions, this study follows the framework below, where the Internet acts as the macro-institution, while discourse or social media interactions are the micro-institutions. Applying the concept familiar to social institution theory, where institutions affect other institutions, we further expand on the idea that other macro-institutions can impact the interactions of social media users [3]. Further supporting the need to identify the prominent macro-institutions that can influence online discussions (Fig. 1).

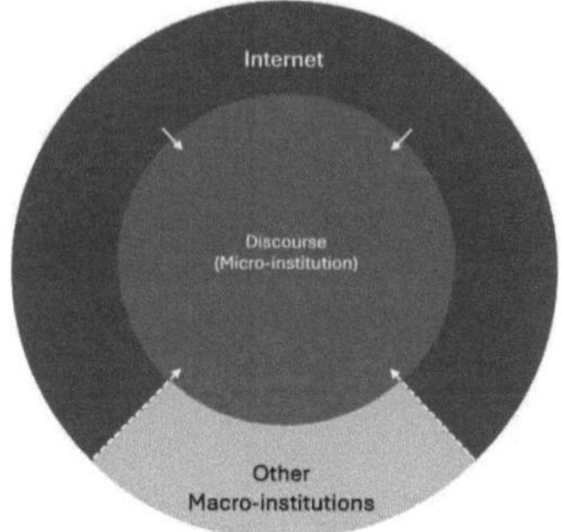

Fig. 1. Technology-Specific Macro-Micro Institutional Framework.

3 Methodology

3.1 Research Design

Qualitative methods vary according to the needs of the studies. Observation has been a prominent research technique for understanding communities for some time [31]. Due to the advent of technological disruptions, communities have now shifted to digital means and have thrived. Standard methodologies such as ethnography have now transcended to virtual locations to accommodate this change.

Netnography, also known as cyberethnography, virtual ethnography, ethnography of the internet, and other names [2, 15], is essentially the online application of ethnography, extending all the practicality to the former [34]. For the sake of simplicity in this study, we will refer to this methodology as netnography.

This study used a passive form of netnography in a subreddit for the LGBTQIA+ community in the Philippines. Through passive observation, the author participated without assimilating his identity and observing without disrupting the dynamics of the social interaction of the community [43]. Using a passive approach also ensures that the individual's representativity is not disturbed while minimizing the author's risk of bias [34].

Guided by Kozinet's five steps [34] and Salzmann-Erikson and Eriksson's LiLEDDA [46], this study will use a six-step process to perform netnography in the social media community to collect the archival data (Fig. 2).

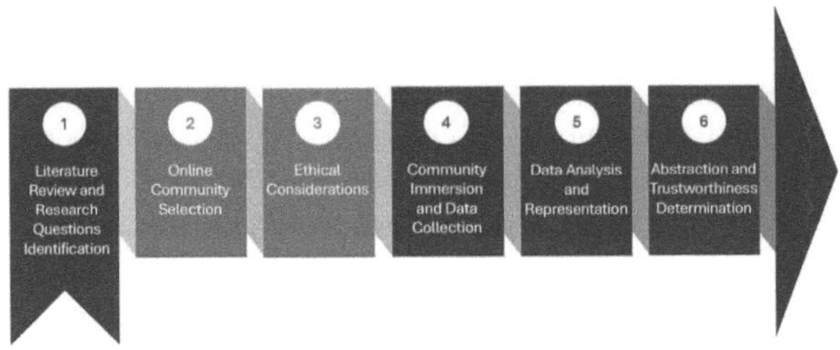

Fig. 2. Social Media Data Steps.

3.2 Data Collection

The corpus of this netnographic study is the subreddit named r/phlgbt, created on December 13, 2014. This subreddit serves as a safe space for the LGBTQIA+ community in the Philippines where they can freely discuss anything under the sun, given they adhere the community rules. At the time of data collection, the community had approximately 12,700 members and has recently grown to 39,000 current members. Although discussions on this subreddit can vary, a significant amount of HIV discussions exist in this digital space.

To collect data from the corpus of this study, this research used a Python program to scrape posts and comments containing the word "HIV". Scraping is a method that automatically captures a considerable dataset of posts using specific tools [41]. This study collected posts, comments, and other relevant information in the subreddit from 2014 to 2024. At the end of extraction, the data kept were posts, poster usernames, comments (including sub-comments), commenter usernames, and corresponding dates. The working dataset includes 3,496 posts in the subreddit r/phlgbt. The researcher searched for specific keywords and included them in the analysis, which aligned with the study's emphasis on HIV-related discussions.

3.3 Data Analysis

The researcher utilized computer-assisted qualitative data analytical software (CAQDAS), Dedoose, to code the themes during the study's analysis. Previous research provided the foundation for using CAQDAS, as it effectively employed these tools to analyze online communities [19, 35]. Archival data from social media allows netnographic studies between big data analysis and discourse analysis that promulgates an understanding of these interactions even with the advancement of technology [40].

In accomplishing the objective of this study, which is to identify the prominent institutions influencing the discussions of the LGBTQIA+ community on Reddit, the research used a reflexive thematic analysis [7]. The researcher consolidated the data sets into an Excel file, representing each discussion by one row of data. Then, the researcher uploaded this file to Dedoose, including the posts, comments, dates, and users involved in the HIV-specific discussions. One Dedoose media represents one discussion thread, including the post's short description, long description or narrative, and comments.

During the data analysis, a second coder joined to further the validity and reliability of the coding process. By fostering a collaborative and reflexive approach between the two coders, the analysis evolves from merely achieving consensus to gaining a deeper understanding of the institutional meanings. To guide the coding process, a codebook was deductively produced with the list of prominent institutions in prior research [7]. However, as the analysis of data set extends, the researcher made inductive adjustments on the codebook allowing an "open-coded" sense which emphasize data-driven results [7]. Throughout the coding process, the researcher employed reflective practices through constant communications and memos that allowed supplementary trustworthiness to the qualitative study. The expected result from this practice is a codebook that attained coding saturation relevant to the social institutions influential in Reddit HIV discussions. This study employs the definition of code saturation, which is the period when a final code added to the codebook does not yield any new codes during subsequent coding sessions [25].

Further ensuring the reliability of this study, the two coders performed inter-rater reliability calculations for multiple sessions. This process checks the coding done by two or more researchers, which helps remove the subjectivity that some qualitative studies encounter difficulty with [16, 29]. This study adopts the available process that improves reliability and transparency, thereby lessening the chance of misinterpreting data meaning [14]. The summary of this data analysis is available in the figure below (Fig. 3).

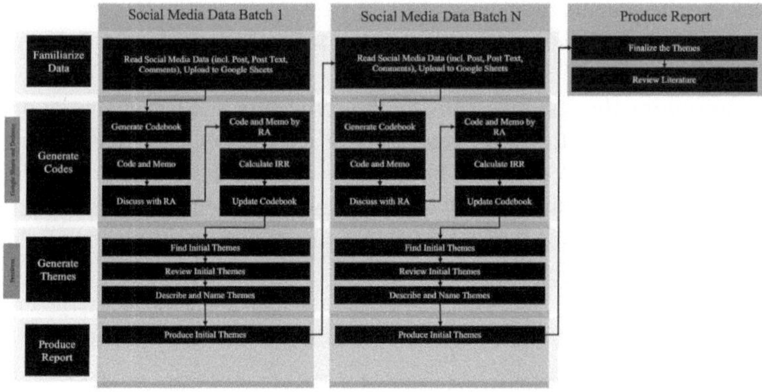

Fig. 3. Summary of Data Analysis.

3.4 Ethical Consideration

Ethical considerations are of considerable importance in the field of netnographic research. The ethical considerations are still debated, particularly whether informed consent is required for conducting a netnographic research study [34, 45].

Although previous Reddit netnographic research posits an exemption on ethical concerns as there is low risk to the participants and the platform already uses anonymity features [8], the researcher still sent a private message to the moderators of the subreddit to request additional guidelines or concerns. Notwithstanding using Reddit's publicly available data and anonymity features, which implicitly protect the ethical rights of participants [33], this study still south ethical approval from the university.

Research on gender and sexually diverse persons has progressed, but not without challenges, as this multitude of research applies traditional ethical notions [37]. In relation to accountability, this research follows the principles presented by Henrickson et al. [26] when the research can. Understandably, this research methodology would not be able to apply all principles; however, it remains to be guided and inspired by the presented considerations.

Lastly, this research acknowledges the ethical intricacies of HIV-related research. Considerably, most ethical frameworks designed for HIV research have pertained to clinical-related studies; this research follows when it can the guiding principles of such frameworks [27]. This study ensures that the discussion's privacy and confidentiality remain safeguarded and preserved only for this purpose.

4 Results and Discussion

The data scraped from the subreddit r/phlgbt totaled 263 media. Each media item contains the thread's subject, a long description, and comments from different users. From these media, excerpts analyzed accumulated to 499. Two coders provided these excerpt codes, which attributed to the macro institutions deductively identified from prior related research [1, 36].

Before presenting the results, to ensure the reliability and transparency of this study, the table below presents the inter-rater reliability information and calculations. As observed, the excerpts coded by the two coders started at 10 but gradually increased as the familiarity and expertise of both coders grew. At the end of the 8th session of IRR, the running cumulative percentage is 94.92%, surpassing the 90% threshold, which is considered a sufficient score [21] (Table 1).

Table 1. Inter-Rater Reliability Calculations and Information.

Batch	Date	Excerpts	Media	Codes Agreed	Codes Disagreed	Total Codes Used	Cumulative Codes Agreed	Cumulative Total Codes Used	Running Cumulative Average
1	December 3, 2024	10	1–10	10	4	14	10	14	71.43%
2	December 10, 2024	12	11–22	12	3	15	22	29	75.86%

(continued)

Table 1. (*continued*)

Batch	Date	Excerpts	Media	Codes Agreed	Codes Disagreed	Total Codes Used	Cumulative Codes Agreed	Cumulative Total Codes Used	Running Cumulative Average
3	December 23, 2024	51	23–46	58	3	61	80	90	88.89%
4	December 23, 2024	52	47–74	60	4	64	140	154	90.91%
5	January 03, 2025	100	75–118	114	4	118	254	272	93.38%
6	January 03, 2025	100	119–154	114	5	119	368	391	94.12%
7	January 10, 2025	100	155–212	119	4	123	487	514	94.75%
8	January 10, 2025	74	213–263	92	4	96	579	610	94.92%

Results indicated that all common macro institutions prevalent in prior research have appeared in HIV discussions on Reddit. As expected, health institution markers, such as testing centers, clinics, and health practitioners, appeared most frequently, comprising 318 excerpts. Next, the Internet, as a social institution, is referenced in 158 excerpts through mentions of social media, websites, and others [36]. Furthermore, other institutions were significantly less mentioned, such as Economy (40), Community (36), and Education (31) (Fig. 4).

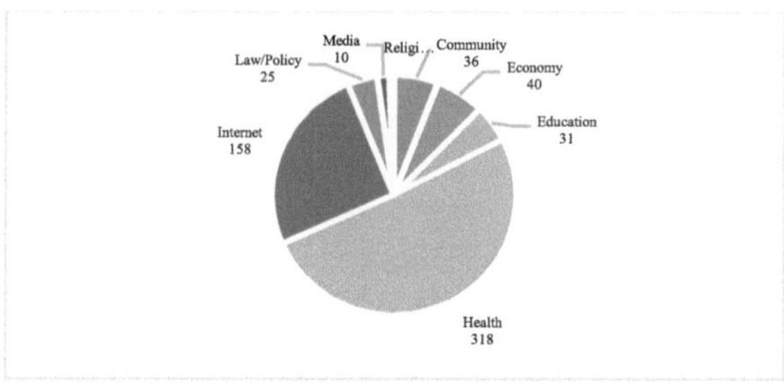

Fig. 4. Code Application of Each Macro Institutions.

The codes applied to the excerpts yielded curious findings when checked for co-occurrence. Code co-occurrence or simultaneous coding is often referred to as "when two or more codes apply to the same passage or sequential passages of text" [48]. The figure below shows the co-occurrence of the codes used during the identification of the macro-institutions most frequently mentioned in the study (Fig. 5).

	Community	Economy	Education	Health	Internet	Law/Policy	Media	Religion
Community		2	5	6	10	0	1	1
Economy	2		0	6	3	4	0	0
Education	5	0		2	6	0	1	0
Health	6	6	2		69	3	2	1
Internet	10	3	6	69		0	5	0
Law/Policy	0	4	0	3	0		0	0
Media	1	0	1	2	5	0		0
Religion	1	0	0	1	0	0	0	

Fig. 5. Code Co-Occurrence of Each Macro Institutions.

In this study, the two institutions or codes that co-occurred the most were health and the internet. These two simultaneously appeared in 69 excerpts, and the next co-occurrence count was significantly lower, at 10, which was for the internet and community.

Frequencies in code co-occurrence often provide insight into the relationship between data, which helps create themes [22]. Considering the prominence of code co-occurrence on the Internet with other macro-institutions, such as health, community, and education, the presence of "techno-social institutions" can be articulated. Techno-social institutions are the integration of technology into other social institutions, such as health, law, and others, due to the prolonged influence of technological advancements on everyday life [11]. In the social media-rich era, interactions through day-to-day discussions help enrich the intersection of technology with other social institutions.

A sample of this intersection between the internet and health is more apparent in discussions where users persuade others to reach out to testing centers, clinics, and healthcare practitioners through social media channels or websites to avail of their services. Excerpts like Media 76, where the user suggested to "try hash clinic too, check their Twitter account first", reinforce the accessibility of these service providers that will help those who are at risk or living with HIV. Another is from Media 23, where another user informed us via a comment that "You can get Prep via SelfCare on FB".

Other excerpts extend beyond suggesting social media platforms to include websites that could serve as another source of information for seekers. In Media 127, one user detailed their experience by sharing, "Hi, in my case I was able to get PEP at myhubcares in Pasig". Then, followed it up with a website suggestion such as "You can visit their website: https://www.myhubcares.com\". This finding supports current studies that investigate online support, focusing on users who also experience the same concerns and cope by helping others online [52].

Other instances of these co-occurrences arise when users attempt to strengthen their claims by backing them up with links that support their assertions. One sample of these declarations is from Media 53, where the comment "For more info regarding transmission and prevention, check this CDC website https://www.cdc.gov/hiv/basics/transmission. html" manifests. Similarly, others would refer to more specific website links, such as Media 49, where the comment goes as "Hello, there are HIV treatment plans by the Saudi government as of 2024. These plans include Pre-exposure prophylaxis. https://www. moh.gov.sa/Ministry/MediaCenter/Publications/Pages/HIV-GUIDELINES.pdf\. I don't know the guidelines for non-citizens, but there you go.". This behavior is consistent with findings that hyperlinks can be used to add credibility and authority by enabling the reader to discern how the original writer or commenter knows what they know [13].

Lastly, some users would still deter others from relying on self-diagnosing using information taken online. An example is from Media 73, where one user warns others that relying solely on Google should not be practiced –"Consult with an expert if you must. DO NOT GOOGLE STUFF." Another sample extends this to not only Google but also social media platforms such as Reddit. A user in Media 98 warns "Just because you saw it in Reddit or international subs, read international papers or better yet ask an actual professional with knowledge with these matters because they studied it for years". This study builds on other findings that integrate the use of technology with healthcare, where perceived trust is still better taken from healthcare practitioners rather than only finding them online [20].

5 Conclusion

This study attempted to understand the institutional dynamics of a social media community. Adding a layer of complexity to that pretense, this study focused on the LGBTQIA+ discussion of one significant issue in the community - HIV. This endeavor answers the necessity raised by other studies to solve the dearth of studies examining the behavior of sexual minorities when using social media [30].

Guided by the social institutional theory, this study explored the influential macro-institutions that hover around the social media interactions of the LGTBQIA+ community during HIV discussions. Findings present that, understandably, health and the Internet dominate these discussions. Even with the recent addition of the Internet as a social institution, it has already become a prominent feature in multiple discussions [36]. Consequently, this study expands the recommendation to leverage historical digital archives, such as Reddit discussions, to further the study of the Internet as a social institution [36].

Furthermore, this study found that, interestingly, the terms "Internet" and "Health" concurrently appear in many individual discussions. This co-occurrence supports the existence of techno-social institutions where technology integrates with other social institutions [11]. Online discussions in the study would observe how users utilize technology to support others and their claims. Alternatively, there will still be users warning others about the dangers of heavily relying on online discussions and information for their health needs.

These findings reveal the existence of these institutions and how social media users balance their interactions in response to these assumed influences.

6 Recommendation

6.1 Micro-institution Focus for Future Studies

This study is not without limitations. In the context of the social institutional framework presented, the study focused on and presented the macro-institutions. Micro-institutions, embodied by social media interactions through discussions, can be further investigated. Future studies can perform an analysis of the dominant discourse of social media communities, which constitutes micro-institutions [50]. In this case, future studies can identify the dominant HIV discourses in the LGBTQIA+ community and extend the current research.

6.2 Beyond the Macro-micro Fixation

Understandably, by following the first recommendation, we are still left with the opportunity to conduct further studies to understand the mechanism of these social interactions [39]. By including the meso layer, future studies can expand the institutional knowledge of the intermediary or interactive space [1, 38]. For example, we already understand that the Internet is the macro-institution, and social media interactions are the micro-institution. Extending on these previous notions, we can assume that social media acts as the meso layer where interactions occurs. The figure below is presented in line with this assumption, which can be further with an understanding that other examples of institutions can interrelate here (Fig. 6).

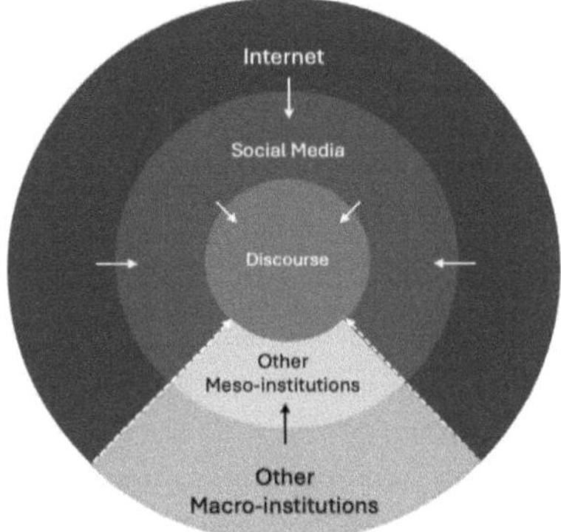

Fig. 6. Extended Technology-Specific Institutional Framework.

6.3 Methodological Approach

Identifying the macro-institutions in the HIV discussions of LGBTQIA+ Reddit users helped further understand the social dynamics of this community; however, future studies can advance this by involving another methodological approach. Considering the passive approach exercised in this study, supplementary interviews can help maximize the benefits of both methods [23]. This approach would also open to the validation and discussion of how these macro-institutions influence their online interactions.

References

1. Abrutyn, S.: Institutional spheres: the macro-structure and culture of social life. In: Abrutyn, S. (ed.) Handbook of Contemporary Sociological Theory. HSSR, pp. 207–228. Springer, Cham (2016). https://doi.org/10.1007/978-3-319-32250-6_11
2. Addeo, F., et al.: Doing social research on online communities: the benefits of netnography. Athens J. Soc. Sci. **7**(1), 9–38 (2019). https://doi.org/10.30958/ajss.7-1-1
3. Agrawal, A., Hockerts, K.: Institutional theory as a framework for practitioners of social entrepreneurship. In: Osburg, T., Schmidpeter, R. (eds.) Social Innovation. CSR, Sustainability, Ethics & Governance, pp. 119–129. Springer, Heidelberg (2013). https://doi.org/10.1007/978-3-642-36540-9_11

4. Angelini, F., et al.: Social media features, perceived group norms, and adolescents' active social media use matter for perceived friendship quality. Front. Psychol. **15** (2024). https://doi.org/10.3389/fpsyg.2024.1222907

5. Baral, R.: Exploring the prominent role of social institutions in society. Int. Res. J. MMC **4**(2), 68–74 (2023). https://doi.org/10.3126/irjmmc.v4i2.56015

6. Berger, M.N., et al.: Social media use and health and well-being of lesbian, gay, bisexual, transgender, and queer youth: systematic review (2022). https://doi.org/10.2196/38449

7. Braun, V., Clarke, V.: Using thematic analysis in psychology. Qual. Res. Psychol. **3**(2), 77–101 (2006). https://doi.org/10.1191/1478088706qp063oa

8. Brewer, C.G.: R/ProtectandServe: an exploration of the virtual canteen culture regarding police misconduct. Polic. Soc. **32**(10), 1193–1208 (2022). https://doi.org/10.1080/10439463.2022.2029434

9. Bronfenbrenner, U.: Toward an experimental ecology of human development (1977)

10. Chandra, S., Hanckel, B.: 'I wouldn't want my family to cop anything': examining the family of origin and its place in LGBTQIA+ young people's social media practices. J. Youth Stud. (2022). https://doi.org/10.1080/13676261.2022.2156781

11. Chayko, M.: Superconnected: The Internet, Digital Media, and Techno-Social Life. Sage, Newcastle upon Tyne (2020)

12. Chinyanganya, T.L., Muguti, J.: Taboos and the pragmatics of teaching HIV and AIDS at primary school: views from selected primary school teachers in Chipadze, Bindura. Greener J. Educ. Res. **3**(2), 046–052 (2013). https://doi.org/10.15580/GJER.2013.2.011613381

13. Coddington, M.: Normalizing the hyperlink: how bloggers, professional journalists, and institutions shape linking values. Digit. J. **2**(2), 140–155 (2014). https://doi.org/10.1080/21670811.2013.785813

14. Cole, R.: Inter-rater reliability methods in qualitative case study research. Sociol. Methods Res. (2023). https://doi.org/10.1177/00491241231156971

15. Costello, L., et al.: Netnography: range of practices, misperceptions, and missed opportunities. Int. J. Qual. Methods **16**, 1 (2017). https://doi.org/10.1177/1609406917700647

16. Creswell, J.: Educational Research: Planning, Conducting, and Evaluating Quantitative, vol. 7 (2002)

17. Devito, M.A., et al.: "Too gay for Facebook": presenting LGBTQ+ identity throughout the personal social media ecosystem. In: Proceedings of the ACM on Human Computer Interaction, vol. 2. CSCW (2018). https://doi.org/10.1145/3274313

18. Ebardo, R., Payawal, B.: Unveiling the pride in social media: a review of LGBTQIA+ use of online social networks. In: Asian CHI 2024. ACM (2024). https://doi.org/10.1145/3704611.3704653

19. Ebardo, R., Suarez, M.T.: Learning affordances of a Facebook community of older adults: a netnographic investigation during COVID-19 (2022)

20. Elinzano, G.B.O., Payawal, B.O., Ebardo, R.A.: Effects of perceived trust, perceived privacy, and technology anxiety to ChatGPT adoption for medical self-diagnosis: a structural equation modeling approach. In: Thiruchelvam, V., Alfred, R., Ismail, Z.I.B.A., Haviluddin, H., Baharum, A. (eds.) ICACSE 2023. LNEE, vol. 1199, pp. 521–536. Springer, Singapore (2024). https://doi.org/10.1007/978-981-97-2977-7_33

21. Graham, M., et al.: Measuring and promoting inter-rater agreement of teacher and principal performance ratings (2012)

22. Guest, G., et al.: Applied Thematic Analysis. SAGE Publications, Inc. (2014). https://doi.org/10.4135/9781483384436

23. Hanell, F., Severson, P.J.: Netnography: two methodological issues and the consequences for teaching and practice (2022)

24. van Heijningen, M., van Clief, L.: Enabling online safe spaces: a case study of love matters Kenya. IDS Bull. **48**(1), 7–22 (2017). https://doi.org/10.19088/1968-2017.103

25. Hennink, M.M., et al.: Code saturation versus meaning saturation: how many interviews are enough? (2017). https://doi.org/10.1177/1049732316665344
26. Henrickson, M., et al.: Research ethics with gender and sexually diverse persons (2020). https://doi.org/10.3390/ijerph17186615
27. Hlongwa, P.: Current ethical issues in HIV/AIDS research and HIV/AIDS care. Oral Dis. **22**, 61–65 (2016). https://doi.org/10.1111/odi.12391
28. Hong, J.S.: Understanding Vietnamese youth gangs in America: an ecological systems analysis (2010). https://doi.org/10.1016/j.avb.2010.01.003
29. Jnanathapaswi, S.G.: Thematic analysis & coding: an overview of the qualitative paradigm (2021). https://doi.org/10.6084/m9.figshare.17159249
30. Kaiser, S., et al.: A comparison of social media behaviors between sexual minorities and heterosexual individuals. Comput. Hum. Behav. **116** (2021). https://doi.org/10.1016/j.chb.2020.106638
31. Kaoukaou, M.: Netnography: towards a new sociological approach of qualitative research in the digital age. In: SHS Web of Conferences, vol. 119, p. 01006 (2021). https://doi.org/10.1051/shsconf/202111901006
32. King, J.L., et al.: Institutional factors in information technology innovation (1994)
33. Kozinets, R.: The field behind the screen: using netnography for marketing research in online communities. J. Mark. Res. (2002)
34. Kozinets, R.V.: Netnography: redefined (2015)
35. Lawless, M., et al.: Dementia on Facebook: requesting information and advice about dementia risk-prevention on social media. Discourse Context Media **25**, 44–51 (2018). https://doi.org/10.1016/j.dcm.2018.01.011
36. Longo, G.M.: The Internet as a social institution: rethinking concepts for family scholarship. Fam. Relat. **72**(2), 621–636 (2023). https://doi.org/10.1111/fare.12825
37. Meezan, W., Martin, J.I.: Handbook of Research with Lesbian, Gay, Bisexual, and Transgender Populations
38. de Mello, A.M., et al.: Meso-institutions as systemic intermediaries in sustainable transitions governance. Environ. Innov. Soc. Transit. **52** (2024). https://doi.org/10.1016/j.eist.2024.100870
39. Ménard, C.: Embedding organizational arrangements: towards a general model (2014). https://doi.org/10.1017/S1744137414000228
40. Morais, G.M., et al.: Netnography: origins, foundations, evolution and axiological and methodological developments and trends. Qual. Rep. **25**(2), 441–455 (2020). https://doi.org/10.46743/2160-3715/2020.4227
41. Norman Adams, N.: 'Scraping' Reddit posts for academic research? Addressing some blurred lines of consent in growing internet-based research trend during the time of Covid-19. Int. J. Soc. Res. Methodol. (2022). https://doi.org/10.1080/13645579.2022.2111816
42. Nova, F.F., et al.: "Facebook promotes more harassment": social media ecosystem, skill and marginalized Hijra identity in Bangladesh. In: Proceedings of the ACM on Human-Computer Interaction, vol. 5. CSCW1 (2021). https://doi.org/10.1145/3449231
43. Nunes, G.S., Arruda Filho, E.J.M.: Consumer behavior regarding wearable technologies: Google glass. Innov. Manag. Rev. **15**(3), 230–246 (2018). https://doi.org/10.1108/INMR-06-2018-0034
44. O. Alichie, B.: Communication at the margins: online homophobia from the perspectives of LGBTQ + social media users. J. Hum. Rights (2022). https://doi.org/10.1080/14754835.2022.2104116
45. Porter, N., et al.: Hen Dos and Don'ts: lifting the veil on tensions in consumer rituals. J. Mark. Manag. **39**(13–14), 1197–1219 (2023). https://doi.org/10.1080/0267257X.2023.2219691
46. Salzmann-Erikson, M., Eriksson, H.: LiLEDDA: a six-step forum-based netnographic research method for nursing science (2012)

47. Sam, C.H.: Shaping discourse through social media: using foucauldian discourse analysis to explore the narratives that influence educational policy. Am. Behav. Sci. **63**(3), 333–350 (2019). https://doi.org/10.1177/0002764218820565
48. Scharp, K.M.: Thematic co-occurrence analysis: advancing a theory and qualitative method to illuminate ambivalent experiences. J. Commun. **71**(4), 545–571 (2021). https://doi.org/10.1093/joc/jqab015
49. Scott, W.R.: The adolescence of institutional theory (1987)
50. Serpa, S., Ferreira, C.M.: Micro, meso and macro levels of social analysis. Int. J. Soc. Sci. Stud. **7**(3), 120 (2019). https://doi.org/10.11114/ijsss.v7i3.4223
51. Statista: Number of social network users worldwide as in 2025 (2025)
52. Stehr, P.: The benefits of supporting others online – how online communication shapes the provision of support and its relationship with wellbeing. Comput. Hum. Behav. **140** (2023). https://doi.org/10.1016/j.chb.2022.107568

Content Themes and Self-presentation of Virtual Influencers - Exploring the Impact on User Engagement and Sentiment

Laura Tölle[(✉)] [iD], Torben Rehmer, Fynn Ruppel, Johann Müller, and Matthias Trier [iD]

Paderborn University, Warburger Straße 100, 33098 Paderborn, Germany
{laura.toelle,trier}@upb.de, {torreh,fynrup,
mjohann}@mail.uni-paderborn.de

Abstract. Virtual Influencers (VIs) are computer-generated characters that imitate human behavior. Especially highly realistic human-like VIs blur the line between human and non-human appearances. Many VIs secured advertising partnerships with major brands due to advantages like control, risk-free brand-consistent storytelling, scalability, and cost-efficiency. This study investigates the impact of different types of Instagram postings by VIs on user sentiment and engagement. Twelve VIs were selected based on pre-defined criteria. The analysis comprised three main steps: First, posts were categorized into content themes. Second, we assessed agency and identity using Llama3.1-405B. User reactions were then analyzed for engagement and sentiment distributions. Emotion classification was conducted by assigning comments to Ekman's six basic emotions. Keyword frequency analysis identified prominent terms associated with specific sentiments. The results of the sentiment analysis indicate that visually engaging content themes, such as fashion and travel-related posts, tend to elicit more positive reactions. In contrast, personality-driven content themes, particularly posts related to family, are more likely to evoke lower sentiment and negative emotions. Moreover, posts emphasizing agency or identity do not necessarily enhance user engagement or sentiment. The study lays the groundwork for examining how digital personas influence consumer behavior. Our findings have implications for digital marketing strategies, highlighting the effectiveness of visually compelling content while underscoring the need for a cautious approach to personality-driven themes.

Keywords: Virtual Influencer · Agency · Identity · Sentiment · Instagram

1 Introduction

Social media influencers have become a central element of online marketing [15]. A more recent phenomenon emerging in this landscape is that of virtual influencers (VIs). VIs are defined as computer-generated characters that act as influencers by mimicking human behaviors and engaging in advertising. They possess anthropomorphized appearances, distinct identities, and social roles but are ultimately controlled by humans or algorithms, offering brands and companies a high degree of control over their public image

A. Coman et al. (Eds.): HCII 2025, LNCS 16337, pp. 82–101, 2026.
https://doi.org/10.1007/978-3-032-12801-0_6

[4]. Their visual styles range from minimalist, cartoon-like, or anime-inspired designs to highly realistic, human-like representations. A particularly prominent category within this domain is the "high-realistic human-like" VI. These influencers challenge the perceptual boundary between human and non-human appearances [5]. An increasing number of VIs on social media have amassed significant followings and secured advertising partnerships with major brands. A prominent example is Lil Miquela, a VI with over 2.4 million followers on Instagram, who starred in a commercial collaboration with BMW. VIs are of growing relevance to businesses due to their potential advantages over traditional human influencers [22]. Unlike human influencers, VIs can be entirely controlled, eliminating risks associated with personal scandals, hence allowing for risk-free, brand-consistent storytelling [28]. Furthermore, they offer high scalability and cost-efficiency, particularly as advancements in artificial intelligence and the metaverse continue to expand their potential applications.

However, despite their strategic advantages, understanding how VIs are perceived is crucial, particularly in terms of brand safety and user engagement. A key factor in influencer marketing success is authenticity. Previous research has consistently highlighted that VIs struggle to be perceived as authentic. Users are aware that VIs are not real individuals but are instead controlled by external actors, which may impact their credibility and effectiveness in influencer marketing campaigns [21]. Parasocial Interaction Theory [12, 13], the Computers Are Social Actors (CASA) [25] paradigm, and Anthropomorphism [27] suggest that VIs seem more authentic when displaying human-like traits, triggering positive sentiment [2]. However, the Uncanny Valley suggests that while greater human resemblance improves perception, near-perfect features can cause discomfort [24]. Besides perceived visual human-likeness (VHL), perceived mental human-likeness (MHL) is crucial [22]. High VHL may be negatively perceived if MHL is low [14]. In this context, agency (self-directed behavior) and identity (consistent traits and personalities) are central [28].

To date, most research has focused primarily on the effects of perceived VHL and how the design of VIs influences these perceptions. In contrast, perceived MHL and how self-presentation of VIs shape this perception has received less attention. While some studies have considered autonomy as a mediating variable [20], little research has investigated how specific actions of VIs, as an independent variable, influence user acceptance [22] and sentiment. Given that VIs do not physically exist, their presence and activities are primarily manifested through the content they produce (e.g., images, videos, and posts).

This study closes this gap by exploring how VIs' content themes, agency, and identity impact user sentiment and engagement. Additionally, this study investigates how sentiment in user comments varies across different types of posts by VIs, providing insights into their marketing effectiveness and potential challenges in the digital marketing landscape. The insights provide guidance for informing marketing strategies, ensuring that campaigns align with audience expectations regarding authenticity, credibility, and ethical transparency. After presenting the theoretical background and related work, we describe the methodological approach used to obtain our results. This is followed by a discussion of the findings and a concluding outlook on future research.

2   Theoretical Background

Research on the perception of VIs is shaped by several theoretical concepts. The CASA paradigm [25] suggests that humans naturally respond to computers in social ways. Incorporating human-like features or behaviors, i.e., anthropomorphic design, amplifies these social responses [26]. Human-like VIs tend to elicit stronger social responses from users [25, 27]. Users may develop one-sided emotional connections with VIs, much like those formed with media personalities or human influencers. This phenomenon, known as parasocial interaction, creates a sense of closeness and familiarity [7, 12]. Parasocial relationships can foster trust, acceptance, and engagement. However, the potential lack of social-emotional depth in VIs can impede the development of such relationships [23]. The aforementioned frameworks support the hypothesis that VIs despite users' awareness that they are not real individuals are perceived as more authentic when they display human-like cues (e.g., realistic appearances, emotional expressions). Consequently, stronger human cues should lead to more positive sentiment toward VIs.

Baudier and de Boissieu [2] indicate that anthropomorphism, emotional content, the attractiveness of posts, and the physical appearance of VIs enhance perceived credibility. However, studies have also suggested that an excessive presence of human-like cues can, in certain cases, result in negative perceptions, contradicting the initial hypothesis. Lim and Lee [19] found that explicitly labelling a VI as computer-generated reduces perceived humanness. This effect was particularly pronounced when VIs expressed negative emotions, which led to unfavorable user reactions. In contrast, positive emotions were better received. Human influencers, however, were evaluated more favorably when expressing negative emotions. Similarly, Ham et al. [10] analyzed emotional expressions and found that joy was generally well received, whereas sadness and particularly lust were perceived as inauthentic, leading to negative reactions. In this context, the Uncanny Valley effect is frequently referenced. This concept suggests a generally positive correlation between human-likeness and favorable perceptions; however, near-perfect human resemblance with minor imperfections can evoke discomfort and be less well-received than a slightly less realistic appearance [24]. Research on the Uncanny Valley effect in VIs has produced mixed results. Some studies found that highly realistic VIs are perceived more negatively than less realistic ones [1, 29]. In contrast, newer studies suggest that the perception of realism and likability follows a linear pattern, with more realistic influencers being rated more favorably [20, 33]. These contradictory findings suggest additional influencing factors. One study proposes that, in addition to perceived VHL, perceived MHL (i.e., the extent to which the influencer is seen as having a human-like mind or traits) also plays a crucial role. A high level of VHL may be perceived negatively if MHL is perceived low [14]. The concepts of agency and identity are particularly relevant in this regard. While VIs are not truly autonomous due to technological limitations and are controlled by humans, their perceived agency (i.e., the extent to which they appear self-directed) and perceived identity (i.e., whether they exhibit consistent traits and personalities) are expected to be significant factors in authenticity perception [28].

3   Research Methods

Since Instagram is a major platform used by VIs to engage with their audiences [30], we chose Instagram users as the target research group. We apply a netnographic approach, focusing on people's experiences on social media [17, 18] to investigate how different content themes posted by VIs and their self-presentation influence user sentiment and engagement. Doing so, we address the following research questions:

1. How are the content themes of VI posts distributed in terms of topics covered and the proportion of sponsored content?
2. How do VIs present themselves in their posts in terms of agency and identity?
3. How do content themes and the self-presentation of VIs influence user engagement and user sentiment?

3.1   Data Collection and Selection of VIs

The goal of the data collection process is to capture both the content of posts produced by VIs and the reactions of Instagram users to these posts. We collected the full captions of VIs' posts, including all characters such as emojis; the number of comments and likes per post; and all first-level comments under each post. Replies to other comments were excluded because they reflect responses to prior comments rather than direct reactions to the original post, making them unsuitable for the following analyses. All comments were anonymized.

For the creation of the dataset, influencers were selected based on specific criteria. To be included in our dataset, the VI must be active on Instagram; have a realistic, human-like appearance rather than an anime-style or non-human representation; have a certain number of followers (100,000 or more) to ensure a sufficient number of comments; must have a minimum of 100 posts to provide a solid data foundation; and the majority of comments under the posts must be in English, as the models used for sentiment analysis have been trained on English texts. To identify suitable VIs, the primary source was VirtualHumans.org, a platform managed by industry insiders that documents and analyzes VIs and related topics. As a result, twelve VIs were identified that met all selection criteria: bermudaisbae, blawko22, fit_aitana, imma.gram, kyraonig, leyalovenature, lilmiquela, millasofiafin, naina_avtr, rozy.gram, shudu.gram, and thalasya_. From each VI, the 100 most recent posts were extracted between February 1 and February 16, 2025. The data extraction process was carried out manually. A preprocessing script was applied to structure the data by extracting key information from each post and transferring it to a database. This included the post description, the number of likes if available, the influencer's name, the post URL, and the content of the comments. In total, 117,324 comments were collected.

3.2   Data Cleaning

To allow for an informative analysis, the collected post and comment data underwent a cleaning process. First, a language categorization was performed on the comments using the transformer model papluca/xlm-roberta-base-language-detection. With an average accuracy of 99.6%, it reliably classifies text into 20 predefined languages. In our dataset,

47,671 comments were identified as English. Additionally, a large number of comments, consisting exclusively of emojis, were separately marked for further analysis. A new language category labelled 'Emoji' was introduced for classification purposes when a comment contained only emojis. This classification was conducted using the emoji Python package, identifying 30,504 such comments. All other comments were not considered for further analysis.

A central aspect of the analysis was the categorization of posts into different content themes. Since post descriptions are often unstructured and usually do not solely contain meaningful information, comprehensive preprocessing of the textual data was conducted to enhance the quality of the texts for the subsequent content analysis. Initially, general cleaning measures were applied to all post descriptions to create a more consistent and structured dataset. This included removing the names of the respective influencers from the descriptions to prevent biases caused by personalized elements. Additionally, special characters and automatically generated additions like "and more" which were introduced during extraction when a post was created in collaboration with other influencers, were removed. Unnecessary line breaks were also eliminated to ensure a uniform text structure. Beyond these general cleaning steps, additional preprocessing was conducted to facilitate the subsequent classification of post descriptions. Descriptions originally written in other languages were translated into English using the model meta-llama/Llama-3.3-70B-Instruct. Unlike traditional translation methods, this process employed a large language model to preserve the linguistic style of the original texts as accurately as possible. Additionally, all non-ASCII characters were removed to avoid potential processing issues. This included non-Latin characters, such as Korean script and emojis, which would be transformed into Unicode in text processing models, thereby negatively impacting classification accuracy. Another important preprocessing step involved the analysis and cleaning of hashtags. A frequency analysis of the hashtags used was conducted to identify those appearing in at least 25% of an influencer's posts (≥ 25 occurrences). These were classified as "standard hashtags", which did not provide additional thematic value to the respective post but rather served as recurring markers. Consequently, these hashtags were removed from the descriptions. For all remaining hashtags, the hashtag symbol (#) was eliminated, particularly to clean empty hashtags that may have resulted from non-Latin characters. Since the analysis focused on the entire caption rather than individual hashtags, removing the symbol contributed to text homogenization and emphasized the content-related aspects of the captions.

These preprocessing steps ensured that the post descriptions maintained a high level of internal consistency, allowing subsequent analyses to be conducted on a cleaned and optimized textual dataset. The cleaned dataset serves as the foundation for the subsequent analyses in this study.

3.3 Data Analysis

The analysis of the collected data comprised three central steps. First, the posts were categorized into content themes. Second, user reactions and their sentiments were examined in relation to these content themes, allowing for insights into how different types of content influence audience engagement and perception. Third, an exploratory analysis was conducted to assess the level of agency and identity that users attribute to VIs, shedding light on how these digital personas are perceived in comparison to human influencers.

Classification Based on Content Themes and Sponsored Posts. All posts were assigned to one of the following categories: Beauty, Family, Fashion, Fitness, Food, Interior, Pet, and Travel, based on the classification framework proposed by Tricomi et al. [31]. These categories were chosen because comprehensive datasets exist for posts made by human influencers, allowing for a comparative analysis of the extent to which VIs post about different content themes compared to human influencers [16]. Due to the preprocessing steps, some post descriptions were empty (e.g., those consisting solely of emojis or non-Latin characters), resulting in a total of 1,165 posts being successfully classified to the content themes. To achieve this classification, a zero-shot classification approach was employed, calculating a confidence value for each post to determine its most likely category. For this task, we utilized the model MoritzLaurer/deberta-v3-large-zeroshot-v2.0, as it demonstrated superior performance in sample evaluations compared to facebook/bart-large-mnli, which is often considered the state-of-the-art model for zero-shot classification tasks. Each post was assigned to the category with the highest confidence value. If the highest confidence value across all categories was below 0.7 (70% certainty), the post was classified into an "Other" category. Various algorithms, including BERTopic [9], Latent Dirichlet Allocation [3], and classical keyword extractors, even after numerous attempts, did not yield satisfactory results, leading us to exclude them from further analysis.

To classify the posts into sponsored and non-sponsored, the post descriptions were matched against an extensive list of keywords that come up in sponsored posts. If one of the keywords was part of the post description, the post was classified as sponsored.

Classification Based on presented Agency and Identity. The posts were classified into the following categories: Agency & Identity, Agency, Identity, and None. To achieve this classification, a system prompt for the large language model Llama3.1-405B was developed based on the theoretical background of agency and identity. The model was instructed to categorize posts according to the extent to which they suggest agency and/or identity. While rule-based or conventional machine learning approaches typically rely on predefined keywords or manually crafted features, a large language model can flexibly interpret various writing styles and expressions, even when agency or identity is implied rather than explicitly stated. This capability is particularly crucial when dealing with high-level concepts such as agency and identity, which often require contextual interpretation beyond simple keyword matching. This enables a more precise and robust classification without the need for extensive curated training data or manual feature engineering.

Analysis of User Reactions and Sentiment. After grouping the posts based on content themes and the agency/identity labelling, user reactions were analyzed to understand engagement patterns and sentiment distributions. The analysis consisted of three steps. The number of likes and comments per post was compared within each influencer's account to determine variations in engagement across the different groups. Patterns and deviations in like counts were identified to understand which themes generated higher or lower engagement levels. User comments were analyzed using two sentiment analysis methods. To categorize user comments based on their emotional content, we employed the emotion classification model j-hartmann/emotion-english-distilroberta-base. This model assigns comments to one of the six basic emotions defined by Ekman: joy, sadness, fear, surprise, anger, and disgust [8] plus a neutral sentiment. One significant limitation of this approach is its inability to effectively process emojis, often resulting in misclassification of emoji-containing comments as neutral. To mitigate this issue, all emojis were filtered out prior to classification. To complement the emotion classification, a separate sentiment analysis was conducted using the transformer model cardiffnlp/twitter-roberta-base-sentiment-latest, which was trained on Twitter data and is capable of incorporating emoji sentiment into its classifications. This model categorized comments into positive, negative, or neutral sentiments. Unlike the previous approach, this method allowed for a complete analysis of comments, including those composed entirely of emojis, thus ensuring a more comprehensive understanding of the sentiment conveyed in user reactions. By combining these two sentiment analysis approaches, a more comprehensive understanding of emotional reactions to different content themes was achieved. To identify the most frequently used keywords in user comments, a keyword frequency analysis was conducted for each influencer. The process involved several steps: The comments were filtered by the highest emotion scores for the three base sentiments. The extracted text was then preprocessed by converting it to lowercase, removing punctuation, and excluding common stopwords. Subsequently, keyword frequencies were calculated to determine the most prominent terms used by commentators. This approach provides a concise overview of the dominant keywords and their associated sentiments.

4 Results

The following section presents the findings of this study, structured according to the research questions.

4.1 Distribution of Content Themes

The first research question focuses on determining how the selected VIs distribute their posts across the eight identified content themes, based on the theoretical background: Beauty, Family, Fashion, Fitness, Food, Interior, Pet and Travel.

Table 1. Distribution of posts per content theme.

Content Theme	Fashion	Travel	Beauty	Interior	Food	Family	Fitness	Pet	Other
Number of Posts	175	128	44	20	19	15	11	8	745

In Table 1, we see how posts are distributed across the content themes. A large majority (745 posts) fall into the "Other" category, indicating that most captions did not meet the criteria for the pre-defined content themes. Among the remaining themes, Fashion holds the highest number of posts (175), followed by Travel (128) and Beauty (44). The other categories represent smaller portions of the dataset.

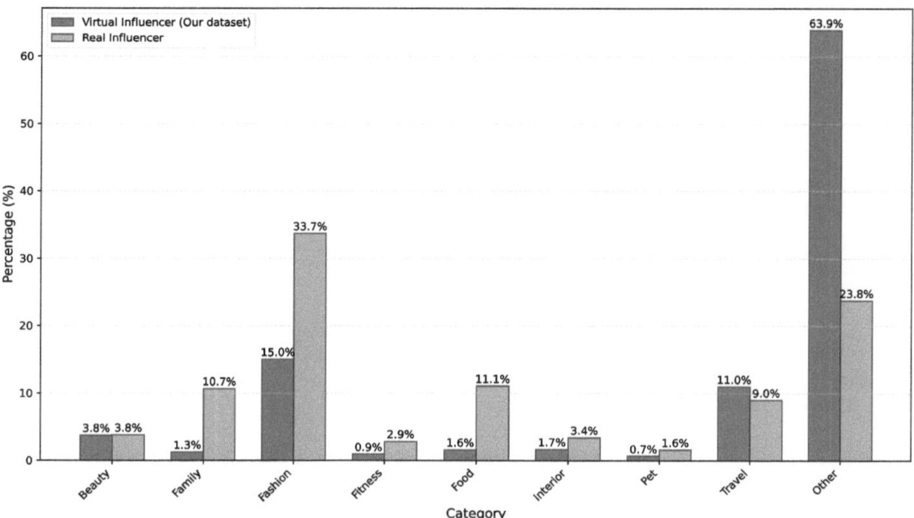

Fig. 1. Content theme distribution comparison between VI and human influencers.

The bar chart in Fig. 1 shows the percentage distribution of categories in our dataset (left bars) compared with a dataset about human influencers (right bars) by Kim et al. [16]. Notably, "Other" which includes all posts that did not meet the 70% confidence threshold for any given topic, is much higher in our dataset (63.9%). In contrast, Family and Food appear at roughly one-tenth the rate reported in the literature with real influencers. Fashion stands at 15.0% in our dataset compared to 33.7% in the literature, while Beauty remains nearly the same in both sources.

Figure 2 highlights the distribution of sponsored vs. non-sponsored posts per content theme. Overall, around 6.5% (77 out of 1,185) of the posts are classified as sponsored. Beauty stands out with the largest proportion of sponsored posts (8 out of 44). In the Fashion category, 15 out of 160 posts are sponsored. For Interior, 2 out of 20 posts are sponsored, making it the second-most sponsored content theme (percentage-wise). In the Other category, 48 posts (6.4%) are sponsored.

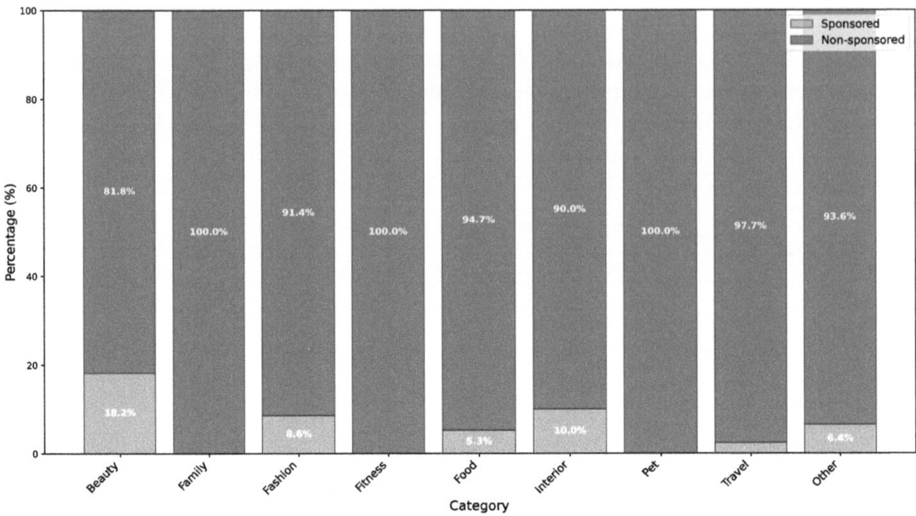

Fig. 2. Sponsored posts vs. non-sponsored posts per content theme.

4.2 Agency-Identity Classification

To analyze how VI present themselves in their posts, focusing on agency and identity, a post classification was conducted, grouping the posts into "Agency" (A), "Identity" (I), "Agency and Identity" (AI), and "None" based on their descriptions. Table 2 shows the distribution of comments per Agency-Identity classification. The median number of comments per Agency-Identity is rather equally distributed, with "None" showing the least comments per posts. As the mean is notably larger than the median for all classifications, some outlier posts got a lot more comments. Posts which neither pose "Agency" or "Identity" result in having the lowest number of comments per post with a median of 43.5. The concept of "Agency" alone displays the fewest posts (127), whereas "Agency and Identity" depicts the largest number of posts (401).

Table 2. Average and median number of comments per classification.

Classification	Mean Number of Comments per Post	Median Number of Comments per Post	Number of Comments overall	Number of Posts
I	72.08	49.0	26381	366
A	65.57	50.0	8328	127
AI	63.03	47.0	25274	401
None	62.73	43.5	18192	290

Table 3 shows sample post descriptions for each Agency-Identity classification, illustrating how each post fits into the corresponding category.

Table 3. Sample post descriptions by Agency-Identity classification.

Classification	Exemplary Post Description
I	I love vegetables and fruits in all shapes and colors, and I wanted to know more about how they are planted and grown. Did you know that they are all unique and have individual wishes and demands, just like us humans? I am slowly realizing that it takes a whole life to really learn about the cultivation and care of plants and the soil. But… there's so much more I want to see and experience! (https://www.instagram.com/p/CcsYNO2qIYS/)
A	Wrapping up my week with the most adorable picnic rendezvous! Ready to soak up the sunshine, munch on yummy treats, and just bask in good vibes. Wanna join?! (https://www.instagram.com/p/C577bHZstnO/)
AI	"I'm in my Trusting my Gut era and thanks to yall I am feeling confident and engaged with the follower who's been in my comments and DMs (as some of you already know). They want to meet up and disclose something (but the last time I did that, @bermudaisBae hacked my account and told me my whole life was a lie SOOO…) Keeping it strictly virtual (https://www.instagram.com/p/DC68WxjRfiW/)
None	Merry Christmas! (https://www.instagram.com/p/DD9PwOJiqWX/)

4.3   User Engagement and Sentiment

To address the third research question, we present our observations on the observed effect in this section.

Content Themes. The bar chart in Fig. 3 illustrates the average number of comments per post, categorized by content theme. The dashed line represents the overall average of 98.46 comments across all categories. Fitness stands out with the highest average (144.8, $n = 11$), followed by Interior (118.3, $n = 20$) and Family (106.5, $n = 15$). Travel (101.8, $n = 128$) and the large "Other" category (99.5, $n = 745$) hover around or slightly above the overall mean, while Food (96.9, $n = 19$), Pet (96.9, $n = 8$), Fashion (89.7, $n = 175$), and Beauty (88.2, $n = 44$) fall below the average.

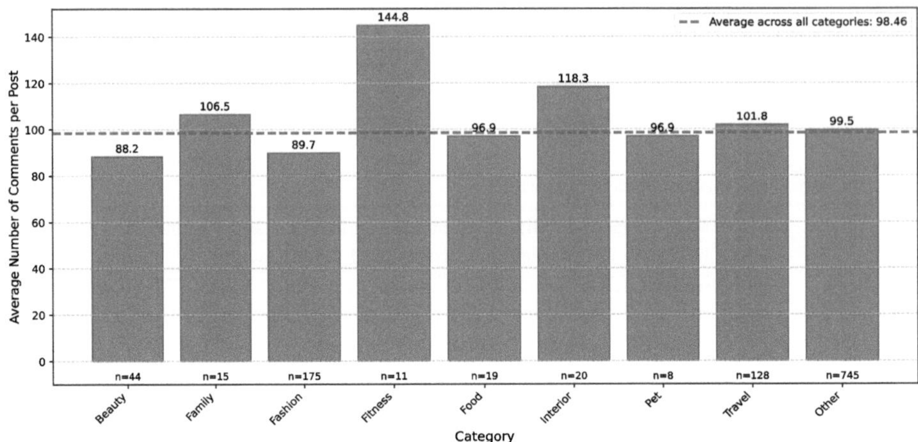

Fig. 3. Average number of comments per content theme, n = number of posts per content theme.

The box plots in Fig. 4 show that the number of likes varies by content theme. Categories such as Fashion and Other display particularly wide ranges, reaching above 20,000 likes in the upper whiskers. Fitness and Pet have narrower ranges and lower median likes, while Beauty, Food and Travel each have medians around the mid-range of likes. Interior and Family fall between, with moderately broad distributions. The overall spread within each category suggests that some content themes, e.g., Fashion, can attract very high like counts, whereas Fitness and Pet tend to remain relatively lower.

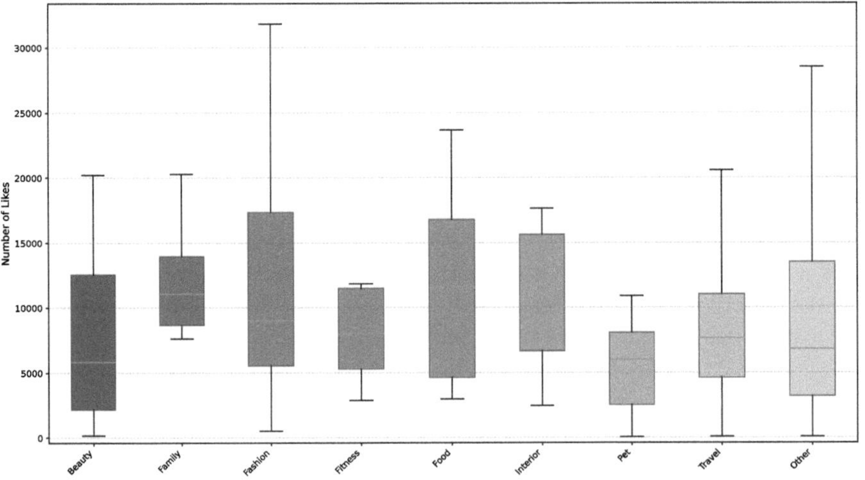

Fig. 4. Distribution of likes per content theme. Outliers removed.

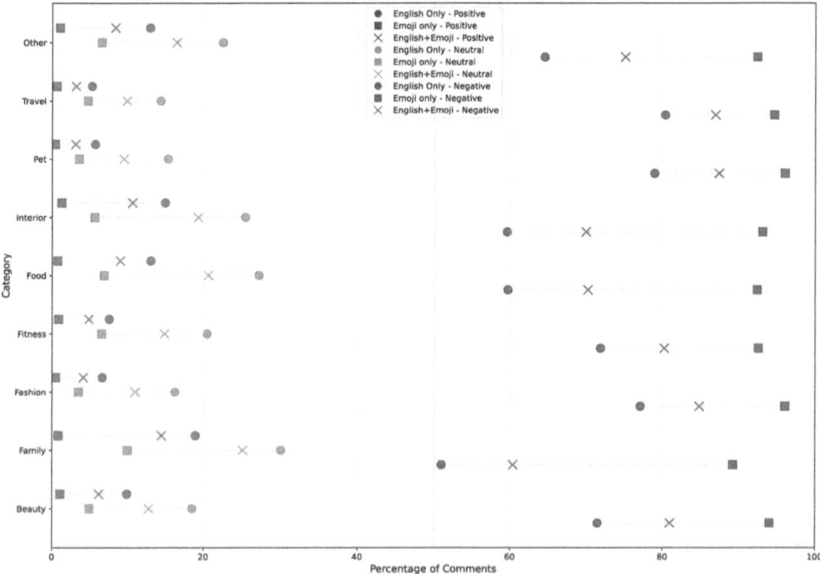

Fig. 5. Sentiment distribution by content theme and language.

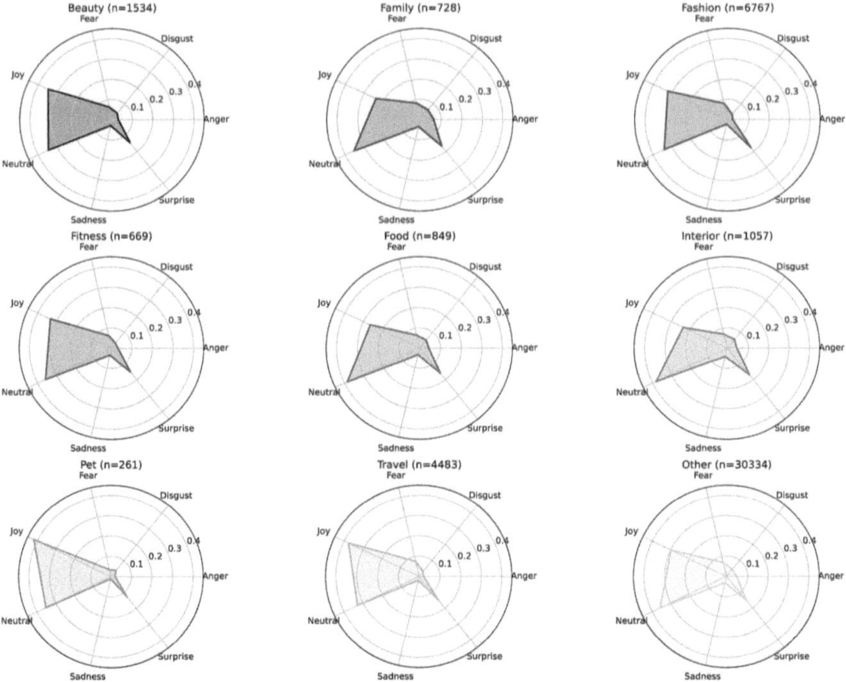

Fig. 6. Ekman's emotions by content theme.

A notable insight from Fig. 5 is that English comments in general are significantly less positive than Emoji-only comments. This is especially true for the Family content-theme, where 89.1% of Emoji-only comments are positive, whereas only 50.9% of English comments are positive. Only roughly 1% of all Emoji comments were classified as negative, whereas this number increases notably for English comments. This discrepancy can also be observed for neutral comments, where the neutral sentiment makes up a larger percentage for English comments compared to Emoji-only comments. Overall, Emoji-only comments are mostly positive whereas English comments are more diverse regarding their sentiment.

The nine radar charts in Fig. 6 illustrate the distribution of Ekman's six basic emotions (joy, sadness, fear, surprise, anger, disgust) plus a neutral category. Each chart corresponds to one content theme and visualizes the relative frequency of each emotion.

The data reveals an increased occurrence of the emotion joy in comments on posts within the content themes Pet (41.8%), Travel (37.7%), Beauty (34.7%), and Fashion (32.6%). In contrast, comments on posts within the Family content theme, while still showing an overall low absolute proportion, exhibited a relatively higher occurrence of fear (8.2%) and disgust (6.0%) compared to the other categories.

Agency-Identity Classification. The distribution of comments per base sentiment per Agency-Identity classification (Fig. 7) acts like the distribution of sentiments per content themes (Fig. 5). English comments are significantly less positive across all groups compared to the Emoji-only comments. The English comments make up more of the negative and neutral comments consistently across all groups in comparison with the Emoji-only comments. Whereas notable differences between English and Emoji-only comments per content theme could be recognized, we did not find any difference in the distribution for the Ekman emotions across all groups for English comments, see Fig. 8. The kind of post regarding Agency-Identity does not seem to have any influence on the comment's emotion distribution at all.

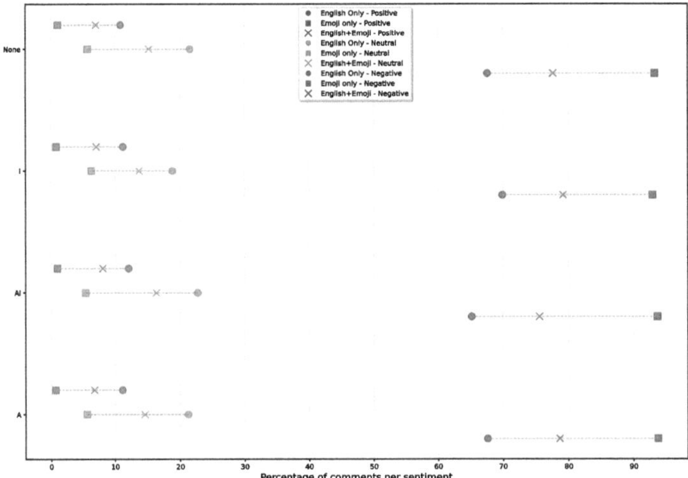

Fig. 7. Base sentiment comparison of comments per Agency-Identity classification.

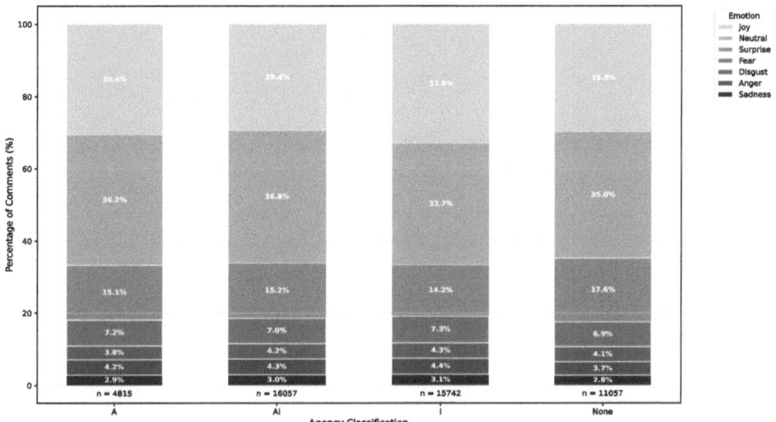

Fig. 8. Distribution of Ekman's emotions for English comments by Agency-Identity classification, n = number of comments per group.

Most Used Key Words Per Sentiment. In Fig. 9, word clouds were generated from comments classified with negative, neutral, or positive base sentiment. Each word cloud displays the terms that, based on this analysis, occur most frequently within its respective sentiment group. In the neutral sentiment word cloud, the terms "robot", "ai", "real", "look" and "human" dominate. Illustrative comments in this category include "It's AI girl not original" and "This is an ai girl she's not real people".

The positive sentiment word cloud features words like "beautiful", "love", "amazing", "wow" and "cute". Corresponding sample comments are "Hey naina you look so beautiful" and "Beautiful looking". Like the neutral sentiment, "robot" or "ai" appear often in the negative sentiment as well, followed by stronger words like "shit" or "fuck" or "hate". Representative comments are: "Fuck you bot", "I'm so fucking sick of you", "This is soooo fucking horrible". Overall, the neutral and negative sentiment language is rather similar, talking about the fact that VIs are robots or artificial, whereas the positive sentiment highlights the visual appearance of the VI.

Fig. 9. Word clouds of comments with neutral (left), positive (middle) and negative (right) base sentiment.

5 Discussion

We argue that user sentiment toward VIs is influenced by multiple factors, including content strategy, self-presentation, and mental processing mechanisms.

5.1 Content Strategy

Our study provides evidence that the content themes of VIs influence user sentiment and engagement. While our analysis shows that emoji-based comments were almost exclusively positive, sentiment differences were observed in text-based comments. Although the overall sentiment of comments was predominantly positive across all categories, we identified notable variations among different content themes. Specifically, posts related to Fashion, Pets, and Travel exhibited the highest average sentiment scores, whereas posts in the categories of Family, Food, and Interior had the lowest average sentiment scores, meaning that for those content themes, more comments were negative or neutral. These findings suggest that visually appealing content themes tend to generate more positive sentiment, whereas themes centred on the influencer's personal experiences often provoke neutral or even negative reactions. This aligns with theoretical expectations that VIs primarily attract user engagement through their visual appeal and the novelty of their digital existence [22]. However, their lower perceived human-likeness reduces their authenticity in the eyes of users, leading to a diminished emotional connection [10]. Consequently, users appear to find VI-generated content that focuses on personal experiences or emotions less enjoyable, frequently reacting with more negative sentiment. Especially when VIs express negative emotions, it often results in unfavorable audience responses [10, 19]. Relating to Attribution Theory [11], the behavior of VIs is attributed to the character itself, but also externally controlled. Hence, users may feel manipulated or deceived, particularly if the creators' identity or the commercial motives concerning the VI are not transparently communicated [23]. Xie-Carson et al. [32] further noted that users raised ethical concerns about the use of artificial digital personas, for example in contexts of social comparison and body image. Besides, VIs are often seen as lacking credible expertise, particularly authentic experiences with the products or services they promote, which undermines their effectiveness in shaping consumer decisions [21, 23]. Negative reactions frequently centered on concerns about authenticity and discomfort with hyperrealistic representations [1]. A perceived lack of authenticity notably reduces audience trust and openness to VIs' recommendations. This phenomenon can be explained by the Uncanny Valley hypothesis [24], which suggests that entities that closely resemble humans, but are not fully human, may evoke feelings of discomfort, eeriness, or aversion [1]. Furthermore, a lack of authenticity impedes the development of parasocial relationships. According to Parasocial Interaction Theory [12], audiences form emotional bonds with media figures who appear authentic and relatable. However, the tension between the human-like appearance of a VI and their non-human nature can create a feeling of dissonance. In this regard, Lou et al. [21] found through interviews that consumers often perceive VIs as emotionally superficial, which hinders the formation of genuine parasocial relationships. The hypothesis that negative sentiment is driven by a lower perceived human-likeness is further supported by our word-frequency analysis, which revealed that comments with a non-positive sentiment frequently contained terms such as "Robot" or "AI". This suggests that users may perceive VIs as artificial and emotionally detached, which in turn influences their reactions to content that typically relies on human relatability.

Furthermore, our content analysis indicates that the overall proportion of sponsored posts among VIs remains relatively low. However, promotional content is more prevalent in categories such as Fashion, Beauty, and Interior, reinforcing the idea that VIs perform better in visually driven content spaces.

5.2 Self-presentation

Contrary to expectations from the literature, our study did not find a significant effect of perceived agency or identity on user engagement (measured by average likes and comments per post) or sentiment (measured through sentiment analysis and emotion categorization). Several explanations may account for this result.

First, we categorized posts based on their descriptions. It is possible that the wording of post descriptions does not strongly influence users' perceptions of agency and identity in VIs. If this is the case, users may not be affected by whether a VI presents itself as an autonomous and intentional entity in its post descriptions.

Second, an alternative explanation is that VIs are generally perceived as artificial, leading users to dismiss their self-ascribed agency and identity. This problem can be understood through the Self-Determination Theory [6], which emphasizes the human preference for actors perceived as autonomous and self-directed. To further investigate this possibility, future research could employ experimental studies and surveys to examine whether the self-ascription of agency and identity by VIs effectively increases perceived agency and identity among users.

A third possible explanation is that perceived agency and identity do have an impact but function as mediating factors for other variables. Prior literature suggests that perceived VHL significantly influences user sentiment and engagement but is itself mediated by other factors. We theorize that perceived agency and perceived identity contribute to perceived MHL. Based on existing theoretical models, we hypothesize that perceived MHL mediates the effect of perceived VHL on user sentiment. A highly human-like VI that exhibits numerous human-like cues may evoke discomfort unless it also exhibits high MHL, which is a promising avenue for future research.

5.3 Mental Processing Model

Based on our findings and the theoretical background, we propose the following model to explain how user sentiment toward VIs is formed (Fig. 10). This model integrates key factors such as content themes, perceived human-likeness, and emotional responses to illustrate the mechanisms underlying user engagement and sentiment formation in interactions with VIs. Furthermore, future research should explore how these factors interact and contribute to users' overall perception of VIs in digital environments.

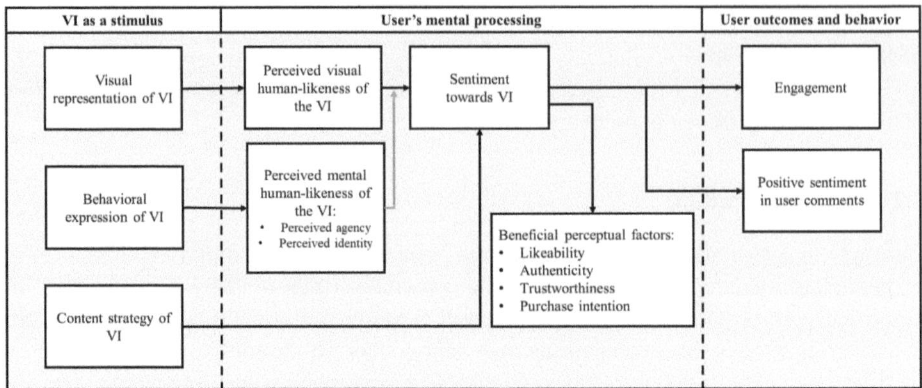

Fig. 10. Mental processing model.

6 Conclusion and Outlook

This study explored how different themes of posts by VIs influence user reactions. By employing a combination of zero-shot classification for content themes and large language model-based classification for self-presentation in terms of agency and identity, this research examined how these factors impact sentiment and engagement levels. Sentiment analysis and engagement metrics were subsequently applied to assess differences across categories. The findings indicate that sentiment and engagement levels vary depending on the content theme of the posts. Visually appealing themes, such as fashion or travel, tend to elicit higher positive sentiment. In contrast, themes emphasizing the VI's personality, such as family-related posts, are more likely to generate less positive sentiment and emotions such as disgust. Furthermore, posts in which VIs exhibit agency, identity, or both, do not necessarily lead to increased engagement or more positive sentiment. An important observation was that negative sentiment in user comments frequently included terms such as "robot", "AI", or "fake". This suggests that negative sentiment is particularly pronounced among users who do not perceive VIs as human-like actors. The results challenge existing research that suggests increasing MHL (e.g., through agency and identity) automatically enhances sentiment toward VIs. Instead, this study highlights the need for further exploration of MHL as a mediating factor rather than a direct predictor of positive user reception.

This study acknowledges several limitations that arise due to the nature of data collection and the constraints imposed by the Instagram platform. One limitation concerns the classification of posts into distinct content themes. Our approach relies solely on post descriptions, which may not always provide sufficient contextual information to accurately categorize a post. A more comprehensive classification would necessitate an analysis of image and video content in addition to the textual description. Given the current restrictions on data accessibility, such an approach was not feasible. Another limitation relates to the analysis of user engagement with VI content. Our study relies on comments as a primary indicator of user perception, however, we cannot guarantee that all comments originate from genuine human Instagram users. A portion of these interactions may be generated by bots or other VIs, which could introduce biases into our findings. Our anecdotal observations suggest that VI accounts seemed to receive a higher proportion of comments by non-humans. An analysis of the influence of bots on the engagement and sentiment distribution and polarizedness of debates provides a promising avenue for future research.

Our findings contribute to a better understanding of how users respond to VIs and how their content strategies can be optimized to enhance engagement and positive sentiment. From a marketing perspective, content strategies for VIs should leverage their visual strengths, focusing on themes such as fashion and travel rather than content that emphasizes their personality. Additionally, brands and marketers must critically address user expectations, as VIs are not perceived in the same way as human influencers. A strategic approach to content curation, accounting for user perceptions of authenticity and human-likeness, could enhance engagement and sentiment outcomes. Future research should incorporate qualitative analyses of user comments to further investigate how users articulate their perception of VIs as artificially generated entities. Additionally, integrating visual content analysis into the study of VIs by incorporating image and video data could yield further insights into the multimodal impact of VIs on audience perception.

Disclosure of Interests. The authors have no competing interests to declare that are relevant to the content of this article.

References

1. Arsenyan, J., Mirowska, A.: Almost human? A comparative case study on the social media presence of virtual influencers. Int. J. Hum. Comput. Stud. **155**, 102694 (2021). https://doi.org/10.1016/j.ijhcs.2021.102694
2. Baudier, P., de Boissieu, E.: Are social media robot influencers credible? A cross-continental analysis in a fashion context. Comput. Hum. Behav. **162**, 108447 (2025). https://doi.org/10.1016/j.chb.2024.108447
3. Blei, D.M., Ng, A.Y., Jordan, M.I.: Latent Dirichlet allocation. In: Advances in Neural Information Processing Systems, vol. 14, pp. 601–608. The MIT Press (2022). https://doi.org/10.7551/mitpress/1120.003.0082
4. Byun, K.J., Sun Joo, G.A.: A systematic review of virtual influencers: similarities and differences between human and virtual influencers in interactive advertising. J. Interact. Advert. **23**(4), 293–306 (2023). https://doi.org/10.1080/15252019.2023.2236102
5. Da Silva Oliveira, A.B., Chimenti, P.: "Humanized robots": a proposition of categories to understand virtual influencers. Australas. J. Inf. Syst. **25** (2021). https://doi.org/10.3127/ajis.v25i0.3223
6. Deci, E.L., Ryan, R.M.: Self-determination theory: a macrotheory of human motivation, development, and health. Can. Psychol. **49**(3), 182–185 (2008). https://doi.org/10.1037/a0012801
7. Dibble, J.L., Hartmann, T., Rosaen, S.F.: Parasocial interaction and parasocial relationship: conceptual clarification and a critical assessment of measures. Hum. Commun. Res. **42**(1), 21–44 (2016). https://doi.org/10.1111/hcre.12063
8. Ekman, P.: An argument for basic emotions. Cogn. Emot. **6**(3–4), 169–200 (1992). https://doi.org/10.1080/02699939208411068
9. Grootendorst, M.: BERTopic: neural topic modeling with a class-based TF-IDF procedure (2022). https://doi.org/10.48550/arXiv.2203.05794

10. Ham, J., Li, S., Looi, J., Eastin, M.S.: Virtual humans as social actors: investigating user perceptions of virtual humans' emotional expression on social media. Comput. Hum. Behav. **155**, 108161 (2024). https://doi.org/10.1016/j.chb.2024.108161

11. Heider, F.: The Psychology of Interpersonal Relations. Wiley, New York (1958)

12. Horton, D., Wohl, R.R.: Mass communication and para-social interaction: observations on intimacy at a distance. Psychiatry **19**(3), 215–229 (1956/2016). https://doi.org/10.1080/003 32747.1956.11023049

13. Hwang, K., Zhang, Q.: Influence of parasocial relationship between digital celebrities and their followers on followers' purchase and electronic word-of-mouth intentions, and persuasion knowledge. Comput. Hum. Behav. **87**, 155–173 (2018). https://doi.org/10.1016/j.chb.2018. 05.029

14. Jin, D., Abas, W.A.W., Kamarudin, S.: Instagram users' para-social interactions with virtual influencers: the mediating role of human-likeness, perceived similarity, and wishful identification. Int. J. Bus. Technol. Manag. **5**(2), 114–126 (2023). https://doi.org/10.55057/ijbtm. 2023.5.2.11

15. Kim, D.Y., Kim, H.Y.: Trust me, trust me not: a nuanced view of influencer marketing on social media. J. Bus. Res. **134**, 223–232 (2021). https://doi.org/10.1016/j.jbusres.2021.05.024

16. Kim, S., Jiang, J.Y., Nakada, M., Han, J., Wang, W.: Multimodal post attentive profiling for influencer marketing. In: Proceedings of the Web Conference 2020 (WWW 2020), pp. 2878–2884 (2020). https://doi.org/10.1145/3366423.3380052

17. Kozinets, R.V.: Click to connect: netnography and tribal advertising. J. Advert. Res. **46**(3), 279–288 (2006). https://doi.org/10.2501/S0021849906060338

18. Kozinets, R.V.: Netnography: Doing Ethnographic Research Online. Sage Publications, Thousand Oaks (2010)

19. Lim, R.E., Lee, S.Y.: "You are a virtual influencer!": understanding the impact of origin disclosure and emotional narratives on parasocial relationships and virtual influencer credibility. Comput. Hum. Behav. **148**, 107897 (2023). https://doi.org/10.1016/j.chb.2023.107897

20. Liu, F., Wang, R.: Fostering parasocial relationships with virtual influencers in the uncanny valley: anthropomorphism, autonomy, and a multigroup comparison. J. Bus. Res. **186**, 115024 (2025). https://doi.org/10.1016/j.jbusres.2024.115024

21. Lou, C., Kiew, S.T.J., Chen, T., Lee, T.Y.M., Ong, J.E.C., Phua, Z.: Authentically fake? How consumers respond to the influence of virtual influencers. J. Advert. **52**(4), 540–557 (2023). https://doi.org/10.1080/00913367.2022.2149641

22. Mo, Z., Zhou, M.: Don't like them but take what they said: the effectiveness of virtual influencers in public service announcements. J. Theor. Appl. Electron. Commer. Res. **19**(3), 2269–2288 (2024). https://doi.org/10.3390/jtaer19030110

23. Molin, V., Nordgren, S.: Robot or human? The marketing phenomenon of virtual influencers: a case study about virtual influencers' parasocial interaction on Instagram (2019)

24. Mori, M., MacDorman, K., Kageki, N.: The uncanny valley [from the field]. IEEE Robot. Autom. Mag. **19**(2), 98–100 (2012). https://doi.org/10.1109/MRA.2012.2192811

25. Nass, C., Moon, Y.: Machines and mindlessness: social responses to computers. J. Soc. Issues **56**(1), 81–103 (2000). https://doi.org/10.1111/0022-4537.00153

26. Nowak, K.L., Rauh, C.: The influence of the avatar on online perceptions of anthropomorphism, androgyny, credibility, homophily, and attraction. J. Comput. Mediat. Commun. **11**(1), 153–178 (2005). https://doi.org/10.1111/j.1083-6101.2006.tb00308.x

27. Reeves, B., Nass, C.: The media equation: How people treat computers, television, and new media like real people. Bibliovault OAI Repos. **10**(10), 19–36 (1996)

28. Robinson, B.: Towards an ontology and ethics of virtual influencers. Australas. J. Inf. Syst. **24** (2020). https://doi.org/10.3127/ajis.v24i0.2807

29. Sands, S., Ferraro, C., Demsar, V., Chandler, G.: False idols: unpacking the opportunities and challenges of falsity in the context of virtual influencers. Bus. Horiz. **65**(6), 777–788 (2022). https://doi.org/10.1016/j.bushor.2022.08.002

30. Shen, Z.: Shall brands create their own virtual influencers? A comprehensive study of 33 virtual influencers on Instagram. Humanit. Soc. Sci. Commun. **11**(1), 1–14 (2024). https://doi.org/10.1057/s41599-024-02698-y

31. Tricomi, P.P., Chilese, M., Conti, M., Sadeghi, A.R.: Follow us and become famous! Insights and guidelines from Instagram engagement mechanisms. In: Proceedings of the 15th ACM Web Science Conference 2023, pp. 346–356 (2023). https://doi.org/10.1145/3578503.3583623

32. Xie-Carson, L., Benckendorff, P., Hughes, K.: Keep it# unreal: exploring Instagram users' engagement with virtual influencers in tourism contexts. J. Hosp. Tour. Res. **48**(6), 1006–1019 (2024). https://doi.org/10.1177/109634802311809

33. Zourrig, H., Park, J., Becheur, I.: How does humanoid virtual influencers' appearance convey social presence? The underlying process and path to purchase intention. Int. J. Consum. Stud. **49**(1), 1–19 (2025). https://doi.org/10.1111/ijcs.70013

Analysis of Combined Impact of Information and Emotional Content on User Engagement Based on Social Media Data

Zhenzhen Xu[1] , Ruichen Cong[2] , and Qun Jin[2]($\boxtimes$)

[1] Graduate School of Human Sciences, Waseda University, Tokorozawa, Japan
[2] Faculty of Human Sciences, Waseda University, Tokorozawa, Japan
jin@waseda.jp

Abstract. This study examines the impact of information and emotional content on user engagement in social media, focusing on ten Japanese cosmetic brands on X (formerly Twitter). To classify content types, we conduct an annotation task with three human evaluators to label 1,000 contents, which then served to train a Support Vector Machine (SVM) classifier. Using text analytics, the emotional content ratio of each content is quantified and its impact on user engagement is analyzed. The correlation analysis revealed a positive association between emotional content and engagement for most brands, with one exception. Furthermore, we divided the emotional content ratio into ten equally sized groups from 0 to 1. A one-way ANOVA demonstrated that the effect of different emotional content ratio on user engagement is statistically significant. Moreover, content with an emotional content ratio between 0.6 and 0.7, paired with an information content ratio of 0.3 to 0.4, achieves the highest engagement compared to contents with lower or higher emotional ratios.

Keywords: Social Media · User Engagement · Machine Learning · Text Analytics · Information Content · Emotional Content

1 Introduction

With the rapid growth in users of social networking services (SNS), platforms such as X (formerly known as Twitter) and Instagram are becoming important for brand marketing. Social media enables companies to connect with a vast consumer base and serves as a primary mechanism for enhancing user engagement. Batra and Keller [1] observed that marketing professionals leverage social media to build interactions with consumers. Gavilanes et al. [2] showed a clear relationship between social media advertising and user engagement. Metrics commonly found in social media applications, including likes, shares, and comments, function as indicators of user engagement—defined as users' observable responses to content. User engagement can involve various forms, ranging from two-way interactions like commenting or replying to one-way responses, such as likes, and shares. These quantifiable responses hold significant importance for social media marketing, prompting extensive research into content strategies.

A. Coman et al. (Eds.): HCII 2025, LNCS 16337, pp. 102–113, 2026.
https://doi.org/10.1007/978-3-032-12801-0_7

Previous studies have investigated content types that influence engagement. For instance, Lee and Park [3] found that information content can improve user engagement, while providing additional links to external information may reduce its effectiveness. Similarly, Swani et al. [4] pointed out that emotional content captures attention and promotes engagement. However, existing studies provided a limited quantitative exploration of how information and emotional content interact. Specifically, the combined impact of these two content types on user engagement remains underexamined.

To address this gap, this study aims to uncover the interactive relationship between information and emotional content. We analyze the ratio of these two content types within social media data and assess their combined impact on user engagement. Our approach involves analyzing the number of likes and retweets across different ratios of information and emotional content to reveal the combined impact of these two content types.

The remainder of this paper is organized as follows. In Sect. 2, related work on content strategies for social media marking is reviewed. In Sect. 3, our proposed method for analyzing the combined impact of information and emotional content is introduced. Section 4 describes the experiments that analyze user engagement in different ratios of emotional content and discusses the results. Finally, this paper is summarized, and future directions are highlighted in Sect. 5.

2   Related Work

2.1   Customer Engagement and User Engagement

Customer Engagement (CE) refers to behaviors that extend beyond purchasing, reflecting either loyalty or disapproval toward a brand [5]. In social media, customers play an increasingly active role in shaping brand narratives through actions like turning company hashtags into 'bashtags.' This concept has been expanded to include a wide variety of customer behaviors that influence brand perception online [6, 7].

Moreover, this study makes a distinction between 'users' and 'customers.' Users on social media may interact with brand content without necessarily making purchases, broadening the scope of engagement beyond traditional customer definitions. This broader perspective allows brands to develop more effective marketing strategies aimed at increasing engagement by reaching a wider user base.

2.2   Information and Emotional Content in Social Media.

Social media content is typically divided into two categories: information and emotional [8]. Information content focuses on delivering factual data, such as product details, promotions, and other objective descriptions. Emotional content, on the other hand, seeks to engage users by evoking feelings like excitement or humor, often through branding strategies such as celebrity endorsements or emotional storytelling. Previous research, such as the work of Lee et al. [9], has shown that emotional content tends to increase user engagement by making the brand more relatable and appealing.

2.3 Emotion and Information Proportion in Engagement Research

While the binary classification of content into emotional or informational styles is common, recent research highlights the importance of content characteristics in predicting user engagement. Lee, Hosanagar, and Nair [10] conducted a large-scale analysis of Facebook brand posts and demonstrated that emotionally rich messages tend to drive higher user engagement—such as likes, shares, and comments—compared to purely informational content. Their findings suggest that emotional appeal plays a particularly influential role in encouraging user interaction, especially when tailored to platform-specific norms and user expectations. This supports the notion that the effectiveness of brand content is shaped not only by its emotional or informational nature, but also by the balance and delivery of these content types.

Stieglitz et al. [11] analyzed over 165,000 tweets using lexicon-based sentiment analysis and demonstrated that emotionally charged posts, especially negative ones, tend to be retweeted more frequently and rapidly than neutral ones. From a methodological perspective, Timoshenko and Hauser [12] employed deep learning on Amazon review data to detect customer needs through convolutional neural networks (CNNs) and clustering techniques. Their study supports the notion that user-generated content can be quantitatively analyzed for nuanced emotional and informational patterns.

Building on these previous works, this study examines how varying emotional-informational content ratios affect user engagement, using a proportional approach to uncover optimal balance points.

3 Analyzing Combined Impact of Information and Emotional Content

3.1 Definition of Information and Emotional Content

In this study, we adopt the definition proposed by Lee et al. [8] to categorize social media content into two primary types: information content and emotional content. This distinction is critical for understanding how different types of content affect user engagement on platforms such as X.

Information content typically comprises objective and fact-based posts. It aims to inform users about specific features, promotions, or technical specifications, generally exhibiting a more straightforward and less personalized tone compared to emotional content. In contrast, emotional content refers to material designed to evoke feelings, such as joy, excitement, surprise, or empathy. This type of content often incorporates personal stories, humor, and emotional appeals intended to resonate with users on a personal level. Emotional content may also integrate visual elements, including emojis, images, or videos, which often enhance its emotional impact. Table 1 provides a detailed definition for each of these content types.

3.2 Scoring System for Human Evaluation

To classify the two types of content—information and emotional—we first define a five-point scale for human evaluation, ranging from -2 (representing fully informational

Table 1. The Definition of Information and Emotional Content [8].

Category	Informational Content	Emotional Content
Definition	Provides objective information about a product or service, aiming to convey specific facts, data, or features.	Aims to evoke emotional responses such as happiness, excitement, or empathy, using storytelling, emotions, or building emotional connections with users.
Characteristics	- Product prices - Promotions - Technical specifications - Service descriptions - Purchase guides	- Positive experiences - Humor - Motivational language - Charity or social cause-related stories - Visual elements like emojis or images
Common Strategies	- Clearly communicate product features or discounts - Outline practical details or product specifications	- Use humor or motivational language - Engage users emotionally through storytelling - Highlight charitable activities or causes aligned with brand values
Goals	- Attract users with practical needs for the product/service - Encourage users to make a purchase decision	- Build emotional connections with users - Strengthen brand loyalty and identity - Increase user engagement, such as likes, comments, and shares

content) to $+2$ (representing fully emotional content). Human evaluation then serves to construct the training dataset for content classification. Table 2 presents examples of content classified using this scale.

As shown in Table 2, these example contents originate from Japanese cosmetic brand accounts on X. For example, the first example uses emotionally charged language, emojis, and visual imagery to evoke excitement and anticipation, resulting in its classification as fully emotional content with a score of $+2$. In contrast, the fourth example provides clear information regarding pricing and promotions, resulting in its classification as information content with a score of -2.

Building on the classification scoring method introduced in Table 2, we proceeded to calculate the emotional content ratio for each post. This ratio represents a normalized value derived from the five-point scale, and the corresponding informational content ratio is then determined as its complement. Since emotional and informational scores were assigned along a single continuum from -2 to $+2$, the emotional content ratio was calculated as a normalized value on this scale.

The emotional content ratio is defined as the proportion of characters identified as emotional in a post relative to the total number of characters as shown in Eq. (1).

$$Emotional\ Content\ Ratio = \frac{Number\ of\ Characters\ Identified\ as\ Emotional}{Total\ Number\ of\ Chracters\ in\ a\ Post} \quad (1)$$

Specifically, emotional characters include expressive punctuation (e.g., exclamation marks), emojis, and emotionally charged words. This ratio allows for a continuous measurement of emotional expression, enabling more nuanced analysis than binary classification.

The informational content ratio is derived as the complement (1 − emotional ratio) in Eq. (2), and our analysis considers this balance rather than emotional content alone.

$$Information\ Content\ Ratio = 1 - Emotional\ Content\ Ratio. \tag{2}$$

Table 2. Examples of Human Evaluation.

Evaluation Item	-2	-1	0	1	2
This summer's must-have beauty product is finally here! ✨ Experience the joy of glowing skin like never before! #NewArrival 😊	✓				
Are you ready with your summer essentials to protect your skin from the intense sunlight?		✓			
With Elixir's morning emulsion,				✓	
Our latest product is now available for only 1,990 yen! Special offer: Get 20% off your first purchase!					✓
In addition to SPF50+ UV protection, it also works as a makeup primer to prevent your makeup from smudging. ✨	✓				

−2 indicates fully informational content (e.g., specific product parameters, ingredients).
−1 indicates mostly informational content.
0 indicates neutral content.
1 indicates mostly emotional content (e.g., user experience, emotional guidance).
2 indicates fully emotional content (e.g., content that evokes emotional resonance).

3.3   Content Classification Using SVM

After human evaluation by using the above scoring method, Cohen's Kappa coefficient is used to investigate the evaluation reliability among human evaluators. The Kappa coefficient is a widely used statistical measure that assesses the level of agreement between multiple raters, adjusting for the possibility of agreement [13]. It can be used to demonstrate that the content classification by our human evaluators is a great agreement or poor agreement.

Thereafter, the data evaluated by evaluators, as the labeled data, are used as training data to conduct a Support Vector Machine (SVM) classifier [14]. Specifically, the term frequency-inverse document frequency (TF-IDF) is used to transform the text into numerical vectors that represent the importance of each word relative to its frequency in the dataset.

3.4 Statistical Analysis Using ANOVA

Following content classification by the SVM model, we obtain the emotional ratio for each piece of content. Then, we conduct a correlation analysis to explore the relationship between the emotional ratio of content and user engagement.

To further examine the impact of emotional ratio on user engagement, we divide the content into ten equally sized groups based on emotional ratios from 0 to 1 (e.g., 0–0.1, 0.1–0.2,..., 0.9–1.0). Then, we employ a one-way Analysis of Variance (ANOVA) and Tukey's Honest Significant Difference (HSD) test to statistically analyze the impact of these emotional ratio groups on user engagement.

This segmentation strategy allows for the observation of more nuanced variations in engagement metrics, such as likes and retweets, across changes in emotional content. By utilizing an equal interval classification method, we ensure that each group represents a consistent range of emotional content, thereby providing a basis for comparing engagement outcomes across the spectrum of emotional expression. It enables us to identify potential optimal ranges of emotional content that may enhance user engagement, as well as to observe how both lower and higher levels of emotional content influence user responses within these ten categories.

4   Experiment and Results

4.1   Content Classification

For the experiment, we collected 5,000 pieces of social media content from ten Japanese cosmetic brands on X posted between June 2022 and June 2023. First, 1,000 contents were selected randomly as a training dataset and were manually labeled by three undergraduate students using the five-point scale as mentioned above.

Each content was independently evaluated by all three evaluators. Based on their evaluation results, a Kappa coefficient of 0.70 was calculated, indicating a high level of consistency among the evaluators. Therefore, the consistency of labeling results was validated. The data evaluated by evaluators were used as training data to train the classifier. After training, the SVM classifier was applied to the unlabeled dataset and achieved an accuracy of 72.87%. Subsequently, the emotional ratio of each post was computed.

4.2   Correlation Analysis Between Ratio of Emotional Content with Likes and Retweets

After calculating the emotional content ratio for each content, we performed a correlation analysis between the emotional ratio with the number of likes and retweets. As shown in Table 3, the results indicated a positive correlation between the emotional content ratio and the number of likes across all brands. This suggests that contents with a higher emotional content ratio tend to receive more likes.

In addition, the emotional content ratio was also found to be positively correlated with the number of retweets for most brands. However, for Brand C, the correlation coefficient was lower and negative, indicating a negative relationship between emotional content ratio and retweets. For further investigation, we conducted a test of no correlation, and the results confirmed that only for Brand C, there was no statistically significant relationship between emotional content ratio with likes and retweets.

The results demonstrate a generally positive impact of emotional content on user engagement, while also pointing to potential differences in how emotional content influences engagement metrics across different brands.

Table 3. Results of Correlation Analysis Between Emotional Ratio with Likes and Retweets.

Brand	And Number of likes	And Number of retweets
Brand A	0.210***	0.175***
Brand B	0.237***	0.277***
Brand C	0.046 n.s.	−0.003 n.s.
Brand D	0.199***	0.186***
Brand E	0.313***	0.323***
Brand F	0.336***	0.307***
Brand G	0.191**	0.163*
Brand H	0.260***	0.164**
Brand I	0.217***	0.191***
Brand J	0.193***	0.145***

*Note: *$p < 0.05$, **$p < 0.01$, ***$p < 0.001$, n.s.: not significant*

4.3 Comparative Analysis on Emotional Content Ratios

A one-way ANOVA was conducted to evaluate the effect of different emotional content ratio, which are 0–0.1, 0.1–0.2,..., 0.9–1.0, on number of likes. The analysis showed a significant effect with $F = 14.518$, $p < 0.05$. Then, the Tukey's HSD test was performed to conduct a multiple comparison analysis between the ten groups. The results revealed significant differences between several groups. We found that the emotional content group of 0.6–0.7 was significantly different from groups with lower ratios, which are 0.0–0.1, 0.1–0.2 and 0.2–0.3, with $p < 0.05$, and higher ratio, which is 0.9–1.0, with $p < 0,01$. It indicates the importance of a balanced emotional content ratio for driving user engagement.

To further analysis, we conducted a line graph to visualize the distribution of likes across the ten emotional content ratio groups. Figure 1 presents the overall trend. As shown in Fig. 1, the contents with an emotional content ratio between 0.6 and 0.7 attract the highest average number of likes, suggesting that this is the optimal ratio range of emotional content for enhancing user engagement. On the other hand, the contents with lower emotional content ratios, which are less than 0.3, may lack emotional appeal to capture attention, whereas those with high emotional content ratios, which are more than 0.8, might distract users from the message, thereby reducing engagement.

In addition, according to Eq. (1), we calculated when the emotional content ratio is 0.6–0.7, the information content ratio is 0.3–0.4. This combination can provide the most effectiveness on user engagement, indicating that more emotional content combined with few information content resonates best with users. Contents that maintain this emotional-information balance show higher engagement, whereas deviations toward either extreme—overly emotional or overly information—tend to reduce user interactions.

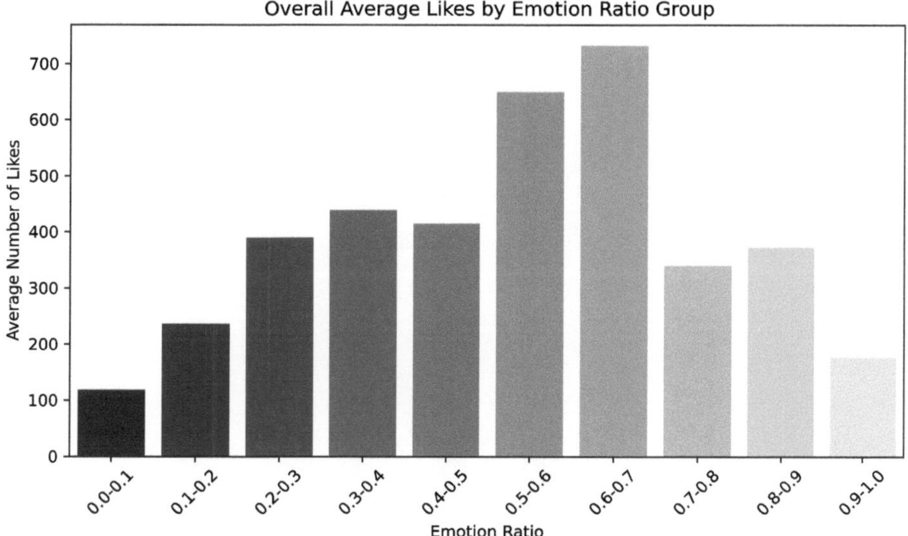

Fig. 1. Average Number of Likes by Emotion Ratio

To further explore how individual brand dynamics align with or deviate from the overall engagement trend, we analyzed three representative brands—Brand C, Brand E, and Brand F—as shown in Fig. 2. These were selected to highlight both consistency and variation in how emotional content ratios relate to average likes, relative to the aggregate pattern presented in Fig. 1.

Brand F most closely resembles the overall trend. In both cases, user engagement peaks when the emotional content ratio falls within the 0.6–0.7 range, indicating that moderately high levels of emotional expression are most effective for maximizing likes. This consistency suggests that Brand F's audience behavior is well aligned with broader platform-wide preferences.

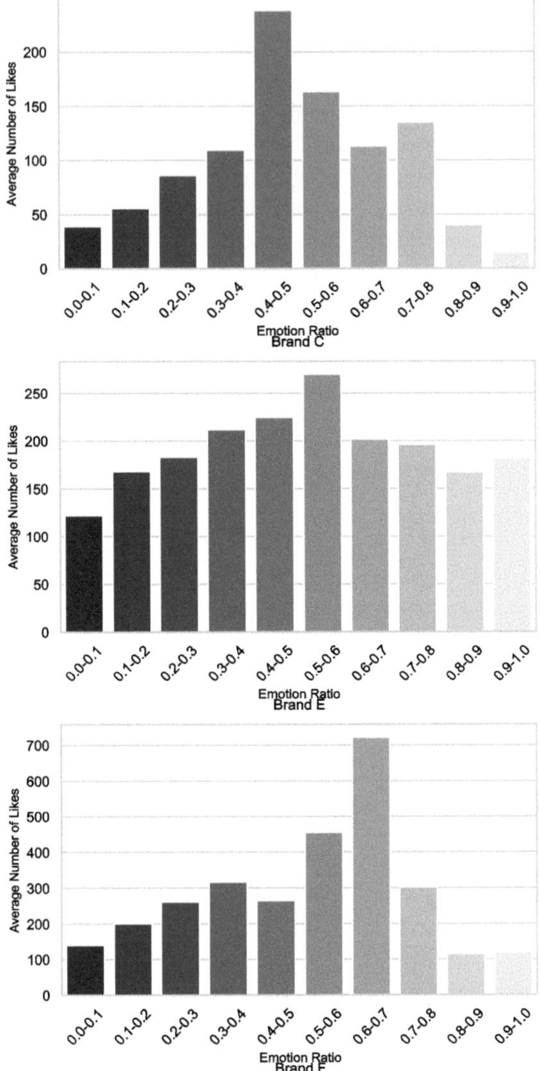

Fig. 2. Average Number of Likes by Emotion Ratio Group for Three Selected Brands

In contrast, Brand C demonstrates a notably different pattern. Its highest engagement occurs at the 0.4–0.5 emotional content ratio, which is lower than the overall peak. The number of likes drops sharply beyond this point, indicating that the audience may prefer moderately emotional content and respond less positively to higher emotional intensity. This implies that for Brand C, excessive emotional expression may diminish engagement.

Brand E presents a more uniform distribution of engagement across a wider range of emotional content ratios, with relatively high likes sustained between 0.2 and 0.7. The absence of a sharp peak suggests that its audience is more tolerant of varying emotional tones and that content effectiveness may depend less on emotional intensity and more on other factors such as message clarity or brand consistency.

These findings emphasize the importance of tailoring emotional content strategies at the brand level. While the 0.6–0.7 range appears optimal in aggregate, audience sensitivities and engagement dynamics vary across brands, requiring customized approaches to emotional expression on social media.

4.4 Discussion

Optimal Emotional Content Ratio (0.6–0.7) with Corresponding Information Content (0.3–0.4). From the results, we observed that the highest user engagement for posts with an emotional content ratio between 0.6 and 0.7 and a corresponding informational content ratio of 0.3 to 0.4. From a psychological perspective, content in this range likely achieves an effective "emotional activation threshold"—eliciting emotional arousal strong enough to prompt action (e.g., liking or sharing) without overwhelming the user or compromising perceived credibility. Concurrently, the presence of informational value reinforces cognitive engagement. This balance allows users to feel emotionally connected while still perceiving the post as meaningful and purposeful, which may account for the high performance observed in this combination.

This finding aligns with dual-processing theories such as the Elaboration Likelihood Model (ELM) [15] and the Heuristic–Systematic Model (HSM) [16], which propose that persuasive content is processed via both affective (heuristic) and cognitive (systematic) routes.

Decreased Engagement at Extreme Emotional Ratios. A notable decrease in engagement levels occurs when emotional content ratios reside at either extreme (0.8–1.0) or are very low (0–0.3). Contents characterized by excessive emotional content and minimal information value may appear overly sentimental, potentially lacking credibility or perceived substance. Users might interpret such contents as emotionally manipulative or clickbait, which can reduce willingness to engage. Conversely, contents predominantly featuring information content with limited emotional expression may seem impersonal or unengaging, failing to capture attention or stimulate affective resonance. In dynamic social media environments, such content risks being overlooked due to its low emotional salience.

These patterns indicate that extreme imbalances in content type may undermine engagement by overly emphasizing one processing route while underutilizing the other. Whether attributed to emotional saturation or cognitive fatigue, both extremes appear to constrain users' ability or motivation to interact. This further supports the idea that content effectiveness depends not only on information conveyed but also on the effective proportioning of emotional and information elements.

Stable Engagement in Balanced Ratios (0.4–0.6). For contents where emotional and information content ratios both fall between 0.4 and 0.6, engagement exhibits a stable pattern across user interactions. While these levels do not reach the peak observed in the 0.6–0.7 emotional range, this band consistently generates moderate user response.

According to Reber et al. [17], messages that are neither excessively complex nor overly simplistic are more likely to be processed fluently, leading to positive affective and increased receptivity. Additionally, from a cognitive balance perspective, content that offers both emotional and rational cues in equal measure may feel psychologically harmonious. This suggests that while these contents may not elicit strong emotional responses, their structural symmetry and moderate tone provide a reliable baseline for consistent engagement—a particularly valuable characteristic in long-term content strategies.

Limitations. One limitation of this study is the lack of control over whether contents were sponsored. Sponsored content often receives enhanced visibility and engagement due to algorithmic promotion, a factor that operates independently of the content's emotional or information quality. Without metadata indicating promotion status, it is difficult to fully isolate the effects of content type on user engagement. Future work should consider incorporating sponsorship information—such as advertising labels or business account data—where available, to better account for this potential confounding factor.

5 Conclusion

In this study, we examined the combined impact of information and emotional content on user engagement based on social media data. First, we defined a five-point scale for human evaluation. Then, we conducted an SVM model for content classification. Thereafter, we investigate the correlation between emotional ratio and the indicators of use engagement. Finally, we used ANOVA and Tukey's HSD to investigate the statistical significance between each emotional ratio group. The results showed that the contents with an emotional content ratio between 0.6–0.7, corresponding to an informational ratio around 0.3–0.4 as the optimal combination for contents, received the highest user engagement. Furthermore, the study indicates a decrease in user engagement at extreme emotional content ratios (above 0.8 or below 0.3). Specifically, Overly emotional contents often appear to lack substance, while highly information contents may seem impersonal, collectively reducing user interest.

By quantifying emotional and information content ratios, this study offers a more refined understanding of how content balance affects user engagement. Future work will incorporate additional engagement dimensions, such as comment sentiment, and further examine the influence of sponsored content. Moreover, the role of visual content, including images and videos, will be further explored. Expanding the study to different industries could also yield more insights into effective content strategies.

References

1. Batra, R., Keller, K.L.: Integrating marketing communications: new findings, new lessons, and new ideas. J. Mark. **80**(6), 122–145 (2016). https://doi.org/10.1509/jm.15.0419
2. Gavilanes, J.M., Flatten, T.C., Brettel, M.: Content strategies for digital consumer engagement in social networks: why advertising is an antecedent of engagement. J. Advert. **47**(1), 4–23 (2018). https://doi.org/10.1080/00913367.2017.1405751
3. Lee, J., Park, C.: Social media content, customer engagement and brand equity: US versus Korea. Manag. Decis. **60**(8), 2195–2223 (2022). https://doi.org/10.1108/MD-12-2020-1595

4. Swani, K., Milne, G.R., Brown, B.P., Assaf, A.G., Donthu, N.: What messages to post? Evaluating the popularity of social media communications in business versus consumer markets. Indust. Market. Manage. **62**, 77–87 (2017). https://doi.org/10.1016/j.indmarman.2016.07.006

5. Harmeling, C.M., Moffett, J.W., Arnold, M.J., Carlson, B.D.: Toward a theory of customer engagement marketing. J. Acad. Mark. Sci. **45**(3), 312–335 (2016)

6. Doorn, J.V., et al.: Customer engagement behavior: theoretical foundations and research directions. J. Serv. Res. **13**(3), 253–266 (2010)

7. Dhaoui, C., Webster, C.M.: Brand and consumer engagement behaviors on Facebook brand pages: let's have a (positive) conversation. Int. J. Res. Mark. **38**(1), 155–175 (2021)

8. Lee, D., Kartik, H., Harikesh, N.: The effect of social media marketing content on consumer engagement: evidence from facebook, Working paper, pp. 1–51. The Wharton School, University of Pennsylvania (2014)

9. Lee, D., Hosanagar, K., Nair, H.S.: Advertising content and consumer engagement on social media: evidence from Facebook. Manage. Sci. **64**(11), 5105–5131 (2018)

10. Advertising content and consumer engagement on social media: Evidence from Facebook

11. Stieglitz, S., Dang-Xuan, L., Bruns, A., Neuberger, C.: Emotions and information diffusion in social media—sentiment of microblogs and sharing behavior. J. Manag. Inf. Syst. **29**(4), 217–248 (2013)

12. Timoshenko, A., Hauser, J.R.: Identifying customer needs from user-generated content. Mark. Sci. **38**(1), 1–20 (2019)

13. Steinijans, V.W., Diletti, E., Bömches, B., Greis, C., Solleder, P.: Interobserver agreement: Cohen's kappa coefficient does not necessarily reflect the percentage of patients with congruent classifications. Int. J. Clin. Pharmacol. Ther. **35**(3), 93–5 (1997)

14. Joachims, T.: Text categorization with support vector machines: learning with many relevant features. In: Proceedings of ECML-98 10th European Conference on Machine Learning (1998)

15. Petty, R.E., Cacioppo, J.T.: The elaboration likelihood model of persuasion. Adv. Exp. Soc. Psychol. **19**, 123–205 (1986)

16. Chaiken, S.: Heuristic versus systematic information processing and the use of source versus message cues in persuasion. J. Pers. Soc. Psychol. **39**(5), 752–766 (1980)

17. Reber, R., Schwarz, N., Winkielman, P.: Processing fluency and aesthetic pleasure: is beauty in the perceiver's processing experience? Pers. Soc. Psychol. Rev. **8**(4), 364–382 (2004)

LLMs and Intelligent Agents in Social Computing and Security

Retrieval-Augmented Generation for Secure Environments: Theoretical Foundations, Agent Architectures, and Local Deployment with FAIRD

Eric Gaida, Nicholas Grund, Nicolas Ventulett, Stefan Böbel,
Artur Gibert, Marius Schanné, Eugen Staab, Dieter Wallach,
and Jan Conrad[✉]

University of Applied Sciences Kaiserslautern, 66482 Zweibrücken, Germany
{eric.gaida,nicholas.grund,nicolas.ventulett,stefan.boebel,eugen.staab,
dieter.wallach,jan.conrad}@hs-kl.de, {argi0001,masc1032}@stud.hs-kl.de

Abstract. Retrieval-Augmented Generation (RAG) systems offer an efficient approach to integrating Large Language Models (LLMs) with external knowledge sources, but they often raise significant data privacy concerns, especially when relying on cloud-based services. This paper introduces FAIRD (Fair AI Research and Education), a novel on-premises RAG framework designed for secure environments that addresses privacy and security risks associated with cloud-based LLMs. FAIRD improves data protection by storing and processing sensitive information locally and within secure networks, mitigating vulnerabilities linked to third-party services. This paper presents a comprehensive analysis of the FAIRD pipeline architecture, focusing on its ability to reduce model hallucinations through structured information retrieval and context augmentation. The framework is evaluated through local deployment at the University of Applied Sciences Kaiserslautern, demonstrating its efficacy in maintaining data sovereignty and compliance with regulatory standards such as GDPR. Critical security challenges, including indirect prompt injection and reconstruction attacks, are addressed and minimized through design principles that restrict external access and enforce local control. The modular design of FAIRD supports scalable and privacy-preserving LLM applications, offering a robust foundation for agentic systems in research, education, and industries requiring secure AI deployment. This work bridges theoretical advances in RAG with practical implementation, highlighting pathways for future research in autonomous, explainable, and secure AI systems.

Keywords: AI · RAG · Agentic AI · Data Sovereignty · Secure LLM Deployment

1 Introduction

The rising popularity and advancements of LLMs have changed the way people search and access information. This is reflected, inter alia, in the increasing

A. Coman et al. (Eds.): HCII 2025, LNCS 16337, pp. 117–134, 2026.
https://doi.org/10.1007/978-3-032-12801-0_8

adoption of AI tools by students in their academic work [1]. The time-consuming process of manually searching through documents, sources, and search engine results has been transformed, enabling users to retrieve specific information via natural language prompts. Furthermore, the capabilities of LLMs extend far beyond information retrieval. They extend into analytical tasks, playing crucial roles in summarization [2] and decision-making scenarios [3]. These functionalities and the ease of using LLMs encourage both private and business users to delegate such tasks to services like OpenAI's ChatGPT, Anthropic's Claude or Microsoft's Copilot to accelerate various workflows [4]. This evolution in information retrieval enables simplified ways of research, analysis, and information management.

However, this development also presents significant risks. One primary drawback is that the tools, models, and technical resources utilized for these purposes are typically controlled entirely by third-party services. This extends to the processing of sensitive information, raising substantial data-protection concerns.

In addition, some of the major LLM providers include user requests as part of their LLM training data. As previously observed with OpenAI's ChatGPT, users may also lack sufficient transparency in relation to data processing practices [5]. Consequently, the processing of confidential or proprietary information becomes impossible. The most secure alternative to cloud-based LLM services are self-hosted solutions, such as Meta's Llama or Google's Gemma models. However, depending on the intended use cases, these models require not only powerful hardware but also specialized interfaces that enable users to interact with LLMs effectively.

1.1 Contribution of This Paper

This paper proposes an architecture for a secure LLM environment. The approach is named FAIRD, which stands for **F**air **AI R**esearch and **E**ducation. FAIRD focuses primarily on RAG, an approach that enhances LLMs with additional information from external data sources. The contribution examines the functionality and architecture of RAG systems, exploring how custom resources are stored, processed, and retrieved locally. This methodology enables enhanced data protection by maintaining the entire system on private hardware within secure networks while simultaneously reducing model hallucinations. Additionally, the approach demonstrates the role of RAG agents, which provide an automated layer for the retrieval process, and analyzes the comprehensive pipeline architecture for information retrieval.

1.2 Related Work

Related work on the topic of RAG has demonstrated the overall functionality of how RAG operates and how it can improve the accuracy of domain-specific tasks, as discussed by Lewis et al. [6]. RAG architecture is characterized by its utilization of external data sources to augment LLM inputs, granting users enhanced control over information processing. Zhao et al. discuss the general use of these systems, which is to incorporate information from external sources into the input prompt that contains the necessary information for the LLM to fulfill a given task [7].

2 Theoretical Foundations of RAG

RAG represents an architecture that enhances the performance of LLMs by incorporating external knowledge sources into the generation process [6]. Unlike purely parametric models, RAG decouples knowledge retrieval from response generation, allowing dynamic access to up-to-date and contextually relevant information [8]. This design addresses several known limitations of LLMs, including hallucination, limited context length, and lack of verifiability [10].

2.1 Core Concept of RAG

At its core, a RAG system comprises three principal components: a retriever, an external memory index, and a generator [11]. The retriever maps an incoming user query into a dense semantic embedding, which is used to locate relevant documents from an indexed corpus through approximate nearest-neighbor search algorithms such as Maximum Inner Product Search (MIPS) or Maximum Cosine Similarity Search (MCSS). The generator, typically a decoder-only transformer, then produces a response conditioned jointly on the query and the retrieved documents [6]. This modular architecture allows RAG systems to integrate structured or unstructured knowledge at runtime, without requiring model retraining [12]. To address the constraints imposed by limited context windows in modern LLMs, advanced pre-processing techniques - such as relevance filtering, passage compression, and evidence re-ranking - are commonly applied [13]. These ensure that only the most important information is retained for generation, thus improving coherence, factual accuracy, and user trust in the output [8].

2.2 RAG-Pipeline

The RAG pipeline comprises four tightly integrated stages [14].

$$\textbf{\textit{Query}} \rightarrow \textbf{\textit{Retrieval}} \rightarrow \textbf{\textit{Augmentation}} \rightarrow \textbf{\textit{Generation}}$$

First, user input is encoded into a high-dimensional vector using a query encoder. This embedding enables the search for semantic similarity against an external document index, retrieving the relevant main passages [6]. These retrieved chunks are then injected into the model prompt during context augmentation. This process can be structured through templating, which uses predefined prompt formats with placeholders for the retrieved content. Alternatively, the process can be structured through pre-contextualization, which provides the model with additional background information or task instructions before the main input. A third option is chain-of-thought prompting, which guides the model to generate intermediate reasoning steps before providing a final answer [15]. Finally, a transformer-based LLM generates a response conditioned on both the retrieved evidence and its parametric knowledge, ensuring contextual relevance and factual grounding [16].

2.3 RAG in Human-Computer Interaction Contexts

The integration of RAG into interactive systems opens new research frontiers in HCI. For instance, in conversational agents and decision-support systems, RAG enables contextual adaptation while maintaining epistemic traceability [9]. Empirical studies indicated that users perceive AI-generated explanations as more trustworthy when they are backed by external evidence [17,18]. Moreover, by externalizing part of the model's "memory", RAG architectures support novel interface affordances such as clickable evidence snippets or user-verifiable source chains - which align with the principles of explainable and cooperative AI [19]. However, including a retrieval step leads to various challenges, including potential mismatches between retrieved and intended context, increased latency, and complex failure modes [20]. These demand careful evaluation from a user-experience perspective, especially when applied in high-stakes domains such as healthcare, law, or finance [21].

2.4 Advanced Retrieval Approaches

A core component of augmented generative AI systems is the information retrieval mechanism, which determines the relevance and quality of the external information provided to the language model. If the retrieval method fails to select relevant documents, retrieval precision is affected negatively and the likelihood of model hallucination increases. Vector-based retrieval approaches can be classified into three categories: sparse retrieval, dense retrieval, and a combined hybrid retrieval.

Sparse Retrieval. Sparse retrieval methods, such as BM25, rely on classic information retrieval techniques that represent documents and queries as high-dimensional, sparse vectors based on term frequency, inverse document frequency (TF-IDF), and document length [22]. These methods are computationally efficient, making them well-suited for environments with limited resources. However, while showing high precision in keyword-based search, they are limited in their ability to capture semantic similarity between a query and a document. They depend on exact or near-exact term matching, which can lead to lower recall in linguistically diverse or paraphrased queries [27].

Dense Retrieval. Dense retrieval approaches address the limitations of keyword-based retrieval methods and have shown to capture deep semantic relationships by reducing both data and queries to dense, low-dimensional vectors within a shared semantic embedding space [25]. Embedding vectors are generated using pre-trained or fine-tuned transformer models, such as BERT [23] or BGE-M3 [24]. During search execution, the vector proximity (e.g., cosine or dot product similarity) is used to retrieve a number of semantically most relevant entities for the given query. Dense retrieval excels in semantic matching and is particularly advantageous in open-domain or cross-lingual scenarios compared to sparse models [27]. However, in certain use cases, dense retrieval may fail to prioritize documents containing critical exact-match terms present in queries [26]. Dense methods require greater computational resources for vector embedding, a factor that must be considered for RAG architectures in local environments.

Hybrid Retrieval. Hybrid retrieval leverages both search approaches and combines the strengths of sparse and dense methods. They are able to select a more diverse and relevant set of documents than either method alone [8]. Furthermore, it has been demonstrated that they reduce hallucinations in RAG systems [30]. Two possible strategies are widely adopted for hybrid retrieval: multi-stage ranking, which applies sparse and dense methods sequentially, and score fusion, which combines their outputs in parallel [25].

In a multi-stage strategy, the sparse retrieval method is typically employed first to extract a broad candidate set of potentially relevant documents. Subsequently, a more computationally expensive semantic similarity search is applied to re-rank or filter the reduced set of candidate documents based on their contextual relevance to the query [29].

The fusion strategy applies a dense and a sparse retriever on the same query in parallel and independently. Each retriever returns a ranked list of candidate documents along with their respective relevance scores. To combine the search results and obtain a single list of entities, Reciprocal Rank Fusion (RRF) is commonly used [28]. Rather than relying on the raw relevance scores, the algorithm assigns higher importance to documents that are frequently ranked high. By summing the reciprocal ranks across the different result sets, a unified ranking is produced. The combined list is re-ranked based on the aggregated scores, and the top documents are selected for augmentation.

3   Agentic RAG Architectures

Agentic Retrieval-Augmented Generation (agentic RAG) systems represent an evolution in the integration of LLMs with external tools and resources. Traditional RAG architectures typically rely on static and preconfigured pipelines for retrieval and generation. In contrast, agentic RAG systems empower LLMs with the autonomy to dynamically decide what to do, allowing them to adapt flexibly to a wide range of tasks. The motivation behind agentic RAG systems stems from the increasing demand for AI systems capable of handling multi-step workflows involving multiple sources of information and/or other specialized capabilities. Agentic RAG architectures offer greater flexibility and robustness by enabling the LLM to act as an agent that can assess task requirements, select and execute tools, and refine outputs iteratively. This autonomy is necessary in complex environments or when problems cannot be fully anticipated in advance. The aim of agentic RAG is to extend the problem-solving capabilities of LLMs, making them more versatile and effective collaborators in autonomous or semi-autonomous workflows.

3.1   Core Components

The architecture of an agentic RAG system comprises several interconnected components that allow the LLM to function as an autonomous agent (see Fig. 1).

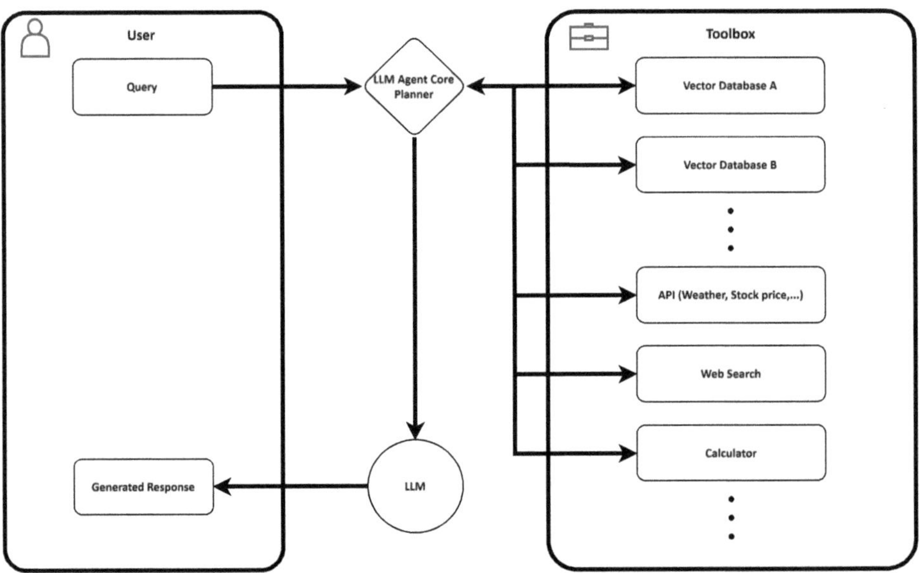

Fig. 1. How an LLM Agent Processes Queries: From user input to generated response, the system leverages vector databases, APIs, web search, calculators and/or more to provide informed answers.

LLM as the Core Planner. At the core is the LLM itself. It serves not just as a normal text generator, but as the central "brain" responsible for understanding the task, deciding the sequence of actions, selecting which tools to use and interpreting the tools outputs, evaluating progress, and formulating the final response with the gathered information.

Toolbox. This is a curated set of external resources that the agent can access to enhance its capabilities beyond the training data it was trained on.

The agent determines the tool to be called and the parameters to be used. Tools can include:

- **Information Retrieval Modules** that enable the agent to find relevant information dynamically: Vector stores, web searches, knowledge graphs, databases, etc.
- **Specialized Functions** that provide abilities that LLMs do not possess: Calculators, code executors, data analysis tools, real-time data APIs such as those for weather.
- **Action Modules** that allow the agent to act in real-world or digital environments: These include sending emails, executing commands in a terminal and controlling devices via APIs.

Action Selection Mechanism. This is the decision-making process by which the LLM agent, based on its reasoning and task context, selects which specific tool from the toolbox to invoke next. It involves generating structured requests (e.g., specific function calls with arguments) to interact with the chosen tool.

Tool Integration and Output Handling. Once a tool is selected and invoked (often via predefined functions or APIs), the system must integrate the tool's output back into the LLM's context. This involves parsing potentially complex results (JSON, text, code output, images, etc.) and presenting them in a format the LLM can understand and utilize for subsequent reasoning or generation.

Feedback Loops and Iteration. A defining characteristic of agentic systems is their ability to iteratively refine their approach. Based on the outputs of the tools or intermediate results, the agent can reassess its plan, correct errors, seek clarification (potentially from a user or another system), try alternative tools, or execute multiple cycles of tool usage before arriving at the final answer. This iterative refinement loop is key to handling complexity and ambiguity.

Model Context Protocol. The Model Context Protocol (MCP) [31] is a structured format used to maintain and exchange context across tool calls, reasoning steps and iterations in agentic RAG systems. MCP is similar to Representational State Transfer (REST), but for agentic systems. While REST defines how clients communicate with services via HTTP, the MCP establishes a standardized method to connect LLMs to various tools and data sources. It specifies how context is maintained and passed between steps, as well as how it is updated as the agent progresses through planning, tool invocation and feedback integration. The protocol standardizes the representation of task states, tool outputs, and intermediate reasoning, enabling the LLM to remember previous steps and adapt dynamically.

3.2   Challenges

Agentic RAG systems introduce added complexity compared to traditional pipelines. Managing evolving context, ensuring the reliable use of tools, and maintaining coherence across multistep workflows are all challenging tasks. These systems also face challenges related to latency, debugging, and safety, especially when interacting with external APIs or performing real-world actions. Importantly, LLMs are prone to errors and hallucinations [32] Excessive autonomy without appropriate constraints may result in unpredictable system behavior. Careful design is needed to balance flexibility with control.

3.3   Agentic RAG Summary

In general, the agentic architecture extends the capabilities of traditional RAG systems by enabling LLMs to plan, select tools, and iteratively solve complex tasks. With components like the Model Context Protocol (MCP), they support dynamic, multi-step workflows that can adapt to changing requirements. Agentic systems like AlphaEvolve [33] have demonstrated the practical viability and scientific impact of agentic systems.

A notable example of the power of agents is AlphaEvolve, which *"developed a search algorithm that found a procedure to multiply two 4×4 complex-valued matrices using 48 scalar multiplications, offering the first improvement, after 56 years, over Strassen's algorithm in this setting"* [33, abstract].

4   FAIRD System Architecture and Deployment Guide

FAIRD (see Fig. 2) is an on-premises chat application that uses LLMs in combination with RAG to answer user queries about locally stored documents. It is designed for the University of Applied Sciences Kaiserslautern.

As seen in Fig. 3, all documents, chat histories, and processed data remain on the user's local machine, ensuring full data sovereignty. The only interaction outside the local machine occurs with the university's on-premises inference server for the hardware intensive LLM inference. Data are not transmitted or stored externally and all communication is restricted to the university's secure internal network. Other LLM hosting services can be connected, but only if configured by the user and at their own discretion.

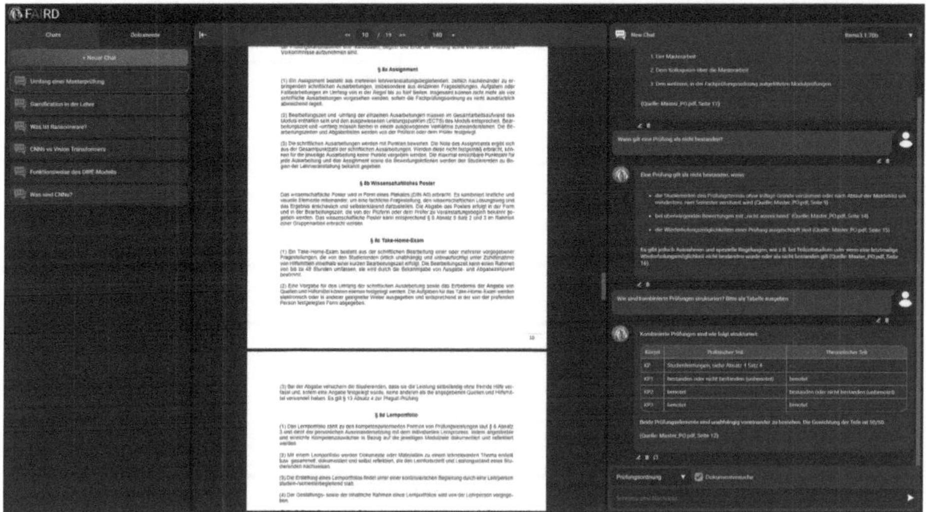

Fig. 2. Example of the FAIRD UI

4.1   Design Principles

FAIRD follows an on-premises-first philosophy. All user data remain on the local machine. When a document is uploaded, it is divided into smaller sections and embedded using a model hosted on the on-premises inference server. These embeddings are then stored in a local Qdrant vector database. Chat histories are saved locally using SQLite, which ensures persistent storage without relying on external services. In order to reduce the computationally intensive aspect of LLM inference on the user's device, this process is transferred to the inference server.

Network exposure is minimized by design. The inference server is exclusively accessible from within the internal network of the University of Applied Sciences Kaiserslautern. The system does not employ any external APIs, cloud services, or remote storage. This stringent isolation protocol is designed to fortify the security and confidentiality of the user's data.

4.2   Deployment Architecture

On the local user machine, FAIRD hosts the frontend using a combination of Electron, Node and Vue.js to provide a responsive, real-time user interface. It also handles local document processing and sessions, as well as file uploads. It stores chat histories using SQLite, and maintains the hybrid Qdrant vector database for efficient semantic retrieval.

The on-premises inference server is responsible for executing LLM inference. It operates models such as Llama, Mistral, and Deepseek within Docker containers and exclusively accepts inference requests from internal university IP

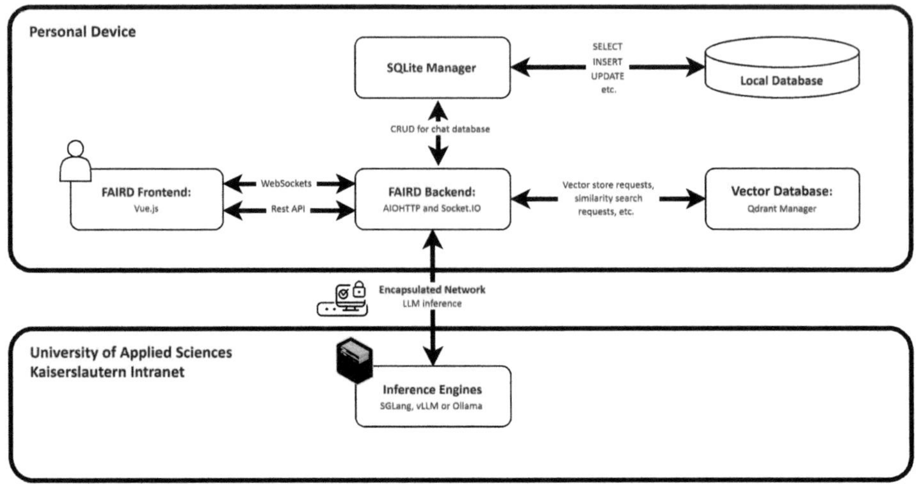

Fig. 3. FAIRD architecture: The backend manages data, performs searches, and uses local LLMs (SGLang, vLLM, Ollama) for fast inference at the University of Applied Sciences Kaiserslautern.

addresses. This ensures that no external traffic reaches the system, and its use is restricted to members of the university.

4.3   System Workflow

The FAIRD system follows a clear and structured workflow. Document ingestion is a one-time process for each document. In Fig. 4 we show the current workflow.

1. A user begins by selecting or creating a document collection
2. Documents are then uploaded to the collection
3. An embedding model breaks the file into chunks and vectorizes them on the inference server.
4. These embeddings are subsequently stored in the local Qdrant database to enable fast and accurate hybrid retrieval during later interactions.

The FAIRD process flow is shown in a simplified form in Fig. 5.

1. User chooses a collection he wants to chat with and submits a query
2. The system retrieves context of relevant document chunks from Qdrant using a local hybrid RAG system (score-fusion, see **2.4**)
3. The query and retrieved context are sent to the inference server for LLM inference
4. The interaction is saved in the local SQLite database
5. The generated response is returned to the user

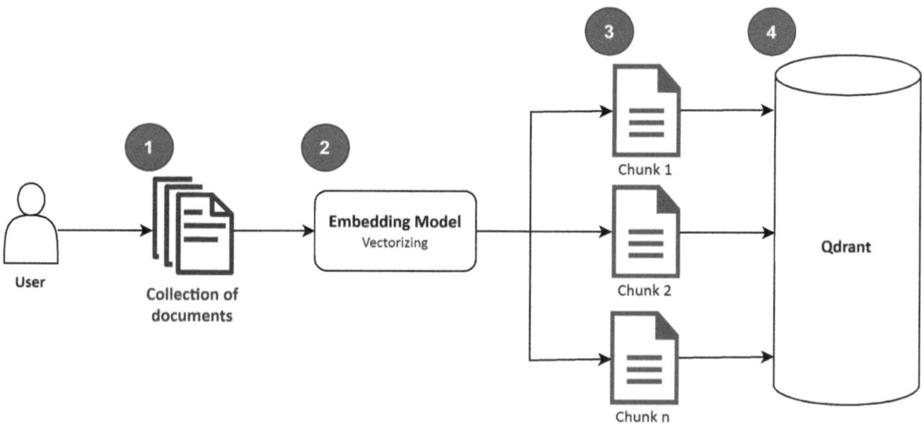

Fig. 4. FAIRD document embedding workflow

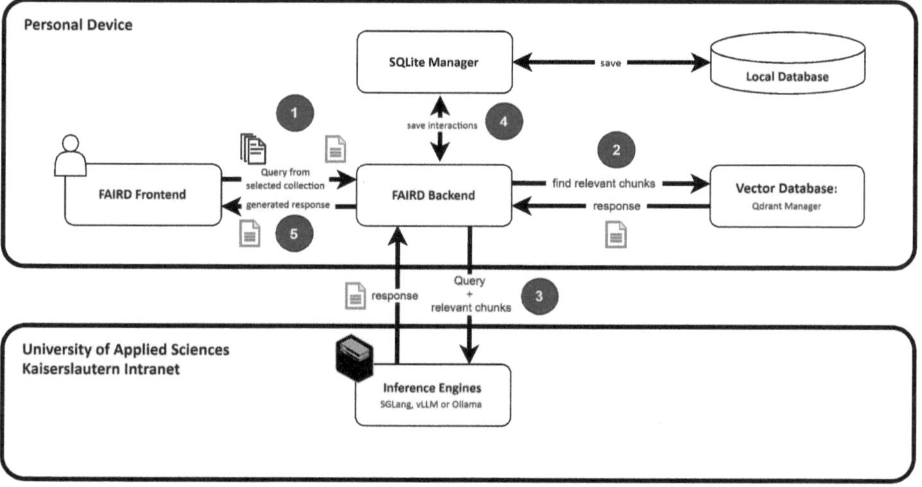

Fig. 5. FAIRD query processing

4.4   Retrieval Performance

Only computational expensive LLM inference operations of vector embedding and text generation are deployed on dedicated on-premises inference servers, while all retrieval tasks are executed directly on the end-user's own device. In this setup, the user device could represent a critical performance bottleneck, particularly with respect to latency as the vector database grows in size.

To evaluate system performance under these constraints, we conducted insert and search benchmarks on the local vector store, comparing two configurations with magnitude differences in hardware (see Fig. 6). The primary test scenario involved a low-end consumer device (Intel(R) Core(TM) i3-8130U 2-core CPU,

Internal Graphics, 8 GB RAM), representing the minimum expected technical baseline for end-user hardware. It reflects a representative deployment condition in which the vector store itself must run on resource-limited devices. For comparison, identical experiments were run on a high-performance server (Intel(R) Xeon(R) Platinum 8362 128-core CPU, 500 GB RAM, 4 NVIDIA A100).

A total of 35,000 data points (vector embeddings) generated from a test corpus consisting of 10,500 distinct pages of research papers were continuously added to the database to simulate realistic growth. For each insertion, we measured the time required both to perform insert, chart **(a)**, and search, chart **(b)**, on the evolving vector store. As illustrated in Fig. 6, insertion and search latency increase linearly with the number of stored data points. As expected, the high-end server outperforms the low-end consumer device in both operations. However, the performance of the consumer hardware remains well within acceptable limits for practical use. It can be assumed that slightly more capable client hardware would further narrow the performance gap to the high-end system.

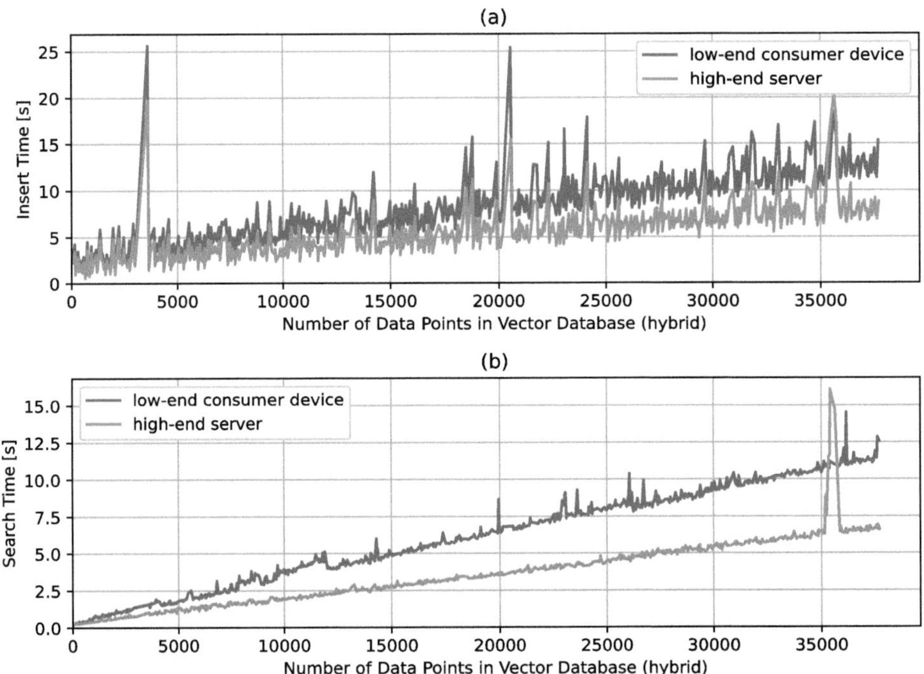

Fig. 6. Time per insert operation (a) and time per search operation (b) for a hybrid vector database, measured on a low-end consumer device and a high-end server as the number of stored data points increases.

5   Software Stack

As can be seen in Fig. 3, FAIRD uses the following open-source components.
Backend Components:

- **aiohttp + Socket.IO**: Asynchronous HTTP server and real-time communication framework for API interactions and live updates (LLM answer streaming).
- **Qdrant**: Local vector database for semantic search and document embeddings.
- **SQLite**: Lightweight, persistent storage for chat histories and metadata.
- **LangChain**: Python-based RAG pipeline orchestration (document retrieval, context augmentation).
- **Docker**: Containerization for LLM inference environments (SGLang and Ollama).
- **Ollama**: Lightweight inference engine for rapid model testing.
- **SGLang**: High-performance inference engine for stable, production-grade models.

Frontend Components:

- **Vue.js**: Interactive UI for chat interfaces and document management.
- **Electron**: Cross-platform desktop app framework (compatible with Windows/macOS/Linux).

6   Data Protection and Privacy

In the context of AI, data protection and privacy are often given high priority, especially since regulations such as the General Data Protection Regulation (GDPR) and the EU AI Act impose strict requirements. Although the processing of sensitive data by AI itself has to be individually assessed based on the application case, data privacy and security mechanisms can help mitigate general risks in this domain.

If run locally, RAG applications facilitate a higher level of data sovereignty as soon as uninstallation allows you to delete the local vector store database, as there are no cloud issues.

6.1   Security Threats and Mitigations in RAG Systems

FAIRD's on-premises design principles, as outlined in Subsect. 4.1, minimize privacy risks by storing sensitive data on the client device, thereby enabling full local control and secure deletion.

In the following, we assume that the documents to be uploaded are stored on the client device and that this device may still be susceptible to certain attacks. This is an inherent risk for any system that accesses private data locally. That is why we do not address general attacks targeting client devices. Instead, we focus on two significant attack vectors relevant to our system and discuss the corresponding mitigation strategies.

Indirect Prompt Injection. Indirect Prompt Injection [34] is a security vulnerability in which an attacker embeds malicious prompts into external data sources, which are later retrieved and unknowingly executed by an LLM-integrated application, allowing the attacker to manipulate the model's behavior without direct access. Running a RAG locally, by itself, does not prevent this attack. This attack is ranked first in the Top 10 list of the most critical vulnerabilities in LLM applications from the Open Worldwide Application Security Project (OWASP) [35].

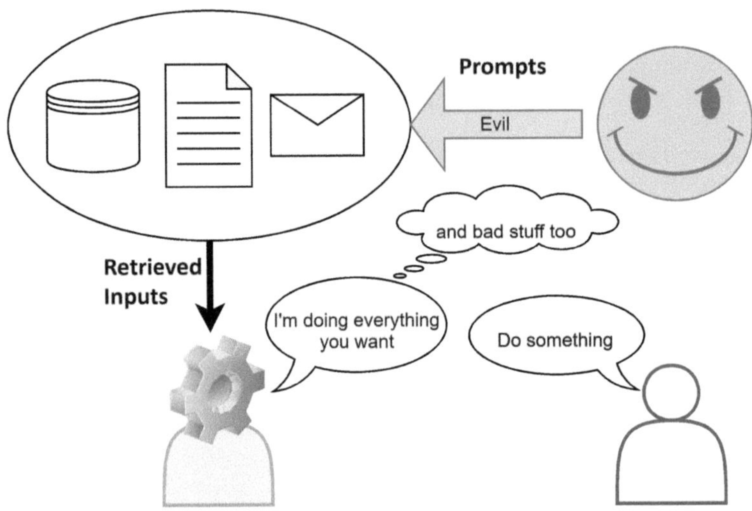

Fig. 7. How a malicious prompt gets injected.

The attack is executed in the following manner (see Fig. 7). A potential threat arises if a document contains a malicious prompt previously injected by an attacker. This could be an article on Wikipedia or a PDF to which the attacker has access. The user uploads the document and once the prompt is retrieved by RAG and inserted into the context, the malicious prompt is executed, can manipulate the LLM and eventually exert control over the system. This can happen independently of whether the retrieval or generation parts of the RAG application are executed locally or remotely. To counteract this attack, FAIRD does not retrieve external content from the Internet. This requires the attacker to inject a malicious prompt into a PDF document uploaded by the user. This cannot be prevented in general, so we further mitigate the effects of this attack by intentionally decoupling FAIRD from external tools such as browsers or email clients. This limits the effects of such an attack to the output of the LLM. Still, this output could contain text that instructs the user to copy a malicious URL to the browser and open it. To mitigate this, users are shown a hint to not simply trust URLs generated by FAIRD.

Reconstruction Attack. Processing the retrieved context on the server remains a weak spot. In a reconstruction attack, documents could be reconstructed from the processed fragments based on the chunks found in the context. In order to do this, an attacker would need access to the inference server. This attack could be completely mitigated by shifting the inference part of FAIRD to the client side. However, running state-of-the-art LLMs with user-friendly performance would require powerful hardware.

7   Conclusion

The rapid advancement and increasing popularity of LLMs have revolutionized the way information is searched and accessed. This transformation is evident in the growing adoption of AI tools by students for academic purposes, significantly accelerating workflows and simplifying research, analysis, and information management. However, this development also presents substantial risks, particularly concerning data protection and the handling of sensitive information. The reliance on third-party services for these tools raises significant concerns about data privacy and transparency.

This paper introduces FAIRD, an architecture for a secure LLM environment that addresses these challenges by focusing on RAG. FAIRD enhances LLMs with additional information from external data sources while maintaining the entire system on private hardware within secure networks. This approach not only improves data protection but also reduces model hallucinations. Our work explores the functionality and architecture of RAG systems, demonstrating how custom resources are stored, processed, and retrieved locally. Additionally, the role of RAG agents are analyzed, highlighting their automated layer for the retrieval process and the comprehensive pipeline architecture for information retrieval.

FAIRD's on-premises-first philosophy ensures that all user data remains on the local machine, minimizing network exposure and strengthens the security and confidentiality of the user's data. The deployment architecture, system workflow, and retrieval performance were discussed, highlighting the system's efficiency and practicality. The software stack and data protection were also outlined, emphasizing the system's commitment to security and data sovereignty.

In conclusion, FAIRD proposes an architecture for a secure and efficient environment for Large Language Models. By combining the benefits of RAG and agentic architectures, FAIRD provides a dependable solution for better data protection, fewer model inaccuracies, and improved efficiency in information retrieval and processing. Future work includes optimizing hybrid retrieval strategies for resource-constrained environments and expanding the agentic capabilities by expanding FAIRD's toolset. By bridging theoretical advancements in RAG with practical implementation, this work paves the way for secure, explainable, and trustworthy AI systems.

Disclosure of Interests. The authors have no competing interests to declare that are relevant to the content of this article.

References

1. von Garrel, J., Mayer, J.: Künstliche Intelligenz im Studium - Eine quantitative Längsschnittstudie zur Nutzung KI-basierter Tools durch Studierende (2023 u. 2025). https://doi.org/10.48444/h_docs-pub-533

2. Singh, G., Bali, K.K.: Enhancing decision-making in optimization through LLM-assisted inference: a neural networks perspective. In: 2024 International Joint Conference on Neural Networks (IJCNN), Yokohama, Japan, pp. 1–7. IEEE (2024). https://doi.org/10.1109/IJCNN60899.2024.10649965

3. Jin, H., Zhang, Y., Meng, D., Wang, J., Tan, J.: A comprehensive survey on process-oriented automatic text summarization with exploration of LLM-based methods. arXiv preprint arXiv:2403.02901 (2024)

4. Musazade, N., Mezei, J., Wang, X.: Exploring the performance of large language models for data analysis tasks through the CRISP-DM framework. In: Rocha, Á., Adeli, H., Dzemyda, G., Moreira, F., Poniszewska-Marańda, A. (eds.) *Good Practices and New Perspectives in Information Systems and Technologies – WorldCIST 2024*, LNNS, vol. 989, pp. 56–65. Springer, Cham (2024). https://doi.org/10.1007/978-3-031-60227-6_5

5. Pollina, E., Armellini, A.: Italy fines OpenAI over ChatGPT privacy rules breach. Reuters (2024), https://www.reuters.com/technology/italy-fines-openai-15-million-euros-over-privacy-rules-breach-2024-12-20/

6. Lewis, P., et al.: Retrieval-augmented generation for knowledge-intensive NLP tasks. arXiv preprint arXiv:2005.11401, https://arxiv.org/abs/2005.11401 (2021)

7. Zhao, P., et al.: Retrieval-augmented generation for AI-generated content: a survey. arXiv preprint arXiv:2402.19473, https://arxiv.org/abs/2402.19473 (2024)

8. Gao, Y., et al.: Retrieval-augmented generation for large language models: a survey. arXiv preprint arXiv:2312.10997, https://arxiv.org/abs/2312.10997 (2024)

9. Zhou, Y., et al.: Trustworthiness in retrieval-augmented generation systems: a survey. arXiv preprint arXiv:2409.10102, https://arxiv.org/abs/2409.10102 (2024)

10. Ni, B., et al.: Towards trustworthy retrieval augmented generation for large language models: a survey. arXiv preprint arXiv:2502.06872, https://arxiv.org/abs/2502.06872 (2025)

11. Zhao, S., Yang, Y., Wang, Z., He, Z., Qiu, L.K., Qiu, L.: Retrieval augmented generation (RAG) and beyond: a comprehensive survey on how to make your LLMs use external data more wisely. arXiv preprint 19473, https://arxiv.org/abs/2409.14924 (2024)

12. Gan, A., et al.: Retrieval augmented generation evaluation in the era of large language models: a comprehensive survey. arXiv preprint arXiv:2504.14891, https://arxiv.org/abs/2504.14891 (2025)

13. Gupta, S., Ranjan, R., Singh, S.N.: A comprehensive survey of retrieval-augmented generation (RAG): evolution, current landscape and future directions. arXiv preprint arXiv:2410.12837, https://arxiv.org/abs/2410.12837 (2024)

14. Merola, C., Singh, J.: Reconstructing context: evaluating advanced chunking strategies for retrieval-augmented generation. arXiv preprint arXiv:2504.19754, https://arxiv.org/abs/2504.19754 (2025)

15. Wang, L., Chen, H., Yang, N., Huang, X., Dou, Z., Wei, F.: Chain-of-retrieval augmented generation. arXiv preprint arXiv:2501.14342, https://arxiv.org/abs/2501.14342 (2025)

16. Sharma, C.: Retrieval-augmented generation: a comprehensive survey of architectures, enhancements, and robustness frontiers. arXiv preprint arXiv:2506.00054, https://arxiv.org/abs/2506.00054 (2025)

17. Song, M., Sim, S.H., Bhardwaj, R., Chieu, H.L., Majumder, N., Poria, S.: Measuring and enhancing trustworthiness of LLMs in RAG through grounded attributions and learning to refuse. arXiv preprint arXiv:2409.11242, https://arxiv.org/abs/2409.11242 (2025)
18. Zhou, H., et al.: TrustRAG: enhancing robustness and trustworthiness in retrieval-augmented generation. arXiv preprint arXiv:2501.00879, https://arxiv.org/abs/2501.00879 (2025)
19. Lauro, Q.R., Shankar, S., Zeighami, S., Parameswaran, A.: RAG without the lag: interactive debugging for retrieval-augmented generation pipelines. arXiv preprint arXiv:2504.13587, https://arxiv.org/abs/2504.13587 (2025)
20. Barnett, S., Kurniawan, S., Thudumu, S., Brannelly, Z., Abdelrazek, M.: Seven failure points when engineering a retrieval augmented generation system. arXiv preprint arXiv:2401.05856, https://arxiv.org/abs/2401.05856 (2024)
21. Ammar, A., Koubaa, A., Nacar, O., Boulila, W.: Optimizing retrieval-augmented generation: analysis of hyperparameter impact on performance and efficiency. arXiv preprint arXiv:2505.08445, https://arxiv.org/abs/2505.08445 (2025)
22. Robertson, S., Zaragoza, H.: The probabilistic relevance framework: BM25 and beyond. Found. Trends Inf. Retr. **3**(4), 333–389 (2009). https://doi.org/10.1561/1500000019
23. Devlin, J., Chang, M.W., Lee, K., Toutanova, K.: Bert: pre-training of deep bidirectional transformers for language understanding (2019), https://arxiv.org/abs/1810.04805
24. Chen, J., Xiao, S., Zhang, P., Luo, K., Lian, D., Liu, Z.: Bge m3-embedding: Multi-lingual, multi-functionality, multi-granularity text embeddings through self-knowledge distillation (2024), https://arxiv.org/abs/2402.03216
25. Zhao, W.X., Liu, J., Ren, R., Wen, J.R.: Dense text retrieval based on pretrained language models: a survey (2022), https://arxiv.org/abs/2211.14876
26. Sawarkar, K., Mangal, A., Solanki, S.R.: Blended rag: improving rag (retriever-augmented generation) accuracy with semantic search and hybrid query-based retrievers. In: 2024 IEEE 7th International Conference on Multi-media Information Processing and Retrieval (MIPR), pp. 155–161 (2024), https://doi.org/10.1109/MIPR62202.2024.00031
27. Karpukhin, V., et al.: Dense passage retrieval for open-domain question answering (2020), https://arxiv.org/abs/2004.04906
28. Cormack, G.V., Clarke, C.L.A., Buettcher, S.: Reciprocal rank fusion outperforms condorcet and individual rank learning methods. In: Proceedings of the 32nd International ACM SIGIR Conference on Research and Development in Information Retrieval, SIGIR 2009, pp. 758–759. ACM, New York, NY, USA (2009), https://doi.org/10.1145/1571941.1572114
29. Sasazawa, Y., Yokote, K., Imaichi, O., Sogawa, Y.: Text retrieval with multi-stage re-ranking models (2023), https://arxiv.org/abs/2311.07994
30. Mala, C.S., Gezici, G., Giannotti, F.: Hybrid retrieval for hallucination mitigation in large language models: a comparative analysis (2025), https://arxiv.org/abs/2504.05324
31. Hou, X., Zhao, Y., Wang, S., Wang, H.: Model context protocol (MCP): landscape, security threats, and future research directions (2025), https://arxiv.org/abs/2503.23278
32. Huang, L., et al.: A survey on hallucination in large language models: principles, taxonomy, challenges, and open questions. ACM Trans. Inf. Syst. **43**(2), Article 42, 55 (2025), https://doi.org/10.1145/3703155

33. Novikov, A., et al.: AlphaEvolve: a coding agent for scientific and algorithmic discovery arXiv:2506.13131, https://arxiv.org/abs/2506.13131 (2025)
34. Greshake, K., Abdelnabi, S., Mishra, S., Endres, C., Holz, T., Fritz, M.: Not what you've signed up for: compromising real-world LLM-integrated applications with indirect prompt injection. arXiv:2302.12173, https://arxiv.org/abs/2302.12173 (2023)
35. OWASP foundation: OWASP top 10 for LLM applications 2025. OWASP GenAI project (2025), https://genai.owasp.org/resource/owasp-top-10-for-llm-applications-2025/, Accessed 25 Jun 2025

An Investigation into the Use of LLM-Based Features for Multimodal Estimation of Elderly Engagement in Active Listening

Hung-Hsuan Huang[✉] and Koichi Takahashi

Faculty of Informatics, The University of Fukuchiyama, Kyoto 620-0886, Japan
hhhuang@acm.org

Abstract. Lack of communication increases health risks such as depression and dementia, making conversational partners essential for elderly support. Conversational agents or robots have the potential to assist in this area. To achieve natural human-agent listening interactions, appropriate responses to the human speaker's level of *engagement* are essential. This study investigates the effectiveness of integrating recently emerging LLM-based features into engagement estimation. Three machine learning experiments are conducted to compare various architectural designs using non-verbal video and audio features (facial expressions, gaze, head movements, and prosody), partial or full utterances, and time-series or flattened fixed-size vectors.

Keywords: Engagement estimation · Large-scale language model · Multimodal machine learning · Recurrent neural network

1 Introduction

Japan's aging rate has already reached nearly 30% and continues to rise, making it the highest in the world [14]. As the elderly population increases, nuclear family structures have become more common, resulting in a growing number of elderly individuals living alone. Additionally, due to the decline of community ties and the effects of chronic illness, elderly people tend to belong to fewer communities and have fewer opportunities for communication compared to younger generation... In this context, a lack of communication increases health risks such as depression and dementia, making conversational partners essential for elderly support.

In 2017, the Ministry of Health, Labour and Welfare of Japan included "assistive devices using robotic technology for communication with elderly people" as a priority area in its policy on "Development and Promotion of Nursing Care Robots." By 2024, the definition of this area was revised to include the phrase "activate communication among elderly people through interactive information exchange." Human communication is not limited to verbal exchanges, but also involves multiple non-verbal cues such as auditory and visual information, as illustrated by the well-known Mehrabian's rule [13]. Therefore, for robots to engage in human-like conversations, transmitting diverse types of information is essential and may help mitigate communication deficits. Conversational agents are systems expected to fulfill this role.

Conversational agents are interactive systems that integrate technologies such as speech recognition and natural language processing. Earlier work in Japan, such as that by Shitaoka et al. [18], conducted experiments using a system capable of speech recognition and response generation, enabling dialogue between robots and humans. Although response accuracy was high, user satisfaction remained low. Feedback suggested that one reason for dissatisfaction was the system's inability to respond to participants' actual conversational needs. Moreover, it has been suggested that low satisfaction may cause users to lose interest in continuing the conversation. Therefore, it is important for conversational agents to estimate the speaker's state to effectively address communication issues.

This study aims to estimate elderly *engagement* based on information provided by elderly participants. By estimating engagement, conversational agents are expected to generate more natural, human-like responses and further improve communication with their target users. Multimodal machine learning has been shown to be effective in various tasks, including active listening. Our group also has been working on this topic for years. In addition to non-verbal signals such as facial expression, prosodic characteristics and body movements, verbal features are also supposed to be essential in the estimation of engagement. However, due to the lack of a powerful tool, earlier works usually could only utilize the verbal signal by hand-crafted features such as the number of words or the composition of part of words [22].

In recent years, advances in deep learning technologies have led to the development of numerous large language models (LLMs), whose effectiveness has been demonstrated across a wide range of tasks. In this paper, we report the results of our investigation into the effectiveness of LLM-based features for estimating engagement during conversations with elderly individuals.

2   Related Works

Engagement refers to the process of establishing, maintaining, and terminating communication, and it is used as an indicator of the degree of interest and willingness to participate in a conversation, as well as whether the speaker desires to continue the interaction. While numerous studies on engagement have been conducted since Goffman [6], its definition varies widely. Sidner et al. [19] define engagement as the process of establishing, maintaining, and ending the connection among two or more participants. They argue that in order to make interactions with robots more natural, it is necessary to pay attention to engagement activities during conversations. Yu et al. [21] define engagement as the extent to which participants are interested, attentive, and involved in the conversation. They classify voice data exchanged between users in voice communication systems into levels representing conversational engagement. O'Brien et al. [17] critically deconstruct the concept of engagement to provide a broader explanation of its definition. Their study focuses on the inconsistency in how engagement has been defined in previous research, classifying its components into four stages and defining it through the concept of the quality of user experience. Glas et al. [5] summarize how engagement has been interpreted in prior studies, highlighting similarities and differences. A common element across definitions is the connection and relationship among participants in conversation, though the definition often varies depending on the research objective. They also clarify related concepts and behaviors, explaining the breadth of engagement interpretation as a complex concept.

In related studies, engagement is often not clearly defined and is typically used in terms of high or low levels. While there has been discussion around attempting to define the concept of engagement, its components are not simple— differences arise depending on the situation and the individual—making it difficult to formulate a single, unified definition. This ambiguity stems from the wide range of interpretations of engagement, necessitating definitions tailored to the specific objectives of each study. The goal of this research is to address the issue of insufficient communication among the elderly using conversational agents. Engagement is defined as a concept that represents the conversation process itself and evaluates or explains that process based on speaker information. Specifically, it refers to the speaker's level of active participation and attentiveness in the conversation.

Various approaches have been explored to estimate engagement by examining which types of information are associated with it and whether it can be predicted. Goffman [6] discusses the role of eye contact, gaze, and facial expressions in engagement through facial cues. Yu et al. [21] estimate engagement by first predicting emotional states from acoustic features of speech. Noroozi et al. [16] utilize body language such as gestures for engagement estimation. As for modeling engagement estimation, Yu et al. [21] analyze acoustic speech features using machine learning methods such as Support Vector Machines (SVM) and Hidden Markov Models to estimate engagement. Tu et al. [20] perform engagement estimation using multimodal learning. Multimodal learning is a machine learning approach that combines multiple modalities, such as speech content, body movements, and facial expressions. By combining modalities previously used in engagement estimation research, it becomes possible to infer engagement that could not be fully explained by a single modality, thereby enabling higher-accuracy predictions through the use of comprehensive information.

Regarding the construction of a corpus of elderly speech for speech recognition, Iribe et al. [9] had subjects respond to four pairs of emotional labels as nonverbal information to objectively assess emotions inferred from speech. They used a previously established emotional model with a five-point scale. They point out that acoustic characteristics of elderly speech differ from those of younger people. Generally, speech recognition models are trained on the voices of healthy, non-elderly individuals, resulting in a mismatch between the acoustic characteristics of elderly speech and the models, thereby reducing recognition accuracy. They also note that intonation varies by age and region, with a marked decline in speech rate due to aging. Hence, they emphasize the need for age-matched voice data in analysis. In related studies estimating speaker engagement via machine learning, data are often collected from younger individuals or randomly sampled populations. While this enhances model generalization, mismatches similar to those seen in emotional inference models may also occur in engagement estimation, rendering the models less effective for elderly users. This applies not only to speech features but also to other feature types. Since the goal of this study is to estimate engagement specifically in elderly individuals, there is no need to include data from younger speakers. Therefore, machine learning will be performed using only elderly data to develop a model specialized for this target group.

3   Dataset

3.1   Corpus

To estimate engagement, we perform multi-class classification using multimodal learning. The elderly data used for training come from an in-door dialogue corpus [8]. The corpus consists of one-on-one conversations recorded online via Skype between four elderly speakers (aged 69–73, average 71) and four university student listeners (average age 22), with two males and two females in each group. All participants were Japanese speakers and engaged in free-form conversation as first-time acquaintances. Each speaker had a session with every student and formed 16 sessions in the dataset, each lasting 14–27 min (average 17 min). The elderly speakers made a total of 2,835 utterances, ranging from 0.10 to 17.72 s in length (average 2.80 s), totaling 7,943.58 s of speech. Given the total dialogue corpus duration of 272 min, elderly participants spoke for about half of the time, indicating sufficient participation in the conversations.

As this study aims to generate natural, human-like responses after the elderly person speaks, we target data recorded during elderly speech. The dataset is segmented with VAD (Voice Activity Detection) function of ELAN (EUDICO Linguistic Annotator) [11] to extract speech segments from the elderly. The corpus is then annotated to three levels of engagement by one of the authors following the criteria below:

Lv0: refers to situations where speech content is poor, negative in tone, frequently interrupted, with little change in facial expression or body movement, and flat or low-pitched voice.

Lv1: the speech is moderately contentful and emotionally neutral, occasional speech disfluencies are present, and some variation in facial expression, body movement, and voice is observed.

Lv2: refers to rich, positive speech content delivered fluently, accompanied by noticeable facial expressions, active body movements, and a modulated, higher-pitched voice.

Overall, all conversations were friendly and there were no really negative emotions observable from the elderly speakers. That is why we denote the engagement level starting from level 0 (Lv0) and toward level 2 (Lv2). Level 0 merely indicates that the conversation is relatively not lively, and does not mean that any negative emotions were observed. Table 1 shows the distribution of resulted engagement level labels. Generally, the utterance at Lv0 occupies most part of the conversation through all of the speakers. Among these speakers, A and B are male while C and D are female. From the results, it can be found that Female speakers tend to speak more and exhibit higher engagement levels. The relatively small proportion of engagement Lv0 may be due to the fact that both speakers and listeners participated with the intention to engage in conversation, often maintaining high engagement throughout. Figure 1 depicts the histogram showing the distribution of the number of tokens extracted from the speakers' utterances. The maximum number of tokens extracted from one single utterance is 49. The most frequent token length among all utterances is four (462 instances, 16.3%). 80.0% (2,257 instances) of utterances have length within 15 tokens.

Table 1. Distribution of engagement levels regarding to the gender of speakers

	A	B	C	D	Total	Ratio
Lv0	145	116	119	54	434	15.3%
Lv1	289	327	364	499	1,479	52.2%
Lv2	178	193	195	356	922	32.5%
Total	612	636	678	909	2,835	100.0%

3.2 Feature Extraction

Based on the labeled conversation corpus, features including verbal (speech content) signals and non-verbal (visual and audio) ones are extracted. The details of feature extraction in these modalities are as below:

Visual: All participants' facial expressions are extracted with an open source tool, OpenFace 2.2.0 [1]. It detects head postures (three-axes values of head positions and rotations are used in this work, six values), 2D and 3D gaze directions (eight values), and facial action units (AU, 17 out of 46 in the original definition) in accordance with Ekman's Facial Action Coding System (FACS) [3]. This resulted in 31 features at 30 fps for the visual modality.

Audio: As described below, depending on the experimental settings, both fixed-length features and features with a fixed sampling rate (proportional to the utterance length) are required; therefore, we used both Low-level Descriptors (LLD) features and functional features extracted with openSMILE 3.0 [4] for audio modality. ComParE_2016 feature set is

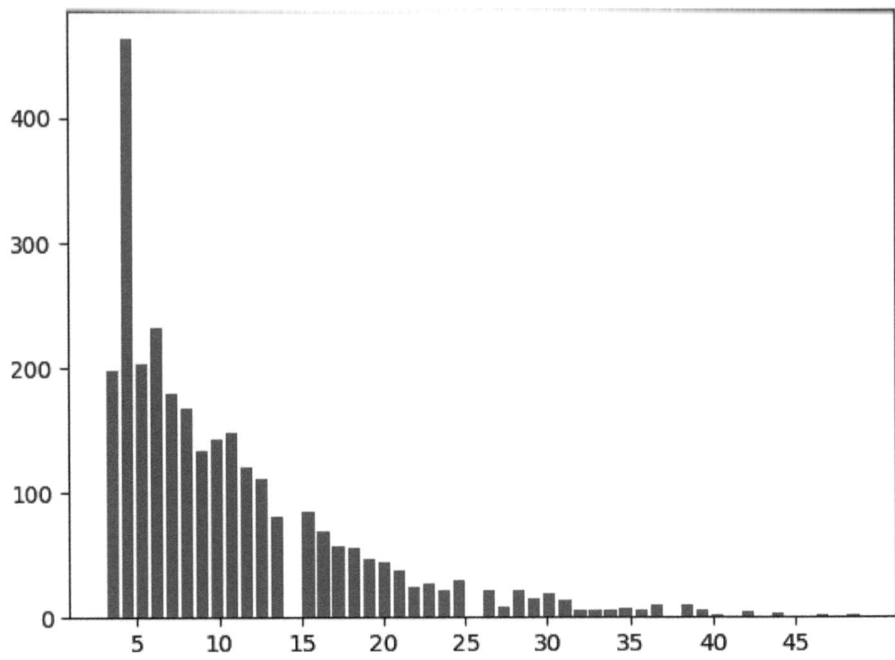

Fig. 1. Histogram showing the distribution of the number of tokens extracted from the speakers' utterances

chosen because of its richer features. This resulted in 65 features per 0.01 s (LLD) or a fixed-length 6,373 feature set for an audio segment.

Verbal: It has been shown that large pre-trained language models (LLMs), such as BERT [2], demonstrate high performance across various tasks. This study aims to investigate whether LLMs are also effective in our active listening corpus involving Japanese elderly individuals. Although many LLMs have been developed for Japanese, their performance varies depending on the task, and no single model is universally superior. In this study, we adopt the RoBERTa [12]-based model developed by Waseda University[1], which achieved the highest average score across five tasks in JGLUE, a Japanese LLM benchmark proposed by Kurihara et al. [10]. The encoder part of this model is used to extract verbal information from manually transcribed audio recordings of the corpus. Juman++ [15] is used as the tokenizer of this model and this model embeds each token into a 768 dimension vector.

The feature extraction procedure resulted in 30,359 tokens of verbal modality, 238,079 frames of visual modality, and 794,358 samples of audio modality.

---

[1] https://huggingface.co/nlp-waseda/roberta-large-japanese.

4   Experiment

4.1   Conditions

Based on the dataset explained in the previous section, we would like to investigate the effectiveness of using LLM-based features in the estimation of engagement. Our research questions are as below:

RQ1: Does the inclusion of LLM-based verbal features improve the performance of the estimation of engagement?

RQ2: Since the number of tokens in an utterance is variable, there are two ways to integrate the verbal modality like treating it as a time series or packing it in a fixed-size embedding. Which way will achieve better performance?

RQ3: If the answer of RQ1 is true, does the estimation require the whole utterance or a part of it is sufficient? If partial information of an utterance is sufficient, which part is more effective?

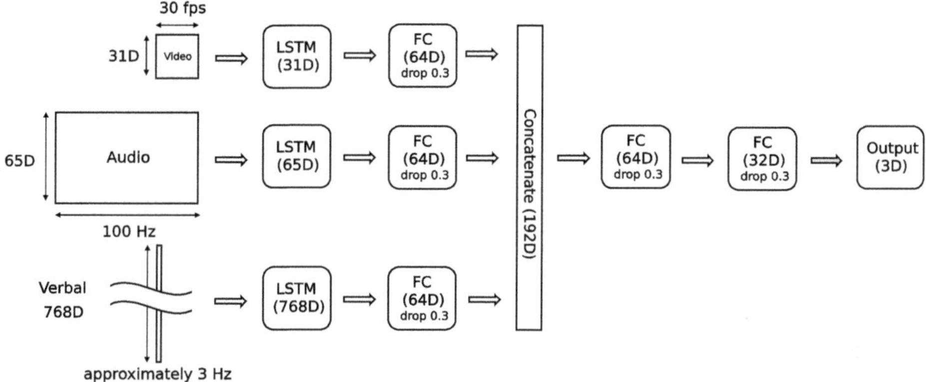

Fig. 2. LSTM based network configuration for Experiment I and II

Experiment I: In order to investigate RQ1, we would like to compare the performance of the following three models: a multimodal model with both verbal and non-verbal (video and audio) inputs, a uni-modal model with verbal inputs only, a multimodal model with non-verbal inputs only. The inputs are processed as a trunk of an utterance and a time series. For audio modality, the raw LLDs of ComParE_2016 feature set are used (65 dimensions × 100 Hz). For video modality, the raw values of the 31-dimension OpenFace features are used (30 fps). The maximum length of non-verbal modalities is 16.1 s for one data point (one utterance). For verbal modality, the raw RoBERTa embeddings are used (768 dimension/token). The maximum length for one sentence is 49 tokens. To be directly compared with other experiments, relatively simple Long Short-term

Memory (LSTM) [7] based networks are chosen. Figure 2 shows the LSTM based network configuration for Experiment I and II. In experiment I, the input data are fed with full information of one sentence where the maximum length of video feature is 499 frames, the one of audio feature is 1,722 samples, and the one of verbal feature is 49 tokens. When a shorter utterance is fed to the network, padding is applied to make it have the equal length with the longest one.

Experiment II: In order to investigate RQ2, the simple multi-layer perceptron counterparts of LSTM-based networks of Experiment I are used to conduct this experiment. The data from all three modalities are extracted to fix-length vectors despite the utterance length varies. For the audio modality, the functional features of ComParE_2016 feature set are used (6,773 dimensions). For the video modality, the root mean squared deltas (RMSD) of each OpenFace feature of consecutive frames are used (31 dimensions). For verbal features, two feature sets, the average and the sum of the raw RoBERTa features (768 dimensions each) are prepared for comparison. The network configuration for Experiment II is the same as Experiment I (Fig. 2). Instead of the full length of an utterance, the features are fed with the length of one second, two seconds, or three seconds, either from the head of the utterance or from the tail of it. Padding is applied to shorter utterances to make them meet the length of other data. Since the timing information of the words within one utterance is not available, the length of verbal inputs is approximated as three tokens per second.

Experiment III: In order to investigate RQ3, instead of the information from the whole utterance in Experiment I, the performance of first one, two, and three seconds and the last one, two, three seconds are compared. The same network organization as Experiment I is adopted. The corresponding segments of non-verbal modalities are extracted from the dataset. Since there is no timing information of each word in the transcription, we approximated that each single token lasts for one third second (a rounded average of utterance period / token number in our dataset). Figure 3 shows the simple multi-layer perceptron (MLP) network configuration for Experiment III. Basically identical to the one for Experiment I and II. Instead of the LSTM units which extract the temporal characteristics of the hand-crafted fixed-length features are fed to the fully-connected layer behind the LSTM layer.

Experiment setups: All of the experimental trials share the same settings:

- All trials run for 200 epochs and the best model during the training process is adopted as the final model. The number is chosen after a few test trials where we found the training converges around 150 or less epochs. The best model is validated with the accuracy of 5% of the training set.
- Adam is used as the optimizer, and ReLU is used as the activation function except for LSTM and output layers.

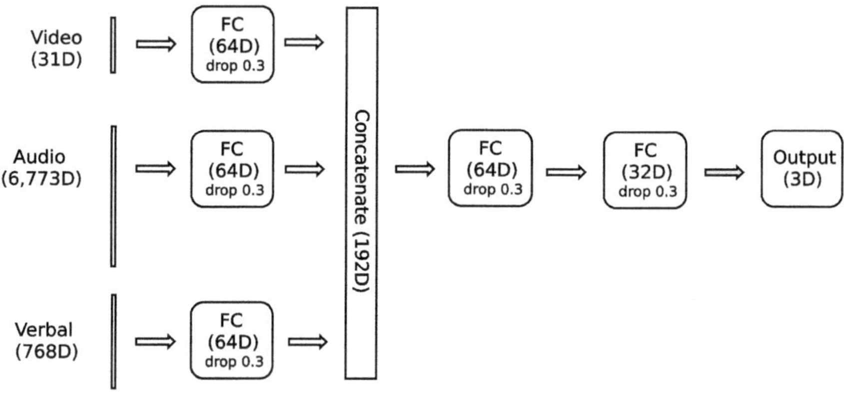

Fig. 3. Network configuration for Experiment III. Basically identical to the one for Experiment I and II

– Since the dataset is imbalance where engagement Lv1 occupies more than half of data points (52.3%), random over sampling is conducted on the two minor classes (Lv0: 15.3%, Lv2: 32.5%) to make them have equal number as Lv1 in the training set but not the test set during each trial.
– Leave-one-speaker-out cross validation is conducted so there are four folds in each trial.

The experiments are conducted with the programs implemented in Keras 3.6[2] and Tensorflow 2.17[3] as the backend. The training time varies regarding different sizes of different trials while the longest one ran for four hours and 50 min on a Nvidia RTX A6000 GPU with an AMD Threadripper 3960X CPU.

5   Results

Metrics. After each trial the macro averages of the precision, recall, and F-measure of all three engagement classes are computed. Since the number of the utterances of each speaker is different, weighted averages among all speakers are computed as the final results.

Table 2 shows that the full multimodal model is a clear winner than verbal-only or non-verbal-only ones in the condition of using full utterances. Considering this is a three-class classification problem where the chance level is 33.3%, the performance is not satisfying. The performance of uni-modal models are below chance level, still, the verbal-only model performs better than the non-verbal only model.

Table 3 shows the results of Experiment II where fixed-length feature trunks capturing the whole utterances are tested. The non-verbal only model actually

---

[2] https://keras.io/.
[3] https://www.tensorflow.org/.

Table 2. Results of Experiment I. The first column denotes the input modalities where V means verbal and NV means non-verbal (video and audio)

Model	Precision	Recall	F-measure	Lv0-F1	Lv1-F1	Lv2-F1
$V - NV$	**0.396263**	**0.421934**	**0.368182**	**0.361468**	**0.413072**	**0.396967**
NV	0.158296	0.332857	0.167631	0.082627	0.125040	0.318967
V	0.332748	0.333733	0.228522	0.160968	0.352042	0.207154

performed best among the five tested combinations. Neither of the two ways to integrate token embeddings to capture one utterance (sum and average) contributed to the final performance. They just behaved like noises and degraded the performance, and the results are contradictory to Experiment I. A possible explanation is: the embedded verbal contents does contribute to the estimation of engagement, but neither summing or averaging could preserve the valuable temporal characteristics. On the other hand, the lengths of utterances vary drastically and actually most utterances are much shorter than the longest one (16.1 s). This causes sparse data and therefore did not contribute to the performance as expected.

Table 3. Results of Experiment II. The first column denotes the input modalities where V means verbal and NV means non-verbal (video and audio). V_S means the verbal modality is computed as the sum of token values while V_A means that it is computed as the average of token values

Model	Precision	Recall	F-measure	Lv0-F1	Lv1-F1	Lv2-F1
NV	**0.654236**	**0.603875**	**0.592413**	**0.587279**	0.62385	**0.604012**
$V_S - NV$	0.551791	0.456086	0.437759	0.348403	**0.706049**	0.298088
$V_A - NV$	0.584393	0.567776	0.531092	0.563146	0.554195	0.574121
V_S	0.128951	0.332262	0.180109	0.082459	0.362944	0.094483
V_A	0.149519	0.331473	0.175812	0.082459	0.267712	0.177260

Table 4 shows the results of Experiment III. The network configuration is the same as Experiment I but with fixed-length segments as its inputs. From the results, it implies that generally longer inputs yield higher performance and the last seconds contribute more in the estimation. Between these two factors, the position where the features are extracted seems to play a more important role. In most but not all cases, the integration of verbal modalities slightly improved the performance, especially in longer segments. It may imply that the verbal information diverse a lot or oppositely similar to each other (e.g. just back channels) in short utterances, so there are no sufficient coherent characteristics found. The overall performance is better than that in Experiment I. This may be because the short inputs are less sparse and more informative to distinguish their characteristics.

Table 4. Results of Experiment III. The first column denotes the input modalities where V means verbal and NV means non-verbal (video and audio)

Model	Precision	Recall	F-measure	Lv0-F1	Lv1-F1	Lv2-F1
Last 3s, $V - NV$	0.599198	0.545746	**0.534651**	0.498544	0.539211	**0.602635**
Last 2s, $V - NV$	0.572315	**0.546109**	0.521189	0.500228	0.506237	0.583521
Last 1s, $V - NV$	0.540891	0.519643	0.511535	0.438199	**0.574574**	0.551631
First 3s, $V - NV$	**0.604096**	0.545194	0.514037	0.534765	0.498704	0.579953
First 2s, $V - NV$	0.566286	0.531952	0.509882	**0.541815**	0.479914	0.552021
First 1s, $V - NV$	0.526398	0.484370	0.445913	0.471294	0.452875	0.489880
Last 3s, NV	0.582863	0.530370	0.511086	0.502565	0.533927	0.572661
Last 2s, NV	0.570882	**0.540106**	**0.531485**	0.499250	**0.559778**	0.576556
Last 1s, NV	0.534103	0.529844	0.515371	0.495050	0.554191	0.536428
First 3s, NV	**0.624004**	0.533894	0.505078	0.509036	0.497733	0.568870
First 2s, NV	0.574317	0.539254	0.504753	**0.542118**	0.455428	**0.576948**
First 1s, NV	0.609463	0.500180	0.479098	0.504189	0.477589	0.504197
Last 3s, V	0.178080	0.331344	**0.201135**	**0.151195**	**0.386304**	0.076330
Last 2s, V	0.154281	**0.334943**	0.163888	0.065991	0.265663	0.123587
Last 1s, V	0.112404	0.333333	0.165001	0.082459	0.125352	**0.311808**
First 3s, V	**0.184507**	0.331960	0.152213	0.095876	0.173294	0.169111
First 2s, V	0.129218	0.333333	0.180601	0.082459	0.364497	0.094483
First 1s, V	0.063845	0.333333	0.103096	0.096413	0.000000	0.181482

6   Conclusion

This study aimed to address the issue of insufficient communication among the elderly by estimating their engagement levels using multimodal learning. Engagement was defined as the degree of activeness and attentiveness toward conversation. By estimating this, we aim to enable conversational agents to respond more naturally, similar to humans.

Using multimodal learning, we compared multiple models incorporating verbal (speech content), visual (head movements, facial expressions, gaze), and audio (prosodic) features. The integration of all three modalities improved estimation performance, demonstrating the effectiveness of multimodal fusion.

In time-series models, engagement-related information tended to be concentrated toward the end of each utterance, and more extensive segments led to better performance. In contrast, statistical models applied to entire utterances showed that non-verbal features had a particularly strong influence, outperforming time-series models in some cases.

Due to the small size of the dataset (four speakers and 16 conversations), drawing definitive conclusions is difficult. As future work, we plan to collect more data with a wider variety of speaker-listener combinations. This study used only one type of LLM-based feature; future research will explore additional models, such as sentence- or document-level embeddings.

References

1. Baltrusaitis, T., Zadeh, A., Lim, Y.C., Morency, L.P.: Openface 2.0: facial behavior analysis toolkit. In: IEEE International Conference on Automatic Face and Gesture Recognition (2018)
2. Devlin, J., Chang, M.W., Lee, K., Toutanova, K.: Bert: pre-training of deep bidirectional transformers for language understanding (2018). arXiv:1810.04805
3. Ekman, P., Friesen, W.V., Hager, J.C.: Facial Action Coding System (FACS). Website (2002). http://www.face-and-emotion.com/dataface/facs/description.jsp
4. Eyben, F., Wöllmer, M., Schuller, B.: opensmile - the munich versatile and fast open-source audio feature extractor. In: Proceeding of the ACM Multimedia, pp. 1459–1462 (2010)
5. Glas, N., Pelachaud, C.: Definitions of engagement in human-agent interaction. In: 2015 International Conference on Affective Computing and Intelligent Interaction (ACII), pp. 944–949 (2015)
6. Goffman, E.: Behavior in Public Places: Notes on the Social Organization of Gatherings. Free Press (1966)
7. Hochreiter, S., Schmidhuber, J.: Long short-term memory. Neural Comput. **9**(8), 1735–1780 (1997)
8. Huang, H.H., Fukuda, M., Nishida, T.: An investigation on the effectiveness of multimodal fusion and temporal feature extraction in reactive and spontaneous behavior generative rnn models for listener agents. In: Proceedings of the 7th International Conference on Human-Agent Interaction (HAI'19), pp. 89–96 (2019)
9. Iribe, Y., Kitaoka, N., Segawa, S.: Speech corpus spoken by young-old, old-old and oldest-old japanese. In: Proceedings of the Tenth International Conference on Language Resources and Evaluation (LREC'16), pp. 4674–4677 (2016)
10. Kurihara, K., Kawahara, D., Shibata, T.: Jglue: Japanese general language understanding evaluation. In: Proceedings of the 13th Language Resources and Evaluation Conference, pp. 2957–2966. Marseille, France (2022)
11. Lausberg, H., Sloetjes, H.: Coding gestural behavior with the NEUROGES–ELAN system. Behav. Res. Methods **41**(3), 841–849 (2009). https://archive.mpi.nl/tla/elan
12. Liu, Y., et al.: RoBERTa: A robustly optimized bert pretraining approach (2019). arXiv:1907.11692
13. Mehrabian, A.: Silent Messages: Implicit Communication of Emotions and Attitudes. Wadsworth Publishing Company (1972)
14. Ministry of Internal Affairs and Communications: Statistics on the elderly in Japan (2024). https://www.stat.go.jp/data/topics/pdf/topics142.pdf
15. Morita, H., Kawahara, D., Kurohashi, S.: Morphological analysis for unsegmented languages using recurrent neural network language model. In: Proceedings of EMNLP 2015: Conference on Empirical Methods in Natural Language Processing, pp. 2292–2297 (2015)
16. Noroozi, F., Corneanu, C.A., Kaminska, D., Sapinski, T., Escalera, S., Anbarjafari, G.: Survey on emotional body gesture recognition. IEEE Trans. Affect. Comput. **12**(2), 505–523 (2018)

17. O'Brien, H.L., Toms, E.G.: What is user engagement? a conceptual framework for defining user engagement with technology. J. Am. Soc. Inform. Sci. Technol. **59**(6), 938–955 (2008). Apr
18. Shitaoka, K., Tokuhisa, R., Yoshimura, T., Hoshino, H., Watanabe, N.: Active listening system for a conversation robot. Nat. Lang. Proc. **24**(1), 3–47 (2017). (In Japanese)
19. Sidner, C., Dzikovska, M.: Human-robot interaction: engagement between humans and robots for hosting activities. In: 4th IEEE International Conference on Multimodal Interfaces, pp. 123–128 (2002)
20. Tu, V.N., et al.: Dctm: Dilated convolutional transformer model for multimodal engagement estimation in conversation. In: Proceedings of the 31st ACM International Conference on Multimedia (MM '23:), pp. 9521–9525 (2023)
21. Yu, C., Aoki, P.M., Woodruff, A.: Detecting user engagement in everyday conversations. In: Proc. 8th Int'l Conference on Spoken Language Processing (ICSLP), pp. 1329–1332 (2004)
22. Zhang, L., Huang, H.H., Kuwabara, K.: Estimating speaker's engagement from non-verbal features based on an active listening corpus. In: HCI International 2018, Las Vegas, USA (2018)

SNS Search System that Uses a Large Language Model to Display Posts on an Interactive Map from Various Perspectives

Tomonari Kamba[(✉)] [iD]

Information Networking for Innovation and Design, Toyo University,
1-7-11 Akabanedai, Kita-ku, Tokyo 115-8650, Japan
`kamba@iniad.org`

Abstract. Filter bubbles and echo chambers on social networking services (SNS) often limit users' exposure to diverse perspectives. To address this issue, we propose a method for extracting multiple viewpoints in real time during SNS searches and presenting them on an interactive positioning map displayed alongside the list of posts. This map visually organizes posts along axes that represent diverse perspectives, which are generated by a large language model (LLM) based on search keywords and retrieved content. The system, developed using the X (formerly Twitter) API and GPT-4o API, was evaluated in a user study involving 10 university students and 17 search keywords, each retrieving 100 posts. The study revealed a significant change in user behavior: participants explored posts primarily through interactions with the map rather than by scrolling through traditional lists.

Keywords: Social Networking Service · Interactive Map · Large Language Model

1 Introduction

The phenomena of filter bubbles and echo chambers on social networking services (SNS) have raised concerns about their potential to narrow individual perspectives and exacerbate social divisions and conflicts. This issue is critical, with possible consequences such as increased polarization, disputes, and even societal instability.

SNS platforms often facilitate the rapid spread of intentionally biased opinions and misinformation, as users tend to evaluate posts based on whether they agree or disagree, often without deeper reflection. The fundamental challenge lies in recognizing the existence of alternative viewpoints—an inherently more complex and creative task than simply reacting to information in a binary manner.

This study proposes a system that presents diverse perspectives within an SNS viewer by visualizing the positioning of posts on an interactive map based on search keywords and retrieved content. By leveraging a large language model (LLM), the system identifies and verbalizes multiple perspectives extracted from the search results. While some

A. Coman et al. (Eds.): HCII 2025, LNCS 16337, pp. 148–160, 2026.
https://doi.org/10.1007/978-3-032-12801-0_10

individuals may resist exposure to opposing views, those with more open or reflective mindsets could benefit from enhanced awareness of diverse perspectives, which may ultimately contribute to mitigating societal divisions.

2 Related Research

2.1 Filter Bubble, Echo Chamber, and Serendipity

The phenomena of filter bubbles [1] and echo chambers [2] pose significant challenges on SNS, compounded by the increasing ease of generating fake information using AI [3] and the rapid dissemination capabilities of these platforms. Technologies such as personalization, recommendation, and targeting further contribute to these issues. For example, early attempts to personalize online news based on user browsing behavior [4] highlighted the risks of over-personalization—risks that remain pressing concerns today [5, 6]. Targeting and recommendation systems, widely employed in advertising and e-commerce, use methods such as content-based filtering and social filtering, the latter recommending content based on shared preferences among users [7].

To counteract the narrowing of user interests, recent research has emphasized the importance of serendipitous encounters with off-topic content. For instance, studies comparing recipe recommendations based on user preferences versus those emphasizing high-surprise factors demonstrated the value of serendipity in enhancing user experience, although food choices are inherently influenced by complex personal factors [8]. Similarly, balancing positive and negative product reviews has been shown to improve user satisfaction [9]. Other studies have investigated serendipity in various contexts, such as measuring it in physical libraries [10], adapting such metrics for digital environments [11], and designing systems to promote serendipitous discovery [12–14].

However, while serendipity is valuable, users often overlook such opportunities or fail to act on them unless internally motivated [15, 16]. Our approach aims to stimulate this internal motivation by presenting users with diverse perspectives, thereby encouraging deeper exploration and understanding.

2.2 Search and Visualization of SNS

Most SNS platforms, including X (formerly Twitter), offer keyword search APIs that support features such as result count, geographic codes, and time frames [17]. Although these APIs do not always enable real-time visualization, substantial research has been conducted on analyzing and visualizing the dissemination of information on SNS [18].

For example, Hwang et al. visualized information diffusion through user interactions, analyzing emotive language and changes in follower counts [19]. Toriumi et al. investigated retweet behavior during crises, demonstrating how critical information was disseminated following an earthquake and identifying user clusters based on retweet patterns [20, 21]. Cheng et al. inferred the geographic locations of tweet senders based on message content, enabling the visualization of user distribution across regions [22].

2.3 Document Classification and Sentiment Analysis

In this study, we extract and position various perspectives from SNS search results. Prior research has extensively explored document classification and sentiment (positive-negative) analysis based on content. Supervised methods such as support vector machines (SVM) [23], and unsupervised techniques including K-means clustering [24] and Latent Dirichlet Allocation (LDA) [25], are commonly used for document classification. More advanced approaches, including Word2Vec [26] and language models such as BERT [27], have further enhanced performance in these tasks.

Sentiment analysis, which identifies positive and negative sentiments, has been successfully applied to datasets such as movie reviews [28] and Twitter posts [29]. Notably, Faridani et al.'s Opinion Space visualized diverse opinions on online articles using principal component analysis, encouraging users to engage with differing viewpoints [30].

This study leverages a large language model (LLM), based on the Transformer architecture [31], to extract diverse perspectives from SNS search results and keywords. Even with limited datasets, the LLM's extensive internal knowledge enables it to generate insightful perspectives, making it a powerful tool for this application.

3 Developed System

Building on the findings and techniques discussed in the previous section, this chapter describes the system we developed to present diverse perspectives extracted from SNS search results.

3.1 User Interface

Figure 1 illustrates the user interface as displayed in a web browser. It is divided into the following sections:

- **Keyword Input Area (Upper Left):** Allows users to enter search keywords.
- **Post List Display Area (Lower Section):** Displays a list of retrieved posts, with options to show 15, 30, 50, or 100 posts at a time.
- **Interactive Map Area (Right Section):** The LLM identifies three axes to classify the search results, scores each post based on these axes, and plots them on a two-dimensional plane using the default X and Y axes. The initial map appears within approximately 2 s, and individual posts are plotted sequentially at a rate of 0.5 to 1 s per post.

Figure 1 presents an example of a search conducted on August 4, 2024, using the keyword *"presidential election."* The search retrieved 50 posts, and the system automatically generated axes such as *"Legitimacy of Election," "Candidate Support,"* and *"Election-related Media Influence."* These axes adapt dynamically to the search results. For instance, earlier searches conducted on the same day yielded different axes such as *"Election Integrity," "Candidate Perception,"* and *"Impact of Misinformation."*

Users can interact with the map through the following features:

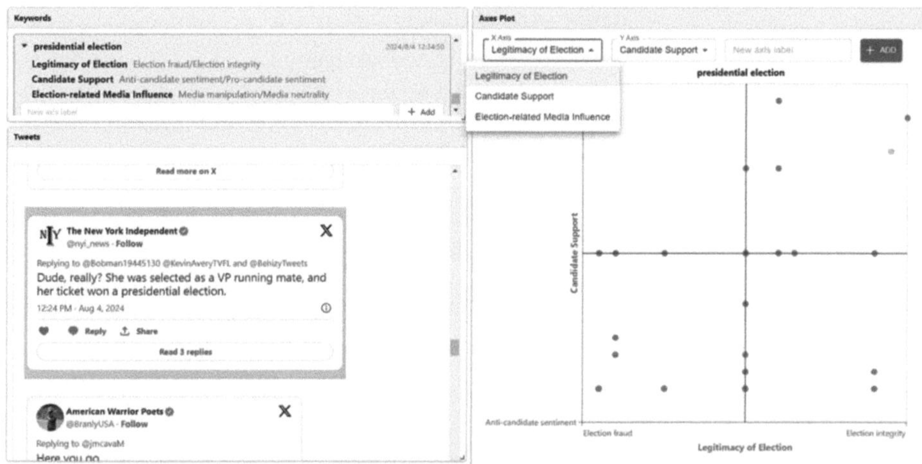

Fig. 1. User Interface.

- **Axis Selection:** Users can switch the X and Y axes via dropdown menus. Selecting the same axis for both X and Y causes all nodes to align along a single line.
- **Custom Axis Input:**

1. Enter a new classification axis in the text input field next to the dropdown menu.
2. Click the "Add" button to prompt the LLM to recalculate and score all search results based on the new axis.

   Additional interactive features include:

- **Highlighting and Linking:** Scrolling through the post list highlights the topmost post in yellow, and the corresponding map node is also highlighted. Hovering over a node displays the associated user's account, while clicking on it moves the corresponding post to the top of the list, highlighting both the post and the node.
- **Handling Multiple Posts at the Same Location:** When multiple posts share the same position on the map, hovering over the node cycles through the associated user accounts. The post list updates accordingly.

3.2 System Workflow and Processing

Following the user interface described in the previous section, this section details the underlying system workflow that enables real-time post visualization and classification.

When a user initiates a keyword search, the system retrieves posts via the X (Twitter) API. The keywords and retrieved posts are processed by the LLM (GPT-4o from OpenAI [32]) to generate three classification axes. Each post is then scored along these axes, with values ranging from -1.0 to 1.0. A map is created using the first two axes to spatially position the posts.

If a user adds a new axis via natural language input, the system processes the input and recalculates scores, updating the positions of the posts accordingly. Posts ranked at the top of the search results are linked to their corresponding nodes on the map, and both are highlighted in yellow to improve visibility and navigation.

All search results are stored in a database along with timestamps, axis names, and score values. To ensure user privacy and minimize storage requirements, only post IDs are retained—post content is discarded after scoring. This approach aligns with data minimization principles while maintaining necessary references to external content.

The LLM is prompted in a structured manner to optimize the visual layout of posts, ensuring that positive values correspond to the right/top regions of the map and negative values to the left/bottom. An excerpt from the prompt used to determine classification axes is shown below:

Analyze the following tweets and propose axes for discussion.

- The number of axes to propose is {axis_count}. For each axis, provide the axis name and the names of both poles.
- Assign {pole1} to the negative direction and {pole2} to the positive direction.
- Select axes that best represent the content of the tweets and encourage meaningful discussion.
- Use concise and easy-to-understand names for the axes.
- Clearly express opposing concepts or opinions in the pole names.
- Avoid overlap by proposing axes from different perspectives.

This structured prompt ensures that the generated axes are relevant, diverse, and semantically meaningful, enabling users to explore search results visually across distinct, non-overlapping dimensions. By scoring and plotting posts along these axes, the system helps users quickly identify contrasting viewpoints and latent themes. This visualization not only highlights differences in opinion but also fosters deeper engagement with diverse perspectives.

4   Evaluation

4.1   Setting and Scoring Axes Using LLM

This section evaluates the ability of the ChatGPT API to generate meaningful axes and assign scores to posts based on search keywords and results. The objective is to demonstrate how the LLM generates axes that extend beyond simple categorization to capture deeper contextual relationships within the data.

Table 1 presents examples of three axes automatically generated by the LLM. These axes highlight contrasting viewpoints or thematic elements, enabling nuanced exploration of the search results. Table 2 shows the scores assigned to individual posts, ranging from −1.0 to 1.0, which determine their positions on the interactive map described in Sect. 3. These scores quantitatively represent each post's alignment with the corresponding axes, thus visualizing the diversity of perspectives present in the search results.

The axes and scores produced by the LLM serve as the foundation for the system's interactive visualization. These outputs demonstrate the LLM's ability to synthesize meaningful dimensions of discussion and assist users in navigating complex information spaces through visual exploration.

Table 1. Example Axes and Poles Generated by the LLM.

Search Word	Time-stamp	Axis	Pole 1	Pole 2
Global warming (50 results)	2024-08-04 03:47	Climate Change Perception	Acknowledgement	Denial
		Emotional Response	Concern	Indifference
		Action on Climate Change	Proactive Measures	Inaction
GPU (100 results)	2024-08-04 04:00	Sentiment Towards GPU Technology	Excitement/Satisfaction	Frustration/Dissatisfaction
		Technical Knowledge and Usability	Ease of Use/Solutions	Technical Challenges/ Complexities
		Impact of GPU on Gaming Experience	Positive Impact	Negative Impact
GPU (10 results)	2024-08-06 01:02	Sentiment on GPU Technology	Supportive	Critical
		Performance Expectations	High	Low
		Market Impact	Positive	Negative
GenerativeAI (30 results)	2024-08-06 01:22	Ethical Implications of AI	AI Ethical Practices	AI Unethical Concerns
		AI Impact on Industries	Transformative Industry Impact	Minimal Industry Impact
		Community and AI Development	Community Engaged	Community Ignored

4.2 Experiments on College Students

The experiment was conducted with 10 university students, including third-year undergraduates and master's students from the Faculty of Informatics. Participants were recruited from a user experience course and were compensated with a $10 gift card for approximately 30 min of participation. All participants were experienced users of X (formerly Twitter).

Experiment Setup. The system retrieved and displayed search results for individual keywords instantly; however, posts appeared on the interactive map sequentially at a rate of 0.5 to 1 s per post, requiring approximately two minutes to display 100 results. To prevent delays due to potential LLM response variability, the search results—100 posts for each of 34 keywords—were preprocessed two hours before the experiment. During the experiment, participants accessed these preprocessed results by selecting keywords from their search history.

Procedure. After a three-minute tutorial, participants completed two tasks (10 min each), followed by a questionnaire:

- Task A: Browse 100 search results for each of 17 keywords *without* the interactive map visible.
- Task B: Browse another set of 100 search results for 17 *similar but distinct* keywords *with* the interactive map visible. Posts were presented in Japanese regardless of whether the keyword was written in Japanese or Roman characters.

Data Collection. With participants' consent, the following data were recorded:

- Keywords selected from the search history.
- Posts activated via scrolling or interaction with the map.
- Click positions and corresponding timestamps on the interactive map.

Additionally, a questionnaire was administered to collect subjective evaluations regarding:

1. The relevance and clarity of the axes generated by the system.
2. The perceived usefulness and accuracy of the nodes displayed on the map.

4.3   Results

Table 2. Examples Post Scores Assigned by the LLM.

Search Word	Post text	Axis and score
Global warming	I remember the summers of my childhood, playing outside without care. Now, I worry about the future of our planet. Global warming before it's too late.	Perception: +1.0 (Acknowledgement) Emotional Response: +0.9 (Concern)
	"Global warming" and "climate change" are shams.	Perception: −1.0 (Denial) Emotional Response: −0.8 (Indifference)
	The problem of global warming is nothing compared to radical Islamic-fascists.	Perception: −0.9 (Denial) Emotional Response: +0.8 (Concern)

(*continued*)

Table 2. (*continued*)

Search Word	Post text	Axis and score
GPU	Get at least a 4070 GPU and an i7 14700K and 64GB RAM. Rest of the components won't really effect performance.	Technological Development 0.8 (Emerging Technologies) User Experience (Satisfactory) 0.6
	Can't stream a game because my CPU and GPU max out while playing… this is HELL.	Technological Development: −0.7 (Obsolete Technologies) User Experience (Frustrating)
	(A spec and price for a second-hand GPU machine)	Technological Development: 0 User Experience 0

Table 3. Average User Interactions per 10 min (n = 10, SD in parentheses).

	Search words selected	Unique words	Posts viewed		View per Word
			list	map	
No map	8.1 (3.7)	7.1 (2.5)	65.8 (9.8)	–	9.3 (3.8)
With map	8.3 (5.3)	5.3 (1.8)	11.1 (9.1)	62.3 (17.8)	13.8 (8.5)

Comparison of User Interactions With and Without the Map. Table 3 compares user interactions in conditions with and without the interactive map. On average, participants selected eight keywords, although repeated selections led to fewer unique choices. Without the map, users viewed an average of 9.3 posts per keyword, which increased to 13.8 when the map was available—indicating higher engagement. Furthermore, users selected 62.3 posts directly via the map, compared to only 11.1 from the list view, meaning approximately 85% of the posts viewed were accessed through map interactions. This shift suggests that the map interface encouraged more deliberate exploration. Overall, participants viewed an average of 73.4 posts per session with the map, compared to 65.8 without it.

User Feedback on Axes and Engagement. A post-experiment questionnaire assessed participants' perceptions of the axes and overall engagement. Most participants considered two or three axes sufficient: four preferred three axes, four preferred two, and two preferred more than three. On average, participants switched axes 6.9 times during the 10-min map-enabled task (SD = 4.9), indicating active exploration. Qualitative comments emphasized the map's utility in providing control and clarity. For example, some users noted they could "see both positive and critical things" (Users 1, 4), "pick and choose what I want to see" (Users 2, 6, 9), and "avoid things I don't like or spam" (Users 3, 5, 6, 8). Several participants also appreciated the clarity of the posts displayed (Users 2, 5, 9).

Heatmap Analysis of User Behavior. Table 4 presents a heatmap of user click interactions on the map. As designed, positively scored posts appeared in the upper-right quadrant and negatively scored posts in the lower-left, consistent with the LLM's scoring instructions. The heatmap, generated using kernel density estimation, highlights areas of high activity in red and low activity in blue. Users averaged 62.3 clicks per session. Those with diagonally distributed red areas (e.g., Users 1, 2, 4, 5) explored a range of perspectives, while others who concentrated clicks in localized areas (e.g., Users 3, 7, 8) appeared to avoid negative content.

Synthesis of Results. The map-based interface had a notable impact on user behavior, encouraging focused and intentional exploration of search results. Interaction with axes and map nodes provided users with greater control over content navigation, supporting individualized preferences to either explore diverse viewpoints or filter out undesirable content.

Table 4. Heatmap of Click Interactions and Representative User Comments.

	User 1: I can view a wide variety of posts according to my interests. I think it is useful for investigating slander and libel, as it correctly reflects the emotional expression of the posts.		**User 6:** Maps reduce the amount of spam and other useless stuff I see. I don't see as much slander and negativity.
	User 2: I can pick and choose what I want to see. I can read a single post more carefully. I can look at for example elections from multiple angles, but noot so useful for everyday words (e.g. "sushi restaurant").		**User 7:** I can see only the posts that interest me and not the ones I don't like. Influencers will not have to ego search and look at comments they don't like.
	User 3: I did not want to see the negative ones, so I could selectively look at them, excluding them.		**User 8:** I never get tired of looking at the same keywords. I don't have to look at the posts that I don't like, such as imps, bots, spam, etc.
	User 4: I could see both the positive and the critical. It is useful to see what is going on in the world and how stock prices react to news.		**User 9:** If a map is available, browse only the ones you are interested in, if not, browse from the top. I can grasp the contents in a short time. I don't have to look at the negative ones.
	User 5: Maps make it easier to understand what is posted. Influencers will not have to look at comments about themselves they don't like.		**User 10:** It is easy to see similar opinions together. It is easy to understand different opinions.

5 Discussion and Future Work

5.1 Contributions and Observed User Behaviors

The central aim of this study was to develop a system that exposes users to diverse perspectives by presenting social media posts along automatically generated semantic axes. The interactive map, powered by an LLM, served as the primary interface for this purpose. The system's design emphasized flexibility, with axes dynamically generated for each search session—even when the same keyword was reused—highlighting the model's adaptability to contextual nuances.

User behavior during the experiment strongly supported the effectiveness of this approach. Approximately 85% of post selections were made through interactions with the map, while only 15% originated from the traditional post list. This substantial shift suggests that the visual interface encouraged more deliberate and exploratory engagement with content clusters, aligning well with the goal of promoting viewpoint diversity.

However, user comments revealed a nuanced reality: several participants used the map not only to explore diverse opinions but also to selectively avoid undesirable or negative content. While the system increased awareness of alternative perspectives, this did not always translate into engagement with them. This highlights a key design challenge: how to preserve user autonomy while gently encouraging encounters with contrasting viewpoints. Future iterations may benefit from incorporating soft nudges, intelligent recommendations, or visual cues to support balanced exploration without overwhelming users.

5.2 Model-Specific Issues and Prompt Engineering

This study employed GPT-4o, released by OpenAI in May 2024 [32], as the sole LLM for generating axes and scoring posts. While other state-of-the-art models—such as Llama 3 [33], Gemini [34], and Claude 3 [35]—offer comparable functionality, their differences in training data, architecture, and alignment processes can lead to divergent outputs [36, 37].

One potential concern with LLM-based systems is the propagation of biases through the selection and naming of axes, or the scoring of posts. Nevertheless, user feedback in this study suggested that participants generally valued the variety of perspectives generated, even when the semantic positioning of posts did not entirely match their expectations. This tolerance may reflect a recognition of the system's exploratory intent rather than evaluative precision.

Prompt engineering played a pivotal role in shaping the model's outputs. Carefully structured prompts guided the LLM to generate interpretable, distinct axes and to distribute posts meaningfully along them. Continued refinement of prompt strategies—such as dynamically adjusting instructions based on keyword category or user behavior—could further improve thematic diversity and reduce the risk of skewed representations.

5.3   Future Directions and Broader Applications

Several promising directions for future development have emerged from this study. One is the introduction of adaptive features, such as personalized axis recommendations, subtle gamification elements, or curiosity-driven prompts to encourage engagement with underrepresented views. These could enhance the user experience and promote deeper reflection.

Another avenue is the comparative evaluation of multiple LLMs, such as Llama 3 and Gemini, to assess how model-specific characteristics influence axis generation, scoring behavior, and user interaction. Such studies could inform the selection or fine-tuning of models for specific application domains.

In addition, longitudinal research is essential to determine whether repeated exposure to diverse viewpoints through this system leads to measurable shifts in user attitudes, openness, or content consumption habits. Addressing this question could significantly extend the social impact of this work.

Finally, the system's design principles are applicable beyond SNS browsing. Domains such as education, journalism, civic discourse, and social issue analysis can benefit from interactive, LLM-driven visualizations that make complex discussions more accessible. In these contexts, promoting perspective-taking is not just desirable but essential for informed decision-making and democratic engagement.

6   Conclusion

This study introduced a system that leverages a large language model to extract semantic axes from SNS keyword search results, score posts accordingly, and visualize them on an interactive positioning map. By enabling users to navigate content along multiple dimensions, the system supports the discovery of diverse perspectives within familiar search contexts.

Experimental findings demonstrated that the interactive map effectively shifted user behavior from passive scrolling to more intentional exploration. While many participants engaged with varied viewpoints, others used the map to filter out undesired content, highlighting its dual function as both an exploratory and selective tool.

Future improvements will aim to better balance openness to diverse perspectives with user preferences. These include exploring alternative LLMs, enhancing prompt design, and integrating adaptive features to support critical thinking in increasingly polarized information environments.

Acknowledgments. This study was supported by JSPS KAKENHI Grant Number JP23K11205.

References

1. Pariser, E.: The Filter Bubble: what the Internet is hiding from you. Penguin UK (2011)
2. Ruiz, C.D., Nilsson, T.: Disinformation and echo chambers: how disinformation circulates on social media through identity-driven controversies. J. Public Policy Mark. **42**(1), 18–35 (2023). https://doi.org/10.1177/07439156221103852

3. Ozbay, F.A., Alatas, B.: Fake news detection within online social media using supervised artificial intelligence algorithms. Phys. A: Statist. Mech. Appl. **540**, Article 123174 (2020). https://doi.org/10.1016/j.physa.2019.123174
4. Kamba, T., Bharat, K., Albers, M.C.: The Krakatoa Chronicle - An Interactive, Personalized, Newspaper on the Web. In: Proceedings of the Forth International Conference on World Wide Web, pp. 159–170 (1995). https://doi.org/10.1145/3592626.3592638
5. Thurman, N.: Personalization of News. The International Encyclopedia of Journalism Studies. Wiley-Blackwell, Massachusetts, USA (2018)
6. Bozdag, E.: Bias in algorithmic filtering and personalization. Ethics. Inf. Technol. **15**, 209–227 (2013). https://doi.org/10.1007/s10676-013-9321-6
7. Shardanand, U., Maes, P.: Social information filtering: algorithms for automating the "Word of Mouth". CHI 1995 Proceedings, pp. 210–217 (1995)
8. Grace, K., Finch, E., Gulbransen-Diaz, N., Henderson, H.: Q-Chef: the impact of surprise-eliciting systems on food-related decision-making. CHI '22 Proceedings, Article No. 11, pp. 1–14 (2022). https://doi.org/10.1145/3491102.3501862
9. Jasim, M., Collins, C., Sarvghad, A., Mahyar, N.: Supporting serendipitous discovery and balanced analysis of online product reviews with interaction-driven metrics and bias-mitigating suggestions. CHI'22 Proceedings, Article No. 9, pp. 1–24 (2022). https://doi.org/10.1145/3491102.3517649
10. Björneborn, L.: Serendipity dimensions and users' information behavior in the physical library interface. Inform. Res. **13**(1), paper 370 (2008)
11. McCay-Peet, L., Toms, E.: Measuring the dimensions of serendipity in digital environments. Inform. Res. **16**(3) paper 483 (2011). https://informationr.net/ir/16-3/paper483.html
12. Thudt, A., Hinrichs, U., Carpendale, S.: The bohemian bookshelf: supporting serendipitous book discoveries through information visualization. CHI '12 Proceedings, pp. 1461–1470 (2012). https://doi.org/10.1145/2207676.2208607
13. Palmonari, M., Uboldi, G., Cremaschi, M., Ciminieri, D., Bianchi, F.: DaCENA: serendipitous news reading with data contexts. ESWC (Satellite Events) **2015**, 133–137 (2015). https://doi.org/10.1007/978-3-319-25639-9_26
14. Beale, R.: Supporting serendipity: using ambient intelligence to augment user exploration for data mining and web browsing. J. Hum.-Comput. Stud. **65**(5), 421–433 (2007)
15. Deci, E.L., Ryan, R.M.: Intrinsic motivation and self-determination in human behavior. Springer New York (1985). https://doi.org/10.1007/978-1-4899-2271-7
16. Ryan, R.M., Deci, E.L.: Self-determination theory: basic psychological needs in motivation, development, and wellness. The Guilford Press (2017)
17. X developer API. https://developer.x.com/docs/twitter-api
18. Conover, M.D., Ratkiewicz, J., Francisco, M., Goncalves, B., Flammini, A., Menczer, F.: Political polarization on twitter. In: Proceedings of the Fifth International AAAI Conference on Weblogs and Social Media, vol. 5(1), pp. 89–96 (2021)
19. Hwang, D., Jung, J.E., Park, S., Nguyen, H.T.: Social data visualization system for understanding diffusion patterns on twitter: aa case study on Korean enterprises. Comput. Inform. **33**, 591–608 (2024)
20. Toriumi, F., Sasaki, T., Shinoda, K., Kazama, K., Kurihara, S., Noda, I.: Information sharing on twitter during the 2011 catastrophic earthquake. WWW 2013 Companion, May 13–1,(2013)
21. Toriumi, F., Baba, S.: Real-time tweet classification in disaster situation. WWW'16 Companion, April 11–15 (2016)
22. Cheng, Z., Caverlee, J., Lee, K.: You are where you tweet: a content-based approach to geo-locating twitter users, CIKM'10, October 26–30 (2010)
23. Cristianini, N., Shawe-Tayler, J.: An introduction to support vector machines and other kernel-based learning methods, p. 204. Cambridge University Press (2000)

24. Jain, A.K.: Data clustering: 50 years beyond K-means. Pattern Recogn. Lett. **31**(8), 651–666 (2010)
25. Blei, D.M., Ng, A.Y., Jordan, M.I.: Latent dirichlet allocation. J. Mach. Learn. Res. **3**, 993–1022 (2003)
26. Mikolov, T., Chen, K., Corrado, G., Dean, J.: Efficient estimation of word representations in vector space, arXiv: 1301.3781 https://doi.org/10.48550/arXiv.1301.3781
27. Devlin, J., Chang, M.-W., Lee, K., Toutanova, K.: BERT: pre-training of deep bidirectional transformers for language understanding, arXiv: 1810.04805 https://doi.org/10.48550/arXiv.1810.04805
28. Pang, B., Lee, L., Vaithyanathan, S.: Thumbs up? Sentiment classification using machine learning techniques. EMNLP **2002**, 79–86 (2002)
29. Go, A., Bhayani, R., Huang, L.: Twitter sentiment classification using distant supervision, CS224N project report, Stanford (2009)
30. Faridani, S., Bitton, E., Ryokai, K., Goldberg, K.: Opinion space: a scalable tool for browsing online comments. Proceedings of CHI **1175–1184**, 2010 (2010)
31. Vaswani, A., et al.: Attention is all you need. Advances in neural information processing systems
32. OpenAI API. https://openai.com/index/openai-api/. Accessed 8 Aug 2024
33. Llama. https://llama.meta.com/. Accessed 8 Aug 2024
34. Gemini. https://gemini.google.com/. Accessed 8 Aug 2024
35. Claude. https://www.anthropic.com/claude. Accessed 8 Aug 2024
36. Zhao, W.X., et al.: A survey of large language models. arXiv:2023.1823 https://doi.org/10.48550/arXiv.2303.18223
37. Hofmann, V., Kalluri, P.R., Jurafsky, D., King, S.: Dialect prejudice predicts AI decisions about people's character, employability, and criminality. arXiv:2403.00742, https://doi.org/10.48550/arXiv.2403.00742
38. Sahoo, P., Singh, A.K., Saha, S., Jain, V., Mondal, S., Chadha, A.: A systematic survey of prompt engineering in large language models: techniques and applications. arXiv:2402.07927 https://doi.org/10.48550/arXiv.2402.07927

ChatGPT Usability. An Exploratory Study in Higher Education

Jenny Morales[1]([✉]) [iD], Fabián Silva-Aravena[1] [iD], Héctor Cornide-Reyes[2] [iD], and Guisselle Muñoz[2] [iD]

[1] Facultad de Ciencias Sociales y Económicas, Universidad Católica del Maule, Talca, Chile
jmoralesb@ucm.cl, fasilva@ucm.cl

[2] Departamento de Ingeniería Informática y Ciencias de la Computación, Facultad de Ingeniería, Universidad de Atacama, Copiapó, Chile
hector.cornide@uda.cl, guisselle.munoz@uda.cl

Abstract. Artificial intelligence and its approach to people's daily lives have been rapid and sustained, from the use of virtual assistants that use natural language processing on commonly used devices such as smartphones to more complex artificial intelligence based on deep learning techniques, such as Generative Pre-trained Transformer (ChatGPT). In education, there is a lot of expectation about using this artificial intelligence correctly, taking advantage of its benefits, and minimizing the risks that its use can entail. Since many users with different interests can use this AI, it is interesting to identify perceived usability. Usability is an essential aspect of user experience; it considers the extent to which a product, system, or service can be used to complete specific tasks, considering the context of use. Usability in a tool used for education is critical since it will allow users to achieve their objectives, thus facilitating learning. In this work, we applied a survey to evaluate undergraduate students' perceptions of ChatGPT usability and identify whether, from the point of view of usability, it is a good tool to use in education. The survey was applied to undergraduate students from two Chilean universities that belonged to two programs related to business and computer science. The survey was conducted online during October 2024. The questionnaire was divided into two sections. The first section was a characterization, and the second section contained the System Usability Scale questionnaire (SUS), widely used to evaluate the perceived general usability of different system interfaces. This work has a quantitative approach with an exploratory scope. The characterization information will be descriptively analyzed in percentages and frequencies. Data from the second part of the questionnaire were analyzed based on the usability categories defined and established in SUS. We had 117 participants, and the perceived usability score was 69.7, which is favorable for ChatGPT. In the analysis by gender and program on the perceived usability of ChatGPT (using the T-student test), we found that men have a better perception of usability than women; in turn, we found that students in computer science have a better perception of usability than those in business. This indicates that it may be a good tool to use in education. In future work,

A. Coman et al. (Eds.): HCII 2025, LNCS 16337, pp. 161–174, 2026.
https://doi.org/10.1007/978-3-032-12801-0_11

we want to expand the sample and focus the results on the positive use of this artificial intelligence tool in teaching and learning.

Keywords: ChatGPT · User eXperience · System Usability Scale · Student perception

1   Background

Generative Artificial Intelligence (GenAI), according to Feuerriegel et al. [1], refers to computational techniques capable of generating seemingly new and meaningful content, such as text, images or audio, from training data. These techniques rely on models trained on large amounts of data [2], which are then used to produce coherent content tailored to the characteristics of the inputs provided by the user. GenAI is a broad field that focuses on creating systems capable of generating new content rather than simply analyzing existing data, distinguishing it from traditional AI models [3,4].

Deep generative models (DGMs) form the backbone of GenAI by leveraging deep learning to model the underlying probability distributions of data [5,6]. DGMs use neural networks to capture complex, high-dimensional relationships within data [7]. These models enable GenAI systems to produce realistic and contextually appropriate content [8], with applications ranging from natural language generation and image synthesis to scientific modeling. There are four ways to classify DGMs [9], which have shaped the evolution of GenAI [8], namely: variational autoencoders (VAEs), generative adversarial networks (GANs), latent diffusion models (LDMs), and transformer models.

VAEs are probabilistic models that map data into a continuous latent space by regularizing the latent space using Gaussian distributions [10], making them efficient but sometimes prone to producing blurry data due to their reliance on reconstruction-based loss functions. GANs, in contrast, use a competition approach between a generator and a discriminator [11], allowing them to produce visually compelling data. However, they present stability challenges during training and a lack of diversity in results. LDMs represent a significant evolution by modeling reversible stochastic processes to generate data from noise [12]. These models are computationally intensive but achieve highly detailed results, especially in image generation tasks. Finally, transformer models have expanded the field by using attention-based architectures that capture long-term dependencies [13], allowing them to successfully handle sequential and multimodal data.

Transformer models, particularly GPT (Generative Pre-trained Transformer), represent one of the most advanced architectures in generative artificial intelligence. ChatGPT is an application of the GPT model designed specifically for conversational text generation. Like its base model, GPT, ChatGPT is trained with large amounts of textual data [2], allowing it to generate responses based on the context of the conversation, making it useful in applications such as virtual assistants, content generation, personalized tutoring, and customer support. The system combines the power of pre-trained deep learning models with a programmability layer to provide a solid foundation for generating natural language conversations [14] answering questions, providing explanations, and adjusting to the user's tone and style. It is currently composed of the GPT-3.5, GPT-4, GPT-4o mini, and GPT-4o models and their previews GPT-o1 and GPT-o1 mini, which are detailed below in Table 1.

Language translation, text creation, emotion analysis, and question-solving are just a few of the many tasks of natural language processing (NLP) where GPT models have emerged as cutting-edge tools [16]. Their flexibility in handling human interactions has proven to be a powerful tool in multiple sectors, such as healthcare [17], finance [18], research [19], and education [20], among others. The influence of ChatGPT on society has generated a growing interest in the educational and training field [20]. Notable benefits include research support, automated classification, and improved human-computer interaction [21].

In education and business research, according to the study by Cribben and Zeinali [22], it is highlighted that ChatGPT offers multiple benefits for both teachers and students, standing out as an innovative tool to optimize learning and teaching processes. For teachers, it facilitates the creation of teaching materials, course design, and automation of tasks such as grading, allowing a more efficient and personalized approach to teaching. From the students' perspective, ChatGPT becomes a valuable resource for understanding complex concepts in a simplified way, generating summaries of long texts, writing and debugging code, and preparing exams with customized questions and answers. On the other hand, the study's results by Elbaz et al. [23] show that the perception of usefulness, ease of use, and convenience of ChatGPT positively influence business students' attitudes towards its use. These attitudes, in turn, strongly impact the intention to adopt the tool, which improves academic performance. However, personal moral values and religious ethics moderate this relationship, generating feelings of responsibility and guilt in the event of uses that compromise academic integrity.

In the field of computer science education, the research work of Dempere et al. [21] is based on the design of an experiment that consisted of dividing students of an introductory course on object-oriented programming into two groups: one with access to ChatGPT to perform practical tasks and another without access, adopting a controlled study methodology. Specific adjustments will be implemented, such as modifying the tasks to minimize direct responses from ChatGPT and introducing interactive defenses of the assignments. The results showed that there were no statistically significant differences in performance between both groups in practical tasks, midterm exams, and final grades, suggesting that the measures adopted guarantee equitable learning. On the other hand, in the study of Singh et al. [24], a survey designed to explore students' perceptions of ChatGPT was used, focusing on aspects such as familiarity, frequency of use, academic impact, and potential threats. The survey included 12 questions and was administered to 430 computer science masters students at the University of Hertfordshire. The results revealed that, although most students are familiar with ChatGPT, more than 50% do not use it regularly in academic

Table 1. ChatGPT model comparison [15].

Model	Main features	Context window	Input/output	Advanced tools	Price	Speed	Availability
GPT-4o	Latest, fastest and most advanced model	128k (average novel or longer)	Text, image, audio	Data analysis, file uploads, navigation, viewing, etc.	$5M tokens in, $15M tokens out. 50% cheaper than GPT-4 Turbo	2x faster than GPT-4 Turbo	Available on all plans incl. Free, Plus, Team, Enterprise
GPT-4o Mini	Light version of GPT-4o, without access to advanced tools	128k (average novel or longer)	Text, image, audio	It does not have access to data analysis, navigation, vision, among others	Included in the free plan and accessible to all levels	Slower than GPT-4o	Available for free and paid users when GPT-4o is not available
GPT-4	Previous model of high intelligence	128k (average novel or longer)	Text, image, audio	Limited advanced tools compared to GPT-4o	More expensive than GPT-4o; pricing based on subscription level	Slower than GPT-4o	Accessible to Chat-GPT Plus, Team and Enterprise users
GPT-3.5	Fast model for routine and simple tasks	16k (1–2 dozen articles or short story)	Text, audio	Does not have access to advanced tools or vision	Cheaper; only available via API	Faster than GPT-4o on simple tasks	Available exclusively through the OpenAI API
GPT-o1	Preliminary version for evaluation before GPT-4o	Not specified	Text	Does not include advanced tools	Available in experimental mode for developers	Similar performance to GPT-4o	Accessible in test mode with API and Playground
GPT-o1 Mini	Compact version of GPT-o1	Not specified	Text	No access to advanced tools	Cheaper than GPT-o1	Slower than GPT-o1	Used for initial testing and experimentation on resource-constrained devices

activities. Among the uses identified were code generation and obtaining explanations for complex concepts.

However, despite the above, ChatGPT presents significant limitations, such as possible errors in answers, lack of originality in solutions, and reliance on training data that may contain biases [2,16]. Furthermore, the use of ChatGPT raises ethical concerns related to plagiarism and academic integrity, requiring a balanced approach to maximize its potential without compromising educational quality [22]. Valcea et al. [25] warn against the potential loss of critical thinking skills due to students' over-reliance on AI for basic tasks.

ChatGPT stands out for its ease of use and efficiency in content generation [26], making it a valuable tool for complex tasks such as academic writing. For example, in the study by Zhai [27], an experiment is documented where ChatGPT was used to write an academic paper. The results are analyzed in terms of coherence, accuracy, and systematicity. The author points out that the process of interacting with the tool took approximately 2–3 h and required limited intellectual effort, as ChatGPT organized and presented the information in a coherent and well-structured manner. Furthermore, the model's ability to respond to diverse queries with consistency and clarity reflects its user experience (UX)-focused design, allowing even users with limited knowledge in the area to obtain high-quality results. The study by Wulandari et al. [28] emphasizes that user experience and ease of use are key to improving efficiency and emotional impact in the interaction with ChatGPT.

User experience (UX) is defined as the perceptions and responses of users resulting from the use or anticipation of the use of a product, system, or service [34]. One of the essential aspects of the UX is usability, defined "extent to which a system, product or service can be used by specified users to achieve specified goals with effectiveness, efficiency and satisfaction in a specified context of use" [35]. The usability of an interface can be evaluated in various ways, such as through inspections, which are carried out by experts (for example, heuristic evaluations and cognitive walkthroughs) or through user test, a user experience of the system is generally carried out, and then a questionnaire or interview related to the perception of use is answered. There are several questionnaires to evaluate usability and UX, such as System Usability Scale (SUS), Questionnaire for User Interface Satisfaction (QUIS), User Experience Questionnaire (UEQ), among others [36].

In educational contexts, the usability and UX of support tools are essential factors, for instance, in the design of educational software [37,38], in the virtual learning objects, which favor the effectiveness of learning processes [39], as well as for learning experiences that consider artificial intelligence and improve student outcomes [40]. In this way, the usability and UX of the tools used become essential and relevant since they will facilitate learning and the achievement of objectives simply. For this reason, this study focused on the usability evaluation of ChatGPT with SUS, a widely used questionnaire [32]. We aim to establish its usability and support its use in education.

This article is organized as follows: Sect. 2 presents the methodology used, exposing the questionnaire and participants. Section 3 shows the results obtained, and Sect. 4 presents the Conclusion.

2   Methodology

We focused on the usability perception of ChatGPT-4o mini by students from two undergraduate programs belonging to different areas, one associated with Business and the other related to Computer Science. The programs belong to different universities.

To evaluate this perception, we used the System Usability Scale questionnaire (SUS). SUS is a questionnaire with 10 items ordered according to positive statements (favorable perception) in odd items and negative statements (unfavorable perception) in even items. It also has a 5-point Likert scale where 1 is "strongly disagree" and 5 is "strongly agree". The scores for odd items are calculated considering the score obtained minus 1 and for even items 5 minus the score obtained. Finally, the sum of the items is multiplied by 2.5, which gives a range of scores up to 100 [29]. 68 is the minimum SUS score to consider good usability (the objective to be achieved). Values lower than this score indicate that the system, interface, or product has elements that need improvement in usability. This questionnaire is widely used to evaluate the general perception of usability associated with a system, interface, or product [30,31].

The questionnaire and its items are shown in Fig. 1. We applied the questionnaire using an online tool between October 14 and November 14, 2024. We introduced them to the questionnaire and asked if they would like to participate. All responses were obtained through voluntary participation. Students of all levels were considered in both undergraduate programs. It is important to note that when socializing the focus of this study, all students reported having used ChatGPT for some assignment or work in their undergraduate programs.

3   Results

We obtained responses from 117 undergraduate students from the two participating programs. Of these, 47 students were from the Computer Science (40%) and 70 from the Business (60%). See Fig. 2.

Regarding the gender distribution, 42 women participated in the study (36%), 73 men (62%) and 2 participants stated that they had another gender (2%). Figure 3 shows the distribution by gender and program. The lowest number of participating women belong to Computer Science.

The participants of both programs belong to different entry years, which helps to have a more representative sample. As shown in Fig. 4, both programs have a higher participation frequency with the entry years 2023 and 2024.

The SUS score for the perceived usability of all participants in both programs (117 participants) was 69.7, which is favorable for ChatGPT. It places it slightly above average, leaving it in the "C" range at the center of the gradient-curve scale [32].

Analyzing the results by item, we found that items 4, 6, 9, and 10 did not reach the target average score (set for a SUS score 68). Table 2 shows the scores obtained and the target scores established according to [30]. This means that these are the items with the lowest perceived usability. Lewis in 2009 established that SUS has two factors: usability and learning. Items 4 and 10 are aligned with the learning factor, and items 1, 2, 3, 5, 6, 7, 8, and 9 are aligned with the usability factor [33]. Therefore, we can indicate that ChatGPT's score in this evaluation is slightly below the average for elements 4 and 10. This could be reflected in some difficulty learning it. On the other hand, scores below the average of items 6 and 9 indicate a perception of low consistency and little confidence when using chatGPT.

Table 2. The SUS scoring target (68) by item and the results obtained.

Item	Target SUS score 68	Score obtained
I4	<=1.85	1.91
I6	<=2.20	2.71
I9	>=3.72	3.29
I10	<=2.09	2.22

Considering the score obtained broken down by program and gender, Table 3 shows that students in Computer Science perceive greater usability than Business students (76.0 and 65.4, respectively). In turn, if we consider it by gender, men perceive greater usability than women (scores of 73.0 and 64.4, respectively).

Table 3. SUS score.

Program	Female	Male	Other	Total
Business	60.7	69.4	00.0	65.4
Computer Science	76.3	76.9	58.8	76.0
Total	64.4	73.0	58.8	69.7

To identify whether the differences in perceptions are significant by gender and program, the Kolmogorov-Smirnov normality test was initially performed, identifying as:

H_0 that the SUS result variable has a normal distribution;

H_1 that the SUS result variable does not have a normal distribution. We considered a p-value <0.05 as a decision rule. Table 4 we can see the result of the Kolmogorov-Smirnov normality test, obtaining a p-value of 0.251, which

Table 4. 1-sample Kolmogorov-Smirnov test.

1-sample Kolmogorov-Smirnov test		SUS score
N		117
Normal parameters[a,b]	Mean	69.658
	Std. deviation	14.9601
Most extreme differences	Absolute	0.094
	Positive	0.094
	Negative	−0.053
Kolmogorov-Smirnov Z		1,018
Asymp. sig. (2-tailed)		0.251

[a] Test distribution is normal
[b] Calculated from data

leads to the conclusion that the SUS result variable has a normal distribution, and H_0 is accepted.

Table 5 shows the group statistics separated by gender, where the number of female and male participants (42 and 73, respectively). It is important to note that for this analysis, respondents who answered "other" in the case of gender were not considered because it is a minimum number to be included in the study. In addition, Table 5 also shows the average obtained for the female 64.405 and the male 72.979, so it can be considered that men have a better perception of the usability of ChatGPT than women.

Table 5. Group statistics by gender.

	Gender	N	Mean	Std. deviation	Std. error mean
SUS score	Female	42	64.405	13.758	2.123
	Male	73	72.979	14.905	1.745

To verify if there is a significant difference between the means of the independent samples, the T-student test was performed, establishing that:

H_0: There are no significant differences in students' perceptions based on gender.

H_1: There are significant differences in students' perceptions based on gender.

According to the results shown in Table 6, Levene's test shows homogeneity of variances with a significance level of 0.626 (using a p-value <0.05 as a rule). The T-student test indicates a significant difference between the groups based on a p-value of 0.003 (considering a p-value <0.05 as a rule). This confirms H_1, so there are differences between the groups. By reviewing the means, it is possible to identify that men perceive ChatGPT as more usable than women.

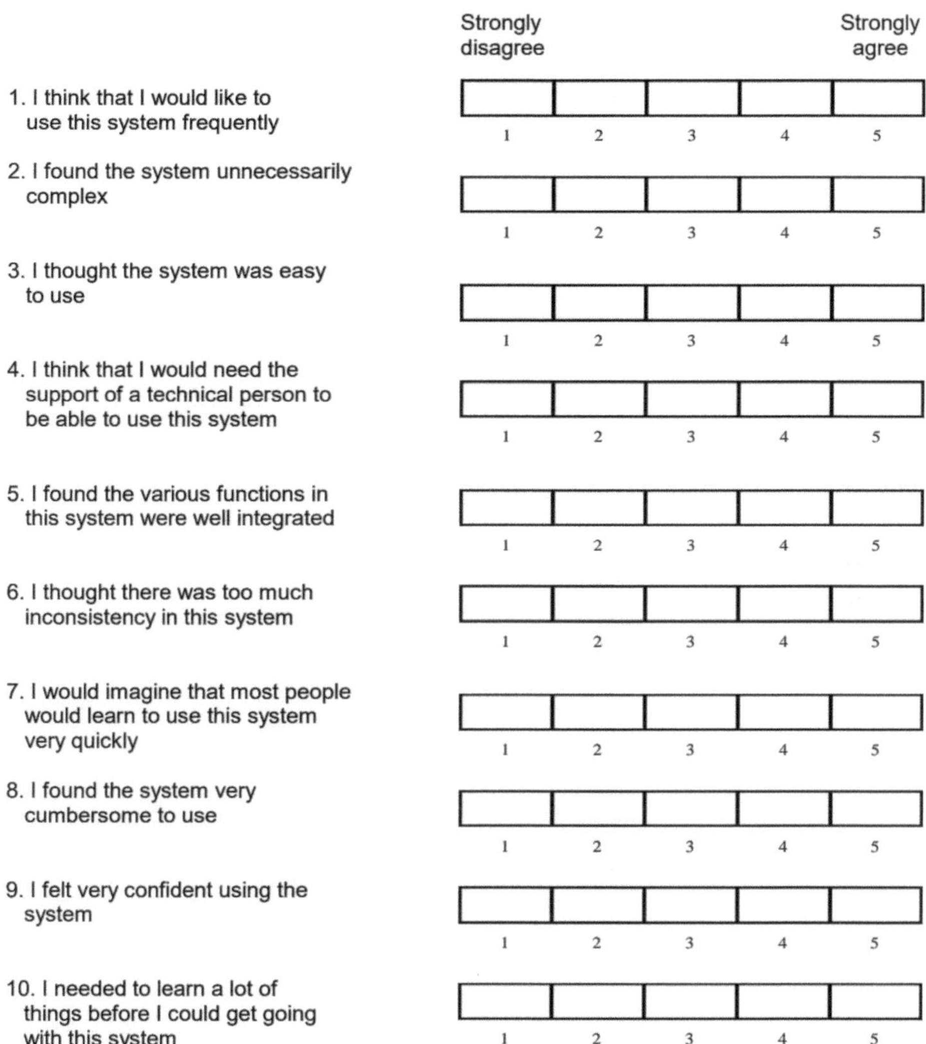

Fig. 1. System Usability Scale [29].

Table 6. Independent sample test (gender).

	Levene's test for equality of var.		t-test for equality of means					95% CI diff.	
	F	Sig.	t	df	Sig. (2-tailed)	Mean diff.	Std. error diff.		
SUS score	0.239	0.626	−3.054	113	0.003	−8.5747	2.8081	−14.1380	−3.0114
			−3.121	91.351	0.002	−8.5747	2.7477	−14.0323	−3.1170

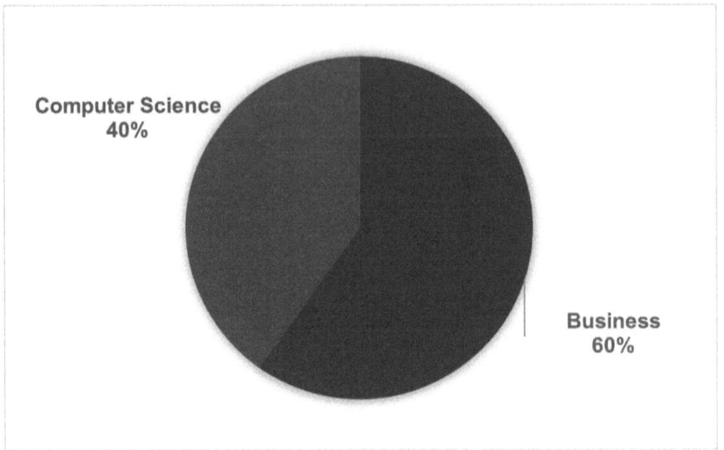

Fig. 2. Distribution of participant by program.

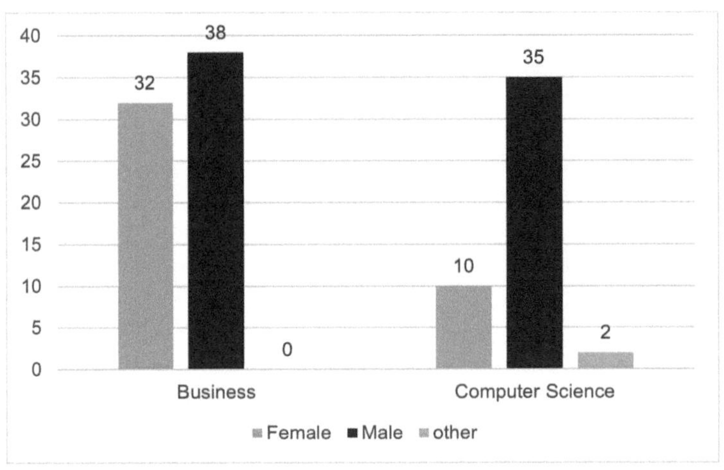

Fig. 3. Distribution of participant by gender.

Table 7 shows the groups' statistics separated by the program. The Business program had 70 participants, and the mean was 65.429. The Computer Science program had 47 participants, and the mean was 75.957. Considering the above, it can be observed that the mean of Computer Science students is 10 points higher than that of Business students. To verify whether the differences are significant, we performed the T-student test, establishing that.

H_0: There are no significant differences in students' perceptions based on the program.

H_1: There are significant differences in students' perceptions based on the program.

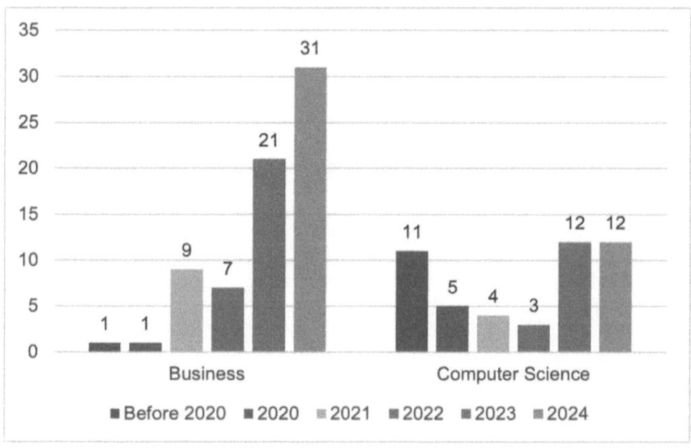

Fig. 4. Distribution of participant by entry years.

In Table 8, we can see the results of Levene's test, which indicated homogeneity of variances with a significance level of 0.891 (using a p-value <0.05 as a rule). On the other hand, the T-student test indicates a significant difference between the groups with a p-value of 0.000 (considering a p-value <0.05 as a rule). This confirms H_1, so there are differences between the groups. It is possible to identify that students in Computer Science programs perceive ChatGPT as more usable than students in Business programs.

Table 7. Group statistics by program.

	Program	N	Mean	Std. deviation	Std. error mean
SUS score	Business	70	65.429	14.039	1.678
	Computer Science	47	75.957	14.176	2.068

Table 8. Independent sample test (program).

	Levene's test for equality of var.		t-test for equality of means						
	F	Sig.	t	df	Sig. (2-tailed)	Mean diff.	Std. error diff.	95% CI diff.	95% CI diff.
SUS score	0.001	0.981	−3.961	115	0.000	−10.5289	2.6579	−15.7936	−5.2642
			−3.954	98.154	0.000	−10.5289	2.6630	−15.8134	−5.2444

4   Conclusions

Considering the interest generated by Generative AI in several areas, we used the System Usability Scale questionnaire to collect information on the usability of ChatGPT in two undergraduate programs. The score obtained by ChatGPT-4o mini was 69.7, which means a good score. We found in the analysis by groups that there are significant differences in that (i) students in the Computer Science program perceive greater usability than students in the Business program and (ii) men perceive greater usability than women. Given the usability obtained from ChatGPT, we consider that there is an auspicious future in the use of this type of AI in teaching, making it easier for students to achieve their objectives in a simple way. However, specific guidelines will have to be established depending on the type of students who use it. Although Computer Science students perceived greater usability in our case, it may be necessary to guide and support students from other degrees. This study only considered two groups of students. In future work, we should analyze the causes or factors that affect gender differences in usability perception, include students from different courses, and focus on specific teaching and learning activities that improve the learning experience.

Acknowledgments. We thank all the students who participated voluntarily and freely in the study.

Disclosure of Interests. The authors have no competing interests to declare that are relevant to the content of this article.

References

1. Feuerriegel, S., Hartmann, J., Janiesch, C., Zschech, P.: Generative AI. Bus. Inf. Syst. Eng. **66**(1), 111–126 (2024)
2. Yenduri, G., et al.: GPT (generative pre-trained transformer)—a comprehensive review on enabling technologies, potential applications, emerging challenges, and future directions. IEEE Access **12**, 54608–54649 (2024)
3. Yehia, E.: Developments on generative AI. In: AI and Emerging Technologies, pp. 139–160. CRC Press (2025)
4. Jebara, T., Jebara, T.: Generative versus discriminative learning. In: Machine Learning: Discriminative and Generative, pp. 17–60 (2024)
5. Tomczak, J.M.: Why deep generative modeling? In: Deep Generative Modeling, pp. 1–13. Springer International Publishing, Cham (2024)
6. Lehmann, F., Buschek, D.: Examining autocompletion as a basic concept for interaction with generative AI. i-com **19**(3), 251–264 (2021)
7. Ruthotto, L., Haber, E.: An introduction to deep generative modeling. GAMM-Mitt. **44**(2), e202100008 (2021)
8. Banh, L., Strobel, G.: Generative artificial intelligence. Electron. Mark. **33**(1), 63 (2023)
9. Strobel, G., Banh, L., Möller, F., Schoormann, T.: Exploring generative artificial intelligence: a taxonomy and types. In: Proceedings of the 57th Hawaii International Conference on System Sciences, pp. 4546–4555 (2024)

10. Kingma, D.P., Mohamed, S., Jimenez Rezende, D., Welling, M.: Semi-supervised learning with deep generative models. Adv. Neural Inf. Process. Syst. (NIPS) **27** (2014). https://doi.org/10.48550/arXiv.1406.5298
11. Goodfellow, I., et al.: Generative adversarial nets. Adv. Neural Inf. Process. Syst. (NIPS) **27** (2014)
12. Rombach, R., Blattmann, A., Lorenz, D., Esser, P., Ommer, B.: High-resolution image synthesis with latent diffusion models. In: Proceedings of the IEEE/CVF Conference on Computer Vision and Pattern Recognition, pp. 10684–10695 (2022)
13. Vaswani, A.: Attention is all you need. Adv. Neural Inf. Process. Syst. (2017)
14. Bahrini, A., et al.: ChatGPT: applications, opportunities, and threats. In: 2023 Systems and Information Engineering Design Symposium (SIEDS), pp. 274–279. IEEE (2023)
15. OpenAI: How can I access GPT-4, GPT-4 Turbo, GPT-4o, and GPT-4o mini? OpenAI Help Center (s.f.). https://help.openai.com/en/articles/7102672-how-can-i-access-gpt-4-gpt-4-turbo-gpt-4o-and-gpt-4o-mini. Accessed 2025/01/10
16. Khadka, B., Aryal, R.: ChatGPT: applications, opportunities and challenges. Int. J. Adv. Eng. Manag. (IJAEM) **5**(11), 396–407 (2023)
17. Li, J., Dada, A., Puladi, B., Kleesiek, J., Egger, J.: ChatGPT in healthcare: a taxonomy and systematic review. Comput. Methods Programs Biomed. **245**, 108013 (2024)
18. Khan, M.S., Umer, H.: ChatGPT in finance: applications, challenges, and solutions. Heliyon **10**(2) (2024)
19. Lehr, S.A., Caliskan, A., Liyanage, S., Banaji, M.R.: ChatGPT as research scientist: probing GPT's capabilities as a research librarian, research ethicist, data generator, and data predictor. Proc. Natl. Acad. Sci. **121**(35), e2404328121 (2024)
20. Sánchez, O.V.G.: Uso y percepción de ChatGPT en la educación superior. Rev. Investig. Tecnol. Inf. **11**(23), 98–107 (2023)
21. Dempere, J., Modugu, K., Hesham, A., Ramasamy, L.K.: The impact of ChatGPT on higher education. Front. Educ. **8**, 1206936 (2023)
22. Cribben, I., Zeinali, Y.: The benefits and limitations of ChatGPT in business education and research: a focus on management science, operations management and data analytics. In: Operations Management and Data Analytics, 29 Mar 2023. Available at SSRN: https://ssrn.com/abstract=4404276. https://doi.org/10.2139/ssrn.4404276
23. Elbaz, A.M., Salem, I.E., Darwish, A., Alkathiri, N.A., Mathew, V., Al-Kaaf, H.A.: Getting to know ChatGPT: how business students feel, what they think about personal morality, and how their academic outcomes affect Oman's higher education. Comput. Educ. Artif. Intell. **7**, 100324 (2024)
24. Singh, H., Tayarani-Najaran, M.H., Yaqoob, M.: Exploring computer science students' perception of ChatGPT in higher education: a descriptive and correlation study. Educ. Sci. **13**(9), 924 (2023)
25. Valcea, S., Hamdani, M.R., Wang, S.: Exploring the impact of ChatGPT on business school education: prospects, boundaries, and paradoxes. J. Manag. Educ. **48**(5), 915–947 (2024)
26. Shaikh, S., Yayilgan, S.Y., Klimova, B., Pikhart, M.: Assessing the usability of ChatGPT for formal English language learning. Eur. J. Investig. Health Psychol. Educ. **13**(9), 1937–1960 (2023)
27. Zhai, X.: ChatGPT User Experience: Implications for Education, 27 Dec 2022. Available at SSRN: https://ssrn.com/abstract=4312418. https://doi.org/10.2139/ssrn.4312418

28. Wulandari, A.A., Nurhaipah, T., Ohorella, N.R.: Perceived ease of use, social influencers, facilitating conditions, user experience on the influence of human-machine interaction on interaction efficiency, emotional impact of using chat GPT. J. Digit. Media Commun. **2**(2), 61–75 (2024)
29. Brooke, J.: SUS—a quick and dirty usability scale. Usabil. Eval. Ind. **189**(194), 4–7 (1996)
30. J. User Exp. https://uxpajournal.org/item-benchmarks-system-usability-scale-sus/. Accessed 2024/12/04
31. Morales, J., Rusu, C.: Usability perception of visual programming language: a case study. In: Proceedings of the CEUR Workshop, vol. 2747, pp. 83–88 (2020)
32. Measuring Usability with the System Usability Scale (SUS). https://measuringu.com/sus/. Accessed 2024/12/04
33. Lewis, J.R., Sauro, J.: The factor structure of the system usability scale. In: Human Centered Design: First International Conference, HCD 2009, Held as Part of HCI International 2009. LNCS, vol. 5619, pp. 94–103. Springer, Berlin Heidelberg (2009). https://doi.org/10.1007/978-3-642-02806-9_12
34. ISO 9241-210:2019 (en) Ergonomics of human-system interaction—part 2010: human-centred design for interactive systems. https://www.iso.org/obp/ui/es/#iso:std:iso:9241:-210:ed-2:v1:en. Accessed 2024/12/04
35. ISO 9241-11:2018 (en) Ergonomics of human-system interaction—part 11: usability: definitions and concepts. https://www.iso.org/obp/ui/en/#iso:std:iso:9241:-11:ed-2:v1:en. Accessed 2024/12/04
36. Morales, J., Rojas, G., Cerda, G.: Towards a methodology to evaluate user experience with personalized questionnaires for the developments of custom systems. In: Kurosu, M., et al. (eds.) HCI International 2022—Late Breaking Papers. Design, User Experience and Interaction. HCII 2022. Lecture Notes in Computer Science, vol. 13516. Springer, Cham (2022)
37. elázquez, I., Sosa, M.: La usabilidad del software educativo como potenciador de nuevas formas de pensamiento. Rev. Iberoam. educ. **50**(4), 1–12 (2009)
38. Rodríguez, A.H.: Usabilidad de un software educativo como medio instruccional para el proceso de enseñanza-aprendizaje de una asignatura. Rev. Iberoam. Investig. Desarro. Educ. (11) (2015). ISSN: 2007-2619
39. Rincón, O.I.C., Castellanos, L.A.M., Villa, J.J.B.: Importancia de la medición y evaluación de la usabilidad de un objeto virtual de aprendizaje. Panorama **13**(25), 23–37 (2019)
40. St-Hilaire, F., et al.: A new era: intelligent tutoring systems will transform online learning for millions. arXiv preprint arXiv:2203.03724 (2022)

Assessing AI-Based System Acceptance Through the Design of a Trustworthiness Estimation Tool for Machine Learning Models

Jonathan Ugalde[1,2](✉) [iD], Rodrigo Salas[2,3] [iD], Aurelio F. Bariviera[4] [iD], and María Paz Godoy[5] [iD]

[1] Faculty of Engineering, Informatics Engineering School, Universidad de Valparaíso, Valparaíso, Chile
[2] Millennium Institute for Intelligent Healthcare Engineering (iHealth), Santiago, Chile
jonathan.ugalde@postgrado.uv.cl
[3] Faculty of Engineering, Biomedical Engineering School, Universidad de Valparaíso, Valparaíso, Chile
[4] Department of Business and ECO-SOS, Universitat Rovira i Virgili, Reus, Spain
[5] Carrera de Información y Control de Gestión, Facultad de Ciencias Económicas y Administrativas, Universidad de Valparaíso, Valparaíso, Chile

Abstract. The widespread adoption of machine learning (ML) models in high-stakes decision-making underscores the need for rigorous trustworthiness assessments. Ensuring trustworthy AI requires evaluating multiple dimensions, including performance, fairness, and interpretability, to support reliable and ethical decision-making. This paper introduces a framework for systematically estimating the trustworthiness of ML models by aggregating diverse quantitative metrics into a unified trustworthiness score. The proposed design consists of modular components that assess key dimensions—performance, fairness, and interpretability—each contributing to an overall evaluation. A flexible weighting mechanism allows customization based on domain-specific priorities and regulatory requirements.

The primary contribution of this work is a structured approach to integrating multiple trustworthiness dimensions into a single assessment framework. By offering a quantitative comparison of ML models, this framework enables researchers and practitioners to make informed decisions about model selection and deployment.

While this framework remains in the design phase, future research will focus on implementation, empirical validation using real-world ML models, and refining metric selection strategies to enhance robustness. The broader implications of this work extend to regulatory compliance, model auditing, and trustworthiness benchmarking, fostering greater transparency and accountability in AI-driven systems.

Keywords: Trustworthiness · Fairness · Interpretability · Artificial intelligence

A. Coman et al. (Eds.): HCII 2025, LNCS 16337, pp. 175–186, 2026.
https://doi.org/10.1007/978-3-032-12801-0_12

1   Introduction

The rapid advancement of artificial intelligence (AI) has led to its integration across a wide range of industries, including healthcare [22], finance [6], autonomous systems [11], and legal applications [3]. At the core of these AI-driven solutions are machine learning (ML) models, which enable sophisticated capabilities in prediction, decision-making, and automation. Despite their remarkable achievements, concerns regarding their trustworthiness continue to hinder widespread adoption [18].

Trustworthiness in AI-based systems is a multifaceted concept, encompassing several key dimensions that determine the reliability of ML models in real-world applications. Performance is a fundamental aspect, as stakeholders require AI systems that consistently deliver accurate predictions across various conditions [18]. However, high performance alone does not guarantee trustworthiness. Fairness is another critical factor, ensuring that AI systems do not perpetuate or amplify biases, particularly in high-stakes domains such as healthcare and finance [6]. Research has shown that biased training data and suboptimal model design can lead to systemic discrimination, disproportionately impacting marginalized groups [17]. To address these concerns, fairness metrics such as demographic parity, equalized odds, and disparate impact analysis have been developed to evaluate and mitigate bias in machine learning models.

In addition to fairness, interpretability plays a key role in fostering trust. Many high-performing models, such as deep neural networks, function as black boxes, making it difficult for users to understand how specific decisions are made [18]. This opacity can undermine trust and limit adoption, especially in regulated sectors where transparency is essential. To enhance interpretability, various techniques have been proposed, including SHAP (Shapley Additive Explanations) [16] and LIME (Local Interpretable Model-agnostic Explanations). These methods provide insights into model behavior, helping stakeholders understand decision-making processes and build confidence in AI outputs. Beyond improving transparency, interpretability also contributes to accountability by enabling developers and regulators to detect errors or unethical patterns before large-scale deployment.

Beyond performance, fairness, and interpretability, other aspects such as robustness and ethical considerations further influence the trustworthiness of AI systems. Robustness refers to a model's ability to maintain reliable performance under adversarial conditions, data distribution shifts, and unexpected environmental changes [11]. Adversarial attacks, where small input perturbations drastically alter predictions, pose significant risks in critical domains such as autonomous driving and medical diagnostics [22]. To mitigate these vulnerabilities, AI models must incorporate defense mechanisms such as adversarial training and out-of-distribution detection. Ethical considerations, on the other hand, address broader societal implications, including AI governance, legal compliance, and alignment with human values [3]. The responsible development of AI requires adherence to well-established principles such as fairness, accountability, transparency, and privacy (FAT), which have gained widespread recognition among policymakers and researchers. Ensuring ethical AI deployment often involves collaboration between computer scientists, ethicists, and legal experts to align AI models with regulatory frameworks and societal expectations.

Given the complexity of trustworthiness, a single metric cannot capture all its dimensions. Instead, comprehensive evaluation frameworks are needed to provide a holistic assessment of AI trustworthiness. This highlights the necessity of a standardized trustworthiness estimation tool that integrates multiple metrics across key dimensions, allowing stakeholders to systematically compare AI models and assess their deployment readiness [17]. A structured evaluation approach would not only improve AI adoption but also reduce risks associated with untrustworthy deployments, promoting responsible and sustainable AI integration across industries.

In this paper, we argue that the trustworthiness of ML models can be effectively assessed through three primary dimensions: performance, fairness, and interpretability. While other aspects such as accountability and transparency are important, they often emerge as consequences of these core elements. The lack of standardized tools to evaluate these dimensions has posed challenges for both AI developers and stakeholders seeking to deploy reliable AI solutions.

To bridge this gap, we propose a framework for a trustworthiness estimation tool that quantitatively assesses ML models based on predefined metrics spanning performance, fairness, and interpretability. This tool provides a structured method to compare models from a trustworthiness perspective, identify potential areas for improvement, and estimate their likelihood of acceptance before deployment. By establishing a systematic evaluation framework, we aim to enhance the trustworthiness of AI systems and facilitate broader acceptance of ML models by decision-makers and end users.

The remainder of this paper is structured as follows: Sect. 2 provides an overview of existing tools used to assess AI trustworthiness. Section 3 details the design of the proposed trustworthiness estimation tool, including key metrics, software components, and core functionalities. Finally, Sect. 4 summarizes our contributions and discusses potential applications, challenges, and future research directions.

2   Related Work

The evaluation of AI trustworthiness has garnered significant attention in recent years, leading to the development of various frameworks and toolkits aimed at assessing key aspects such as fairness, interpretability, and robustness. This section provides an overview of existing methodologies and examines their contributions to the broader landscape of AI trustworthiness.

Ensuring fairness in machine learning models is a key component of trustworthiness. Several frameworks have been developed to detect and mitigate bias in AI systems. One of the most prominent tools is AI Fairness 360 (AIF360) by IBM [4], an open-source toolkit that offers over 70 fairness metrics and multiple bias mitigation algorithms, enabling researchers and practitioners to evaluate and improve model fairness.

Another significant framework is Fairlearn, developed by Microsoft [26]. This Python library provides fairness assessment metrics and mitigation techniques that can be seamlessly integrated into ML pipelines, making it particularly useful for organizations seeking to balance trade-offs between accuracy and fairness in real-world applications. Additionally, Google's ML Fairness Gym [9] offers a simulation environment where developers can explore the long-term impact of fairness interventions in reinforcement learning settings, facilitating more robust fairness evaluations.

Interpretability is another key dimension of AI trustworthiness, as it enables stakeholders to understand how models generate their predictions. IBM's AI Explainability 360 (AIX360) [2] is a comprehensive toolkit that provides a range of interpretability techniques, including surrogate models, feature importance methods, and counterfactual explanations. These techniques help enhance model transparency and build user confidence in AI systems. Other widely adopted interpretability frameworks include LIME (Local Interpretable Model-Agnostic Explanations) [24] and SHAP (Shapley Additive Explanations) [16]. LIME generates locally faithful approximations of complex models to produce human-interpretable explanations, while SHAP employs cooperative game theory to assign importance scores to input features. Both frameworks have been extensively used in industry and academia to enhance AI transparency and accountability. Google's TCAV (Testing with Concept Activation Vectors) [13] is another powerful interpretability tool that quantifies the influence of high-level human concepts in deep learning models, offering insights beyond standard feature-level explanations.

Robustness is essential to ensure that AI models perform reliably under varying conditions, including adversarial attacks and data distribution shifts. The Adversarial Robustness Toolbox (ART) by IBM [20] is a leading framework for evaluating model resilience against adversarial attacks, providing tools for attack simulation, defense mechanisms, and robustness testing. Similarly, Google's What-If Tool (WIT) [27] enables users to analyze AI models under different scenarios, helping identify vulnerabilities related to fairness and robustness. WIT is particularly valuable for debugging AI models and enhancing their resilience before deployment. Another notable tool, DeepXplore [21], performs automated white-box testing of deep learning models, ensuring robustness against adversarial examples and unexpected failures. TensorFlow's Responsible AI Toolkit [1] also integrates functionalities for fairness, explainability, and robustness assessments, making it a valuable resource for deep learning practitioners aiming to incorporate responsible AI practices into their workflows.

Beyond individual aspects of trustworthiness, broader initiatives focus on ethical AI development. The Ethical AI Toolkit by the Alan Turing Institute [15] offers a set of tools and guidelines to ensure AI systems align with ethical principles, including fairness, transparency, and accountability.

While these frameworks provide valuable tools for assessing specific aspects of AI trustworthiness, most focus on isolated dimensions rather than offering a holistic evaluation. For example, fairness toolkits like AIF360 and Fairlearn excel at detecting and mitigating bias but lack interpretability or robustness assessments. Conversely, interpretability frameworks like LIME and SHAP do not provide mechanisms for assessing fairness or robustness.

This gap highlights the need for a comprehensive trustworthiness estimation tool that integrates multiple dimensions into a unified framework. By leveraging insights from existing methodologies, our proposed tool aims to bridge this divide, providing a systematic approach to evaluating AI models across performance, fairness, and interpretability.

3   Framework Design

This section describes the design of a software component aimed at estimating the level of trustworthiness offered by the predictions of a machine learning model. The design approach focuses on complementing various metrics from different dimensions of trustworthiness to generate a general trustworthiness metric. This overall metric takes into account both the value of the metrics associated with each dimension and the weight assigned to each metric. Consequently, the level of trustworthiness is conditioned by the values and weights associated with each metric, a concept illustrated in the force diagram in Fig. 1.

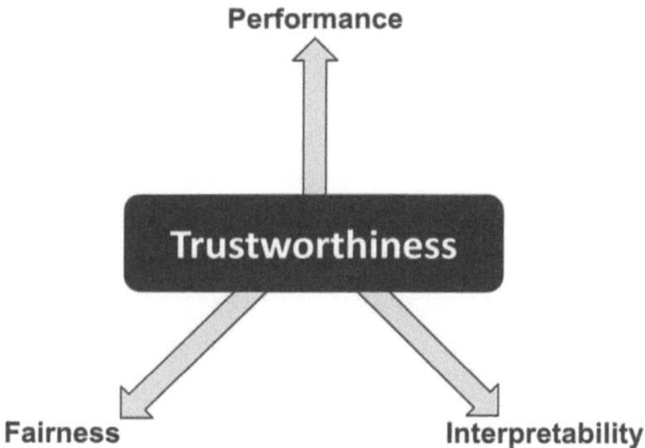

Fig. 1. Trustworthiness force diagram with three interacting forces: performance, fairness, and interpretability.

3.1   Metrics Selection

The integration of different trustworthiness components is achieved through the aggregation of various metrics, which must be selected based on their significance and utility for inclusion in the computation of the overall trustworthiness indicator. The following guidelines are provided for selecting suitable metrics for use in the software component.

As an initial approach, the selected metrics should be quantitative and ideally have a numerical domain within the range [0, 1] or be transformable through mathematical operations to align their values within this interval. This ensures that the software component can operate in a standardized manner with normalized values in [0, 1].

Regarding performance metrics, classical metrics such as accuracy, precision, recall, or F1-score meet the criteria of having a well-defined numerical domain. Therefore, the selection of a performance metric can be based on the specific performance focus required by the application domain or the perspective adopted by the researcher. For instance, in medical applications where minimizing false negatives is critical, recall should be prioritized [23], as it reduces the risk of diagnosing a person as healthy when they actually have a condition. Conversely, in applications such as spam email identification, minimizing false positives leads to avoid filtering out important emails. In such cases, maximizing precision is the preferred approach [23]. Hence, the choice of performance metrics depends on the specific problem that the machine learning model aims to solve or the researcher's preferences.

For fairness metrics, although numerous fairness definitions and associated metrics exist, the proposed framework recommends using metrics derived from confusion matrices for both the protected and unprotected groups. These include statistical parity [10], predictive parity [7], predictive equality [8], equal opportunity [14], equalized odds [12], overall accuracy equality [5], and treatment equality [5], among others [25]. Since these fairness metrics are computed as differences between two probabilities, their values typically lie within the [0, 1] range, making them highly suitable for integration with performance and interpretability metrics.

Regarding interpretability, it is advisable to consider metrics that evaluate different aspects of the quality of explanations generated by a machine learning model. In this context, feature attribution-based metrics such as monotonicity, non-sensitivity, and effective complexity [19] can be utilized. These metrics focus on aspects such as soundness, clarity, and parsimony, respectively.

3.2 Software Components

The implementation of the proposed framework is structured into multiple software components, each responsible for evaluating different aspects of trustworthiness in machine learning models. For simplicity, these components are organized into distinct classes, each of which provides specialized methods for computing trustworthiness metrics, some performance, fairness and interpretability metrics has been included as examples. As shown in Fig. 2, the proposed design follows a modular approach ensuring that each software component can be independently evaluated and extended. The following subsections provide a detailed description of each class and its principal functions, highlighting their role in the overall framework.

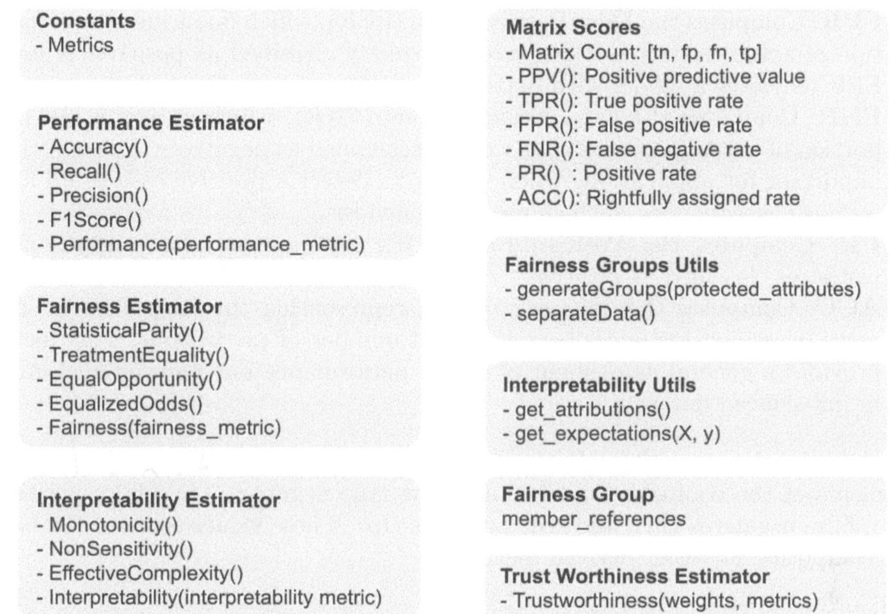

Fig. 2. Proposed framework classes.

Constants. The Constants class defines a set of predefined metrics that serve as a standard reference across different estimators. These metrics are essential for evaluating multiple aspects of trustworthiness, including performance, fairness, and interpretability. By centralizing metric definitions within this class, the framework ensures consistency across computations and facilitates the reuse of well-established measurement criteria.

Matrix Scores. The MatrixScores class provides a foundational set of functions for computing values derived from the confusion matrix. The confusion matrix is a fundamental statistical tool in machine learning evaluation, as it summarizes the classification performance by presenting counts of true positives, true negatives, false positives, and false negatives. The class includes the following core functions:

- **PPV**: Computes the Positive Predictive Value (PPV), also known as precision. This metric quantifies the proportion of true positive predictions out of all positive predictions made by the model, providing insight into the reliability of positive classifications.
- **TPR**: Computes the True Positive Rate (TPR), commonly referred to as recall or sensitivity. This metric measures the proportion of actual positives correctly identified by the model, which is particularly important in applications where missing positive cases is costly.

- **FPR**: Computes the False Positive Rate (FPR), which quantifies the proportion of actual negatives that were incorrectly classified as positive. A lower FPR indicates a model with better specificity.
- **FNR**: Computes the False Negative Rate (FNR), which measures the proportion of actual positives that were misclassified as negatives. This metric is important for applications where failing to detect a positive case could have serious consequences, such as medical diagnosis.
- **PR**: Computes the Positive Rate (PR), representing the proportion of instances classified as positive.
- **ACC**: Computes the accuracy metric, representing the proportion of correctly classified instances over the total number of predictions. This metric provides a general assessment of model performance but may be misleading in imbalanced datasets.

Additionally, the MatrixScores class maintains a count of the fundamental elements of the confusion matrix, including true negatives (tn), false positives (fp), false negatives (fn), and true positives (tp). These values serve as the basis for computing all other derived metrics.

Performance Estimator. The PerformanceEstimator class focuses on evaluating the model's predictive performance through various widely used metrics. The class includes the following functions:

- **Accuracy**: Computes the overall accuracy of the model, which is the ratio of correctly classified instances to the total number of predictions. While accuracy is useful in balanced datasets, it may not be sufficient for imbalanced classification problems, and other metric can be selected.
- **Recall**: Measures the proportion of actual positive instances that were correctly classified by the model. This metric is especially important in scenarios where missing a positive case (e.g., a disease diagnosis) is more costly than predicting a false positive.
- **Precision**: Computes the proportion of positive predictions that were actually correct. This metric is important when false positives need to be minimized, such as in fraud detection systems.
- **F1-Score**: Computes the F1-score, which is the harmonic mean of precision and recall. This metric provides a balanced assessment of model performance, particularly in cases where precision and recall must be jointly optimized.
- **Performance(performance_metric)**: Allows for the computation of a user-specified performance metric, providing flexibility in the evaluation process.

Fairness Estimator. The FairnessEstimator class is responsible for assessing fairness-related aspects of the model's predictions. Fairness evaluation is essential to ensure that machine learning models do not produce biased outcomes across different demographic groups. The class provides the following fairness metrics:

- **StatisticalParity**: Computes statistical parity, which measures whether different demographic groups receive similar positive prediction rates. This metric ensures that no group is disproportionately favored or disadvantaged by the model's decisions.
- **TreatmentEquality**: Evaluates treatment equality, which examines whether the ratio of false positives and false negatives is consistent across groups. A disparity in treatment equality may indicate bias in the decision-making process.
- **EqualOpportunity**: Computes equal opportunity fairness, which assesses whether the true positive rate is equal across different demographic groups. This metric is particularly relevant in scenarios where ensuring fair access to positive outcomes is required.
- **EqualizedOdds**: Measures equalized odds, which ensures that both false positive and true positive rates are balanced across groups. This is one of the most stringent fairness criteria.
- **Fairness(fairness_metric)**: Computes a generalized fairness metric based on the selected criterion, allowing for flexible fairness assessments.

Fairness Group and Fairness Groups Utils. The FairnessGroup class defines the structure of fairness groups, which categorize individuals based on demographic attributes relevant to fairness analysis. It should includes references to the members into the original dataset, which allow to perform group-based computations in other classes.

The **FairnessGroupsUtils** class should provide utility functions for managing fairness groups, including:

- **generateGroups(g)**: Generates fairness groups based on a specified attribute g, enabling systematic group-based fairness evaluation.
- **separateData()**: Segments the dataset into different fairness-related groups for independent assessment.

Interpretability Estimator and Interpretability Utils. The InterpretabilityEstimator class focuses on assessing the interpretability of machine learning models. Interpretability metrics allows to determine that model predictions are understandable and explainable. The class provides the following functions:

- **Monotonicity**: Evaluates whether the model's predictions follow a consistent pattern with respect to input features.
- **NonSensitivity**: Measures how sensitive the model's explanations are to small perturbations into the input features.
- **EffectiveComplexity**: Assesses the complexity of the model's decision-making process.
- **Interpretability(interpretability_metric)**: Computes a generalized interpretability metric based on the selected criterion.

The **InterpretabilityUtils** class provides functions for extracting and visualizing explanations, including:

- **get_attributions()**: Obtains feature attributions using a determined technique (e.g., permutation-based variable importance method).
- **get_expectations(X, y)**: Retrieves model expectations given input features and targets, defined in some studies [19]. These expectations are then used to compute interpretability metrics.

Trustworthiness Estimator. The TrustworthinessEstimator class aggregates performance, fairness, and interpretability metrics to compute an overall trustworthiness score using the Trustworthiness(weights, metrics) function. The objective of this function is to merge performance, fairness and interpretability metrics into the trustworthiness score, to provide a comprehensive assessment of the trustworthiness of a model for AI-driven decision-making processes. In addition to these metrics, this function also receives a set of weights (with one weight for every metric), allowing to distribute the importance of a metric and a certain trustworthines dimension into the computation of the overall trustworthiness metric.

4   Conclusions and Future Work

This paper has presented the conceptual design of a framework aimed at estimating the trustworthiness of machine learning (ML) models by integrating multiple evaluation metrics from different dimensions of trustworthiness. The proposed design provides a structured methodology to quantitatively assess key aspects such as performance, fairness, and interpretability, offering a holistic perspective on the reliability of ML predictions. By defining a modular architecture composed of distinct software components, including estimators for each trustworthiness dimension and a centralized trustworthiness estimator, this work lays the foundation for a systematic approach to trustworthiness evaluation.

One of the key contributions of this framework design is its ability to provide a quantitative and comparable trustworthiness score, making it possible to contrast different ML models based on a unified trustworthiness assessment. The approach outlined in this paper allows researchers and practitioners to incorporate multiple metrics and assign customizable weights to reflect domain-specific requirements. This flexibility ensures that the framework can be adapted to a wide range of application scenarios, from healthcare to finance and beyond, where trustworthiness is a critical concern.

Despite these contributions, it is important to acknowledge that this paper presents a framework design rather than an implemented system. As such, several challenges remain before this design can be translated into a fully operational tool. One key challenge is the implementation and empirical validation of the framework to ensure that the aggregation methodology effectively captures meaningful trustworthiness insights. Future work should focus on developing a prototype implementation and conducting empirical evaluations on real-world ML models to refine the trustworthiness estimation approach.

In conclusion, this paper has outlined a comprehensive design for a trustworthiness estimation framework that has the potential to significantly improve the evaluation and comparability of ML models. While the framework remains at the conceptual stage, its structured approach, modular architecture, and flexible metric aggregation provide a strong foundation for future development. Moving forward, implementing, validating, and expanding this design will be key steps in advancing the field of trustworthy AI and enabling more reliable and interpretable machine learning systems.

Acknowledgments. This study was partially founded by the Chilean Fondecyt 1221938 Project. Also, J. Ugalde was partially funded by the Escuela de Ingeniería Informática, Universidad de Valparaíso, Chile, through grant No. 101.016/2020.

Disclosure of Interests. The authors have no competing interests to declare that are relevant to the content of this article.

References

1. Abadi, M., et al.: TensorFlow: large-scale machine learning on heterogeneous systems. https://www.tensorflow.org/ (2015). Software available from tensorflow.org
2. Arya, V., et al.: AI explainability 360 toolkit. In: Proceedings of the 3rd ACM India Joint International Conference on Data Science & Management of Data (8th ACM IKDD CODS & 26th COMAD), pp. 376–379 (2021)
3. Bell, G., Brandimarte, P.: AI and the law: navigating responsibility and trust in automated decision-making. AI Soc. (2022). https://doi.org/10.1007/s00146-022-01462-6
4. Bellamy, R.K., et al.: AI fairness 360: an extensible toolkit for detecting and mitigating algorithmic bias. IBM J. Res. Dev. **63**(4), 4:1–4:15 (2019). https://doi.org/10.1147/JRD.2019.2942287
5. Berk, R., Heidari, H., Jabbari, S., Kearns, M., Roth, A.: Fairness in criminal justice risk assessments: the state of the art. Sociol. Methods Res. **50**(1), 3–44 (2021)
6. Bussmann, N., Giudici, P., Marinelli, D., Papenbrock, J.: Explainable AI in fintech: a taxonomy of existing methods, challenges and future directions. J. Risk Financ. Manag. **14**(6), 272 (2021). https://doi.org/10.3390/jrfm14060272
7. Chouldechova, A.: Fair prediction with disparate impact: a study of bias in recidivism prediction instruments. Big Data **5**(2), 153–163 (2017)
8. Corbett-Davies, S., Pierson, E., Feller, A., Goel, S., Huq, A.: Algorithmic decision making and the cost of fairness. In: Proceedings of the 23rd ACM SIGKDD International Conference on Knowledge Discovery and Data Mining, pp. 797–806 (2017)
9. D'Amour, A., Srinivasan, H., Atwood, J., Baljekar, P., Sculley, D., Halpern, Y.: Fairness is not static: deeper understanding of long term fairness via simulation studies. In: Proceedings of the 2020 Conference on Fairness, Accountability, and Transparency, pp. 525–534 (2020)

10. Dwork, C., Hardt, M., Pitassi, T., Reingold, O., Zemel, R.: Fairness through awareness. In: Proceedings of the 3rd Innovations in Theoretical Computer Science Conference, pp. 214–226 (2012)
11. Grigorescu, S., Trasnea, B., Cocias, T., Macesanu, G.: A survey of deep learning techniques for autonomous driving. J. Field Robot. **38**(8), 1305–1322 (2021). https://doi.org/10.1002/rob.21918
12. Hardt, M., Price, E., Srebro, N.: Equality of opportunity in supervised learning. Adv. Neural Inf. Process. Syst. **29** (2016)
13. Kim, B., et al.: Interpretability beyond feature attribution: quantitative testing with concept activation vectors (TCAV). https://arxiv.org/abs/1711.11279 (2018)
14. Kusner, M.J., Loftus, J., Russell, C., Silva, R.: Counterfactual fairness. Adv. Neural Inf. Process. Syst. **30** (2017)
15. Leslie, D.: Understanding artificial intelligence ethics and safety: a guide for the responsible design and implementation of AI systems in the public sector (2019). https://doi.org/10.5281/zenodo.3240529
16. Lundberg, S.M., Lee, S.I.: A unified approach to interpreting model predictions. Adv. Neural Inf. Process. Syst. **30** (2017). https://arxiv.org/abs/1705.07874
17. Mehrabi, N., Morstatter, F., Saxena, N., Lerman, K., Galstyan, A.: A survey on bias and fairness in machine learning. ACM Comput. Surv. (CSUR) **54**(6), 1–35 (2021)
18. Molnar, C.: Model-agnostic interpretable machine learning. Ph.D. thesis, LMU (2022)
19. Nguyen, A.P., Martínez, M.R.: On quantitative aspects of model interpretability. arXiv preprint arXiv:2007.07584 (2020)
20. Nicolae, M.I., et al.: Adversarial robustness toolbox v1. 0.0. arXiv preprint arXiv:1807.01069 (2018)
21. Pei, K., Cao, Y., Yang, J., Jana, S.: DeepXplore: automated whitebox testing of deep learning systems. In: Proceedings of the 26th Symposium on Operating Systems Principles, pp. 1–18 (2017)
22. Rajpurkar, P., et al.: Deep learning for chest radiograph diagnosis: a retrospective comparison of the CheXNeXt algorithm to practicing radiologists. PLoS Med. **15**(11), e1002686 (2018). https://doi.org/10.1371/journal.pmed.1002686
23. Raschka, S., Liu, Y.H., Mirjalili, V.: Machine Learning with PyTorch and Scikit-Learn: Develop Machine Learning and Deep Learning Models with Python. Packt Publishing Ltd (2022)
24. Ribeiro, M.T., Singh, S., Guestrin, C.: "Why should I trust you?" Explaining the predictions of any classifier. In: Proceedings of the 22nd ACM SIGKDD International Conference on Knowledge Discovery and Data Mining, pp. 1135–1144 (2016)
25. Verma, S., Rubin, J.: Fairness definitions explained. In: Proceedings of the International Workshop on Software Fairness. FairWare '18, pp. 1–7. Association for Computing Machinery, New York, NY, USA (2018). https://doi.org/10.1145/3194770.3194776
26. Weerts, H., Dudík, M., Edgar, R., Jalali, A., Lutz, R., Madaio, M.: Fairlearn: assessing and improving fairness of AI systems. J. Mach. Learn. Res. **24**(257), 1–8 (2023)
27. Wexler, J., Pushkarna, M., Bolukbasi, T., Wattenberg, M., Viégas, F., Wilson, J.: The what-if tool: interactive probing of machine learning models. IEEE Trans. Vis. Comput. Graph. **26**(1), 56–65 (2019)

A Comparison of the Coverage of Chat GPT in *China Daily* and *The New York Times* Based on Frame Theory and Content Analysis

Yang Wang[1] (iD) and Zengquan Fang[2](✉)

[1] School of Marxism, Beijing Normal University, Beijing 100875, China
[2] School of Journalism and Communication, Beijing Normal University, Beijing 100875, China
Fangzq@bnu.edu.cn

Abstract. On November 30, 2022, OpenAI released Chat GPT, a chatbot in the field of artificial intelligence. This thesis examines coverage of Chat GPT in *China Daily* and *The New York Times* between December 1, 2022, and April 30, 2023. This thesis uses frame theory and content analysis to study the differences in reporting and points out that there are significant differences between *China Daily* and *The New York Times* in reporting quantity, reporting topics, information sources, re-porting frames, and reporting attitudes. This difference is related to the national policies, cultural backgrounds, values, and media traditions of China and the United States.

Keywords: Chat GPT · *China Daily* · *The New York Times* · Comparison

1 Introduction

Artificial Intelligence (AI) has emerged as a transformative force with global implications, shaping economies, politics, culture, education, and military strategies. The field's origins trace back to the 1956 Dartmouth Conference, where visionaries like McCarthy and Minsky laid the foundation for AI as a scientific discipline (McCarthy et al. 2006). Since the early 2000s, AI has evolved at an accelerated pace, with countries such as the U.S., Japan, and China implementing national strategies to foster technological and industrial growth (Radu 2021; Executive Office of the President, National Science and Technology Council & Committee on Technology 2016).

AI development can be divided into distinct phases. In the 1970s, early research focused on knowledge processing and pattern recognition (Lu 2019). The 1990s marked significant milestones, such as IBM's Deep Blue defeating Garry Kasparov in 1997, signaling a new era for AI (Campbell 1999). By the 2010s, deep learning algorithms became widely adopted, with leading companies like Facebook, Google, and Baidu driving advancements (Cade 2013; Wang 2023). AI technologies are now embedded across sectors including smart cities, autonomous vehicles, and healthcare (Pan 2016).

However, the rapid expansion of AI raises critical ethical concerns, such as privacy violations and algorithmic bias (Zuiderveen Borgesius 2020; Hristov 2016). The media

A. Coman et al. (Eds.): HCII 2025, LNCS 16337, pp. 187–198, 2026.
https://doi.org/10.1007/978-3-032-12801-0_13

plays a pivotal role in shaping public perceptions of AI, especially in the context of emerging technologies like Chat GPT, released by OpenAI in 2022 (Baidoo-Anu & Owusu Ansah 2023). How AI is framed and discussed in the media significantly influences the public's understanding of its potential benefits and risks (Goodman & Goodman 2006; Nerlich & Halliday 2007).

Given that the U.S. and China are at the forefront of AI technological development (Saveliev & Zhurenkov 2021), this study compares the media coverage of Chat GPT in *The New York Times* and *China Daily* from December 2022 to April 2023. It focuses on the differences in framing, topics, and attitudes, aiming to highlight how the media in these two influential nations shape the public's understanding of AI.

2 Literature Review

2.1 Chat GPT

OpenAI released Chat GPT, powered by the GPT-3.5 model, in November 2022. This model utilizes generative pre-trained transformers (GPT), a natural language processing (NLP) technology designed for advanced text comprehension and generation (Pavlik 2023). Chat GPT enables continuous, human-like conversations, offering features such as language translation, text summarization, and programming assistance (Mijwil et al. 2023). It quickly became the fastest-growing consumer app, reaching 100 million users by January 2023 (Alexandra 2023).

However, several concerns have emerged, particularly regarding security risks and academic integrity, including the potential for malicious use and biased outputs (Derner & Batistic 2023; Eke 2023). Scholars like Floridi (2023) emphasize that while large language models like Chat GPT excel at processing text, they lack true cognitive abilities and understanding, limiting their potential for deeper insight.

From a journalistic perspective, the ethical implications of Chat GPT's use, including concerns about accuracy, accountability, and bias, have been widely discussed (Biswas 2023; Chan 2023). Despite these critical discussions, limited research has focused on how media outlets in different countries frame Chat GPT, especially in terms of social, ethical, and technological impacts.

2.2 China Daily

China Daily is the most widely read English-language newspaper in China and plays a key role in shaping global perceptions of China's political, economic, and cultural landscape (Thussu et al. 2017). As a mouthpiece of the Chinese Communist Party (CPC), it frequently reflects the official stance of the Chinese government on various issues, including technological developments (Chen 2012). With its vast readership across print and digital platforms, *China Daily* is frequently cited by international media, serving as a primary tool for China's foreign propaganda (Duan & Takahashi 2017).

2.3 The New York Times

The New York Times is regarded as one of the most influential and credible newspapers in the United States, with significant impact on public opinion and U.S. foreign policy (Samaie & Malmir 2017). Known for its journalistic excellence, including 132 Pulitzer Prizes, it plays a central role in shaping narratives both within the U.S. and internationally (Pulitzer Prize Winners and Finalists n.d.).

2.4 China vs. The U.S. on Artificial Intelligence

Artificial Intelligence (AI) has become a central area of competition between the U.S. and China. Historically, the U.S. has been a leader in technological innovation, but China has rapidly developed its own AI capabilities, positioning itself as a global tech power (Freeman 2006; Scharre 2019). As both countries vie for dominance, AI development has emerged as a strategic focal point that influences their political, economic, and security dynamics (Wang & Chen 2018). The media plays a significant role in shaping these national narratives, and the ideological differences between China and the U.S. heavily influence how AI technologies are reported (Ha et al. 2020).

3 Methodology

This study applies frame theory and content analysis to compare the coverage of Chat GPT by *The New York Times* and *China Daily* from December 1, 2022, to April 30, 2023.

3.1 Theoretical Foundations

Frame Theory. Frame theory, introduced by Goffman (1974), emphasizes how media shape perceptions by highlighting specific aspects of an issue. Framing involves selecting certain facts and organizing them to promote particular perspectives (Tuchman 1973; Entman 1993). Shoemaker & Reese (1996) argue that news frames are shaped by various factors such as journalistic preferences and political ideologies. In media content studies, frames are central themes that give meaning to events (Gamson & Modigliani 1987).

Content Analysis. Content analysis, a method used to systematically analyze media texts, allows researchers to quantify and interpret the content of communication (Berelson 1952). This method is widely applied to study media coverage of topics like AI (Chuan et al. 2019). Content analysis is valuable when direct data collection is not feasible and helps identify recurring themes, biases, or attitudes in media (Holsti 1969).

3.2 Research Design

Research Question. This study examines how and why *The New York Times* and *China Daily* differ in their coverage of Chat GPT between December 1, 2022, and April 30, 2023, focusing on frames, topics, and attitudes.

Data Collection. The GALE ACADEMIC ONEFILE database, accessed through the University of Melbourne Library, was used for sourcing articles. The search was limited to the period from December 1, 2022, to April 30, 2023, with the document type set to article, the publication filtered to *The New York Times*, and the keyword set as "Chat GPT". A total of 102 articles were retrieved. After filtering out irrelevant data and stories that only mentioned Chat GPT briefly, 53 valid articles were retained.

As *China Daily* is not available in academic databases, articles were retrieved directly from its official website. The search period was also set from December 1, 2022, to April 30, 2023, using an advanced search with the keywords "Chat GPT" in both the title and the article. This yielded 29 articles. After removing duplicates and excluding video content, 27 valid articles were obtained.

Category Construction. To analyze media reports, the study categorizes data into:

Report Topics: Includes Technology and Business, Politics and Policy, Risks and Regulation, Education and Culture, and Others (Chuan et al. 2019).

Sources of Information: Classified into officials, industry companies, experts, media, and individuals.

Attitudes: Articles were classified as positive, negative, or mixed based on their portrayal of Chat GPT.

Frames of Coverage: An article may contain multiple frames depending on its content. This typology draws from previous studies (Nisbet & Lewenstein 2002; Chuan et al. 2019), adapted for this study's specific context. This study categorized the reporting framework into Social Development, Risk Concern and Ethics and Regulation.

Social Development: Highlights the benefits and opportunities of Chat GPT technology.

Risk Concern and Ethics: Focuses on potential risks, ethical issues, and the human-machine relationship.

Regulation: Discusses legal and policy responses to AI, with an emphasis on government actions.

4 Analysis

4.1 Findings

Number of Reports. Between December 1, 2022, and April 30, 2023, *The New York Times* published 53 articles on Chat GPT, while *China Daily* published 27. *The New York Times* maintained consistent coverage, peaking in February and March 2023. In contrast, *China Daily* had no reports in December 2022 and January 2023, with coverage intensifying in February 2023. (See Fig. 1).

Report Topics. Both newspapers focused on technology & business and risk & regulation, but with different emphases. *China Daily* prioritized technology & business (over 60% of reports), whereas *The New York Times* concentrated on risk & regulation (over 80%). Other topics such as politics, policy, education, and culture were covered to a lesser extent (Fig. 2 and Table 1).

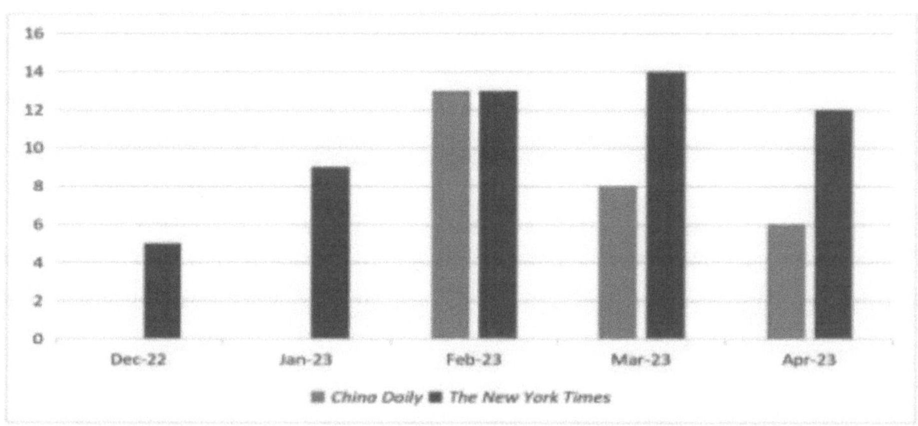

Fig. 1. Distribution of the number of reports about Chat GPT in *China Daily* and *The New York Times*.

Table 1. Number of articles on topics covered by Chat GPT in *China Daily* and *The New York Times*

Report Topics	Technology & Business	Risk & Regulation	Politics & Policy	Education & Culture	Others
Number of topics covered by *China Daily* for Chat GPT	17	8	4	4	0
Number of topics covered by *The New York Times* for Chat GPT	29	46	7	12	7

Sources of Information. The most cited sources in *The New York Times* were industry companies (80%), followed by experts & scholars (70%), while *China Daily* relied mainly on industry companies (60%) and officials (30%). *The New York Times* used a broader range of sources, including media (30%), individuals (20%), and others (20%), suggesting a more diverse perspective (Fig. 3 and Table 2).

Report Frames. Both newspapers framed Chat GPT within social development, risk concerns & ethics, and regulation, but *China Daily* emphasized social development (70%), while *The New York Times* focused on risk concerns & ethics (90%). Regulation received the least attention in both outlets (Fig. 4 and Table 3).

Report Attitudes. *China Daily* exhibited a predominantly positive attitude (63%) toward Chat GPT, aligning with China's pro-technology stance. In contrast, *The New York Times* presented a mixed stance (62%), reflecting concerns about AI risks and ethical implications (Figs. 5, 6 and Table 4).

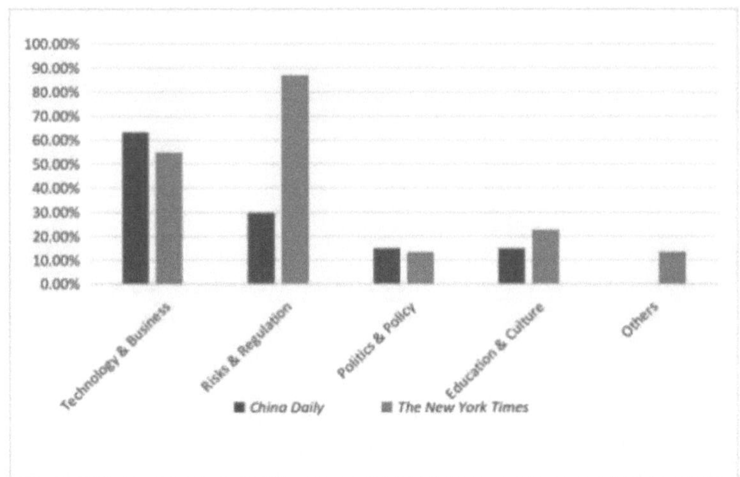

Fig. 2. Percentage Distribution of topics covered by *China Daily* and *The New York Times* on Chat GPT.

Table 2. Number of articles on information source covered by Chat GPT in *China Daily* and *The New York Times*.

Sources of information	Industry Companies	Experts & Scholars	Media	Officials	Individuals	**Others**
Number of information sources covered by *China Daily* for Chat GPT	17	7	4	8	1	4
Number of information sources covered by *The New York Times* for Chat GPT	46	37	20	12	17	15

4.2   Discussion

The surge in Chat GPT coverage coincided with its rapid adoption, surpassing 100 million users by January 2023. The New York Times began reporting on Chat GPT from its launch in November 2022, while China Daily delayed coverage due to concerns over potential misinformation.

China's AI policies, particularly the 2017 NGAI Development Plan, underscore AI's pivotal role in driving economic growth, which is reflected in *China Daily*'s emphasis on industry advancements and government perspectives. In contrast, *The New York Times*

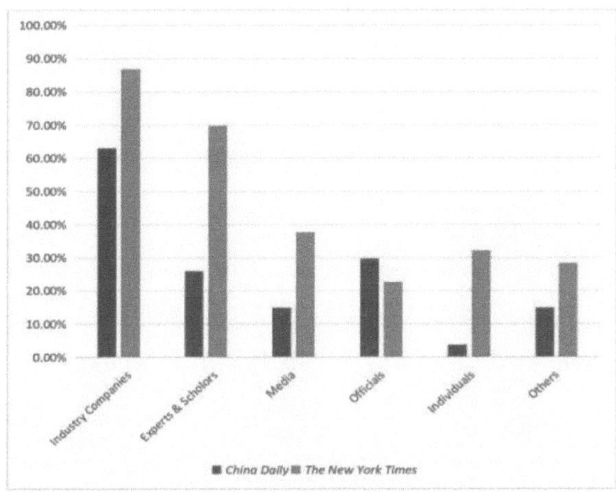

Fig. 3. Percentage Distribution of sources of information on Chat GPT in *China Daily* and *The New York Times*.

Table 3. Number of articles on frames covered by Chat GPT in *China Daily* and *The New York Times*.

Frames	Social Development	Risk Concern &Ethics	Regulation
Number of frames in *China Daily* on Chat GPT	20	9	7
Number of frames in *The New York Times* on Chat GPT	37	48	7

adopts a more critical stance, focusing on AI risks, privacy concerns, and regulatory challenges, consistent with broader U.S. government concerns about the ethical implications of AI.

These distinct reporting frameworks and attitudes underscore broader geopolitical and ideological differences. While *China Daily* frames AI as a tool for national progress, *The New York Times* presents a more cautious perspective, emphasizing potential threats and ethical concerns.

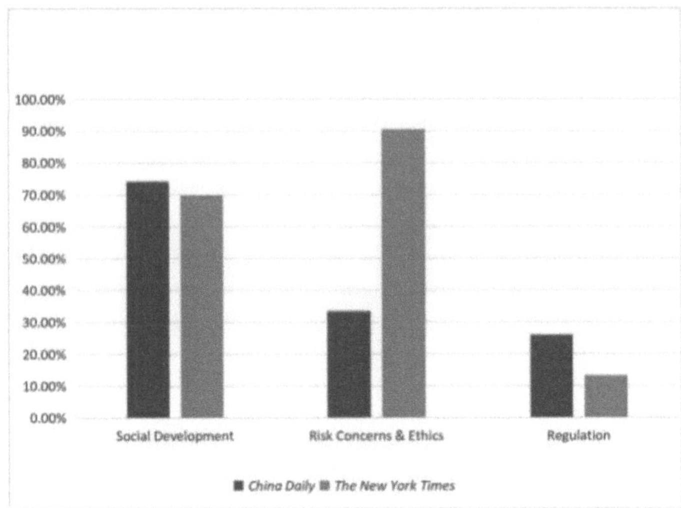

Fig. 4. Percentage Distribution of frames in *China Daily* and *The New York Times* on Chat GPT.

Table 4. Number of articles on attitude covered by Chat GPT in *China Daily* and *The New York Times*.

Attitude	Positive	Negative	Mixed
Distribution of attitude in *China Daily* on Chat GPT	17	6	4
Distribution of attitude in *The New York Times* on Chat GPT	5	15	33

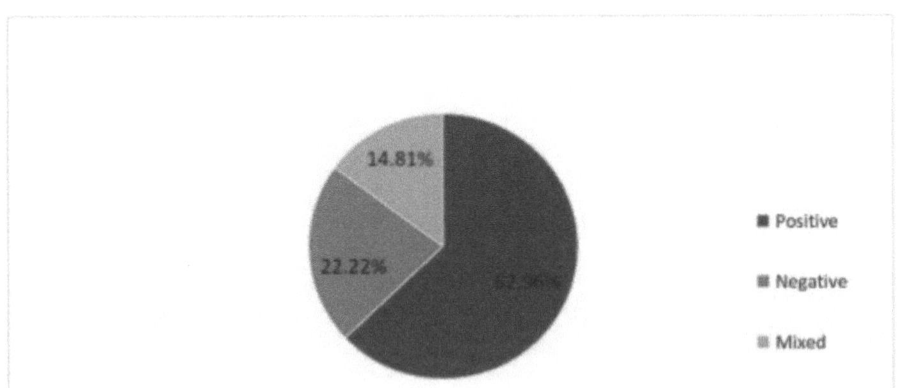

Fig. 5. Distribution of Attitudes of *China Daily* in Chat GPT.

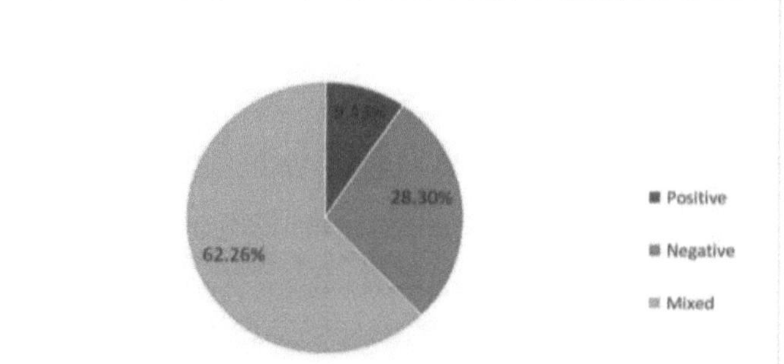

Fig. 6. Distribution of Attitudes of The *New York Times* in Chat GPT.

5   Conclusion

5.1   Summary of Findings

This study compared the coverage of Chat GPT in China Daily and The New York Times from December 1, 2022, to April 30, 2023. Initially, China Daily had no coverage of Chat GPT, but as its popularity surged, the coverage increased. Meanwhile, The New York Times consistently reported on the topic, with coverage peaking in February and March 2023.

Topics: *China Daily* predominantly focused on technology & business, while *The New York Times* emphasized risk & regulation, reflecting concerns over democratic values and the societal implications of AI (Barton et al. 2017; Roberts et al. 2021).

Sources of Information: Both newspapers relied on industry companies and experts, but *China Daily* included more official sources, consistent with China's centralized control of information (Brady 2017). In contrast, *The New York Times* integrated more individual perspectives, aligning with U.S. values of individualism (Vandello & Cohen 1999).

Frames & Attitudes: *China Daily* framed Chat GPT as a tool for social development, while *The New York Times* focused on risk & ethics. *China Daily* exhibited a predominantly positive attitude, while *The New York Times* had a mixed stance, reflecting concerns about AI's potential risks and ethical implications (Schmidt et al. 2021; Dang & Liu 2021).

5.2   Shortcomings

The study is limited by a short timeframe (6 months) and a small sample size (80 articles), which may affect the generalizability of the findings.

Manual content analysis introduces potential subjectivity, and the absence of automated tools may affect consistency.

Focusing on only two newspapers limits the ability to draw broader conclusions about the differences in mainstream media between China and the U.S..

5.3 Future Research Directions

Future research could expand AI journalism studies by analyzing other technologies such as VR, AR, and Metaverse, going beyond just Chat GPT.

Comparing coverage across a wider range of media outlets from multiple countries would provide a more comprehensive understanding of international perspectives on AI.

Investigating how media organizations construct discourse on emerging technologies can help improve public understanding and inform policy-making (Donk et al. 2012; Cui & Wu 2021).

Acknowledgments. This research was supported by the Senior Think Tank of Beijing Normal University (110590104).

Disclosure of Interests. The authors have no competing interests to declare that are relevant to the content of this article.

References

Alexandra, B.: Chat GPT statistics 2023: trends and future perspectives. Gitnux (2023). https://blog.gitnux.com/chat-gpt-statistics/

Baidoo-Anu, D., Owusu Ansah, L.: Education in the Era of Generative Artificial Intelligence (AI): Understanding the Potential Benefits of Chat GPT in Promoting Teaching and Learning. J. AI **7**(1), 52–62 (2023). https://dergipark.org.tr/en/pub/jai/issue/77844/1337500

Barton, D., Woetzel, J., Seong, J., Tian, Q.: Artificial intelligence: implications for China (2017). http://dln.jaipuria.ac.in:8080/jspui/bitstream/123456789/1888/1/MGI-Artificial-intelligence-implications-for-China.pdf

Biswas, S.: Role of chat GPT in journalism: according to chat GPT. J. Alsalam Univ. **6**(1), 39–41 (2023)

Brady, A.M.: Plus, ça change? Media control under Xi Jinping. Problems Post-Communism **64**(3–4), 128–140 (2017). https://doi.org/10.1080/10758216.2016.1197779

Cade, M.: Facebook Taps 'Deep Learning' Giant for New AI Lab. WIRED (2013). https://www.wired.com/2013/12/facebook-yann-lecun/

Campbell, M.: Knowledge discovery in Deep Blue. Commun. ACM **42**(11), 65–67 (1999). https://dl.acm.org/doi/pdf/10.1145/319382.319396

Chan, A.: GPT-3 and InstructGPT: technological dystopianism, utopianism, and "Contextual" perspectives in AI ethics and industry. AI Ethics **3**(1), 53–64 (2023). https://doi.org/10.1007/s43681-022-00148-6

Chen, L.: Reporting news in China: evaluation as an indicator of change in the *China Daily*. China Inform. **26**(3), 303–329 (2012). https://doi.org/10.1177/0920203X12456338

Chuan, C.H., Tsai, W.H.S., Cho, S.Y.: Framing artificial intelligence in American newspapers. In: Proceedings of the 2019 AAAI/ACM Conference on AI, Ethics, and Society, pp. 339–344 (2019). https://doi.org/10.1145/3306618.3314285

Cui, D., Wu, F.: The influence of media use on public perceptions of artificial intelligence in China: evidence from an online survey. Inf. Dev. **37**(1), 45–57 (2021). https://doi.org/10.1177/02666669198934

Dang, J., Liu, L.: Robots are friends as well as foes: ambivalent attitudes toward mindful and mindless AI robots in the United States and China. Comput. Hum. Behav. **115**, 106612 (2021). https://doi.org/10.1016/j.chb.2020.106612

Donk, A., Metag, J., Kohring, M., Marcinkowski, F.: Framing emerging technologies: risk perceptions of nanotechnology in the German press. Sci. Commun. **34**(1), 5–29 (2012). https://doi.org/10.1177/107554701141789

Derner, E., Batistič, K.: Beyond the safeguards: Exploring the security risks of Chat GPT (2023). arXiv preprint arXiv:2305.08005. https://doi.org/10.48550/arXiv.2305.08005

Duan, R., Takahashi, B.: The two-way flow of news: a comparative study of American and Chinese newspaper coverage of Beijing's air pollution. Int. Commun. Gaz. **79**(1), 83–107 (2017). https://doi.org/10.1177/174804851665630

Eke, D.O.: Chat GPT and the rise of generative AI: threat to academic integrity? J. Respon. Technol. **13**, 100060 (2023). https://doi.org/10.1016/j.jrt.2023.100060

Entman, R.M.: Framing: Toward clarification of a fractured paradigm. J. Commun. **43**(4), 51–58 (1993)

Executive Office of the President, National Science and Technology Council & Committee on Technology. (2016). Preparing for the future of artificial intelligence. https://obamawhiteho use.archives.gov/sites/default/files/whitehouse_files/microsites/ostp/NSTC/preparing_for_ the_future_of_ai.pdf

Freeman, R.B.: Does globalization of the scientific/engineering workforce threaten US economic leadership? Innov. Policy Econ. **6**, 123–157 (2006). https://doi.org/10.1086/ipe.6.25056182

Goodman, J.R., Goodman, B.P.: Beneficial or biohazard? How the media frame biosolids? Public Underst. Sci. **15**(3), 359–375 (2006). https://doi.org/10.1177/0963662506062468

Ha, L., et al.: How US and Chinese media cover the US–China trade conflict: a case study of war and peace journalism practice and the foreign policy equilibrium hypothesis. Negot. Confl. Manage. Res. (2020). https://doi.org/10.1111/ncmr.12186

Holsti, O.R.: Content analysis for the social sciences and humanities. Addison-Wesley, Reading, MA (1969)

Hristov, K.: Artificial intelligence and the copyright dilemma. Idea **57**, 431 (2016)

Lu, Y.: Artificial intelligence: a survey on evolution, models, applications, and future trends. J. Manage. Anal. **6**(1), 1–29 (2019). https://doi.org/10.1080/23270012.2019.1570365

McCarthy, J., Minsky, M.L., Rochester, N., Shannon, C.E.: A proposal for the Dartmouth summer research project on artificial intelligence, August 31, 1955. AI Mag. **27**(4), 12 (2006). https://doi.org/10.1609/aimag.v27i4.1904

Nerlich, B., Halliday, C.: Avian flu: the creation of expectations in the interplay between science and the media. Sociol. Health Illn. **29**(1), 46–65 (2007). https://doi.org/10.1111/j.1467-9566. 2007.00517.x

Nisbet, M.C., Lewenstein, B.V.: Biotechnology and the American media: the policy process and the elite press, 1970 to 1999. Sci. Commun. **23**(4), 359–391 (2002). https://doi.org/10.1177/ 107554700202300401

Pan, Y. (2016). Heading toward artificial intelligence 2.0. *Engineering*, 2(4), 409–413. https://doi. org/10.1016/J.ENG.2016.04.018

Pavlik, J.V.: Collaborating with Chat GPT: considering the implications of generative artificial intelligence for journalism and media education. J. Mass Commun. Educ. **78**(1), 84–93 (2023). https://doi.org/10.1177/10776958221149577

Pulitzer Prize Winners and Finalists. (n.d.). https://www.nytco.com/award-collection/2019-pul itzer-prize-winners/

Radu, R.: Steering the governance of artificial intelligence: national strategies in perspective. Policy Soc. **40**(2), 178–193 (2021). https://doi.org/10.1080/14494035.2021.1929728

Roberts, H., et al.: Achieving a 'Good AI Society': comparing the aims and progress of the EU and the US. Sci. Eng. Ethics **27**, 1–25 (2021). https://doi.org/10.1007/s11948-021-00340-7

Samaie, M., Malmir, B.: US news media portrayal of Islam and Muslims: a corpus-assisted Critical Discourse Analysis. Educ. Philos. Theory **49**(14), 1351–1366 (2017). https://doi.org/10.1080/ 00131857.2017.1281789

Saveliev, A., Zhurenkov, D.: Artificial intelligence and social responsibility: the case of the artificial intelligence strategies in the United States, Russia, and China. Kybernetes **50**(3), 656–675 (2021). https://doi.org/10.1108/K-01-2020-0060

Scharre, P.: Killer apps: the real dangers of an AI arms race. Foreign Aff. **98**, 135 (2019)

Schmidt, E., et al.: The final report. The National Security Commission on Artificial Intelligence. https://reports.nscai.gov/final-report/table-of-contents/

hussu, D.K., De Burgh, H., Shi, A. (eds.). China's media go global. Routledge (2017)

Tuchman, G.: Making news by doing work: routinizing the unexpected. Am. J. Sociol. **79**(1), 110–131 (1973). https://doi.org/10.1086/225510

Vandello, J.A., Cohen, D.: Patterns of individualism and collectivism across the United States. J. Pers. Soc. Psychol. **77**(2), 279–292 (1999). https://doi.org/10.1037/0022-3514.77.2.279

Wang, Y., Chen, D.: Rising Sino-US competition in artificial intelligence. China Quar. Int. Strat. Stud. **4**(02), 241–258 (2018). https://doi.org/10.1142/S2377740018500148

Wang, Y.: Synergy in silicon: the evolution and potential of academia-industry collaboration in AI and software engineering. TechRxiv Preprint (2023). https://doi.org/10.36227/techrxiv.239 61540.v1

Zuiderveen Borgesius, F.J.: Strengthening legal protection against discrimination by algorithms and artificial intelligence. Int. J. Hum. Rights **24**(10), 1572–1593 (2020).https://doi.org/10. 1080/13642987.2020.174397

Understanding User Behavior in Social Computing

Representating Negative State of a Robot's Abdominal/Thoracic Breathing Accompanied Movement System

Ryousuke Fujii[1], Yuto Nishiguchi[1], Kuya Moriyama[1], and Tomoko Yonezawa[1,2,3(✉)]

[1] Kansai University, 2-1-1, Ryozenji-Cho, Takatsuki, Osaka 569-1095, Japan
{k543861,yone}@kansai-u.ac.jp
[2] ATR Interaction Science Laboratories, 2-2-2, Hikaridai, Soraku-gun, Kyoto 619-0288, Japan
[3] Keio University, 5322, Endo, Fujisawa, Kanagawa 252-0882, Japan

Abstract. This paper presents an upper-body robot system that expresses involuntary abdominal and thoracic (chest) breathing. The system employs servomotors to generate breathing-related movements in both the shoulder and abdominal regions in response to the robot's breathing parameters. By adjusting the speed, stability, and range of motion of each servomotor, the system aims to enhance nonverbal communication by expressing emotional and physical states such as excitement, anxiety, panic, fatigue, and debility. Experimental results suggest that combining multiple elements of breathing expression can improve the robot's ability to evoke empathetic responses through emotionally expressive physical behavior.

Keywords: Interaction · Usage state · Robot crisis · Robot ethics · Psychophysiological internal model · Involuntary expressions

1 Introduction

In today's aging society, robots are increasingly being used in the medical and nursing care fields to address labor shortages caused by the declining birthrate and aging population. In particular, robots with empathic communication functions are playing a significant role in collaborating with humans to provide services.

Weak robots are characterized by their limited capabilities and are designed to naturally engage users by evoking a sense of "wanting to help" [1]. Therefore, weak robots are considered to have a healing effect and to promote conversation, which can also help prevent dementia in the elderly [2–4].

However, strong and complex emotional expressions have received little attention so far due to the dominance of juvenile and weak expressions. As a result, challenges remain in developing deeper relationships that incorporate negative emotions.

A. Coman et al. (Eds.): HCII 2025, LNCS 16337, pp. 201–215, 2026.
https://doi.org/10.1007/978-3-032-12801-0_14

In addition, actual human emotional behavior is always a complex interplay of emotions such as joy and sadness, among which minute changes occur [5–7]. The ability of a robot to express such complex emotional changes in its internal state will enable richer emotional communication in its interaction with the user, and the robot will play a role as a provider of emotional support, changing the relationship with the user to a richer one.

To naturally influence and shape user behavior, conveying emotions through nonverbal expressions is effective [8]. Additionally, dynamic modeling of a robot's internal emotional transitions has the potential to enable more intuitive and effective human-robot interactions.

In this study, we focused on "breathing" as a form of physical emotional expression and adopted the transmission of emotional states solely through breathing as a core design principle. While conventional modalities such as facial expressions, voice, gestures, and changes in skin color convey rich emotional information, they may also lead to overinterpretation by users. To naturally elicit unconscious empathy and spontaneous intervention from humans, we intentionally limited the expressive modality to breathing alone.

Breathing is a nonverbal and autonomic behavior that inherently reflects internal emotional states without being overtly assertive. This subtlety allows for the formation of human-robot relationships that leave interpretive space for the observer. By restricting the robot's emotional expression to only breathing— excluding facial expressions, vocal tones, or gestures—we aimed to investigate how minimal cues can evoke emotional interpretation and empathy from users.

This approach has significant implications for the design of weak interfaces, which operate on limited informational output yet still foster intervention behaviors in humans. By exploring how such understated expressions can generate affective engagement, we contribute to the understanding of minimalistic yet effective emotional communication in human-robot interaction.

In line with this goal, we developed an upper-body robot system that varies its breathing patterns—specifically in terms of instability, depth, region (thoracic and abdominal), and rate—with the aim of constructing an internal transition model.

2   Related Studies

2.1   Involuntary Expressions of Robots

The study of involuntary representations plays an important role in facilitating smoother communication with humans [9].

Several studies suggest that such representations can improve message clarity and enhance familiarity with agents. It has been demonstrated that the intensity of physiological needs can be expressed through both the agent's behavior and heartbeat expressions, using an internal representation model that combines voluntary behaviors—such as eye movement, gaze, and approaching an object— with involuntary physiological expressions such as pulsation [10].

Moreover, it has been shown that when an agent first meets a user and exhibits breathing and breath-like expressions while speaking in close proximity, it increases discomfort and gives a negative impression of intimacy [11].

These previous studies are based on the assumption that the robot is located near the user. In contrast, the present study aims to enable communication based on spatial distance by implementing physiological expressions that can be perceived and interpreted by users even from a distance.

2.2   Interaction by Breathing

Using a stuffed robot system capable of representing breathing, heart rate, body temperature, and body movement, we demonstrated that the rate of abdominal movement is interpreted as an indicator of the robot's arousal level [12].

We also found that users' heart rate and respiratory rate were significantly lower when petting a breathing robot compared to a non-breathing one [13].

However, these previous studies did not clarify the effects of the specific region about robot's breathing.

In this study, we utilize respiratory expressions in the shoulder and thoracic regions to explore not only the perceived level of arousal but also internal emotional states such as anxiety. Furthermore, we examine how the location of these respiratory movements influences users' impressions.

3   Proposed System

This research aims to enhance user empathy by simulating the robot's breathing motion. We developed an upper-body robot that exhibits involuntary breathing expressions based on a combination of breathing parameters (Fig. 2).

The system comprises two sections: (1) an internal emotion control module, which determines the robot's breathing parameters, and (2) a body expression module, which controls servo motors in the abdominal and thoracic region to generate breathing movements. The robot's body is constructed from a 2-L drinking water bottle, with servo motors controlled by an Arduino. Abdominal breathing is simulated using a soft substrate and a servo motor placket. To enhance its human-like appearance, the robot is covered with quilt batting and dressed in infant clothing. The breathing motions are governed by the robot's internal state representation system.

The internal emotion control system regulates the robot's breathing state using four parameters: instability (randomness of movement), depth (motor movement magnitude), region (breathing area), and rate (motor movement speed). Each parameter is assigned a binary value (0 or 1), leading to 16 possible combinations. Instability randomly increases during the breathing motion, with the servomotor moving from the maximum angle back to $0°$.

The body expression module executes breathing movements using servo motors located in the abdominal and shoulder (thoracic) regions. In this system, abdominal movement is defined as abdominal breathing, while shoulder movement is defined as thoracic (chest) breathing.

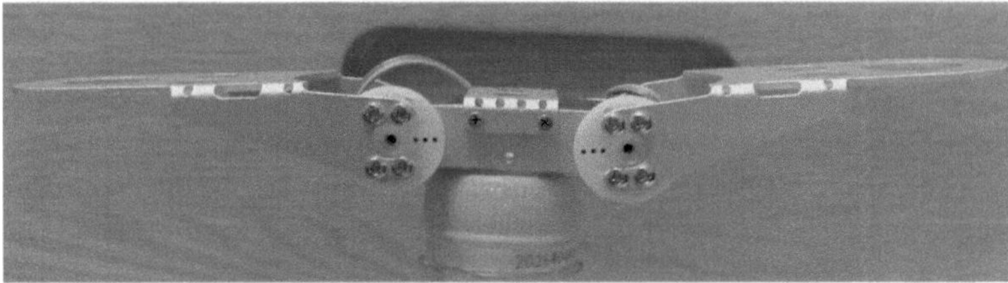

(a) Normal (without shoulder motion)

(b) During thoracic breathing (with shoulder motion)

Fig. 1. Shoulder motion of breathing expression robot

Inhalation occurs when the servo motors move to positions determined by the breathing parameters, while exhalation returns them to their initial state. This integrated system enables the robot to express its emotional state through breathing patterns.

Figures 1 and 3 show the exhalations of shallow and deep breathing in the shoulder and abdomen, respectively (Table 1).

Table 1. Breathing characteristics classification

Factor	Classification	Description
Factor A:	A1: Weak	Instability 30%
Breathing Instability (BI)	A2: Strong	Instability 50%
Factor B:	B1: Shallow	Thoracic: 60°–80° Abdomen: 100°–140°
Breathing Depth (BD)	B2: Deep	Thoracic: 60°–100° Abdomen: 100°–170°
Factor C:	C1: Thoracic	Mainly thoracic moves
Breathing Region (BR)	C2: Abdomen	Mainly abdomen moves
Factor D:	D1: Slow	13 breaths/min
Breathing Rate (RR)	D2: Fast	27 breaths/min

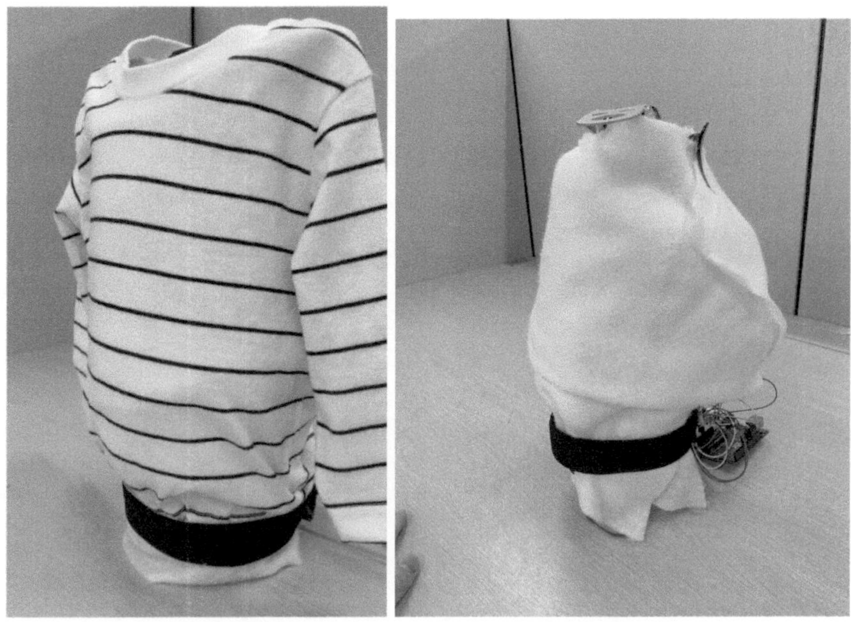

(a) Robot Appearance (Dressed)   (b) Robot Body

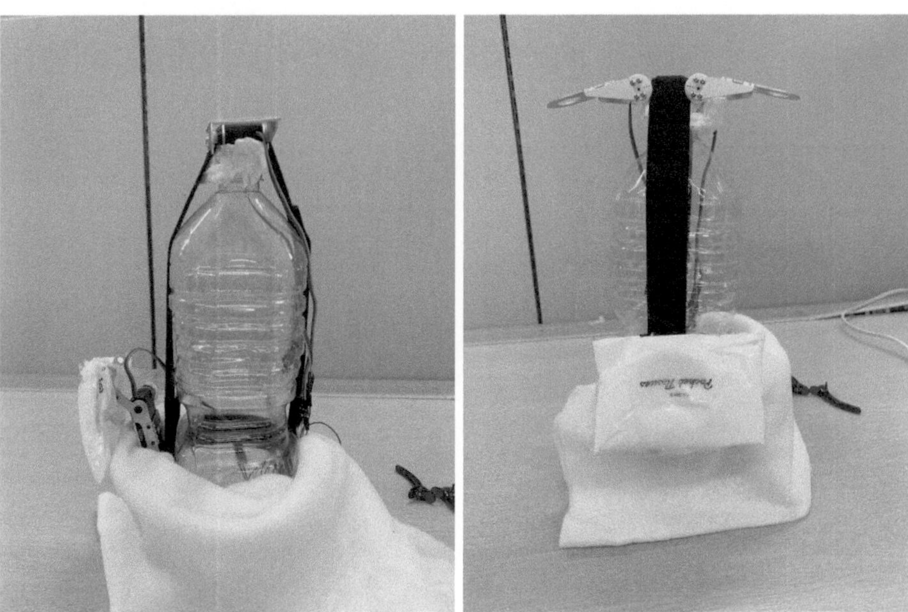

(c) An upper-body Robot (Abdomen)   (d) Abdomen Wrapped with Celtic Core

Fig. 2. Breathing expression robot

(a) Normal (without abdominal motion)

(b) During belly breathing (with belly movement)

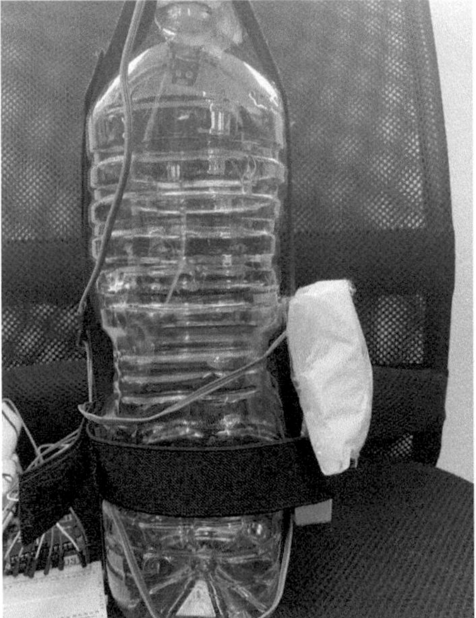

(c) Normal (no abdominal movement) during experiment

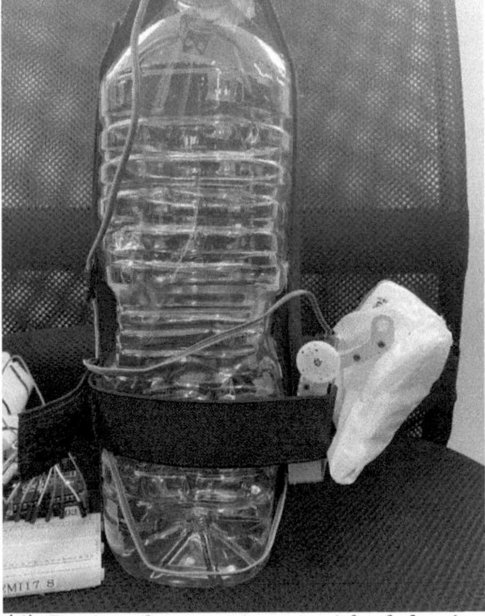

(d) During the experiment with abdominal breathing (with abdominal motion)

Fig. 3. Abdominal servo motor movement

4   Experiment

4.1   Purpose

Using the proposed robotic system, we will examine how it relates to the impressions of "excitement," "anxiety," "panic," "fatigue," and "debility".

4.2   Hypotheses

H1: Faster breathing enhances the impression of excitement.

– Previous studies have shown that respiratory rate increases with sympathetic nervous system activation [14], and such physiological changes contribute to emotional impressions of tension and activity perceived by others [15].

H2: Deeper breathing amplifies all emotional states.

– There are reports that the amplitude of breathing affects the perceived intensity of emotional states, thus deep and pronounced breathing may be interpreted as an exaggeration of emotional expression [16].

H3: Thoracic breathing strengthens impressions of fatigue and debility.

– Thoracic breathing is commonly observed in states of anxiety, tension, and fatigue. It is considered inefficient and stress-inducing in clinical psychology and somatic therapy [17].

H4: Greater breathing instability increases perceptions of anxiety and panic.

– Irregular breathing patterns and rhythmic disruptions are characteristic of clinical conditions such as panic disorder, and can evoke emotional agitation and a sense of crisis in observers [18].

4.3   Methodology

Fifteen participants (9 males and 6 females, mean age 25.3 years) watched a 15-second robotic video clip of breathing states. Using the Visual Analog Scale (VAS, 0–99), the degree to which a total of 16 breathing patterns conveyed five emotional states was assessed. As an evaluation method, participants were asked to respond to a questionnaire covering the following items.

Q1: The robot appeared to be experiencing excitement.
Q2: The robot seemed to be showing signs of anxiety.
Q3: The robot appeared to be in a state of panic.
Q4: The robot looked as if they were suffering from fatigue.
Q5: The robot appeared to be in a condition of debility.

An analysis of variance (ANOVA) was performed on the obtained assessment data to examine the main effect of emotional state on breathing patterns and whether there was an interaction between them.

4.4 Results

An analysis of variance was performed on the results of each subjective evaluation at a significance level of $\alpha = 0.05$. Tables 2, 3, 4, and Fig. 4 show the results of the variance analysis for the experiment.

First, in Q1 (Excitement assessment items), significant differences in the main effects appeared for factors B(BD), C(BR), and D(RR) (B2(Deep) > B1(Shallow), C1(Thoracic) > C2(Abdomen), D2(Fast) > D1(Slow)). This result indicates that deep, thoracic, and fast breathing respectively represent the state of excitement.

Next, for Q2 (Anxiety assessment items), the main effects of B, C, and D were significant, as was the interaction between CDs (Fig. 5). In other words, thoracic respiration is still strongly associated with anxiety, while abdominal respiration is associated with anxiety when the speed is fast. These results indicate that thoracic (chest) breathing can strongly express anxiety, and that speed can also express anxiety even if it is not thoracic breathing.

In Q3 (Panic assessment items), the main effects of all factors—A(BI), B, C, and D—were significant, and the interaction between A and C showed a significant difference. Specifically, significant differences were found in the AC interaction when C1 > C2 at A1(Weak), C1 > C2 at A2(Strong), and A2 > A1 at C1 (Fig. 6). In other words, thoracic-movement breathing tends to make subjects feel panic, especially when their breathing is unstable.

In Q4 (Fatigue assessment items), significant interactions were observed for BC, ABD, and ABCD, in addition to significant main effects for factors A and C. Notably, significant differences in the BC interaction occurred when C1 > C2 at B1, C1 > C2 at B2, and B2 > B1 at C2 (Fig. 7). This suggests that thoracic breathing may be associated with perceptions of poor physical condition, while deep abdominal breathing may also reflect such a state. A significant difference in the ABD interaction was observed when D2 > D1 at A2B2. This implies that deep or shallow breathing with high instability can make subjects feel unwell, whereas deep abdominal breathing may serve to express such unwellness.

In Q5 (Debility assessment items), the main effects of factors A, C, and D were significant. The findings—A2 > A1, C1 > C2, and D2 > D1—indicate that unstable, thoracic, and fast breathing, respectively, are perceived as signs of a life-threatening condition.

Regarding hypothesis testing, the results of Q1 indicated that deep, thoracic, and fast breathing each represented excited states, supporting Hypotheses 1 and 2. Q2 showed that thoracic and fast abdominal breathing conveyed anxiety, supporting Hypothesis 4. Q3 revealed that unstable thoracic breathing evoked perceptions of panic, further supporting Hypothesis 4. In Q4, no significant interaction was observed regarding breathing depth, partially rejecting Hypothesis 2. However, the results also suggested that thoracic and deep abdominal breathing indicated a sense of being unwell, supporting Hypothesis 3. Finally, Q5 indicated that unstable, thoracic, and rapid breathing were associated with life-threatening conditions, supporting Hypothesis 3. In summary, while Hypothesis 2 was partially rejected, the remaining hypotheses were supported.

Table 2. ANOVA results

	A		B		C		D	
	F	p	F	p	F	p	F	p
Q1: excitement	0.057	0.815	17.056	0.001*	123.352	<0.001*	17.917	<0.001*
Q2: anxiety	0.752	0.4	5.533	0.034*	24.024	<0.001*	6.255	0.025*
Q3: panic	14.256	0.002*	6.525	0.023*	174.358	<0.001*	23.719	<0.001*
Q4: fatigue	7.971	0.014*	2.392	0.144	21.491	<0.001*	2.776	0.118
Q5: debility	9.453	0.008*	2.858	0.113	22.11	<0.001*	8.403	0.012*

*:<0.05

Table 3. Two-way interaction in ANOVA

	AB		AC		BC		AD		BD		CD	
	F	p	F	p	F	p	F	p	F	p	F	p
Q1: excitement	0.171	0.685	2.291	0.152	0.196	0.665	0.841	0.375	0.08	0.782	0.543	0.473
Q2: anxiety	0.115	0.739	0.113	0.742	3.248	0.093	2.499	0.136	0.55	0.471	5.774	0.031*
Q3: panic	0.953	0.345	8.52	0.011*	1.12	0.308	3.877	0.069	0.415	0.53	0.435	0.52
Q4: fatigue	1.578	0.23	0.057	0.815	5.878	0.029*	0.864	0.368	0.923	0.353	4.16	0.061
Q5: debility	0.281	0.604	2.628	0.127	0.063	0.805	4.569	0.051	4.569	0.051	0.007	0.934

*:<0.05

Table 4. ANOVA three-way and four-way interactions

	ABC		ABD		ACD		BCD		ABCD	
	F	p	F	p	F	p	F	p	F	p
Q1: excitement	0.159	0.697	1.555	0.233	2.259	0.155	1.739	0.208	0.048	0.83
Q2: anxiety	0.011	0.916	0.327	0.577	0.745	0.402	0.326	0.577	2.549	0.133
Q3: panic	0.056	0.816	0.733	0.406	0.186	0.673	0.785	0.391	0.023	0.881
Q4: fatigue	2.943	0.108	5.11	0.04*	0.189	0.67	0.111	0.744	6.186	0.026*
Q5: debility	0.878	0.365	0.161	0.694	0.481	0.499	0.001	0.972	0.217	0.648

*:<0.05

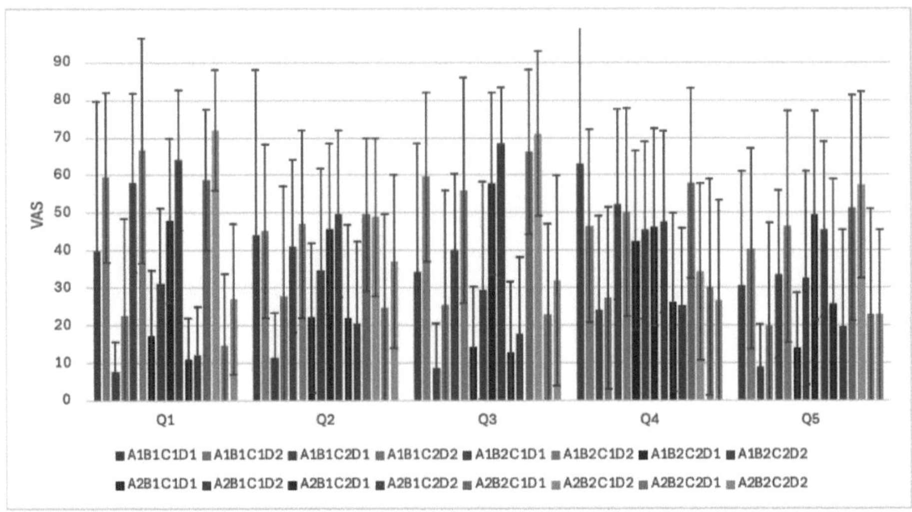

Fig. 4. Dispersion analysis table

5   Discussion

5.1   Effectiveness of Proposed Method

The results revealed that, in general, thoracic breathing conveyed stronger impressions of negative abnormality compared to abdominal breathing. This is likely because thoracic breathing, which involves prominent shoulder movement, is more visually noticeable and therefore perceived as a stronger indicator of internal distress.

Deep breathing increased evaluations of abnormal mental states (Q1–Q3), suggesting that greater surface movement due to breathing is associated with perceived psychological disturbance. Fast breathing also elevated impressions for all items except Q4. These findings imply that both deep and fast breathing are perceived as physically demanding, possibly because they involve larger movements and simulate states requiring greater air intake.

Furthermore, increased instability in breathing was associated with higher evaluations of abnormal physical condition (Q3–Q5), indicating that irregular breathing patterns signal physical distress. A common feature among these expressive breathing states is their resemblance to the breathing patterns of humans experiencing heavy physical strain.

Several interactions among the expressive elements demonstrated that combining parameters enhances the robot's expressiveness. This highlights the necessity of designing a system that integrates multiple respiratory features, rather than simply adjusting individual elements.

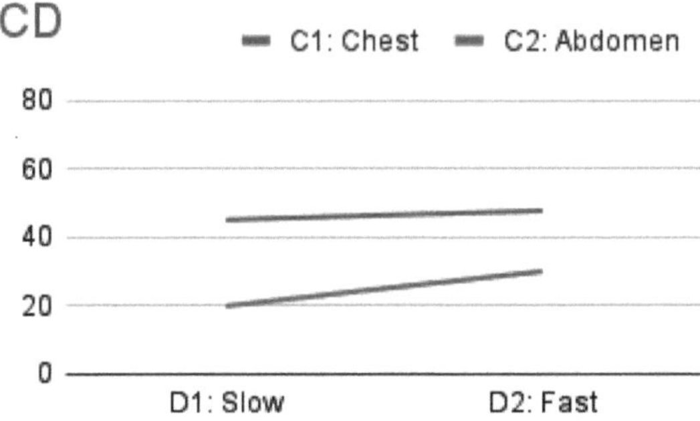

Fig. 5. Breathing parameter experiment: interaction between CDs in Q2 (anxiety state assessment)

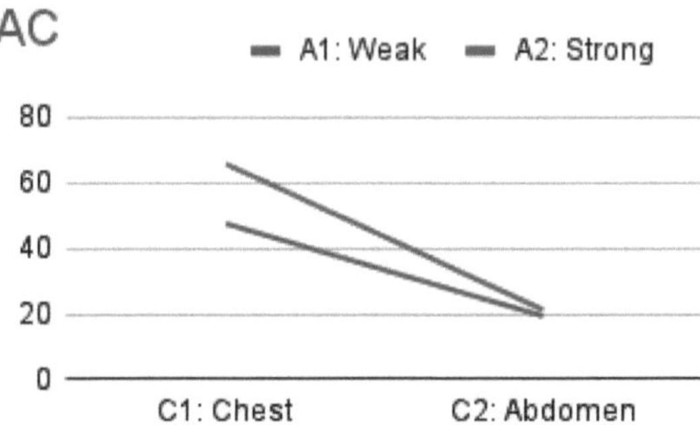

Fig. 6. Respiratory parameter experiment: interaction between ACs in Q3 (panic state assessment)

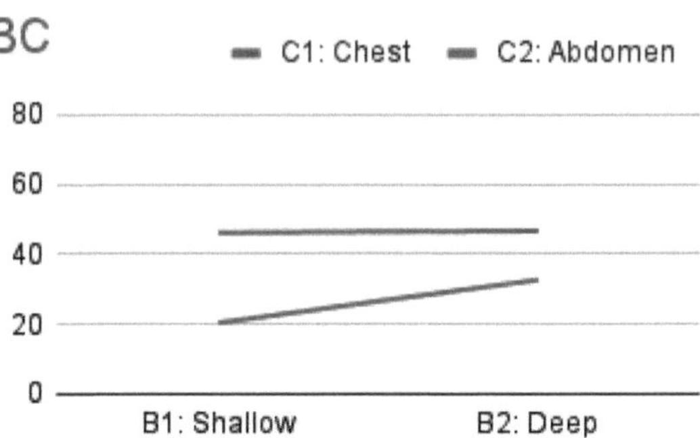

Fig. 7. Respiratory parameter experiment: interaction between BCs in Q4 (fatigue state assessment)

5.2   Limitation

The above results may not necessarily apply to all robots that exhibit breathing behavior. For instance, the proposed robot is driven by servo motors and lacks actual pulmonary respiration or accompanying airflow. Although lung-based breathing mechanisms, such as those found in inflatable robots [12,19] present challenges due to their delicate control systems and structural complexity, the presence of air enables uniform and natural expansion.

Additionally, in humans, shoulder movement during respiration is thought to result from spinal motion associated with thoracic breathing. Since the proposed robot does not replicate such anatomical structures, there is a risk that its breathing may be perceived as superficial.

Furthermore, the robot used in this study was limited in size; different effects are expected when the robot is scaled to the size of an adult or a child around eight years old.

Finally, impressions of breathing are likely to differ between animal-type [12] and human-type robots. In particular, human breathing can involve both involuntary and intentional expressions, which may lead to differing perceptions regarding the biological authenticity of such behaviors.

Based on these considerations, it is essential to enhance the perceived animacy of the robot through broader investigation into natural and trustworthy biological expressions.

5.3   Ethical Viewpoint

Biological expressions, such as those implemented in this robot, aim to pursue a level of biological realism that humans naturally trust and empathize with. This realism is expected to play a crucial role in the development of partner robots that can express emotions strongly. For instance, such robots could serve as walk-through companions in attractions like haunted houses.

However, the higher the perceived trustworthiness of these robots, the greater the concern that they may be exploited in scenarios where they could deceive humans. There is a potential risk of their use in malicious contexts such as fraud, theft, or robbery, where they might take advantage of human vulnerability. Therefore, the development of robots capable of eliciting human trust must be subject to appropriate restrictions depending on their intended use.

6   Conclusion

In this study, we developed an upper-body robot that performs involuntary breathing expressions by combining abdominal/thoracic respiratory parameters. The aim was to achieve natural and effective non-verbal communication through involuntary movements associated with the robot's breathing. From the results of the evaluation,

1: Thoracic (Chest) breathing was associated with anxiety, while fast abdominal breathing also conveyed anxiety (interaction between factors C and D).
2: Thoracic breathing strongly indicated panic, particularly when combined with unstable breathing (interaction between A and C).
3: Thoracic breathing and deep abdominal breathing both signaled poor physical condition.

4: Unstable and rapid thoracic breathing suggested a life-threatening condition.

These findings suggest that it is necessary to design a system that integrates multiple respiratory expression parameters in a complex and coordinated manner, rather than adjusting each element in isolation for effective implementation of an internal transition model. We can also derive the following insights from these results:

1: Chest breathing, which involves noticeable shoulder movement, is likely to be more visually prominent. As a result, it may be more readily interpreted as a sign of internal distress.
2: Deep breathing led to higher ratings of abnormal mental states (Q1–Q3), suggesting that greater surface movement caused by breathing is associated with the perception of psychological disturbance.
3: This trend may be explained by the fact that both deep and rapid breathing mimic a physiological condition requiring increased air intake. These patterns may thereby evoke impressions of elevated arousal or stress.
4: Unsteady breathing was associated with higher ratings of abnormal physical states (Q3–Q5), indicating that irregular respiratory rhythms resemble those seen in individuals experiencing intense physical strain, and are therefore perceived as indicators of physical distress.

These observations underscore the importance of designing a system that integrates multiple aspects of respiratory expression, rather than relying on the isolated manipulation of individual elements. A more holistic approach may yield expressions that are perceived as more natural, believable, and emotionally communicative.

Since the robot in this study has not yet reached the stage of autonomous control based on the verified breathing expression elements, it is necessary to implement an automatic control system that responds to both normal and abnormal internal states. Specifically, the system should distinguish between negative mental abnormalities and negative physical abnormalities, expressing them through appropriate and differentiated breathing behaviors.

To achieve this, we aim to develop an internal transition model that dynamically visualizes and intuitively communicates the robot's internal emotional states. This model is intended to enable natural and effective interaction by continuously updating the robot's internal state in response to external stimuli and linking it with involuntary physiological expressions. Furthermore, in situations where the robot experiences temporary malfunctions, the model will include mechanisms to clearly convey its condition to the user, promoting timely intervention and support.

This internal transition model is expected to improve user understanding of the robot's internal state and enhance feelings of empathy and intimacy. By expressing stress and anxiety, it may naturally encourage the user to assist the robot, reinforcing the core concept of "weak robots." The robot's ability to adapt its internal state in real-time based on environmental and user input is also anticipated to contribute to more context-sensitive interaction.

The other kinds of involuntary expressions such as sweat [20] or heartbeat [21] would help the people understand the robot's insistence or fatal situation. The design of the changes in robots' breathing and facial color can be used to communicate discomfort or boundary violation such as when the user enters the robot's personal space.

Acknowledgement. This work was supported in part by JSPS Grants-in-Aid for Scientific Research 24K02977, 23K11202, 21K11968, 23K11278, 22K19792.

This research was supported in part by JST Moonshot R and D Program (Grant Number JPMJMS2215), JST CREST Grant Number JPMJCR18A1 Japan, and JSPS KAKENHI 24K02977, 22K19792, 23K11202, 23K11278, 21K11968. JPMJMS2215 supported investigating the proposed system's safety and security, and the others supported the system implementation and the experiment. We thank to the participants in the experiment.

References

1. Okada, M.: Development of weak robots aimed at human interaction and its evolution. J. Robot. Soc. Jpn. **34**(5), 299–303 (2016)
2. Shibata, T., Wada, K.: Clinical and empirical studies on the effects of robot therapy using seal robot 'Paro'. J. Robot. Soc. Jpn. **29**(3), 246–249 (2011)
3. Okubo, H., Inoue, K., Maruyama, J., Hamada, T., Taisei, H.: Study on robot motion design in recreation for elderly people with dementia. Trans. Soc. Instrum. Control Eng. **44**(5), 450–457 (2008)
4. Moyle, W., Bramble, M., Jones, C.J., Murfield, J.E.: She had a smile on her face as wide as the Great Australian Bight: a qualitative examination of family perceptions of a therapeutic robot and a plush toy. Gerontologist **59**(1), 177–185 (2019)
5. Fukuda, M.: The hierarchy of emotions and brain evolution: evolutionary positioning of social emotions. Jpn. J. Res. Emot. **16**(1), 25–35 (2008)
6. Umeda, S.: Interaction between brain and body in generating emotions. Cogn. Neurosci. **22**(1), 35–39 (2020)
7. Kono, T.: Emotion and psychological categorization. Philos. Sci. **52**(2), 1–19 (2020)
8. Yuasa, M., Takekawa, N.: Human impression management and non-verbal behavior expression models for guiding user behavior with anthropomorphic agents. IEICE Trans. Electron. **94**(1), 124–137 (2011)
9. Yonezawa, T., Yamazoe, H.: Wearable partner agent with anthropomorphic physical contact with awareness of user's clothing and posture. In: Proceedings of the 2013 International Symposium on Wearable Computers, pp. 77–80 (2013)
10. Yoshida, N., Ueno, K., Mase, K., Yonezawa, T.: Arousal and valence in robot's emotional expression of breathing and heartbeat. In: Human-Agent Interaction Symposium, G-6 (2020)
11. Nakatani, Y., Yoshida, N., Yonezawa, T.: Breathing expression for intimate impression corresponding to the positional relationship. In: Human-Agent Interaction Symposium, P-14 (2014)
12. Yoshida, N., Yonezawa, T.: Investigating breathing expression of a stuffed-toy robot based on body-emotion model. In: Proceedings of the Fourth International Conference on Human Agent Interaction, pp. 139–144 (2016)

13. Sefidgar, Y.S., MacLean, K.E., Yohanan, S., Van der Loos, H.F.M., Croft, E.A., Garland, E.J.: Design and evaluation of a touch-centered calming interaction with a social robot. IEEE Trans. Affect. Comput. **7**(2), 108–121 (2015)
14. Levenson, R.W.: Blood, sweat, and fears: the autonomic architecture of emotion. Ann. N. Y. Acad. Sci. **1000**(1), 348–366 (2003)
15. Boiten, F.A., Frijda, N.H., Wientjes, C.J.E.: Emotions and respiratory patterns: review and critical analysis. Int. J. Psychophysiol. **17**(2), 103–128 (1994)
16. Philippot, P., Chapelle, G., Blairy, S.: Respiratory feedback in the generation of emotion. Cogn. Emot. **16**(5), 605–627 (2002)
17. Gilbert, C.: Interaction of psychological and emotional variables with breathing dysfunction. In: Recognizing and Treating Breathing Disorders: A Multidisciplinary Approach, 2nd edn., pp. 79–91. Churchill Livingstone Elsevier (2014)
18. Abelson, J.L., Nesse, R.M., Weg, J.G., Curtis, G.C.: Persistent respiratory irregularity in patients with panic disorder. Biol. Psychiat. **49**(7), 588–595 (2001)
19. Zhang, Y., et al.: Extracorporeal closed-loop respiratory regulation for patients with respiratory difficulty using a soft bionic robot. IEEE Trans. Biomed. Eng. (2024)
20. Yonezawa, T., Meng, X., Wan, X.: Physiologically expressive robotic hand as a lifelike presence. In: Proceedings of the International Conference on Human-Computer Interaction (HCII 2024): Social Computing and Social Media, pp. 61–77 (2024)
21. Yoshida, N., Yonezawa, T.: Honne and Tatemae: expression of the agent's hidden desire through physiological phenomena. Hum. Interface Soc. J. **26**(2), 249–258 (2024)

Towards a Formal Methodology for Evaluating Information Consumer Experience at Work

María Paz Godoy[1]([✉]) [iD], María Angélica S. Piñones[1], Cristian Rusu[2] [iD], and Jonathan Ugalde[3] [iD]

[1] Carrera de Información y Control de Gestión, Facultad de Ciencias Económicas y Administrativas, Universidad de Valparaíso, Valparaíso, Chile
`mariapaz.godoy@uv.cl`
[2] Escuela de Ingeniería en Informática, Pontificia Universidad Católica de Valparaíso, Valparaíso, Chile
[3] Informatics Engineering School, Faculty of Engineering, Universidad de Valparaíso, Valparaíso, Chile

Abstract. In modern work environments, the ability to effectively access, interpret, and act upon information is a key driver of productivity and well-being. However, traditional evaluation approaches often fail to capture the nuanced experiences of information consumers navigating complex information systems. This paper introduces a comprehensive methodology for evaluating the Information Consumer Experience (ICX) in real-world organizational contexts. Grounded in principles from Human-Computer Interaction (HCI), Customer Experience (CX), and workplace studies, we present a conceptual model of ICX alongside a structured evaluation framework. The methodology integrates both qualitative and quantitative techniques—including interviews, surveys, and data analysis—to provide a holistic understanding of how individuals engage with information. It unfolds across three interrelated stages: the Characterization Stage, the Experimentation Stage, and the Analysis Stage, each comprising sequential sub-stages aligned with key phases of the evaluation process. To our knowledge, this is the first formal approach designed to evaluate ICX across diverse organizational settings, offering actionable insights and recommendations for enhancing the information consumer experience.

Keywords: Information Consumer Experience · Evaluation Methodology · Customer Experience

1 Introduction

In today's competitive business environment, organizations constantly seek new strategies to attract and retain customers [14]. This shift has led to increased attention on Consumer Experience (CX), which captures expectations, satisfaction, and challenges during customer-brand interactions [18]. Improving CX

A. Coman et al. (Eds.): HCII 2025, LNCS 16337, pp. 216–235, 2026.
https://doi.org/10.1007/978-3-032-12801-0_15

benefits both sides: organizations gain loyalty and performance, while customers receive better service and products. Achieving this requires optimizing all touchpoints throughout the customer journey, making CX management a key competitive advantage [14].

A comparable dynamic exists within organizations, where employees interact with internal information systems, services, and products. These internal consumers rely on efficient and positive experiences to perform their duties effectively. As with external CX, the quality of these internal interactions significantly impacts productivity and satisfaction. Organizations typically have information management departments that oversee and support access to these systems across different areas.

Conventional evaluation methods often emphasize usability or efficiency, failing to capture the full, subjective experience of information consumers. Addressing this gap, this paper presents a formalized methodology to evaluate the Information Consumer Experience (ICX) in organizational settings. The approach focuses on identifying pains, needs, and perceptions across information interactions, shifting the evaluation lens from system performance to user-centered experience.

This methodology introduces a novel tool for researchers and practitioners, incorporating Customer Experience (CX) techniques to extend beyond models like User Experience (UX) [2,6,11,20] and the Technology Acceptance Model (TAM) [12,13,15,22]. As a refinement of our previous work [8,9,19], it uses Business Process Modelling Notation (BPMN) to formalize its structure and tasks, allowing validation by HCI experts. This final version stands as the first generalizable framework for assessing ICX across diverse organizations with high information demands.

This paper is structured as follows: Sect. 2 introduces key concepts. Section 3 outlines the methodology, and Sects. 4, 5, and 6 detail its three stages. Finally, Sect. 7 presents our conclusions.

2 Background

2.1 Customer Experience (CX)

Customer Experience (CX) refers to the perception formed by customers during interactions with a brand's products, systems, or services [16]. This perception spans six dimensions: Emotional, Sensory, Cognitive, Pragmatic, Lifestyle, and Relational [7]. In this work, the concept of Information Consumer Experience (ICX) is framed as a specific extension of CX, limited to interactions with information products, systems, or services.

2.2 Information Consumer Experience (ICX)

ICX focuses on how employees interact with information resources within organizations [10]. These include using information for reports, decision-making, collaboration, or interdepartmental exchanges. Like CX, these interactions generate touchpoints that influence work experience. ICX inherits and adapts CX evaluation methods for organizational contexts where information is central to daily tasks.

2.3   Customer Journey Map (CJM)

The Customer Journey Map (CJM) visualizes all customer interactions—called touchpoints—with products or services [24]. It helps understand the full CX by identifying key elements such as Persona, Touchpoints, Channels, and Emotions [17]. CJMs are valuable for mapping expectations and emotions across the customer journey and serve as inspiration for ICX analysis.

2.4   Data Quality

In organizations, data producers, managers, and consumers play key roles in ensuring data quality. Quality is defined by its suitability for use and is assessed across four dimensions: intrinsic, accessibility, contextual, and representational [23]. These include attributes such as accuracy, security, relevance, and interpretability—all critical to the ICX.

2.5   Business Process Model and Notation

Business Process Model and Notation (BPMN) provides a standardized graphical language for modeling and communicating business processes [21]. Its clarity and structure make it ideal for representing the ICX methodology, supporting a consistent understanding of evaluation stages and activities across organizational stakeholders.

3   ICX Evaluation Methodology

The proposed methodology for evaluating the Information Consumer Experience (ICX) consists of three sequential stages, each comprising interrelated sub-stages. Each stage or sub-stage may produce one or more documents as inputs or outputs of its execution. Additionally, each sub-stage includes activities that need to be carried out to implement the methodology. As previously mentioned, BPMN modeling notation was used to represent the methodology, with the aim of making it easily understandable for all users. Figure 1 presents the general diagram of the methodology, clearly identifying the three stages, each assigned a unique ID (EI, EII, EIII). Figure 1 presents a general description of the methodology, along with its respective inputs and outputs.

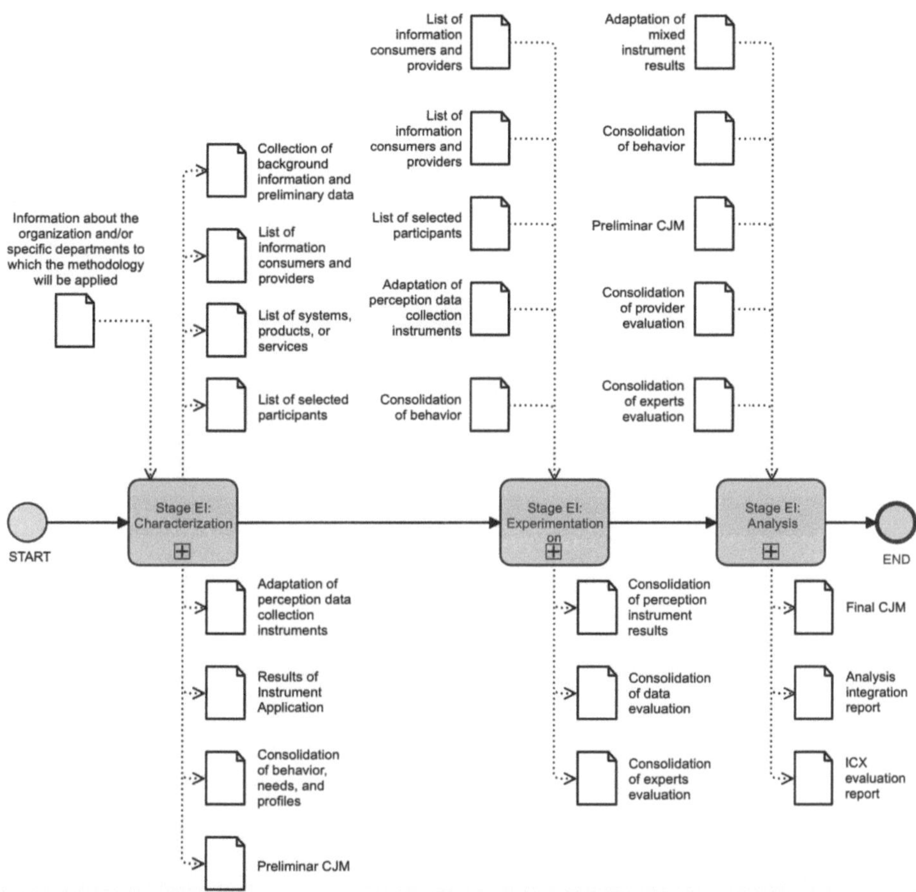

Fig. 1. BPMN Diagram - General description of the methodology

4   Stage I: Characterization Stage

The objective of this first stage is to conduct an exploratory diagnosis aimed at analyzing the organization, its information consumers, and information providers. In this stage, it is essential to gather necessary information from the organization and/or departments to which the methodology will be applied, such as the functions of the organization and/or department, characteristics, information acquisition processes, and any additional information considered necessary (Fig. 2).

4.1   Sub-stage I.1: Planning

The planning sub-stage is fundamental to developing the Information Consumer Experience (ICX) evaluation methodology. In this sub-stage, participants, products, systems, or services to be evaluated are consolidated. The first step is

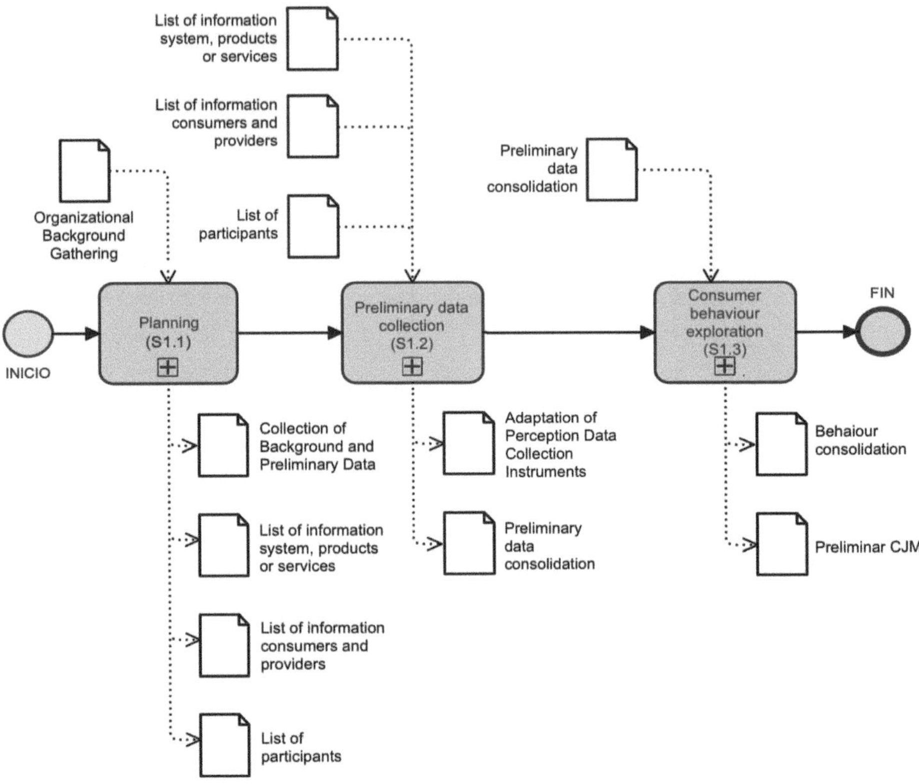

Fig. 2. Stage I - Characterization Stage

to gather background information about the organization, which provides the necessary context for analysis. Next, this background information is analyzed, and information consumers and providers within the organization are identified. Clearly defining these roles is crucial for properly selecting participants. Once identified, the information products, systems, or services subject to evaluation are chosen. Finally, participants, providers, and selected information elements are consolidated. The result of this sub-stage is a compilation of background information and preliminary data, along with detailed lists of systems, products or services, information consumers and providers, and the final selection of participants for the study (Fig. 3).

To carry out these activities, the following recommendations are made:

- Among the professionals selected to apply the information consumer experience evaluation methodology, it is recommended to appoint a leader, who will oversee each of the stages and ensure compliance.
- When selecting participants, it is strongly suggested to include representative participants, ensuring a balanced number of information consumers per

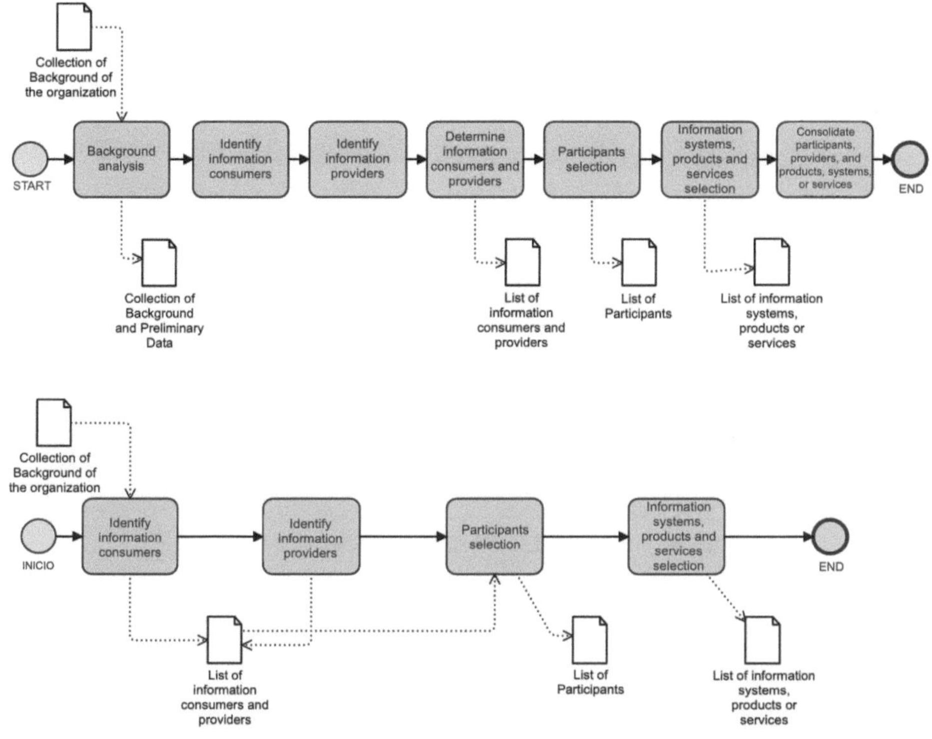

Fig. 3. Sub-stage I.1: Planning

department or area of the organization, or those with the most interactions
with other departments.
- When selecting information products, systems, or services, it is recommended
  to include a reasonable number of products, systems, or services to conduct
  a complete organizational-level analysis.

4.2 Sub-stage I.2: Preliminary Data Collection

The sub-stage of preliminary data collection focuses on gathering initial information that will allow a better understanding of the context and informational
dynamics of the organization. To start this sub-stage, it is essential to have lists
of systems, products, or services, as well as information consumers and providers,
along with the selection of participants. Activities include analyzing these lists
to select a subgroup of participants, adapting data collection instruments to capture the perception of information consumers, and applying these instruments in
an exploratory manner. Subsequently, the remaining participants are identified,
and the mass data collection instruments are applied. Finally, the preliminary
data obtained is consolidated. The result of this sub-stage is the adaptation of

data collection instruments and the consolidation of preliminary data, providing a solid foundation for subsequent phases of the evaluation (Fig. 4).

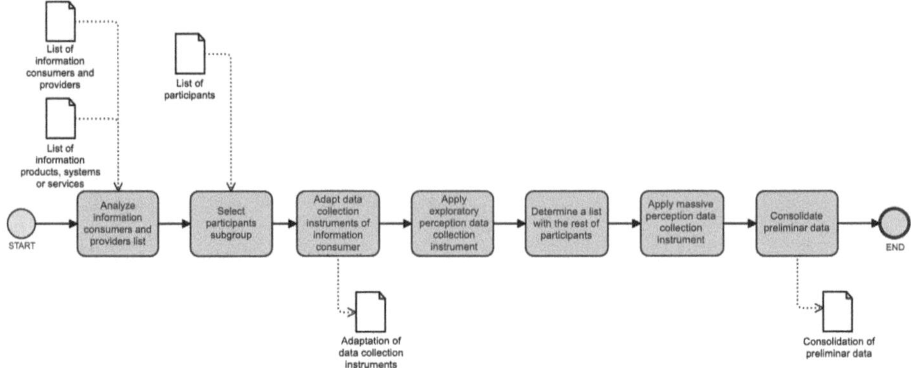

Fig. 4. Sub-stage I.2: Preliminary Data Collection

The recommendations for this sub-stage are as follows:

- Once the information consumers selected for the preliminary data collection are identified, it is recommended to conduct a brief induction for the participants to explain key concepts, the purpose, and the confidentiality of the information obtained during each of the stages.
- Evaluators' information should be managed anonymously.
- Exploratory perception data collection instruments refer to qualitative information collection tools such as interviews.
- It is recommended to section interviews into stages, each with a specific objective to be achieved through a series of questions.
- Mass perception data collection instruments refer to quantitative information collection tools such as surveys.
- For the aforementioned instruments, those presented in "Information Consumer eXperience: A Chilean Case Study" are considered.

4.3 Sub-stage I.3: Exploration of Consumer Behavior

The sub-stage of exploring consumer behavior focuses on analyzing and understanding how information consumers interact with information systems, products, or services. Starting with the consolidation of preliminary data collected, the initial behavior of these consumers is explored to identify their needs and preferences. Additionally, touchpoints and channels used by consumers are analyzed, and different types of information consumers are identified and profiled.

This phase also includes consolidating observed behaviors and analyzing expectations and emotions at touchpoints. The final result of this sub-stage is the creation of a preliminary version of the consumer journey map, providing a comprehensive view of the journey and interactions of consumers with information (Fig. 5).

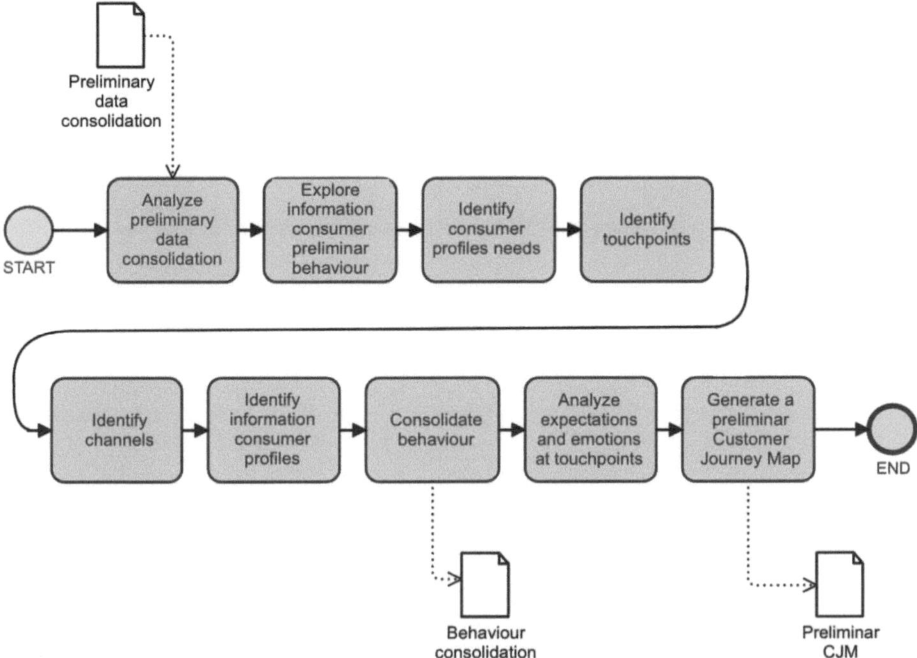

Fig. 5. Sub-stage I.3: Exploration of Consumer Behavior

The recommendations for this sub-stage include:

− When identifying information consumer profiles according to the identified needs, it is recommended to document the information in detail, including descriptions and needs. For this documentation, it is suggested to use Tables 1, 2, and 3. For guidance on this form of documentation, previously used in earlier studies, refer to Table 4, "Consolidated Behavioral Documentation." [9]

Table 1. Example of a list of information consumer needs.

List of Information Consumer Needs		
Need ID	Name of Need	Description
N1	Centralized Information Service	Consumers indicate a need for up-to-date data at all times, to use reliable inputs in their daily work, especially for decision-making processes.

Table 2. Example of a list of information consumer profiles.

List of Information Consumer Profiles		
Profile ID	Information Consumer Profile	Description
C1	Executive Consumer	Profile of information consumers at the executive level, generally belonging to the executive tier and using data as inputs for high-level strategic, policy, and organizational management decision-making processes.

Table 3. Example of associations between needs and profiles of information consumers.

Associations between Needs and Information Consumer Profiles				
		Priority for the Profile		
ID	Need	P1	P2	P3
A1	N1	High	Medium	Low

- For the preliminary consumer journey map, special attention should be paid to touchpoints along with their channels, expectations, and emotions that information consumers associate with each interaction. The map is typically represented as a two-dimensional axis where touchpoints are plotted horizontally, and a perception level scale is plotted vertically, usually ascending from negative to positive perception. This allows each touchpoint to be assigned a perception level, helping to identify the best and worst-rated touchpoints by consumers, enabling the organization to take appropriate measures.
- For exploring preliminary consumer behavior, it is recommended to use narrative analysis or phenomenological analysis, depending on expert criteria.

Table 4. Documentation of Needs, Profiles, and Associations

Inputs	(4) Consolidation of preliminary data
Steps	- Analyze the document of consolidated preliminary data obtained in the previous stage. - Explore preliminary consumer behavior. - Identify touchpoints. - Identify needs that impact the work of information consumers. - Fill out the table "Example of a list of information consumer needs." - Identify needs shared by certain groups of information consumers. - Define information consumer profiles. - Fill out the table "Example of a list of information consumer profiles." - Analyze the information in each table. - Use the associations identified in step 6 to establish connections between needs and consumer profiles, following the table "Example of associations between needs and profiles of information consumers."
Outputs	Behavioral Consolidation

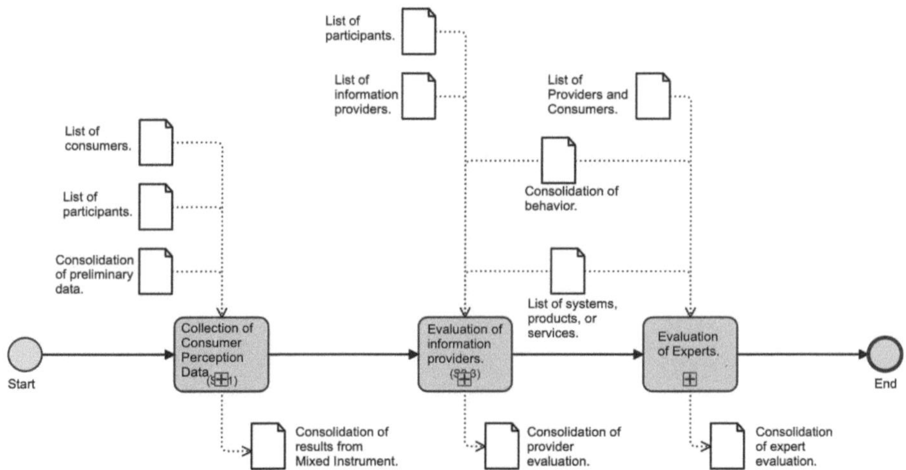

Fig. 6. Stage II - Experimentation Stage

5   Stage II: Experimentation Stage

The experimentation stage is crucial for the effective evaluation of information systems, products, or services. In this phase, evaluation methods are implemented to obtain detailed data on the expectations and perceptions of information consumers. Using a mixed approach, both qualitative and quantitative data are collected, including perceptions of information providers and details of the information acquisition process. Additionally, the quality of data associated with each product, system, or service is evaluated individually, and a cognitive simulation is conducted with experts to gain a deeper perspective. At the end of this stage, the results from perception instruments, data evaluation, and expert evaluation are consolidated, providing a comprehensive and well-founded view of the performance and experience of information consumers (Fig. 6).

Consider the following recommendations:

- In each of the sub-stages, confidentiality must be emphasized, informing participants that their actions may be recorded, their identities will not be disclosed, and reminding them of the purpose of the evaluation.
- The methods proposed in this methodology can be used to evaluate a variety of systems, products, or services, and information consumer perceptions; therefore, any necessary adjustments should be considered.

5.1   Sub-stage II.1: Data Collection on Consumer Perception

The sub-stage of data collection on consumer perception focuses on applying a mixed instrument designed to capture the expectations and perceptions of information consumers across various measurement dimensions. Building on

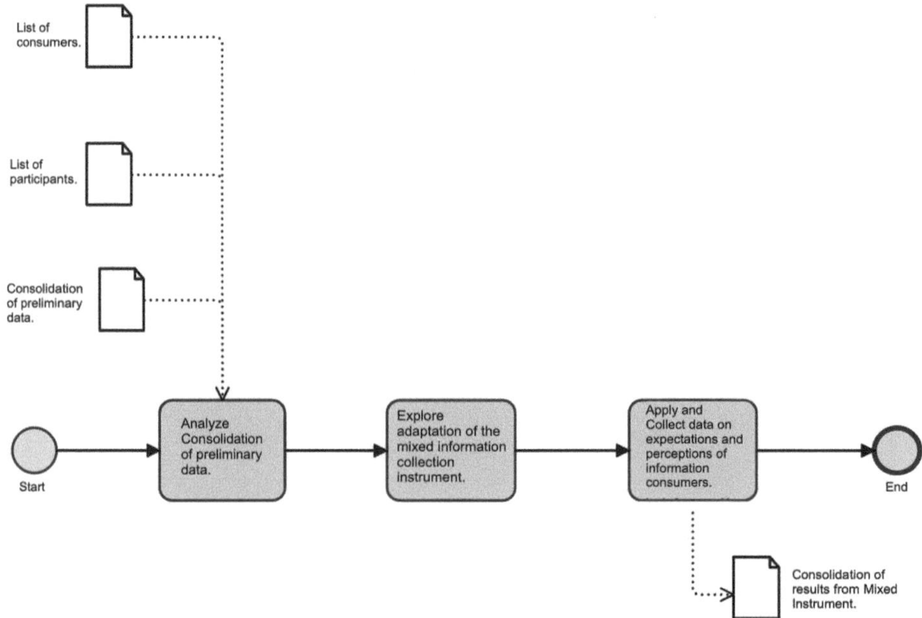

Fig. 7. Sub-stage II.1: Data Collection on Consumer Perception

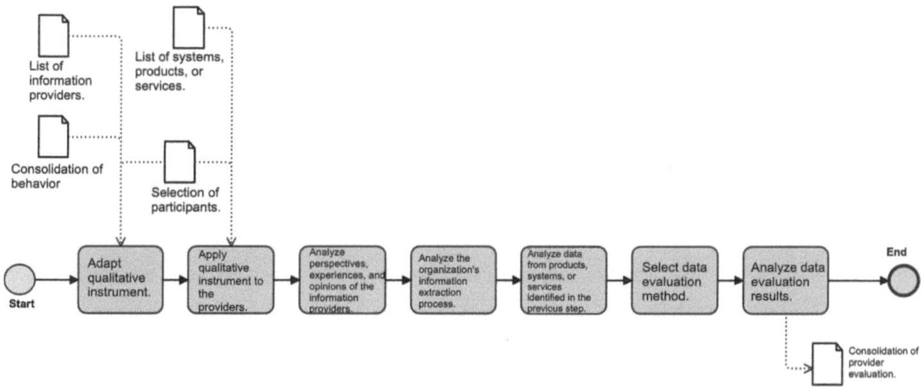

Fig. 8. Sub-stage II.2: Evaluation of Information Providers

the behavioral consolidation obtained in the previous stage, this instrument is adapted to ensure accurate and detailed data collection. For data collection, adapted surveys based on specialized questionnaires used in the literature related to employee experience can be utilized, such as the Job Satisfaction Survey [1], perception surveys about the work environment like the Quality of Work Life Scale Questionnaire [4], and the Work Environment Impact Scale-Self Rating (WEIS-SR Questionnaire) [5], as well as surveys related to working with information systems, such as Quality of Self-Service Technology (SSTQUAL) [3].

These surveys can be adapted with a focus on information work (ICX) and the specific context of the organization. It is recommended to consolidate a single survey that includes aspects of the types of surveys mentioned above, for a data collection that covers the greatest amount of information. Additionally, the application of this survey should be followed by a subsequent interview, structured based on the findings from the survey, to delve deeper into the perceptions and needs of information consumers.

The result of this sub-stage is the consolidation of results obtained through the mixed instrument, providing a solid foundation for analyzing the information consumer experience. (Fig. 7).

5.2   Sub-stage II.2: Evaluation of Information Providers

The sub-stage for evaluating information providers focuses on obtaining a detailed understanding of the information extraction process and the perceptions of providers within the organization. Based on the behavioral consolidation and the list of providers and participants, a qualitative instrument is adapted and applied to explore in depth the perspectives, experiences, and opinions of information providers. This analysis covers not only the extraction of information but also the quality of the data managed by the organization (Fig. 8).

For this sub-stage, it is recommended to consider the following:

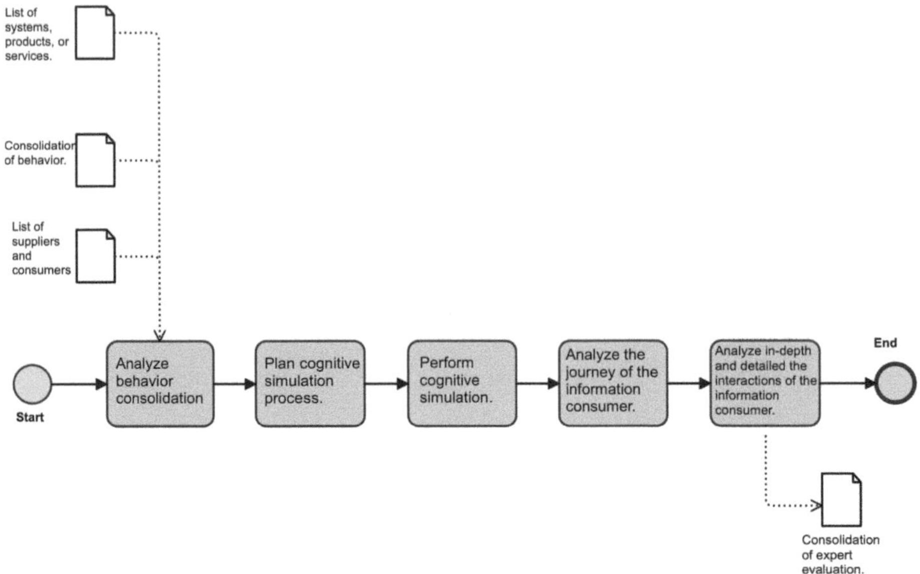

Fig. 9. Sub-stage II.3: Expert Exploration Evaluation

- The qualitative instrument employed in this stage should aim to provide a detailed understanding of the information extraction process and the perception of providers, exploring their experiences and opinions. Therefore, the instrument should align with this purpose. Instruments that can be chosen include semi-structured interviews, focus groups, direct non-participative observation, perspective-based inspection, surveys, adaptations of previously conducted surveys or interviews, among others. It is essential to choose an instrument that best serves the purpose of the stage.
- For data quality evaluation, it is recommended to analyze data through data profiling, assessing data integrity, usability, and other aspects that can estimate the quality of the data managed within the organization.

5.3   Sub-stage II.3: Expert Exploration

The expert exploration sub-stage focuses on conducting cognitive simulations guided by experts in consumer experience (CX) to analyze in depth the behavior of information consumers. Using the behavioral consolidation document and considering the identified information products, systems, services, and consumer profiles, this simulation is planned and executed (Fig. 9).

t!

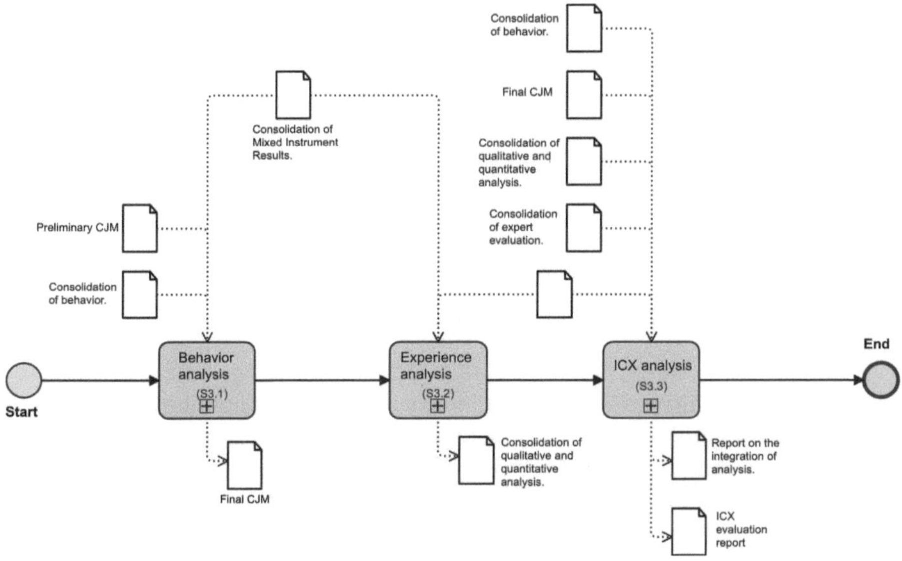

Fig. 10. Stage III - Analysis Stage

6 Stage III: Analysis Stage

The analysis stage is crucial for interpreting and synthesizing all the information collected throughout the process. Starting with the consolidation of results obtained from mixed instruments, consumer behavior, the preliminary CJM, and evaluations from providers and experts, an in-depth analysis is conducted. Definitive maps of the information consumer journey are created, adjusted according to identified profiles. Qualitative and quantitative methods are applied, including statistical analysis, to integrate and understand the data holistically. Based on this analysis, specific indicators are defined by profile and at the organizational level, and concrete recommendations are developed. Finally, all this information is consolidated into a detailed ICX evaluation report, which includes the definitive CJM and the analysis integration report, providing a comprehensive and actionable view of the information consumer experience within the organization (Fig. 10).

6.1 Sub-stage III.1: Behavior Analysis

The behavior analysis sub-stage focuses on deepening the understanding of the behavior of information consumers through the analysis of consolidated data and the creation of definitive consumer journey maps (CJM). Starting with the consolidation of results from mixed instruments, the preliminary CJM, and behavior consolidation, a detailed analysis is conducted to identify touchpoints and specific consumer profiles. This process includes comparing the preliminary

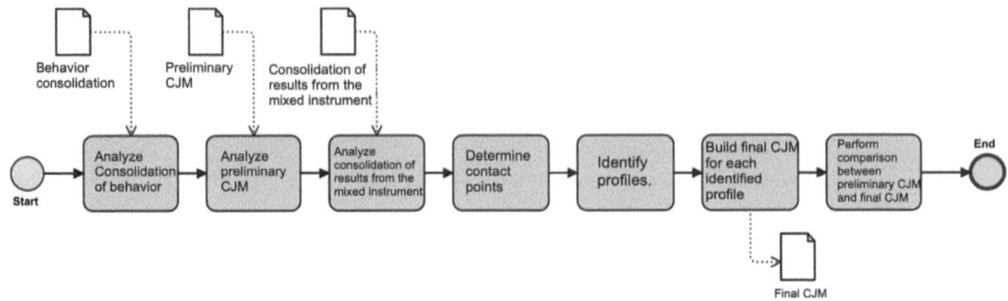

Fig. 11. Sub-stage III.1: Behavior Analysis

CJM with the definitive CJM, enriching the analysis through narrative and phenomenological techniques to capture consumer perceptions of their experiences. The goal is to construct a definitive CJM for each identified profile, providing an accurate and comprehensive representation of the consumer's journey. This sub-stage concludes with the definitive CJM, which integrates and reflects all mapped interactions and experiences throughout the process (Fig. 11).

During this behavior analysis, the definitive consumer journey map is constructed, providing the final version of this tool and establishing a comparison with the preliminary version. Recommendations include:

- Organize the information documented in the behavior consolidation document to complete Table 5, facilitating the creation of the definitive CJM.
- Following the recommendation given in Sub-stage S1.3: Exploration of Consumer Behavior, create the preliminary Consumer Journey Map to show information consumers' perceptions of each touchpoint.
- Develop a specific map for each profile identified in the previous stage.
- While analyzing and developing the definitive CJM, it is recommended to take notes of relevant data that capture attention, to later analyze these notes and consider them in the recommendations that need to be developed in the following stages.

6.2   Sub-stage III.2: Experience Analysis

The experience analysis sub-stage is dedicated to integrating and evaluating the data collected to gain a deep understanding of the information consumer experience. Starting with the consolidation of results from mixed instruments and provider evaluations, a thorough analysis is conducted. This process includes both a qualitative analysis of the obtained results, providing a detailed and contextual view of the experiences, and a quantitative analysis using statistical methods to validate and generalize the findings. The combination of these approaches allows for a complete and robust analysis, offering a holistic and precise view of the consumer experience within the organization (Fig. 12).

Table 5. Touchpoints of information consumers during their interaction with the organization.

ID	Scenario	Touchpoint	Category	Components	Description
TP01	Consumption	Response to information services and access credentials	Own brand request	Technological interaction between employee-client	Whether in response to a report request or access credentials to an information service, the consumer receives an email with a link to a report or their access credentials, allowing them to access the service. It is important to note that this touchpoint can be optional, as once the request is answered, the consumer can use the response for future access.

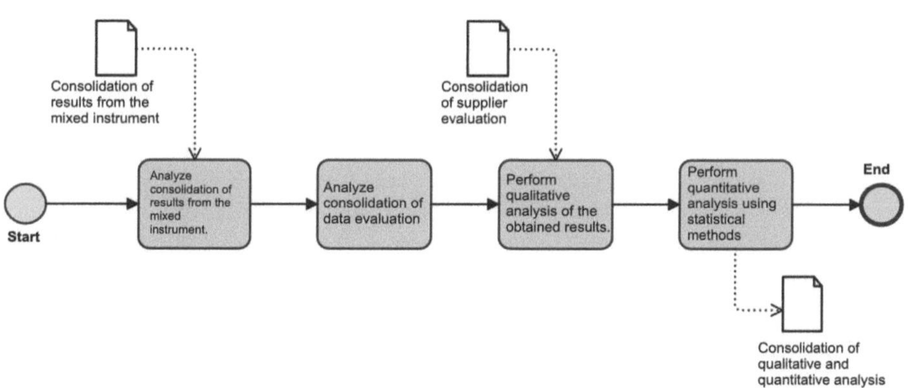

Fig. 12. Sub-stage III.2: Experience Analysis

Consider the following recommendations:

- It is recommended to use an adapted SERVQUAL evaluation for assessing the information consumer experience, which can be divided into two sections: gathering information consumers' perceptions and gathering their expectations. Subsequently, responses should be measured using a five-point Likert scale, applying a percentage transformation function to each scale value, allowing for quantitative analysis of the information consumer experience. Table 6 presents the Likert scale used for the SERVQUAL adaptation.

Table 6. Proposed Likert Scale for SERVQUAL Adaptation.

Likert Scale for SERVQUAL Adaptation				
Strongly Dis-agree	Disagree	Neither Agree nor Disagree	Agree	Strongly Agree
0% - 20%	20% - 40%	40% - 60%	60% - 80%	80% - 100%

- Organize and graph the information captured through Likert scales to obtain a visual representation of participants' perceptions.
- Depending on the limitations for implementing the methodology, the combination of statistical methods previously used in the literature should be evaluated.
- Include interpretations of each graph created with the evaluation data.
- It should be noted that other techniques, such as variance analysis, factor analysis, among others, can enrich the quantitative analysis.
- It is also recommended to generate a list of relevant data and interpretations for the subsequent analysis integration.

6.3   Sub-stage III.3: ICX Analysis

The ICX analysis sub-stage is the final sub-stage of the methodology, focusing on consolidating and synthesizing all previously conducted analyses to comprehensively evaluate the information consumer experience. Starting from the definitive CJM, behavioral consolidation, qualitative and quantitative analyses, and expert and provider evaluations, an exhaustive analysis is conducted. Recommendations are made to improve the evaluated aspects, and the analysis integration document is complemented. Additionally, specific indicators are created for each consumer profile, and a global ICX indicator that integrates these profiles is developed. Finally, all these elements are compiled into a detailed ICX evaluation report, which includes profile-specific indicators, the global indicator, and recommendations, providing a comprehensive tool for improving the information consumer experience in the organization (Fig. 13).

Consider the following:

- Maintain a global and critical perspective on each of the previously completed stages and sub-stages, focusing on integration rather than specifics to achieve a complete analysis integration.
- When integrating analysis results into a deliverable report for the stakeholders of the proposed methodology application, recommendations should be provided for each touchpoint analyzed and graphed in the definitive CJM, suggesting improvements for those with negative experiences and perceptions, and highlighting aspects to maintain or improve for those with positive evaluations to prevent negative evaluations over time.

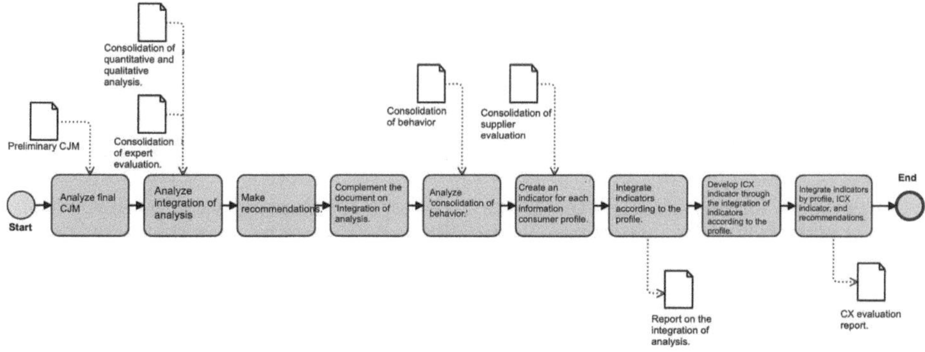

Fig. 13. Sub-stage III.3: Experience Analysis

- It is recommended that the global ICX indicator be derived directly from the previous quantitative experience analysis sub-stage (e.g., Service Quality Index obtained through the SERVQUAL application), while ICX indicators by profile are constructed from the quantitative analysis broken down by each profile (e.g., an ICX indicator for a specific consumer profile can be derived from the Service Quality Index (SERVQUAL) considering only responses from consumers belonging to that specific profile).
- For ICX indicators by profile, clarity in naming, a clear evaluation metric, and interpretable results are essential to obtain a consistent diagnosis of the state of each specific profile, encompassing their satisfaction levels.
- Providing explanations of each indicator, considering the aspects mentioned above, benefits the understanding of all parties (stakeholders - person measuring using this indicator information consumer profile).
- All analyses should integrate positive and negative aspects identified by the evaluators.

Once this stage is completed, the outputs, such as the "definitive CJM," "Analysis Integration," and "ICX Evaluation Report," should be available for use by different stakeholders of the organization or the specific study unit. The results should be delivered responsibly to ensure that the provided recommendations are implemented effectively.

7 Conclusions

In this paper, we presented a formal methodology for evaluating the Information Consumer Experience (ICX) in real-world organizational contexts. Recognizing the limitations of traditional evaluation approaches, our work proposes a user-centered framework that captures the experiential, cognitive, and affective dimensions of information interactions in the workplace. By adapting principles and techniques from Customer Experience (CX) studies, our methodology offers a novel perspective for analyzing the quality and effectiveness of information consumption within organizations.

The proposed methodology is structured into three interconnected stages —Characterization, Experimentation, and Analysis— each designed to support the systematic identification of pains, needs, and perceptions of information consumers. Through the integration of qualitative and quantitative techniques such as interviews, surveys, and data analysis, our approach provides a comprehensive view of ICX, enabling organizations to generate actionable insights and develop strategies aimed at improving both working conditions and organizational outcomes.

To ensure practical applicability and clarity, we modeled the entire evaluation process using Business Process Model and Notation (BPMN), facilitating its implementation across diverse organizational contexts. As the first formal and generalizable framework for evaluating ICX, this methodology contributes both theoretically and practically to the fields of Human-Computer Interaction (HCI), organizational studies, and information management. Future work includes empirical validation across various industries, refinement based on expert feedback, and the development of supporting tools to streamline its application.

References

1. Ahmad, K.Z.B., Jasimuddin, S.M., Kee, W.L.: Organizational climate and job satisfaction: do employees' personalities matter? Manag. Decis. **56**(2), 421–440 (2018). https://doi.org/10.1108/md-10-2016-0713
2. Alhendawi, K.M., Baharudin, A.S.: The impact of interaction quality factors on the effectiveness of web-based information system: the mediating role of user satisfaction. Cogn. Technol. Work **16**(4), 451–465 (2013). https://doi.org/10.1007/s10111-013-0272-9
3. Considine, E., Cormican, K.: The rise of the prosumer: an analysis of self-service technology adoption in a corporate context. Int. J. Inf. Syst. Project Manag. **5**(2), 25–39 (2022). https://doi.org/10.12821/ijispm050202 https://doi.org/10.12821/ijispm050202 https://doi.org/10.12821/ijispm050202 https://doi.org/10.12821/ijispm050202 https://doi.org/10.12821/ijispm050202
4. Dhamija, P., Gupta, S., Bag, S.: Measuring of job satisfaction: the use of quality of work life factors. Benchmarking Int. J. **26**(3), 871–892 (2019). https://doi.org/10.1108/bij-06-2018-0155
5. Dorsey, J., et al.: Using the WEIS-SR to evaluate employee perceptions of their college work environment. Work **54**(1), 103–111 (2016). https://doi.org/10.3233/wor-162281
6. Ganeshan, M.K., Vethirajan, C.: Electronic human resource management practices and employees perception towards information technology industry. Int. J. Sci. Technol. Res. **9**, 86–90 (2020)
7. Gentile, C., Spiller, N., Noci, G.: How to sustain the customer experience: an overview of experience components that co-create value with the customer. Eur. Manag. J. **25**(5), 395–410 (2007)

8. Godoy, M., Rusu, C., Ugalde, J.: A preliminary methodology for information consumer experience evaluation. In: International Conference on Human-Computer Interaction, pp. 506–519. Springer (2023)

9. Godoy, M.P., Rusu, C., Ugalde, J.: Information consumer experience: a Chilean case study. In: International Conference on Human-Computer Interaction, pp. 248–267. Springer (2022)

10. Godoy, M.P., Rusu, C., Ugalde, J.: Information consumer experience: a systematic review. Appl. Sci. **12**(24) (2022). https://doi.org/10.3390/app122412630

11. Gunadham, T., Thammakoranonta, N.: Knowledge management systems functionalities enhancement in practice. In: Proceedings of the 5th International Conference on Frontiers of Educational Technologies - ICFET 2019. ACM Press (2019). https://doi.org/10.1145/3338188.3338213

12. Hossain, M.E., Mahmud, I., Idrus, R.M.: Modelling end users' continuance intention to use information systems in academic settings: expectation-confirmation and stress perspective. Interdiscipl. J. Inf. Knowl. Manag. **16**, 371–395 (2021). https://doi.org/10.28945/4841 https://doi.org/10.28945/4841 https://doi.org/10.28945/4841 https://doi.org/10.28945/4841

13. Hou, A.C., Chen, Y.C., Shang, R.A.: Mutual relations in ERP implementation: the impacts of work alienation and organizational support in state-owned enterprise. Procedia Comput. Sci. **100**, 1289–1296 (2016). https://doi.org/10.1016/j.procs.2016.09.244

14. Keiningham, T., et al.: Customer experience driven business model innovation. J. Bus. Res. **116**, 431–440 (2020)

15. Kumar, S., Verma, P., Patel, P., Rajesh, J.I.: Perceptions of Indian managers on the impact of convergent technologies on work and resultant organisational performance in service industry. Int. J. Emerg. Mark. **17**(2), 550–573 (2020). https://doi.org/10.1108/ijoem-06-2020-0658

16. Lemon, K.N., Verhoef, P.C.: Understanding customer experience throughout the customer journey. J. Mark. **80**(6), 69–96 (2016)

17. Marquez, J.J., Downey, A., Clement, R.: Walking a mile in the user's shoes: customer journey mapping as a method to understanding the user experience. Internet Ref. Serv. Q. **20**(3–4), 135–150 (2015)

18. Meyer, C., Schwager, A., et al.: Understanding customer experience. Harv. Bus. Rev. **85**(2), 116 (2007)

19. Olivares, M.P.G., Rusu, C., Granollers, T.: Hacia una metodología de evaluación de la experiencia del consumidor de información. Rev. AIPO **4**(2), 9–18 (2023)

20. Pigg, S., Lauren, B., Keller, E.J.: Designing for learning experiences. In: Proceedings of the 35th ACM International Conference on the Design of Communication. ACM (2017). https://doi.org/10.1145/3121113.3121127

21. S. D. Organization: BPMN specification - business process model and notation (2023). https://www.bpmn.org/

22. Shamsi, M., Iakovleva, T., Olsen, E., Bagozzi, R.P.: Employees' work-related well-being during COVID-19 pandemic: an integrated perspective of technology acceptance model and JD-r theory. Int. J. Environ. Res. Public Health **18**(22), 11888 (2021). https://doi.org/10.3390/ijerph182211888

23. Strong, D.M., Lee, Y.W., Wang, R.Y.: Data quality in context. Commun. ACM **40**(5), 103–110 (1997)

24. Temkin, B.D.: Mapping the customer journey. Forrester Res. **3**, 20 (2010)

Unlocking Multilingualism: Thoughts Shaped by Tools?

Carina Ulrika Groener and Anna Zanina

University of St. Gallen, Dufourstrasse 50, 9000 St. Gallen, Switzerland
`{carina.groener,anna.zanina}@unisg.ch`

Abstract. This paper analyses how the persuasive form of AI-generated editing suggestions for language and style in academic writing can manipulate the usage of AI-tools from supporting learning processes to outsourcing sub-tasks - especially for multilingual writers. In a qualitative analysis comparing an undergraduate student draft introduction with a fully AI-generated and two AI-edited versions (one where AI-editing has a dominator function, i.e. there are no explanations and the user only needs to control the output and one with an operator function, with marked changes and explanations also supporting critical evaluation and learning processes). The results show that AI-editing as dominator produces a larger number of changes compared to AI-editing as operator, and these changes also affect content and meaning. Together with the persuasive phrasing of AI outputs and the writers' expectation of efficiency, this contributes to support an uncritical way of usage. This can be problematic for undergraduate multilingual writers in particular, as they still lack the language skills and knowledge about academic writing conventions to be able to critically evaluate the AI-suggested output they are responsible for. In addition to that, the comparison also shows that changes through AI-editing stay on the language surface. Argumentation-related effects or errors indicating the learning level like mentioning academic titles of authors or very generalized method descriptions stay unchanged in the AI-editing process. These errors can serve as valuable indicators to discriminate AI-edited from fully AI-generated texts especially at undergraduate level.

Keywords: Academic Writing · Undergraduate Level · AI-editing of Language and Style · ChatGPT for Editing · Multilingual Writing · Discrimination of AI-edited and Completely AI-generated Texts · Interrelation of Language and Thought · Writing and Thinking

1 Introduction

Many researchers and students worldwide engage in multilingual educational environments due to English as a lingua franca for academic discourse. Although being used to writing in more than one language, reading academic texts, building arguments and expressing ideas in a foreign language often seems difficult for multilingual writers (Amano et al. 2024). This is because academic writing courses for multilingual writers often focus on "fixing mistakes" in the target language language but only rarely include multilingual approaches into the writing processes (Brinkschulte et al. 2015, p. 20).

© The Author(s), under exclusive license to Springer Nature Switzerland AG 2026
A. Coman et al. (Eds.): HCII 2025, LNCS 16337, pp. 236–254, 2026.
https://doi.org/10.1007/978-3-032-12801-0_16

Therefore, AI-tools based on Large Language Models (LLMs) are raising hopes of many multilingual writers to make writing processes faster and more efficient than ever before through the options of AI translation, editing and text generation. In educational and research environments recommendations for the use of AI-tools emphasize that these tools must be used in compliance with academic integrity standards. Such recommendations for education often emphasize that using AI-tools should support learning processes instead of outsourcing processes completely to these tools (Rickert 2024, Steinhoff 2025). However, the persuasive form AI- generated text-outputs have and are presented with could possibly undermine this recommendation.

This paper investigates how LLM outputs, here Chat GPT 4o (Open AI 2024), are presented and how different ways of using them for editing encourage methods of utilisation that rather outsource work steps in multilingual academic writing instead of supporting learning processes. Therefore, we use a qualitative analysis and compare four different undergraduate term paper draft introductions - one fully AI-generated, one human draft introduction and two different AI-edited versions (one with marked changes and explanations for the changes and one without). This comparison focuses on typical characteristics of academic language and style, in order to draw conclusions about how AI usage could be influenced by the persuasive form of these outputs and how the use of AI as an editing tool can provide valuable insights into students' learning processes.

First, we explain the interrelation between language and thought grounded on Bühler's concept of language as a tool (Buehler 1982) and Vygotsky's concept of "higher mental functions" (Kozulin 2012, xi) to show the differing perceptions of language influence on thought. Second, we introduce multilingual text production using Knorr's (2025) cascading model for academic text production as well as her language-sensitive competence model for academic writing to show that over longer periods of the writing process, heuristic thinking and idea generation run parallel to reading, text drafting and editing. Multilingual writers then use their whole repertoire of languages in these processes especially when it comes to aspects of argumentation, formulating ideas, re-reading and editing their own texts (Knorr 2025, pp. 100–101). Here, we assume that the use of AI-tools by multilingual writers for text formulation and editing can influence thoughts and ideas presented in argumentation significantly, because multilingual writers often do not feel very articulate in their writing language and thus tend to accept the AI-proposed improvements. Third, in order to analyze changes through AI-editing, we conducted two sets of AI-language editing processes using Chat GPT4o with an anonymized undergraduate student draft text example, one using a short zero-shot prompt only asking for an improved text output. In the second editing process we designed a simple tutor function and asked to mark the proposed changes and explain them. This comparative setting allows us to analyze the amount and the type of changes. In this context the persuasive form of AI-generated text or unexplained proposed changes together with the multilingual writers' insecurity and wish to improve efficiency can lead to immediate acceptance instead of critical evaluation and learning. This can be problematic when multilingual writers bear full responsibility for compliance with the codes of conduct of academic integrity and correctness of content as responsible authors (Brommer et al. 2023) without having necessary language competencies to control these outputs. Because in the end, it is the final text that is graded or perceived as the authors' thoughts.

2 Language, Thought and Multilingual Academic Writing

2.1 Acquisition of Language and Academic Discourse

By approaching the instrumental character of human language in the context of computer-generated language, we address two scholars who have investigated the ontogenesis of thought, reasoning and the verbalisation of thought. Karl Buehler presented a language model of thinking as a synthesis of language and logos. Furthermore, he positioned human speech within the category of speech acts, from which a linguistic product is generated (Buehler 1982/1934, p. 53). Buehler's organon model - referring to Aristotle - conceives of language as a tool with which the sender conveys and communicates topics and facts to the receiver through representation, expression and appeal. The speech acts and their products form linguistic concepts.

Lev Vygotsky, for his part, recognised the central significance of language to the formation of terms for cognitive development. He conceived the theory that language itself contains a semantic argumentative structure which shapes and determines human thoughts (Kozulin 2012, p. lvi). This led him to assert that thought evolves through language - a consecutive continuation of Buehler's view (Vygotsky 2003/1925, pp. 129–174). Vygotsky examined academic language particularly with regard to its role in cognitive development and the way it influences thinking. In his work 'Thought and Language' (2012/1934), he emphasises that what he calls "scientific" language plays a crucial role in the developmental process of thinking. For him, it is not just an extension of everyday language, but a separate form of language that is linked to specific thought processes and cognitive structures (Vygotsky 2002/1934). Vygotsky regarded the language of science as a special form of language that promotes abstract and theoretical thinking. It differs fundamentally from everyday language, which is primarily focussed on direct, concrete experiences and social interactions. Academic language, on the other hand, makes it possible to develop abstract concepts that are not directly linked to specific objects or experiences. This leads to a higher level of categorisation and generalisation and promotes the development of abstract, systematic thinking. Vygotsky also characterised academic language as a central element of development. He emphasised that the acquisition of academic concepts and the ability to use them correctly play a central role in learning and the advancement of cognitive skills. Introduction to academic language enables learners to engage with abstract concepts, generalise and think systematically - skills that are essential for later scientific and intellectual success. Academic language, according to Vygotsky, is a tool that enables the individual to organise and structure thinking. By changing the language of thought - from concrete, everyday language to abstract, scientific language - the individual's cognitive abilities are brought to a higher level. This change in the use of words is therefore not only a linguistic process, but also a profound cognitive one. Through the confrontation with terminology, these terms become increasingly precise and abstract. The transition from every day to academic language is therefore a gradual process that is closely linked to the development of higher mental functions. Vygotsky emphasises that this change in word use can bring about a change in thinking because language acts as a tool for thinking (Vygotsky 2012/1934, p. 155–221).

Examples from communicative practice in academia and academic writing support the proposition of multilingualism manifesting itself not only in the minimal form of a hybrid lingua franca at the cutting edge of the publication language. Indeed, many publications in English are only monolingual on the surface and conceal layers of verbalization in other languages. Vygotsky's concepts highlight the importance of linguistic frameworks for reasoning to evolve. Since a rapidly computer-generated text supersedes autonomous phrasing and frees the users from the need to construct a sentence as an entire syntactic sequence, users are more likely to adopt simplified constructions from an AI-proposed text.

Language plays a crucial role in organizing and processing knowledge, by being implemented in interaction and cognitive processing, highlighting two key assertions: the potential limitations of a single linguistic structure in encompassing diverse perspectives, and the centrality of language to cognitive processes and social interaction. Linguistic structures categorize and represent different types of information (e.g., spatial relations, causality, a change in an attribute of one of the verb's arguments), which affects how individuals conceptualize the world. If a particular linguistic structure dominates a text, it might restrict the way in which individuals from diverse cultural or linguistic backgrounds can express and understand particular cognitive concepts, limiting cognitive flexibility and cultural expression.

In academic context, thoughts and ideas are conventionally presented in written form, the terminology of which belongs to the category of specialised languages. Galbraith and Torrence (1999) emphasize that academic writing involves multiple local and global cycles of constraint satisfaction, where each cycle represents a self-driven process of idea generation, refinement, and articulation. These cycles are iterative, allowing the writer's implicit knowledge, dispositions, and current thoughts to interact dynamically, leading to the emergence of new understanding or perspectives as the writer progresses through drafts and revisions (p. 141). Galbraith's model indicates that during each cycle, the writer's mental network experiences constraint satisfaction processes - activating, inhibiting, and resolving various elements - resulting in the creation and reshaping of ideas. Inhibitory feedback mechanisms facilitate transitions between stable states, supporting the evolution of ideas across cycles. Knowledge is viewed as an active, dynamic construct, continuously shaped through these cyclical processes where ideas are reorganized, refined, and expanded, ultimately producing coherent written work (Galbraith 1999, p. 143). Work cycles - comparable to Vygosky's formation's way description of connection between thought and word, "which is neither preformed nor constant and emerges in the course of development" (Vygotsky 2012/1930, pp. xlvi/p. 110) - serve as operational frameworks within which implicit knowledge is dynamically constructed, transformed, and articulated in writing, highlighting the active and iterative nature of knowledge development.

There are several models for academic text production, such as Flower and Hayes (1981) who identify "planning, translating and reviewing" as the three central aspects of the writing process (p. 370). They define writing "as a set of distinctive thinking processes which writers orchestrate or organize during the act of composing" (p. 366), a definition underlining the interrelation of thinking and writing in the writing process. Another one is Kruse's (2007) circular model of the writing process that includes four phases: "planning and coordinating", "collecting material and data", "working on the text and reviewing" and "finalizing and publishing" (p. 112).

Knorr's (2025) cascade model of text production contains seven overlapping phases: "discovery phase, data collection and analysis phase, text production phase, revision phase, completion phase, examination phase and publication phase" which correspond with also overlapping writing-related activities like "reading texts by other authors, epistemic-heuristic writing, data collection, preparation and analysis, formulating one's own text, reading texts by other authors, reading one's own text" (p. 85). This model shows that defining a research question, reading other author's texts, drafting one's own text and reviewing often overlap in writer's text production and contribute to the process of developing ideas and building arguments. In her language-sensitive competence model for academic writing, she includes the dimension of language including all linguistic and literal experiences of an individual into the textual and linguistic requirements for academic writing. Within the fields of knowledge, the dimension of language influences the field of declarative knowledge, e.g., when realizing text-structures or authorship, academic language and technical terminology or using grammar and vocabulary. The field of procedural knowledge is largely based on the dimension of language. e.g., how one's own claims and positions are communicated, how readers' needs, text structures, subject specific conventions, citations and paraphrases are realized and how different linguistic properties of written language are encoded. This language-sensitive competence model for academic writing can help to understand and describe individual writers' literal and linguistic levels of knowledge (pp. 99–101), and thus including multilingualism into text production.

2.2 Multilingual Text Production with or Without AI-Tools

Multilingualism can generally be understood as "the ability of societies, institutions, groups and individuals to engage, on a regular basis, with more than one language in their day-to-day lives" (EPRS 2022, p. 2). In higher education multilingualism becomes more and more important, due to multilingual students, student mobility and many English Medium Language study programs worldwide, which lead to a multilingual learning environment. In these multilingual learning environments students use translingual practices, such as navigating fluidly between different language repertoires (Canagarajah 2013) not only for speaking but also in order to manage complex communication tasks like academic writing. Nevertheless, most multilingual writers have at least one dominant or strong language, their most proficient language (Silva-Corvalán & Treffers-Daller 2016). However, Brinkschulte et al. (2015) showed that many standard writing courses do not include translingual practices, but they focus more on improving students' study language skills "in a very product-oriented manner" (p. 20). This strong focus on the study language supports these students' insecurity during the writing process because it focuses on the mistakes made in the study language and can cause difficulties for multilingual students to express their ideas and thoughts in the drafting process (Rohmah & Muslim 2021). Multilingual writers' texts often contain typical mistakes like a lack of clarity, uncommon grammatical structures, deviations in technical terms and reduced vocabulary or redundant phrases (Saber et al. 2020). Especially in drafts of inexperienced writers, grammatical structures of the dominant language are adapted, an effect called "cross linguistic transfer" (Berzak, et al. 2014). In this context, the rise of LLMs can bear great advantages especially for multilingual writers, as they can easily translate or rephrase text parts in order to help express and formulate one's own ideas and arguments. But it can also be tempting to use AI-tools to formulate ideas, without paying much attention to precise terminology or meaning. Therefore, the use of AI-tools heavily influences and maybe even promotes translingual practices, like mixing languages while thinking, paraphrasing, building arguments or drafting a text, when used carefully for specific tasks in the writing process.

2.3 Aspects of Academic Writing Conventions, Language and Style

One sub-task, where AI-tools are often used in academic writing, is editing, for conciseness, academic language and style. Academic writing conventions are subject-specific, like preferred citation-styles, or language-specific, like the use of "I", "we" or the frequency of passive voice in different academic text genres. Macgilchrist (2014) names six general conventions of academic writing:" Key structures: Writing paragraphs and topic sentences, Key directions: Using signposts, Key persons: Writing "I", "we" or in passive voice, Key actions: more verbs, less nouns, Key genders: Using gender-inclusive language, Key sources: Citing other research" (p. 5). Most undergraduate multilingual writers feel insecure about these conventions of academic writing. Especially multilingual writers do not only need to adapt to the conventions of academic research and learn subject-specific technical terms and discourse in their study language, but they need to navigate between different languages to do so. This is why they hope that AI-tools can support them.

Criteria of academic language and style include a detached and authoritative voice for presenting the authors' positions for objectivity, logically structured texts, conciseness and density realized through formal, objective and precise terminology and complex grammar (Snow & Ucelli 2009, pp. 118–119). This includes longer sentences with more subordinate clauses and nominalization, but also the correct linking and structure words to underline the logical and organized structure of the argumentation as well as precise technical terminology and hedging. Hedging means using expressions, limiting the scope of a claim within academic argumentation, in order to express insights as precisely as possible. Most common in English are adjective or adverbial hedges like "presumably", but also modal verbs like "can" or "should", quantifiers like "some" and conversational phrases like "sort of" can be used to limit the scope of a statement (Hinkel 2003, pp. 316–324).

From these above-mentioned general conventions, higher order concerns (HOC), such as logically structured reasoning, hedging and writing in paragraphs including topic sentences as well as choosing correct discipline-specific terminology directly impact content, argumentation quality and also the final text's evaluation (Beals 2016 p. 119). Multilingual writers often focus on the logical structure of the text and the argumentation when editing and are therefore working with HOC. Lower order concerns (LOC) focus on basic rules of language, like correct grammar, spelling, punctuation or the mechanical consistency of citations - it is necessary to check these LOCs through proofreading

(Beals 2016, p. 118). Especially for second language or multilingual writers, language insecurities and insufficient writing practice can be important reasons for writing anxiety (Kusumaningputri, et al. 2018).

2.4 AI Usage Between Ghostwriting and AI-Tutoring

Using AI-tools in academic writing and education is still discussed controversially: One the one hand AI-tools are seen as a promising aid to improve the quality of writing especially for second language or multilingual writers (Faisal & Carabella 2023), on the other hand there are concerns about possible negative effects of AI usage, like decreasing capability of critical thinking and cognitive offloading (Gerlich 2025), "deskilling" as dequalification with a loss of competence (Reimann 2023, p. 4) or "unauthorized content generation" (Foltynek et al. 2023, p. 2). In this context "hiding the use of AI or automated tools in the creation of content or drafting of publications" (ALLEA 2023, p. 10) is seen as a violation of research integrity. With regard to positive or negative effects of AI usage, it seems to be crucial how exactly AI is used in academic writing as Buck and Wessels (2025) point out. They emphasize "AI-Leadership" (p. 868) as one of the most important future skills and differentiate between three stages of AI agency and human responsibility: As dominator AI creates texts and content more or less independently and humans' control and correct if necessary. As facilitator, AI-tools and humans collaborate closely and equally, while AI makes suggestions and humans improve and refine. As an operator AI is used as a support tool offering proposals or analysis and only humans decide about the content (pp. 869–870). Building on Hayes' (1996) model of the writing process, Buck and Limburg (2024) differentiate four categories of using AI-tools: an unreflected use, where AI-tools replace thinking and learning. Another way of usage can be seen, where AI-tools relieve cognition through offloading lower order concerns to an AI-tool, like stylistic or language corrections of a draft text, or where they support cognition, for example when AI-tools explain technical terminology or help to find synonyms. The most advanced way to use AI-tools is to expand human thought in a metacognitive use, e.g., when AI-tools give feedback on human arguments (pp. 11–15). Especially when AI-tools are used to support or enhance human thinking, a high level of writing competencies is necessary and time-saving effects are only minor (Buck 2025, p. 84). In educational contexts these different ways of using AI-tools from unreflected to metacognitive use are reflected in ethical guidelines, most of which require acknowledging the use of AI-tools (Foltynetk et al. 2023, p. 2). Rickert (2023) summarizes the different possible roles of AI-tools in the writing process as tutor, co-author or ghostwriter. In educational contexts it is recommended to use AI-tools as tutors to enhance the learning process instead of using them as a ghostwriter. However, the persuasive form of AI-generated outputs together with language insecurity and significant time-saving effects rather undermine a reflected use of AI-tools that enhances learning especially for undergraduate multilingual writers.

3   Comparison of AI-Generated, AI-Edited and Human Draft Introduction

3.1   Materials and Methods

In order to be able to analyse this persuasive effect, we chose an explorative approach of qualitative analysis, where we compare an undergraduate student draft introduction with two different AI-edited versions and a completely AI-generated introduction. This qualitative approach allows us to analyse the number and linguistic quality of the AI text outputs. The anonymized student example is a draft introduction of an undergraduate term paper with English level B2 in the Common European Reference Framework (CERF). With this authentic human draft, we conducted two sets of AI-language editing processes using Chat GPT4o (Open AI 2024). We chose an introduction as a formali-zed text part for comparison, because it has three steps, a first passage to gain the readers' attention, a second to introduce the research question and a third for the description of the procedure. The human draft contains different typical mistakes, which we expected to be corrected in the editing process: mistakes of spelling, grammar and technical termi-nology, but also mistakes regarding the conventions of academic criteria and style, like missing hedges, unclear or inconsistent terminology, inconsistent structure or a vague method description or academic degrees for authors when introducing paraphrases.

In order to come close to current undergraduate student AI usage, we worked with a simple prompting technique, which uses simple zero-shot prompts. We conducted two sets of AI-editing attempts: First, we prompted: "Please refine this introduction of an academic term paper regarding logical argumentation, text coherence and grammar and spelling" only asking for an improved text output. This prompt does not contain a role, context or detailed descriptions of academic language criteria, because many undergraduate students do not yet know which prompting technique to use for which purpose or which criteria exactly academic language and style need to fulfill. In this way of AI-editing the tool is used as a dominator (Buck & Wessels 2025, pp. 869–870) to whom one outsources the editing process and only checks if it sounds "good". In the second attempt we used the prompt "Act like a tutor for academic writing at university level. Please refine this introduction of an academic term paper regarding logical argumentation, text coherence and grammar and spelling. Please mark all changes in a track change mode and explain why you proposed these changes." In this prompt the tool serves as an operator (Buck& Wessels 2025, pp. 869–870), comparable to a human editor, who should leave the final decision about changes to the responsible author and provide explanations for the proposed changes and therefore help to improve writing competencies and to keep full responsibility about the changes in the text.

For the fully AI-generated text, we used the original research question for the human draft with the prompt: "Act like an undergraduate student of business studies. Create an introduction for an academic term paper about the research question: How can genetic engineering ensure the food supply for the world's population?"

3.2   Comparison of Undergraduate Introductions

All undergraduate introductions, fully AI-generated, AI-edited either as dominator or as operator, as well as the human draft version, share a similar argument structure: They contain three paragraphs, starting with a general statement about the relevance of the overall topic, then lead to the more specific subject "genetically modified food". After that, they present the research question and describe the following text structure. The human draft contains typical effects of multilingual writing and inexperience with the conventions of academic writing, like reduced and redundant vocabulary ("new" is used twice in the same sentence), the usage of unusual grammatical structures like passive often adapted from the first or dominant language, ("are increasingly being discussed"), or unnecessary citations meant to prove general statements "(UNFPA 2018)". Looking at the fully AI-generated introduction, we see no word repetitions, an extended vocabulary like "limited arable land, and water scarcity" (Open AI 2024) unusual for undergraduate writers, no unusual grammar and a mentioning of statistical numbers ("expected to reach nearly 10 billion by 2050", Open AI 2024), which can be seen as matching characteristics of academic style and language. However, for statistical numbers a citation would be required. Comparing the human draft and the AI-generated introduction for the same research question, the AI-generated text shows a native-like language level with extended technical terminology. This huge difference in language performance alone must have a very impressive effect on undergraduate multilingual academic writers, making their own draft texts look even more deficient and support their wish to have their language and style improved by AI-tools (Table 1).

In the AI-edited version without markings and explanations, AI serves as dominator (Buck & Wessels 2025, pp. 869–870). After the prompt "Please refine this introduction of an academic term paper regarding logical argumentation, text coherence and grammar and spelling", the tool presents its output with the following phrase claiming to have exactly done what it was asked for: "Here is a refined version of your introduction, improved for logical flow, coherence, academic tone, grammar, and spelling" (Open AI 2024). This presentation phrase alone has a strong persuasive function, as it claims to have precisely fulfilled the user's advice. Without markings and explanations it is up to the user to critically check if this is really the case, what exactly was changed and how, a task requiring advanced linguistic and academic knowledge and counteracting efficiency.

In the first paragraph we observe that an unusual passive construction originally transferred from the dominant language German was changed into a more natural English nominal construction "are increasingly a topic of" (Open AI 2024). Also choosing "public and scientific discourse" (Open AI 2024) instead of "discussed in the media" (undergraduate student draft) matches academic terminology and style more precisely as the human original. However, the aspect of "scientific" (Open AI 2024) is added as a completely new aspect of meaning, which had not been part of the human original. The redundant, but objective usage of "new" in "new challenges that raise new questions" in the human draft becomes "unprecedented challenges, prompting critical questions" (Open AI 2024), a strong intensification of meaning caused by these different adjectives, which cannot be found in the original. At the end of the paragraph, the unnecessary citation is missing. In this first paragraph we see improved grammar and terminology, and a removed citation, but also two cases of changed meaning compared to the original.

When treated as an operator and asked to mark the changes in a track change mode and explain the proposed changes, we count 7 passages changed, instead of 9 changes

Table 1. Comparison of authentic human, AI-generated, AI-edited (as dominator or operator) introductions, first paragraph.

human original	The current changes of the environment on earth are increasingly being discussed in the media. The growing population of the world and climate change are presenting humanity with new challenges that raise new questions, such as how to deal with increasing periods of drought or what resources are available to meet the food needs of the growing world population. (UNFPA 2018).
AI-generated (Open AI 2024)	In today's world, securing a stable food supply is one of the most pressing global challenges. As the global population continues to grow—expected to reach nearly 10 billion by 2050—the demand for food will increase dramatically. Traditional agricultural methods may not be sufficient to meet this rising demand, especially considering factors like climate change, limited arable land, and water scarcity. This has led scientists, policymakers, and businesses to explore innovative solutions, among which genetic engineering has emerged as a particularly promising technology.
AI-edited, as dominator, (Open AI 2024) changes underlined	The ongoing environmental changes on Earth are increasingly a topic of public and scientific discourse. Global population growth and climate change are presenting humanity with unprecedented challenges, prompting critical questions such as how to manage prolonged droughts and how to meet the rising demand for food.
AI-edited as operator (Open AI 2024) with marked changes and explanations	The current changes of the environment on earth [**environmental changes affecting the Earth**] are increasingly being discussed in the media. The growing population of the world [**global population**] and climate change are presenting humanity with new challenges that raise new [**critical**] questions, such as how to deal with increasing periods of drought [**prolonged droughts**] or what resources are avail-able [**available**] to meet the food needs [**nutritional demands**] of the growing world population [**global population**] (UNFPA 2018).

in the unmarked version. The output is presented again claiming to have precisely done what was asked for: "Below is your introduction with tracked changes using brackets and explanations following each change. I've focused on improving logical argumentation, text coherence, academic tone, and grammar/spelling" (Open AI 2024). All changes are marked as asked for, but explanations are short and exemplary, not every change proposed is provided with an explanation. This effect can most likely be improved by using more elaborate prompting techniques, like Chain-of- Thought prompting or using specialized AI-tools especially designed for editing purposes. However, on the one hand many undergraduate students do not yet know which specialized tools to use for which steps in the writing process and many universities do not yet provide student licenses for such tools.

Again, unusual grammatical expressions, which are representations of the student writers' dominant language are replaced by natural English: "environmental changes affecting the Earth" (Open AI 2024) instead of "The current changes of the environment on earth" in the human original. Chat GPT's explanation for this change is not really helpful for learning purposes because it depicts the linguistic effect of the change, not the grammatical reason: "Clarity and conciseness: Replaced vague or redundant expressions (e.g., "changes of the environment on earth") with more precise academic language" (Open AI 2024). Other changes of more precise academic terminology like "nutritional demands" (Open AI 2024) instead of "food needs" (human original) are not listed. Compared with the undocumented AI-editing version, the redundant "new" (human original) is replaced once by "critical challenges" (Open AI 2024), which changes the original meaning much less compared to the uncommented version. In addition to that, at the end of the paragraph the unnecessary citation remains and also keeps this version much closer to the original.

When comparing the second paragraph of the undergraduate student draft and the fully AI-generated text the huge difference between language levels of an undergraduate human multilingual writer and AI-generated text becomes even more obvious regarding the range of technical and academic vocabulary, grammar and academic style. This could contribute to multilingual authors being tempted to have texts generated and formulated by the AI instead of putting thoughts into words themselves.

In the AI-edited versions, there are 12 changes in the AI as dominator version and 9 changes in the operator version with marked changes. Mistakes in spelling are corrected, as well as unusual formatting of the in-text citation in both versions. Also in the AI-editing as dominator version more precise subject specific terminology is used: "potentially reducing environmental impact" (Open AI 2024) instead of "be more envirnonmentally freindly" (human original) and an additional sentence to underline the weighing between two positions is introduced: "However, genetically modified foods remain controversial" (Open AI 2024). This additional sentence cannot be found in the AI as operator version (Table 2).

Again, the fully AI-generated passage shows a remarkable range of technical terminology and balanced argumentation: "the widespread use of genetically modified organisms (GMOs) raises important economic, ethical, and regulatory questions" (Open AI 2024). Most remarkable in this paragraph is the introduction of stronger and more frequently used hedges through AI-editing as dominator like in "One potential solution

Table 2. Comparison of human, AI-generated, AI-edited (as dominator or operator) introductions, second paragraph.

human original	For food industry it can be genetically modified foods, which are seen as a promise for a better future. They should ensure food security and be more envirnomentally [sic!] freindly [sic!] (Gu X. (2023). pp. 170–173) At the same time, critics like Professor Lappé argue that the cultivation of genetically modified foods not only pollutes the environment, but also plunges farmers into social dependency (Lappé et al. 1998).
AI-generated (Open AI 2024)	Genetic engineering involves altering the DNA of crops to improve their yield, resistance to pests and diseases, tolerance to harsh environmental conditions, and nutritional value. However, while the scientific potential is clear, the widespread use of genetically modified organisms (GMOs) raises important economic, ethical, and regulatory questions. From a business perspective, it is also important to consider how genetic engineering can contribute to food security while balancing public trust, market dynamics, and international trade policies.
AI-edited as dominator (Open AI 2024)	One potential solution discussed in the context of the food industry is the development and use of genetically modified (GM) foods. These are often regarded as a promising approach to ensuring food security while potentially reducing environmental impact (Gu 2023, pp. 170–173). However, genetically modified foods remain controversial. Critics, such as Professor Lappé, argue that the cultivation of GM crops can harm the environment and lead to socio-economic dependencies among farmers (Lappé et al. 1998).

(continued)

Table 2. (*continued*)

AI-edited as operator, incl. Documentation and explanation (Open AI 2024)	For food industry it can be [**In the food industry,**] genetically modified foods [**(GM) foods**] which are seen as a promise for a better future [**are viewed by some as a potential solution for a more sustainable future**]. They should ensure [**are expected to improve**] food se-curity [**security**] and be more envirnomentally freindly [**environmentally friendly**] (Gu, X. (2023). p. 170–173 [**2023, pp. 170–173**]). At the same time, critics like Pro-fessor [**Professor**] Lappé argue that the cultivation of genetically modified foods [**crops**] not only pollutes the environment, but also plunges farmers into social dependency [**leads to social and economic dependency among farmers**] (Lappé et al. 1998).

discussed in the context of food industry" (Open AI 2024) instead of "For food industry it can be" (human original and Open AI 2024, operator) or "These are often regarded" (Open AI 2024) instead of "They should ensure" (human original and Open AI, 2024, Operator), the student draft uses simpler words and interestingly enough these are also preserved in the AI-editing as operator version. These changes show that multilingual writers with limited knowledge of academic phrasing and vocabulary rather use modal verbs like "can" or "should" for hedging instead of passive phrases including adjectives and adverbs with restrictive meaning. Here the student draft clearly shows the learning process: on the one hand the use of modal verbs shows that the student tries to use hedging and more precise language to express the scope of the argument, on the other hand as undergraduate the student cannot yet use more grammatically complex and variable academic hedges. This process of academic socialisation can also be observed in the use of undergraduate students' phrases introducing foreign positions such as "critics, such as Professor Lappé" (human original), where the academic position of the author cited is mentioned to underline the authority argument function. This phenomenon can be observed in the student draft as well as in both AI-edited versions. Although mentioning academic positions is unusual in academic texts, common "mistakes" like this clearly show the learning process of students just starting their socialisation with academic discourse conventions and finding them in undergraduate texts could possibly help to differentiate AI-edited from fully AI-generated texts.

The last paragraph of the undergraduate introduction presents the research question and introduces the basic structure. The student draft version starts with the research question "How can genetic engineering ensure the food supply for the world's population?" This research question is also a part of the AI-generated version, as it was a part of the prompt used to generate the introduction. For an undergraduate term paper this research question would be too broad, as its attempt is to solve a global problem, it needs to be refined to a much more limited scope. In the AI-generated text this leads to a very extensive description of procedure. The paper wants to "analyze the benefits and risks of using genetic engineering in agriculture, examine case studies where genetically modified crops have impacted food production, and consider the role of businesses and governments in promoting sustainable and responsible biotechnological innovations" (Open AI 2024). This sounds academic on the surface but includes at least three different aspects of the topic, each of which would be enough for a thesis at least. The student draft describes the research method used as "To answer this question academic literature will be used" (human original). Again, this typical undergraduate phenomenon shows that students have learned to include the research method into the introduction, but they are not yet aware how to precisely do that in their subject or genre.

Table 3. Comparison of human, AI-generated, AI-edited (as dominator or operator) introductions, third paragraph.

human original	The present work focuses on the question: "How can genetic engineering ensure the food supply for the world's population?" To answer this question academic literature will be used. The first chapter begins by explaining what exactly genetically modified food is. In addition, this chapter explains both the opportunities and the dangers of genetically modified food. It then explains the legal framework in the US. The last chapter answers the actual research question. It explains how genetically modified food can ensure the supply of food for the world's population and what the future of these technologies will look like.
AI-generated (Open AI 2024)	This term paper explores the research question: **How can genetic engineering ensure the food supply for the world's population?** It will analyze the benefits and risks of using genetic engineering in agriculture, examine case studies where genetically modified crops have impacted food production, and consider the role of businesses and governments in promoting sustainable and responsible biotechnological innovations. Understanding these dynamics is crucial for developing effective strategies that address food security in a rapidly changing world.

(continued)

Table 3. (*continued*)

AI- edited as dominator (Open AI 2024)	This paper investigates the central question: How can genetic engineering contribute to ensuring the global food supply? To address this question, academic literature will be critically examined. The first chapter defines genetically modified food and outlines both the potential benefits and risks associated with its use. The second chapter provides an overview of the legal and regulatory framework in the United States. The final chapter directly addresses the research question by exploring how genetic engineering can help secure the global food supply and discusses possible future developments in this field.
AI- edited as operator (Open AI 2024), incl. documentation and explanation	**This paper explores the research question:** ***How can genetic engineering contribute to ensuring the global food supply?***] To answer this question[,] academic literature will be used **[academic literature will be analyzed]**. The first chapter begins by explaining what exactly genetically modified food is **[provides a definition of genetically modified food]**. In addition, this chapter explains both the opportunities and the dangers of genetically modified food **[GM foods]**. It then explains **[The following chapter outlines]** the legal framework in the US **[United States]**. The last chapter answers the actual research question. It explains how genetically modified food can ensure the supply of food for the world's population and what the future of these technologies will look like **[directly addresses the research question by examining the role of GM food in securing global nutrition and discussing the future prospects of genetic engineering technologies]**.

When explaining the basic structure of the following text the student draft uses the verb" explains" for the four different aspects mentioned, but it only speaks of "the first chapter" and "the last chapter" (student draft). The fully AI-generated text uses "analyze", "examine" and "consider" (Open AI 2024) and thus shows a larger range in terminology (Table 3).

When comparing the AI-edited versions, the AI-editing as dominator version shows 12 changed words or phrases, whereas the AI-edited as operator version including explanations has only 8 marked changes.

Again, we see the effects of hedging especially in the formulation of the research question in both AI-edited versions: "How can genetic engineering ensure" (student draft) becomes "How can genetic engineering contribute to ensure" (Open AI 2024, operator), a change that limits the scope of the question. This is also mentioned in the explanation for the changes: "Refinement of research question presentation: Italicized and reworded the research question to match academic conventions" (Open AI 2024). In addition to that, both AI-edited versions contain the description of the research method as "academic literature will be critically examined" (Open AI 2024) in the dominator and "academic literature will be analyzed" (Open AI 2024) in the operator version containing explanations, which is more precise than the human original "used", but would still be considered to be too general for a theoretical approach, while at the same time showing an important step in academic socialization. Therefore, such learning level indicator errors can serve as indicators to discriminate AI-edited from fully AI-generated texts.

In the student draft, only two chapters are mentioned with four content aspects to be covered in the description of the structure. The AI-editing as dominator version changes this into three chapters, which is a much more logical structure. In the AI as operator edited version with explanations, there is only "The first chapter" and "The last chapter", just two like in the student draft. This structural mistake is only fixed in the AI as dominator edited version. Not all proposed changes could be found in the explanations of the AI as operator edited version with explanations, instead these explanations were quite general: "Spelling and grammar: Corrected typos (e.g., "avail-able," "freindly") and standardized phrasing" (Open AI 2024).

When looking at the explanations for the marked changes given by ChatGPT 4o, explanations are only exemplary, not every change is explained, which impedes the controlling process and prevents learning. The aspect of logic is not improved in the AI-editing as operator version although mentioned in the presentation of the generated text. Especially in the AI-editing as operator, the changes are concerning grammar, spelling and style, aspects covered by proofreading, while content-related improvements of logic could only be found in the AI-editing as dominator version. At the same time changes of meaning could also only be found in the AI as dominator version.

To sum up, when analyzing the AI-edited versions of the human draft introduction, we see 33 words or phrases changed in the dominator AI-edited version and we only observe 24 changes using the AI-editing as operator version asking for markups and explanations. This means, in the AI-editing as operator version less changes are made and there are no significant changes in content and meaning, but also no improvements of logic. This is basically what proofreading does. The use of academic terminology and hedging is better and more suitable in the AI-editing as dominator version, also the proposed change for the structure. This means that for multilingual users at an undergraduate level of studies, who do not yet know much about the conventions of academic writing and their study subject, outputs of AI-editing as dominator must seem more persuasive, because the changes are more numerous and also affecting logic. This promise to quickly "fix" grammar, language and academic style instead of using a seemingly less efficient operator function with marked changes and explanations. A strong wish for efficiency and believing in superiority of AI-technique seems to correspond with a lack of trust in multilingual writers' language skills and supports a way of usage that outsources AI-editing to the tool using it in its dominator function and reducing possible learning effects and human control.

4 Conclusion

While for a long time, fluent language and a wide range of terminology was a valuable indicator also for the quality of arguments, working with AI-generated or AI-edited hybrid texts require to look behind the language surface. In our comparison the fully AI-generated version shows extensive technical terminology and correct and natural English phrases and grammar, the content and the mentioned methodology, here visible in the scope of the paper, is much too large for an undergraduate term paper.

Comparing two versions of AI-editing, one using AI-editing as a dominator, where the task of editing is done by AI and the human's role is to correct and the other using AI as operator, where the human has full control, in this case realized though the prompt asking for marking all the changes and for explanations, we observe that the number of changes was bigger in the dominator function and also the quality of changes had more influence on content and meaning, positive through fixing a logical inconsistency and negative through changes in meaning.

Typical effects of multilingually written draft texts, like unusual grammatical structures, redundant vocabulary and grammar and spelling mistakes as well as inconsistent in-text citations are corrected. In this context, AI-editing processes, as tested in this explorative setting, work well for "fixing language mistakes" on the language surface level. However, this would be considered proofreading instead of editing.

In contrast to fully AI-generated texts, AI-edited human texts still show argumentation-related effects or mistakes showing the writers' socialization with academic discourse, like redundant simple modal verbs as hedges, mentioning academic titles of authors or very generalized method descriptions. These errors indicating the learning level can serve as valuable indicators to discriminate AI-edited from fully AI-generated texts especially at undergraduate level.

As the use of AI-tools is more and more reflected and discussed also in the context of academic integrity, writers will become more aware of which tool to use, how and when and what kind of prompting techniques are needed for what kind of task. But for the current state, this qualitative approach can provide some explanations why AI-generated texts, fully generated or edited seem so persuasive for multilingual writers and therefore can also significantly influence these writers' thoughts and ideas.

As this qualitative analysis of an undergraduate human draft introduction compared with a fully AI-generated introduction and two different AI-edited versions show, AI outputs, not only fully generated, but also as AI-edited versions appear persuasive especially for multilingual writers feeling less secure in their writing language and hoping for efficiency in writing and editing processes. This persuasive effect consists of two main aspects: On the one hand it is the linguistically correct, fluent and discourse-adapted appearance of the generated or edited text-output in the AI-editing as dominator function showing a larger number of changes compared to the operator function with less changes. On the other hand, the persuasive appearance is created by the way AI-tools present their output, where they state that the required task was fulfilled, when the text output is presented. And it is up to the users to critically evaluate the output and find mistakes, a requirement that can be very difficult for undergraduate and multilingual writers who are still learning these academic writing criteria and their study language. This means that students need to be educated in how to communicate ideas with multilingual resources and how to use AI-tools responsibly in the drafting, writing and revisioning process.

References

ALLEA: The European Code of Conduct for Research Integrity (revised edition) (2023). https://doi.org/10.26356/ECOC

Amano, T., et al.: The manifold costs of being a non-native English speaker in science. PLOS Biol. **21**(7) (2023). https://doi.org/10.1371/journal.pbio.3002184

Beals, K.A.: Thinking through writing: guidelines for planning learner-centered instruction. Rowman & Littlefield Publishers, USA (2016)

Berzak, Y., Reichart, R., Katz, B.: Reconstructing native language typology from foreign language usage. In: Proceedings of the Eighteenth Conference on Computational Natural Language Learning, pp. 21–29, Ann Arbor, Michigan. Association for Computational Linguistics (2014)

Brinkschulte, M., Stoian, M.-E., Borges, E.: Resource-focused research for multilingual competence in scientific writing. J. Acad. Writ. **5**(1), 17–28 (2015). https://doi.org/10.18552/joaw.v5i1.159

Brommer, S., et al.: Wissenschaftliches Schreiben im Zeitalter von KI gemeinsam verantworten. Diskussionspapier Nr. 27. Berlin: Hochschulforum Digitalisierung (2023) https://hochschulforumdigitalisierung.de/wp-content/uploads/2023/11/HFD_DP_27_Schreiben_KI.pdf. Accessed 2 May 2025

Buck, I.: Wissenschaftliches Schreiben mit KI. Paderborn Brill/Schoeningh

Buck, I., Limburg, A.: KI und Kognition im Schreibprozess: Prototypen und Implikationen. Journal für Schreibwissenschaft **26**(1). 8–23 (2024)

Buck, I., Wessels, D.: Gut geführt = gut geschrieben? AI Leadership als relevante Kompetenz in der Kollaboration mit KI-Tools. In: Braegger, G. & Hans-Guenter, R. (Hrsg.): Handbuch Lernen mit digitalen Medien. Wege der Transformation. 3., aktualisierte und erweiterte Auflage, pp. 863–880 (2025)

Buehler, K.: Sprachtheorie. Fischer, Stuttgart (1982/ 1934)

Canagarajah, S.: Translingual practice. Global englishes and cosmopolitan relations. Routledge, Milton Park, Abingdon, Oxon (2013)

EPRS (European Parliamentary Research Service: "Multilingualism: than Language of the European Union. EPRS_BRI (2019)642207 (2022). https://www.europarl.europa.eu/RegData/etudes/BRIE/2019/642207/EPRS_BRI(2019)642207_EN.pdf. Accessed 18 April 2025

Faisal, F., Carabella, P.A.: Utilizing grammarly in an academic writing process: higher-education students' perceived views. J. English Lang. Teach. Linguist. **8**(1), 23 (2023). https://doi.org/10.21462/jeltl.v8i1.1006

Flower, L., Hayes, J.R.: A Cognitive Process Theory of Writing. Coll. Compos. Commun. **32**(4), 365–387 (1981). https://doi.org/10.2307/356600

Foltynek, T., et al.: ENAI Recommendations on the ethical use of Artificial Intelligence in Education. Int. J. Educ. Integr. **19**, 12 (2023). https://doi.org/10.1007/s40979-023-00133-4

Galbraith, D., Torrance, M.: Writing as a knowledge-constituting process. In: Knowing What to Write. Ams-terdam, NL. Amsterdam University Press, pp. 137–157 (1999)

Gerlich, M.: AI tools in society: impacts on cognitive offloading and the future of critical thinking. Societies **15**, 6 (2025). https://doi.org/10.3390/soc15010006

Hayes, J.R.: A new framework for understanding cognition and affect in writing. In: Levy, C.M., Ransdell, S. (eds.) The Science of Writing: Theories, Methods, Individual Differences, and Applications, pp. 1–27. Lawrence Erlbaum Associates, Inc. (1996)

Hinkel, E., Hinkel, E.: Teaching academic ESL writing: practical techniques in vocabulary and grammar, 1st edn. Routledge. New York (2003) https://doi.org/10.4324/9781410609427

Kozulin, A: Foreword. In: Hanfmann, E, Vakar, G., Kozulin, A. (eds.) Lev Vygotsky. Thought and Language. Revised and expanded edition, pp. ix–xxiii. Cambridge Massachusetts MIT Press (2012)

Kozulin, A.: Vygotsky in context. In: Hanfmann, E., Vakar, G., Kozulin, A. (eds.) Lev Vygotsky. Thought and Language. Revised and expanded edition, pp. xxv–lxxvii, Cambridge Massachusetts MIT Press (2012/1986)

Kusumaningputri, R., Ningsih, T.A., Wisasongko, W.: Second language writing anxiety of Indonesian EFL students. Lingua Cultura **12**(4), 357 (2018) https://doi.org/10.21512/lc.v12i4.4268

Knorr, D.: Schreibberatung. Eine Systematik. Boehlau, Wien (2025)

Kruse, O.: Keine Angst vor dem leeren Blatt. Ohne Schreibblockaden durchs Studium. Campus Verlag, Frankfurt a.M. (2007)

Macgilchrist, F.: Academic writing. Ferdinand Schoeningh Paderborn (2014)

Open AI: ChatGPT 4o [Large language model]. https://chat.openai.com/chat

Reinmann, G.: Deskilling durch Künstliche Intelligenz? Potenzielle Kompetenzverluste als Herausforderung für die Hochschuldidaktik. Diskussionspapier Nr. 25. Berlin: Hochschulforum Digitalisie-rung (2023). https://hochschulforumdigitalisierung.de/publikationen/diskussionsp apier-25-deskilling-durch-kuenstliche-intelligenz/. Accessed 15 May 2025

Rickert, A.: Wissenschaftliches Schreiben – KI als Ghost, Partner oder Tutor. Blog PHZH (2024). https://blog.phzh.ch/zhe/wissenschaftliches-schreiben-ki-als-ghost-partner-oder-tutor/?pk_vid=0594c108e7320ae417460128724ec8ba. Accessed 04 June 2025

Rohmah, N., Muslim, A.B.: Writing anxiety in academic writing practice. Advances in Social Science, Education and Humanities Research (2021). https://doi.org/10.2991/assehr.k.210 427.053

Saber, A., Cartron, A., Kloppmann-Lambert, C., Louis, C.: Towards a typology of linguistic and stylistic errors in scientific abstracts written by low-proficiency doctoral students in France. Fachsprache. J. Profess. Sci. Commun. **42.3–4**, 90–114 (2020)

Silva-Corvalán, C., Treffers-Daller, J.: Digging into dominance: a closer look at language dominance in bilinguals. In: Silva-Corvalán, C., Treffers-Daller, J. (eds.) Language Dominance in Bilinguals: Issues of Measurement and Operationalization, pp. 1–14. Cambridge University Press, Cambridge (2016)

Snow, C., Ucelli, P.: The Challenge of Academic Language. In: Olsen, D.R., Torrence, N.: The Cambridge Handbook of Literacy. Cambridge University Press. 112–133 (2009)

Steinhoff, T.: Kuenstliche Intelligenz als Ghostwriter, Writing Tutor und Writing Partner. In: Albrecht, C., Brueggemann, J., Kretschmann, T., Meier, C. (eds.) Personale und funktionale Bildung im Deutschunterricht. Deutschdidaktik., pp. 85–99. J.B. Metzler, Berlin, Heidelberg (2025). https://doi.org/10.1007/978-3-662-69640-8_7

Vygotsky, L.: Thought and language. The Miss Press, Cambridge, London (2012/1934)

Vygotskij, L.S.: Denken und Sprechen. Ed. and transl. by Joachim Lompscher and Georg Rückriem. Beltz, Weinheim und Basel (1934/2002)

Vygotsky, L.: On psychological systems. In the Collected Papers, vol. 1. (1930). Cited from Kozulin, A: Vygotsky in context. In: Lev Vygotsky. Thought and Language. Revised and expanded edition, ed. and transl. by Hanfmann, E., Vakar, G., Kozulin, A., pp. xxv-lxxvii, Cambridge Massachusetts MIT Press. (2012/1986)

Vygotskij, L.: Ausgewaehlte Schriften - Band 1. Ed. by Lompscher J., Lehmanns Media-LOB.de, Berlin (2003/1925)

Estimating Subjective Evaluation on Drinking Experiences Using fNIRS Sensing

Hung Le[1], Duc Tran Minh[1], Takeshi Amiya[2], Satoshi Tezaki[2], Takashi Iimure[3], Toru Shioi[2], Kazunori Miyata[1], and Shogo Okada[1]

[1] Japan Advanced Institute of Science and Technology, Nomi, Ishikawa, Japan
{hungle,s2110437,miyata,okada-s}@jaist.ac.jp
[2] Value Creation Frontier Laboratories, Sapporo Breweries Ltd, Yaizu, Shizuoka, Japan
{takeshi.amiya,satoshi.tezaki,tooru.shioi}@sapporobeer.co.jp
[3] Quality Assurance Department, Sapporo Breweries Ltd, Tokyo, Japan
takashi.iimure@sapporobeer.co.jp

Abstract. Understanding how the body reacts to different types of drinks could help companies develop healthier drinks while keeping customers satisfied. Functional near-infrared spectroscopy (fNIRS) can be used to provide objective information about how neurons respond to taste stimuli. In this study, we collected two datasets using two fNIRS devices to measure hemoglobin concentration changes in the prefrontal cortex and salivary gland regions during the consumption of alcoholic drinks. Machine learning models were utilized to predict the hedonic aspects of participants based on the collected data. The best model achieved 64% balanced accuracy on one of the datasets. The results suggested that the perception of taste is encoded in hemodynamic signals.

Keywords: fNIRS · Machine learning · Neuroimaging · Tasting

1 Introduction

1.1 Background

As people's lives are getting better, we start to explore methods to improve the quality of daily activities, including the dining experience [1]. Sensory analysis is one of such methods used to assess how a product is perceived through the senses. The sensory tests give companies a preview of how the market will react to new foods or beverages. To overcome the subjectivity of the tests, some studies analyze the changes in brain activities while individuals are consuming foods or beverages. Using neuroimaging methods, such as functional magnetic resonance imaging (fMRI) or positron emission tomography (PET), studies have shown that subjective pleasantness coincides with activity in the cortex region of the brain [10].

© The Author(s), under exclusive license to Springer Nature Switzerland AG 2026
A. Coman et al. (Eds.): HCII 2025, LNCS 16337, pp. 255–265, 2026.
https://doi.org/10.1007/978-3-032-12801-0_17

PET or fMRI, however, are expensive techniques, and the participant's head needs to be stationary for these assessments to work well. On the other hand, fNIRS provides the flexibility needed for this task at a reasonable price. fNIRS is a noninvasive optical method that measures cortical activity based on the properties of hemoglobin absorption of near-infrared light [15]. The measurements that can be obtained by fNIRS include changes in the concentrations of oxyhemoglobin (HbO), de-oxyhemoglobin (HbR), and total hemoglobin in brain tissue (HbT = HbO + HbR).

This work aimed to investigate the relationships between drinking experience and hemodynamic responses in different head regions. Our two main contributions were as follows: (1) We collected two new fNIRS datasets for taste-related cognitive studies, and (2) we described a new task for objectively predicting drinking experience via fNIRS and presented our preliminary results.

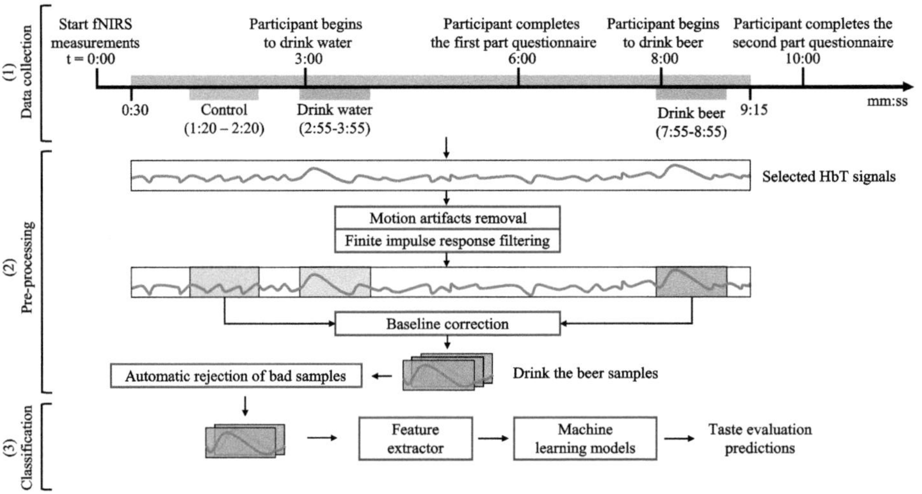

Fig. 1. Overall structure of the task: (1) the data collection process, (2) the preprocessing steps conducted in this paper, (3) the classification step

1.2   Related Work

Several previous works have aimed to study the hedonic aspects of taste using fNIRS measurements, but the results have largely been inconclusive. In [12], human cortical taste cognitive processing was studied via fNIRS. To the best of our knowledge, [12] is the first work to propose the use of fNIRS as a tool for taste-related cortical studies. In [14], the authors used fNIRS to indirectly measure human saliva secretion. They found a correlation between hemodynamics and saliva volume, suggesting that it is feasible to measure hemodynamic signals accompanying stimulated saliva secretion. The activity of hemoglobin in the frontal pole cortex and its relationship with the pleasantness of consuming a drink was also investigated in [10]. More recently, [8] aimed to assess whether it is possible to detect the differences among oat milk, almond milk, and water samples using HbO changes from the dorsolateral prefrontal cortex, but their attempt was not successful.

In recent years, machine learning methods have been widely adopted in many fields such as natural language processing and image processing. Increasing numbers of fNIRS studies are incorporating machine learning algorithms as well. In [16], the authors used support vector machines to predict speech imagery with four different tones. A context-aware graph neural network was proposed to classify an auditory task in [7]. While deep neural networks are powerful, they require large datasets to work well. Unlike text or images, collecting a large neuroimaging dataset is impractical due to the cost involved. Therefore, for this paper, we resorted to classical machine learning approaches with time series transformation methods to make predictions from fNIRS data.

2 Methods

2.1 Participants

Twenty-three healthy adults between the ages of 25 and 62 were asked to participate in the experiments. There were 18 males and 5 females, all of whom were Japanese. This study was performed after receiving approval from the Research Ethics Committee of Sapporo Breweries LTD in accordance with the Declaration of Helsinki. The participants were legally allowed to consume alcoholic beverages after a health check, and they provided written consent for the use of the data collected in the experiments for further analysis. Participants were asked to fast at least one hour before the time of the experiment.

During the experiment, participants sampled five different commercial beers. To prevent health issues, the quantity of beer consumed was minimized. Each participant tasted one to two beers per day, spaced out to allow for the consumption of 30 to 40 ml of beer, which had an alcohol content of 5 to 5.5%. This amount is significantly lower than the standard daily limit for adult drinking. To maintain consistent experimental conditions, both the laboratory's humidity and temperature, as well as the temperature of the beer, were controlled to remain as stable as possible.

2.2 Data Acquisition Devices

Two near-infrared spectroscopy systems, HOT-2000 and WOT-S20 (NeU Corporation, Tokyo, Japan), were used to determined HbO, HbR, and HbT concentration changes. Both devices can capture blood flow activity via two channels, which we denoted as the L (left) and R (right) channels. Based on the available literature, we narrowed our search in two regions of the head - the prefrontal cortex and the parotid glands - for which no single device can capture these signals simultaneously. The optode positions of both devices are shown in Fig. 2.

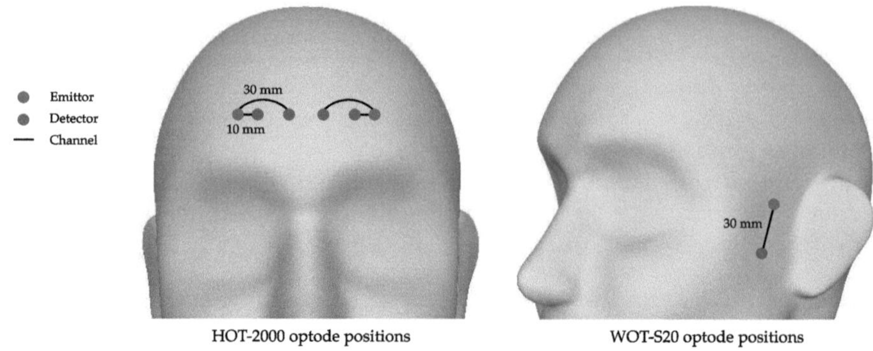

Fig. 2. Positions of the optodes

HOT-2000. The HOT-2000 system captures the blood flow activity in the prefrontal cortex with a 10 Hz sampling frequency. This device contains two emitters and four detectors, forming two long channels (emitter-detector distance is 3 cm) and two short channels (emitter-detector distance is 1 cm). The two emitters were positioned 40 mm horizontally apart from the center of the forehead, and detectors were placed between each emitter and the center of the forehead. The output of this device is the HbT, and separate HbO and HbR signals were not available. We used the "subtracted-HbT" signals (the difference between HbT data collected via the short channel and the long channel) for the experiments.

WOT-S20. The WOT-S20 system captures the blood flow activities in the parotid glands with a 5 Hz sampling frequency. This device contains two pairs of emitter and detector probes, the optodes were positioned on the right and left areas anterior to the ears. The distance between emitters and detectors is 30mm. All HbO, HbR, and HbT signals were available, but we used only the total Hb change from this device to obtain comparable results with those obtained with the HOT-2000 system.

2.3   Experimental Design and the Labeling Process

Before the experiment, participants were briefed about the experimental procedures and were asked to sit quietly during the experiment except when they had to perform a task. After the fNIRS device was securely positioned on the heads of the participants, the experiment's timer started at $t_0 = 0 : 00$ (0 minutes: 0 seconds), and the fNIRS device initiated. Every 30 seconds thereafter, three different devices (a throat microphone, a camera, and an infrared camera, in that order) were activated. Combining the modalities collected by these three devices is intended for future work. At 3:00, participants were asked to drink a glass of water, which was placed by a staff member 30 seconds earlier. At

4:30, a staff member placed a glass of beer to be tasted in front of the participants. At 6:00, participants were instructed to observe the beer placed in front of them and complete part of the questionnaire. This part included questions about the beer's appearance and its perceived tastiness, as well as the participant's current physical and emotional comfort and relaxation levels. At 8:00, participants tasted the beer as instructed. At 9:30, the beer was removed from the table by the staff. At 10:00, participants were asked to fill out another part of the questionnaire. This section included questions about the beer's flavor profile (strength of taste, odor, flavor, acidity, sweetness, and bitterness), the beer's deliciousness, the participant's preference for the beer, and again, the participant's physical and emotional comfort and relaxation levels. The total length of each trial was approximately 12 minutes. Part (1) of Fig. 1 summarizes the data collection process.

The list of questions and their corresponding English translations are shown in Table 1. The responses were recorded using a 7-point Likert scale, with 7 being the most favorable score. Figure 3 shows the Spearman's rank correlation coefficient among all collected data. There can be seen that there is an high correlation between the "Like" and "Taste" labels.

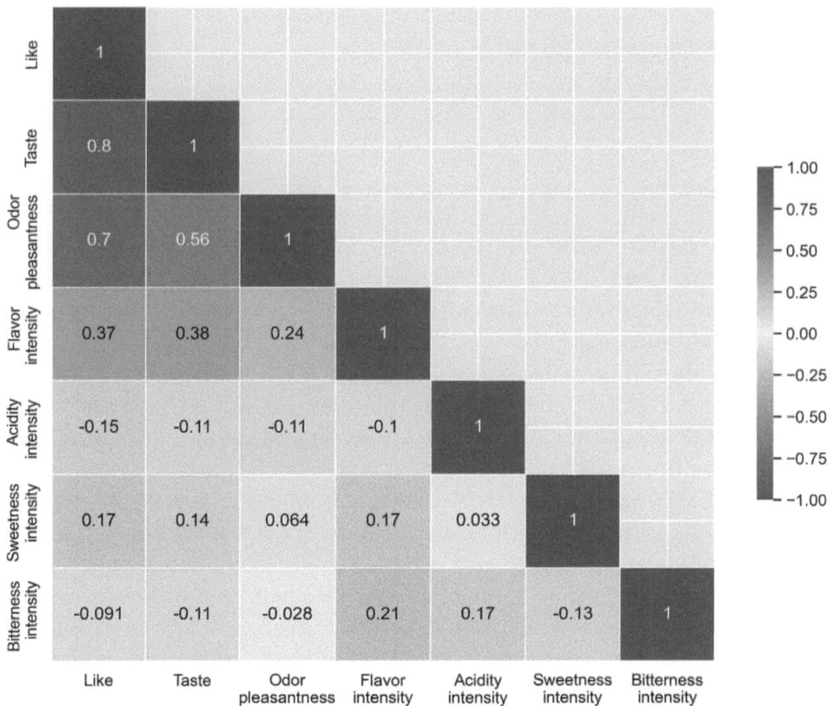

Fig. 3. Spearman's rank correlation coefficient matrix of the labels among all the collected samples

Table 1. The list of questions in the questionnaire

Question ID	Question
1	総合評価として、このビールは美味しかったですか。嗜好の度合を7段階評価してください。 (Overall, did you think this beer was delicious? Please rate your level of preference on a 7-point scale.)
2	味について、このビールの嗜好の度合を7段階評価してください。 (Please rate your level of preference for this beer in terms of taste on a 7-point scale.)
3	香りについて、このビールの嗜好の度合を7段階評価してください。 (Please rate your level of preference for this beer in terms of aroma on a 7-point scale.)
4	味の濃さを7段階評価してください。 (Please rate the strength of the flavor on a 7-point scale.)
5	酸味の強さを7段階評価してください。 (Please rate the strength of the sourness on a 7-point scale.)
6	甘味の強さを7段階評価してください。 (Please rate the strength of the sweetness on a 7-point scale.)
7	苦味の強さを7段階評価してください。 (Please rate the strength of the bitterness on a 7-point scale.)

2.4 Preprocessing and Feature Extraction

fNIRS signals contain noise due to the flexible movement of the head. In an attempt to remove bad data points and unwanted artifacts, we applied the following processing techniques (illustrated in part (2) of Fig. 1). First, we removed motion artifacts, such as spikes and baseline shifts, by applying the temporal derivative distribution repair algorithm [3] to all the time series data, which was 8 minutes and 45 seconds in duration. Then, irrelevant periodic physiological signals, such as changes in blood pressure and heart rate, were removed by a bandpass filtering between 0.01 and 0.5 Hz with a transition bandwidth of 0.1 and 0.5, respectively. Next, we used the 60-second resting phase as the baseline period for conducting the baseline correction during the drinking phase (we calculated the mean of the resting phase and subtracted this mean from the drinking phase). Each sample now contained only the 60-second baseline corrected drinking phase. Then, we removed bad samples with the autoreject algorithm [6], which uses peak-to-peak thresholds to detect outlier data points. After the automatic removal of bad samples, 93 samples (out of 116 samples) were obtained from the HOT-2000 device, and 107 samples (out of 110 samples) were obtained from the WOT-S20 device. The preprocessing steps were conducted with the help of the MNE-Python package[1] introduced in [4].

---

[1] https://doi.org/10.5281/zenodo.592483.

Once the fNIRS signals were processed, we treated our problem as a multivariate time series classification problem. Formally, let us say $X = \{x_1, x_2, ..., x_n\}$ and $Y_i = \{y_{i1}, y_{i2}, ..., y_{in}\}$ are the sets of samples and their corresponding classes. Note that each sample was annotated with multiple labels, so there was a set of m labels $\{Y_1, Y_2, ..., Y_m\}$. In our scenario, each sample $x_i \in X$ consisted of two-time series variables $L = \{l_{t1}, l_{t2}, ..., l_{tp}\}$ and $R = \{r_{t1}, r_{t2}, ..., r_{tp}\}$ representing p time steps of the HbT signals from the left and right channels, respectively. First, we applied a feature extractor function e to x_i to extract discrete representations of the time series signals. The objective was to learn a classifier f that maximizes the likelihood that $f(e(x_j)) = y_{ij}$ for each label Y_i. We next describe the two algorithms that we used as the feature extractor function e.

The first extractor function was *catch22* [9], which is a set of 22 CAnonical Time-series CHaracteristics reduced from 4791 features in the *hctsa* feature library. The features span a wide range of representations of time-series characteristics including distribution, simple temporal statistics, linear autocorrelation, nonlinear autocorrelation, successive differences, and fluctuation analysis. For the comprehensive list of the features, we refer readers to [9].

The second method we use for extracting time series signals is called ROCKET (RandOm Convolutional KErnel Transform) [2]. ROCKET uses many random convolutional kernels to capture features relevant to time series. By leveraging different aspects of kernel architecture (length, weights, bias, dilation, and padding), ROCKET can reduce the computational time significantly compared to similar methods such as InceptionTime or TS-CHIEF.

2.5   Machine Learning Models

Two classical machine learning models which are random forest (RF) and naive Bayes (NB) were chosen as the classifiers. We relied on the *scikit-learn* library [13] for the implementation of these models. RF is an ensemble learning method that makes use of decision trees, while NB is based on Bayes' theorem. A grid hyperparameter search was conducted for both models since they have relatively short computational time. We formulated the problem as a classification task by converting the Likert scores to binary classes using the median as the threshold. For evaluation, we report the average 5-fold cross-validation results. The balanced accuracy and weighted F1 score were chosen as the evaluation metrics. Both of these metrics take into account the imbalanced nature of the datasets, so a biased classifier will not obtain a high score.

3   Results

In Tables 2, 3 and 4, 5, we present the results of the *Like* and *Taste* labels ($\pm$ 95% confident interval across folds), along with the baseline results (majority voting). For the label *Like*, the combination of ROCKET and NB achieves the best performance with a balanced accuracy of 64.14% and a weighted F1 score of 67.85%. For the label *Taste*, the combination of ROCKET and RF achieved

Table 2. Balanced Accuracy scores (%) of the prediction results

Label	Device	Balanced Accuracy		
		Baseline	catch22 + NB	catch22 + RF
Like	WOT-S20	50.0 ± 0.0	49.19 ± 8.68	49.19 ± 8.68
	HOT-2000	50.0 ± 0.0	58.97 ± 11.81	58.97 ± 11.81
Taste	WOT-S20	50.0 ± 0.0	58.92 ± 8.86	47.44 ± 6.68
	HOT-2000	50.0 ± 0.0	57.52 ± 9.43	50.96 ± 9.9

Table 3. Balanced Accuracy scores (%) of the prediction results with catch22 features

Label	Device	Balanced Accuracy		
		Baseline	ROCKET + NB	ROCKET + RF
Like	WOT-S20	50.0 ± 0.0	46.67 ± 10.9	43.21 ± 14.85
	HOT-2000	50.0 ± 0.0	**64.14 ± 7.83**	62.6 ± 12.27
Taste	WOT-S20	50.0 ± 0.0	51.87 ± 8.71	44.35 ± 8.18
	HOT-2000	50.0 ± 0.0	60.69 ± 15.14	**64.3 ± 17.26**

a balanced accuracy of 64.3% and a weighted F1 score of 70.5%. These results were obtained on the HOT-2000 dataset. For the WOT-S20 dataset, the results are not as promising. The best balanced accuracy and F1 score on the WOT-S20 dataset is 58.92% and 66.68% (the combination of *catch22* and RF for the *Taste* label).

In Table 6, we used the same best methods found in Tables 2, 3, 4 and 5, but replaced the input signals with the period signals for drinking water. For the labels *Like* and *Taste*, using the drinking water data did not yield better results than random guesses. The results obtained using signals captured by the HOT-2000 system suggest that the models were able to learn the effect of the drinks on the brain and not just exploit artifacts in the signal. For other labels including *odor pleasantness, flavor intensity, acidity intensity, sweetness intensity,* and *bitterness intensity,* our methods did not yield a high accuracy (above 60%).

Table 4. F1-score (%) of the prediction results with catch22 features

Label	Device	Weighted F1 score		
		Baseline	catch22 + NB	catch22 + RF
Like	WOT-S20	42.49±1.59	48.47±9.92	46.37±8.11
	HOT-2000	53.35±3.39	64.57±11.66	62.73±14.06
Taste	WOT-S20	42.49±1.59	61.86±9.0	50.23±7.69
	HOT-2000	53.35±3.39	66.68±10.95	62.56±12.65

Table 5. F1-score (%) of the prediction results with ROCKET features

Label	Device	Weighted F1 score		
		Baseline	ROCKET + NB	ROCKET + RF
Like	WOT-S20	42.49±1.59	46.73±10.14	43.95±15.77
	HOT-2000	53.35±3.39	**67.85±5.77**	66.1±10.98
Taste	WOT-S20	42.49±1.59	54.59±8.86	45.65±9.14
	HOT-2000	53.35±3.39	68.04±13.17	**70.5±17.29**

Table 6. Balanced Accuracy scores (%) when using drinking beer vs. drinking water as the input

Label/Device	Condition	Model	
		ROCKET + NB	ROCKET + RF
*Like*HOT-2000	Beer	**64.14 ± 7.83**	**62.6 ± 12.27**
	Water	39.7 ± 12.63	43.01 ± 15.71
*Taste*HOT-2000	Beer	**60.69 ± 15.14**	**64.3 ± 17.26**
	Water	50.21 ± 19.98	46.69 ± 14.15

The reason could be that the hemodynamic responses in the regions we studied did not capture these perceptions, but further analysis is needed.

4 Discussion

In [5], the researchers found that processing sweet taste involved the prefrontal cortex, and fNIRS can be used to study this region. However, later research [10] suggested that there is no significant difference in Hb response for sweet and bitter stimulation. In this work, our models were also not able to reliably classify *bitterness* and *sweetness* perception from the prefrontal cortex Hb response, as well as other tastes like *flavor* intensity or *acidity* intensity. This finding aligned with previous research, which stated that differences in Hb responses to basic tastes are unknown [11]. With that being said, we are optimistic that more advanced machine learning models could detect these differences.

A common finding in many fNIRS studies is that Hb responses vary widely among different participants and within the same participant across different trials (e.g., [5,10]). We observed the same characteristic in our collected datasets. This characteristic of fNIRS signals makes it challenging to analyze them using statistical models, such as generalized linear models. Our work found that machine learning methods provide an alternative approach, offering hope that favorable results can be achieved, particularly in the task of evaluating subjective drinking experiences. A limitation of our work is that the differences between participants and between the drinks were not deeply incorporated into models.

Future models should consider this limitation, as the incorporation could provide the models with useful information to make more accurate predictions.

5   Conclusion

In this work, we collected two novel datasets to determine whether it is possible to infer a person's drinking preference from hemoglobin activity. Two devices were used to capture hemoglobin concentration changes in two different regions of interest. By applying different machine learning models and time series transformation methods, we were able to predict whether a person thinks a drink is tasty with a balanced accuracy of 64%, and whether they like the drink with a similar accuracy. In addition, our results suggested that some differences between water and beer can be captured using fNIRS devices.

In future work, we plan to extend the datasets to improve the stability of the models and conduct single-participant analysis to investigate how different types of people react to different types of beer and flavors. For labels other than *Like* and *Taste*, we plan to conduct extensive experiments with more advanced machine learning models. Lastly, other modalities obtained from different devices were not utilized in this research. Using multimodal deep learning models to combine these sources, in addition to fNIRS signals, is an interesting research direction to be explored.

Acknowledgment. The authors sincerely appreciate Fumito Ishida and Nanako Ishinabe for their support for this study.

References

1. Bocanegra, M., Lemke, M., de Vries, R.A., Ludden, G.D.: Commensality or Reverie in Eating? Exploring the Solo Dining Experience. In: Proceedings of the 2022 International Conference on Multimodal Interaction, pp. 25–35. ICMI '22. Association for Computing Machinery, New York, NY, USA (2022). https://doi.org/10.1145/3536221.3556577
2. Dempster, A., Petitjean, F., Webb, G.I.: ROCKET: exceptionally fast and accurate time series classification using random convolutional kernels. Data Min. Knowl. Disc. **34**(5), 1454–1495 (2020). https://doi.org/10.1007/s10618-020-00701-z
3. Fishburn, F.A., Ludlum, R.S., Vaidya, C.J., Medvedev, A.V.: Temporal Derivative Distribution Repair (TDDR): A motion correction method for fNIRS. Neuroimage **184**, 171–179 (2019). https://doi.org/10.1016/j.neuroimage.2018.09.025
4. Gramfort, A., Luessi, M., Larson, E., Engemann, D., Strohmeier, D., Brodbeck, C., Goj, R., Jas, M., Brooks, T., Parkkonen, L., Hämäläinen, M.: MEG and EEG data analysis with MNE-Python. Front. Neurosci. **7** (2013)
5. Hu, C., Kato, Y., Luo, Z.: An fnirs research on prefrontal cortex activity response to pleasant taste. J. Behav. Brain Sci. **03**, 617–623 (2013). https://doi.org/10.4236/jbbs.2013.38065

6. Jas, M., Engemann, D.A., Bekhti, Y., Raimondo, F., Gramfort, A.: Autoreject: automated artifact rejection for MEG and EEG data. Neuroimage **159**, 417–429 (2017). https://doi.org/10.1016/j.neuroimage.2017.06.030

7. Kumar, C., Rahimi, N., Gonjari, R., McLinden, J., Hosni, S.I., Shahriari, Y., Shao, M.: Context-aware multimodal auditory BCI classification through graph neural networks. In: 2023 45th Annual International Conference of the IEEE Engineering in Medicine & Biology Society (EMBC), pp. 1–4 (2023). https://doi.org/10.1109/EMBC40787.2023.10339984. ISSN: 2694-0604

8. Laves, K., Mehlhose, C., Risius, A.: Sensory Measurements of Taste: Aiming to Visualize Sensory Differences in Taste Perception by Consumers–An Experiential fNIRS Approach. J. Int. Food & Agribusiness Mark. **35**, 1–21 (2022). https://doi.org/10.1080/08974438.2022.2064027

9. Lubba, C.H., Sethi, S.S., Knaute, P., Schultz, S.R., Fulcher, B.D., Jones, N.S.: catch22: CAnonical Time-series CHaracteristics. Data Min. Knowl. Disc. **33**(6), 1821–1852 (2019). https://doi.org/10.1007/s10618-019-00647-x

10. Minematsu, Y., Ueji, K., Yamamoto, T.: Activity of frontal pole cortex reflecting hedonic tone of food and drink: fNIRS study in humans. Sci. Rep. **8**(1), 16197 (2018). https://doi.org/10.1038/s41598-018-34690-3, number: 1 Publisher: Nature Publishing Group

11. Minematsu, Y., Ueji, K., Yamamoto, T.: Activity of frontal pole cortex reflecting hedonic tone of food and drink: fNIRS study in humans. Sci. Rep. **8**(1), 16197 (2018). https://doi.org/10.1038/s41598-018-34690-3, number: 1 Publisher: Nature Publishing Group

12. Okamoto, M., Dan, I.: Functional near-infrared spectroscopy for human brain mapping of taste-related cognitive functions. J. Biosci. Bioeng. **103**(3), 207–215 (2007). https://doi.org/10.1263/jbb.103.207

13. Pedregosa, F., Varoquaux, G., Gramfort, A., Michel, V., Thirion, B., Grisel, O., Blondel, M., Prettenhofer, P., Weiss, R., Dubourg, V., Vanderplas, J., Passos, A., Cournapeau, D., Brucher, M., Perrot, M., Duchesnay, E.: Scikit-learn: machine learning in python. J. Mach. Learn. Res. **12**(85), 2825–2830 (2011)

14. Sato, H., Obata, A.N., Moda, I., Ozaki, K., Yasuhara, T., Yamamoto, Y., Kiguchi, M., Maki, A., Kubota, K., Koizumi, H.: Application of near-infrared spectroscopy to measurement of hemodynamic signals accompanying stimulated saliva secretion. J. Biomed. Opt. **16**(4), 047002 (2011). https://doi.org/10.1117/1.3565048

15. Villringer, A., Chance, B.: Non-invasive optical spectroscopy and imaging of human brain function. Trends Neurosci. **20**(10), 435–442 (1997). https://doi.org/10.1016/S0166-2236(97)01132-6

16. Zhang, H., Guo, Z., Chen, F.: The Effects of Different Brain Regions on fNIRS-based Task-state Detection in Speech Imagery. In: 2023 45th Annual International Conference of the IEEE Engineering in Medicine & Biology Society (EMBC), pp. 1–4 (2023). https://doi.org/10.1109/EMBC40787.2023.10340896. ISSN: 2694-0604

Internet of Things (IoT) for Weather Monitoring Systems in Rural Zones: Literature Review

Sandro Nieto[1]([⊠]) and Sandra Cano[2]

[1] Doctorate of Intelligent Industry, Pontificia Universidad Católica de Valparaíso, Valparaíso, Chile
sandro.nieto.m@mail.pucv.cl
[2] School of Informatics Engineering, Pontificia Universidad Católica de Valparaíso, Valparaíso, Chile
sandra.cano@pucv.cl

Abstract. Climate monitoring systems using IoT (Internet of Things) are crucial because they provide real-time data that directly benefits the areas to be monitored. The use of IoT in climate monitoring for rural areas faces challenges due to the characteristics of the area, technological, economic and social limitations. This study aims to conduct a literature review of IoT technologies that have been recently implemented using IoT for climate monitoring. This literature review explores the state of the art of IoT-based concepts for climate monitoring in rural areas. In this review, 9 studies were selected from the SCOPUS and Web of Science databases between 2019 and 2024. The selected studies attempt to answer three research questions related to technological challenges, climate monitoring variables and climate sensors.

Keywords: Internet of Things (IoT) · Climate Monitoring · Remote Areas · Weather Sensors

1 Introduction

Climate change and extreme weather events have had a significant impact on agricultural production in rural areas, leading to the need for reliable weather monitoring systems to support decision-making and improve resilience [1, 2]. Therefore, Internet of Things has revolutionized the way we approach weather monitoring, offering a cost-effective and scalable solution for real-time data collection and analysis in remote rural areas [3].

The Internet of Things has emerged as a powerful technology for addressing various challenges in diverse domains, including environmental monitoring and agriculture. In the context of rural areas, IoT-based weather monitoring system can play a crucial role in providing real-time meteorological information to farmers, enabling them to make informed decisions regarding crop management and reducing the risks associated with adverse climatic conditions [4].

The application of IoT technology in rural weather monitoring systems has gained significant attention in recent years. IoT-based systems leverage a network of interconnected sensors, cloud-based data processing, and advanced analytics to provide farmers

A. Coman et al. (Eds.): HCII 2025, LNCS 16337, pp. 266–277, 2026.
https://doi.org/10.1007/978-3-032-12801-0_18

with accurate, real-time weather data, including temperature, humidity, rainfall, and wind patterns [4, 5].

These systems can help farmers make informed decisions on planting, irrigation and pest management, thereby improving agricultural productivity and resilience to climate change. IoT-based weather monitoring systems in rural zones offer several advantages over traditional weather monitoring methods. First the integration of low-cost sensors and wireless communication technologies enables to deployment of distributed sensor networks, providing a more comprehensive and granular understanding of local weather conditions. Second, the real-time data collection and dissemination capabilities of IoT systems allow farmers to access critical information promptly, enabling them to respond to changing weather patterns and make timely decisions [4, 6]. Thridly, the incorporation of data analytics and predictive models in IoT-based systems can help farmers anticipate and prepare for extreme weather events, reducing the risks of crop losses and financial impacts [6, 7].

The objective of this literature review is to analyze the recent developments of IoT systems applied to climate monitoring, focusing on the implementation challenges, the variables measured, the types of sensors used, and the communication technologies used. This literature review is conducted to answer the following research questions:

RQ1: What are some of the key challenges in deploying IoT-based weather stations in remote areas?

RQ2: What meteorological variables and IoT sensors are used to monitor weather in remote areas?

RQ3: What communication protocols are most used to monitor weather in remote areas?

This article is structured as follows. Section 2, an overview of IoT concepts for weather monitoring. Section 3, PRISMA methodology that has been applied to carry out the literature review. Section 4, results obtained and answers to the research questions that have been formulated. Section 5 discussion. Finally, Sect. 6 conclusions.

2 Background

2.1 Internet of Things

The Internet of Things (IoT) is an emerging paradigm that describes an environment where everyday objects are equipped with communication and computing capabilities, allowing their integration within the Internet infrastructure to facilitate advanced services [8] IoT refers to the interconnection of physical devices, objects, and systems over the internet, allowing them to collect and share data to perform specific actions [9] According to the Institute of Electrical and Electronics Engineers (IEEE), IoT is an expanding interconnected network infrastructure, comprised of physical and virtual devices, which use various technologies to interact and communicate with each other and with the external environment via the internet.

According to [10] every object in an IoT system is "smart" in the sense that it provides computational capabilities, allowing for interaction and data transfer within the IoT network.

2.2 IoT Climate Monitoring Systems

An IoT climate monitoring system is defined as an integrated network of devices and sensors that collect real-time data on environmental conditions such as temperature, humidity, air quality, and other climatic factors [11]. This data is transmitted over the internet to analytics and visualization platforms, where it can be monitored and used to make informed decisions. IoT systems allow continuous and detailed monitoring, facilitating the early detection of possible problems and contributing to a more dynamic and proactive environmental management. The main elements of these systems include environmental monitoring sensors, connectivity, gateways/base stations, network management systems, and environmental monitoring data applications.

3 Methodology

This review was carried out through a systematic search of the available literature published in databases such as Scopus and Web of Science, applying a search string with keywords adjusted to the theme. Scientific articles published between 2019 and 2024 that offer empirical or experimental solutions in remote areas of difficult access, with energy and telecommunications limitations, were selected, this entire process was carried out according to the guidelines of suggested reporting elements for systematic reviews and meta-analyses [12].

3.1 Study Selection Process

For the systematic review of IoT systems applied to climate monitoring in remote areas, the PICOS framework (Participants, Interventions, Comparisons, Outcomes, and Study Design) was adopted to structure the selection of relevant studies. This framework helped to narrow down the inclusion and exclusion criteria, ensuring that the most relevant studies were collected for analysis. Here's how each component of the PICOS framework was applied:

Participants (P). The participants in the studies analyzed are remote areas that are difficult to access, where climate monitoring is especially critical. These areas lack adequate infrastructure and are characterized by geographic isolation and a scarcity of resources to install conventional monitoring systems.

Intervention (I). The intervention refers to the implementation of systems based on IoT technologies for climate monitoring, which include the use of sensors for the collection of environmental data and its transmission to analysis platforms. These systems are designed to operate autonomously in remote environments, optimizing energy and communication use in areas with limited infrastructure.

Comparisons (C). The review focuses on identifying and analyzing the different technologies used in climate monitoring in remote areas. The various technological solutions implemented in these environments are explored and the challenges associated with their implementation are compared, along with the strategies adopted to overcome such limitations.

Outcomes (O). The results obtained in the studies provide a comprehensive view of the key components of IoT systems applied to climate monitoring in remote areas, highlighting the main challenges in implementation, such as energy management, connectivity and the adaptation of technologies to the restrictive conditions of these environments.

Study design (S). The systematic review focuses on observational studies, case studies, and experimental studies that study the implementation and evaluation of IoT systems in climate monitoring in remote areas. These studies explore how environmental monitoring technologies have been used in contexts with limited access to infrastructure, highlighting issues in integrating sensors, communications, and energy solutions in harsh environments.

3.2 Search Strategy

A search was carried out in the Scopus and Web of Science databases, selected for their relevance to technical and scientific topics related to the IoT. Using keywords combined using Boolean operators, the following string was used:

("Internet of Things" OR "IoT") AND ("weather monitoring" OR "climate monitoring" OR "environmental monitoring" OR "weather station") AND ("sensors" OR "communication protocols") AND ("remote areas" OR "rural areas").

3.3 Screening and Eligibility

The process of selecting articles for this systematic review began with the obtaining of articles through academic databases. We searched Scopus, where we initially obtained 49 articles, and Web of Science, where we found 12 relevant articles. To ensure that only relevant studies were included, the following inclusion and exclusion criteria were established.

The Inclusion Criteria. Articles that apply IoT technologies for climate monitoring in remote areas. Articles describing practical applications of IoT sensors for measuring climate variables in hard-to-reach environments. Articles published in English and accessible in full format.

Exclusion Criteria. Articles that do not deal directly with climate monitoring or IoT use. Literature reviews, meta-analyses, or repeated articles.

After applying the inclusion and exclusion criteria, articles that met the requirements established for the final analysis were selected.

3.4 Analysis Process

Initial Review. The titles and abstracts of the retrieved articles were reviewed to determine their relevance to the research questions and the objectives of the study. This made it possible to exclude items that did not comply with the main focus of climate monitoring in remote areas using IoT systems.

Detailed Reading. The selected articles were read and analyzed in depth to extract key information related to the meteorological variables monitored, the sensors used, the communication protocols employed, and the technical challenges faced and overcome. This reading allowed us to identify common patterns and highlight the solutions proposed in the implementation of these systems.

Summary of Results. The information extracted from the articles was organized into key categories to highlight trends, challenges, and opportunities in the use of IoT technologies for climate monitoring. This synthesis facilitated the identification of gaps in research and areas that require further attention in future studies (Fig. 1).

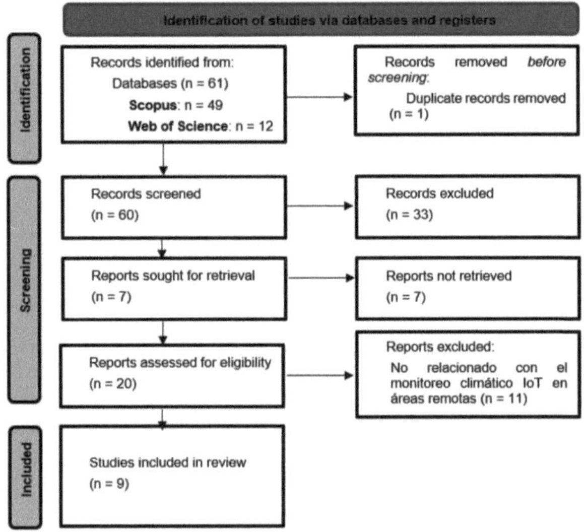

Fig. 1. Flow Diagram of Article Selection Process Based on PRISMA Guidelines.

4   Results of the Literature Review

This section presents the results obtained from the literature review, organized around the research questions posed.

RQ1: What are some of the key challenges in implementing IoT-based weather stations in remote areas?

4.1   Energy

One of the most common problems identified in IoT-based environmental monitoring systems in remote areas is the lack of access to reliable energy sources. Energy consumption is the most frequent and critical challenge in the implementation of IoT weather stations in remote areas. Efficient use of energy is critical, as stations often operate autonomously in locations where access to traditional power grids is not available. Several solutions solve this problem, such as the use of low-power components [13] low-power modes in hardware and software [14] and the design of systems that optimize energy use in device idle periods [15]. [16] and [17] also highlight the importance of efficient energy management, using low-power technologies such as LoRa.

However, alternative energies such as solar energy, although effective, are conditioned by climatic factors that can limit the constant availability of energy. In remote areas, adverse weather conditions can affect the performance of solar panels, which in turn impacts the power system and therefore the entire system. This aspect is mentioned in [18] who highlight the dependence on sources such as solar and thermal, but also recognize the limitations they present due to environmental variations.

To solve the problem of lack of access to reliable energy sources in remote areas, one of the most common solutions is the use of renewable energy sources, mainly solar energy. [14] reinforce by pointing out that solar energy is an effective option for weather stations in hard-to-reach areas, allowing IoT devices to operate continuously. However, the effectiveness of solar panels is conditioned by the availability of sunlight, which can be affected by adverse weather conditions, especially in areas with significant weather variability [14].

In addition to solar energy [18] other energy sources stand out, such as thermal energy, which can also be used to power IoT systems in remote environments.

4.2 Connectivity

The problem of connectivity is the second most common challenge. The lack of a telecommunications infrastructure that allows reliable connectivity, especially in regions without access to traditional communication networks, is one of the key problems in IoT environmental monitoring systems in remote areas.

[15] highlight that limited mobile network coverage and lack of adequate infrastructure in rural areas make it difficult to implement effective IoT systems, as devices cannot transmit data constantly. Furthermore, [16] mention that connectivity is even more complex in more remote areas, where cellular networks are not available, forcing devices to rely on less reliable or more expensive alternative solutions.

4.3 Data Storage

Data storage is another crucial challenge, especially in remote areas where connectivity options are limited. Solutions are required that allow large volumes of data to be stored without overloading networks or increasing energy consumption. Local storage systems, such as the use of SD cards, have been proposed [14, 19] and efficient file systems such as simpleFS [13] which store data in binary formats to reduce energy consumption.

RQ2: What meteorological variables and IoT sensors are used to monitor weather in remote areas?

4.4 Temperature

Temperature is one of the most common parameters measured in IoT climate monitoring systems. Measuring air temperature is essential for understanding weather patterns and their impact on other factors. [16] mention that ambient temperature is one of the key variables measured in their monitoring system in remote areas, along with other climatic parameters. [14, 20] use temperature sensors in their climate monitoring system to measure ambient temperature.

4.5 Humidity

Relative humidity is a key parameter for climate studies, as it influences comfort conditions, cloud formation and agricultural production. [14] use sensors such as the DHT11 to measure relative humidity in automatic weather stations in rural areas. [20] also measure relative humidity using the DHT11 sensor, which provides temperature and humidity readings at their weather station, which is part of a low-power environmental monitoring system.

4.6 Wind Speed and Direction

Wind speed and wind direction are important measures for understanding weather phenomena such as storms and high winds. Several studies include these parameters. [20] use an anemometer to measure wind speed and a wind direction sensor in their climate monitoring system, allowing them to study wind behavior in rural areas. [14] also include wind speed measurement in their climate monitoring system in areas with extreme weather events.

4.7 Precipitation

Precipitation is an essential meteorological parameter for climate studies, especially in flood-prone areas. IoT systems typically use rain sensors to measure this parameter. [14] incorporate rain sensors into their automatic weather stations to measure the amount of precipitation in rural areas that may be exposed to flooding. [20] also includes a raindrop sensor to measure precipitation in their weather station, which is part of their low-power IoT system.

4.8 Solar Radiation

Solar radiation is an important parameter for systems that monitor solar energy and other aspects of climate, such as evaporation and photosynthesis. Several articles mention the measurement of this parameter. [20] include solar radiation sensors in their monitoring system, using weather stations to measure solar irradiance in rural areas. [16] do not specify the type of sensors used to measure solar radiation but mention that solar radiation conditions are critical for climate monitoring in remote areas.

4.9 Atmospheric Pressure

Atmospheric pressure is another important variable, especially for predicting changes in weather, such as storms or cold fronts. [20] include the BMP180 sensor, which measures atmospheric pressure, in their weather station. [14] also use pressure sensors to monitor atmospheric conditions, which helps in the assessment of the impact of atmospheric pressure on the local climate.

RQ3: What communication technologies and protocols are most used for weather monitoring in remote areas?

4.10 Communication Technologies

Lora. One of the most prominent communication technologies is LoRa (Long Range), which is used due to its ability to provide low-power and long-range communications. LoRa is a wireless communication technology that operates in unlicensed bands, making it ideal for remote areas where telecommunications infrastructure does not exist. [16] and [20] use LoRa in their IoT systems for the transmission of sensor data over long distances, where energy consumption is a priority. This technology is suitable for transmitting small amounts of data over long distances, even up to 20 km in rural areas under ideal conditions.

Satellites. In extremely remote areas, where terrestrial infrastructure is not available, satellites are a key solution. Low-orbit satellites are used to establish satellite-based IoT networks that enable data transmission from inaccessible areas. [17] implemented a satellite-enabled IoT system to collect environmental monitoring data in places like Tibet, where traditional communication networks do not exist. Satellites enable continuous data transmission from distributed IoT stations, providing a reliable solution even in the most inhospitable environments.

4.11 Communication Protocols

LoRaWAN. The LoRaWAN protocol is one of the most widely used in IoT climate monitoring systems due to its ability to manage long-range networks and low energy consumption. [20] and [16] use LoRaWAN for data transmission between sensors and gateways (base stations) that act as intermediaries between end devices and data collection platforms. LoRaWAN provides a star network architecture, where sensor nodes connect directly to a gateway, optimizing the power efficiency of devices. It offers three classes of devices (A, B and C), each with different transmission capacities and power consumption, adapting to the needs of each application.

MQTT (Message Queuing Telemetry Transport). The MQTT protocol is commonly used in IoT systems due to its lightness and efficiency for small message transmission and real-time data management. This protocol is particularly useful for climate monitoring because it allows for the efficient transmission of data between sensors and central platforms, using a publish/subscribe model that minimizes network overhead. [14] mention that MQTT is ideal for systems with low-power devices, as it facilitates the fast and reliable transmission of data over low-capacity and long-range networks.

HTTP/HTTPS. This protocol is widely used for data transmission in web applications. Although it is not as efficient as LoRaWAN or MQTT in terms of low power consumption, it is used in systems where devices are connected to monitoring platforms accessible via the internet. [20] implement HTTP in their system to enable real-time visualization of data collected from weather stations on the ThingSpeak platform, facilitating remote access to information.

5 Discussion

The implementation of IoT weather stations in remote areas faces several challenges, one of the most critical being the management of energy consumption. The difficulty in guaranteeing the autonomy of stations in areas without access to stable electricity grids has been identified as a fundamental challenge in various studies. The most common solution to this problem is the use of renewable energy sources, such as solar, supplemented by efficient energy storage in batteries or supercapacitors. However, the performance of solar panels can be affected by climatic factors, limiting the constant availability of energy, especially in regions with adverse weather conditions [14, 18] Despite these difficulties, the design of IoT devices with low-power components and the implementation of technologies such as LoRa, which optimize energy use during idle periods, has proven to be an effective solution for extending the lifespan of weather stations [13, 20].

Another relevant challenge is connectivity in remote areas, where the lack of telecommunications infrastructure makes it difficult to constantly transmit data. In regions where mobile network coverage is limited or non-existent, the use of communication technologies such as LoRa, which allows efficient transmission over long distances with low energy consumption, is presented as a viable solution [15, 16]. However, in even more isolated areas, such as mountainous areas or extreme regions such as Tibet, the use of unmanned aerial vehicles (UAVs) and satellites has been proposed to ensure connectivity, thus ensuring real-time data transmission, regardless of the limitations of local infrastructure [17].

Data storage also represents a significant challenge in these systems, as in many cases, IoT devices must store large volumes of data locally before they can transmit it to central platforms. This challenge is exacerbated in areas where connectivity is limited, increasing the need for efficient storage solutions that minimize energy consumption. Current solutions include the use of SD cards and optimized file systems such as simpleFS, which allow data to be stored in binary formats, thus reducing energy consumption and avoiding network overload [13, 14].

As for the meteorological variables recorded in IoT systems for climate monitoring in remote areas, temperature, humidity and atmospheric pressure are the most measured. Sensors such as DHT11 and DS18B20 are used to obtain accurate temperature and humidity readings [14, 20] Other important parameters such as wind speed and direction, as well as precipitation, are also monitored using sensors such as anemometers and rain gauges, which makes it possible to predict extreme weather phenomena such as storms and heavy rainfall [20] In addition, some systems include solar radiation sensors, which is crucial for assessing evaporation and renewable energy generation [14].

The selection of communication protocols and technologies is critical to the successful implementation of IoT systems in remote areas. Among the most widely used protocols are LoRa and LoRaWAN, which stand out for their ability to transmit data over long distances with low energy consumption [16, 20] In regions where LoRa is not viable due to lack of coverage, the use of satellites has emerged as an effective solution, as observed in the case of Tibet [17] In addition, the MQTT protocol is widely used for its efficiency in transmitting small messages, facilitating real-time data management with low-power devices [14] These protocols are critical to ensure connectivity in remote areas, ensuring that weather data can be sent for analysis and visualization on cloud-based platforms.

5.1 Areas for Future Research

The analysis of the reviewed articles leads us to express some areas for future research.

Lack of Standardization in IoT Solutions. The studies reviewed have revealed several recurring findings in the implementation of IoT climate monitoring systems in remote areas. One of them is the lack of standardization in IoT solutions, which affects interoperability between different solutions. Several authors, such as [20] and [16] highlight the importance of developing a common framework that facilitates the integration and replicability of these systems, which is essential to ensure their expansion and use globally. Without a clear standard, IoT systems tend to be customized solutions tailored to local conditions, limiting their applicability and making replicability a challenge.

Lack of a Standardized Methodology for the Development of IoT Solutions. The lack of a standardized methodology for the development of IoT solutions is another relevant finding. [18] mention that there is no common methodological framework for the implementation of IoT systems in remote areas, which leads to the creation of ad-hoc solutions. This approach hinders scalability and increases costs, as each project must face and solve similar problems independently. [14] underline the need for a standardized methodology that guides developers in the selection of technologies, sensors, and communication platforms, and in the way, data is managed. Without a clear methodology, the replicability of systems is compromised, and the quality and efficiency of development are affected.

Lack of Standardization of Data. The lack of standardization of data is another critical issue affecting the interoperability of environmental monitoring IoT systems. [20] highlight that, due to the lack of standards in the format of meteorological data, IoT systems cannot effectively share their data with other platforms or networks, which limits the possibility of obtaining a holistic and real-time view of environmental conditions. This can also cause problems in comparing data between different regions or projects. [16] stress that, in order to improve data interoperability between different IoT devices, it is essential to develop standards that ensure that data can be shared, integrated, and analyzed without the need for constant customization. Standardizing data not only facilitates interoperability but also improves the accuracy and quality of analyses made from that data, enabling informed decisions in real-time.

6 Conclusion

In this literature review on IoT systems for climate monitoring in remote areas, several findings have been identified:

The most common technologies to ensure connectivity in remote areas are LoRa WAN and GSM. These technologies allow for long-distance data transmission, but their effectiveness depends on the availability of adequate infrastructure.

Temperature, humidity, and atmospheric pressure sensors are the most used in IoT climate monitoring systems. Other parameters such as wind speed and direction; precipitation and solar radiation are also measured less frequently.

IoT systems in remote areas rely on alternative energy sources, mainly solar and thermal power. The combination of these sources together with battery energy storage and optimal energy use are essential to ensure the autonomous operation of the devices. A lack of standardization in data and communication protocols has been identified, which limits interoperability between different IoT systems and platforms, making their integration and scalability difficult.

Given the findings identified, it is inferred that the implementation of a standardized framework could offer a comprehensive solution. This framework would be a structured guide that allows developers and IoT experts to address technical and operational issues more efficiently. By providing clear guidelines on selecting appropriate technologies, device integration, and data management, a standardized framework would help mitigate issues related to interoperability and lack of data standardization. In addition, it would offer a common approach to optimize energy consumption, using renewable energies in a combined way and improving energy storage.

References

1. Chew, K.T., Jo, R.S., Lu, M., Raman, V., Hui Then, P.H.: Organic Black Soldier Flies (BSF) Farming in rural area using libelium waspmote smart agriculture and internet-of-things technologies. In: 2021 IEEE 11th IEEE Symposium on Computer Applications & Industrial Electronics (ISCAIE), pp. 228-232. IEEE, Penang, Malaysia (2021). https://doi.org/10.1109/ISCAIE51753.2021.9431801
2. Zhang, Y., et al.: Research on soil moisture detection and remote precision irrigation of seedlings based on internet of things. INMATEH Agric. Eng. pp. 449–460 (2023). https://doi.org/10.35633/inmateh-69-42
3. Mittal, A., Sarangi, S., Ramanath, S., Bhatt, P.V., Sharma, R., Srinivasu, P.: IoT-based precision monitoring of horticultural crops — a case-study on cabbage and capsicum. In: 2018 IEEE Global Humanitarian Technology Conference (GHTC), pp. 1–7. IEEE, San Jose, CA (2018). https://doi.org/10.1109/GHTC.2018.8601908
4. Bhatti, U.A., Masud, M., Bazai, S.U., Tang, H.: Editorial: investigating AI-based smart precision agriculture techniques. Front. Plant Sci. **14**, 1237783 (2023). https://doi.org/10.3389/fpls.2023.1237783
5. Tzounis, A., Katsoulas, N., Bartzanas, T., Kittas, C.: Internet of Things in agriculture, recent advances and future challenges. Biosyst. Eng. **164**, 31–48 (2017). https://doi.org/10.1016/j.biosystemseng.2017.09.007
6. Antony, A.P., Leith, K., Jolley, C., Lu, J., Sweeney, D.J.: A review of practice and implementation of the Internet of Things (IoT) for smallholder agriculture. Sustainability **12**(9), 3750 (2020). https://doi.org/10.3390/su12093750
7. Ruan, J., et al.: Agriculture IoT: emerging trends, cooperation networks, and outlook. IEEE Wirel. Commun. **26**(6), 56–63 (2019). https://doi.org/10.1109/MWC.001.1900096

8. Lin, J., Yu, W., Zhang, N., Yang, X., Zhang, H., Zhao, W.: A survey on internet of things: architecture, enabling technologies, security and privacy, and applications. IEEE Internet Things J. **4**(5), 1125–1142 (2017). https://doi.org/10.1109/JIOT.2017.2683200
9. Madakam, S., Ramaswamy, R., Tripathi, S.: Internet of Things (IoT): a literature review. J. Comput. Commun. **03**(05), 164–173 (2015). https://doi.org/10.4236/jcc.2015.35021
10. Bassi, A., et al. (eds.): Enabling Things to talk. Springer Berlin Heidelberg, Berlin, Heidelberg (2013). https://doi.org/10.1007/978-3-642-40403-0
11. IoT Environmental Monitoring - Everything you need to know, IoT Environmental Monitoring - Everything you need to know. Accedido: 23 de junio de 2024. [En línea]. Disponible en: https://www.loriot.io/blog/environmental-monitoring-01.html
12. PRISMA statement, PRISMA statement. Accedido: 13 de febrero de 2025. [En línea]. Disponible en: https://www.prisma-statement.org
13. Ďuďák, J., Gašpar, G., Budjač, R., Sládek, I., Husár, P.: A low-power data logger with simple file system for long-term environmental monitoring in remote areas. IEEE Sens. J. **23**(24), 31178–31195 (2023). https://doi.org/10.1109/JSEN.2023.3328357
14. Gaspar, P.N., Magalhães De Lima, J.P., Sousa, L.M.C., Pinto, V.P.: Development of a meteorological data acquisition prototype: a low-cost and mobile proposal. E3S Web Conf. **546**, 01015 (2024). https://doi.org/10.1051/e3sconf/202454601015
15. Hidayat, M.S., Nugroho, A.P., Sutiarso, L., Okayasu, T.: Development of environmental monitoring systems based on LoRa with cloud integration for rural area. IOP Conf. Ser. Earth Environ. Sci. **355**(1), 012010 (2019). https://doi.org/10.1088/1755-1315/355/1/012010
16. Andreadis, A., Giambene, G., Zambon, R.: Low-power IoT for monitoring unconnected remote areas. Sensors **23**(9), 4481 (2023). https://doi.org/10.3390/s23094481
17. Chen, Y., et al.: Satellite-enabled Internet of Remote Things network transmits field data from the most remote areas of the tibetan plateau. Sensors **22**(10), 3713 (2022). https://doi.org/10.3390/s22103713
18. Prauzek, M., Konecny, J., Borova, M., Janosova, K., Hlavica, J., Musilek, P.: Energy harvesting sources, storage devices and system topologies for environmental wireless sensor networks: a review. Sensors **18**(8), 2446 (2018). https://doi.org/10.3390/s18082446
19. Sunehra, D.: Raspberry pi based pollution and climate monitoring system using internet of things. Int. J. Adv. Res. Eng. Technol. **10**(2) (2019). https://doi.org/10.34218/IJARET.10.2.2019.005
20. Murdyantoro, E., Setiawan, R., Rosyadi, I., Nugraha, A.W., Susilawati, H., Ramadhani, Y.: Prototype weather station uses LoRa wireless connectivity infrastructure. J. Phys. Conf. Ser. **1367**(1), 012089 (2019). https://doi.org/10.1088/1742-6596/1367/1/012089

Key Factors in Patient Satisfaction: A Random Forest Strategy

Fabián Silva-Aravena[1]([✉]) [iD], Jenny Morales[1] [iD], Paula Sáez[1] [iD], Sergio Baltierra[2] [iD], and Héctor Cornide-Reyes[3] [iD]

[1] Facultad de Ciencias Sociales y Económicas, Departamento de Economía y Administración, Universidad Católica del Maule, Talca, Chile
{fasilva,jmoralesb,pfsaez}@ucm.cl
[2] Facultad de Ciencias de la Ingeniería, Universidad Católica del Maule, Talca, Chile
sbaltierra@ucm.cl
[3] Facultad de Ingeniería, Departamento de Ingeniería Informática y Ciencias de la Computación, Universidad de Atacama, Copiapó, Chile
hector.cornide@uda.cl

Abstract. Patient satisfaction is a key quality indicator in healthcare, influencing the adherence to treatment and the overall perception of the service. However, analyzing satisfaction is complex due to multiple factors, such as quality of care, waiting times, and the environment. This study introduces an optimized Random Forest (RF) model to classify satisfaction based on survey data from 1,000 users in a public hospital in Pakistan. The analysis focuses on registration processes, medical care, laboratory and pharmacy services, and hospital environment quality. The methodology identifies influential variables that affect satisfaction and achieves the precision of the prediction 87%. It involves transforming the target variable to classify satisfaction into three levels: low, medium and high; normalizing predictors; balancing classes using SMOTE; optimizing RF hyperparameters; and extracting decision rules. The key factors identified include the attitude of the medical personnel, waiting times, availability of medication, and hospital cleanliness. The proposed model improves understanding of key drivers of patient satisfaction and offers healthcare managers a practical tool to improve service delivery effectively. By addressing the most critical aspects, this approach supports targeted interventions to improve patient experiences and overall service quality.

Keywords: Patient satisfaction · Healthcare quality · Decision support management · Random forest optimization · SMOTE balancing

1 Introduction

Patient satisfaction is essential to evaluate the quality of healthcare services and serves as a cornerstone in hospital management [1,2]. It not only reflects the patient's perception of the care received but also their willingness to continue

A. Coman et al. (Eds.): HCII 2025, LNCS 16337, pp. 278–290, 2026.
https://doi.org/10.1007/978-3-032-12801-0_19

using the services and recommend them to others [3,4]. In addition, patient satisfaction influences treatment adherence and health outcomes, making it a critical factor in the design of healthcare policies [5]. The patient experience includes factors such as quality of care, environmental conditions, waiting times, and process efficiency [6].

Patient satisfaction models have been extensively studied, employing various methodologies to evaluate and improve healthcare quality. Satisfaction generally depends on tangible factors, such as facilities and cleanliness, as well as intangible aspects such as communication [1,7]. However, satisfaction determinants vary between cultural contexts and user expectations, which requires adaptive approaches [8,9].

The application of Machine Learning (ML) to analyze patient satisfaction has gained prominence, offering the ability to manage large datasets and uncover complex patterns [23,24]. Among these techniques, classification models have proven effective in identifying the most influential factors affecting satisfaction [25]. Predictive models based on ML facilitate targeted interventions in critical areas such as quality of care, waiting times, and resource availability [26].

Decision trees (DT) and Random Forest (RF) models are particularly effective in analyzing patient satisfaction in healthcare due to their high interpretability and ability to extract concrete decision rules [27,28]. These models enable the segmentation of patients by satisfaction level and the identification of specific areas for improvement [29]. However, such analyses face challenges, including response heterogeneity and class imbalance, which can be addressed through techniques such as SMOTE [30,31].

The contribution of our study lies in the development of a methodology based on an ML model to classify patient satisfaction, employing an optimized RF strategy to maximize prediction accuracy [30,32]. The proposed model categorizes satisfaction into three levels (that is, low, medium, and high) and highlights the variables that most strongly influence satisfaction perception. The methodology consists of five stages: transformation of the target variable, normalization of the predictor variables, class balancing using SMOTE, hyperparameter optimization, and extraction of decision rules from the optimized model [28].

This article is structured as follows. Section 2 reviews related work, followed by Sect. 3, which details the methodology. Section 4 presents the main results and Sect. 5 discusses the findings. Finally, Sect. 6 concludes the study and outlines the future implications of improving patient satisfaction with healthcare services.

2   Related Work

Patient satisfaction has become a critical focus of healthcare research, due to its impact on health outcomes and its influence on continued utilization of services [1]. The literature highlights that factors such as quality of care, hospital environment, and process efficiency are key components of the patient experience [6]. This multidimensional nature of patient satisfaction requires analytical approaches capable of capturing the interplay between these factors and their influence on the perception of overall service.

During the past decade, the analysis of patient satisfaction has advanced through the application of ML techniques, which offer the ability to handle large datasets and uncover complex patterns [24,33]. Classification methods, including DT and RF, have been widely adopted in healthcare satisfaction studies due to their high interpretability and predictive accuracy [28,34]. These models are particularly effective for identifying specific factors that influence satisfaction and for categorizing satisfaction levels, which facilitates targeted interventions in areas of high impact [35,36].

A common limitation in patient satisfaction analysis is the heterogeneity of responses and class imbalance, as surveys often exhibit a high concentration of responses at specific satisfaction levels, such as low or high, making it difficult to accurately represent all levels [30]. To address this issue, class-balancing techniques such as SMOTE have been employed, enhancing the performance of the model by generating synthetic observations for minority classes [30,37]. Previous studies have shown that incorporating SMOTE with supervised models significantly improves the classification of satisfaction levels compared to models without balancing techniques [38,39].

In addition to methodological advances, the literature emphasizes the importance of tailoring satisfaction models to the cultural context and patient expectations. Studies indicate that factors that influence patient perceptions vary substantially depending on the hospital setting, geographic region, and type of healthcare institution [40,41]. For example, while timely service delivery is critical in western contexts, accessibility and staff courtesy are more influential in others. This variability underscores the need for adaptive and personalized satisfaction models to accurately reflect patient expectations in different contexts.

Recent research on patient satisfaction also highlights a trend towards integrating quantitative and qualitative data, providing a more comprehensive view of the patient experience [42,43]. Incorporating qualitative elements, such as open-ended survey responses, captures subjective factors that influence satisfaction but may not be evident in the numerical data. This integration enables the development of hybrid models that combine supervised and unsupervised techniques, providing deeper insights and a more nuanced understanding of patient satisfaction. Such methodological advancements present a significant opportunity for future research in healthcare care, paving the way for predictive and explanatory satisfaction models that optimize the quality and experience of hospital services.

3   Methodology

In this paper, we present a strategy for classifying patient satisfaction in a public hospital using an optimized RF model. The methodology encompasses data exploration, class balancing of the target variable, and hyperparameter optimization, enabling the identification of key factors that influence patient satisfaction.

3.1   Context

In our study, we analyze overall patient satisfaction (Overall Satisfaction Index, OSI) based on a survey of 1,000 anonymous patients from a public hospital in Pakistan. The survey evaluates multiple dimensions across administrative services, medical consultations, laboratory services, pharmacy, and hospital physical facilities. Each area includes specific attributes that measure service quality, such as courtesy of staff, waiting times, and cleanliness, among others. These attributes were assessed on an ordinal scale from 1 to 4, capturing patients' experiences as categorical values. To facilitate statistical analysis and predictive modeling, we standardized the responses into numerical values.

3.2   Data Preprocessing

We performed a transformation of the target variable and a normalization procedure for the predictor variables, following these steps:

- First, we reduced the target variable, OSI, from 5 to 3 satisfaction levels to minimize class variability, enhance interpretability, and improve prediction quality. The transformation of OSI (Y) was defined as follows:

$$Y = \begin{cases} 1 \text{ (Low)} & ; \text{if } 1 \leq \text{OSI} \leq 2, \\ 2 \text{ (Medium)} & ; \text{if } 3 \leq \text{OSI} \leq 4, \\ 3 \text{ (High)} & ; \text{if } \text{OSI} = 5, \end{cases} \tag{1}$$

  where 1, 2, and 3 correspond to low, medium, and high satisfaction levels, respectively. Using this classification, we identified 11 patients in the low satisfaction level, 679 in the medium level, and 310 in the high level.
- Next, we normalized the predictor variables to ensure the dataset was on the same measurement scale [10]. This step enhances the performance of the model. The normalization was performed as follows:

$$Z^s = \frac{Z - \mu}{\sigma} \tag{2}$$

  where Z represents the original values of the variables in the dataset, Z^s denotes the normalized values, μ is the mean of each variable in the dataset, and σ is the standard deviation of each variable.

3.3   Class Balancing: SMOTE Strategy

To address the class imbalance in Y, we applied the SMOTE strategy, which generates synthetic instances for all minority classes by interpolating existing instances [11,12]. Let $v_{\min}$ represent the set of instances in the minority class. The process is defined as follows:

- For each instance $v_i \in v_{\min}$, we selected the k-nearest neighbors using the Euclidean distance [12], $d(v_i, v_j)$, defined as:

$$d(v_i, v_j) = \sqrt{\sum_{f=1}^{F}(v_{i,f} - v_{j,f})^2} \qquad (3)$$

  where F represents the number of features in the dataset, $v_{i,f}$ is the value of feature f for instance v_i, and $v_{j,f}$ is the value of feature f for instance v_j.
- Among the k-nearest neighbors, we randomly selected one, denoted as v_{nei}.
- Next, we generate a new synthetic instance, $v_{\mathrm{new},f}$, by linearly interpolating between v_i and v_{nei}, using a random coefficient, $\lambda \in [0,1]$. The value $v_{\mathrm{new},f}$ was obtained as follows:

$$v_{\mathrm{new},f} = v_{i,f} + \lambda \cdot (v_{\mathrm{nei},f} - v_{i,f}) \qquad (4)$$

- We repeated this process for all the features f in the dataset and for all instances in $v_{\min}$.

3.4 Dataset Splitting for Model Training and Evaluation

Subsequently, we split the balanced data set into 70% for training and 30% for testing, as follows:

$$Z^s = \left\{ Z^s_{\mathrm{train}}, Z^s_{\mathrm{test}} \right\}, \quad Y = \{y_{\mathrm{train}}, y_{\mathrm{test}}\} \qquad (5)$$

where Z^s_{train} and y_{train} were used to build and optimize the model, while Z^s_{test} and y_{test} were reserved for final evaluation.

3.5 Model Selection: Random Forest Strategy

For the classification of Y, we selected the RF model due to its suitability to handle the heterogeneous nature and class imbalance present in our study data [13,14]. In addition, RF was chosen for its strong predictive performance and its ability to identify the variables that contribute to patient satisfaction, facilitating interpretation and decision making for healthcare teams.

The RF model consists of a set of n decision trees $h_1(Z^s)$, $h_2(Z^s)$,...,$h_n(Z^s)$ where each tree h_i is trained on a random subset of data $\mathcal{D}$ and features F [15].

The final prediction, $\hat{Y}$, obtained from the RF model corresponds to the mode of the individual predictions of each tree, defined as follows:

$$\hat{Y} = \mathrm{mode}\{h_i(Z^s) \mid i = 1, \ldots, n\} \qquad (6)$$

For each tree h_i we selected a random subset $\mathcal{D}_i \in \mathcal{D}$. The observations not included in $\mathcal{D}_i$, were reserved to evaluate the performance of the tree h_i.

$$\mathcal{D}_i \subset \mathcal{D}, \quad |\mathcal{D}_i| = |\mathcal{D}| \tag{7}$$

Next, for each tree node, we randomly select a subset of f_s characteristics from the available F, where $f_s = \sqrt{F}$. Based on this subset, the splits of the nodes were determined by maximizing the information gain $\Delta G(t)$, which in turn minimized the impurity of the nodes using the Gini index G, calculated as:

$$G = 1 - \sum_{c=1}^{C} p_c^2 \tag{8}$$

where p_c represents the proportion of observations belonging to class c. Subsequently, we calculated $\Delta G(t)$ by splitting node t into two child nodes (t_L, t_R), as follows:

$$\Delta G(t) = I(t) - \left(\frac{|t_L|}{|t|} I(t_L) + \frac{|t_R|}{|t|} I(t_R) \right) \tag{9}$$

where I_t represents the impurity of the original node, and $|t|$, $|t_L|$, and $|t_R|$ denote the number of observations in the original node and the left and right child nodes, respectively.

3.6 Optimizing Random Forest Hyperparameters

To maximize the precision of the RF model, we optimize its hyperparameters using the GridSearchCV strategy combined with 5-fold cross-validation [16]. The evaluated hyperparameters were as follows:

$$
\begin{aligned}
n_{\text{trees}} &\in \{50, 100, 150, 200\} \quad \text{(number of trees)} \\
\text{max\_depth} &\in \{10, 15, 20, \text{None}\} \quad \text{(maximum depth)} \\
\text{min\_samples\_split} &\in \{2, 5, 10\} \quad \text{(minimum samples to split a node)} \\
\text{min\_samples\_leaf} &\in \{1, 2, 4\} \quad \text{(minimum samples to form a leaf)} \\
\text{max\_features} &\in \{\sqrt{F}, \log_2(F), \text{None}\} \quad \text{(number of features per split)}
\end{aligned}
$$

Using the hyperparameter search strategy, which maximizes the weighted F1 score, $\mathcal{F}_1^{\text{w}}$, we identified the optimal combination, θ_{opt}, defined as follows:

$$\theta_{\text{opt}} = \underset{\theta}{\operatorname{argmax}} \, \mathcal{F}_1^{\text{w}}(\text{RF}(Z_{\text{train}}, \theta)) \tag{10}$$

3.7 Evaluation of the Optimized Random Forest Model

We evaluated the optimized RF model on the test set using the following metrics: precision ($\mathcal{P}$), recall ($\mathcal{R}$), and weighted F1 score ($\mathcal{F}_1$), calculated as follows:

$$P = \frac{TP}{TP + FP}, \quad R = \frac{TP}{TP + FN}, \quad \mathcal{F}_1 = \frac{2 \cdot \mathcal{P} \cdot \mathcal{R}}{\mathcal{P} + \mathcal{R}} \tag{11}$$

where TP (true positives) represents the number of instances correctly classified for a given class, FP (false positives) denotes the instances incorrectly classified as belonging to that class, and FN (false negatives) refers to the instances incorrectly classified as belonging to other classes [17].

To evaluate the overall performance of the model, we used $\mathcal{F}_1^{\text{w}}$ [18]. This metric is defined as:

$$\mathcal{F}_1^{\text{w}} = \sum_{i=1}^{C} \frac{n_i}{N} \cdot \mathcal{F}_{1,i} \tag{12}$$

where C is the number of classes, n_i is the number of instances in class i, and N is the total number of instances. Additionally, we evaluated the RF model's ability to differentiate between classes by calculating the True Positive Rate ($\mathcal{T}$) and False Positive Rate ($\mathcal{F}$) for each class:

$$\mathcal{T} = \frac{TP}{TP + FN}, \quad \mathcal{F} = \frac{FP}{FP + TN} \tag{13}$$

For each class i, we generated the Receiver Operating Characteristic (ROC) curve by plotting $\mathcal{T}$ against $\mathcal{F}$ at various probability thresholds. The area under the curve (AUC) was defined as

$$\text{AUC} = \int_0^1 \mathcal{T}(\mathcal{F}) \, d\mathcal{F} \tag{14}$$

where the AUC value ranges from 0.5 (random model) to 1 (perfect classification). We calculated an AUC for each class predicted by the model. Finally, we reported the weighted average as the overall performance metric.

We used these metrics, along with the confusion matrix and the ROC curve, to comprehensively evaluate the optimized RF model on the test set.

4 Results

In this section, we present the study results, which were conducted using Google Colab Research and implemented in Python.

To enhance the interpretability of the optimized RF model, the methodology emphasized the importance of class balancing using SMOTE, hyperparameter optimization with GridSearchCV, and the extraction of decision rules. The results are presented below.

4.1 Synthetic Data Generation with SMOTE

After applying the SMOTE strategy, we successfully balanced the dataset with a total of 450 observations per class, generating 1,037 synthetic instances and achieving a total dataset size of 2,037 observations (see Fig. 1).

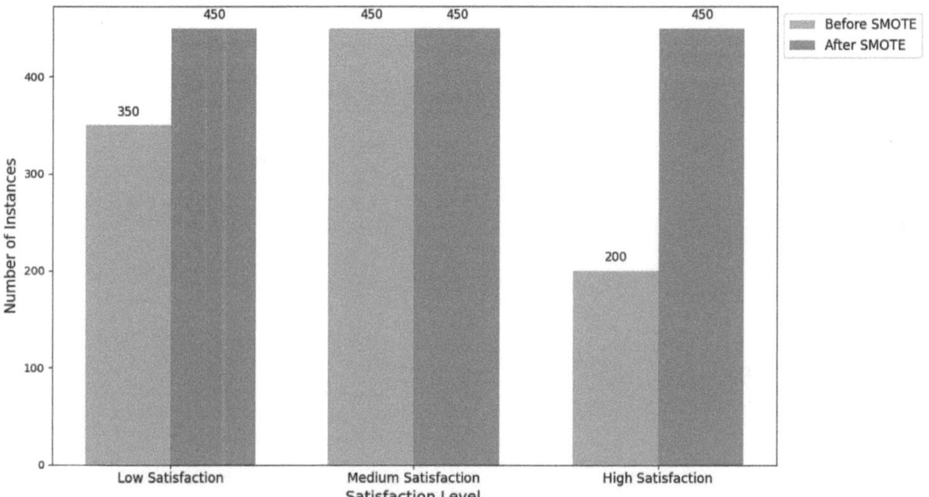

Fig. 1. Class distribution before and after applying SMOTE

4.2 Optimized Random Forest Performance

Our methodology enhances prediction accuracy and generalization capability by determining optimal hyperparameters (θ_{opt}): `max_depth`: 10, `max_features`: `sqrt`, `min_samples_leaf`: 1, `min_samples_split`: 2, and `n_estimators`: 150. With this configuration, the optimized RF model achieved a weighted $\mathcal{F}_1^{\mathrm{w}}$ score of 87%. The results are presented in Table 1 and Fig. 2.

Table 1. Confusion matrix for optimized RF model

True Class	Low	Medium	High
Low	197	1	0
Medium	9	156	38
High	3	30	178

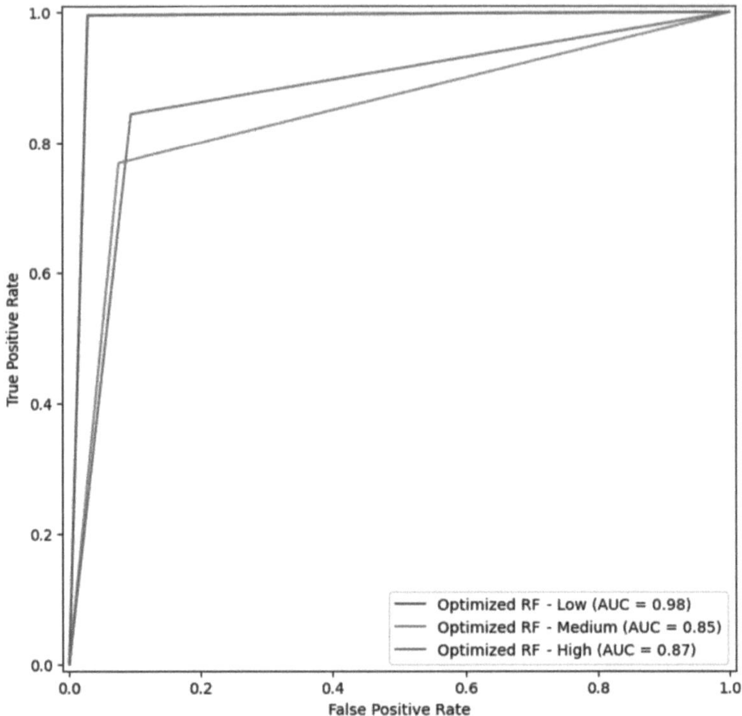

Fig. 2. ROC curves for the optimized RF model

4.3   Key Decision Rules Extraction

From the optimized RF model, we extracted a representative tree to identify the most relevant decision rules that determine patient satisfaction levels. These rules are designed to be interpretable, facilitating their application by healthcare managers. Table 2 summarizes the key decision rules.

Table 2. Decision Rules from the Optimized RF Model

Rule Description	Class Predicted
If Doctor_Attitude > 3 (good) and Registration_Waiting ≤ 2 (no delay)	High
If Lab_Staff_Attitude > 3 (excellent) and Lab_Waiting_Time ≤ 2 (short)	High
If Lab_Report_Quality > 3 (very good) and Doctor_Attitude > 3 (good)	High
If Medicine_Delivery_Time > 3 (quick) and Reception_Staff_Assistance > 3 (excellent)	Medium
If Environment_Cleanliness ≤ 2 (poor) and Medicine_Availability ≤ 2 (low)	Low
If Bathroom_Cleanliness ≤ 2 (poor) and Doctor_Guidance ≤ 2 (poor)	Low
If Pharmacist_Attitude ≤ 2 (poor) and Medicine_Availability ≤ 2 (low)	Low

5   Discussion

In this study, we develop a methodology based on an optimized RF model to classify patient satisfaction (Y) into three levels: low, medium, and high. The approach included normalizing predictor variables (Z^s), balancing classes using SMOTE, and optimizing hyperparameters (θ_{opt}), resulting in an effective and interpretable model.

One of the key strengths of the RF model is its ability to handle imbalanced and heterogeneous data, common in satisfaction surveys. Incorporating SMOTE to balance the classes of Y addressed the inherent data bias, improving the representation of minority classes. This is critical, as previous studies have highlighted that imbalanced responses can significantly reduce a model's predictive performance [19]. Furthermore, the interpretability of the RF model, through the use of decision trees, facilitates the identification of critical variables such as staff attitude, waiting times, medication availability, and hospital cleanliness. This contrasts with approaches such as deep neural networks, which offer limited interpretability [20].

However, there are limitations. The model relies on the quality of the collected data, which can introduce subjective biases based on patients' individual perceptions. While our approach focuses on quantitative variables derived from standardized responses, other studies have emphasized the value of including qualitative data and contextual observations to enrich the assessment [21]. Furthermore, preprocessing and optimization, including the computation of metrics like Gini and $\Delta G(t)$, may be resource-intensive for hospitals with limited technical capabilities. Hybrid approaches combining supervised and unsupervised models have shown promise in reducing this burden [22].

Compared to previous studies, our model stands out for its precision $(\mathcal{F}_1^{\mathrm{w}} = 87\%)$, surpassing traditional approaches and demonstrating the effectiveness of optimization strategies based on θ_{opt}. Nonetheless, the results should be interpreted cautiously, considering the limitations of the hospital context and the potential biases in the survey data.

6   Conclusions

In this paper, we developed a five-stage methodology to classify patient satisfaction (Y) in a hospital setting using an optimized Random Forest (RF) model. The process included normalizing predictor variables (Z^s), balancing classes with SMOTE, and optimizing hyperparameters (θ_{opt}). This approach enabled the construction of a robust and interpretable model, highlighting critical factors in the hospital experience.

The results indicate that the optimized model achieved a weighted $\mathcal{F}_1^{\mathrm{w}}$ score of 87%, identifying variables such as staff attitude, waiting times, medication availability, and hospital cleanliness as the most influential in overall patient satisfaction. The class balancing and optimization strategies significantly enhanced the model's ability to classify satisfaction levels, providing clear decision rules for healthcare managers.

To further improve this methodology, we propose integrating qualitative data, such as open-ended patient feedback, and exploring hybrid approaches that combine supervised and unsupervised techniques, reducing reliance on intensive pre-processing. Incorporating longitudinal data would allow for an analysis of how satisfaction evolves over time, offering a more dynamic and adaptive perspective.

From a management standpoint, this model serves as a practical tool for optimizing service quality, enabling healthcare managers to prioritize interventions based on empirical data. For future studies, we aim to apply this methodology in diverse hospital contexts and explore its integration into real-time feedback systems, fostering continuous improvement in the patient experience.

References

1. Fatima, A., Ali, M.: Hospital management and patient satisfaction. Int. J. Healthcare Res. **12**(4), 123–134 (2018)
2. Ferrand, D., Jean, M.: Patient perceptions of service quality in hospitals. Healthcare Rev. **30**(2), 89–101 (2016)
3. Stein, S.M., Day, M., Karia, R., Hutzler, L., Bosco, J.A., III.: Patients' perceptions of care are associated with quality of hospital care: a survey of 4605 hospitals. Am. J. Med. Qual. **30**(4), 382–388 (2015)
4. Gishu, T., Weldetsadik, A.Y., Tekleab, A.M.: Patients' perception of quality of nursing care; a tertiary center experience from Ethiopia. BMC Nurs. **18**, 1–6 (2019)
5. Nwosu, N.T., Babatunde, S.O., Ijomah, T.: Enhancing customer experience and market penetration through advanced data analytics in the health industry. World J. Adv. Res. Rev. **22**(3), 1157–1170 (2024)
6. Berkowitz, B.: The patient experience and patient satisfaction: measurement of a complex dynamic. Online J. Issues Nurs. **21**(1) (2016)
7. Hussain, A., Sial, M.S., Usman, S.M., Hwang, J., Jiang, Y., Shafiq, A.: What factors affect patient satisfaction in public sector hospitals: evidence from an emerging economy. Int. J. Environ. Res. Public Health **16**(6), 994 (2019)
8. Larson, E., Sharma, J., Bohren, M.A., Tunçalp, Ö.: When the patient is the expert: measuring patient experience and satisfaction with care. Bull. World Health Organ. **97**(8), 563 (2019)
9. Mpinga, E.K., Chastonay, P.: Satisfaction of patients: a right to health indicator? Health Policy **100**(2–3), 144–150 (2011)
10. Singh, D., Singh, B.: Investigating the impact of data normalization on classification performance. Appl. Soft Comput. **97**, 105524 (2020)
11. Hassanzadeh, R., Farhadian, M., Rafieemehr, H.: Hospital mortality prediction in traumatic injuries patients: comparing different SMOTE-based machine learning algorithms. BMC Med. Res. Methodol. **23**(1), 101 (2023)
12. Mohammed, A.J., Muhammed Hassan, M., Hussein Kadir, D.: Improving classification performance for a novel imbalanced medical dataset using SMOTE method. Int. J. Adv. Trends Comput. Sci. Eng. **9**(3), 3161–3172 (2020)
13. Bader-El-Den, M., Teitei, E., Perry, T.: Biased random forest for dealing with the class imbalance problem. IEEE Trans. Neural Netw. Learn. Syst. **30**(7), 2163–2172 (2018)
14. More, A.S., Rana, D.P., Agarwal, I.: Random forest classifier approach for imbalanced big data classification for smart city application domains. Int. J. Comput. Intell. & IoT **1**(2) (2018)

15. Lyu, S.H., He, Y.X., Zhou, Z.H.: Depth is more powerful than width with prediction concatenation in deep forest. Adv. Neural. Inf. Process. Syst. **35**, 29719–29732 (2022)
16. Handoyo, S., Chen, Y. P., Wibowo, R. B. E., Widodo, A. W.: Finding Optimal Models of Random Forest and Support Vector Machine through Tuning Hyperparameters in Classifying the Imbalanced Data. Preprints (2024)
17. Wang, X., Zhai, M., Ren, Z., Ren, H., Li, M., Quan, D., Chen, L., Qiu, L.: Exploratory study on classification of diabetes mellitus through a combined Random Forest Classifier. BMC Med. Inform. Decis. Mak. **21**, 1–14 (2021)
18. Gumaei, A., Ismail, W.N., Hassan, M.R., Hassan, M.M., Mohamed, E., Alelaiwi, A., Fortino, G.: A decision-level fusion method for COVID-19 patient health prediction. Big Data Res. **27**, 100287 (2022)
19. Ghorbani, R., Ghousi, R., Makui, A., Atashi, A.: A new hybrid predictive model to predict the early mortality risk in intensive care units on a highly imbalanced dataset. IEEE Access **8**, 141066–141079 (2020)
20. ElShawi, R., Sherif, Y., Al-Mallah, M., Sakr, S.: Interpretability in healthcare: A comparative study of local machine learning interpretability techniques. Comput. Intell. **37**(4), 1633–1650 (2021)
21. Berger, S., Saut, A.M., Berssaneti, F.T.: Using patient feedback to drive quality improvement in hospitals: a qualitative study. BMJ Open **10**(10), e037641 (2020)
22. Baker, S., Xiang, W., Atkinson, I.: Continuous and automatic mortality risk prediction using vital signs in the intensive care unit: a hybrid neural network approach. Sci. Rep. **10**(1), 21282 (2020)
23. Khanbhai, M., Anyadi, P., Symons, J., Flott, K., Darzi, A., Mayer, E.: Applying natural language processing and machine learning techniques to patient experience feedback: a systematic review. BMJ Health & Care Informatics **28**(1) (2021)
24. Avula, R., et al.: Data-driven decision-making in healthcare through advanced data mining techniques: A survey on applications and limitations. Int. J. Appl. Mach. Learn. Comput. Intell. **12**(4), 64–85 (2022)
25. Patil, K., Patil, S., Danve, R., Patil, R.: Machine learning and neural network models for customer churn prediction in banking and telecom sectors. In: Editor, F., Editor, S. (eds.) ICACECS 2021, Proceedings of Second International Conference on Advances in Computer Engineering and Communication Systems, pp. 241–253. Springer, Heidelberg (2022)
26. Yanamala, A.K.Y.: Cost-sensitive deep learning for predicting hospital readmission: enhancing patient care and resource allocation. Int. J. Adv. Eng. Technol. Innov. **1**(3), 56–81 (2022)
27. Valdes, G., Luna, J.M., Eaton, E., Simone, C.B., Ungar, L.H., Solberg, T.D.: MediBoost: a patient stratification tool for interpretable decision making in the era of precision medicine. Sci. Rep. **6**(1), 37854 (2016)
28. Doubleday, K., Zhou, H., Fu, H., Zhou, J.: An algorithm for generating individualized treatment decision trees and random forests. J. Comput. Graph. Stat. **27**(4), 849–860 (2018)
29. Rafid, A.K.M.R.H., Azam, S., Montaha, S., Karim, A., Fahim, K.U., Hasan, M.Z.: An effective ensemble machine learning approach to classify breast cancer based on feature selection and lesion segmentation using preprocessed mammograms. Biology **11**(11), 1654 (2022)
30. Yan, Y., Chen, Z., Xu, C., Shen, X., Shiao, J., Einck, J., Chen, R. C., Gao, H.: An Oversampling-enhanced Multi-class Imbalanced Classification Framework for Patient Health Status Prediction Using Patient-reported Outcomes (2024). arXiv:2411.10819

31. Wang, L., Zhao, Z., Luo, Y., Yu, H., Wu, S., Ren, X., Zheng, C., Huang, X.: Classifying 2-year recurrence in patients with DLBCL using clinical variables with imbalanced data and machine learning methods. Comput. Methods Programs Biomed. **196**, 105567 (2020)
32. Ahmed, A., Ashour, O., Ali, H., Firouz, M.: An integrated optimization and machine learning approach to predict the admission status of emergency patients. Expert Syst. Appl. **202**, 117314 (2022)
33. Ahmed, Z., Mohamed, K., Zeeshan, S., Dong, X.: Artificial intelligence with multifunctional machine learning platform development for better healthcare and precision medicine. Database **2020**, baaa010 (2020)
34. Banegas-Luna, A.J., Peña-García, J., Iftene, A., Guadagni, F., Ferroni, P., Scarpato, N., Zanzotto, F.M., Bueno-Crespo, A., Pérez-Sánchez, H.: Towards the interpretability of machine learning predictions for medical applications targeting personalised therapies: A cancer case survey. Int. J. Mol. Sci. **22**(9), 4394 (2021)
35. Al Hammadi, F.: Evaluation of Patient Satisfaction in Telemedicine Using Machine Learning Algorithms (2022)
36. Almaazmi, S.: Evaluation of Patient Experience in Healthcare. PhD thesis, Khalifa University of Science (2020)
37. Xu, Y., Park, Y., Park, J.D., Sun, B.: Predicting nurse turnover for highly imbalanced data using SMOTE and machine learning algorithms. Healthcare **11**(24), 3173 (2023)
38. Ishaq, A., Sadiq, S., Umer, M., Ullah, S., Mirjalili, S., Rupapara, V., Nappi, M.: Improving the prediction of heart failure patients' survival using SMOTE and effective data mining techniques. IEEE Access **9**, 39707–39716 (2021)
39. Xu, Z., Shen, D., Nie, T., Kou, Y.: A hybrid sampling algorithm combining M-SMOTE and ENN based on Random Forest for medical imbalanced data. J. Biomed. Inform. **107**, 103465 (2020)
40. Young, G.J., Meterko, M., Desai, K.R.: Patient satisfaction with hospital care: effects of demographic and institutional characteristics. Med. Care **38**(3), 325–334 (2000)
41. Mourshed, M., Zhao, Y.: Healthcare providers' perception of design factors related to physical environments in hospitals. J. Environ. Psychol. **32**(4), 362–370 (2012)
42. Grondahl, V.A., Wilde-Larsson, B., Karlsson, I., Hall-Lord, M.L.: Patients' experiences of care quality and satisfaction during hospital stay: a qualitative study. Eur. J. Pers. Cent. Healthc. **1**(1), 185–192 (2013)
43. Luo, J.Y.N., Liu, P.P., Wong, M.C.M.: Patients' satisfaction with dental care: a qualitative study to develop a satisfaction instrument. BMC Oral Health **18**, 1–10 (2018)

Security, Privacy, and Trust in Digital Environments

Improving Security and Privacy of Cognitive Digital Twins Through Dynamic Consent for Healthcare and Resilient Societies

Sabarathinam Chockalingam[1]($\boxtimes$), Sandeep Pirbhulal[2], and Habtamu Abie[2]

[1] Department of Risk and Security, Institute for Energy Technology, Halden, Norway
`Sabarathinam.Chockalingam@ife.no`
[2] Norwegian Computing Center, Oslo, Norway
`{sandeep,Habtamu.Abie}@nr.no`

Abstract. Cognitive Digital Twins (CDTs) are virtual models of physical systems that integrate cognitive functions with real-time Internet of Things (IoT) data to support simulation, decision-making, and cyber resilience. In domains such as healthcare and smart cities, CDTs enable advanced capabilities but also introduce significant privacy and security risks, especially due to continuous, real-time data exchange and automated decision-making. This paper presents DC-TWIN, a dynamic consent-enabled CDT framework that addresses the limitations of static, one-time consent models in real-time, data-intensive environments. DC-TWIN introduces a multi-layered architecture consisting of: (i) a multi-layered architectural stack, including user control, policy management, dynamic trust, and data governance layers, that supports compliance monitoring, risk-aware user interfaces, consent history tracking, federated identity and role binding, and adaptive trust modeling, and (ii) a dynamic consent reasoning engine that uses contextual signals (e.g., user role, device status, network activity) and human factors (e.g., cognitive load, trust calibration, fatigue) to assess data access requests in real time, issuing granular decisions (grant, deny, prompt) or escalating for clarification. We highlight key use cases in healthcare, welfare technologies, and smart cities. The framework empowers users with real-time, contextual control over how their data is accessed, shared, and reused through adaptive interfaces and personalized consent mechanisms. By integrating dynamic consent reasoning, trust calibration, and continuous feedback loops, DC-TWIN supports transparent, compliant, and user-aligned data governance. It contributes to the secure and ethical deployment of CDTs by reinforcing user autonomy, enhancing risk communication, and enabling responsive consent management in critical domains such as healthcare.

Keywords: Digital Twins · Dynamic Consent · Healthcare · Privacy · Security · Social Robots

A. Coman et al. (Eds.): HCII 2025, LNCS 16337, pp. 293–305, 2026.
https://doi.org/10.1007/978-3-032-12801-0_20

1 Introduction

1.1 Motivation and Background

Cognitive Digital Twins (CDTs) are virtual representations of physical systems, processes, or entities that integrate key cognitive functions, including attention, perception, learning, memory, and decision-making [1–3]. In our context, CDTs denote virtual replicas of Internet of Things (IoT)-based systems used in healthcare and resilient societies, incorporating cognitive capabilities and a human-in-the-loop approach [2]. This allows for the collection of real-time data and insights from IoT devices without disrupting ongoing operations, while also simulating human behavior, interactions, and decision-making processes. By simulating critical events in a virtual environment, CDTs support performance optimization, enable proactive mitigation of cyber threats, and allow testing of how privacy issues could occur and be managed. On one hand, CDTs can play an important role in strengthening the security of critical applications such as healthcare, social robotics, and smart city infrastructures [4]. On the other hand, CDTs effectively double the attack surface, posing severe challenges related to data privacy and security, particularly in areas such as consent, trust, and identity management [5].

In healthcare and other critical applications, CDTs handle not only sensitive data such as medical records and personal information but also simulate key cognitive aspects of human behavior and decision-making. This dual role highlights the need for adaptive approaches to data protection and identity verification. As regulatory focus intensifies around frameworks like General Data Protection Regulation (GDPR), ISO/IEC standards, and NIS2 directive, there is a growing need to embed privacy-by-design principles into CDT platforms, particularly around consent management. Moreover, empowering users over their personal data, including specifying who can access it, reduces the risk of unauthorized access and strengthens trust in CDT systems, ultimately, these measures support the development of a more transparent, secure, and resilient digital ecosystem [6].

An effective consent mechanism is a cornerstone of privacy-by-design, essential for maintaining user autonomy and trust in systems like CDTs. Traditional static consent, where individuals provide one-time permission for data use without the ability to update or withdraw it, falls short in the dynamic context of CDTs [7]. As CDT systems evolve over time, often adapting to new analytical capabilities and broader use cases, static consent limits user control and fails to reflect the changing landscape of data use. For instance, a CDT developed for personalized healthcare. A patient may initially consent to the use of their medical data to monitor a chronic illness. However, as the CDT system expands, the same data might later be used to evaluate new treatment responses or even contribute to anonymized datasets for public health research. Without a mechanism for updating their consent, the patient loses control over how their data is repurposed, undermining both privacy and autonomy.

Despite the critical need for adaptable consent mechanisms, research on integrating dynamic consent frameworks into CDTs remains limited. This study aims to fill that gap by addressing the following Research Question (RQ):

RQ. How can dynamic consent be integrated into Cognitive Digital Twins (CDTs) to enhance user control and privacy in healthcare and other critical applications?

To address the limitations of static and one-time consent in dynamic and data-intensive environments like healthcare and smart cities, we introduce DC-TWIN, a dynamic consent-enabled CDT framework. DC-TWIN integrates real-time, user-driven consent management into CDT architecture, allowing individuals to retain control over how their data is accessed and used as system contexts evolve. Moreover, consent policies can adapt dynamically to contextual factors such as user role, device status, and environment, enabling responsive and situation-aware data governance. To enhance security, dynamic consent can also incorporate periodic identity verification, ensuring that access rights are continuously aligned with authorized user intent. This helps mitigate risks such as impersonation, and unauthorized data access. Beyond privacy protection, dynamic consent supports the flexible and responsible data sharing needed for continuous CDT development. It ensures that user trust and ethical data practices scale alongside the increasing sophistication of CDTs in sectors like healthcare and smart cities.

Unlike traditional IoT systems, where dynamic consent typically governs isolated data collection and sharing, such as a smartwatch transmitting heart rate data to an application, dynamic consent in CDTs extends to how data is processed and reused inside an evolving virtual model. In CDTs, data is not only collected but also continuously processed, aggregated, and repurposed within an evolving virtual model. This model generates insights and supports decision-making based on real-time updates, contextual inputs, and behavioral simulations. As a result, consent management in CDTs must account for ongoing, multi-layered data interactions, making it significantly more demanding, and essential, for ensuring user autonomy, privacy, and trust.

1.2 Our Contributions

In this paper, we present DC-TWIN, a dynamic consent-enabled CDT framework for healthcare and resilient society applications. The main contributions are as follows:

- A lightweight, federated dynamic consent architecture integrated into CDTs, enabling real-time, user-driven access control.
- A context-aware consent reasoning model that dynamically evaluates data access requests based on contextual factors, while also accounting for human factors to determine when consent is needed, from whom, and at what level (e.g., pre-approved, prompt, or deny).
- Demonstration of representative use cases within healthcare and resilient society contexts.

1.3 Organization of the Paper

The remainder of this paper is organized as follows: Sect. 2 presents literature review. Section 3 introduces our proposed dynamic consent-enabled CDT framework. Section 4 demonstrates the approach through representative use cases. Conclusions and future work directions are provided in Sect. 5.

2 Literature Review

2.1 Security and Digital Twins

DTs enhance the understanding of cyber risks by continuously monitoring vulnerabilities and attack-vectors, thereby enabling greater resilience in physical systems [8–10]. As such, DTs possess significant potential for supporting secure, reliable, and responsive services in domains such as healthcare and resilient societies [8]. They have also been applied to strengthen cyber security, especially in areas such as autonomous attack detection [9], cyber security training [10], among others. For instance, DTs have the potential to develop new prevention, detection, and response strategies without disturbing real-world operations [2]. In [2], Pirbhulal et al. introduce DTs with cognitive capabilities and a human-in-the-loop approach referred as CDTs. This support intelligent, real-time decision making for improving security in Information Technology (IT) – Operational Technology (OT) integrated CIs. The convergence of IT and OT in sectors such as healthcare and resilient societies significantly expands the threat surface, making CDT-based approaches particularly valuable. However, while DTs and CDTs can strengthen system resilience, they also raise new security concerns. The virtual communication and synchronization between physical and digital entities can increase the attack surface and introduce new vulnerabilities [11]. Alcarez et al. present the significance of secure data flow within DTs by restricting unauthorized access which raise the necessity for efficient data sharing security strategies in virtual systems [12].

2.2 Privacy and Digital Twins

While DTs provide enhanced capabilities for system performance and resilience, they also introduce complex privacy challenges. Notably, DTs process large volumes of real-time, often sensitive data, raising concerns about how that data is collected, stored, and reused. Some efforts have explored the use of DTs for privacy enhancement. For example, [13] presents a DT-based demonstrator capable of simulating privacy-preserving scenarios in smart ecosystems. However, protecting the privacy of data within DT environments remains a critical issue [14, 15]. Modern systems must adhere to increasingly stringent data protection frameworks, including ISO/IEC 27000:2018, GDPR, and the NIS2 Directive. However, achieving compliance is particularly challenging in practice. These regulatory frameworks provide limited guidance on how to implement privacy safeguards in complex, interconnected environments like DT infrastructures.

Since its enforcement, GDPR has compelled organizations, both within [16] and beyond the EU [17], to demonstrate compliance or face significant penalties. Nonetheless, the technical interpretation and operationalization of GDPR requirements remain ambiguous [18], especially when applied to emerging technologies such as DTs. These systems may involve automated, data-driven decision-making processes that use sensitive personal information, creating a grey area for consent management, user control, and accountability.

Given the evolving and often opaque nature of data processing within DTs, especially CDTs, there is a need for adaptive, user-centric privacy mechanisms that can respond to changing contexts. This highlights the importance of embedding dynamic consent capabilities directly into CDT architecture to ensure transparency, compliance, and user autonomy.

2.3 Dynamic Consent: Foundations, Challenges, and Relevance for CDTs

As CDTs evolve into complex, data-intensive systems that continuously collect, process, and repurpose sensitive information, traditional static consent mechanisms prove insufficient. Static consent, typically obtained once at the point of data collection, lacks the flexibility to reflect changes in data use, operational context, or user intent over time. This rigidity risks undermining user autonomy, transparency, and compliance, particularly in domains where data is reused across evolving services and scenarios. Dynamic consent has emerged as a user-centric alternative that addresses these limitations. It enables individuals to modify, revoke, or grant consent in real time, promoting continuous engagement and transparency. First widely articulated in the context of biomedical research [19], dynamic consent has since been adopted in healthcare, and IoT domains, where it enables adaptive privacy management and user-centric data governance.

A recent systematic literature review [20] identifies key themes in dynamic consent research, highlighting its role in supporting privacy, user control, trust, and transparency. However, the review also finds that while privacy and control are widely addressed, security and risk communication remain underexplored, especially in the context of emerging digital ecosystems like CDTs. Studies such as [21] and [22] emphasize the benefits of dynamic consent, including personalization, continuous user control, and improved trust. Others (e.g., [23, 24]) explore technical architectures, such as blockchain-based solutions, to ensure auditability and integrity of consent transactions. However, challenges persist around consent fatigue, usability, and the lack of standardized consent enforcement frameworks.

Despite growing interest, dynamic consent has not been clearly explored in the context of DTs, where continuous simulation, real-time data use, and human interaction create a need for context-aware and flexible consent mechanisms. This gap motivates our work, which introduces a conceptual framework for integrating dynamic consent into DTs to support ethical, secure, and user-controlled data sharing in healthcare and other critical domains.

3 Proposed Dynamic Consent-Enabled Cognitive Digital Twins Framework (DC-TWIN)

3.1 Physical Twin

The physical twin component of the proposed DC-TWIN architecture focuses on real-world, IoT-based systems in healthcare and resilient society domains, such as clinical trials, smart cities, welfare robotics, and health data-sharing infrastructures (Fig. 1). These systems generate rich, heterogeneous streams of sensitive data (e.g., patient vitals, sensor readings from elderly-care robots, real-time environmental data from smart city infrastructure), which are transmitted via wireless networks (e.g., 5G, Wi-Fi) to authorized entities including healthcare professionals, social workers, and municipal services.

As outlined in Sect. 2.1, such environments are increasingly targeted by cyber threats due to the convergence of IT and OT layers. Wireless communication channels in particular are vulnerable to eavesdropping, spoofing, and data tampering. Given the high sensitivity of medical and behavioural data, these risks demand not only technical protections, but also privacy-aware consent governance, as discussed in Sect. 2.2. To support this, the physical twin continuously synchronizes with its virtual counterpart, receiving feedback from simulated threat scenarios, policy testing, and context-sensitive privacy evaluations. For instance, if an unusual access pattern is detected during a remote clinical consultation (e.g., a third-party application trying to access sensor data from a smart health device), the CDT can simulate the threat, evaluate it against consent policies, and recommend mitigation (e.g., deny access or prompt the user). This enables real-time, proactive threat mitigation without interrupting ongoing care services.

In addition, physical twins serve not only as data collectors and actuators but as gateways for embedding human-centric considerations, such as user preferences, interaction comfort, and ethical constraints, into CDT workflows. For example, in a welfare robotics scenario, a user may predefine specific boundaries for when and how their interactions can be recorded and used for system learning. These preferences are enforced downstream through the CDT's dynamic consent engine (Sect. 3.4), ensuring that physical context, autonomy, and privacy norms are tightly intertwined.

In this way, the physical twin contributes to both technical resilience and ethical governance, aligning real-world system behaviours with the adaptive and user-aligned principles central to DC-TWIN.

3.2 Virtual Twin

The virtual twin component of the DC-TWIN architecture mirrors its physical counterpart in a continuously synchronized digital environment enriched with cognitive and adaptive capabilities. As illustrated in the Fig. 1, it serves as an intelligent control and simulation layer, enabling real-time analysis, system-wide resilience, and context-aware decision-making. The virtual twin operates through three tightly interlinked functions:

- **Monitoring Security and Integrity Events:** The virtual twin constantly monitors for security threats and integrity violations, such as unauthorized access, data tampering, and/or device anomalies. For example, in a smart hospital setting, it can detect irregular login patterns to electronic health records or flag anomalies in vital sign sensors that may indicate tampering or device malfunction. This monitoring function combines real-time sensing with cognitive modeling to support anticipatory threat detection and early risk mitigation.
- **Analyzing Access and Consent Policies:** This module dynamically evaluates access control rules and user consent conditions to determine whether a specific actor (e.g., physician) is permitted to access a given dataset or trigger an operation. These evaluations are informed by privacy regulations such as GDPR, ISO/IEC 27000, and the NIS2 Directive (see Sect. 2.2), as well as user-defined consent preferences established through DC-TWIN's user control layer. For instance, a CDT may block a routine data query from an external service if the user has recently updated their consent to restrict data sharing to in-house teams.

- **Integrating Dynamic Inputs:** The virtual twin integrates diverse contextual signals (e.g., device type, network conditions, access time) and human-centric factors (e.g., trust calibration, user fatigue, interaction history) to drive adaptive system behaviour. This may include adjusting verification thresholds during high-risk scenarios or streamlining consent prompts for cognitively burdened users. As detailed in Sect. 3.4, this fusion supports personalized, responsive, and trust-sensitive decision-making.

Collectively, these three layers position the DT not just as a passive simulation tool but as a proactive, privacy-aware, and human-aligned cognitive system. It operates at the intersection of cyber security, consent governance, and user trust, core to the ethical use of CDTs in healthcare, smart cities, and other critical domains.

3.3   Integration of Dynamic Consent into Digital Twins

At the core of DC-TWIN is a modular, multi-layered dynamic consent framework seamlessly integrated into the CDT architecture as shown in Fig. 1. This framework enables real-time, adaptive, and human-aligned consent governance by distributing responsibilities across four key architectural layers:

- **User Control Layer:** This layer provides a user-facing consent dashboard, enabling individuals (e.g., patients, caregivers, or citizens) to grant, modify, or revoke consent in real time. Integrated feedback loops keep users informed about access activities and evolving system contexts, promoting transparency and trust. For instance, a patient can review which clinicians accessed their data during an emergency and adjust future consent preferences accordingly.
- **Policy Management Layer:** This layer hosts a dynamic consent reasoning engine, which evaluates access requests based on user roles, data sensitivity, and operational context (e.g., emergency vs. routine care). For example, during routine hours, access to genomic data may require explicit patient approval, whereas in emergencies, pre-defined policy rules may allow limited access without user prompt, ensuring timely care without compromising ethical safeguards.
- **Dynamic and Trust Layer:** This layer enhances decision-making by incorporating federated identity management and role binding, and adaptive trust modeling. It accounts for factors like device reputation, access history, or user trust scores. For instance, access requests from verified hospital devices may be approved automatically, while those from unfamiliar sources may trigger additional verification or consent prompts.
- **Data Governance Layer:** This layer ensures the enforcement of consent decisions, once granted or denied, through run-time access control. It also manages consent metadata, such as timestamps and usage context, making the process auditable and compliant with regulatory requirements (e.g., GDPR, NIS2). This ensures that both system-level integrity and user-defined boundaries are preserved during ongoing data exchanges.

By distributing consent management across these layers, DC-TWIN supports fine-grained, context-sensitive, and user-centric control over data access and sharing. This ensures that consent is not treated as a one-time static agreement, but as a living, adaptable process aligned with evolving system behavior and human expectations, critical for trustworthy DT operations in sensitive domains like healthcare and smart society services.

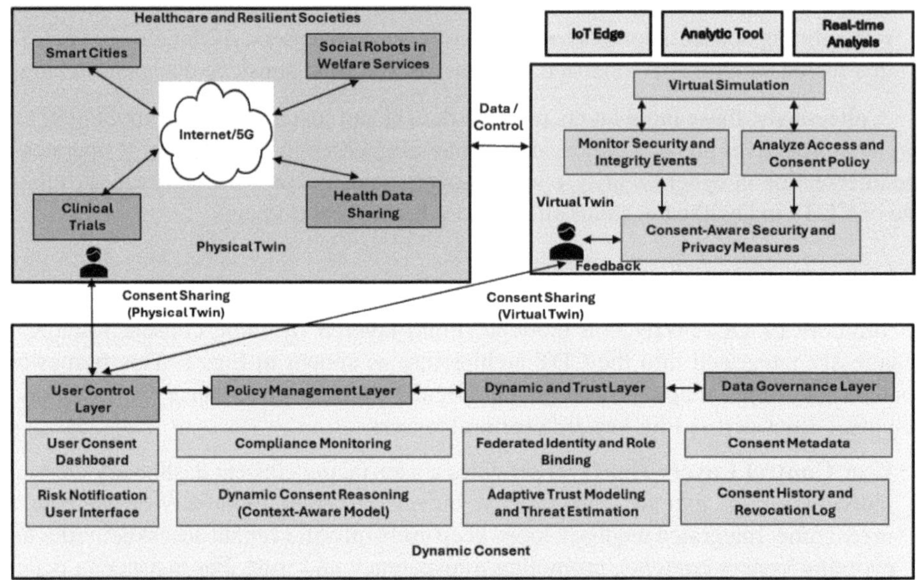

Fig. 1. DC-TWIN Architecture Integrating Dynamic Consent into CDTs

3.4 Adaptive Context Aware Consent Model

At the core of DC-TWIN's architecture is an adaptive, context-aware consent model, operationalized through the Dynamic Consent Reasoning Engine. This engine acts as the model's cognitive core, evaluating access requests in real time by integrating system-level context (e.g., user roles, device and network status, environment, time) with human-centric factors (e.g., cognitive load, trust calibration, UI preferences, and fatigue). This adaptive model is designed to overcome the rigidity of static consent approaches, enabling personalized and situation-sensitive decisions that adjust to evolving user needs and operational conditions. For instance, in high-stress scenarios such as emergency care, the engine may issue pre-approved access decisions to ensure responsiveness, whereas in routine or low-trust conditions, it may prompt users to use explicit input or deny access entirely.

As highlighted in Sect. 2.3, static consent fails to accommodate the evolving nature of data use and user expectations in DTs. Drawing from these insights, the proposed model builds on key principles from dynamic consent research (e.g., [19, 22, 25]), but adapts them to the unique demands of CDTs.

The model evaluates a range of contextual inputs, including:

- User role (e.g., patient, clinician, technician).
- Device and network conditions (e.g., secure hospital device vs. public mobile).
- Environmental and temporal cues (e.g., emergency care vs. scheduled visits).

For example, a nurse accessing patient vitals during an emergency may be automatically granted access under predefined high-priority policies. The same request during non-emergency hours from a personal device may trigger a consent prompt.

Simultaneously, the system incorporates human-centric variables such as:

- Cognitive load and user fatigue.
- Trust calibration and previous interactions.
- Interface personalization preferences (e.g., grouped vs. granular consent prompts).

For instance, users flagged as cognitively overloaded (e.g., through rapid navigation or repeated errors) may receive streamlined consent prompts to prevent fatigue and disengagement, challenges well recognized in the dynamic consent literature ([21, 23]).

Based on the combination of these context and user state signals, the consent engine generates one of three decisions:

- Grant – for known, low-risk, or pre-approved operations.
- Prompt – when user input is needed due to new, high-risk, or ambiguous conditions.
- Deny – when requests violate policy, context mismatches occur, or trust is insufficient.

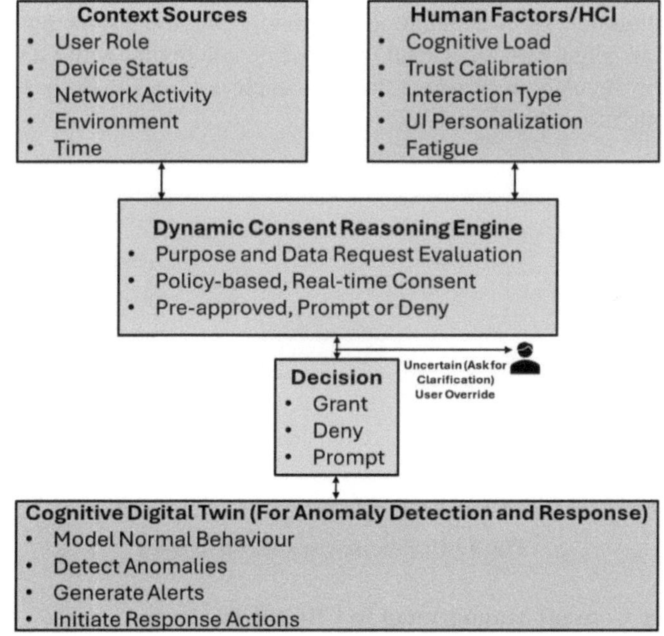

Fig. 2. Adaptive Context-Aware Consent Model: Integrating System Context and Human Factors for Dynamic Consent Decisions in CDTs

These decisions are automatically enforced through CDT's access control policies, ensuring that data processing remains aligned with user intent, regulatory compliance, and system-level governance rules. Importantly, the consent logic remains application-agnostic: while downstream CDT functions (e.g., anomaly detection or robotic actuation) may rely on this consent filtered data, the adaptive model focuses purely on data access and control, not application logic (Fig. 2).

4   Representative Use Cases

4.1   Privacy Aware Personal Health Data Sharing

In healthcare settings, dynamic consent plays a vital role in preserving individual autonomy, particularly as personal health data is used across diagnostic, monitoring, and research applications [22]. For example, a patient managing diabetes via a wearable glucose monitor may initially consent to share data with their primary care provider. However, during a routine check-up, the device may prompt the patient for consent to share the same data with a remote endocrinologist or a research registry studying long-term outcomes. Without dynamic consent, such secondary data sharing would either require prior over-permission or create legal and ethical risks.

DC-TWIN addresses this gap by embedding real-time, context-aware consent controls directly into CDT workflows. Patients are provided with a user-friendly dashboard to update or revoke consent as needed, supported by policy rules that consider device context (e.g., secure hospital Wi-Fi vs. public hotspot) and operational context (e.g., emergency admission vs. scheduled consultation). Our framework ensures that data access decisions align with individual intent while complying with GDPR and health data sovereignty regulations. Figure 3 shows example use cases in the healthcare context detailed in both Subsects. 4.1 and 4.2.

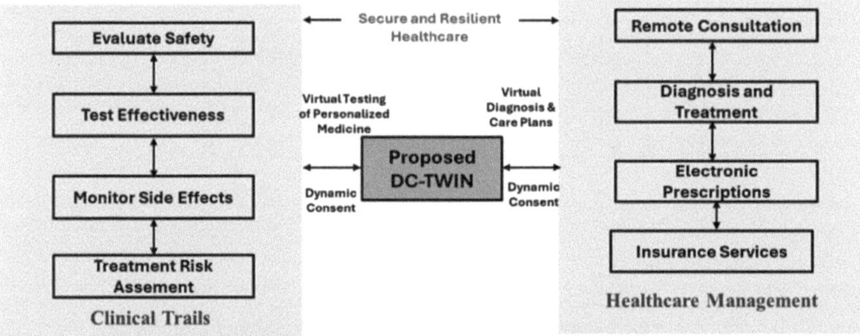

Fig. 3. Healthcare Use Case: Examples

4.2   Adaptive Consent Management in Clinical Trials

Clinical trials increasingly rely on digital platforms to recruit, monitor, and engage participants. In decentralized or remote trials, participants often interact with mobile applications or wearables to submit health data. For example, in a cardiology study, participants may use a smartwatch to share heart rate variability. Initially, consent may cover this primary use. Later, researchers may wish to analyze sleep patterns or share anonymized data with international collaborators. Static consent models do not accommodate these evolving needs.

With DC-TWIN, researchers can simulate various trial scenarios using a CDT-based environment. For instance, during a simulated emergency alert from a participant's device (e.g., potential arrhythmia), the CDT can test how to invoke predefined consent overrides to notify the trial's clinical response team. Furthermore, the dynamic consent layer allows participants to receive tailored prompts, e.g., "Do you allow your data to be included in cross-national comparative studies?", with options to set time limits or restrict data to specific domains [26].

4.3 Data Privacy and Compliance in Welfare Robotics

Welfare robots deployed in eldercare and assisted living environments frequently collect and act upon sensitive data, such as voice commands, motion patterns, or emotional cues [27]. Consider a social robot assisting an elderly user with daily routines. It may collect audio commands to schedule medication or monitor fall risk based on movement patterns. Over time, as the robot learns user preferences, it may suggest sharing health patterns with caregivers or physicians.

DC-TWIN supports such use cases by embedding dynamic consent mechanisms into the robot's interaction layer. For example, if the user's fatigue level is detected as high (via slowed responses or biometrics), the robot can simplify consent prompts or delay non-urgent data-sharing requests. Likewise, when a new caregiver interacts with the robot, the system can prompt the user to approve or deny access to specific data streams (e.g., activity logs, calendar reminders). By contextualizing consent decisions in real time, based on trust, identity, and risk, the framework promotes both usability and privacy.

5 Conclusions and Future Work Directions

This paper introduced DC-TWIN, a conceptual framework for integrating dynamic consent into CDTs to enhance privacy, user control, and adaptive data governance in healthcare and resilient society applications. By embedding context-aware, real-time consent mechanisms into the CDT architecture, DC-TWIN addresses the limitations of static, one-time consent models and supports ethical, user-aligned data practices. The framework aims to operationalize dynamic consent through layered mechanisms including a Dynamic Consent Reasoning Engine, user control interfaces, and adaptive trust calibration. Through illustrative use cases in health data sharing, clinical trials, and welfare robotics, we demonstrated how dynamic consent can be operationalized to reflect evolving user intent, context, and trust. The framework highlights the importance of aligning consent processes with the continuous, data-intensive nature of CDTs. Future work will involve refining the model through stakeholder feedback and expert consultation, developing prototypes to explore technical feasibility and usability.

Acknowledgments. This research is funded from the Research Council of Norway through, the SFI Norwegian Centre for Cybersecurity in Critical Sectors (NORCICS), with the project number #310105 and User-centred Security Framework for Social Robots in Public Space (SecuRoPS), with the project number #321324 in addition to an INTPART projects, Reinforcing Competence in Cybersecurity of Critical Infrastructures: A Norway-US Partnership (RECYCIN), with the project number #309911 and International Alliance for Strengthening Cybersecurity and Privacy in Healthcare (CybAlliance), with the project number #337316. This work is also supported by the European Union's HORIZON Research and Innovation Programme under grant agreement No 101120657, project ENFIELD (European Lighthouse to Manifest Trustworthy and Green AI).

Disclosure of Interests.   The authors declare that they do not have competing interests.

Use of AI-Assisted Tools.   During the preparation of this work, the authors utilized AI-assisted tools to enhance English language accuracy, including spelling, grammar, and punctuation. The content generated and corrected by these tools was thoroughly reviewed, revised, and edited by the authors to ensure accuracy and originality. The authors accept full responsibility for the originality of the final content of this publication.

References

1. Zheng, X., Lu, J., Kiritsis, D.: The emergence of cognitive digital twin: vision, challenges and opportunities. Int. J. Prod. Res. **60**(24), 7610–7632 (2022)
2. Pirbhulal, S., Chockalingam, S., Abie, H., Lau, N.: Cognitive digital twins for improving security in IT-OT enabled healthcare applications. In: International Conference on Human-Computer Interaction, pp. 153–163. Springer (2024)
3. Du, J., Zhu, Q., Shi, Y., Wang, Q., Lin, Y., Zhao, D.: Cognition digital twins for personalized information systems of smart cities: proof of concept. J. Manag. Eng. **36**(2), 04019052 (2020)
4. Kumar, M.R., Jain, U., Francis, F., Adhvaryu, R., Natrayan, L.: Cognitive digital twin systems for predictive security in AI-enhanced IoT environments. In: 2024 First International Conference on Software, Systems and Information Technology (SSITCON), pp. 1–6. IEEE (2024)
5. Wang, Y., Su, Z., Guo, S., Dai, M., Luan, T.H., Liu, Y.: A survey on digital twins: architecture, enabling technologies, security and privacy, and future prospects. IEEE Internet Things J. **10**(17), 14965–14987 (2023)
6. Evans, B., Frumkin, L., Coopamootoo, K., Jesus, V., Little, S.: Digital technologies, power and control: a review of how organisations can empower individuals and communities to develop trust, uphold their privacy and curate their identity in a secure digital environment. (2022)
7. Dennehy, L., White, S.: Consent, assent, and the importance of risk stratification. Br. J. Anaesth. **109**(1), 40–46 (2012)
8. Pirbhulal, S., Abie, H., Shukla, A.: Towards a novel framework for reinforcing cybersecurity using digital twins in IoT-based healthcare applications. In: 2022 IEEE 95th Vehicular Technology Conference:(VTC2022-Spring), pp. 1–5. IEEE (2022)
9. Yigit, Y., Panitsas, I., Maglaras, L., Tassiulas, L., Canberk, B.: Cyber-twin: digital twin-boosted autonomous attack detection for vehicular ad-hoc networks. In: ICC 2024-IEEE International Conference on Communications, pp. 2167–2172. IEEE (2024)
10. Yigit, Y., Kioskli, K., Bishop, L., Chouliaras, N., Maglaras, L., Janicke, H.: Enhancing cybersecurity training efficacy: a comprehensive analysis of gamified learning, behavioral strategies and digital twins. In: 2024 IEEE 25th International Symposium on a World of Wireless, Mobile and Multimedia Networks (WoWMoM), pp. 24–32. IEEE (2024)
11. Suhail, S., Iqbal, M., Hussain, R., Jurdak, R.: ENIGMA: an explainable digital twin security solution for cyber–physical systems. Comput. Ind. **151**, 103961 (2023)

12. Alcaraz, C., Meskini, I.H., Lopez, J.: Digital twin communities: an approach for secure DT data sharing. Int. J. Inf. Secur. **24**(1), 1–19 (2025)
13. Damjanovic-Behrendt, V.: A digital twin-based privacy enhancement mechanism for the automotive industry. In: 2018 International Conference on Intelligent Systems (IS), pp. 272–279. IEEE (2018)
14. Zemskov, A.D., et al.: Security and privacy of digital twins for advanced manufacturing: a survey. arXiv preprint arXiv:2412.13939 (2024)
15. Wang, C., Ming, Y., Liu, H., Feng, J., Zhang, N.: Secure and flexible data sharing with dual privacy protection in vehicular digital twin networks. IEEE Transactions on Intelligent Transportation Systems (2024)
16. GDPR Enforcement Tracker. https://www.enforcementtracker.com/
17. Statista. Penalties under GDPR for transferring personal data outside the European Union as of January 2025
18. Klymenko, O., Kosenkov, O., Meisenbacher, S., Elahidoost, P., Mendez, D., Matthes, F.: Understanding the implementation of technical measures in the process of data privacy compliance: a qualitative study. In: Proceedings of the 16th ACM/IEEE International Symposium on Empirical Software Engineering and Measurement, pp. 261–271 (2022)
19. Kaye, J., Whitley, E.A., Lund, D., Morrison, M., Teare, H., Melham, K.: Dynamic consent: a patient interface for twenty-first century research networks. Eur. J. Hum. Genet. **23**(2), 141–146 (2015)
20. Chockalingam, S., Kvalvik, P., Sarshar, S.: A position on rethinking HCI practices in dynamic consent: balancing privacy, trust, safety, and risk communication. In: Proceedings of the 35th European Safety and Reliability Conference (ESREL 2025) and the 33rd Society for Risk Analysis Europe Conference (SRA-E 2025) (2025)
21. Lay, W., Gasparini, L., Siero, W., Hughes, E.K.: A rapid review of the benefits and challenges of dynamic consent. Res. Ethics **21**(1), 180–202 (2025)
22. Lee, A.R., Koo, D., Kim, I.K., Lee, E., Yoo, S., Lee, H.-Y.: Opportunities and challenges of a dynamic consent-based application: personalized options for personal health data sharing and utilization. BMC Med. Ethics **25**(1), 92 (2024)
23. Verreydt, S., Yskout, K., Joosen, W.: Security and privacy requirements for electronic consent: a systematic literature review. ACM Trans. Comput. Healthcare **2**(2), 1–24 (2021)
24. Kakarlapudi, P., Mahmoud, Q.: A systematic review of blockchain for consent management. Healthcare. 2021; 9: 137. s Note: MDPI stays neutral with regard to jurisdictional claims in published … (2021)
25. Budin-Ljøsne, I., et al.: Dynamic consent: a potential solution to some of the challenges of modern biomedical research. BMC Med. Ethics **18**, 1–10 (2017)
26. Sahan, K., Wijesurendra, R., Preiss, D., Mafham, M., Sheehan, M.: Towards an understanding of the ethics of electronic consent in clinical trials. Trials **25**(1), 545 (2024)
27. Sarathy, V., Arnold, T., Scheutz, M.: When exceptions are the norm: Exploring the role of consent in hri. ACM Trans. Hum.-Robot Interact. **8**(3), 1–21 (2019)

Method for Evaluating Cyber Risk Management Frameworks

Matheus de Andrade[1,3]([✉]), Amândio Ferreira Balcão Filho[1,2], and Ferrucio de Franco Rosa[1,2]

[1] UNIFACCAMP, Campo Limpo Paulista, SP, Brazil
[2] CTI Renato Archer, Campinas, SP, Brazil
[3] IFSP, Instituto Federal de São Paulo, São Paulo, SP, Brazil
`matheus.7t@gmail.com`

Abstract. The increasing sophistication of cyber threats has guided organizations to adopt cybersecurity risk management frameworks as a key strategy to address these challenges. However, effectively evaluating these frameworks remains a significant challenge. This study introduces the Evaluating Cyber Risk Frameworks (e-CRF) method, a systematic approach for assessing cybersecurity risk management frameworks based on criteria such as comprehensiveness, adaptability, effectiveness, and regulatory compliance. Although e-CRF has been tested with frameworks such as the NIST Cybersecurity Framework and CIS Controls, it is designed to apply to any framework, free or commercial. The e-CRF was validated by information security experts who used a software prototype to assign weights and scores to the evaluation criteria. The results show that e-CRF eases the standardization of the evaluation process, highlighting significant performance differences and providing valuable insights for selecting and continuously improving cybersecurity frameworks.

Keywords: Cybersecurity · Risk management · Framework · Maturity · Comparative analysis · Evaluation · Awareness

1 Introduction

Cyber risk management has become a central concern for organizations across all sectors, driven by the exponential increase in digital threats such as ransomware, phishing, and denial-of-service attacks. In an increasingly digital and interconnected environment, protecting digital assets and ensuring business continuity is a constant challenge [13].

In this context, cybersecurity risk management frameworks have emerged as fundamental tools to guide organizations in identifying, assessing, and mitigating threats. These frameworks provide structured guidelines for implementing robust information security practices, ensuring that organizations are effectively prepared to face cyber risks. However, the wide variety of available frameworks—each with its own specific characteristics and focus—poses a significant challenge in selecting the most appropriate approach for each organization [24].

A. Coman et al. (Eds.): HCII 2025, LNCS 16337, pp. 306–325, 2026.
https://doi.org/10.1007/978-3-032-12801-0_21

We propose the *Evaluating Cyber Risk Frameworks* (e-CRF) method, a systematic and collaborative approach for evaluating cybersecurity risk management frameworks. By integrating criteria such as comprehensiveness, adaptability, effectiveness, cost-benefit, and compliance, the e-CRF aims to standardize the evaluation process and facilitate the identification of the best options to meet specific organizational needs. By incorporating elements from a literature review conducted, this study strengthens the theoretical foundation of the method, highlighting its practical relevance and addressing gaps identified in previous research [17].

The main objective of this study is to provide a systematic and practical approach for evaluating cybersecurity risk management frameworks, supporting organizations in decision-making. The integration of the literature review in this article seeks to consolidate the theoretical foundations of the e-CRF method, addressing both challenges and opportunities in the field of cybersecurity.

2   Literature Review and Related Work

A systematic literature review was carried out, involving a thorough analysis of 30 selected articles. The primary objective of this review was to answer the following research question: *"What recent methods and frameworks have been proposed to evaluate and support cyber risk management, considering criteria such as effectiveness, cost-benefit, and regulatory compliance?"*

This study conducted a systematic literature review based on the protocol proposed by Kitchenham [17], widely adopted in software engineering and adapted here for the cybersecurity context. The objective was to identify key challenges and opportunities in the evaluation of cyber risk management frameworks.

The search was conducted in three well-established databases in the field of Computer Science—IEEE Xplore[1], ACM Digital Library[2], and Springer Link[3]—chosen for their credibility, diversity of content, and focus on technological innovation.

The search covered the years from 2016 to 2024 and used the following string, adapted to each database's syntax: *("All Metadata": cyber risk management) AND ("All Metadata": frameworks) AND ("All Metadata": evaluation) AND ("All Metadata": method).* This string was defined according to the PICOC (Population, Intervention, Comparison, Outcome, Context) model to ensure the recovery of studies relevant to the research objective.

The search strategy was developed using the PICOC model: Population (cybersecurity frameworks), Intervention (evaluation methods), Comparison (not applicable), Outcome (selection and classification), and Context (academic and industrial applications).

---

[1] https://ieeexplore.ieee.org/Xplore/home.jsp.
[2] https://dl.acm.org/.
[3] https://link.springer.com/.

The initial search returned 210 articles. After removing duplicates and applying the inclusion and exclusion criteria through a screening of titles, abstracts, and keywords, 27 articles were selected for detailed analysis.

The inclusion criteria were: (i) journal or conference papers with full-text availability; (ii) publications between 2016 and 2024; and (iii) studies written in English or Portuguese. The exclusion criteria comprised: (i) studies from unrelated fields; (ii) works misaligned with the research question; and (iii) short papers or abstracts lacking methodological description.

Among the selected studies, 8 address continuous cybersecurity awareness strategies (2.1.1 Studies on Solutions Based on Continuous Cybersecurity Awareness), 6 focus on dynamic monitoring approaches (2.1.2 Studies on Solutions Based on Dynamic Monitoring), and 13 explore risk assessment methods and performance metrics (2.1.3 Studies on Solutions Based on Risk Assessment Methods and Performance Metrics). The main findings that support framework selection are discussed in Sect. 2.2 Analysis and Discussion on the Results of the Literature Review, while related works are analyzed in Sect. 2.3 Analysis of Related Work.

2.1   Cyber Risk Management Frameworks

This section presents a systematic analysis of the 27 selected studies on cyber risk management frameworks, categorized into three main groups: (i) eight studies addressing solutions based on continuous cybersecurity awareness strategies, detailed in Subsect. 2.1; (ii) six studies focused on dynamic monitoring approaches, discussed in Subsect. 2.1; and (iii) thirteen studies exploring risk evaluation methods and performance metrics, presented in Subsect. 2.1.

The key findings that support framework selection are consolidated in Subsect. 2.2, while Subsect. 2.3 presents three additional papers closely related to the proposed e-CRF method, totaling 30 analyzed studies.

We highlight that the quality of the guidelines and the effectiveness of the practices are interrelated and complementary—both essential for the proper selection and application of a robust framework. In this context, quality refers to the clarity, completeness, and regulatory compliance of the proposed guidelines. Effectiveness, in turn, refers to the framework's ability to meet organizational needs by supporting practical and efficient risk mitigation.

Studies categorized under continuous cybersecurity awareness emphasize the quality of guidelines as a determining factor. Those focusing on dynamic monitoring approaches highlight the frameworks' effectiveness in practical application. Finally, studies addressing risk assessment methods and performance metrics present structured methodologies supported by quantitative or qualitative indicators. Together, these categories provide a comprehensive and balanced perspective, enabling organizations to select frameworks that best fit their operational and strategic contexts.

Table 1 summarizes the analyzed studies, structured as follows: Objectives— Identification (I), Evaluation (E), Comparison (C), and Suggestion (S); Application Domains—(1) Enterprise, (2) Financial, (3) Government, (4) Cloud, (5)

Table 1. Summary of the analyzed studies

Ref.	Authors	Objectives				App. Domain						Classification
		I	E	C	S	1	2	3	4	5	6	
[1]	(Alghaithi et al.; 2022)		X			X						Performance
[3]	(Ayati & Naji; 2022)		X			X						Performance
[4]	(Billard; 2019)		X			X						Performance
[5]	(Binyamini et al.; 2021)		X			X						Performance
[7]	(Carmichael et al.; 2022)		X					X				Monitoring
[8]	(Couretas; 2019)		X			X					X	Performance
[9]	(Datta; 2020)		X					X				Monitoring
[10]	(Din et al.; 2023)			X					X			Monitoring
[11]	(Feng et al.; 2017)		X			X						Monitoring
[12]	(Fitroh et al.; 2017)	X				X						Awareness
[13]	(Giuca et al.; 2021)		X			X	X					Monitoring
[14]	(Jain et al.; 2022)			X		X	X		X			Awareness
[15]	(Khurana et al.; 2022)		X						X		X	Monitoring
[16]	(Khuvis et al.; 2019)	X						X				Monitoring
[18]	(Levy; 2020)		X			X						Performance
[19]	(Li; 2023)	X							X			Performance
[20]	(Maneerattanasak et al; 2017)		X			X						Awareness
[21]	(Manuja & Shekhawat; 2023)		X			X						Monitoring
[22]	(Moreira et al.; 2021)		X			X	X					Awareness
[23]	(Naumov & Kabanov; 2016)		X			X						Performance
[25]	(Pandurang Gaikwad et al.; 2023)	X				X	X					Awareness
[26]	(Purkait & Damle; 2023)	X	X					X	X	X	X	Awareness
[28]	(Rehman et al.; 2018)		X			X						Monitoring
[29]	(Romansky et al.; 2024)				X	X	X					Monitoring
[30]	(Savold et al.; 2017)				X	X						Performance
[32]	(Waqdan et al.; 2023)		X							X		Monitoring
[33]	(Wu et al.; 2023)		X			X						Performance

Healthcare, and (6) Education; and Classification—Awareness, Monitoring, or Performance.

2.1.1 Studies on Solutions Based on Continuous Cybersecurity Awareness

Continuous awareness is a key pillar in cyber risk management, contributing to the development of a security-oriented organizational culture. Several studies highlight approaches that combine education, organizational structure, and adaptability to emerging technological contexts.

Purkait and Damle [26] emphasize the importance of awareness in light of increasing cyber threats, while Amit et al. [14] highlight the role of big data and artificial intelligence in proactive threat detection. Adaptive architectures that go beyond basic cybersecurity hygiene by incorporating automation and cognitive analysis are proposed by Jerry et al. [8] and Savold et al. [30].

Other authors focus on governance and organizational resilience. For instance, Fitroh et al. [12] employ COBIT 5 to align IT issues with strategic objectives; Khurana et al. [15] apply risk management strategies in distributed Scrum environments; and Romansky et al. [29] introduce an extension of TUF to enhance security in industrial systems.

Finally, Ikram et al. [10] stress the importance of trust in interconnected cyber-physical systems and propose CACMTM to ensure secure communication in dynamic environments.

2.1.2 Studies on Solutions Based on Dynamic Monitoring

Continuous monitoring is essential for evaluating the effectiveness of cyber risk management frameworks, as it enables real-time threat detection, rapid incident response, and ongoing adjustments to security strategies.

Li [19] introduces a comprehensive network security framework leveraging artificial intelligence. This framework integrates objective modeling, defined boundaries, essential security components, and specialized services to facilitate a holistic and unified approach to network security.

Feng et al. [11] present a user-centered machine learning framework designed for cybersecurity operations centers. The primary objective of this framework is to mitigate alert fatigue and reduce the occurrence of false positives, thereby enhancing the efficiency of security analysts and improving overall threat detection capabilities.

Billard [4] introduces the SURE framework, which dynamically and autonomously evaluates security and utility risks. By integrating contextual factors, system requirements, and security decisions, the framework enables the selection of appropriate mitigation strategies, offering greater flexibility compared to traditional static approaches.

Naumov and Kabanov [23] propose a dynamic risk assessment framework based on system dynamics, tailored to address the continuously evolving nature of cyber environments. This approach empowers organizations to adapt their risk management strategies in response to emerging internal and external threats, thereby enhancing resilience and decision-making agility.

Khuvis et al. [16] describe a continuous integration-based framework to manage software environments at the Ohio Supercomputer Center (OSC). This solution integrates tools such as EasyBuild, Spack, and ReFrame to automate testing and installation triggered by GitLab commits, increasing deployment speed and security in high-performance computing (HPC) environments.

Moreira et al. [22] apply the Constructivist Multi-Criteria Decision Aid (MCDA-C) method to develop a risk management plan within a large Brazilian bank, using NIST framework controls as a reference. The study demonstrates that integrating multi-criteria decision-making with qualitative and quantitative data effectively supports the structuring and prioritization of control categories.

2.1.3 Studies on Solutions Based on Risk Assessment Methods and Performance Metrics

Risk assessment frameworks are essential for identifying threats, evaluating impacts, and implementing mitigation actions. The distinction between methodology and framework lies in the level of prescription: methodologies provide clear execution guidelines, while frameworks offer more flexible structures. The definition of metrics, such as KPIs, supports the measurement of security effectiveness, enabling results-oriented management.

Several studies propose frameworks and models aimed at enhancing risk management across diverse technological domains. Ayati et al. [3] introduce a control framework incorporating measurable metrics to ensure continuous quality and performance monitoring. Manuja et al. [21] emphasize the necessity of adapting security standards in response to increasing technological dependence, while Alghaithi et al. [1] investigate software security frameworks with a focus on identifying vulnerabilities in the development lifecycle.

Carmichael [7] discusses the importance of evaluating privacy risks in the context of artificial intelligence and large-scale data processing. Urairat et al. [20] advocate for the integration of IT risk management practices to support comprehensive cybersecurity strategies.

Levy et al. [18] present a risk assessment framework tailored for critical data centers. Mofareh et al. [32] propose a dynamic model for evaluating risks associated with IoT devices in healthcare settings. In a related effort, Soumya et al. [9] introduce the DRAFT framework, which combines risk assessment with resilience planning for IoT environments. Additionally, Binyamini et al. [5] suggest an automated rule-generation model based on textual vulnerability descriptions, and Rehman et al. [28] present the CPS Framework for managing risks in cyber-physical systems, validated through a real-world case study.

Emerging technologies are also addressed through innovative risk management models. Zhongdai et al. [33] propose a deep learning-based approach to enhance cybersecurity in maritime digital systems, while Pandurang et al. [25] explore the role of machine learning in detecting interdependent risks, particularly in phishing attacks. Finally, Giuca et al. [13] provide a critical review of existing risk frameworks, identifying key gaps in their adaptability and practical implementation, underscoring the need for more flexible and actionable approaches in evolving threat landscapes.

2.2   Analysis and Discussion on the Results of the Literature Review

The literature analysis revealed five recurring key criteria in cybersecurity risk management frameworks: comprehensiveness, adaptability, effectiveness, cost, and compliance. A trend toward the adoption of adaptable solutions was observed, although there remains a lack of empirical validation, particularly in low-cost frameworks.

The reviewed studies range from broad sectoral proposals to more specific approaches, but all reinforce the focus on digital asset protection and risk mitigation. A notable trend is the increasing integration of technologies such as artificial intelligence and machine learning, which enable more effective and predictive responses to anomalous behavior.

Gaps persist regarding the definition of performance metrics, such as response time, mitigation rate, and vulnerability reduction. The absence of such indicators hampers objective comparisons between frameworks.

The conducted review allowed for the identification of distinct approaches to evaluating cybersecurity risk management frameworks, with emphasis on criteria such as effectiveness, adaptability, cost-benefit, and compliance. However, the lack of standardization hinders objective comparisons between methodologies.

The identified approaches range from qualitative, quantitative, to hybrid methods. While qualitative approaches are flexible and contextual, they tend to be subjective; quantitative ones offer precision but require data and higher complexity. Hybrid approaches are emerging as a promising alternative by balancing both dimensions. A gap was also observed in the consideration of human factors, such as organizational culture, level of awareness, and resistance to adopting security practices—critical elements to the effectiveness of frameworks, yet rarely quantified.

Lastly, the constant evolution of threats demands dynamic and updatable frameworks. Examples such as the NIST Cybersecurity Framework have advanced in this direction, but could still benefit from the integration of real-time intelligence and adaptive feedback loops.

Given these limitations, the need for a structured and comparable method is reinforced. The e-CRF proposal aims to fill this gap by integrating technical and organizational criteria, enabling a more accurate evaluation aligned with organizational needs.

2.3   Analysis of Related Work

In this review, three studies were considered related work due to presenting similar objectives or contributions, or because they address the same application domain. Table 2 presents a summary of the related works, categorizing them according to their objectives (Identification, Evaluation, Comparison, Suggestion) and applications (Enterprise, Financial, Governmental, Cloud, and Education). The following paragraphs provide a comparative analysis of these studies.

Palia et al. [24] highlight the importance of control effectiveness in programs and projects to ensure consistent achievement of objectives. They propose an adaptable control structure, accompanied by measurable metrics to assess program performance. The authors adopt a case studybased approach to demonstrate the applicability of the proposed structure in a corporate environment. The article identifies a problem with traditional control maturity models, which often focus on operational efficiency while neglecting direct evaluation of control effectiveness. As a result, programs may fail due to the lack of effective controls. The solution offered by the authors aims to overcome this limitation by providing a structured approach to improving outcomes and mitigating risks. Unlike Radu et al. [27], who analyze multiple approaches to framework evaluation, Palia et al. focus specifically on applying metrics to individual projects. However, the study does not address the adaptation of the structure to different sectors, which may limit its applicability across varied contexts.

Radu et al. [27] analyze cybersecurity risk management frameworks, highlighting the importance of comprehensive evaluation to ensure that organizations select the most appropriate approach for their needs. They conduct a comparative analysis between qualitative and quantitative risk assessment methods, identifying the limitations of each approach. The authors perform a comparative review of existing frameworks, considering factors such as adaptability, cost-effectiveness, and regulatory compliance. The article notes that while qualitative methods are widely used, they can be subjective and inconsistent; in contrast, quantitative methods offer greater precision but require large volumes of data and can be complex. As a solution, the authors propose a hybrid model that combines the strengths of both approaches, allowing for a more balanced and reliable evaluation. The study provides practical guidelines for choosing frameworks, supporting informed decision-making by organizations. In contrast to Palia et al. [24], which focus on metrics for specific projects, this work adopts a broader and comparative approach. However, the practical implementation of the hybrid model has not yet been carried out, which represents a limitation of the study.

Wang et al. [31] explore the importance of continuous awareness as a critical factor in mitigating cyber risks, recognizing that the human factor is one of the greatest vulnerabilities within organizations. The authors propose a cybersecurity awareness framework that integrates regular training, educational campaigns, and evaluation metrics to measure the impact of these initiatives. They used a qualitative research approach and interviews with information security experts to develop the framework. The article identifies a problem with traditional security approaches, which often focus on technical solutions while neglecting human behavior as a key element in preventing incidents. The suggested solution aims to overcome this limitation by providing a systematic approach that encourages continuous employee engagement and the development of a security-oriented organizational culture. Although the study by Wang et al. [31] provides a valuable framework for cybersecurity awareness, it does not address direct integration with technical risk management frameworks, which may limit its applicability in highly regulated environments.

Related works were classified according to their objectives and application domains, as shown in Table 2.

Table 2. Summary of the related work

Ref.	Authors	Objectives				Application Domain						Classification
		I	E	C	S	1	2	3	4	5	6	
[24]	Abhinav et al. (2021)		X			X	X					Performance
[27]	Radu et al. (2020)	X	X			X	X		X	X		Performance
[31]	Wang et al. (2018)				X	X						Awareness
–	This Work (2024)	X	X	X	X	X	X	X		X	X	Performance

Legend: Objectives—Identification (I), Evaluation (E), Comparison (C), Suggestion (S)
Application Domains—(1) Enterprise, (2) Financial, (3) Government, (4) Cloud, (5) Healthcare, (6) Education
Classification—Awareness, Monitoring, Performance

2.4   Key Differentials of e-CRF Compared to Related Work

The *Evaluating Cyber Risk Frameworks* (e-CRF) method introduces advancements over previous studies. Its main differentials include: customization of criteria, integration of qualitative and quantitative metrics, process automation, support for framework comparison, a collaborative approach, and inclusion of human and organizational factors.

e-CRF allows each organization to define specific weights for criteria and subcriteria—an aspect not addressed in Palia et al. (2021) [24] and only partially considered in Radu et al. (2020) [27]. It also enables a more comprehensive evaluation by combining technical metrics with organizational dimensions, overcoming limitations highlighted in Wang et al. (2018) [31] and again in Radu et al. (2020) [27], which do not integrate both perspectives.

Its implementation as a software platform reduces the manual effort seen in Palia et al. (2021) [24] and addresses the lack of practical application mentioned in Radu et al. (2020) [27]. The capability to directly compare frameworks, not explored by Wang et al. (2018) [31], increases the method's relevance across diverse organizational contexts.

Another important distinction is the involvement of multiple evaluators, which fosters a collaborative perspective and reduces individual bias—a common limitation in previous approaches. Lastly, e-CRF stands out for including human and cultural factors as integral components of the evaluation process, which are often missing or insufficiently incorporated in related work. The consolidation of these aspects demonstrates that e-CRF offers a more comprehensive, practical, and context-aware approach for evaluating cyber risk management frameworks. Table 3 summarizes these comparisons.

Table 3. Comparative summary of related work

Ref.	Studies	PC	IM	AT	CF	AC	FH
[24]	Palia et al. (2021)	No	Qualit.	No	No	No	No
[27]	Radu et al. (2020)	Partial	Quantit.	No	Partial	No	No
[31]	Wang et al. (2018)	No	Qualit.	No	No	No	Yes
This Work	Proposed Method	Yes	Qualit. and Quantit.	Yes	Yes	Yes	Yes

Legend: PC = Customization of Criteria, IM = Integration of Metrics, AT = Automation, CF = Framework Comparison, AC = Collaborative Approach, FH = Human Factor Considered

3 The e-CRF Method

We propose the *Evaluating Cyber Risk Frameworks* (e-CRF) method, a collaborative evaluation approach involving multiple evaluators. In this method, each criterion C_i is weighted and assessed across different frameworks N. The method allows evaluators to assign specific weights to each subcriterion, reflecting the relative importance of each aspect, and to use a weighted average to calculate the final score for each framework based on the evaluations received.

3.1 Evaluation Method Description

The performance indicator ICRF (Indicator for Cybersecurity Risk Frameworks) is calculated using Eq. 2 and represents the final outcome of the e-CRF method.

Each criterion C_i is evaluated by E evaluators across N frameworks. The final weighted score for each criterion is calculated as the weighted average of the scores assigned by all evaluators. For each criterion C_i, the weighted score $N(C_i, F_k)$ of a framework F_k is obtained using the average of the weighted scores assigned by the E evaluators, as described in Eq. 1.

$$N(C_i, F_k) = \frac{1}{E} \sum_{e=1}^{E} \left(\frac{\sum_{j=1}^{n} (N_e(sc_{ij}, F_k) \times W_e(sc_{ij}))}{\sum_{j=1}^{n} W_e(sc_{ij})} \right) \tag{1}$$

In this equation, $N_e(sc_{ij}, F_k)$ represents the score given by evaluator e to subcriterion sc_{ij} for the framework F_k. The value $W_e(sc_{ij})$ corresponds to the weight assigned to subcriterion sc_{ij} by evaluator e.

The final score $NF(F_k)$ of a framework F_k, considering all criteria and evaluators, is calculated as described in Eq. 2:

$$NF(F_k) = \frac{\sum_{i=1}^{n} (N(C_i, F_k) \times W(C_i))}{\sum_{i=1}^{n} W(C_i)} \tag{2}$$

Here, $N(C_i, F_k)$ represents the average weighted score for criterion C_i for the framework F_k, considering all evaluations. The value $W(C_i)$ refers to the overall weight of criterion C_i, which can be assigned globally or calculated as the average of the weights defined by all evaluators. Figure 1 presents the flowchart of the e-CRF method.

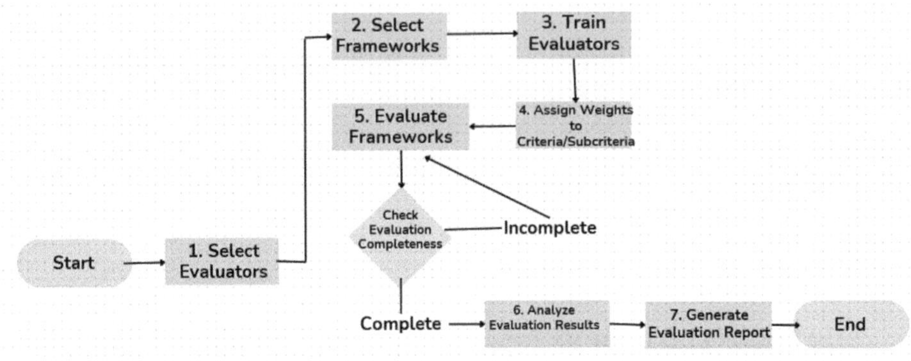

Fig. 1. Flowchart of the e-CRF methodFlowchart of the e-CRF method

This flowchart organizes the evaluation process into sequential steps, from the selection of evaluators to the generation of the final report. The flow includes framework definition, evaluator training, assignment of weights to criteria and subcriteria, completion of evaluations, completeness verification, result analysis, and the automatic generation of reports with consolidated indicators.

3.2   Calculation Example

To illustrate the calculation process using the e-CRF method, consider three main criteria: Cost, Information Security, and Efficiency. These criteria were evaluated by two evaluators (E_1 and E_2) with the following detailed data for the subcriteria:

Cost Criterion: E_1 assigned scores of 4 and 5, with weights 2 and 3, respectively. E_2 assigned scores of 3 and 4, with weights 1 and 2, respectively.

Information Security Criterion: Both E_1 and E_2 assigned scores of 3 and 4, with weights equal to 1.

Efficiency Criterion: E_1 assigned scores of 2 and 5, with weights 2 and 1, respectively. E_2 assigned scores of 3 and 4, with weights 1 and 2, respectively.
    The general weights for the criteria are:

$$W(\text{Cost}) = 2, \quad W(\text{Information Security}) = 1, \quad W(\text{Efficiency}) = 1.$$

Criterion Score Calculations

Cost: The average weighted score for the Cost criterion $N(\text{Cost}, F_k)$ is calculated as:

$$N(\text{Cost}, F_k) = \frac{1}{2}\left(\frac{4 \times 2 + 5 \times 3}{2 + 3} + \frac{3 \times 1 + 4 \times 2}{1 + 2}\right)$$

$$= \frac{1}{2}(4.6 + 3.67) = 4.14. \tag{3}$$

Information Security: The average weighted score for the Information Security criterion $N(\text{Information Security}, F_k)$ is:

$$N(\text{Information Security}, F_k) = \frac{1}{2}\left(\frac{3 \times 1 + 4 \times 1}{1 + 1} + \frac{3 \times 1 + 4 \times 1}{1 + 1}\right)$$

$$= \frac{1}{2}(3.5 + 3.5) = 3.5. \tag{4}$$

Efficiency: The average weighted score for the Efficiency criterion $N(\text{Efficiency}, F_k)$ is:

$$N(\text{Efficiency}, F_k) = \frac{1}{2}\left(\frac{2 \times 2 + 5 \times 1}{2 + 1} + \frac{3 \times 1 + 4 \times 2}{1 + 2}\right)$$

$$= \frac{1}{2}(3.0 + 3.67) = 3.34. \tag{5}$$

Final Score of the Framework The final score $NF(F_k)$ of framework F_k, considering all criteria, is calculated as:

$$NF(F_k) = \frac{4.14 \times 2 + 3.5 \times 1 + 3.34 \times 1}{2 + 1 + 1}$$

$$= \frac{15.12}{4} = 3.78. \tag{6}$$

Based on the calculated final score, framework F_k achieves a score of 3.78, reflecting its performance according to the evaluated criteria and assigned weights.

This example demonstrates the flexibility of the e-CRF method, allowing adjustments to weights and criteria to meet the specific needs of each organization. Furthermore, the inclusion of multiple evaluators adds robustness and reliability to the assessment process.

3.3   Justification for the Choice of Aggregation Function

The aggregation function ($\sum$) employed in the e-CRF method is the weighted average—a widely adopted approach in multi-criteria decision analysis due to its simplicity, flexibility, and ability to incorporate the relative importance of individual subcritoria. By assigning greater influence to more significant criteria through weighting, this method enhances the coherence and representativeness of the overall assessment.

Although alternative aggregation strategies - such as simple weighted sum, maximization/minimization functions, and hybrid models can be employed depending on the specific context; the geometric mean was ultimately excluded due to its propensity to distort representativeness in scenarios of high variability among inputs values. Future versions of e-CRF may incorporate the option to select from a menu of aggregation functions, thereby enabling greater flexibility and customization in accordance with organizational requirements.

3.4   Criteria and Subcriteria

The method proposes the evaluation of cybersecurity risk management frameworks based on the following criteria and subcriteria:

Cost (Implementation, Licensing, Training, Maintenance, Consulting), **Information Security** (Data Protection, Intrusion Detection, Incident Response, Recovery, Prevention), **Efficiency** (Resource Optimization, Response Time, Automation, Scalability, Integration), **Performance** (Effectiveness of Security Measures, Threat Detection Rate, Risk Mitigation, Operational Impact, Recovery Time), **Complexity** (Ease of Implementation, Learning Curve, Technical Requirements, Compatibility with Existing Systems, Maintenance Complexity), **Flexibility/Adaptability** (Adaptation to Different Sectors, Customization, Scalability, Integration with Other Tools, Configuration Adjustments), **Compliance** (Regulation, Internal Policies, Auditing, Reporting, Certification), **Support and Documentation** (Documentation Quality, Availability of Technical Support, User Community, Learning Resources, Documentation Updates), **Scalability** (Growth Capacity, Performance at Scale, Expansion Flexibility, Growth Management, Multinational Support), **Community and Adoption** (Popularity, Community Feedback, Real Use Cases, Collaborations and Partnerships, Continuous Development), **Integration with Other Tools** (Compatibility, APIs and Connectors, Interoperability, Ease of Integration, Support for Open Standards), and **Innovation and Updates** (Update Frequency, Incorporation of New Technologies, R&D, Market Feedback, Continuous Improvement).

4   Case Study

A case study was conducted at a medium-sized educational institution characterized by complex operational processes and the use of multiple legacy systems, which demand efficient cybersecurity risk management—particularly to ensure compliance with Brazil's General Data Protection Law (Lei Geral de Proteção de Dados - LGPD) [6]. The institution was selected due to the critical nature of the data it handles and the urgency to strengthen its information security practices.

To support the empirical validation of the e-CRF method, a prototype software application [2] was developed. This prototype adopts a three-tier architectural model, comprising: (i) a presentation layer (React.js and Chart.js), (ii) a business logic layer (Node.js with Express.js and JWT-based authentication), and (iii) a persistence layer (Supabase with PostgreSQL). Key functionalities of the e-CRF include user authentication, framework registration, assignment of weights and scores, and automated generation of reports in XLSX and PDF formats. Additional features include comparative analysis reports, integrated technical support, and iterative improvements based on user feedback. To ensure data integrity and system security, the platform employs multiple protection mechanisms, such as password encryption using bcrypt, authentication via JSON Web Tokens (JWT), and automated backups managed through Supabase.

The system supports three distinct user roles: the *evaluator*, responsible for assigning scores; the *manager*, tasked with analyzing evaluation reports; and the *administrator*, who manages the system and user access.

The evaluation process followed a standardized procedure composed of: (1) evaluator identification, (2) selection of cybersecurity frameworks, (3) definition of weights, (4) scoring, and (5) generation of evaluation reports. For empirical validation, three information security specialists were consulted: one from a public institution, one from a multinational company, and one from a large financial institution. This diversity ensured a comprehensive analysis across different organizational contexts.

The e-CRF prototype was tested and validated in real-world scenarios by the three experts, who assessed the system's performance in practical settings. The evaluators highlighted the system's effectiveness in structuring cyber risk assessments, its intuitive interface, and its utility in supporting informed decision-making regarding cybersecurity framework adoption.

The primary goal of the evaluation was to determine how effectively the e-CRF supports the selection of cybersecurity risk management frameworks, focusing on usability, evaluator engagement, and the quality of generated reports. A five-stage workshop was conducted: (1) expert selection, (2) training on the e-CRF, (3) practical evaluation of three frameworks per evaluator, (4) automatic report generation, and (5) collection of structured feedback.

The frameworks evaluated were the NIST Cybersecurity Framework, ERM OECD, C2M2, CMMI, and CIS Controls, considering criteria such as cost, effectiveness, flexibility, and regulatory compliance.

The results demonstrated that the implementation of the e-CRF methodology significantly reduced the time required for risk framework evaluations, enhanced the accuracy of risk analysis, and improved transparency throughout the assessment process. Furthermore, the approach facilitated more effective prioritization of cybersecurity investments by providing a structured and data-driven evaluation mechanism. Feedback collected from users corroborated the applicability of the e-CRF across diverse organizational contexts, emphasizing the platform's user-friendly interface and the clarity and interpretability of the generated reports. These findings underscore the potential of the e-CRF to support informed decision-making in cybersecurity risk management.

Among the challenges encountered were initial user resistance to change, the need for training, and the demand for customized evaluation criteria. Lessons learned include the importance of continuous support and the need to adapt the methodology to the specific needs of each organization.

4.1 Discussion and Analysis of the Case Study Results

The results obtained in the case study demonstrated that the application of e-CRF provided significant improvements in the process of evaluating cybersecurity risk management frameworks. Through the assessments conducted, the evaluators were able to compare different frameworks in a structured and objective way, allowing the identification of strengths and weaknesses in relation to the main criteria. Table 4 presents the comparative scores of the evaluated frameworks, covering criteria such as cost, security, and efficiency, among others. These results offer a clear overview of the main characteristics of each framework, supporting the prioritization of cybersecurity investments and the selection of the most suitable approach for each organization.

Table 4. Comparative scores of frameworks across evaluation criteria.

Framework	C	S	E	D	Cx	F	Cf	Sp	Es	Cm	I	In	e-CRF
NIST Cybersecurity Framework	3.67	4.80	3.93	4.80	3.73	3.80	4.20	4.60	3.67	4.00	4.22	4.60	4.17
CIS Controls	3.60	4.73	4.00	4.26	3.73	3.86	4.20	4.66	3.66	4.00	4.00	4.00	4.06
C2M2	3.12	4.00	4.02	3.86	4.00	3.13	5.00	4.00	3.00	3.85	3.00	4.00	4.01
CMMI	3.00	3.00	3.00	3.00	2.00	3.00	4.00	3.00	3.00	4.00	3.00	4.00	3.24
ERM OECD	3.00	3.00	3.00	4.00	2.00	3.00	4.00	3.00	3.00	3.00	3.00	3.00	3.10

Legend: Cost (C), Security (S), Efficiency (E), Performance (D), Complexity (Cx), Flexibility (F), Compliance (Cf), Support (Sp), Scalability (Es), Community (Cm), Integration (I), Innovation (In), Final e-CRF Score

The use of e-CRF allowed evaluators to standardize the analysis process, minimizing subjective variations and ensuring greater consistency in results. Furthermore, the platform facilitated understanding of the evaluation criteria and subcriteria, providing a more intuitive user experience. The integrated help section in the system was highlighted as a critical factor for understanding the parameters used, contributing to a faster and more accurate evaluation process.

One of the most relevant findings was the system's ability to automatically generate reports and comparative charts that highlight performance differences between evaluated frameworks. These reports provided valuable insights for the participating organization's managers, enabling them to identify the frameworks with the best cost-benefit ratio and prioritize critical security areas. The generated reports also helped visualize the limitations of each framework, offering practical information for continuous improvement in risk management practices.

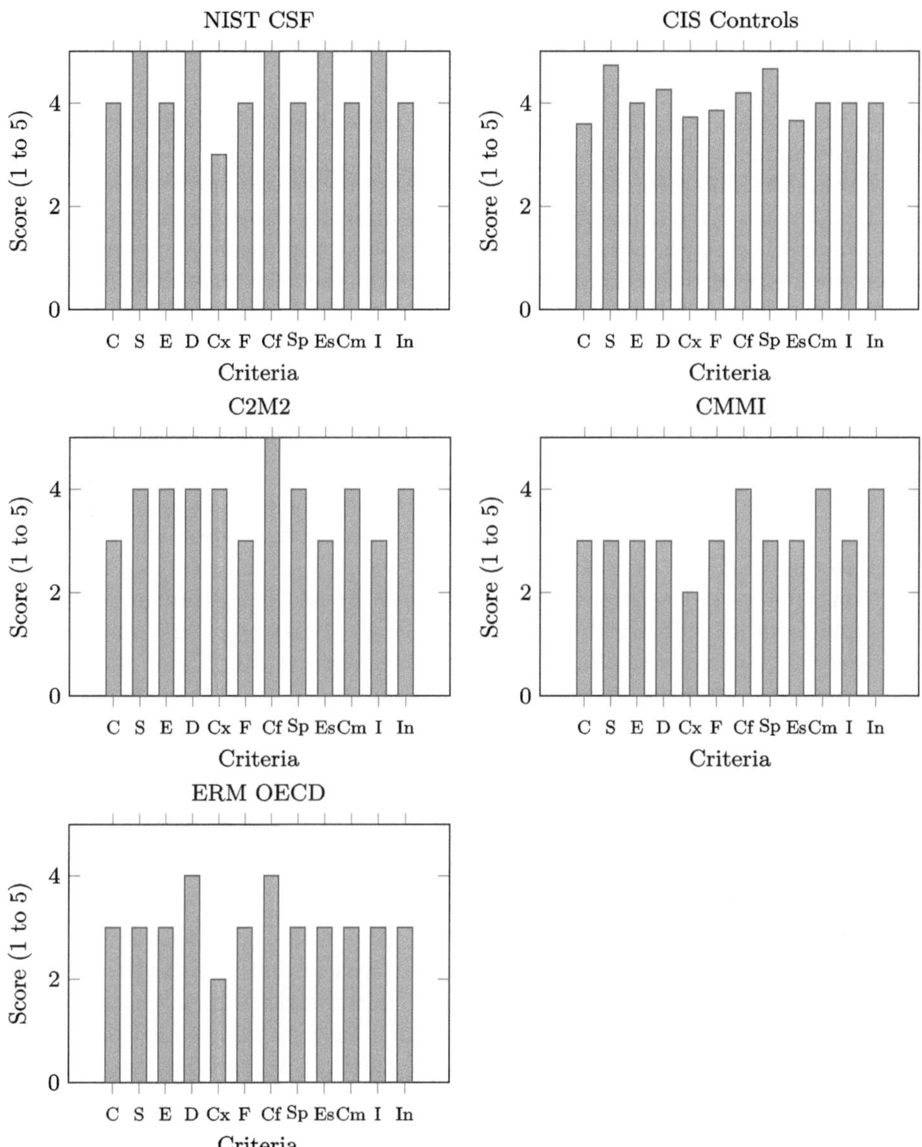

Legend: C - Cost, S - Security, E - Efficiency, D - Performance, Cx - Complexity, F - Flexibility, Cf - Compliance, Sp - Support, Es - Scalability, Cm - Community, I - Integration, In - Innovation.

Fig. 2. Comparison of framework scores by evaluation criteria.

The application of the method directly influenced the decision-making process within the organization. Managers reported that the platform helped visualize key gaps in the analyzed frameworks, allowing for the identification of improvement opportunities and necessary adjustments to meet the organization's specific needs. Additionally, the system highlighted frameworks with greater flexibility and adaptability, which proved to be more effective in dynamic and constantly evolving environments.

The results indicated that e-CRF contributes to the standardization of framework evaluation, increasing the reliability of analyses. However, it became clear that the method needs to be adapted to the particularities of each organization to ensure more effective application. The importance of providing continuous support to users during the early stages of implementation was emphasized.

Additionally, the case study showed that the developed platform helped reduce the time required to perform evaluations and increased the accuracy of the analyses. Participants reported that using the platform facilitated the comparison between different frameworks and boosted confidence in decisions based on the generated reports.

To illustrate the results, Fig. 2 presents the scores of each framework by evaluation criterion, allowing for easier performance comparison and supporting the selection of the most suitable option.

In summary, the analysis demonstrates that the e-CRF method and the developed platform are effective tools for evaluating cybersecurity risk management frameworks. The study reinforces the importance of adopting a standardized and objective approach in framework selection, contributing to the strengthening of cybersecurity practices within organizations. Despite the challenges encountered, the benefits observed outweigh the difficulties, positioning e-CRF as a practical and efficient solution for cyber riskmanagement.

5   Conclusion

This study presented the development and validation of the Evaluating Cyber Risk Frameworks (e-CRF) framework, a systematic and standardized method for assessing cybersecurity risk management frameworks. The practical application of the framework, demonstrated through a case study, revealed that e-CRF serves as an effective tool to support organizations in selecting and adopting risk management frameworks aligned to their specific operational and regulatory requirements, enhancing both the security posture and efficiency of organizational risk management processes.

The use of e-CRF contributed to the standardization of the evaluation process, improving the reliability, transparency, and efficiency of the analyses performed. The prototype developed for e-CRF proved to be intuitive and practical, facilitating the application of the framework while generating comprehensive reports that aid strategic decision-making in cybersecurity governance.

Although challenges were identified, such as the need for user training and the demand for customized evaluation criteria, the results indicate that e-CRF is a robust and adaptable solution with the potential for a positive impact in various organizational contexts.

The study reinforces the importance of adopting structured approaches for evaluating cybersecurity risk management frameworks, thereby contributing to the strengthening of security practices in organizations and the continuous improvement of risk mitigation processes.

During the application of the e-CRF framework, several limitations were identified. These included initial resistance from evaluators toward adopting this new tool, the necessity for training to ensure effective utilization of the tool, and the demand for increased flexibility in customizing evaluation criteria. Additionally, refinements to the calculation model and data visualization features were recognized as key areas for enhancement. Future work will focus on expanding the application of the e-CRF framework across diverse business sectors, integrating it with widely used risk management systems, and incorporating advanced analytical functionalities.

References

1. Alghaithi, S., Alkaabi, A., Al Hamadi, H., Al-Dmour, N.A., Ghazal, T.M.: A study of risk management frameworks and security testing for secure software systems. In: 2022 International Conference on Electrical, Computer, Communications and Mechatronics Engineering (ICECCME), pp. 1–4 (2022). https://doi.org/10.1109/ICECCME55909.2022.9988363
2. de Andrade, M., Rosa, F.F., Balcão Filho, A.F.: e-CRF prototype repository (2025). https://github.com/TeteuSensei/avaliadorFramework
3. Ayati, S.A., Naji, H.R.: A novel it-based lightweight risk management framework for metering networks in smart grids. In: 2022 12th Smart Grid Conference (SGC), pp. 1–5 (2022). https://doi.org/10.1109/SGC58052.2022.9998887
4. Billard, A.K.: Decision model for the security and utility risk evaluation (SURE) framework. In: Proceedings of the Australasian Computer Science Week Multiconference, ACSW '19. Association for Computing Machinery, New York, NY (2019). https://doi.org/10.1145/3290688.3290694. https://doi.org/10.1145/3290688.3290694
5. Binyamini, H., Bitton, R., Inokuchi, M., Yagyu, T., Elovici, Y., Shabtai, A.: A framework for modeling cyber attack techniques from security vulnerability descriptions. In: Proceedings of the 27th ACM SIGKDD Conference on Knowledge Discovery and Data Mining (KDD '21), pp. 2574–2583 (2021). https://doi.org/10.1145/3447548.3467159
6. Brasil: Lei Geral de Proteção de Dados Pessoais (LGPD) – Lei n° 13.709, de 14 de agosto de 2018 (2018). https://www.planalto.gov.br/ccivil_03/_ato2015-2018/2018/lei/l13709.htm
7. Carmichael, L., Atmaca, U.I., Maple, C., Taylor, S., Pickering, B., Surridge, M., Epiphaniou, G., Le, A.T., Murakonda, S.K., Weller, S., Mcmahon, J., Hall, W., Boniface, M.: Towards a socio-technical approach for privacy requirements analysis for next-generation trusted research environments. In: Competitive Advantage in the Digital Economy (CADE 2022), vol. 2022, pp. 169–180 (2022). https://doi.org/10.1049/icp.2022.2061
8. Couretas, J.M.: Cyber Security—An Introduction to Assessment and Maturity Frameworks, pp. 9–18 (2019). https://doi.org/10.1002/9781119420842.ch2

9. Datta, S.K.: Draft—a cybersecurity framework for IoT platforms. In: 2020 Zooming Innovation in Consumer Technologies Conference (ZINC), pp. 77–81 (2020). https://doi.org/10.1109/ZINC50678.2020.9161441

10. Din, I.U., Awan, K.A., Almogren, A.: Secure and privacy-preserving trust management system for trustworthy communications in intelligent transportation systems. IEEE Access **11**, 65407–65417 (2023). https://doi.org/10.1109/ACCESS.2023.3290911

11. Feng, C., Wu, S., Liu, N.: A user-centric machine learning framework for cyber security operations center. In: 2017 IEEE International Conference on Intelligence and Security Informatics (ISI), pp. 173–175 (2017). https://doi.org/10.1109/ISI.2017.8004902

12. Fitroh, Siregar, S., Rustamaji, E.: Determining evaluated domain process through problem identification using COBIT 5 framework. In: 2017 5th International Conference on Cyber and IT Service Management (CITSM), pp. 1–6 (2017). https://doi.org/10.1109/CITSM.2017.8089281

13. Giuca, O., Popescu, T.M., Popescu, A.M., Prostean, G., Popescu, D.E.: A survey of cybersecurity risk management frameworks. In: Balas, V.E., Jain, L.C., Balas, M.M., Shahbazova, S.N. (eds.) Soft Computing Applications, pp. 240–272. Springer International Publishing, Cham (2021)

14. Jain, A.K., Misra, T., Tyagi, N., Suresh Kumar, M.V., Pant, B.: A comparative study on cyber security technology in big data cloud computing environment. In: 2022 5th International Conference on Contemporary Computing and Informatics (IC3I), pp. 235–241 (2022). https://doi.org/10.1109/IC3I56241.2022.10072552

15. Khurana, S.K., Wassay, M.A., Verma, K.: A review on risk management framework for large scale scrum. In: 2022 International Conference on Computational Modelling, Simulation and Optimization (ICCMSO), pp. 394–400 (2022). https://doi.org/10.1109/ICCMSO58359.2022.00082

16. Khuvis, S., You, Z.Q., Na, H., Brozell, S., Franz, E., Dockendorf, T., Gardiner, J., Tomko, K.: A continuous integration-based framework for software management. In: Proceedings of the PEARC '19, pp. 1–7 (2019). https://doi.org/10.1145/3332186.3332219

17. Kitchenham, B.: Procedures for performing systematic literature reviews. Joint Technical Report, Keele University TR/SE-0401 and NICTA TR-0400011T.1, vol. 33 (2004)

18. Levy, M.: A novel framework for data center risk assessment. In: 2020 11th IEEE Annual Ubiquitous Computing, Electronics & Mobile Communication Conference (UEMCON), pp. 0148–0154 (2020). https://doi.org/10.1109/UEMCON51285.2020.9298072

19. Li, X.: Research on network information security service model based on user requirements under artificial intelligence technology. In: 2023 IEEE 3rd International Conference on Power, Electronics and Computer Applications (ICPECA), pp. 1568–1572 (2023). https://doi.org/10.1109/ICPECA56706.2023.10075946

20. Maneerattanasak, U., Wongpinunwatana, N.: A proposed framework: an appropriation for principle and practice in information technology risk management. In: 2017 International Conference on Research and Innovation in Information Systems (ICRIIS), pp. 1–6 (2017). https://doi.org/10.1109/ICRIIS.2017.8002513

21. Manuja, P., Shekhawat, R.S.: It security frameworks: risk management analysis and solutions. In: Proceedings of the 4th International Conference on Information Management and Machine Intelligence (ICIMMI '22), pp. 1–7 (2023). https://doi.org/10.1145/3590837.3590881

22. Moreira, F.R., Da Silva Filho, D.A., Nze, G.D.A., de Sousa Júnior, R.T., Nunes, R.R.: Evaluating the performance of NIST's framework cybersecurity controls through a constructivist multicriteria methodology. IEEE Access **9**, 129605–129618 (2021). https://doi.org/10.1109/ACCESS.2021.3113178
23. Naumov, S., Kabanov, I.: Dynamic framework for assessing cyber security risks in a changing environment. In: 2016 International Conference on Information Science and Communications Technologies (ICISCT), pp. 1–4 (2016). https://doi.org/10.1109/ICISCT.2016.7777406
24. Palia, A., Devlin, C., Yelorda, M., Morrison, A.: Program controls effectiveness measurement framework and metrics. In: 2021 2nd International Conference on Computation, Automation and Knowledge Management (ICCAKM), pp. 369–373 (2021). https://doi.org/10.1109/ICCAKM50778.2021.9357724
25. Pandurang Gaikwad, A., Balram Kakpure, K., Ambadas Landge, A., Gunderao Kulkarni, S., PramodJadhav, M., Tiwari, M.: Cybersecurity risk management: a complete framework for it enterprises. In: Proceedings of the 10th IEEE UPCON, pp. 602–607 (2023). https://doi.org/10.1109/UPCON59197.2023.10434767
26. Purkait, S., Damle, M.: Cyber security and frameworks: a study of cyber attacks and methods of prevention of cyber attacks. In: 2023 International Conference on Sustainable Computing and Data Communication Systems (ICSCDS), pp. 1310–1315 (2023). https://doi.org/10.1109/ICSCDS56580.2023.10104823
27. Radu, R., Săndescu, C., Grigorescu, O., Rughiniş, R.: Analyzing risk evaluation frameworks and risk assessment methods. In: 2020 19th RoEduNet Conference: Networking in Education and Research (RoEduNet), pp. 1–6 (2020). https://doi.org/10.1109/RoEduNet51892.2020.9324879
28. Rehman, S., Allgaier, C., Gruhn, V.: Security requirements engineering: a framework for cyber-physical systems. In: 2018 International Conference on Frontiers of Information Technology (FIT), pp. 315–320 (2018). https://doi.org/10.1109/FIT.2018.00062
29. Romansky, B., Mazzuchi, T., Sarkani, S.: Extending the update framework (TUF) for industrial control system applications. In: SoutheastCon 2024, pp. 1571–1576 (2024). https://doi.org/10.1109/SoutheastCon52093.2024.10500028
30. Savold, R., Dagher, N., Frazier, P., McCallam, D.: Architecting cyber defense: a survey of the leading cyber reference architectures and frameworks. In: Proceedings of the IEEE CSCloud, pp. 127–138 (2017). https://doi.org/10.1109/CSCloud.2017.37
31. Wang, Y., Qi, B., Zou, H.X., Li, J.X.: Framework of raising cyber security awareness. In: 2018 IEEE 18th International Conference on Communication Technology (ICCT), pp. 865–869 (2018). https://doi.org/10.1109/ICCT.2018.8599967
32. Waqdan, M., Louafi, H., Mouhoub, M.: An IoT security risk assessment framework for healthcare environment. In: 2023 International Symposium on Networks, Computers and Communications (ISNCC), pp. 01–08 (2023). https://doi.org/10.1109/ISNCC58260.2023.10324002
33. Wu, Z., Wang, J., Shi, Q., Zhang, J., Liu, J., Zhang, X.: An attack-aware shipping enterprise cybersecurity framework based on deep learning. In: Proceedings of the 11th International Conference on Information Systems and Computing Technology (ISCTech), pp. 115–119 (2023). https://doi.org/10.1109/ISCTech60480.2023.00028

Blockchain-Based Microlending for Financial Inclusivity: A Literature Review of Its Privacy and Trust

Gian-Luca Gücük[1]([⊠]) [iD], Stephan Leible[1] [iD], Yining Shi[2],
Constantin von Brackel-Schmidt[1], and Janick Edinger[1] [iD]

[1] University of Hamburg, Hamburg, Germany
`gian-luca.guecuek@studium.uni-hamburg.de`, `{stephan.leible,`
`constantin.schmidt,janick.edinger}@uni-hamburg.de`
[2] University of Mannheim, Baden-Württemberg, Germany
`yining.shi@students.uni-mannheim.de`

Abstract. Access to affordable and trustworthy financial services remains limited for billions of people worldwide, particularly in low-resource countries. Peer-to-peer (P2P) microlending has emerged as a promising approach to help bridge this gap by directly connecting borrowers and lenders without reliance on traditional financial intermediaries. However, conventional P2P microlending platforms face persistent challenges related to user trust, data privacy, and institutional dependence; issues that hinder their broader adoption and impact. This study investigates the potential of blockchain technology to address these limitations by enabling decentralized, transparent, and privacy-preserving microlending systems. Through a systematic literature review, we analyzed 35 papers in the final dataset existing work at the intersection of blockchain, P2P lending, microfinance, and financial inclusion. The findings suggest that blockchain technology can enhance trust through transparent record-keeping and programmable smart contracts, while supporting privacy via technical approaches (e.g., zero-knowledge proofs). However, implementation requires careful attention to socio-technical conditions, including governance, user literacy, and system interoperability. We propose a research agenda that focuses (1) on foundational blockchain-related challenges and (2) on platform design and real-world deployment. Our study offers conceptual grounding and practical direction for future research on inclusive, secure, and context-sensitive financial technologies.

Keywords: Peer-to-Peer Microlending · Blockchain · Financial Inclusion · Microfinance · Peer-to-Peer Lending Platforms

1 Introduction

Over the past decades, financial exclusion has remained a global issue, with over 1.4 billion adults unbanked and lacking access to formal financial services, particularly in developing countries [1]. Traditional banking systems often fail to reach marginalized

A. Coman et al. (Eds.): HCII 2025, LNCS 16337, pp. 326–342, 2026.
https://doi.org/10.1007/978-3-032-12801-0_22

populations due to factors such as high operational costs, dependence on centralized intermediaries, and security risks [2]. In response, microfinance and peer-to-peer (P2P) microlending platforms have emerged as promising alternatives, facilitating direct interactions between lenders and borrowers without the need for traditional financial intermediaries [3]. These systems aim to democratize financial access and empower underbanked individuals and small businesses [4]. However, despite their potential, conventional P2P microlending systems face several critical challenges. Trust and privacy are recurring concerns that hinder the platform economy and user retention [5]. In this context, privacy refers to the protection of user identity and sensitive data from unauthorized disclosure, particularly on publicly visible systems. It involves minimizing data exposure while still enabling platform functionality. Trust, on the other hand, pertains to users' confidence in the fairness, reliability, and security of the platform, especially in environments with limited regulatory oversight.

However, issues such as fraudulent behavior, data leaks, and asymmetric information remain largely unresolved [6]. Furthermore, platform providers often act as centralized gatekeepers, holding sensitive data and determining creditworthiness, which introduces potential bias and security risks [7]. Blockchain technology (BT) has been proposed as a transformative solution that can address these persistent issues in the finance sector. Characterized by decentralized architecture, cryptographic security, and transparent record-keeping, BT offers mechanisms to enhance both privacy and trust in financial transactions [8, 9]. In particular, features such as smart contracts and zero-knowledge proofs allow for automated loan processing and privacy-preserving verification, respectively [10, 11]. These characteristics can mitigate the inefficiencies of centralized platforms while enabling trustless transactions in environments, such as developing countries with low institutional trust or limited infrastructure [12, 13]. Despite this potential, the integration of BT into P2P microlending platforms introduces new technical, regulatory, and usability challenges. The public visibility of blockchain transactions based on the blockchain type can compromise user privacy, while the absence of central oversight raises concerns around data protection and privacy [14, 15].

While numerous studies have explored blockchain's application in financial services (e.g., [16, 17]), few have systematically examined how these systems balance privacy and transparency in microlending contexts of low-resource countries. This gap is particularly relevant, as design decisions of blockchain architecture within digital microlending platforms have profound implications for inclusivity, data protection, and user trust. Therefore, in this paper, we address this gap and investigate how blockchain-based microlending platforms can navigate the inherent trade-offs between privacy and trust, particularly in the context of financial inclusivity. Guided by this challenge, our research question (RQ) is:

How can blockchain-based microlending platforms balance the need for privacy and trust in peer-to-peer financial transactions while maintaining user accessibility and inclusivity in low-resource environments?

To address this RQ, we synthesize the current academic discourse, identify relevant case studies, and use cases, and outline a research agenda that can support the development of inclusive and secure blockchain-based microlending platforms. Accordingly, we conducted a literature review based on the approach of vom Brocke et al. [18] and integrated insights from existing research on BT, P2P (micro)lending, and microfinance. We aim to provide a structured overview of the potential of BT in microlending, shed light on contemporary technological approaches, and outline directions for future research and system design of microlending platforms with BT.

2 Background

This section begins by outlining the origins and evolution of microfinance as an approach for advancing financial inclusion (Sect. 2.1). Next, it examines the rise of P2P lending platforms and their contribution to expanding credit access, particularly for underserved populations (Sect. 2.2). Finally, it discusses the critical challenges of trust and privacy in P2P microlending (Sect. 2.3), setting the stage for exploring blockchain-based P2P microlending platforms in subsequent sections.

2.1 Microfinance

Microfinance plays a foundational role in the development of P2P microlending by providing small-scale financial services to populations excluded from traditional banking [19]. These services are especially critical in developing countries, where low-income individuals and microenterprises often lack credit history, formal documentation, or collateral [20, 21]. Microfinance institutions (MFIs) emerged to bridge this gap, offering non-traditional loans without collateral or using substitutes. Initially dependent on non-governmental organizations (NGOs) and donor funding, many MFIs, such as the Grameen Bank, have evolved into financially self-sufficient entities [22]. This shift has attracted the interest of commercial banks like Deutsche Bank, which have established their own microfinance arms. MFIs are typically evaluated by two criteria: outreach and financial sustainability. While smaller loans tend to reach poorer populations, they also generate higher proportional costs, making long-term sustainability more difficult [23, 24]. Although concerns have been raised about a shift toward profitability undermining the social mission, studies show that efficient, self-sustaining MFIs can improve both reach, by serving more low-income clients, and impact, by achieving greater poverty reduction (e.g., [25, 26]). Despite reaching over 211 million borrowers at the end of 2013 [27], accessibility remains a challenge, particularly in rural or infrastructure-poor regions. Mobile money services, such as M-Pesa, have expanded financial access by enabling users, for example, in Kenya, to make payments and withdraw funds through local agents, even in remote areas [28]. Such technological advancements underscore the ongoing importance of digital innovation and ecosystems in microfinance, demonstrating how they can significantly expand financial reach [29].

2.2 P2P Lending and Financial Inclusivity

P2P lending platforms have reshaped microfinance and the financial services landscape by enabling direct transactions between individual lenders and borrowers, bypassing traditional banking institutions as intermediaries [30]. The launch of platforms like

Zopa in the UK in 2005 and Prosper in the US in 2006 marked the beginning of this model's global diffusion [31, 32]. With annual growth rates exceeding 50% in some markets, P2P lending constitutes a substantial segment of alternative finance [33]. Key drivers behind this growth include cost efficiency, attractive interest rates, and improved access to credit for micro, small, and medium-sized enterprises [34, 35]. Unlike banks, which often impose strict lending criteria, P2P platforms leverage technological infrastructure to reduce administrative overhead and offer flexible credit terms. This structure enhances financial inclusivity by serving borrower segments that are usually underserved or excluded by traditional financial institutions, such as freelancers, gig workers, and individuals lacking credit histories. Thus, by lowering barriers to entry, P2P platforms have contributed to expanding access to the financial market, especially in regions where banking infrastructure is limited or costly.

Nevertheless, several challenges persist. Most platforms act as intermediaries that verify borrower identity, determine credit scores, often based on proprietary or third-party algorithms, and process the transfer of funds. These centralized structures can introduce bias, raise trust concerns, and pose challenges, for example, in terms of transparency [36]. Therefore, information asymmetry can be a critical issue as lenders often lack comprehensive data to assess borrower risk accurately [36, 37]. While platforms employ methods ranging from credit scoring to external verifications, uncertainty regarding creditworthiness, fraud, and repayment behavior continues to limit trust and scalability [38, 39]. Furthermore, in low-resource environments or developing countries, users may lack the technological literacy, financial experience, or institutional trust required to engage confidently with P2P platforms [17, 40]. The absence of collateral, limited access to digital identities, and insufficient mechanisms for dispute resolution can further exacerbate these issues. As a result, the potential of P2P microlending remains unevenly realized and often inaccessible to those most in need.

2.3   Trust and Privacy Challenges in P2P (Micro) Lending

Trust and privacy of users are central success factors for P2P lending platforms. These platforms, while offering increased accessibility and disintermediation, often struggle with information asymmetry, lack of transparency, and data security risks [37, 39]. Also, the absence of face-to-face interactions and institutional guarantees leads to increased uncertainty for both borrowers and lenders. Lenders risk misjudging creditworthiness based on limited or unverifiable borrower information (e.g., income data), while borrowers risk exploitation through opaque platform algorithms and data practices [36, 40]. Fraudulent activity, adverse selection, and identity misrepresentation can further erode platform trust [15, 34, 41]. Privacy concerns arise from the centralized handling of sensitive user data, including income, identification, and behavioral profiles. Platforms usually require users to disclose personal and financial information, which is stored on centralized servers that can be compromised. This is particularly critical in low-resource environments, where regulatory protections may be weak or inconsistently enforced. At the same time, the need for transparency to ensure fair lending and mitigate fraud adds further complexity to managing user privacy. These challenges highlight the need for technological innovations that not only enhance accessibility but also uphold users' rights to privacy and autonomy. Some platforms use BT and its unique characteristics, attempting to balance the trade-off between privacy and transparency issues by integrating cryptographic techniques such as zero-knowledge proofs [8, 13]. However, adoption remains limited, and many platforms still lack robust approaches to guarantee user trust and privacy.

3 Method

We employed a literature review in this study to investigate how blockchain-based P2P microlending platforms can address the dual challenges of trust and privacy, particularly in low-resource environments. Following the five-step approach proposed by vom Brocke et al. [18], this review aimed to provide an overview of the current state of research, synthesizing insights from academic and practitioner sources. The five steps of the literature review were conducted as follows:

1. **Definition of review scope:** The review focused on the scholarly and practical discourse surrounding blockchain-based P2P microlending systems. Particular attention was given to works discussing privacy-preserving mechanisms, trust building, and system design in the context of financial inclusivity and low-resource environments. In addition, studies addressing transparency challenges and the balance between openness and data protection were considered essential to the review.
2. **Conceptualization of topic:** A preliminary, unstructured literature review was conducted to identify relevant keywords to construct search queries. These included word combinations of "blockchain," "microlending," "microfinance," "peer-to-peer lending," "financial privacy," "trust," and "decentralized finance."
3. **Literature search:** Search queries were applied across the academic databases IEEE Xplore, ACM Digital Library, ScienceDirect, AISeL, and complementary Google Scholar. After removing duplicates, results were screened regarding their relevance to the RQ and topic through a three-stage analysis process: title, abstract, and full-text. A total of 35 sources were selected for in-depth analysis, including both conceptual and empirical studies as well as illustrative case studies.
4. **Literature analysis and synthesis:** The selected 35 sources were analyzed to extract and compare different case studies, use cases, approaches to balancing privacy and transparency, and fostering trust without centralized intermediaries in financially excluded populations. Approaches such as smart contracts, zero-knowledge proofs, and AI-based credit scoring were categorized as recurring patterns.
5. **Research agenda development:** Building on the findings, we identified promising research possibilities and divided them into five general, blockchain-related, and four platform-related opportunities. They focus, for example, on balancing transparency and privacy, designing blockchain-based microlending platforms, and providing needed technological literacy, particularly in developing countries and economies.

The insights gathered served as a foundation for evaluating how BT can be deployed to build trustworthy, privacy-preserving, and inclusive microlending platforms.

4 Literature Review

This section is structured in two parts. It starts with the examination of P2P microlending (platform) challenges, including issues of trust and privacy (Sect. 4.1). After that, it explores how BT has been applied in the microlending context, illustrating its potential and limitations through identified use cases and case studies (Sect. 4.2).

4.1 P2P Microlending (Platform) Challenges

Many P2P microlending platforms share the overarching mission of MFIs: improving financial inclusion, for example, by enabling access to capital for underserved populations. Digital platforms such as Zidisha and Kiva aim to simplify cross-border microlending by directly connecting individual lenders in high-income countries with entrepreneurs in low-resource environments [42]. Unlike traditional MFIs, these platforms seek to minimize the role of intermediaries and create transparent, donor-independent lending ecosystems. However, in practice, many platforms, particularly Kiva, continue to rely on MFIs as local (field) partners for borrower vetting, loan disbursement, and repayment management [43].

Kiva exemplifies this hybrid model. It has facilitated loans to millions of borrowers across many countries [44], often starting from as little as $25 per lender. Although the platform portrays itself as a P2P marketplace, most loans involve intermediation: MFIs collect and manage borrower data, disburse funds, and absorb loan interest as compensation [25]. Lenders receive only the principal upon loan maturity, making their involvement philanthropic rather than investment-based. This structure raises questions around trust, accountability, and data control. Lenders must trust both the platform and its partner MFIs to fairly represent borrower needs and manage funds transparently, yet they typically lack the means to verify outcomes or repayment details independently.

These limitations extend to privacy and fairness. Borrowers must share personal and financial information with both MFIs and the central platform, raising concerns over how data is stored, accessed, and potentially exploited, especially in jurisdictions with weak data protection laws. Meanwhile, lenders often rely on simplified borrower profiles and filters (e.g., gender or sector) to guide their lending decisions. This can reinforce platform-driven biases and unintentionally marginalize certain groups [42, 45].

A further concern lies in the partial reintermediation created by relying on MFIs. While local partners provide essential contextual knowledge, they may also engage in opportunistic behavior, such as retaining low-risk loans for themselves and redirecting higher-risk clients to P2P platforms. This practice, observed on Kiva, has led to lower average repayment rates compared to traditional MFI portfolios [42]. Consequently, the platform design falls short of the full potential promised by digital disintermediation and trustless technology.

In summary, while P2P microlending platforms aspire to promote financial inclusion through disintermediation and transparency, their practical implementations reveal significant design and operational challenges. These include persistent dependencies on intermediaries, issues of trust and accountability, privacy risks, and potential biases in borrower selection. Table 1 provides an overview of several identified key challenges, highlighting their implications for P2P microlending (platforms).

Table 1. Challenges of P2P microlending (platforms).

Challenge	Description
Intermediation and trust	Despite aiming for disintermediation, platforms like Kiva rely on MFIs, creating dependence on intermediaries for trust and accountability. This undermines digital disintermediation and the trustless design promised by P2P platforms [42–44].
Data privacy risks	Borrowers must disclose sensitive personal and financial data to multiple parties (platform and MFI), with risks of misuse, especially in weak regulatory contexts [31, 42].
(Platform-driven) Bias	Simplified borrower profiles and categorical filters may unintentionally reinforce biases or exclude certain groups from fair access to credit [36, 42].
Lack of transparency	P2P microlending platforms often provide limited visibility into how borrower information is verified, funds are managed, and repayments are tracked, making it difficult for lenders to independently assess the lending process [31].
Opportunistic behavior	For example, MFIs or lenders may channel higher-risk borrowers to P2P platforms while retaining safer loans, leading to poorer repayment performance on P2P loans [31, 42].
Costs of hybrid models	The reliance on MFIs reintroduces some of the costs and delays associated with traditional systems, limiting the full efficiency potential of P2P microlending [25, 44].

4.2 Blockchain Technology and P2P Microlending (Platforms)

Building on the status quo, we observe that while traditional P2P lending and microlending systems offer new avenues for financial inclusion, they continue to grapple with structural limitations, particularly regarding trust, privacy, and centralized control. BT emerges as a potential response to these issues, offering features such as decentralization, transparency, and cryptographic security that can address some of the documented weaknesses of current P2P microlending (platforms).

Much of the existing blockchain literature focuses on applications such as remittances, crowdfunding, and initial coin offerings [46, 47], with P2P lending often discussed in the context of industrialized economies and fintech [41, 48]. However, researchers have also begun exploring the potential of BT in development finance, including microfinance and P2P microlending [12, 49, 50]. While promising, these discussions often do not focus on the socio-technical nuances and privacy-trust trade-offs inherent in decentralized lending ecosystems.

Addressing this gap, we identified key blockchain features as enablers for building trust while safeguarding sensitive user data. Table 2 illustrates specific BT potentials derived from its characteristics, which can help address some of the challenges described in P2P microlending platforms. The challenges "(platform-driven) bias" and "costs of hybrid models" are less directly addressable through BT; they require broader socio-technical or economic measures.

Table 2. BT potentials to address specific challenges of P2P microlending (platforms).

Challenge	BT Potentials
Intermediation and trust	Blockchain can enable direct, peer-to-peer transactions recorded on a tamper-resistant ledger, reducing dependence on, for example, MFIs as intermediaries and supporting trustless interactions (e.g., with the support of smart contracts) [8, 12, 14].
Data privacy risks	Blockchain can incorporate privacy-preserving technologies (e.g., zero-knowledge proofs, decentralized identity) to minimize unnecessary data sharing while ensuring compliance and verification [10, 11, 16].
Lack of transparency	Blockchain's distributed ledger provides auditable, immutable records of transactions (e.g., loan terms and repayments), increasing visibility for lenders and borrowers alike [2, 14].
Opportunistic behavior	The data integrity and auditable records on blockchain can limit the ability of intermediaries to game the system (e.g., by misrepresenting borrower risk levels) [13, 51].

The technical features of a blockchain implementation must be critically evaluated in context, as they shape how effectively microlending platforms can balance transparency, privacy, and trust. Public blockchains increase transparency but may risk exposing sensitive borrower data, whereas private or federated blockchains can limit visibility to enhance privacy [9]. In that way, BT offers alternative architectures for P2P microlending platforms by enabling transparent record-keeping, decentralized identity management [52], and privacy-preserving verification, thereby reducing reliance on central intermediaries and enhancing trust and control [53]. Realizing these benefits, however, requires adjustable platform architectures tailored to specific regulatory, cultural, and socio-technical environments, particularly in low-resource countries.

Table 3 illustrates a selection of conceptual and practical use cases and case studies identified in the reviewed literature. Each case provides insights into how BT is currently used, or could be expanded, to support and foster P2P microlending (platforms) regarding several of the described challenges in this field. These cases demonstrate the growing potential and the fragmentation of blockchain-based microlending ecosystems.

Table 3. Selection of blockchain-based use cases and case studies from the literature review.

Case Source	Case Description
Lane et al. [54]	White_paper for the Everex financial ecosystem that runs on Ethereum and facilitates loans by pegging digital currencies to national ones. Smart contracts automate loan processes, reducing transaction costs in cross-border lending.

(*continued*)

Table 3. (*continued*)

Case Source	Case Description
Kinai et al. [55]	Built on Hyperledger Fabric, this conceptual system connects buyers, sellers, and financial intermediaries via mobile apps, enabling inclusive financing through smart contracts.
Arvanitis [41]	The platform Lendoit uses smart contracts to verify identity and automate loan issuance. It uses multiple verification sources for a kind of credit rating.
Xie et al. [10]	Presentation of the ZeroLender platform for P2P lending in Bitcoin. It uses zero-knowledge proofs for privacy reasons and secure payments against potential malicious behavior.
Zeng et al. [15]	Proposition of HyperP2PLS, a Hyperledger-based P2P lending system with a web application and smart contracts to increase reliability and regulatory oversight.

5 Research Agenda

In light of the findings (e.g., case studies) from our literature review, it is evident that BT holds significant potential for transforming microlending systems, especially in low-resource environments where issues of trust, transparency, and data privacy are particularly pronounced. However, this transformation is still in its infancy, and mature solutions are scarce so far. Therefore, to systematize future research directions, we propose a two-part research agenda. Section 5.1 focuses on research themes related to BT in the microlending and microfinance sector. Section 5.2 addresses the design and configuration of blockchain-based microlending platforms in greater detail.

5.1 Research Directions on Blockchain in Microlending

The unique features and characteristics of the BT, such as distributed ledgers, immutability, smart contracts, and privacy-enhancing technologies, are theoretically well-suited to mitigate trust and data security issues in microlending [9, 54, 55]. Yet empirical evidence remains sparse [13], especially in developing countries, where technological infrastructure and regulatory frameworks vary significantly. Below, we outline five promising research areas for deeper investigation to foster a responsible and effective blockchain adoption for P2P microlending platforms, balancing privacy and trust.

Scalable, Privacy-Preserving Mechanisms.
Guiding question: *How can scalable and context-appropriate privacy-enhancing mechanisms be implemented in blockchain-based microlending systems without compromising verifiability and usability?*

This area explores the integration of privacy-enhancing mechanisms, such as zero-knowledge proofs and homomorphic encryption, into blockchain-based P2P microlending systems. While such approaches promise to protect sensitive borrower data [8, 10], their computational intensity and complexity may hinder adoption in low-resource settings. Research is needed to evaluate the trade-offs between data protection and system verifiability, particularly in environments with limited connectivity, device capacity, or user literacy. Usability studies are crucial to ensure these technologies remain transparent to non-expert users.

Trust Without Intermediaries.

Guiding question: *What mechanisms can build and maintain trust in decentralized financial ecosystems, in the absence of centralized authorities or financial institutions?*

P2P microlending models often rely on MFIs for borrower vetting and monitoring [43], which limits decentralization. This research area examines alternatives, such as cryptographic reputation systems, decentralized identities, or community-based governance models [15, 52]. These mechanisms are intended to foster trust between lenders and borrowers without replicating the gatekeeping functions of centralized entities. Key concerns include mitigating fraud, signaling borrower reliability, and ensuring that trust is both technically and socially verifiable.

Blockchain Governance in Low-Resource Contexts.

Guiding question: *How can governance of blockchain-based microlending systems be structured in environments with limited digital or institutional infrastructure?*

The decentralized nature of the BT introduces challenges around accountability, dispute resolution, and system coordination [11, 15], especially in unregulated or underdeveloped financial ecosystems. Research is needed to explore governance frameworks that enable rule enforcement, user recourse, and adaptable compliance mechanisms. This can include hybrid governance involving local actors, algorithmic arbitration, and smart contract-based enforcement of loan terms. Successful models must be resilient to infrastructure instability and reflect local socio-legal norms.

Interoperability and Standardization.

Guiding question: *How can blockchain-based microlending be integrated with legacy financial infrastructures and digital identity systems?*

For blockchain-based microlending to achieve scale, it must connect with existing financial services, such as mobile money platforms (e.g., M-Pesa), and (national) identity systems. Research should investigate data interoperability and compliance with know-your-customer and anti-money-laundering standards [46, 54, 56]. Studies should also examine how to prevent fragmentation across ecosystems and develop open standards that encourage vendor-neutral adoption and long-term maintainability.

User Inclusivity and Technological Literacy.

Guiding question: *What are the minimum usability and literacy thresholds for adopting blockchain-based microlending systems among underserved populations?*

Even if technically feasible, blockchain-based systems must be understandable and accessible for their users and adopters [51]. Research should map the needed technological and financial literacy and regulatory constraints of the target populations [17]. Particular attention should be paid to low-bandwidth environments and socio-cultural perceptions of automated financial systems. This research area should also consider the co-design of solutions with communities to ensure relevance and adoption.

5.2   Research Directions on Blockchain-Based Microlending Platform Design

While the previous subsection addressed research directions of BT in microlending, the successful realization of blockchain-based P2P microlending also hinges on platform-level implementation. Specifically, systems must not only embed trust and privacy at the protocol level, but also manifest these properties through concrete user interfaces, processes, and incentive structures. This section further outlines the research agenda, with four interrelated focal points addressing platform design, operational dynamics, and real-world integration. The goal is to ensure that the blockchain-based platform design bridges the gap between technical capabilities and inclusive user experiences.

Context-Sensitive Platform Architectures.
Guiding question: *How can blockchain-based P2P microlending platforms be adapted to suit the technological, cultural, and financial realities of different regions?*

Microlending platforms should align with the constraints and expectations of their operating environments. Research should explore modular or layered architectures that allow deployment in both fully online and partially offline contexts, including mobile designs. Customization of smart contract logic to local lending norms, credit cycles, and dispute resolution preferences is also crucial [12, 13, 51].

Incentive Design and Stakeholder Alignment.
Guiding question: *What incentive structures can align borrower, lender, and verifier behavior while sustaining platform viability in blockchain-based P2P microlending?*

Blockchain-based P2P microlending platforms must offer benefits to all stakeholders. This includes dynamic interest rate models or collateral mechanisms and incentives for community participation or loan verification [10]. Research should also analyze how incentives can be designed to minimize misalignment (e.g., moral hazard) while ensuring that platforms remain accessible and fair [13].

Resilience and Risk Management.
Guiding question: *How can blockchain-based P2P microlending platforms manage financial and operational risks without centralized oversight?*

Platform-level mechanisms must address liquidity risks, borrower default, smart contract failures, and reputational abuse [40]. Research is needed on automated fallback protocols, reserve pools, insurance schemes, and decentralized arbitration mechanisms. Cases from existing conceptual or practical platforms (e.g., Lendoit, ZeroLender, and Everex) can inform the design of resilient systems in fragile markets [10, 41, 54].

Deployment and Evaluation Frameworks.
Guiding question: *What methodologies can guide the testing, piloting, and long-term evaluation of blockchain-based P2P microlending platforms in real-world conditions?*

It is promising to provide frameworks for testing of platform prototypes, including simulation environments, stakeholder pilots, and impact evaluations. Special focus should be given to participatory methods and longitudinal studies that capture social and economic outcomes over time. Collaborations with NGOs, local cooperatives, or MFIs can be of significant importance for contextual validation [13, 57].

Together, these platform-focused research areas highlight the complexity of translating blockchain's theoretical advantages into practical P2P microlending solutions. Unlike purely technical innovations, platform design must consider a wide range of contextual, social, and economic factors that influence user engagement and system sustainability. The integration of trust and privacy should occur at both the infrastructure level and through everyday user experiences. Advancing this agenda will necessitate interdisciplinary collaboration and close cooperation with stakeholders in the field.

6 Discussion and Conclusion

This study set out to investigate how blockchain-based P2P microlending (platforms) can balance the dual imperatives of privacy and trust while ensuring inclusivity and accessibility for users. This is significant, especially in low-resource settings. Through a literature review and analysis of found case studies and use cases, we identified general P2P microlending challenges and how BT can address them. Furthermore, we identified technological and design trade-offs that shape the deployment and success of such platforms. One insight is that privacy and trust are not mutually exclusive, but deeply interdependent dimensions: trust is enhanced when privacy protections are visible and enforceable, while privacy mechanisms must be transparent enough to ensure verifiability and accountability [8, 10]. Moreover, our findings highlight that contextual adaptability to digital infrastructures, user literacy levels, and regulatory conditions plays a decisive role in shaping viable platform configurations [17, 40]. The reviewed case studies and use cases illustrate that technical innovations alone are insufficient unless embedded in governance models and social systems that are both comprehensible and trustworthy to the target communities [15, 39, 40]. As such, blockchain-based P2P microlending must be viewed not as a static technological intervention, but as a socio-technical ecosystem requiring co-evolution between technology, users, and institutions.

From a theoretical perspective, our research contributes to the evolving discourse on decentralized finance by challenging the assumption that decentralization alone suffices to build trust in financial ecosystems. The findings suggest that trust in blockchain-based P2P microlending platforms must be actively engineered through verifiable privacy safeguards, localized governance mechanisms, and transparent risk signaling, features that align with broader socio-technical theories of digital infrastructure [6, 39, 58]. Additionally, in line with the work of Spiliotopoulos et al. [59], our results show privacy as a necessary condition, rather than a trade-off, for systems serving a marginalized population with financially vulnerable consumers. This reinforces the need to embed concepts like context-sensitive trust and usable privacy within existing models of fintech adoption and digital credit systems in low-resource environments [13, 57]. Therefore, we suggest a shift from abstract blockchain capability to the institutional and experiential dimensions of real-world environments for financial participation.

From a practical perspective, this study offers actionable insights for platform developers and financial service providers seeking to leverage BT for P2P microlending. The results underscore that privacy and trust are not merely technical add-ons but central design imperatives that shape user adoption. Practitioners should, therefore, prioritize

modular, context sensitive system architectures that can flexibly respond to infrastruc-
tural constraints and local norms and regulations [12, 51]. For example, designing low-
bandwidth-compatible mobile interfaces with clear privacy indicators and simplified
consent flows could enhance adoption among users with limited digital literacy. Furthermore, the insights highlight the potential of decentralized trust mechanisms, such
as verifiable credentials or community-driven reputation systems, to replace traditional
credit evaluation processes, reducing reliance on central intermediaries (e.g., MFIs)
that often act as gatekeepers [15, 52]. Also, development organizations and regulators
should consider the long-term sustainability and accountability of such systems, supporting pilots and audits that balance technological ambition with real-world constraints
and the needs of vulnerable populations [13, 40, 57].

This paper is subject to several limitations. First, the literature review is constrained
by the scope of selected databases and search terms, which may have excluded relevant
but non-indexed sources. Second, while the study synthesizes insights from diverse
domains, such as blockchain, microlending, and digital financial inclusion, it does not
empirically validate the proposed research agenda or the practical feasibility of the
identified technologies in a real-world setting. Third, the analysis primarily reflects
conceptual perspectives; practical insights from current blockchain microlending pilots
or startups may be underrepresented due to limited found and publicly available works.
Lastly, although the paper emphasizes low-resource and developing contexts, it does not
delve deeply into region-specific socio-political dynamics that can shape adoption and
governance.

Taken together, the findings of this study suggest that blockchain-based P2P
microlending holds significant potential, but only if privacy, trust, and inclusion are
treated as foundational, not peripheral, platform design objectives. Priority should be
given to platform designs that have demonstrated practical viability. As seen in other
domains, such as open science [60] and licensing [61], many blockchain solutions remain
conceptual or at the prototype stage, with few moving toward implementation and adoption. The research agenda presented here highlights that both technical foundations
and platform-level decisions must evolve in tandem to meet the complex demands of
underserved financial ecosystems. Addressing these challenges will require interdisciplinary collaboration between researchers of different disciplines (e.g., computer science
and social sciences), as well as iterative, real-world testing in diverse socio-economic
environments. Moreover, the literature synthesis reinforces the importance of context:
solutions that succeed in one region may not translate seamlessly to another, underscoring the need for flexibility and sensitivity to local conditions. Ultimately, BT is not a
silver bullet, but a promising foundation when thoughtfully applied, and can help create
more accountable, transparent, and user-empowering microlending systems, especially
in developing countries.

Disclosure of Interests.
The authors declared no potential conflicts of interest with respect to the research,
authorship, and/or publication of this article.

References

1. The World Bank Group. The Global Findex Database 2021: Financial Inclusion, Digital Payments, and Resilience in the Age of COVID-19 (2021) https://https://documents.worldbank.org/en/publication/documents-reports/documentdetail/099818107072234182. Accessed 16 June 2025
2. Budisteanu, T.-G.: Blockchain and the banking sector: benefits, challenges and perspectives. Open J. Soc. Sci. **13**(3), 288–300 (2025). https://doi.org/10.4236/jss.2025.133019
3. Yum, H., Lee, B., Chae, M.: From the wisdom of crowds to my own judgment in microfinance through online peer-to-peer lending platforms. Electron. Commer. Res. Appl. **11**(5), 469–483 (2012). https://doi.org/10.1016/j.elerap.2012.05.003
4. Verma, S.: Leveraging Fintech peer-to-peer platform to democratize access of easy credit in rural areas of india for sustainable digital economy. SSRN Electronic Journal (2024). https://doi.org/10.2139/ssrn.5204179
5. Marth, S., Hartl, B., Penz, E.: Sharing on platforms: reducing perceived risk for peer-to-peer platform consumers through trust-building and regulation. J. Consum. Behav. **21**(6), 1255–1267 (2022). https://doi.org/10.1002/cb.2075
6. Sampat, B., Mogaji, E., Nguyen, P.N.: The dark side of FinTech in financial services: a qualitative enquiry into FinTech developers' perspective. International Journal of Bank Marketing **42**(1), 38–65 (2024). https://doi.org/10.1108/IJBM-07-2022-0328
7. Salami, I.A., et al.: Addressing bias and data privacy concerns in ai-driven credit scoring systems through cybersecurity risk assessment. Asian Journal of Research in Computer Science **18**(4), 59–82 (2025). https://doi.org/10.9734/ajrcos/2025/v18i4608
8. Christidis, K., Devetsikiotis, M.: Blockchains and smart contracts for the internet of things. IEEE Access **4**, 2292–2303 (2016). https://doi.org/10.1109/ACCESS.2016.2566339
9. Casino, F., Dasaklis, T.K., Patsakis, C.: A systematic literature review of blockchain-based applications: current status, classification and open issues. Telematics Inform. **36**, 55–81 (2019). https://doi.org/10.1016/j.tele.2018.11.006
10. Xie, Y., Holmes, J., Dagher, G.G.: ZeroLender: trustless peer-to-peer Bitcoin lending platform. In: Proceedings of the Tenth ACM Conference on Data and Application Security and Privacy. ACM, pp. 247–258 (2020). https://doi.org/10.1145/3374664.3375735
11. Dai, J., Vasarhelyi, M.A.: Toward blockchain-based accounting and assurance. J. Inf. Syst. **31**(3), 5–21 (2017). https://doi.org/10.2308/isys-51804
12. Schmidt, K., Sandner, P. Solving Challenges in Developing Countries with Blockchain Technology (2017). Accessed 16 June 2025
13. Hoque, M.M., Kummer, T.-F., Yigitbasioglu, O.: How can blockchain-based lending platforms support microcredit activities in developing countries? An empirical validation of its opportunities and challenges. Technological Forecasting and Social Change 203 (2024). https://doi.org/10.1016/j.techfore.2024.123400
14. Cong, L.W., He, Z.: Blockchain disruption and smart contracts. The Review of Financial Studies **32**(5), 1754–1797 (2019). https://doi.org/10.1093/rfs/hhz007
15. Zeng, X., Hao, N., Zheng, J., Xu, X.: A consortium blockchain paradigm on hyperledger-based peer-to-peer lending system. China Communications **16**(8), 38–50 (2019). https://doi.org/10.23919/JCC.2019.08.004
16. Fanning, K., Centers, D.P.: Blockchain and its coming impact on financial services. J. Corporate Accounting & Finance **27**(5), 53–57 (2016). https://doi.org/10.1002/jcaf.22179
17. Adegbite, A.: The role of blockchain technology in enhancing financial inclusion. IOSR Journal of Economics and Finance **15**(5), 19–28 (2024). https://doi.org/10.9790/5933-1505071928

18. vom Brocke, J., et al.: Reconstructing the giant: on the importance of rigour in documenting the literature search process. In: Proceedings of the 17th European Conference on Information Systems (ECIS2009) (2009)

19. Robinson, M.S.: The Microfinance Revolution: Sustainable Finance for the Poor, Washington, D.C., USA (2001)

20. Aghion, B.A., de Morduch, J.: The Economics of Microfinance. The MIT Press, London, England (2005)

21. OECD. FinTech lending in Sub-Saharan Africa (2024) https://www.oecd.org/content/dam/oecd/en/topics/policy-sub-issues/digital-finance/FinTech-lending-in-Sub-Saharan-Africa.pdf. Accessed 11 June 2025

22. Ledgerwood, J., White, V.: Transforming Microfinance Institutions - Providing Full Financial Services to the Poor. World Bank, Washington, DC (2006)

23. Hermes, N., Lensink, R., Meesters, A.: Outreach and efficiency of microfinance institutions. World Dev. **39**(6), 938–948 (2011). https://doi.org/10.1016/j.worlddev.2009.10.018

24. Nurmakhanova, M., Kretzschmar, G., Fedhila, H.: Trade-off between financial sustainability and outreach of microfinance institutions. Eurasian Econ. Rev. **5**(2), 231–250 (2015). https://doi.org/10.1007/s40822-015-0016-7

25. Roberts, P.W.: The profit orientation of microfinance institutions and effective interest rates. World Dev. **41**, 120–131 (2013). https://doi.org/10.1016/j.worlddev.2012.05.022

26. Caballero-Montes, T.: The relationship between financial and social performances in microfinance: Insights from the provision of agricultural loans in Cambodia. Savings and Development **46** (2023)

27. Reed, L.R. Mapping Pathways out of Poverty: The State of the Microcredit Summit Campaign Report. Microcredit Summit Campaign (MCS). (2015) https://www.results.org/wp-content/uploads/SOCR2015_English_Web.pdf. Accessed 16 June 2025

28. Mas, I., Radcliffe, D.: Mobile payments go viral - m-PESA in Kenya. The Capco Institute's Journal of Financial Transformation **32**, 169–182 (2011)

29. Mathison, S. Increasing the Outreach and Sustainability of Microfinance through ICT Innovation (2006). https://www.findevgateway.org/sites/default/files/publications/files/mfg-en-paper-increasing-the-outreach-and-sustainability-of-microfinance-through-ict-innovation-2006.pdf. Accessed 16 June 2025

30. Turguttopbas, N., Kayral, I.E.: Global peer-to-peer lending market. Pressacademia (2023). https://doi.org/10.17261/Pressacademia.2023.1657

31. Chen, D., Lai, F., Lin, Z.: A trust model for online peer-to-peer lending: a lender's perspective. Inf. Technol. Manage. **15**(4), 239–254 (2014). https://doi.org/10.1007/s10799-014-0187-z

32. Bazarbash, M., Beaton, K.: Filling the Gap. IMF Working Papers **20**(150) (2020). https://doi.org/10.5089/9781513552477.001

33. Zhang, B., et al.: The 5th UK Alternative Finance Industry Report (2018). https://www.jbs.cam.ac.uk/wp-content/uploads/2020/08/2018-5th-uk-alternative-finance-industry-report.pdf. Accessed 16 June 2025

34. Gomber, P., Kauffman, R.J., Parker, C., Weber, B.W.: On the fintech revolution: interpreting the forces of innovation, disruption, and transformation in financial services. J. Manag. Inf. Syst. **35**(1), 220–265 (2018). https://doi.org/10.1080/07421222.2018.1440766

35. Abbasi, K., Alam, A., Brohi, N.A., Brohi, I.A., Nasim, S.: P2P lending Fintechs and SMEs' access to finance. Economics Letters **204** (2021). https://doi.org/10.1016/j.econlet.2021.109890

36. Mild, A., Waitz, M., Wöckl, J.: How low can you go? — Overcoming the inability of lenders to set proper interest rates on unsecured peer-to-peer lending markets. J. Bus. Res. **68**(6), 1291–1305 (2015). https://doi.org/10.1016/j.jbusres.2014.11.021

37. Lenz, R.: Peer-to-peer lending - opportunities and risks. European Journal of Risk and Regulation **7**(4), 688–700 (2016). https://doi.org/10.1017/S1867299X00010126

38. Milne, A., Parboteeah, P.: The Business Models and Economics of Peer-to-Peer Lending (2016). https://www.ceps.eu/ceps-publications/business-models-and-economics-peer-peer-lending/. Accessed 16 June 2025

39. Bao, T., Ding, Y., Gopal, R., Möhlmann, M.: Throwing good money after bad: risk mitigation strategies in the P2P lending platforms. Inf. Syst. Front. **26**(4), 1453–1473 (2024). https://doi.org/10.1007/s10796-023-10423-4

40. Gonzalez, L.: Blockchain, herding and trust in peer-to-peer lending. Manag. Financ. **46**(6), 815–831 (2020). https://doi.org/10.1108/MF-09-2018-0423

41. Arvanitis, S.: P2P lending review, analysis and overview of lendoit blockchain platform. International Journal of Open Information Technologies **7**(2), 94–98 (2019)

42. Riggins, F.J., Weber, D.M.: Information asymmetries and identification bias in P2P social microlending. Inf. Technol. Dev. **23**(1), 107–126 (2017). https://doi.org/10.1080/02681102.2016.1247345

43. Paruthi, G., Frias-Martinez, E., Frias-Martinez, V.: Peer-to-peer microlending platforms: Characterization of online traits. In: Proceedings of the 2016 IEEE International Conference on Big Data. IEEE, pp. 2180–2189 (2016). https://doi.org/10.1109/BigData.2016.7840848

44. Choo, J., Lee, C., Lee, D., Zha, H., Park, H.: Understanding and promoting micro-finance activities in kiva.org. In: Proceedings of the 7th ACM international conference on Web search and data mining. ACM, New York, NY, USA, pp. 583–592 (2014). https://doi.org/10.1145/2556195.2556253

45. Ly, P., Mason, G.: Individual preferences over NGO projects: evidence from microlending on Kiva. SSRN Journal (2010). https://doi.org/10.2139/ssrn.1652269

46. Böhme, R., Christin, N., Edelman, B., Moore, T.: Bitcoin: economics, technology, and governance. Journal of Economic Perspectives **29**(2), 213–238 (2015). https://doi.org/10.1257/jep.29.2.213

47. Hartmann, F., Grottolo, G., Wang, X., Lunesu, M.I.: Alternative fundraising: success factors for blockchain-based vs. conventional crowdfunding. In: Proceedings of the 2019 IEEE International Workshop on Blockchain Oriented Software Engineering (IWBOSE). IEEE, pp. 38–43 (2019). https://doi.org/10.1109/IWBOSE.2019.8666515

48. Schweizer, A., Schlatt, V., Urbach, N., Fridgen, G.: Unchaining social businesses – blockchain as the basic technology of a crowdlending platform. In: Proceedings of the 38th International Conference on Information Systems (ICIS2017) (2017)

49. Ammous, S.: Economics beyond financial intermediation: digital currencies' potential for growth, poverty alleviation and international development. The Journal of Private Enterprise **30**(3), 19–50 (2015)

50. Larios-Hernández, G.J.: Blockchain entrepreneurship opportunity in the practices of the unbanked. Bus. Horiz. **60**(6), 865–874 (2017). https://doi.org/10.1016/j.bushor.2017.07.012

51. Renduchintala, T., Alfauri, H., Yang, Z., Di Pietro, R., Jain, R.: A survey of blockchain applications in the fintech sector. Journal of Open Innovation: Technology, Market, and Complexity **8**(4) (2022). https://doi.org/10.3390/joitmc8040185

52. Yan, Z., Zhao, X., Liu, Y., Luo, X.: Blockchain-driven decentralized identity management: an interdisciplinary review and research agenda. Information & Management **61**(7) (2024). https://doi.org/10.1016/j.im.2024.104026

53. Mhlanga, D.: Block chain technology for digital financial inclusion in the industry 4.0, towards sustainable development? Frontiers in Blockchain **6** (2023). https://doi.org/10.3389/fbloc.2023.1035405

54. Lane, A., Leiding, B., Norta, A.: Lowering Financial Inclusion Barriers with a Blockchain-Based Capital Transfer System: Whitepaper (2017). https://doi.org/10.1109/INFCOMW.2019.8845177

55. Kinai, A., Markus, I., Oduor, E., Diriye, A.: Asset-based lending via a secure distributed platform. In: Proceedings of the Ninth International Conference on Information and Communication Technologies and Development. ACM (2017). https://doi.org/10.1145/3136560.313 6594
56. Kumar, D., Phani, B.V., Chilamkurti, N., Saurabh, S., Ratten, V.: A blockchain-based decentralized peer-to-peer lending framework for SMEs. In: Proceedings of the 2023 International Conference on Intelligent Computing and Its Emerging Applications. ACM, pp. 130–140 (2023). https://doi.org/10.1145/3659154.3659188
57. Liu, A., Urquía-Grande, E., López-Sánchez, P., Rodríguez-López, Á.: Research into microfinance and ICTs: A bibliometric analysis. Evaluation and Program Planning **97** (2023). https://doi.org/10.1016/j.evalprogplan.2022.102215
58. Mandić, A., Marković, B., Žigo, I.R.: Risks of the use of fintech in the financial inclusion of the population: a systematic review of the literature. Journal of Risk and Financial Management **18**(5) (2025). https://doi.org/10.3390/jrfm18050250
59. Spiliotopoulos, T., et al.: Identifying and Supporting Financially Vulnerable Consumers in a Privacy-Preserving Manner: A Use Case Using Decentralised Identifiers and Verifiable Credentials. arXiv (2021). https://doi.org/10.48550/arXiv.2106.06053
60. Leible, S., Schlager, S., Schubotz, M., Gipp, B.: A review on blockchain technology and blockchain projects fostering open science. Frontiers in Blockchain **2**(16) (2019). https://doi.org/10.3389/fbloc.2019.00016
61. Schoenhals, A., Hepp, Thomas, Leible, Stephan, Ehret, P., Gipp, B.: Overview of licensing platforms based on distributed ledger technology. In: Proceedings of the Hawaii International Conference on System Sciences (HICCS2019), pp. 4675–4684 (2019)

Mouse Pointing Endpoint Prediction to Distinguish Between Human and Bot Using Kinematic Template Matching

Hafiz Shafiq Ur Rehman Khalil[1], Nisar Ahmed[2], and YiJun Yang[1(✉)]

[1] Xi'an Jiaotong University, Xi'an, People's Republic of China
shafiq_rai@stu.xjtu.edu.cn
[2] Sapienza University of Rome, Rome, Italy

Abstract. Bot detection is a term that refers to the ability of behavioral biometrics to differentiate between humans and bots. Human interactive proofs (HIPs), such as CAPTCHA, are the current approaches for distinguishing between humans and bots. Because most CAPTCHA systems can be solved using state-of-the-art AI approaches, CAPTCHAs are not perfect for bot detection. Bots are getting increasingly intelligent, with the ability to imitate human behavior. In this paper, the proposed method to distinguish between human and bot is based on endpoint prediction of mouse movement utilizing behavioral biometrics and mouse dynamics. First collected human and bot mouse movement data, after data collection, split this data into training and testing parts and build the template libraries, matching these templates libraries with each other and distinguishing between human and bot on the base of endpoint prediction. Different types of experiments were performed to distinguish between human and bot. First, use human data to train prediction model and evaluate prediction performance on both human and bot testing templates and the target hit rate is 10.6% on human testing (Human-Human) templates and 3.5% on bot testing (Human-Bot) templates when 90% of movement is completed. After that use bot data to train prediction model and evaluate prediction performance on both bot and human testing templates and the target hit rate is 11.2% on bot testing (Bot-Bot) templates and 5.2% on human testing (Bot-Human) templates when 90% of movement is completed. Overall, the target hit rate can easily discriminate between human and bot.

Keywords: Bot detection · Mouse Endpoint prediction · Behavior · Biometrics · Template matching

1 Introduction

The research described in this paper addresses the issue of differentiation between bots and humans under realistic conditions. It covers the study of Template Matching (TM) which is a flexible and relatively straightforward technique to use, which makes them one of the most popular methods of prediction and object recognition. We are using TM for endpoint prediction and to distinguish between humans and bots. TM transforms a mouse pointing movement's velocity profile into a 2-D stroke gesture that can be recognized using template matching. A template library is built from prior mouse movements (training and testing), then templates are arranged for comparison, and finally, a best-matched template selected, and the endpoint is predicted using the total distance travelled by the matching template.

1.1 Context

A computer is a basic tool for work in an office and home. At the start, the computer was not very simple and easy. Human Computer Interaction (HCI) was not very simple and it's not easy to improve. Personal computer interface has progressed from command-line interface to graphical user interface (GUI), i.e., windows, icons, menus, pointer, and direct manipulation where users can use joystick, mouse, trackball, or finger to point the required target on the screen. If pointing in the GUI is easy, a large number of users will use the computer more efficiently. Especially for people with dyskinesias, but for people with movement problems, if we can predict the endpoint of the mouse movement and allow the endpoint to be reached more quickly, we can save a lot of time. According to the survey, almost 65% of people use a mouse while working on a computer [1] which is 3–5 times of our keyboard usage [2].

With the introduction of Internet Relay Chat in 1988, people began utilizing bots on computers. Another early bot spotted on the internet was WebCrawler for the first search engines. WebCrawler, launched in 1994, was the first bot to index web sites [3]. Web bots have been responsible for some of the world's most serious and expensive internet security breaches. The term "bot" comes from a robot which is also sometimes called Zombie [4]. A bot is also called a Web bot, spider, or crawler. Typically, online bots are pre-programmed software that, like a robot, executes certain commands when given the appropriate input. These computer program are used to perform simple and repetitive online tasks that would be too difficult or boring for a human to perform on a regular basis [5].

Bots are used for a variety of purposes, normally web bots are used as chat rooms like AirAsia Virtual Allstar (AVA) on Air Asia airline website or for an advertiser on websites. They (called crawlers) can perform web searches to retrieve information, data, or documents from the website and save this information obtained on web pages. Search bots can then create electronic catalogs of "spider" sites, which organize site indexes and display them as search engine results. Many servers allow chatbots to conduct a variety of administrative functions or give users with assistance and information [3].

A web-bot is not only being used for gaining information in the context of science but also for malicious reasons for example, steeling copyrighted substance / licensed property or the execution of a DDoS attack. Malicious bots cause massive losses through site scraping, account takeover, account creation, credit card fraud, denial of service attacks, denial of inventory, and other methods. Bots are also used to influence and divide society (e.g., bots were employed to disrupt the Brexit vote [6] day). Mostly web bots are used for criminal activities because they are easy to scale and adopt human behavior which makes them difficult to detect.

Malicious bots are used for sending spam email, crawl content, or manipulate user comments on websites [7]. The bot can also record keyboard keystrokes and mouse movements or collect passwords and financial information. Zombie bugs have the advantages of worms, but their infection functions are more extensive, and they are generally modified a few hours after the exploitation of the new vulnerability. Malicious bots are a hybrid threat to computers, consisting of both malware and bots. Once malicious software has infected a host computer, it links to one or more central servers that can monitor and control hundreds or thousands of other infected computers. When a group of computers that have been infected with malicious software and cooperating as one entity, this is known as a botnet. This is accomplished through the use of broad-based remote attacks on targets [5].

So, it is very important to stop the malicious and detect these bots so that they cannot steal any information and secure the system. Our goal is to distinguish between human and bot so that we can protect the website, data, and user personal information etc.

1.2 Motivation and Proposed Approach

The objective of this research is to look at a Template Matching (TM) solution for the bot and human session classification problem, using a specific application in a real-world situation. The key research question is, if utilizing computational intelligence approaches, it is possible to get good differentiation outcomes in the task of discriminating between sessions of legitimate, human users and Web bots.

The lack of labelled data, or its limited availability, is a prevalent problem in real-world applications. Labeling is nearly always a costly operation. Furthermore, there is no strong criterion for labeling all possible bots in the specific scenario of interest, so even among accessible labels, a fraction may include inaccurate information.

This work investigates the possibility of structural and behavioral characterization of bots in order to obtain insight into the problem and suggest a feasible solution. If this idea is confirmed, Template Matching might be able to classify the difference between humans and bots.

The proposed approach is particularly well suited to real-time applications. It can make a decision as soon as enough data from the users' mouse movements is gathered; experiments demonstrate that this usually happens within the first few movements.

The fundamental reason for my research was the necessity for accurate computer user identification on any website, and the goal of this work is to identify between human and bot users. For achieving my goal, we have divided the problems into small sub problems by using the divide and conquer rule and try to distinguish between human and bot.

First, we tried to figure out what the basic characteristics of the movement are so that we could understand the pointer movement, pattern of movement, and user behavior of mouse movement. After that, we tried to figure out how the bot works and accomplishes its goals, and finally, we tried to figure out how constraints affect pointing motion. Is there any technique to predict the endpoint of mouse movement or to detect the bot? Is it possible to design a technique for detecting online bots? Make a distinction between a human and a bot and propose a bot detection system to protect websites and reduce server burden.

In experimental work, tried to look at cursor trajectories and other characteristics that measure speed and accuracy during pointing tasks to try to address these issues.

1.3 Contribution

We made the following contributions to detecting web bot and the target direction on the computer interface so that we can predict the endpoint, distinguish between human and bot, and propose web bot detection mechanism.

Use Kinematics to Predict Endpoint Distance. Previously many researchers used kinematics techniques to predict the endpoint of the pointer such as Kinematic endpoint perdition and Kinematic template matching. We are also using Kinematic template matching for the whole screen to predict the endpoint distance for human as well as bot. We characterize the impact of movement distance on the accuracy of the kinematic template matching predictor for both Human and Bot.

Pointing Facilitation and Endpoint Prediction. We are defining the design space for endpoint predictors concerning the proposed pointing facilitation techniques. We are using kinematic template matching which can be used in modern graphical interfaces to facilitate pointing and for the prediction of mouse movement endpoint.

Use Kinematics to Distinguish Human and Bot. We define the design space for human and bot. We are using Kinematics template matching techniques to distinguish between human and bot and from the results analysis propose a bot detection mechanism.

1.4 Paper Organization

The rest of the paper is arranged as follows. Section 2 provides the background information on type of web bots and discusses related studies on approaches for detecting them based on behavioral and different implementation levels. Section 3 introduces the concept of web CAPTCHAs and defines the problem. Section 4 discusses the proposed study approach; Sect. 5 covers the experimental setup with an analysis of the experimental results, and Sect. 6 conclude the paper.

2 Background and Related Work

2.1 Types of Web Bots

Web crawling, which indexes Web information on behalf of search engines, was the earliest and most common bot application. Bots can be good or bad, and there are many kinds of bots on the Internet. Different types of web bots can be distinguished based on their data extraction strategy, which refers to the method of extracting data from a website. A few examples include link checkers that discover broken links, feed fetchers that send Web content to mobile apps, and shopping bots that work for product search engines or price comparison sites with whom a particular online store works. These bots often notify a Web server of their identity by including the bot's name in the user agent field, allowing them to be quickly identified and processed in a special way if necessary. The biggest threat posed by their presence is an increase in network and server traffic, which is generally kept under check by the bots themselves by limiting their own activity pace.

The operation of agents that collect sensitive data and reuse it, such as e-mail harvesters or resource archivers, raises certain concerns regarding privacy and ethics on the Internet. Advanced application-level agents such as social bots [8], blog bots [9] or spambots [10] are even more annoying.

Autonomous agents have also been employed to disturb business activity on the Internet. For example, click bots are a type of network program that simulates clicks on sensitive links such as advertising banners.[11]. They're usually hired to commit "click frauds" in internet advertising, where metrics like impressions (the number of times an ad is seen) and conversions are used to determine how effective an ad is (the number of times a visualized ad is clicked). A click fraud is when the quantity of real impressions and conversions is inflated by intentionally generated impressions and conversions. The advertiser may be targeted by depleting their visualization budget early in the day, causing their advertising to disappear once the daily display limit is met. Sites that host the ads, on the other hand, can boost their own earnings by mimicking more traffic.

Bots that are malicious can harm e-commerce competitiveness and profitability in a variety of ways. Because duplicate information exists on the Internet, scraping and duplicating web content might affect a website's SEO (Search Engine Optimization) rating. Price harvesting enables you to destabilize competitors' prices. Customer accounts may be created or taken over to spam the site's comment sections, take advantage of account promotion credits (discounts, loyalty points, etc.), or purchasing items keep in shopping carts without purchasing them, lowering inventory availability for legitimate consumers. Bots are also used to perform gift card and credit card frauds, as well as mass ticket purchases for unauthorized resale on e-commerce sites.

To crack the CAPTCHA protection, some bots are armed with CAPTCHA cracking capabilities. They do not produce any mouse or keystroke events. This form of bot is currently the most extensively used blog bot on the internet.

2.2 Approaches to Web Bot Detection

Regarding this examination, Bot detection shows the identification of robotized programming, the stimulus behind the removal of information from the website page. The administrator of the site is shielding themselves from web bots by utilizing the web-bot discovery system by watching the guest, searching for indications of the conduct of a web bot. Bots are getting progressively smart, with the ability to imitate human behavior. Sophisticated bots are typically detected using Active Detection and Passive Detection approaches [12].

Active detection methods such as CAPTCHA, determine if a user is human or not by completing a basic online test that is simple for actual humans to complete but complex for software bots to solve. Normally, CAPTCHA systems are based on image completion (puzzle based), character recognition from distorted images (text-based), and object recognition in a set of images (image based).

Passive detection such as detectors are undetectable and analyzes the user's activity as they operate on the device. The Google reCAPTCHA v3 algorithm replaces old-style logical tasks with a transparent algorithm that can distinguish between bots and humans based on their web usage patterns. Other studies describe online users' browsing habits in order to detect DDoS attacks (Distributed Denial of Service).

Despite the fact that these algorithms are frequently used, still they do have significant limitations. Even for humans, bot detection activities are challenging to complete. Second, contemporary techniques can readily solve the majority of CAPTCHA systems. For example, [13] shown that a state-of-the-art voice recognizer's accuracy on the eBay audio captcha is less than 1%, whereas a customized classifier's performance can reach 75%. The CAPTCHA is first pre-processed by the solver to make it easier to analyze, for as by removing colors or applying noise reduction techniques. By using a clustering method on the image, the solver tries to partition the CAPTCHA into fragments containing exactly one character. Finally, a classifier is employed to determine which character is present in each chunk, such as a support vector machine (SVM) or a neural network. Using a machine learning-based approach to segment and detect the text, text-based CAPTCHA was solved with 98 percent accuracy[14].

User Behaviours Based Detection Techniques. The relevance of recognizing human activity throughout the form filling process has been recognized by modern detection systems. If a server detects mouse or keyboard events, it recognizes the user as human. As a result, bot creators are compelled to develop a more complex bot, the Human Mimic Bot. These bots access a blog page in the browser and create keystroke and mouse events using OS API calls. It imitates human browsing behavior in this way, tricking previous detection systems. The bot, for example, repeatedly sends "Press down-key" command to scroll down the page to the bottom. The mouse pointer is then moved into each field of the comment form, and a sequence of keystrokes is used to enter in prepared text content. Finally, the bot makes a mouse click on the submit button to submit the comment. The server is unable to detect whether the UI events are generated by hardware (such as the mouse device and keyboard) or software by simply evaluating the incoming user input data (such as human mimic bot) [15]. If the server depends solely on the existence of UI events to detect bots, it will be fooled by Human Mimic Bot.

According to certain behavioral biometrics study human behavior is more complex than bot behavior. Bots have consistent patterns of little variability, compared to the intrinsic irregularity and burstiness of human activity [15]. Many bots, for example, move the mouse cursor in straight lines at a constant speed or press keys at regular intervals. Humans are incapable of performing such perfect, regular motions. As a result, the server could detect human mimic bot by considering behavioral complexity.

Some academics distinguish between human and bot behavior in online services, based on behavioral complexity. They provide a technique that is both effective and simple to use for differentiating bots from humans. Their suggested detection method has two major components: 1) a client-side logger and 2) a server-side classifier [16]. They collect user behavior events on the client side, such as mouse movement and keyboard data, and send this data back to a server-side classifier, which determines if a user is human or bot.

Similarly, other researchers studied page access behavior and presented two powerful algorithms [17] dependent method, one of which focuses on the page perusing request and the other on the relationship between perusing time and page data. The authors executed their identification system on a test-bed to assess its identification rate. The following are the weakness of these two algorithms. For algorithm 1, even though it can smother the pace of bogus identification of ordinary customers. The algorithm 2 on the other hand, has a high level of assault recognition precision, but it may dismiss some typical users.

Some other researchers proposed counter systems dependent on utilizing approaches Hidden Semi-Markov Models (HSMM) [18] to simulate HTTP requests from ordinary web users to describe the browsing behavior of users to identify HTTP GET flooding assaults against web servers. The utilization of the HSMM algorithm in abnormality discovery is advantageous because it results in highly effective and precise outcomes. But the disadvantage of using the HSMM algorithm in abnormality discovery is its high computational complexity, particularly when the algorithm is executed in online mode.

Bot Detection on Different Implementation Levels. Mostly, a Web server is gotten to by both genuine and ill-conceived users; in this manner, analysts can utilize perusing conduct information assembled on the server-side to detect variant patterns in traffic. Strategies dependent on client perusing conduct comprise one of the best location procedures in the endeavor to recognize one-of-a-kind examples or practices in Web server traffic. Numerous specialists have endeavored to show perusing conduct for the location of HTTP GET flooding assaults in recent years.

The IP or TCP layer, rather than the application layer, is the focus of most current DDoS research. The author created D-WARD, a security mechanism that is deployed in edge routers to detect attacks by monitoring the asymmetry of two-way packet speeds [19]. TTL values [20] and IP addresses [21] (assuming that attack traffic utilizes randomly faked addresses) were also used to detect the DDoS attacks. A DDoS attack is launched by a botnet, A botnet is a collection of network-connected computers that are infected with malware and hand over control of the infected system to a central bot controller. Botnets can be set up in a client-server or peer-to-peer architecture. They can employ a variety of network protocols, but HTTP-based bots are the most common [22] because to the widespread use of web-based services. HTTP-based application layer attacks are exceedingly difficult to deal with [10, 23] in comparison to classic network layer DDoS attacks, which are reasonably straightforward to detect.

On the other hand, HTTP-level traffic features seen on Web servers have shown to be effective bot and actual user distinguishers without interfering with the website or server software [24]. Differences in traffic patterns of humans and bots have been extensively studied, most commonly using data from web server access logs. Bot requests have been found for a variety of websites [25, 26], with the following characteristics: a tendency to overlook picture files, lesser amounts of HTTP response data, greater rates of unassigned referrers, HEAD requests, and erroneous requests.

Bot detection methods based on HTTP features use machine learning techniques or traffic pattern analysis. They are mostly aimed at offline bot detection, which entails categorizing past HTTP data from whole server sessions.

To build probabilistic session models, statistical components of HTTP request data, such as the categories of downloaded resources, are used in traffic pattern-based approaches [27, 28] or inter-arrival periods [29].

On different layers of the OSI-model, which standardizes layered processing of communication between computers, a web-bot can be discovered. For example, if excessive network activity has been tracked from recurring similar IP addresses, a web-bot can be detected on the network layer (or pool of IP addresses) [23].

In the Transport Layer web bots can also be detected based upon TCP traffic on the network. For instance, traffic generation based on click rates (For instance, sending x requests per second). The web-bot stands out above all other network interactions by exceeding incoming TCP packages [30]. Behavioral patterns in traffic, such as a page visit every Monday at 4 p.m., can make a visitor suspicious.

The HTTP protocol in the application layer, which is used to communicate between a web client (browser) and a web server at the application layer, may carry information that reveals the presence of a web bot. To detect DDoS attack at application layer CUSUM algorithm [31] was used.

The literature's high efficacy of bot detection methodologies verified the intrinsic differences between bot and human traffic, as well as human behavior. However, a review of related research revealed that just a few studies addressed the issue of bot identification on the user's side or offline bot detection. These two studies, [32] and [33], looked at the performance of decision tree-based classification algorithms for different quantities of requests seen in a session. They did, however, consider page requests that corresponded to user clicks. On the other hand, in this paper deal with the challenge of detecting Web bots as quickly as possible on the user's side, without requiring any session or server assistance. In addition, we try to predict the end point of mouse moment for both human and bot.

3 Problem Formulation

Bots are getting increasingly smart, with the ability to imitate human behavior online. Algorithms for distinguishing between humans and bots, on the other hand, are becoming increasingly complex. In response to these advanced bots, researchers try to differentiate between two types of bot detection technologies [12]:

- Active Detection. Traditionally known as CAPTCHA, these methods identify whether a user is human or a bot by undertaking online activities that are tough for software bots to solve but simple for actual human users to complete. However, now people create algorithms that overcome web CAPTCHAs. Usually, people solved the web CAPTCHA by using the mouse, thus if we can identify the user of mouse movement, we can simply determine whether the user doing the web captcha is a human or a machine.
- Passive Detection. These detectors are undetectable and assess the user's actions as they interact with the device. Traditional cognitive challenges are replaced with a transparent algorithm capable of distinguishing bots and humans based on their web behavior in the most recent version of Google reCAPTCHA v3. Other researchers [34], documented online users' surfing behavior in order to detect DDoS attacks (Distributed Denial of Service).

CAPTCHA is a user verification mechanism that is commonly used on websites. When a user opens a website, he faced a web captcha, which might take the form of a question, an object orientation, or a puzzle with slider. To begin the project, a slider online captcha was picked and moved using a web bot. To accomplish this, first choose a web site (https://www.geetest.com/en/demo) that offered a slider web captcha, and then attempt to automate that captcha.

The selenium web driver was used to access the website and maximize the website page with selenium to access the web captcha more properly. The selenium web driver has a function to get the location of the web captcha on the screen, and then found element by xpath. Slider web captcha is a captcha that comprises of a picture that is divided into two pieces, one of which is called a puzzle image and the other is called slice. First, grabbed the actual image, and then used HTML site elements to get the puzzle and slider parts. Figure 1 depicts the puzzle and slider portion of the image.

Fig. 1. Puzzle and slider images of the CAPTCHA.

After acquiring the puzzle and slider images, converted them into grayscale and then grayscale images to binary images as shown in Fig. 2.

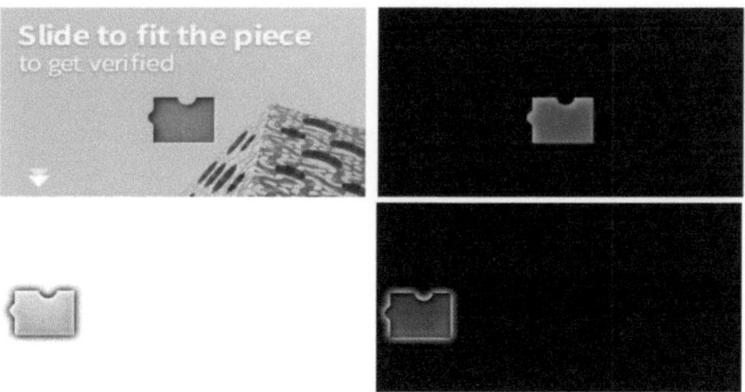

Fig. 2. Convert grayscale images into binary images.

Find the inner boundary of the missing patch of the puzzle and the outer border of the puzzle in the binary image then estimated the distance between the image's outer border and inner border. The pyautogui module was used to easily solve the web captcha by automating mouse movement.

4   Research Methodology

4.1   Methodological Framework

A 2-D stroke gesture was created using the velocity profile of a pointing action, and Kinematic Template Matching (KTM) was used to estimate the endpoint based on previously collected mouse movements.[35]. KTM converts a pointing movement's velocity profile into a 2-D stroke gesture that can be detected through template matching.

On the basis of mouse movement endpoint prediction, the KTM method is used to distinguish between human and bots, however this methodological approach was a little different. For deployment in collaborative contexts, the capacity to predict was critical. Because TM searches the entire library to find the best-matched template, prediction accuracy will increase as the number of templates in the training library grows. However, it was surprising to learn that after reaching a certain number of templates, accuracies did not increase any further. Figure 3 is a methodological framework diagram.

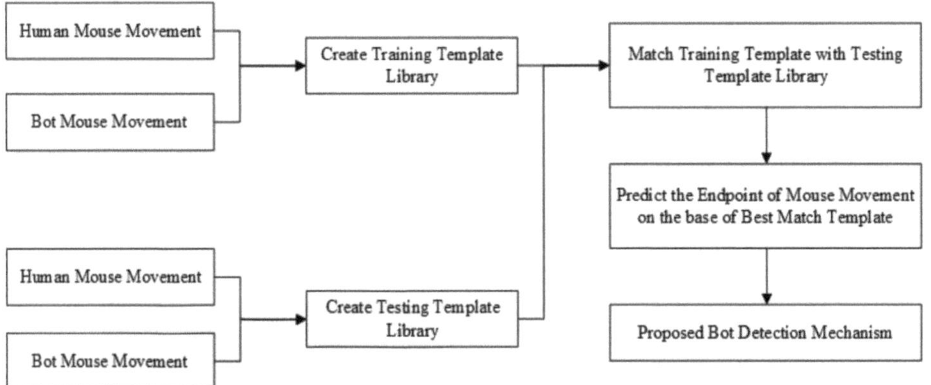

Fig. 3. Methodological framework diagram.

4.2   Building Template Library

Building a Template Library from previously acquired mouse movement data for both humans and bots and separating the data into two portions for human and bot training and testing. After creating both a human and a bot template library, match the templates and predict the endpoint of each movement while distinguishing between the two. Each template was created using a discrete sequence of position-time (x, y, t) points that defined a mouse movement, and these points were then utilized to create a template velocity profile. We need to know the rate at which the position changes in order to calculate the velocity, so finding the change of position is crucial (distance).

$$D = \sqrt{(x_2 - x_1)^2 + (y_2 - y_1)^2} \tag{1}$$

As we know position changing in a specific time interval.

$$\Delta t = t_2 - t_1 \tag{2}$$

Velocity is rate of change of distance with respect to time. So, the velocity of mouse movement calculated by using Eq. 1 and 2.

$$V = \frac{D}{\Delta t} \tag{3}$$

To reduce computational complexity and match other templates, the movement locations, velocity profile, duration, and total distance traveled were all saved as part of the template. All the templates are building on this mechanism. In Fig. 4 (a) showed the mouse movement and (b) velocity-time template.

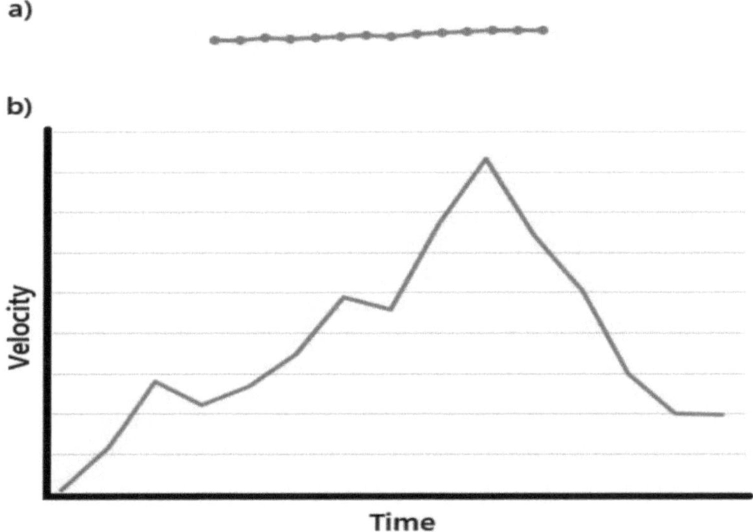

Fig. 4. The raw movement points are (b) the velocity-time profile.

4.3 Template Matching

The velocity profile of each template was designed to represent a complete pointing movement when the library was built. While matching the testing template with training template, to enable for equitable training-testing template comparisons, each training template was changed to reflect its motion at a similar moment in time as the testing template. The goal of matching the velocity-time template is to predict the endpoint of the mouse movement. It is important to note that hitting the endpoint directly isn't possible because the endpoint was so small, and mostly items, icons, buttons, and images on a computer screen are larger than 50 pixels. So, considering our target is at least 50 pixel and as a result, at the end of the mouse movement, create a circle with a radius of 50 pixels. To consider, the predicted point lies in this circle, it means it is hitting the target and if the predicted point is fall out of the circle, it means it is missing the target. As shown in Fig. 5.

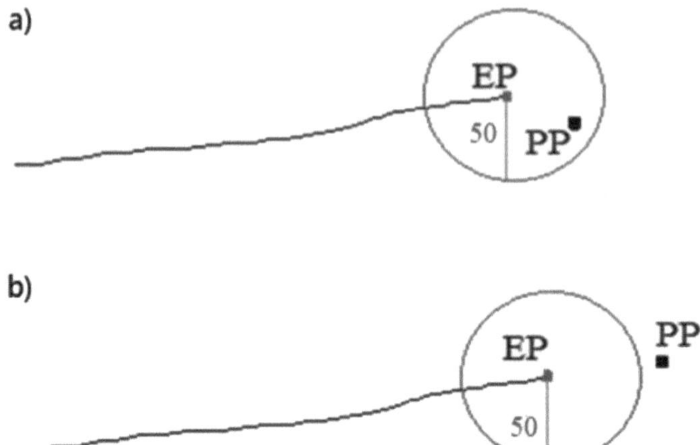

Fig. 5. Endpoint prediction, (a) shows predicted point lies indie the circle and (b) shows us predicted point is outside the circle.

Each testing template TE is compared to each training template TR_i in the library using the following cumulative scoring function S(TR):

$$S(TR_i) = S\left(TR_i^*\right) + \begin{cases} \dfrac{\sum_{k=0}^{n_{te}} \sum_{j=0}^{n_{te}} |TE_j - TR_{ij}|}{n_{te}} & n_{te} \leq n_{tr} \\ \dfrac{\sum_{k=0}^{n_{te}} \left(\sum_{j=0}^{n_{tr}} |TE_{kj} - TR_{ij}| + \sum_{j=n_{tr}+1}^{n_{te}} TE_{kj} \right)}{n_{te}} & n_{te} \geq n_{tr} \end{cases} \quad (4)$$

where TR_i is the library of training templates; $S(TR_i^*)$ is the TRi cumulative score for from all training movement points evaluated thus far; TE_j is the jth velocity value from the testing templates and n_{te} is the number of points in the testing velocity profile. TR_{ij} are the jth velocity values from the training template's velocity profiles and n_{tr} is the number of points in the training template's velocity profile. Once $S(TRi)$ is calculate, it became the next $S\left(TR_i^*\right)$ upon the arrival of the next movement point.

In case 1: $n_{te} \leq n_{tr}$, the score is simply the total difference in velocity values at each timestamp adjusted as illustrated in Fig. 5.

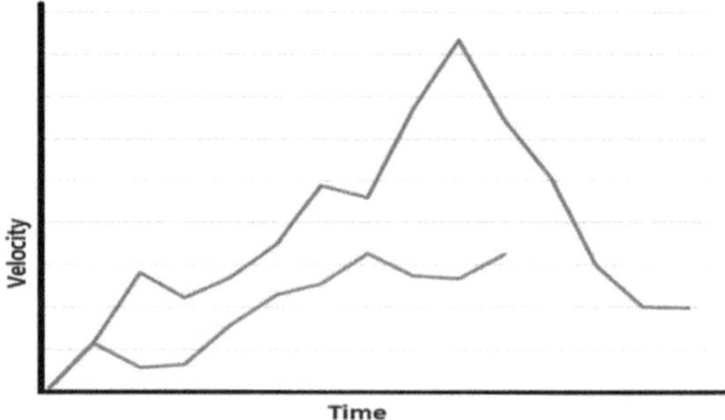

Fig. 6. Comparison of two velocity profile when $n_{te} \leq n_{tr}$.

In case 2: $n_{te} > n_{tr}$ Selecting as the best-matched template produce less likely to yield a favorable predication. To raise the score, the remaining velocity values of the testing templates are added to negatively weight these shorter templates (Figs. 6 and 7).

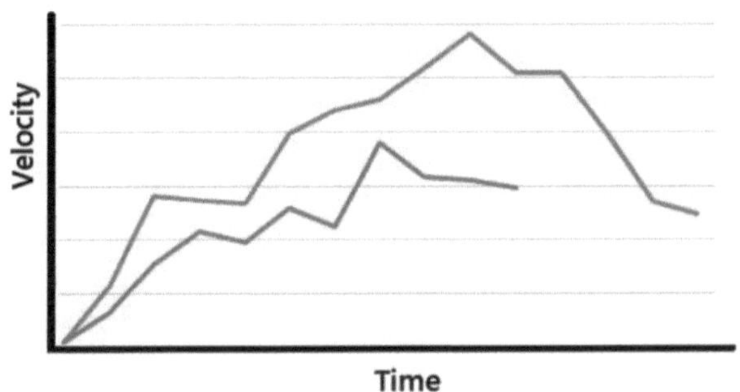

Fig. 7. Comparison of two velocity profile when $n_{te} > n_{tr}$.

4.4 Endpoint Prediction

A cumulative scoring function is essential in the success of TM. Once $S(TR_i)$ is computed in equation number 4, it become the next $S(TR_i^*)$ on the arrival of the next mouse movement. When the testing template has been compared to the whole training template library then a template whose cumulative score is lowest was chosen as the best-matched template. Selected that template as a best match template as shown in Fig. 8 light blue was the testing template and gray was the best match template.

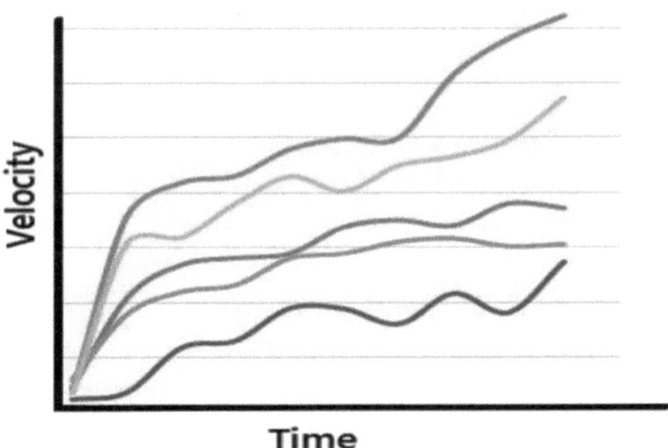

Fig. 8. Gray (best-matched template).

Finally, the entire length of the best-matched template is determined, and the testing template endpoint in the current direction of motion is predicted to be Dt pixels distant from its original start point.

5 Implementation and Results Analysis

5.1 Experimental Setting

In two-dimensional pointing tasks, a study was performed to evaluate the prediction accuracy of KTM. The following steps were taken to differentiate between human and bot, as illustrated in Fig. 9, On the basis of the mouse movement endpoint prediction.

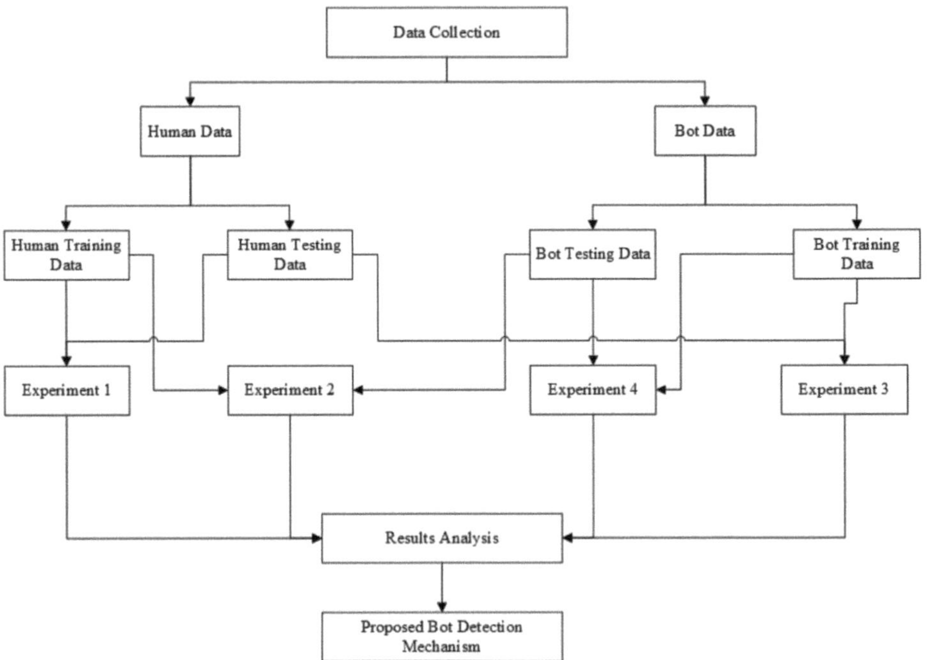

Fig. 9. Experimental workflow diagram.

5.2 Method

Mouse Tracking Environment. A mouse-tracking environment was created in PyCharm by using python language. PyCharm is an integrated development environment (IDE) for computer programming, with a focus on the Python programming language. PyCharm is a free and open-source IDE. To simplify the creation of mouse-tracking experiments inside PyCharm, a simple program was developed in python language and used some libraries. Mouse-tracking experiments were run in full-screen mode.

Participants. Twenty capable volunteers (15 males, 5 females) with an average age of 23 years took part in data gathering. All of the participants were right-handed, and they were all computer science students with extensive computer knowledge and skill.

Human Data Collection. Participants were given 100 trials to complete, with each trial consisting of one click on a single target. In blocks of 11 trials, targets were displayed randomly on the screen. To capture 2-D pointing movements, the target is 50 pixels in diameter. The top-most circle in the ring was chosen as the first target of each block. Each trial consisted of a single click that started the next trial and presented only one target on the screen. Subjects were instructed to click the targets "as rapidly and accurately as possible," with a sound being made if the target was missed, and only that trial being repeated. The distances between each target were chosen at random. It took about 3 to 4 min to finish each batch of 100 trials. To avoid weariness, subjects were allowed to take a break between blocks. The data of user clicks (left or right click), every mouse movement, and the time duration (x, y, t) from one click to the next click was gathered and saved into the log file during this operation. The microsecond time was recorded for this reason in order to determine the time difference between each click and the durations of pixel-to-pixel movement.

Bot Data Collection. For collecting bot mouse movement data, created different types of bots which shows human like behavior in mouse movement e.g., a bot with constant speed and linear motion, a bot with constant speed and curve motion, a bot whose velocity is variable and linear motion, a bot with variable velocity and curve motion, a bot completing its task in fixed time and a bot completing its task in variable time, and a bot which mimic human behavior like as much as possible, so that our comparison was more perfect. Same environment and same application were used to collect the bot mouse movement data.

5.3 Results and Discussion

After collecting Human and Bot mouse movement data. This data was used to create four separate template libraries (training and testing) both for human and bot such like that, Human Training Template Library, Bot Training Template Library, Human Testing Template Library and Bot Testing Template Library. After building the template libraries, matched these template libraries with each other. Four different experiments were performed to predict the endpoint of each template and based on target hit rate distinguish between human and bot. The percentage of directly hit the target maybe very low because the size of the endpoint was very small. So that's why drawing a circle at the end of movement and set the radius of the circle was 50 pixels. If predicted endpoint lies inside the circle, then it is hitting the target and if the predicted endpoint is outside the circle, it means it missed the target.

Human Data for Prediction. In the first two experiments, human training template library was used for prediction model and evaluated prediction performance on both human (human-human) and bot (human-bot) testing templates. The following is how KTM was evaluated, one by one templates were selected from the template library. To simulate a testing movement, the points from the chosen template were employed. The final distance of the simulated testing template was predicted using the KTM algorithm. To determine the accuracy of a prediction, each predicted distance was compared to the movement's ground truth distance. A new template was chosen from the library after the final prediction was made.

First experiment was performed by using human training template library and human testing template library and evaluate the perform. The prediction accuracy of template matching was measured at movement-distance-percentage intervals ranging from 10% to 90% in 10% increments. Evaluate TM based on percent distance complete. Figure 10 box-and-whisker plot of human-human TM prediction accuracy at various percentage movements. The upper and lower quartiles of the error values are shown by boxes, and whiskers extend to the most extreme data point. TM seems to overshoot the endpoint more often than fall short of it.

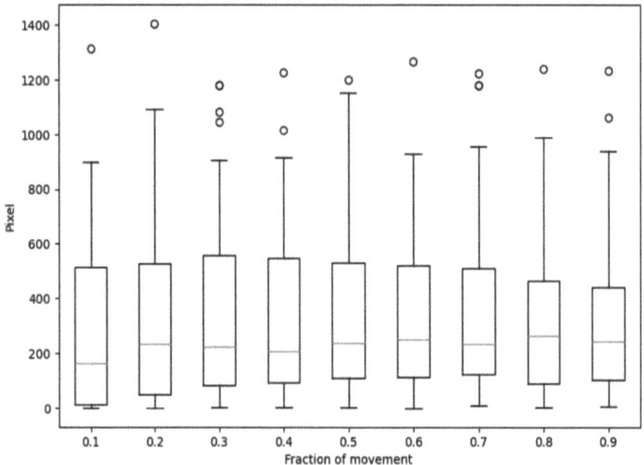

Fig. 10. Distribution of human-human prediction errors in pixels from true endpoint. The percentage of movement completed is based on the distance traveled.

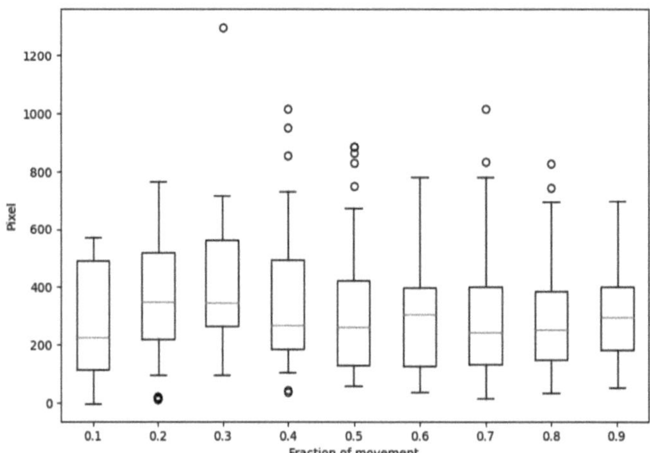

Fig. 11. Distribution of human-bot prediction errors in pixels from true endpoint. The percentage of movement completed is based on the distance traveled.

Second experiment was performed by using human training template library and bot testing template library and evaluate the perform. As shown in Fig. 10, the boxes and whiskers represent a smaller range of values. The prediction accuracy of template matching was evaluated at movement-distance-percentage intervals ranging from 10% to 90% in 10% increments. Figure 11 a box-and-whisker plot of human-human TM prediction accuracy at various percentage movements.

Target hit rate of human and bot testing templates shown in Table 1 while using human data in the training template at different percentage of distance traveled. The predictive accuracy of template matching was evaluated at 10 to 90 percent of movement with a 10% increment each time. It is important to note that experiments were performed by target-agnostic without any knowledge of target locations or dimensions to predict endpoints. This data was collected using 50-pixel-wide targets; the frequency with which the predicted endpoint actually landed within the target is indicated here. The hit-rate for human-human is significantly higher than human-bot. Either these hit rates themselves were not particularly very high but still it was very useful to distinguish between human and bot.

Table 1. Target hit rate on human training template library.

Distance Traveled	Human-Human	Human-Bot
50%	2.5%	1.2%
60%	4.1%	1.8%
70%	6.5%	2.3%
80%	8.2%	2.7%
90%	10.6%	3.5%

Bot Data for Prediction. Here used bot data to train prediction model and evaluate prediction performance on both human (bot-human) and bot (bot-bot) testing templates was same as in first two experiments.

Third experiment was performed by using bot training template library and human testing template library and evaluate the perform. As shown in Fig. 10 the boxes and whiskers represent a same range of values. The predictive accuracy of template matching was evaluated at movement-distance-percentage intervals ranging from 10% to 90% in 10% increments. Figure 12 shows a box-and-whisker plot of the predictive accuracy of bot-human TM at different percentages of movements.

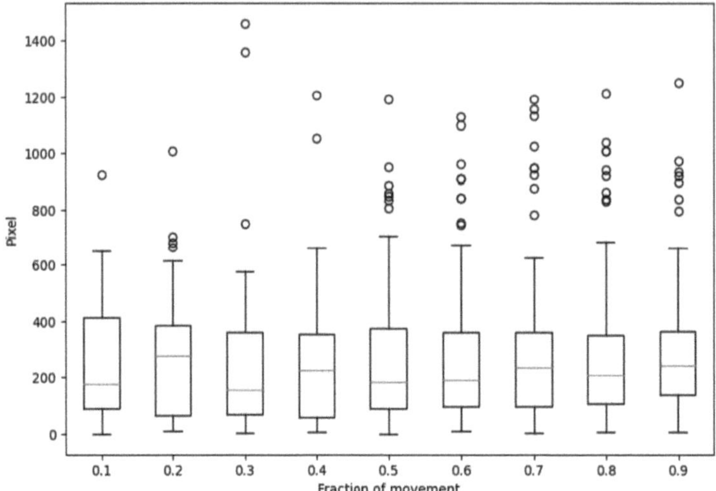

Fig. 12. Distribution of bot-human prediction errors in pixels from true endpoint. The percentage of movement completed is based on the distance traveled.

Fourth experiment was performed by using bot training template library and bot testing template library and evaluate the perform. Same as previously boxes and whiskers shows little less ranges of values as displayed in Fig. 11. The predictive accuracy of template matching was evaluated at movement-distance-percentage intervals ranging from 10% to 90% in 10% increments. Figure 13 shows a box-and-whisker plot of the predictive accuracy of bot-bot TM at different percentages of movements.

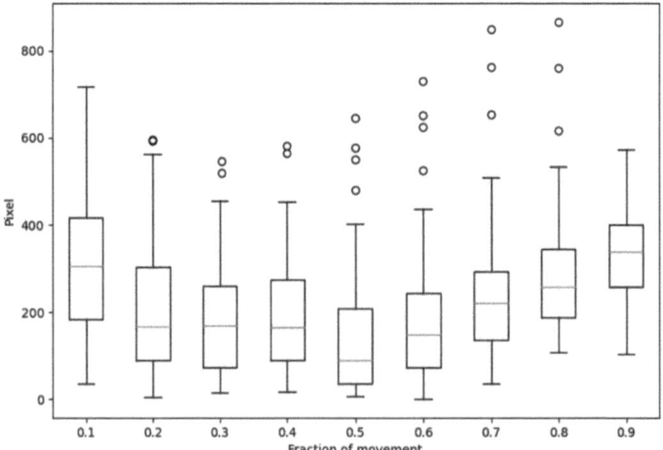

Fig. 13. Distribution of bot-bot prediction errors in pixels from true endpoint. The percentage of movement completed is based on the distance traveled.

Target hit rate of human and bot testing templates shown in Table 2 while using bot data in the training template at different percentage of distance traveled. The predictive accuracy of template matching was evaluated at 10 to 90 percent of movement with a 10% increment each time. It is important to note that experiments were performed by target-agnostic without any knowledge of target locations or dimensions to predict endpoints. This data was collected using 50-pixel-wide targets; the frequency with which the predicted endpoint actually landed within the target is indicated here. The hit-rate for bot-bot is significantly higher than bot-human. Either these hit rates themselves were not particularly very high but still it was very useful to distinguish between human and bot.

Table 2. Target hit rate on Bot training template library.

Distance Traveled	Bot-Human	Bot-Bot
50%	2.8%	3.1%
60%	3.1%	4.4%
70%	4.0%	6.2%
80%	4.5%	8.6%
90%	5.2%	11.2%

Different tests were performed to differentiate between human and bot and the result of our experiments confirming that the assumptions were valid, and the template matching were suitable for distinguishing between human and bot system. KTM is an effective technique for predicting the endpoints of human and bot and effective to distinguish between human and bot. KTM performs with higher accuracy for identical user compared to non-identical user. Although the target accuracies reported are not as impressive, but we think this is mainly due to evaluating KTM on raw data and using target size of 50 pixels, if use larger target size the accuracies and target hit rate will be better.

This approach has distinct advantages over earlier work conducted in this area. Earlier work has been much focused on the server-side verification and many of the features have been developed around that and furthermore in this work the numbers of features captured are far less in earlier implementations. In this implementation, mouse movements and click events are captured using logger system and converted into templates and on templating matching distinguish between human and bot.

The collection of previous movements that we use as templates is the backbone of our work. While endpoint prediction techniques could be developed that are accurate but computationally expensive, the capacity to make predictions in real-time is critical for deployment in interactive situations, just as distinguishing between human and bot at run time is computationally expensive. Because KTM searches the library exhaustively for the best-matching template, the number of templates in the library has a negative impact on the execution time. When KTM algorithm was developing, they find out size of 1000 templates worked well for the given target amplitude range of 100–800 pixels, so if the target amplitude range vary, we need to change the size of library. Here in this case target range varies from 100 to more than 1400 pixel so that's why library size is almost 1200.

Information from the browser, such as mouse and keyboard activities, is used to create behavioral features. Mouse movements, mouse clicks, scrolling, and the time between two consecutive mouse button clicks are just a few examples of events that can be collected using JavaScript. One of behavioral techniques' limitations is the amount of data required to accurately categorize a user as a human or a bot. Differentiating between human and bot on the base of endpoint is possible but in real-time it may require more time because of data collection and endpoint prediction results. Mouse features such as Mouse trajectories, Mouse clicks, Mouse wheel spin/scroll and mouse activity time can also be used to user authentication and moreover, to keep track of a user's behavior during a session, template matching technique is very useful. Despite the fact that experiments confirmed that template matching is a valid technique, but for faster and more efficient bot detection in the future try to use more variable of mouse movements with template matching.

6 Conclusions

The velocity profiles of pointing movements are treated as 2-D stroke gestures in kinematic template matching, which uses template matching to predict movement endpoints. This method is more user-specific, target-independent, and easier to implement. Various types of experiments were carried out during the research to distinguish between humans and bots. Fortunately, after analyzing the results of human and bot, the target rate between identical users and non-identical users was quite astonishing. Identical users had shown a high target rate such as in human-human data, endpoint prediction on 90% movement was 10.6% while, bot-bot data gave endpoint prediction on 90% movement was 11.2%. However, with the non-identical users the target hit rate was quite low such as in human-bot data, endpoint prediction on 90% movement was 3.5% while, bot-human data had shown endpoint prediction on 90% movement was 5.2%. So, the target hit rate easily distinguished between human and bot. The major purpose of choosing this method was simple, and easy to handle.

References

1. Johnson, P.E.: Office ergonomics: motion analysis of computer mouse usage. In: Proceeding of the American Industrial Hygiene Conference and Exposition, pp. 12–13 (1993)
2. Mikkelsen, S., Vilstrup, I., Lassen, C.F., Kryger, A.I., Thomsen, J.F., Andersen, J.H.: Validity of questionnaire self-reports on computer, mouse and keyboard usage during a four-week period. Occup. Environ. Med. **64**(8), 541–547 (2007). https://doi.org/10.1136/oem.2005.026351
3. Knecht, T.: A Brief History Of Bots And How They've Shaped The Internet Today – Abusix. 04 MAY 2021. https://abusix.com/resources/botnets/a-brief-history-of-bots-and-how-theyve-shaped-the-internet-today/. Accessed 18 Nov 2021
4. Pierre-Marc Bureau. Botnet malware: What it is and how to fight it | WeLiveSecurity. 22 Oct 2014. https://www.welivesecurity.com/2014/10/22/botnet-malware-fight/. Accessed 18 Nov 2021

5. E. J. H. Tom's Guide Staff. What Is A Web Bot? – Tom's Guide | Tom's Guide. 28 Nov 2013. https://www.tomsguide.com/us/web-bot-definition,review-1961.html. Accessed 18 Nov 2021

6. Gorodnichenko, Y., Pham, T., Talavera, O.: Social Media, Sentiment and Public Opinions: Evidence From #Brexit And #Uselection," *Nhk技研*, **151**(2), pp. 10–17 (2018). http://www.nber.org/papers/w24631

7. Mishra, S., Jeanneau, E., Berger, M.H., Hochepied, J.F., Daniele, S.: Novel Heteroleptic Heterobimetallic Alkoxide Complexes as Facile Single-Source Precursors for Ta5+ Doped TiO2-SnO2 Nanoparticles **49**(23) (2010)

8. Clark, E.M., Williams, J.R., Jones, C.A., Galbraith, R.A., Danforth, C.M., Dodds, P.S.: Sifting robotic from organic text: a natural language approach for detecting automation on Twitter. J. Comput. Sci. **16**, 1–7 (2016). https://doi.org/10.1016/j.jocs.2015.11.002

9. Chu, Z., Gianvecchio, S., Koehl, A., Wang, H., Jajodia, S.: Blog or block: detecting blog bots through behavioral biometrics. Comput. Networks **57**(3), 634–646 (2013). https://doi.org/10.1016/j.comnet.2012.10.005

10. Kaur, R., Singh, S., Kumar, H.: Rise of spam and compromised accounts in online social networks: a state-of-the-art review of different combating approaches. J. Netw. Comput. Appl. **112**, 53–88 (2018). https://doi.org/10.1016/j.jnca.2018.03.015

11. Haider, C.M.R., Iqbal, A., Rahman, A.H., Rahman, M.S.: An ensemble learning based approach for impression fraud detection in mobile advertising. J. Netw. Comput. Appl. **112**, 126–141 (2018). https://doi.org/10.1016/j.jnca.2018.02.021

12. Acien, A., Morales, A., Fierrez, J., Vera-Rodriguez, R.: BeCAPTCHA-Mouse: Synthetic Mouse Trajectories and Improved Bot Detection (2020). http://arxiv.org/abs/2005.00890

13. Bursztein, E., Bethard, S.: Decaptcha: Breaking 75% of eBay audio CAPTChas. 3rd USENIX Work. Offensive Technol. WOOT 2009, pp. 1–7 (2009)

14. Bursztein, E., Martin, M., Mitchell, J.C.: Text-based CAPTCHA Strengths and Weaknesses. Proc. ACM Conf. Comput. Commun. Secur., pp. 125–137 (2013)

15. Gianvecchio, S., Wu, Z., Xie, M., Wang, H.: Battle of Botcraft. p. 256 (2009). https://doi.org/10.1145/1653662.1653694

16. Chu, Z., Gianvecchio, S., Wang, H.: Bot or human? A behavior-based online bot detection system. vol. 11170 LNCS, no. 2. Springer International Publishing (2018)

17. Yatagai, T., Isohara, T., Sasase, I.: Detection of HTTP-GET flood attack based on analysis of page access behavior. IEEE Pacific RIM Conf. Commun. Comput. Signal Process. - Proc., pp. 232–235 (2007). https://doi.org/10.1109/PACRIM.2007.4313218

18. Ranjan, S., Swaminathan, R., Uysal, M., Knightly, E.: DDoS-resilient scheduling to counter application layer attacks under imperfect detection. Proc. - IEEE INFOCOM (2006). https://doi.org/10.1109/INFOCOM.2006.127

19. . Mirkovic, G.P., Reiher, P.: Attacking DDoS at the source. Proc. - Int. Conf. Netw. Protoc. ICNP, pp. 312–321 (2002). https://doi.org/10.1109/ICNP.2002.1181418

20. Peng, T., Leckie, C., Ramamohanarao, K.: Protection from distributed denial of service attacks using history-based IP filtering. IEEE Int. Conf. Commun. **1**, 482–486 (2003). https://doi.org/10.1109/icc.2003.1204223

21. Jin, C., Wang, H., Shin, K.G.: Hop-Count Filtering: An effective defense against spoofed DDoS traffic. Proc. ACM Conf. Comput. Commun. Secur., pp. 30–41 (2003)

22. Acarali, D., Rajarajan, M., Komninos, N., Herwono, I.: Survey of approaches and features for the identification of HTTP-based botnet traffic. J. Netw. Comput. Appl. **76**, 1–15 (2016). https://doi.org/10.1016/j.jnca.2016.10.007

23. Behal, S., Kumar, K.: Detection of DDoS attacks and flash events using novel information theory metrics. Comput. Networks **116**, 96–110 (2017). https://doi.org/10.1016/j.comnet.2017.02.015

24. Doran, D., Gokhale, S.S.: Web robot detection techniques: overview and limitations. Data Min. Knowl. Discov. **22**(1–2), 183–210 (2011). https://doi.org/10.1007/s10618-010-0180-z
25. Suchacka, G.: Analysis of aggregated bot and human traffic on e-commerce site. 2014 Fed. Conf. Comput. Sci. Inf. Syst. FedCSIS 2014, **2**, pp. 1123–1130 (2014). https://doi.org/10.15439/2014F346
26. Dikaiakos, M.D., Stassopoulou, A., Papageorgiou, L.: An investigation of web crawler behavior: characterization and metrics. Comput. Commun. **28**(8), 880–897 (2005). https://doi.org/10.1016/j.comcom.2005.01.003
27. Doran, D., Gokhale, S.S.: An integrated method for real time and offline web robot detection. Expert. Syst. **33**(6), 592–606 (2016). https://doi.org/10.1111/exsy.12184
28. P. Jędrzejowicz, Akademia Morska w Gdyni. IEEE Poland Section, M. IEEE Systems, and Institute of Electrical and Electronics Engineers. 2015 IEEE 2nd International Conference on Cybernetics (CYBCONF) : proceedings : June 24–26, 2015, Gdynia, Poland (2015)
29. Lu, W.Z., Yu, S.Z.: Web robot detection based on hidden Markov model. 2006 Int. Conf. Commun. Circuits Syst. ICCCAS, Proc., vol. 3, no. 90304011, pp. 1806–1810 (2006). https://doi.org/10.1109/ICCCAS.2006.285024
30. Kakavelakis, G., Beverly, R., Young, J.: Auto-learning of SMTP TCP transport-layer features for spam and abusive message detection. LISA 2011 - 25th Large Install. Syst. Adm. Conf., no. May 2014, pp. 217–226 (2011)
31. Jazi, H.H., Gonzalez, H., Stakhanova, N., Ghorbani, A.A.: Detecting HTTP-based application layer DoS attacks on web servers in the presence of sampling. Comput. Networks **121**, 25–36 (2017). https://doi.org/10.1016/j.comnet.2017.03.018
32. Tan, P.N., Kumar, V.: Discovery of web robot sessions based on their navigational patterns. Data Min. Knowl. Discov. **6**(1), 9–35 (2002). https://doi.org/10.1023/A:1013228602957
33. Balla, A., Stassopoulou, A., Dikaiakos, M.D.: Real-time web crawler detection. 2011 18th Int. Conf. Telecommun. ICT 2011, pp. 428–432 (2011). https://doi.org/10.1109/CTS.2011.5898963
34. Xie, Y., Yu, S.Z.: A large-scale hidden semi-Markov model for anomaly detection on user browsing behaviors. IEEE/ACM Trans. Netw. **17**(1), 54–65 (2009). https://doi.org/10.1109/TNET.2008.923716
35. Pasqual, P.T., Wobbrock, J.O.: Mouse pointing endpoint prediction using kinematic template matching. Conf. Hum. Factors Comput. Syst. - Proc., pp. 743–752 (2014). https://doi.org/10.1145/2556288.2557406

Evaluating the Impact of Insider Threats

Radiah Rivu$^{(\boxtimes)}$ and Joram Bwambale

International University of Applied Sciences, Berlin, Germany
`sheikh-radiah-rahim.rivu@iu.org`

Abstract. Insider threats have become one of the most pressing issues in organizational cybersecurity. They originate from within an organization and are perpetrated by personnel with legal permissions in the system's normal operations. Increasing internal attacks lead to further consequences within the organization. In addition, organizations fail to understand the interplay between psychological, social, and organizational aspects leading to insider threats. In this research proposal, we investigate the various kinds of insider threats organizations face and the effectiveness of the methods adopted to combat threats.

Keywords: cybersecurity · insider threat · data securtiy

1 Introduction

As we adopt new technologies such as virtual reality [1] and artificial intelligence [2] in our workplaces, we are at an increased risk of cybersecurity attacks due to the lack of effective infrastructure protection mechanisms. Although researchers are actively using emerging technologies to investigate other forms of attack, such as shoulder surfing [3], a comprehensive understanding of the causes of insider threats and their effects remains lacking.

Insider threats can result in significant financial losses and reputational damage. There could be various reasons that are interwoven such as job dissatisfaction, workplace stress, and psychological factors. The matter at hand becomes worse due to organizations' failing to understand and tackle such issues. People who are stressed, organisational inequities, or personal conflicts are more likely to rationalise harmful behaviour, including data theft or system sabotage, as acts of revenge or self-defence [7]. Academic research shows that psychological factors play a big role in insider threats, especially with malicious insiders. In addition to psychological factors, an increasing disconnection from ethical standards also leads to such attacks. Ethical disengagement, where employees separate themselves from the ethical implications of their behaviour has relevance to insider wrongdoing [8]. More recent research also shows that when employees experience a higher level of job dissatisfaction or financial stress, they will justify harmful actions as legitimate [9]. This is in line with cognitive dissonance theory where people within an organisation try to reduce the discomfort tied to their unethical actions by changing their perception of the organisation or their role within it

A. Coman et al. (Eds.): HCII 2025, LNCS 16337, pp. 365–374, 2026.
https://doi.org/10.1007/978-3-032-12801-0_24

(Ma et al., 2021). From these psychological studies, there is need for organisations not only to fix the technical aspects but also to create a supportive and engaging work environment by reducing the psychological triggers for insider threats.

In this paper, we investigate the impact of insider threats on organizations and recommend a consolidated approach to incorporate technology-based security together with people-centered security systems. Our work is guided by the following research questions (RQ):

- RQ 1: What organizational, social and psychological factors affect the occurrence of insider threats?
- RQ 2: What actions can be taken to mitigate insider threat attacks?

Our findings show that research based prevention techniques emphasizing a combination of behavioural, technical, and organizational measures are very important. Early identification of at-risk employees is the key to prevention. Behavioural analytics and monitoring systems refer to the dimensions of awareness about abnormal behaviour, such as sudden growth in data access or significant drop in productivity, which means the employee is disengaged or dissatisfied [7]. These systems use machine learning algorithms to monitor user behaviour to identify patterns of activities that are out of the norm. Insider threat detection in this sense is proactive. However, there are training programs to raise awareness on insider threat and ethical conduct that reduce the risk of accidental threat. With more awareness on cybersecurity, simulation exercises will enable employees to detect phishing attempts, observe any suspicious activity, and understand the consequence of their negligence. Additionally, we suggest a framework to act as a guideline for organizations to implement as a mitigation measure.

2   Literature Review

Our work draws from previous work on 1) understanding the causes of insider threats, and 2) the ways to mitigate various types of insider threats.

2.1   Types of Insider Threats

Insider threats are one of the major concerns in cybersecurity; they refer to unauthorized use of authorized access by individuals within an organization. These individuals deliberately or inadvertently compromise the integrity, confidentiality, or availability of organizational data and systems. Unlike external threats, insiders enjoy authorized access, and their actions and activities are not easily detectable or preventable through traditional security measures [7,9]. Insider threats can be divided into two major types: malicious insiders and unintentional insiders.

Insider threats go beyond full-time employees. Contractors, third party vendors and business partners who have access to the organisations' internal systems are also insiders. This broad definition means that organisations need to have comprehensive insider threat frameworks that includes both behavioural and technical controls [8] of members within the organisations as employees and outsiders who have direct access to the internal system of the organisation. In relation to this, working remotely or hybrid adds another block of having internal employees out of the organisation premises. This means that insider threats will go up because working from home may cause an employee to accidentally leak sensitive data to cyber nerds or make the system not secure. To this regard, researchers noted that insider threat management in a remote work environment is harder since traditional monitoring systems may not be sufficient to detect or prevent careless or malicious behaviour. In other words, an insider threat includes both intentional and unintentional activities by people who have access to critical systems. While malicious insiders use the insider position for their own benefit, many times the unintentional ones cause damage due to negligence.

2.2   Relevance to Cybersecurity

As Ma et al. [10] noted, insider-induced data breach in IoT ecosystem can result to multibillion dollar losses. Insider incidents also impact operations by targeting critical systems. The vulnerabilities in IoT identified by Kim et al. [9] can be exploited by an insider to take down physical systems, which can cause failure in interconnected infrastructures. This highlights the need for comprehensive standards that protect both digital and physical assets. The integration of IoT and AI in modern infrastructures has expanded the attack surface from an insider threat perspective. Saxena et al. [8] writes that insiders can now manipulate IoT devices to bypass traditional security measures.

Behavioural analytics has been shown to be key in fighting insider threats. These systems use past trends to identify deviations from normal activity patterns so that organisations can detect threats with a high signal [9]. Other key psychological drivers of malicious insider activity are stress, job dissatisfaction and poor company culture [10]. Feeding this data into the monitoring system makes it much easier for a company to predict and prevent insider incidents. As we have seen, hybrid and remote work has increased the likelihood of insider attacks. Employees using personal devices or unsecured networks to log into company systems can accidentally leak sensitive information, triggering a breach [10]. Advanced monitoring solutions like UEBA are critical to dealing with these risks because they can do real-time anomaly detection in decentralized work environments [9]. Proactive approaches like Zero Trust Architecture (ZTA) and multi-factor authentication (MFA) are becoming more relevant in fighting insider threats. ZTA is based on the concept of continuous verification where no user is trusted automatically even within the internal context of the organization. MFA adds an extra layer of security so even internally compromised personnel cannot access.

3   Methodology

We now present our mixed-methods approach to evaluate insider threat attacks. We provide methodology for a quantitative survey (n=170) and a qualitative interview (n=4). Both the survey and interviews were conducted with approval from the university Ethics board and the data obtained was stored digitally. The data was made accessible only to the researchers involved.

3.1   Survey

For our survey, we targeted the sample population from occupations across various sectors that are likely to be exposed to insider threats, for example, cybersecurity analysts. The survey was conducted online (via Google Forms) with 170 participants and recruitment was done through professional networking sites such as LinkedIn. Participation was voluntary and anonymous.

Participants had to first digitally sign the consent form, fill in the demographics (age, gender, profession, job experience), and then answer the survey questionnaire. The survey questionnaire focused on the prevalence of insider threats, the level of preparation on existing cybersecurity controls, and the impact of psychological, social, and organizational factors.

3.2   Interviews

For our interview, we recruited four participants and conducted a semi-structured interview session. For our sample population, we focused on professional role, years of experience, and industry representation and therefore we can term the participants as"experts" in their respective fields. Participation was voluntary and participants were recruited through a call for participation via LinkedIn.

During registration, participants filled in their demographics and then they set a date to be interviewed. The interviews were conducted virtually through Zoom [4], with each session lasting 45–60 min. The interviews were recorded and transcribed with obtained consent from the participants.

4   Data Analysis and Results

In this section, we present our data analysis on the conducted survey and interviews.

4.1   Survey Results

The survey data were collected through Google Forms. Data was preprocessed, and used for statistical analysis. For statistical analysis, we used SPSS [5]. For our survey, we had 170 participants, with an age range of 18 to 55 years , male = 51%. The professional experience of the participants are shown in Table 1.

Table 1. Job experience in cybersecurity.

Years	Number	Percentage (%)
18–24	16	9.4
25–34	84	49.4
35–44	54	31.8
45–54	13	7.6
55+	3.	1.8

When asked about the prevalence of insider threats, 72.4% of the respondents reported insider threat incidents in the last 12 months. The most common was unintentional threats. Other common threats were malicious insiders, financial mismanagement, and data theft. Our survey also revealed interesting factors that affect the overall state of security. Of the psychological motivators, stress and burnout topped the list at 62.4% , followed by job dissatisfaction at 54.7% , financial pressure at 53.5%, ethical disengagement at 42.4%, lack of recognition at 32.9% and peer pressure/toxic work culture at 56.5%. The results are illustrated in Fig. 1

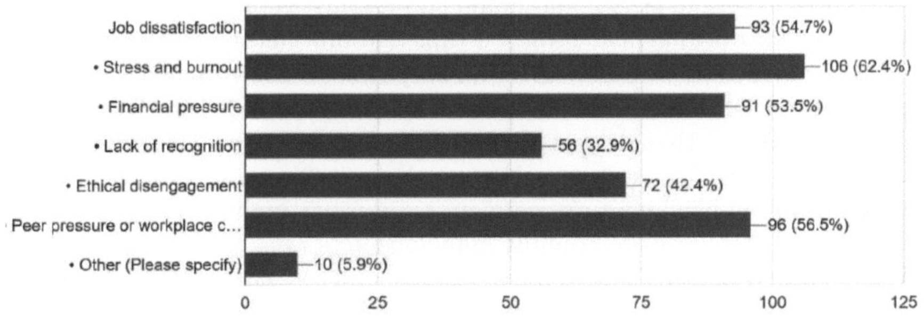

Fig. 1. Factors contributing to Insider Threats.

We also asked about the challenges faced by organizations when trying to mitigate insider threats. Top of the list are a lack of expertise or trained personnel, limited technological infrastructure, and a lack of awareness or training. Privacy concerns and high false positive rates in detection systems were also major hurdles. And when it comes to social engineering tactics, 50.6% said social engineering is a high threat inside their organisation; of those, 22.9% said it's very high.

A Pearson correlation was run to see if there was a relationship between years of experience in cybersecurity and perceived organization's cybersecurity maturity. Results showed a weak statistically significant positive correlation, r (170) =.203, p=.008. This reflects that people with more years of experience in cybersecurity rated their organization's maturity in cybersecurity slightly higher. Another Pearson correlation was run to see the relationship between years of experience in cybersecurity and being prepared to mitigate insider threats. Results showed a weak positive correlation of r (164) =.074, p=.346, which is not statistically significant. From this, we derive that years of experience in cybersecurity cannot positively prepare one to mitigate insider threats.

Insufficient training is associated with more unintentional insider threats. Organisations with no training programs are more likely to have accidental breaches by their employees. Malicious insiders and insufficient training shows a value of 0.237 (p = 0.002), weak positive correlation. Insufficient training may also contribute to more malicious insider threats. From these, we derive that employee training is key to mitigating both unintentional and malicious insider threats. Organisations should focus on improving their training programs to not only address unintentional breaches but also to reduce the chance of malicious activities. This ensures that employees understand the security protocols and the consequences of breaches to minimize both types of threats.

4.2   Interview Results

Thematic analysis of the interview responses showed many key themes related to insider threats. Among the four experts, a major psychological factor discussed was job dissatisfaction, stress, and financial pressure as motivators for insiders to act maliciously or negligently. Expert 1 talked about factors such as the feeling of low value or overwork that may drive an employee to compromise organizational security. Financial strain, usually caused by debt, was identified as one of the common motivators that drive individuals to engage in insider threats; most of these are data theft or system sabotage. Expert 3 and 4 said other external pressures, such as blackmail or coercion, were other main psychological factors that can drive employees to commit malicious acts.

We identified another key area, workplace culture, that affect insider threat. Experts pointed out toxic cultures that can lead to situations that promote insider threats. Expert 2 mentioned poor management and a lack of communication that can create employee disengagement, which would drive them to malicious or negligent actions. Lack of trust and negative organizational culture were mentioned a lot as variables that would increase the risk of insider threats.

All agree that employee training and awareness will be part of any mitigation strategy. In essence, experts said regular training especially on recognizing and avoiding social engineering attacks will reduce insider threats. Simulations of phishing attacks and practical hands-on training were suggested as ways to make employees more vigilant and aware. Expert 3 also said to open communication channels where employees can report suspicious activities without fear of retaliation. The experts know the challenges that organizations face in dealing with insider threats. Expert 2 said one of the biggest challenges is to distinguish normal behaviour from suspicious activities, especially in cases of big data. Limited resources and specialized skills in most organizations, especially in emerging markets were also identified as a big barrier to detecting and mitigating insider threats.

5   Discussion

In this section, we discuss the different factors impacting different organizations. We illustrate the various ways organizations can attempt to mitigate insider threats and the lessons learned.

Our findings converge and diverge with existing literature on insider threats. For example, the prevalence of insider threats and major psychological, social, and organizational drivers identified in this research is consistent with previous research. One divergent point from the literature is employee training and awareness programs. Although they are considered one of the building blocks in addressing insider threats, in this study, only 28% of the respondents rated these programs as highly effective. The challenge is distinguishing normal behavior from suspicious activities, especially regarding big data. Limited resources and specialized skills in most organizations, especially in emerging markets were also identified as a big barrier to detecting and mitigating insider threats. This is contrary to other studies where the importance of training programs in improving employee awareness to prevent insider threats has been emphasized. The low rating for the effectiveness of training in this study means organizations may not be benefitting from training due to poor engagement or lack of coverage over specific threats. This adds to the growing concern that training should be more practical and focused on specific insider threats.

Among the findings are several trends and patterns. The most common trend is the psychological and organizational factors that drive insider threats. Stress, burnout, and dissatisfaction with the job was identified as the most serious determinants, as many said that either one of these was a critical driver of unintentional or malicious insider threats. Advanced technological solutions like UEBA and RBAC although promising has their downsides when they require more rigid employee training programs to be effective. Another leading finding is that there are sectoral challenges: every industry has unique vulnerabilities, hence requires a customized response. This means that while technological solutions will not be less important, it is only a multidimensional approach-which includes a focus on employee well-being, organizational culture, and continuous training-that allows organizations to fully rise to the insider threats challenge. Areas to improve include increasing employee training programs and the organization's preparedness to insider threats.

In general, the findings show that insider threat management is holistic; organisations should not just focus on technological solutions but make sure the welfare of the employees is taken care of, build up a positive organizational culture, and update the training programs according to the ever-evolving nature of insider threats. Results of this study can be very useful for any organization to improve its cybersecurity resilience and reduce the potential for insider threats.

5.1 Framework

We provide the following key features that organisations can implement to mitigate insider attacks.

- **Increased monitoring and technology integration**: As detection and prevention of insider threats is already effective with tools like UEBA and RBAC, investments in security solutions should always be continued. The machine learning system should be updated regularly to improve anomaly detection and false positive takedowns.
- **Continual employee training**: Since the insider threats were mainly psychological and social in nature, organizations need to be more dynamic in creating training sessions that go beyond awareness and create capabilities within the organization. This can include simulated attack opportunities, scenario participations, and response exercise training on real-time threats. Training can make the employee community proactive in identifying the insider threat.
- **Organization culture**: Organizations need to focus on creating a positive work culture in the workplace. Businesses can reduce the chance of malicious and unintentional insider threats by addressing job dissatisfaction, burnout, and peer pressure. A culture of transparency, communication, and recognition creates an environment that deters insider threats.
- **Regular Audits and Incident Response Planning**: Regular audits and incident response planning are key. That's why organizations must make a conscious effort to conduct security reviews and have an incident response plan that is well understood and effective. Most importantly, instill within the staff a sense of responsibility.
- **Industry-specific approaches**: Insider threats are industry-specific. In the healthcare industry, the challenge is access to medical data. In government and defence, it's national security. Designing cybersecurity with industry-specific vulnerabilities will help mitigate threats.

5.2 Limitation

While we provide valuable insights in this field, our evaluation is not without limitation. The scope of the study was limited as we conducted the interview with only four experts. As future work, we look forward to expanding our sample population to better represent various industries where insider attacks take place.

In addition, there lies some methodological limitation as the respondents may have been biased in their responses. The participants may have under or over reported the prevalence of insider threat attacks that may have compromised the quality of the data collected.

6 Conclusion

In this paper, we investigated the impact of insider threats on organizations. We surveyed 170 participants and conducted an expert interview with four experts to understand how different factors play a role in insider threats and what can be done to mitigate such attacks.

Insider attacks are hard to detect because they can access many of the most critical systems and data, which makes it hard to distinguish between calm and malicious activities. So, there is need to combine traditional security mechanisms with advanced technologies for insider threat detection. New tool and technologies have made it possible to detect, mitigate, and prevent insider threats. The core of insider threat detection nowadays is basically machine learning and Artificial Intelligence (AI). These technologies can be used to review past behaviour to identify activities that could be malicious. AI cybersecurity relies on large datasets to identify behaviour patterns and detect anomalies that are well hidden from traditional systems. The advancement of these technologies has moved cybersecurity from traditional rule-based frameworks to more flexible, data-informed methodologies that adapt to the dynamic nature of emerging threats. For example, machine learning algorithms like Random Forest and Support Vector Machines (SVM) have been effective in detecting insider threats by analysing network traffic, system logs, and user activities [11]. The main benefit of these models is that they can differentiate between normal and abnormal behaviours by using both labelled and unlabelled datasets, so they can recognize subtle indicators of compromise that would otherwise go undetected. Moreover, advanced deep learning techniques like Convolutional Neural Networks (CNN) and Recurrent Neural Networks (RNN) have been shown to detect complex and novel threats, especially those related to covert insider actions like data exfiltration or sabotage. These AI techniques can analyse network traffic and other unstructured data in real-time from user interaction logs to find potential threats.

The rise of hybrid and remote work models brings new organizational vulnerabilities that add to insider threat management. With no oversight that comes with working from home, there is increased risk of negligent insider behaviour mishandling of sensitive data, getting phished, or accidentally exposing internal systems to attackers. The implication is simple: when employees are not engaged with the security infrastructure, breakdowns in communication mean weak adherence to security policies. Therefore, organisations will need custom training and monitoring systems for hybrid and remote work.

Our findings show that a combination of policies would be effective in mitigating such attacks. Based on these, we presented a framework to be employed by personnel to address threats from insider attacks.

References

1. Ville, M., et al.: Virtual field studies: conducting studies on public displays in virtual reality. In: Proceedings of the 2020 CHI Conference on Human Factors in Computing Systems (2020). https://doi.org/10.1145/3313831.3376796
2. Pereira, V., Hadjielias, E., Christofi, M., Vrontis, D.: A systematic literature review on the impact of artificial intelligence on workplace outcomes: a multi-process perspective. Hum. Resour. Manag. Rev. (2023)

3. Yasmeen, A., et al.: Understanding shoulder surfer behavior and attack patterns using virtual reality. In: Proceedings of the 2022 International Conference on Advanced Visual Interfaces, pp. 1–9 (2022)
4. Oliffe, J.L., Kelly, M.T., Gonzalez Montaner, G., Yu, K., Wellam, F.: Zoom interviews: benefits and concessions. Int. J. Qual. Methods (2021)
5. Sweet, S.A., Grace-Martin, K.: Data analysis with SPSS. Allyn & Bacon, Boston (1999)
6. Pantelidis, E., Bendiab, G., Shiaeles, S., Kolokotronis, N.: Insider detection using deep autoencoder and variational autoencoder neural networks. arXiv preprint arXiv:2109.02568 (2021)
7. Gupta, M., Akiri, C.K., Aryal, K., Parker, E., Praharaj, L.: From ChatGPT to ThreatGPT: impact of generative AI in cybersecurity and privacy, pp. 80218–80245. IEEE (2023)
8. Saxena, N., et al.: Impact and key challenges of insider threats on organizations and critical businesses. MDPI (2020)
9. Kim, A., Oh, J., Ryu, J., Lee, K.: A review of insider threat detection approaches with IoT perspective, pp. 78847–78867. IEEE (2020)
10. Ma, Q., Sun, C., Cui, B., Jin, X.: A Novel Model for Anomaly Detection in Network Traffic Based on Kernel Support Vector Machine. Elsevier (2021)
11. Raval, M.S., Gandhi, R., Chaudhary, S.: Insider Threat Detection: Machine Learning Way, pp. 19–53. Springer (2018)

Evaluating Security Support Tool for Help Recipients

Ayane Sano[1,2]([✉]) [iD], Yukiko Sawaya[1] [iD], Takamasa Isohara[1] [iD],
and Masakatsu Nishigaki[2] [iD]

[1] KDDI Research, Inc., 2-1-15 Ohara, Fujimino, Saitama 356-8502, Japan
`{ay-sano,yu-sawaya,ta-isohara}@kddi.com`
[2] Shizuoka University, 3-5-1 Johoku, Naka-ku, Hamamatsu, Shizuoka 432-8011, Japan
`nisigaki@inf.shizuoka.ac.jp`

Abstract. To protect users from various cyber-attacks, users take security actions by themselves. Some computer and smartphone users, referred to as "Help Recipients," delegate necessary security actions to their family or friends, referred to as "Helpers". However, Helpers are not always able to be close to Help Recipients. Help Recipients cannot always delegate security actions to Helpers. Therefore, it is important to support Help Recipients in taking security actions by themselves. Our previous work found that there are two reasons why Help Recipients cannot take security actions by themselves. First, many users cannot choose appropriate security actions. It is difficult for them to distinguish appropriate security actions from a large amount of information. Second, they cannot understand technical terms. In this paper, we propose a security support tool for Help Recipients to solve these problems. This tool selects the appropriate method and security system based on the services and applications being used, and provides only the minimum necessary information. Help Recipients do not need to search many websites and only need to confirm the information described in the security support tool. To evaluate the effectiveness of this tool, we developed a prototype and conducted a user experiment. After the experiment, many users would like to use this prototype; however, there is room for improvement in terms of adjusting the amount of information.

Keywords: Security action · Security Support tool

1 Introduction

Recently, various cyber-attacks have increased, and users take security actions by themselves to avoid security damage. Related works [1–5] describe that some computer and smartphone users, referred to as "Help Recipients," delegate necessary security actions to their family or friends, referred to as "Helpers". They cannot take security actions by themselves because they lack sufficient knowledge about IT or/and security. As long as the Helpers take Help Recipients' security actions, the Help Recipients' devices are safe. However, the Helpers do not always have close connections with Help Recipients,

A. Coman et al. (Eds.): HCII 2025, LNCS 16337, pp. 375–390, 2026.
https://doi.org/10.1007/978-3-032-12801-0_25

and the Help Recipients cannot always delegate security actions to Helpers. In addition, bridging the digital divide is required [6], and there are some approaches to support digital utilization, such as smartphone classes and seminars [7–9]. Therefore, it is important to support Help Recipients in taking security actions by themselves.

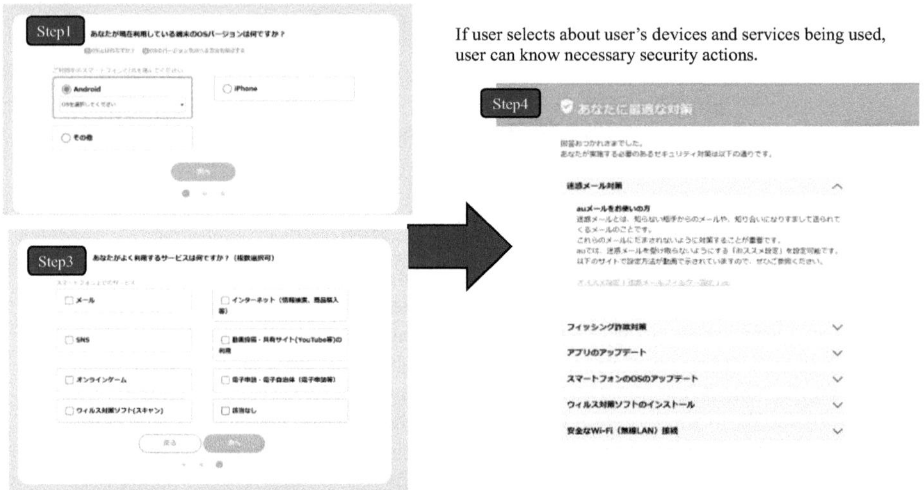

Fig. 1. Image of Security Support Tool.

Related work [1] describes that there are two main reasons why Help Recipients cannot take security action by themselves. First, many users cannot choose the appropriate security actions and security systems because many websites provide a large amount of information for users. Second, they cannot understand technical terms. If they are motivated to take security actions, they may stumble due to the amount of information and the difficulty of the content. We consider that it is difficult for users to find appropriate information on website. In this paper, we propose a security support tool for Help Recipients to solve these problems. Figure 1 shows an image of the tool. All the user needs to do is choose the devices and applications being used. This tool chooses the appropriate method and security system based on the services and applications being used, and provides only the minimum necessary information. This tool includes explanations of technical terms. We created a prototype and set two research questions. We define users who take security actions by oneself as Self-reliant users.

RQ1: How is the level of usability of this prototype for Help Recipients?

RQ2: What are the points for improvement in the prototype?

We conducted a user experiment to evaluate the effectiveness of this prototype by using the services of a research company in Japan. We conducted the experiment on April 5th, 2024. We conducted the screening survey from March 14th to March 18th, 2024. We recruited 48 participants, consisting of 30 Help Recipients and 18 Self-reliant users. The participants had to be smartphone users of a specific communication carrier, aged 20 to 89 years, and users of at least one of the following services: email, internet, social media, video posting sites, online games, and online submissions. The participants actually used the prototype and answered a questionnaire. The questionnaire included questions about the user's impression of the prototype and additional functions for this prototype. As a result of this experiment, the contributions of our paper are as follows.

- Approximately 70% of Help Recipients answered that they would like to use this prototype.
- The improvement points are reducing the amount of information and making this prototype easier to understand.

Based on these findings, many users would like to use this prototype, but there is room for improvement. We found that it is important to adjust the amount of information and the explanation of technical terms according to users' literacy level.

This paper describes related works in Sect. 2 and a proposed method and the experimental method in Sect. 3. We describe the findings of a demonstration experiment in Sect. 4 and discuss the improvement points of the prototype for the Help Recipients and the limitations of this experiment in Sect. 5. Finally, the conclusion and future works are discussed in Sect. 6.

2 Related Works

In this section, we describe related works about user characteristics of Help Recipients and support approaches for Help Recipients. We define Help Recipients as some computer and smartphone users who delegate necessary security actions to their family or friends. Related works do not use the word of "Help Recipients," but we collected related works that describe people who delegate their family, friends, or shop clerks.

2.1 User Characteristics of Help Recipients

Our previous work [1] conducted an online interview with people who had delegated security actions to a Helper before, but now take security actions by themselves. The past experience where the Help Recipient and someone close to them were damaged by security attacks, and the past experience of attending a security seminar influenced on the opportunity that enabled the Help recipients to take security actions by themselves. Moreover, we understand that there are two main reasons why Help Recipients cannot take security actions by themselves. First, many users cannot distinguish appropriate security actions and security systems because many websites provide a large amount of information for users. Second, they cannot understand technical terms.

Kropczynski et al. [2] found the characteristics of Help Recipients and Helpers, the communication methods and support contents between them. Mendel et al. [3, 10] found the characteristics of older people and Helpers, the support process to enhance mobile security for older people. Pacheco [11] investigated the user awareness of older people regarding online safety and cybersecurity. He described that it is necessary to provide a support tool for older people.

These related works describe the characteristics of Help Recipients, but the method to promote security actions by themselves has not been found.

2.2 Support Approaches for Help Recipients

Chouhan et al. [5] developed a mobile application in which Help Recipients request support from Helpers when they need to make decisions about their security and privacy. Mendel et al. [4] developed an application where older people request support from Helpers and evaluated the effectiveness of this application. In addition, there are some related works about UI design for older people, people with low literacy. Salman et al. [12] conducted research in which five experts evaluated the usability of smartphones for elderly people. As a result, "appearance," "language," "dialogue," and "information" have an effect on improving usability. Olwal et al. [13] proposed a prototype framework called OldGen, which provides personalized mobile interfaces for elderly people.

Zajicek [14] described that it is necessary to provide designs considering diversity. Chaudry et al. [15] proposed some recommendations of UI design for people with low literacy, such as large-sized widgets, and starting every task from the same location. Medhi et al. [16] evaluated mobile interfaces for low-literacy users. As a result, textual interfaces are unusable by low-literacy users. Kodagoda et al. [17] described the problems of low-literacy users in terms of seeking information online and proposed design principles for low-literacy users. As described above, support approaches and personalized user interface are needed for Help Recipients.

3 Security Support Tool

In this section, we described the details of security support tool and a demonstration experiment to evaluate this tool.

3.1 Functions

Related work [1] describes that Help Recipients cannot take security actions by themselves because many users cannot choose appropriate security actions and security systems, and they cannot understand technical terms. If they are motivated to take security actions, they may stumble due to the amount of information and the difficulty of the content. It is difficult for them to distinguish appropriate security actions from a large amount of information. In this paper, we propose a security support tool for Help Recipients to solve these problems. Figure 2 shows the image of each step of the tool. All the user needs to do is choose the devices and applications being used. This tool chooses the appropriate method and security system based on the services and applications being used, and provides only the minimum necessary information. This tool includes explanations of technical terms. By using this tool, users with low literacy do not need to search for and judge appropriate information, and they can easily take security actions by themselves. The instructions for using the tool consists of a maximum of four steps as follows. The case of an Android smartphone is shown as an example.

- Step 1. The user selects the OS type and version of their device. e.g., Android, iPhone
- Step 2. The user selects the manufacturer's name if their device is an Android smartphone in Step1. e.g., Sony, Samsung, Sharp, Kyocera.

- Step 3.The user selects the services they are using (multiple choices allowed). e.g., email, internet, social media.
- Step 4.The tool shows the necessary security actions and appropriate methods.

Fig. 2. Each step of Security Support Tool.

In Step 1, user chooses the OS types and the version of their devices from options. The user can see the explanation of the OS and how to confirm the OS version of their device. In Step 2, this step shows only for Android users. The user chooses the manufacturer's name of their device from options. In Step 3, the user chooses the services they are using. This step allows multiple choices. In Step 4, the security support tool shows the necessary security actions and appropriate methods based on the user response from Step1,2, and 3. For example, in the case of the user who has not used the latest OS, the user is shown "updating the OS" as a necessary security action in Step 4. In the case of the user who has not installed anti-virus software, the user is shown "installing anti-virus software" as a necessary security action in Step 4. In the case of the user who has used email, the user is shown "spam email protection" as a necessary security action in Step 4. Moreover, the tool shows different procedures according to each OS types and manufacturer name. For example, the tool shows the website that describes appropriate methods which Android users conducts only for Android users. We give priority to the website that describes each step with images and videos as the appropriate methods.

3.2 Demonstration Experiment

We developed a prototype of a security support tool. We implemented this prototype on a virtual server. The users can use the prototype by accessing the website. To evaluate the effectiveness of this prototype, we set two research questions.

RQ1: How is the level of usability of this prototype for Help Recipients?

RQ2: What are the points for improvement in the prototype?

We conducted a demonstration experiment to evaluate the effectiveness of this prototype by using the services of a research company in Japan. We conducted the experiment at a research company venue on April 5th, 2024. We recruited participants for the screening survey by matching the population composition rate of smartphone users in Japan [18]. We conducted the screening survey from March 14th to March 18th, 2024. We recruited 48 participants, consisting of 30 Help Recipients and 18 Self-reliant users. The participants had to be smartphones users of a specific communication carrier, aged 20 to 89 years, and users of at least one of the following services: email, internet, social media, video posting sites, online games, and online submissions. We did not consider the allocation of the participants, but we prioritized setting the same number of Android users and iPhone users. The participants consist of 21 Help Recipients-Android users, 9 Self-reliant users-Android users, 9 Help Recipients-iPhone users, and 9 Self-reliant users-iPhone users. We recruited Android users who use devices from Google, Sony, Samsung, Sharp, Kyocera and whose OS version ranges from 10 to 14. The OS version of 1 Android user is 7, but this participant assumes OS version is 10. We recruited iPhone users who use iPhone13–15 or SE, and their OS version ranges from 14 to 17. The demographic of participants is shown in Table 1. In Table 1, Help Recipient consist of many older females, and Self-reliant users consist of many males.

The participants actually used the prototype and answered a questionnaire. The questionnaire included questions about the user's impression of the prototype and additional functions for this prototype. In particular, the investigator supported how to use a computer for users who were not accustomed to computers or/and smartphones, and listened to and ghostwrote their open-ended questions. In addition, the investigator conducted additional hearings with the users who answered the differences from the intent of open-ended questions. The questionnaire items are described in Appendix. The questionnaire has been translated from Japanese. The questionnaire consists of 13 items, SUS (System Usability Scale), WUS (Web Usability Scale), the future intention of this tool, the future intention of this tool in the case of requiring a charge, the amount of information, additional information, the intention of this tool in the case of computer and IoT devices, the recommendation level and the reason, the content of convenience and inconvenience, additional function, and other comments. We used the SUS [19], WUS [20] scale and set the recommendation level based on the NPS [21]. In this paper, we did not collect any information that could identify the participants. All responses from the participants were anonymized. In accordance with the regulations of the research company, the participants were paid a fee for attending the experiment. Participants were free to withdraw from the experiment at any time. This experiment was exempt from ethical review according to the guidelines of our organization.

Table 1. The demographic of participants.

Age	Help Recipient			Self-reliant users		
	Male	Female	Total	Male	Female	Total
20–29	0	0	0	2	1	3
30–39	0	1	1	0	2	2
40–49	1	2	3	3	2	5
50–59	0	8	8	3	1	4
60–69	3	7	10	2	0	2
70–79	1	6	7	2	0	2
80–89	0	1	1	0	0	0
Total	5	25	30	12	6	18

4 Evaluation

We describe the analytical method and result of this experiment.

4.1 Analytical Method

We used HAD [22] and BellCurve for Excel [23] as analytical software. To evaluate RQ1, we calculated the average of SUS, WUS and the number of participants who answered each option of other quantitative questions. We confirmed the difference between Help Recipients and Self-reliant users by using test of independence ($p < 0.05$) and Fisher's exact test ($p < 0.05$) when the sample size was small. To evaluate RQ2, we used open-ended questions after Q9 and analyzed them by using after coding. The first person created categories for the data of open-ended question and classified the data by using the categories. The second person classified the data by using the categories created by the first person. In cases where many factors were present in the open-ended question, we classified based only on the factor that appeared first. We calculated the matching degree of the classification results of the first person and the second person by using

Kappa statistics. As a result, Q9 was 0.607, Q10 was 0.675, Q11 was 0.806, Q12 was 0.813, Q13 was 0.738. All results exceeded 0.6 as the standard [24] and we analyzed by using the classification results of the first person.

4.2 Result

We described the results of this experiment as follows. The average SUS score is 55, with Help Recipients scoring is 51 and self-reliant users scoring 61. There is a possibility that the average SUS score on the American site is 68 [25], which differs from the Japan site. The average SUS score for Help Recipients is low and improving the prototype is necessary. The average WUS score is shown as Table 2. We found that this prototype has high content reliability, good response, good understanding of layout. However, the likeability is low, it is necessary to improve.

Table 2. Result of WUS.

Average (out of 5)	Likeability	Usefulness	Content reliability	Understanding of operation	Understanding of layout	Ease of viewing	Level of response
All	3.2	3.5	4.2	3.5	3.9	3.7	4.3
Help Recipients	3.3	3.5	4.2	3.5	3.9	3.7	4.3
Self-reliant users	3.0	3.6	4.2	3.4	3.8	3..8	4.4

Table 3. Intention to use of prototype.

	Yes	Neither	No
All	68.8% (33/48)	12.5% (6/48)	18.8% (9/48)
Help Recipient	70.0% (21/30)	16.7% (5/30)	13.3% (4/30)
Self-reliant users	66.7% (12/18)	5.6% (1/18)	27.8% (5/18)
In the case of requiring a charge			
All	8.3% (4/48)	22.9% (11/48)	68.8% (33/48)
Help Recipient	0% (0/30)	26.7% (8/30)	73.3% (22/30)
Self-reliant users	22.2% (4/18)	16.7% (3/18)	61.1% (11/18)

The number and rate of participant who answered Q3 and Q4 are shown in Table 3. We summarized the number of responses "I would like to use", "I would like to use little" as "Yes" and the number of responses "I do not use", "I do not use much" as "No". The rate of participants interested in using this prototype is about 68.8%. In the case of Help Recipient, about 70.0%, and Self-reliant users about 66.7%. After conducting a test of independence, there was no difference between Help Recipients and Self-reliant users (p > 0.05). We confirmed that many users intend to use this prototype. On the other hand, in the case of requiring a charge, the rate of participants interested in using this prototype is about 8.3%. After conducting Fisher's exact test, there was a difference between Help Recipients and Self-reliant users (p = 0.016). In the case of requiring a charge, none of Help Recipients intended to use it, and it is necessary to improve.

The number and rate of participants who answered Q5 are shown in Table 4. More than 60% of participants answered "Just right" regarding amount of information for both Help Recipients and Self-reliant users. Some participants answered "A little more", so it is important to reduce the amount of information.

Table 4. Amount of information of prototype.

Rate (Number)	Little	A little less	Just right	A little more	More
All	0% (0/48)	4.2% (2/48)	62.5% (30/48)	22.9% (11/48)	10.4% (5/48)
Help Recipient	0% (0/30)	6.7% (2/30)	60.0% (18/30)	20.0% (6/30)	13.3% (4/30)
Self-reliant users	0% (0/18)	0% (0/18)	66.7% (12/18)	27.8% (5/18)	5.6% (1/18)

The number and rate of participants who answered Q6 are shown in Table 5. We found that more than half of participants request how to set the device excluding with security settings as additional information for both Help Recipients and Self-reliant users. In particular, half of Help recipients requested how to use the device. Therefore, the prototype improves usability by adding information such as how to set the device and how to use the device.

Table 5. Request of additional information.

Rate (Number)	How to use the device	How to set the device excluding security settings	Nothing
All	47.9% (23/48)	54.2% (26/48)	37.5% (18/48)
Help Recipient	56.7% (17/30)	56.7% (17/30)	33.3% (10/30)
Self-reliant users	33.3% (6/18)	50.0% (9/18)	44.4% (8/18)

The number and rate of participant who answered Q7 are shown in Table 6. Table 6 shows the intention of using prototype in the case of computer or IoT. The results show only computer users and IoT users, excluding users who do not use these devices. Similar to Q3 and Q4, we summarized the number of responses "I would like to use", "I would like to use little" as "Yes" and the number of responses "I do not use", "I do not use much" as "No". The rate of participants interested in using this prototype is about 60.0% in the case of Help Recipients and computer users, but the rate is about 38.1% in the case of Help Recipient and IoT users. In Table 6, we found that a different rate of the intention to use depending on each device. In particular, in the case of IoT, the rate of the intention to use by Self-reliant users is low, so some ingenuity is necessary.

Table 6. Intention to use prototype in the case of computer/IoT.

Rate (Number)	Yes	Neither	No
Computer			
All	58.1% (25/43)	2.3% (1/43)	39.5% (17/43)
Help Recipient	60.0% (15/25)	4.0% (1/25)	36.0% (9/25)
Self-reliant users	55.6% (10/18)	0% (0/18)	44.4% (8/18)
IoT			
All	40.5% (15/37)	5.4% (2/37)	54.1% (20/37)
Help Recipient	38.1% (8/21)	4.8% (1/21)	57.1% (12/21)
Self-reliant users	43.6% (7/16)	6.3% (1/16)	50.0% (8/16)

Table 7. The reason of answering recommendation level.

Help Recipient	Rate (Number)	Self-reliant users	Rate (Number)
Provide appropriate information, easy to use	20.0% (6/30)	Provide appropriate information, easy to use	27.8% (5/18)
Easy to understand	16.7% (5/30)	Easy to understand	16.7% (3/18)
Recommend people with other literacy levels or in trouble	13.3% (4/30)	Recommend people with other literacy levels or in trouble	11.1% (2/18)
Feel safe	3.3% (1/30)		
Difficult to understand	26.7% (8/30)	Difficult to use	22.2% (4/18)
Do not recommend people with high literacy levels because they are not in trouble	16.7% (5/30)	Do not recommend people with high literacy levels because they are not in trouble	11.1% (2/18)
Other	3.3% (1/30)	Difficult to understand	5.6% (1/18)
		Other	5.6% (1/18)

Table 8. Points of convenience and inconvenience.

Points of convenience			
Help Recipients	Rate (Number)	Self-reliant users	Rate (Number)
Functions (explanation of technical terms and how to take security actions), easy to understand	50.0% (15/30)	Showing only appropriate information for me, displayed as a list	38.9% (7/18)

(continued)

Table 8. (*continued*)

Points of convenience			
Help Recipients	Rate (Number)	Self-reliant users	Rate (Number)
Showing only appropriate information for me, displayed as a list	23.3% (7/30)	Functions (explanation of technical terms and how to take security actions), easy to understand	33.3% (6/18)
Easy to set (possible to set alone)	6.7% (2/30)	Easy to set (possible to set alone)	16.7% (3/18)
Device is safe	6.7% (2/30)	Nothing	5.6% (1/18)
Nothing	10.0% (3/30)	Other	5.6% (1/18)
Other	3.3% (1/30)		
Points of inconvenience			
Difficult to understand	30.0% (9/30)	Difficult to understand	27.8% (5/18)
Cannot be set according to the site	6.7% (2/30)	Design is poor, not unified	16.7% (3/18)
Difficult to view	6.7% (2/30)	Cannot be set according to the site	11.1% (2/18)
Many contents	3.3% (1/30)	Many contents	5.6% (1/18)
Design is poor, not unified	3.3% (1/30)	Nothing	27.8% (5/18)
Nothing	43.3% (13/30)	Other	11.1% (2/18)
Other	6.7% (2/30)		

The average recommendation level is 6.2, with Help Recipients scoring 6.1 and Self-reliant users scoring 6.3. The reasons for answering the recommendation level are shown in Table 7. We found positive and negative opinions were obtained for both Help Recipients and Self-reliant users. As examples of positive opinions, many users answered "Provide appropriate information, easy to use" and" Easy to understand" for both Help Recipients and Self-reliant users. However, as examples of negative opinions, many users answered "Difficult to understand" and" Do not recommend people with high literacy levels because they are not in trouble" for Help-Recipients, and "Difficult to use" for Self-reliant users. We think it is necessary to approach making the prototype easier to understand.

The points of convenience and inconvenience are shown in Table 8. As points of convenience, more than half of Help Recipients answered "Functions (explanation of technical terms and how to take security actions), easy to understand". Subsequently, many users answered "Showing only appropriate information for me, displayed as a list". In the case of Self-reliant users, many users answered "Functions (explanation of technical terms and how to take security actions), easy to understand", "Showing only appropriate information for me, displayed as a list". Therefore, we confirmed that the users perceive the positive points of the prototype. About 43.3% of the Help Recipients answered "Nothing" as points of inconvenience, so some users are satisfied with this prototype. On the other hand, as points of inconvenience, about 30% of users answered "Difficult to understand" for both Help Recipients and Self-reliant users.

The additional functions are shown in Table 9. Many Help Recipients requested "Additional information" and" Case study". Some Help Recipients answered "Nothing", so we confirmed that some Help Recipients are satisfied with this prototype.

Table 9. Additional functions.

Help Recipient	Rate (Number)	Self-reliant users	Rate (Number)
Additional information	16.7% (5/30)	Additional information	22.2% (4/18)
Explanation of technical terms	13.3% (4/30)	Chat, Contact point	16.7% (3/18)
Case study	13.3% (4/30)	Explanation of technical terms	5.6% (1/18)
Chat, Contact point	10.0% (3/30)	Case study	5.6% (1/18)
How to use the smartphone, how to set the smartphone	6.7% (2/30)	Nothing	38.9% (7/18)
Nothing	36.7% (11/30)	Other	11.1% (2/18)
Other	3.3% (1/30)		

5 Discussion

We discuss the effectiveness of the prototype including suggestions for improvement, and the limitations of this experiment.

5.1 Effectiveness of Prototype

As described in Sect. 4.2, we found that security support tool is effective for Help Recipients. The average SUS score is low; however, the reliability of content and understanding of layout in the WUS score are high. Moreover, many users answered that convenience points of the prototype were positive and nothing for inconvenience points. Therefore, we confirmed that the usability of this prototype is high.

However, some users pointed out issues regarding the amount of information and difficulty in understanding. We consider the prototype is needed for improvement. We describe three suggestions for improvement.

1. **Reduce the amount of information**: When developing the prototype, we put the explanations of technical terms into the prototype to make them easier to understand. However, it leads to an increase in the number of sentences and the amount of information. It is necessary to adjust the amount of information in terms of literacy level.
2. **Decrease the contents which the user inputs**: Some users described that operation is difficult and the prototype is difficult to understand. In particular, it is difficult for Help Recipients to select the version of the OS in Step 1. The version of the OS is needed to judge the latest OS, but we will improve the tool by showing "updating the OS" for all users in Step 4.
3. **Limit the number of security actions in Step 4**: The number of security actions shown in Step 4 differs from the contents input by users. Some users may feel that the number of security actions in Step 4 is too many. It is necessary to limit the number of security actions such as prioritizing ranking.

We will improve the prototype based on the upper three suggestions and evaluate the usability in the future.

5.2 Limitation

We describe two limitations of this paper. We conducted the experiment only with smartphones users of a specific communication carrier. There is a possibility that different results would be obtained if an experiment were conducted with a different composition of the population, such as users of different devices. In addition, the participants in the experiment were 48 users, so we will conduct the demonstration experiments with a large number of participants.

6 Conclusion

We proposed a security support tool for promoting security actions for Help Recipients. After conducting a demonstration experiment, we found that the usability of the security support tool is high, but there is room for improvement such as the amount of information, and the level of difficulty of content. We described three suggestions for improving the tool. In the future, we will revise the tool and evaluate its effectiveness by conducting a demonstration experiment with a large number of participants.

Appendix: Questionnaire Items

- Q1: SUS (1: Strongly disagree ~ 5: Strongly agree)

  1. I think that I would like to use this tool frequently.
  2. I found the tool unnecessarily complex.

  3. I thought the tool was easy to use.
  4. I think that I would need the support of a technical person to be able to use this tool.
  5. I found the various functions in this tool were well integrated.
  6. I thought there was too much inconsistency in this tool.
  7. I would imagine that most people would learn to use this tool very quickly.
  8. I found the tool very cumbersome to use.
  9. I felt very confident using the tool.
10. I needed to learn a lot of things before I could get going with this tool.

- Q2: WUS (1: Strongly disagree ~ 5: Strongly agree)

  1. The visual expression of this website is enjoyable.
  2. I am impressed by this website.
  3. I feel familiar with this website.
  4. I find the information I want immediately on this website.
  5. I do not understand many words on this website.
  6. I have much times to use this website.
  7. I trust the content of this website.
  8. I trust this website.
  9. The sentence expression on this website is appropriate.
10. The operating procedure of this website is simple and easy to understand.
11. I can understand how to use this website immediately.
12. I do not get lost what I should do next on this website.

13. The uniformity of this website is perfect.
14. It is easy to understand the layout of the menu on this website.
15. It is easy to understand where I am.
16. I can read the sentences on this website such as between lines, sentence layout.
17. It is difficult to see pictures, tables and figures on this website.
18. My eyes feel tired by using this website.
19. The response time of this website is fast in terms of operation.
20. There are cases where the screen of this website is not correct when I use it.
21. There are cases where the screen of this website is slow and stops midway when I use it.

- Q3: The future intention of this tool (1: I do not use ~ 5: I would like to use)
- Q4: The future intention of this tool in the case of requiring a charge (1: I do not use ~ 5: I would like to use)

  Suppose that the price of this tool is the amount of money you imagine.

- Q5: The amount of information (1: little ~ 5: much)
- Q6: Additional information excluding the information shown in this tool (multiple choices allowed)

  1. I want to see how to use the devices.
  2. I want to see how to set the devices (excluding security settings).

3. Nothing applicable.

- Q7: The intention of this tool in the case of computer and IoT devices (1: I do not use the target device, 2: I do not use ~ 6: I would like to use)

1. The tool in the case of computer
2. The tool in the case of IoT devices

- Q8: The recommendation level of this tool for your friends and family (1: I do not recommend at all ~ 10: I very recommend)
- Q9: The reason of answering Q8 (Open-ended question)
- Q10: The content of convenience (Open-ended question)
- Q11: The content of inconvenience (Open-ended question)
- Q12: The functions that you want to add to this tool (Open-ended question)
- Q13: Other comments (Open-ended question)

References

1. Sano, A. Sawaya, Y, Isohara, T, Nishigaki, M.: Human factors impacting the security actions of help recipients. In: Proceedings of the BWCCA 2023, pp. 81–93 (2023)
2. Kropczynski, J., Anaraky, R.G., et al.: Examining collaborative support for privacy and security in the broader context of tech caregiving. In: Proceedings of the CSCW 2021, pp. 1–23 (2021)
3. Mendel, T., Toch, E.: My mom was getting this popup: understanding motivations and processes in helping older relatives with mobile security and privacy. In: Proceedings of the ACM on Interactive, Mobile, Wearable and Ubiquitous Technologies, pp. 1–20 (2020)
4. Mendel, T., Gao, D., et al.: An exploratory study of social support systems to help older adults in managing mobile safety. In: Proceedings of the MobileHCI 2021, pp.1–13 (2021)
5. Chouhan, C., LaPerriere, C.M., et al.: Co-designing for community oversight: helping people make privacy and security decisions together. In: Proceedings of the CSCW 2019, pp.1–31 (2019)
6. Ministry of Internal Affairs and Communications: WHITE PAPER information and Communications in Japan. https://www.soumu.go.jp/johotsusintokei/whitepaper/eng/WP2021/chapter-3.pdf. Accessed 16 Apr 2025
7. KDDI: Awareness Raising and Education (Connecting Hearts and Minds). https://www.kddi.com/english/corporate/sustainability/educate/. Accessed 16 Apr 2025
8. The Mainichi: Smartphone classes taught by teens attract flood of elderly applicants in central Japan. https://mainichi.jp/english/articles/20220816/p2a/00m/0na/020000c. Accessed 16 Apr 2025
9. Kyodo News: FEATURE: Japan local gov'ts helping aged people learn how to use smartphone. https://english.kyodonews.net/news/2021/11/a52b5f784700-feature-local-govts-helping-aged-people-learn-how-to-use-smartphone.html. Accessed 16 Apr 2025
10. Mendel, T.: Social help: developing methods to support older adults in mobile privacy and security. In: Proceedings of the UbiComp/ISWC 2019, pp. 383–387 (2019)
11. Pacheco, E.: Older adult's safety and security online: a post-pandemic exploration of attitudes and behaviors. J. Digit. Media Interact. 7(17), 107–126 (2024)

12. Salman, H.M., Ahmad, W.F.W., Sulaiman, S.: Usability evaluation of the smartphone user interface in supporting elderly users from expert's perspective. IEEE Access **6**, 22578–22591 (2018)
13. Olwal, A., Lachanas, D., Zacharouli, E.: OldGen: mobile phone personalization for older adults. In: Proceedings of the SIGCHI 2011, pp. 3393–3396 (2011)
14. Zajicek, M.: Interface design for older adults. In: Proceedings of the WUAUC 2001, pp. 60–65 (2001)
15. Chaudry, B.M., Connelly, K.H., Welch, J.L.: Mobile interface design for low-literacy populations. In: Proceedings of the IHI 2012, pp. 91–100 (2012)
16. Medhi, I., Patnaik, S., et al.: Designing mobile interfaces for novice and low-literacy users. In: Proceedings of the TOCHI, vol. 18, no. 2, pp. 1–28 (2011)
17. Kodagoda, N., William Wong, B.L., et al.: Interactive visualization for low literacy users: from lessons learnt to design. In: Proceedings of the CHI 2012, pp. 1159–1168 (2012)
18. Ministry of Internal Affairs and Communications Usage Trend Survey of 2022. https://www.soumu.go.jp/johotsusintokei/statistics/statistics05b1.html. Accessed 18 Apr 2025. (in Japanese)
19. Brooke, J.: SUS: A Quick and Dirty Usability Scale, Usability Evaluation in Industry, pp. 189–194. Taylor and Francis (1996)
20. Nakagawa, K., Suda, T., Zempo, H., Matsumoto, K.: The development of questionnaire for evaluating web usability. J. Tenth Hum. Interface, pp. 421–424. (in Japanese)
21. Reichheld, F.F.: The one number you need to grow. Harv. Bus. Rev. **81**(12), 46–54 (2004)
22. Shimizu, H.: An introduction to the statistical free software HAD: suggestions to improve teaching, learning and practice data analysis. J. Media Inf. Commun., 59–73 (2016)
23. BellCurve for Excel. https://bellcurve.jp/ex/?srsltid=AfmBOopqF_BYkM9emK8fAhf7W9rNegki1CwolNQB6t4I7Ev83RFE_bYF. Accessed 23 Apr 2025. (in Japanese)
24. Landis, J.R., Koch, G.G.: The measurement of observer agreement for categorical data. Biometrics **33**, 159–174 (1977)
25. Nielsen Norman Group: Beyond the NPS: measuring perceived usability with the SUS, NASA-TLX, and the single ease question after tasks and usability tests. https://www.nngroup.com/articles/measuring-perceived-usability/. Accessed 24 Apr 2025

Enhancing Cybersecurity Through User Experience (UX) Design: Bridging Usability and Protection

Charlotte Wiberg[✉]

Department of Informatics, Umeå University, 901 87 Umeå, Sweden
`charlotte.wiberg@umu.se`

Abstract. Balancing effectiveness with usability remains a core challenge in cybersecurity design. While prior research has addressed issues such as password usability and phishing susceptibility, many studies overlook the broader context in which users make security decisions. Cybersecurity models often assume rational behavior, ignoring real-world factors like cognitive load, time pressure, and competing goals. Users frequently bypass security prompts not out of negligence, but because these measures interrupt workflow and reduce efficiency.

User experience (UX)-driven security solutions have been proposed, yet few are systematically evaluated in real-world environments. It remains unclear which UX principles most effectively improve security compliance while minimizing cognitive burden. Additionally, overly complex mechanisms promote circumvention, while overly permissive ones compromise protection. This tension is exacerbated by digitalization and security fatigue—users' mental exhaustion from frequent prompts and warnings.

To address these challenges, this study proposes a UX-integrated cybersecurity framework that aligns security measures with human behavior and cognitive limitations. It emphasizes a shift from rigid enforcement to user-centered design, where security becomes seamless and embedded in everyday tasks.

Using a narrative literature review and empirical studies of user interactions with security features, the study identifies key UX design elements that encourage secure behavior without disrupting productivity. The goal is to promote a culture where users see security not as a barrier, but as an enabler. By prioritizing usability in cybersecurity design, organizations can improve adoption, reduce breaches, and foster a more resilient digital ecosystem.

Keywords: User Experience · UX · Usability · Cybersecurity · literature review

1 Introduction

In today's increasingly digital society, cybersecurity has become a cornerstone of organizational resilience and public trust. While technical safeguards and policy frameworks have advanced significantly, user behavior continues to represent a persistent vulnerability. Human factors are now widely recognized as both a weak link and a potential asset in cybersecurity systems [1]. Nevertheless, today's security designs often position users as obstacles rather than partners, introducing procedures that hinder workflow efficiency, generate frustration, and ultimately reduce compliance.

This paradox—where security measures intended to protect may unintentionally weaken overall security—stems from a lack of attention to usability in cybersecurity systems [2]. Research has identified key usability challenges such as security fatigue [3], alert desensitization, and password overload [4] as symptoms of a disconnect between system design and human capabilities. Despite these findings, there remains a lack of systematic frameworks that integrate principles of user experience (UX) into cybersecurity design [5].

While the literature includes studies on specific security behaviors—such as phishing susceptibility [6] and password management strategies [7]—few works address the broader interaction between security mechanisms and the cognitive and contextual realities users face in their daily environments. Moreover, UX-informed security improvements are rarely tested in real-world settings, leaving questions about their long-term effectiveness and adoption.

This study addresses these research gaps by proposing a user experience-driven framework for cybersecurity design. Drawing on a narrative literature review, qualitative interviews, and heuristic evaluation, the study identifies key UX design elements that promote secure behavior while minimizing cognitive burden. The ultimate goal is to support the development of cybersecurity systems that align with human cognition, motivation, and workflow—transforming security from an obstacle into an enabler.

2 Background

Usable security, situated at the intersection of cybersecurity and human-computer interaction (HCI), has gained increasing attention over the past two decades. It advocates for security systems that are not only technically robust but also cognitively and behaviorally aligned with user needs [11]. Despite this recognition, many security measures remain rooted in design paradigms that prioritize control and enforcement over usability. As a result, users frequently bypass or resist security mechanisms that they perceive as obstructive, irrational, or inconsistent with their work practices [12].

Studies have shown that users often operate under time pressure, cognitive load, and competing priorities—all of which affect their willingness and ability to engage with security features [10]. Yet, cybersecurity models still frequently assume rational actors making optimal security decisions, disregarding the bounded rationality and contextual limitations inherent to human behavior [9]. This mismatch contributes to noncompliance and insecure workarounds, which can ultimately undermine even the most technically sophisticated security systems.

Security fatigue, defined as a state of mental exhaustion caused by repeated security interactions, is increasingly common in environments characterized by frequent authentication prompts, unclear threat communication, and excessive decision-making demands [3]. Similarly, poor feedback, lack of transparency, and inconsistent user interfaces contribute to diminished trust and reduced system engagement [8, 12].

Although UX principles—such as simplicity, feedback, minimal disruption, and contextual clarity—are well established in the broader field of interaction design, their targeted integration into cybersecurity practices is still limited. Few frameworks exist to guide designers in incorporating UX insights into the creation of secure yet usable systems, and even fewer have been empirically validated in operational settings.

2.1 Aim

This study aims to propose a conceptual framework for cybersecurity design that incorporates principles of user experience (UX) to enhance both usability and compliance. By combining insights from a narrative literature review with empirical findings on user interaction with security features, the study seeks to identify which design principles most effectively:

- Support secure user behavior
- Reduce cognitive and operational burden
- Integrate seamlessly into everyday workflows

2.2 Research Questions

The study addresses the following research questions:

1. Which UX principles have the greatest potential to improve compliance with cybersecurity procedures without compromising usability?
2. How do users perceive and interact with current security features in real-world digital environments?
3. How can a UX-based design framework reduce the occurrence of security fatigue and circumventive behavior where users in everyday system use?

3 Methodology

To address the research questions, this study employs a mixed-methods design that integrates a narrative literature review, qualitative user interviews, and heuristic UX evaluation of cybersecurity features in real-world settings. This triangulated approach enables both breadth and depth in exploring how UX principles can be meaningfully integrated into cybersecurity frameworks.

3.1 Research Design

The study follows an exploratory sequential design [14], where the literature review and qualitative data collection inform the development of a conceptual framework. This framework is then validated through expert heuristic evaluation and mapped to user-centered design principles.

3.2 Narrative Literature Review

A narrative literature review [16] was conducted to identify existing UX approaches in cybersecurity, documented challenges, and gaps in the integration of usability and security. Following the PRISMA guidelines [15] for literature reviews in general, the review used the following process:

- **Databases:** Scopus, ACM Digital Library, IEEE Xplore, and Web of Science
- **Search Terms:** "usable security", "user experience AND cybersecurity", "security fatigue", "human factors AND security", "UX design AND secure systems"
- **Inclusion Criteria:** Peer-reviewed journal or conference articles from 2005–2024, in English, with empirical or design-based contributions
- **Exclusion Criteria:** Purely technical solutions with no human factors component
- **Analysis:** Thematic synthesis using qualitative coding [17]

A narrative literature review, also known as a traditional literature review, provides a comprehensive and critical overview of existing research on a specific topic. They are often used as a first step in research, to scope out a research area before embarking on a more focused systematic review. It synthesizes and interprets findings from various sources, often exploring the development of the research over time and identifying gaps in the literature. Unlike systematic reviews, narrative reviews don't adhere to strict methodological protocols and may not include every article on a topic [cf. 16.

The review identified 48 relevant papers and/or books, from which recurring usability challenges and UX principles in security contexts were extracted and categorized. (The reference list of the identified sources is found at the end of the reference list [6–8, 11, 14, 19–62]).

3.3 Qualitative User Interviews

To understand user perceptions and behaviors in relation to security systems, informal semi-structured interviews were conducted with 6 participants across three professional sectors: healthcare, education, and IT services. The recruitment of the participants were conducted with purposive sampling to ensure variation in role (e.g., admin staff, technical staff, management) and security responsibility. An interview guide were used which was focused on daily interaction with security features, perceived disruptions, coping strategies, and suggestions for improvement. The interviews were held via video calls or informal face-to-face meetings (45–60 min each). Notes were taken during sessions (in order to keep the informal narrative). Analysis was conducted by use of reflexive thematic analysis [18] to identify patterns related to usability, compliance, and cognitive load.

3.4 Heuristic UX Evaluation

A heuristic evaluation [46] was conducted on common enterprise security interfaces. A panel of four UX designers and – experts evaluated tools using both Nielsen's usability heuristics and security-specific heuristics [8, 13]. Usability issues were identified, rated, and compared with interview findings to inform framework development.

3.5 Framework Development

Insights from all methods were synthesized to develop a UX-Cybersecurity Design Framework, integrating UX principles with behavioral drivers and system implementation strategies.

4 Findings

The findings from the narrative literature review, qualitative user interviews, and heuristic evaluations revealed three converging themes that illustrate the persistent disconnect between user experience and cybersecurity implementations in organizational contexts. These themes are not isolated, but often reinforce one another, resulting in diminished compliance and increased user burden.

4.1 Cognitive Load and Workflow Interruption

Participants across all three sectors (healthcare, education, and IT services) consistently described multi-factor authentication (MFA), VPN logins, and frequent re-authentication prompts as *disruptive to their primary tasks*. One healthcare professional explained:

> *"When I'm trying to enter patient data and the system logs me out after ten minutes, I lose my focus and it slows everything down."*

Heuristic evaluations corroborated these complaints, identifying interface designs that lacked *persistent session feedback* or seamless re-authentication options. In high-pressure environments, such interruptions contributed not only to productivity loss but also to strategic circumvention, such as using shared workstations to avoid repeated login cycles. This illustrates how poor usability can unintentionally encourage insecure behaviors.

4.2 Security Fatigue and Compliance Behaviors

Many users described *emotional weariness* in dealing with frequent and seemingly redundant security prompts. This phenomenon, commonly referred to as **security fatigue**, manifested in risky coping behaviors: reusing passwords, disabling browser security settings, or saving credentials in plain text documents.

One IT administrator noted:

> *"After being prompted for login credentials five times in a day, I just started leaving some apps open permanently—even if I'm not using them."*

This behavior not only undermines intended security mechanisms but also reflects a breakdown in users' *perceived efficacy*—they begin to view compliance as meaningless, or worse, as obstructive. Literature reviewed in the SLR echoes this, identifying fatigue as a predictor of non-compliance (Sheng et al., 2014; West, 2008).

4.3 Mismatch Between Design and Mental Models

The third theme centers on a *lack of alignment between system behavior and user expectations*. Several participants were confused by features like forced logouts, security timeouts, or ambiguous warning messages. They interpreted these events not as protective measures, but as *system errors* or *poorly implemented software*.

For example, one educator described:

"When my document didn't save because the session timed out, I assumed the system had crashed. No one told me it was about security."

The heuristic evaluation revealed inconsistent UI patterns, especially around authentication messages and error handling. Icons and warning colors were often used without explanation, contributing to a *lack of trust in system logic*. These results underscore the need to *make security behavior visible and interpretable*—a key UX principle missing from many implementations.

4.4 Meta-reflection: Intersections and Systemic Implications

While the themes are analytically distinct, they are deeply interrelated and collectively point to a systemic misalignment between cybersecurity design and the cognitive and emotional realities of users. Cognitive load often acts as a catalyst for security fatigue, especially when users are repeatedly interrupted by poorly integrated security procedures. Similarly, misunderstandings stemming from a mismatch between system behavior and user mental models exacerbate the sense of burden and frustration, reinforcing insecure coping behaviors.

Notably, heuristic evaluations confirmed that many design flaws were not the result of individual system errors, but of *systemic design conventions*—such as default timeout settings or lack of feedback—that are replicated across platforms. This suggests that user frustration is not an anomaly but a foreseeable consequence of neglecting UX principles in security architecture.

The convergence of findings across literature, interviews, and heuristic analysis strengthens the validity of these insights. Moreover, they underscore a key implication: **effective cybersecurity cannot rely solely on enforcement and control—it must engage users as cognitive and emotional agents, not just as risk factors**. This forms the rationale for the UX-Cybersecurity Framework developed in this study, which aims to guide the integration of usability and protection in a mutually reinforcing way.

5 Discussion

The findings from this study demonstrate that cybersecurity design continues to suffer from a fundamental misalignment with user cognition, motivation, and workflow. Across sectors and systems, users encounter security mechanisms that disrupt productivity, erode trust, and contribute to behavioral fatigue. These experiences are not merely anecdotal or sector-specific—they reflect a systemic design problem where usability and protection are treated as trade-offs, rather than as mutually reinforcing design goals.

This section reflects on how these challenges reveal broader implications for cybersecurity design and argues for a shift in perspective: from security as enforcement, to security as interaction. To achieve this, we must design with users' cognitive limitations and behavioral patterns in mind—embracing what Herbert Simon termed **bounded rationality**. The following subsections discuss key strategies derived from the findings.

5.1 Designing for Bounded Rationality

Security systems often assume rational, informed, and compliant users. In reality, users operate under uncertainty, time pressure, and multitasking demands. As revealed in Sect. 4.1, disruptions from authentication or session timeouts frequently occurred during high-stakes tasks, prompting users to circumvent protocols to preserve workflow continuity.

Rather than expect perfect compliance, design must accommodate the heuristics and shortcuts users naturally adopt. Systems should guide behavior through **intuitive affordances** and **predictable patterns**, reducing the need for users to consciously evaluate risk in every interaction. For example, adaptive authentication that adjusts based on context can minimize interruptions without reducing control. Designing for bounded rationality means acknowledging that "perfect security" is less useful than *sufficiently secure systems that support consistent, low-effort compliance* [9, 10].

5.2 Reducing Security Fatigue Through Seamless Integration

As Sect. 4.2 showed, repeated security prompts, unclear feedback, and redundant steps contribute to emotional exhaustion and risky workarounds. Security fatigue is not a sign of user irresponsibility—it is a symptom of poor design. Instead of layering more security steps, organizations should strive to *embed* security into natural workflows.

Examples include **context-aware security measures** that adjust based on user behavior or location, and **single sign-on systems** that reduce redundant credential entry. Seamless integration does not imply weakening security controls, but rather optimizing *when, where, and how* they are presented. Well-integrated mechanisms feel like a part of the task—not an obstacle to it [11].

5.3 Building Transparent and Trustworthy Systems

The third major theme—misalignment between system logic and user mental models—reveals a deeper issue: a lack of transparency and communicative clarity. When users do not understand why systems behave the way they do, trust erodes and control is lost.

To counter this, systems must offer **real-time feedback, plain-language explanations**, and **consistency across interfaces**. These elements build not only trust but also *learned predictability*, enabling users to form accurate expectations of how systems will respond. Transparency, in this sense, is not merely about revealing technical logic, but about enabling users to confidently navigate secure interactions [12].

5.4 Bridging Toward a UX-Centered Security Framework

Taken together, these reflections underscore the inadequacy of traditional control-oriented security models in addressing today's usability challenges. Rather than viewing security as a barrier that must be enforced, this study proposes a reframing: **security as an embedded, experience-driven design objective**. The persistent issues uncovered—cognitive burden, fatigue, and misunderstanding—call for a structured, principle-based response.

In the next section, we introduce the **UX-Cybersecurity Design Framework**: a layered approach that translates these empirical insights into actionable design strategies. The framework synthesizes user experience principles, behavioral drivers, and implementation guidelines to support systems that are both secure *and* usable—by design.

6 UX – Cybersecurity Design Framework

Building on the empirical findings and theoretical insights presented in this study, we propose a structured framework that integrates UX principles into cybersecurity design. The **UX–Cybersecurity Design Framework** is intended as both a conceptual model and a practical tool. It emphasizes that usability, cognitive support, and behavioral understanding must inform the design of security systems—not as peripheral concerns, but as foundational criteria.

The framework is organized into three interrelated layers: **UX Principles**, **Behavioral Drivers**, and **Implementation Guidelines**. Each layer builds on the others, translating design ideals into actionable practices that are sensitive to the realities of users' environments, motivations, and limitations.

6.1 Layer 1 – UX Principles

This foundational layer consists of design heuristics drawn from interaction design and cybersecurity usability literature. These principles serve as the interface between human needs and system behavior:

- **Simplicity**: Eliminate unnecessary complexity from security tasks and interfaces.
- **Feedback**: Provide clear, timely, and context-sensitive responses that reinforce understanding.
- **Minimal Disruption**: Embed security actions within workflows to reduce friction and task-switching.
- **Consistency**: Apply uniform logic and visual language across devices and platforms.
- **User Control**: Allow adjustable settings or opt-out mechanisms in low-risk scenarios to support autonomy.

6.2 Layer 2 – Behavioral Drivers

This layer reflects the cognitive and psychological mechanisms that influence user interaction with security systems. It translates abstract design values into behavioral objectives:

- **Cognitive Load Management**: Streamline tasks to reduce decision fatigue and inattentional errors.
- **Trust and Transparency**: Foster user confidence through predictable, explainable system behaviors.
- **Autonomy Support**: Enable users to feel competent and in control rather than coerced or monitored.

6.3   Layer 3 – Implementation Guidelines

The third layer operationalizes the framework. These are actionable design strategies that translate principles and behavioral goals into real-world practice:

- **Secure Defaults**: Design systems that are secure out of the box without relying on user intervention.
- **Context-Aware Adaptation**: Tailor security prompts and controls to usage patterns and situational risk.
- **Inclusive Co-Design**: Involve end-users and UX specialists from the outset to anticipate usability barriers.
- **Iterative Testing**: Evaluate systems regularly with real users under realistic conditions.

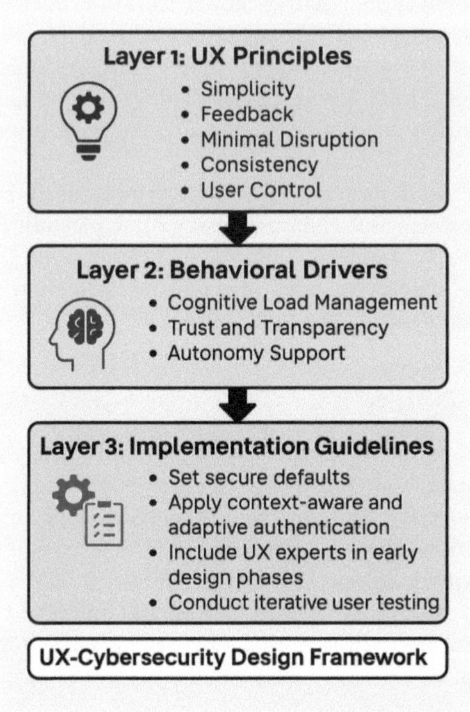

Fig. 1. The UX – Cybersecurity framework.

The framework is visualized in Fig. 1, illustrating how these layers interact. Rather than a linear process, the model encourages continuous feedback between layers—reflecting how user understanding, design refinements, and contextual needs evolve together.

By synthesizing cognitive, behavioral, and design perspectives, this framework aims to bridge the gap between secure technology and usable interaction. It offers a roadmap for practitioners who seek to create cybersecurity systems that not only protect but also empower users.

In the following section, we reflect on the broader implications of this approach, its potential to shift current design paradigms, and its relevance for future research and practice.

7 Conclusion

This study set out to explore how user experience (UX) principles can be systematically integrated into cybersecurity design to bridge the persistent gap between technical protection and human behavior. Through a mixed-methods approach—comprising a narrative literature review, qualitative interviews, and heuristic evaluation—it became evident that current security solutions often fail to account for users' cognitive limitations, emotional responses, and contextual constraints.

Three primary challenges emerged: excessive workflow interruptions, growing security fatigue, and a disconnect between user mental models and system logic. These challenges do not exist in isolation; rather, they reflect systemic shortcomings in the way cybersecurity is conceived, designed, and deployed. Importantly, the findings show that usability and security must not be treated as competing priorities, but as mutually reinforcing objectives.

To address this, the study proposes the **UX-Cybersecurity Design Framework**, a layered model that translates user-centered design principles into practical strategies for secure, usable systems. By promoting simplicity, seamless integration, and contextual clarity, the framework enables security mechanisms that align with user workflows, reduce friction, and foster sustained compliance.

7.1 Implications for Practice

This research emphasizes that cybersecurity is no longer solely a technical domain—it is fundamentally human-centered. Designers, developers, and security architects are encouraged to incorporate UX thinking from the earliest stages of system development. Usability testing, participatory design, and heuristic evaluations should become standard tools in the cybersecurity design process.

Organizations that adopt this mindset can expect improved compliance, reduced error rates, and stronger user trust—all of which contribute to more resilient security environments.

7.2 Future Research

Further research is needed to empirically test and refine the proposed framework across diverse real-world settings. Controlled experiments and longitudinal field studies could help determine which UX interventions most effectively influence secure behavior over time.

In particular, future studies should explore how the framework performs in contexts with varying levels of digital literacy, risk awareness, and organizational culture. Such research would not only validate the model but also expand its applicability across sectors.

Disclosure of Interests. The authors have no competing interests to declare that are relevant to the content of this article.

References

1. Sasse, M.A., Brostoff, S., Weirich, D.: Transforming the 'weakest link'—a human/computer interaction approach to usable and effective security. BT Technol. J. **19**(3), 122–131 (2001)
2. Beautement, A., Sasse, M.A., Wonham, M.: The compliance budget: managing security behaviour in organisations. In: Proceedings of the 2008 Workshop on New Security Paradigms, pp. 47–58 (2008)
3. Sheng, S., Holbrook, M., Kumaraguru, P., Cranor, L., Downs, J.: Who falls for phish? A demographic analysis of phishing susceptibility and effectiveness of interventions. In: Proceedings of the SIGCHI Conference on Human Factors in Computing Systems, pp. 373–382 (2014)
4. Florêncio, D., Herley, C.: A large-scale study of web password habits. In: Proceedings of the 16th International Conference on World Wide Web, pp. 657–666 (2007)
5. Karwowski, W., Ahram, T. Z., Nazir, S.: Advances in Human Factors in Cybersecurity, vol. 1212. Springer, Cham (2020)
6. Downs, J.S., Holbrook, M.B., Cranor, L.F.: Decision strategies and susceptibility to phishing. In: Proceedings of the Second Symposium on Usable Privacy and Security, pp. 79–90 (2006)
7. Bonneau, J., Herley, C., Van Oorschot, P.C., Stajano, F.: The quest to replace passwords: a framework for comparative evaluation of web authentication schemes. In: IEEE Symposium on Security and Privacy, pp. 553–567 (2012)
8. Braz, C., Robert, J.M.: Security and usability: the case of the user authentication methods. In: People and Computers XIX, pp. 199–212 (2006)
9. Camp, L.J.: Designing for trust. In: Trust, Reputation, and Security: Theories and Practice, pp. 9–18. Springer, Berlin (2006)
10. West, R.: The psychology of security. Commun. ACM **51**(4), 34–40 (2008)
11. Furnell, S.: Cybercrime: Vandalizing the Information Society. Addison-Wesley (2010)
12. Norman, D.A.: The Design of Everyday Things (Revised and Expanded Edition). Basic Books (2013)
13. Kainda, R., Flechais, I., Roscoe, A.W.: Security and usability: analysis and evaluation. In: ARES, pp. 275–282 (2010)
14. Creswell, J.W., Plano Clark, V.L.: Designing and Conducting Mixed Methods Research, 3rd edn. SAGE Publications (2018)

15. Page, M.J., et al.: The PRISMA 2020 statement: an updated guideline for reporting systematic reviews. BMJ **372**, n71 (2021)
16. Ferrari, R.: Writing narrative style literature reviews. Med. Writing. **24**, 230–235 (2015)
17. Thomas, J., Harden, A.: Methods for thematic synthesis. BMC Med. Res. Methodol. **8**(1), 45 (2008)
18. Braun, V., Clarke, V.: Using thematic analysis in psychology. Qual. Res. Psychol. **3**(2), 77–101 (2006)
19. Nielsen, J.: Usability Engineering. Morgan Kaufmann (1994)
20. Abomhara, M., Køien, G.M.: Security and privacy in the Internet of Things: current status and open issues. In: International Conference on Privacy and Security in Mobile Systems (PRISMS), Aalborg, Demark (2014)
21. Al-Muhtadi, J., Ranganathan, A., Campbell, R.H., Mickunas, M.D.: Cerberus: a context-aware security scheme for smart spaces. In: Proceedings of the 1st IEEE International Conference on Pervasive Computing and Communications, PerCom 2003, pp. 489–496 (2003)
22. Al Sharnouby, M., Alaca, F., Chiasson, S.: Why phishing still works: user strategies for combating phishing attacks. Int. J. Hum. Comput. Stud. **82**, 69–82 (2015)
23. Beautement, A., Sasse, M.A., Wonham, M.: The compliance budget: managing security behaviour in organisations. In: Proceedings of the 2008 Workshop on New Security Paradigms, pp. 47–58. Association for Computing Machinery, New York (2008)
24. Biddle, R., van Oorschot, P.C., Patrick, A.S.: Graphical passwords: learning from the first twelve years. ACM Comput. Surv. **44**(4), 1–41 (2012)
25. Camp, L.J.: Designing for trust. In: Falcone, R. (ed.) Trust, Reputation, and Security: Theories and Practice, pp. 9–18. Springer-Verlang (Berlin) 2003 (2006)
26. Camp, L.J.: Mental models of privacy and security. IEEE Technol. Soc. Mag. **25**(1), 37–46 (2006)
27. Chiasson, S., Forget, A., Stobert, E., van Oorschot, P.C., Biddle, R.: Multiple password interference in text passwords and click-based graphical passwords. In: CCS 2009: Proceedings of the 16th ACM Conference on Computer and Communications Security, pp. 500–511 (2009)
28. Chowdhury, N., Adam, M., Skinner, G.: The impact of time pressure on cybersecurity behaviour: a systematic literature review. Behav. Inf. Technol. **38**, 1–19 (2019)
29. Das, A., Bonneau, J., Caesar, M., Borisov, N., Wang, X.: The tangled web of password reuse. In: Proceedings of NDSS 2014 Symposium (2014)
30. De Luca, A., Hang, A., Brudy, F., Lindner, C., Hussmann, H.: Touch me once and I know it's you! Implicit authentication based on touch screen patterns. In: CHI 2012: Proceedings of the SIGCHI Conference on Human Factors in Computing Systems, pp. 987–996 (2012)
31. Di Nocera, F., Tempestini, G., Orsini, M.: Usable Security: A Systematic Literature Review (2005–2022) (2023)
32. Egelman, S., Peer, E.: Scaling the security wall: developing a security behavior intentions scale (SeBIS). In: Proceedings of the 33rd Annual CHI Conference on Human Factors in Computing Systems, CHI 2015, 2873–2882 (2015)
33. Felt, A.P., Egelman, S., Wagner, D.: I've got 99 problems, but vibration ain't one: a survey of smartphone users' security habits. In: SPSM 2012: Proceedings of the Second ACM Workshop on Security and Privacy in Smartphones and Mobile Devices, pp. 33–44 (2012)
34. Florêncio, D., Herley, C.: A large-scale study of web password habits. In: Proceedings of the 16th International Conference on World Wide Web, WWW 2007, pp. 657–666 (2007)
35. Garfinkel, S., Lipford, H.R., Yee, K.: Secure User Interfaces: Bridging Security and HCI. Springer-Verlag (2004)
36. Garfinkel, S., Lipford, H.R.: Usable Security. History, Themes, and Challenges. Springer-Verlag, Berlin (2014)

37. Grawemeyer, B., Johnson, H.: Using and managing multiple passwords: a week to a view. Interact. Comput. **23**(3), 256–267 (2011)
38. Greenberg, S., Buxton, B.: Usability evaluation considered harmful (some of the time). In: CHI 2008: Proceedings of the SIGCHI Conference on Human Factors in Computing Systems, pp. 111–120 (2008)
39. Hof, H.-J.: User-centric IT security – guidelines for usable mechanisms. Int. J. Inf. Secur. **14**(6), 531–543 (2015)
40. Hsu, J.S.-C., Hung, Y.W., Hsieh, P.-J., Chiu, C.-M.: Examining formation and alleviation of information security fatigue by using job demands–resources theory. Inf. Syst. J. **34**(6), 2132–2172 (2024)
41. Ion, I., Reeder, R., Consolvo, S.: "… no one can hack my mind": Comparing expert and non-expert security practices. In: Proceedings of the 2015 Symposium on Usable Privacy and Security SOUPS, pp. 327–346 (2015)
42. Jacobs, D., McDaniel, T.: A survey of user experience in usable security and privacy research. In: Moallem, A. (eds.) HCI for Cybersecurity, Privacy and Trust. HCII 2022. Lecture Notes in Computer Science, vol. 13333, pp. 154–172. Springer, Cham (2022). https://doi.org/10. 1007/978-3-031-05563-8_11
43. Kainda, R., Flechais, I., Roscoe, A.W.: Security and usability: analysis and evaluation. In: International Conference on Availability, Reliability and Security (ARES 2010), pp. 275–282 (2010)
44. Karwowski, W., Ahram, T.Z., Nazir, S.: Advances in Human Factors in Cybersecurity. Proceedings of HFE 2020 Virtual Conference on Human factors in Cybersecurity, USA , 16–29 July 2020, vol. 1219. Springer, Cham (2020)
45. Kuzen, E., Strembeck, M.: Security research in ubiquitous computing: a literature review. J. Inf. Secur. Appl. **34**, 271–290 (2017)
46. Naqvi, B., Kävrestad, J., Islam, A.K.M.N.: Inclusive and accessible cybersecurity: challenges and future directions. Computer **57**(6), 73–81 (2024)
47. Norman, D.A.: The Design of Everyday Things (Revised and Expanded Edition). Basic Books (2013)
48. Schechter, S., Brush, A.J.B., Egelman, S.: It's no secret: Measuring the security and reliability of authentication via "secret" questions. In: IEEE Symposium on Security and Privacy, pp. 375–390 (2009)
49. Sheng, S., Holbrook, M., Kumaraguru, P., Cranor, L., Downs, J.: Who falls for phish? A demographic analysis of phishing susceptibility and effectiveness of interventions. In: Annual CHI Conference on Human Factors in Computing Systems, CHI 2014, pp. 373–382 (2014)
50. Stobert, E., Biddle, R.: The password life cycle: user behaviour in managing passwords. In: Tenth Symposium on Usable Privacy and Security, SOUPS, pp. 243–255 (2014)
51. van den Broek, T., van Veenstra, A.F.: Modes of governance in inter-organizational data collaborations. In: ECIS 2015 Completed Research Papers, Paper 188 (2015)
52. Vance, A., Lowry, P.B., Eggett, D.: Using accountability to reduce access policy violations in information systems. J. Manag. Inf. Syst. **29**(4), 263–290 (2013)
53. Wang, Y., Emurian, H.H.: An overview of online trust: concepts, elements, and implications. Comput. Hum. Behav. **21**(1), 105–125 (2005)
54. Wash, R.: Folk models of home computer security. In: SOUPS 2010: Proceedings of the Sixth Symposium on Usable Privacy and Security Article No. 11, pp. 1–16 (2010)
55. Wash, R., Rader, E.: Too much knowledge? Security beliefs and protective behaviors among United States Internet users. In: Eleventh Symposium On Usable Privacy and Security (SOUPS 2015), SOUPS, pp. 309–325 (2015)
56. West, R.: The psychology of security. Commun. ACM **51**(4), 34–40 (2008)
57. Whitten, A., Tygar, J.D.: Why Johnny can't encrypt: a usability evaluation of PGP 5.0. In: Proceedings of the 8th USENIX Security Symposium, August 1999, pp. 169–183 (1999)

58. Wiedenbeck, S., Waters, J., Birget, J. C., Brodskiy, A., Memon, N.: Authentication using graphical passwords: effects of tolerance and image choice. In: Proceedings of the 2005 Symposium on Usable Privacy and Security - SOUPS, pp. 1–12 (2005)
59. Wu, M., Miller, R.C., Garfinkel, S.L.: Do security toolbars actually prevent phishing attacks?. In: CHI 2006: Proceedings of the SIGCHI Conference on Human Factors in Computing Systems, pp. 601–610 (2006)
60. Zhang-Kennedy, L., Chiasson, S., Biddle, R.: Password advice shouldn't be boring: visualizing password guessing attacks. In: Proceedings of the 2013 APWG eCrime Researchers Summit, San Francisco, CA, USA, pp. 1–11 (2013)
61. Zurko, M.E., Simon, R.T.: User-centered security. In: New Security Paradigms Workshop, pp. 27–33 (1996)
62. Zwilling, M., Klien, G., Lesjak, D., Wiechetek, Ł, Çetin, F., Basım, H.N.: Cyber security awareness, knowledge and behavior: a comparative study. J. Comp. Inf. Syst. **62**, 82–97 (2022)

Author Index